BRAIDED
THE ˇ HORSES ARE COMING!

— Meanderings and Memoirs of a Modern Explorer —

by Donald L. Monroe

From top to bottom: Donald and Marion Monroe in Hawaii, Hink with plaiting in her mane, Donald Monroe, and a wild Nevada mustang enjoying just being a horse.

THE BRAIDED HORSES ARE COMING!

— Meanderings and Memoirs of a Modern Explorer —

Is Bigfoot, Sasquatch, or Wild Man Responsible for the Strange Braids in Horses' Manes?

by Donald L. Monroe

Spatial Systems
Billings, Montana
2013

THE BRAIDED HORSES ARE COMING!

Written and edited by Donald L. Monroe.

Book design and additional editing by Thad Mauney

Published by Spatial Systems
P.O. Box 2255
Billings, Montana 59103

"TONIA"

Dedicated to the memory of Tonia Wild Two Feathers Onya Brown.

Either way identified she was especially fond of wild horses, and was ever helpful to current research efforts through arduous travel and many unexpected hardships and became a true part of its documentation. Various colorful/descriptive excerpts and sentiments are included taken slightly edited for content/message from her travel notes done in mixed gender humor, wisdom. and some gender mention of romantic intention of the journey was found in her surprise left behind written covert little green note book. This once private journal was found eighteen months after her untimely death September 4th, 2011. In many ways women by their intuitive contribution continue to inspire and excite my exploring sojourn, as without their undivided and unconditional support and separate uncanny discernment, noted compassion and obvious survival tenacity, etc., at times much less I am sure would often have not been accomplished. Some women by their unpredictable natural ability are sometimes more courageous than men. "Not to say however that women are any better or more adept than men, but they damn well are not any worse!" Lesser men of experience and understanding of their gender share in some contrary opinion; "what we earn guys is what we get," and throughout all of future slated, "Trilogy Manuscripts," courageous women to the last one ever get their due credit!

The book ever writes much of Onya's gender discernment, humor, and patience. There is something here for everyone in human compassion from the heart and soul of man, beast, and unknown hominids. No matter what this sojourn becomes for anyone it is a true sample of the author's lifelong efforts to discover the truth of hidden secrets.

CREDITS

Native American/Asian/Astrology research:
Tonia F. Brown, Wise River Montana.

Thanks for support, interest, and continuing field research, including witness and important photographic evidence of plaiting, editing, and publishing: Thad Mauney, Ph.D., Billings, Montana.

Front Cover Photograph:
Neil Hinck at the N & N Ranch

The cover photo is of world famous wrangler, Neil Hinck, past master horse trainer and proud owner of the once highly renowned, N & N Blazer Horse Ranch, operated until fall 2012, was located near the berg town of Adrian, Oregon. The back cover portrayal of the mounted fantasized/reincarnated Conquistador that now is a hard riding Vaquero... "has in fantasy in our presentation returned back to in time to this new era to be forever chasing after any and all wild horses that may be running away with his fabled legendary beautiful sweet heart, "LA LLORONA," who is said to be forever cursed as the Wailing Women of Mexican legend and song, more of her to be explained when Onya meets the Diablo of Socorro, New Mexico.

Back Cover Artwork
by Phil Jenson

This continuing beautiful western art work was the contribution of Cowboy Artist, wrangler, Phil Jenson of, Owyhee River, Oregon. His art work is as real and true life as himself! If anyone is further interested in his custom depictions, Phil can be contacted through the author; address included ahead in the book.

CONTENTS

PREFACE

Don Monroe is as original as they come. His lifestyle and his writing style are authentically his own. Unlike some, he takes full responsibility for both. Therefore it is a pleasure to participate in publishing this log of a fragment of his adventures and his interpretation of phenomena that seem to have been occurring all around us in plain sight but gone (mostly) unnoticed or trivialized.

Here Monroe brings us a view of the tangles that appear repeatedly in horses' manes and have been written off as annoyances caused by wind and brush. On close inspection these seem far too complex and too often repeated to be mere happenstance. Whether any of Monroe's proposed explanations turn out to be right or wrong, it is worth noticing that this has been occurring both because we should observe the world we live in, and also because we should observe how we, collectively, have been oblivious for so long to such a strange but readily observable phenomenon.

In publishing this work, I am not, personally, subscribing to any particular theory as to how the "braids, plaits, twists, or tangles" (and here the terms are used almost synonymously) get into horses' manes. I can, however, say that I, personally, have seen them, held them in hand, and examined them in the field, on the horse. I have seen them in locations hundreds of miles apart, and it is difficult to conceive any means by which mere wind and chance could have made them all so similarly, and especially when they contain distinct overhand knots. I don't know who or what is making them. If "civilized" humans are doing this, the simplest explanation other than wind, the agents are unusually successful in going unobserved, and in keeping a widespread activity totally secret. If not humans, then who or what is doing it?

As a scientist I must simply report them as unexplained but repeatedly observed phenomena. Despite all conjecture, the actual cause for these is yet to be found. Monroe proposes that wild hominids or feral humans make them. These I have not seen, and so I don't know. I remain open to future evidence. He has plans for further books, and perhaps they will introduce the evidence. We shall see.

In preparing this book for publication I have made the usual corrections of spelling, grammar, and formatting only up to a point. In addition to being an explorer, Monroe is also an artist, and his art includes his language. Rather than adopting everyone else's style, Don finds, or creates, his own solutions to the ever difficult problem of navigating an idea through the narrow passages of language. Don has never been afflicted by overexposure to Strunk & White*. To force conformance to the modern style of short, monotopical, declaratives would be like forcing Joel Chandler Harris to clean up Uncle Remus's grammar and suppress his accent. Or, if you will forgive more grandiose comparisons, it would be like telling James Joyce to take Ulysses' rambling mind out of Finnegan's Wake, or telling Dali that clocks just don't melt. Don's writing style is quite simply his own. It is a record of Americana 2013. Some of his creative solutions to spelling current-day American English, including how to get past the spellchecker, have purposely been left for the reader to enjoy the

---

* Strunk, William, Jr.; White, E.B. The Elements of Style. This little book on English grammar and style has been a favorite guide to formal English for everyone from newspaper editors to university professors, and has appeared in various editions from 1918 to the present. I like their style, but in fact not everyone writes their way, for example one of my friends commented on Don's prose: "Yeah, that's the way you would say it."

play of letters and the multiple entendre, (and don't just stop at double). A few words, such as moot, pseudo, abrupt, and passé are used in ways that should make us re-examine the limitations of our university-groomed grammar. Jump into his flow and enjoy it. And in the course of it, please accept and forgive any errors that I may have introduced, for these I alone am responsible.

Now, I must raise a difficult but important topic: the potential legal status of the beings Monroe suggests as makers of the braids. If the braids/plaits/twists are being made by intelligent and skillful hominids or feral humans, what are their rights? If we ever do encounter Bigfoot or Sasquatch, how shall we treat them? We must consider this carefully. If they are human or nearly so, to kill them—even as scientific specimens—is murder, to capture them, even briefly, is kidnapping, and to coerce them into our 'civilized' conditions would violate the sovereignty of their population to determine its own course of living. If they exist at all, they are not mere animals. I feel strongly that they deserve all the legal protections we now recognize for ourselves, plus one special one—the right to be left alone. If they are real, they have been exceedingly careful to protect their autonomous lifestyle. I think we must respect as innate, and inalienable, their right to do so. Therefore, I invite legal scholars to contemplate how this should be cast in the legal system so as to properly establish the protections they deserve. We should contemplate this now, before the issue arises. If in fact there is a covert population of other beings among us, their natural skills are of value and, who knows, they may be more resilient than, and outlast us nature-ignorant city dwelling hominids.

In closing, let me again invite you to join Don Monroe and his friends in this adventure, and to examine the world he sees. It can be quite fun. As he puts it: "Forward...

Thad Mauney
Billings, Montana
March, 2013

FORWARD

"This is a book that logically explains at least some of the new found plausible answers to help solve the ongoing late night horse mane braiding (Plaiting!) mystery that has dumbfounded everyone's wildest fantasized explanation to think to ever be able to explain any real part of it, nor does most anyone beyond an a very few investigative persons at all realize what sort of an unknown hand to finger adaptable wild being, entity, or humankind, or what sort of a beast looking hominid ("Feral wild people!") are believed by the author to be responsible for the plaiting; or in addition do most anyone remotely realize either what possible strong directive power may be almost as if a magical dictate that has by a continuing abstract requirement remains persuasive of the strange tradition that has likely been passed on down to them almost since the dawn of horses and humanity; a feared dictatative power perhaps able through unmeasurable time, become a highly powerful influence ever insistent of the difficult accomplishment.

This strange tradition/requirement adherence has carried on since the days of the early western settlement of America over much of the urban ranch and remaining wilderness areas of the West, and many vast far places south, north, east, and beyond! What ever sort of an opposed finger to thumb hominid creature continues to accomplish plaiting the hair of horses' manes that upon completion often as not is of a most clever primitive variation just as much as if it were also perhaps intended to be an art form; but still however, all of them are usually much similar; each and every single one, each time no matter where found, is of a much singular design, always arranged "just so-so" done to an obvious and/or often a very same, or a separate creature satisfaction! Each plait is ever done of a very tightly braid, or several of them, or many! As said, almost this has been done in what looks at times as if wanting to have been intended as an artistry accomplishment, or even at times; any number of much similar braids are left hanging down loose tied off at there ends, or next be done in a long string of impossibly tight knotted braids (Plaiting), "that after the fact most always these are left hanging in an unsightly precarious elongated flowing hair mess, all hair ever hanging haphazard and ragged down along side of a horse, just as if all of it for some reason were intended to look like some sort of a raw flitting dragging confusion, best explained; all first impression in my opinion, most part, all looks at first glance to be an all messed-up, highly ugly horses' mane, UN-intentionally (?), messed up enough to the eye to warrant the description of a rag/shag hair mess, flitting off and down to where left hanging, often as not in a long gruff, ruff-shod rag tag oval shape, or last mention, all of it is hard tied down fast close to the skin, in what is definitely an able-done purposeful (?) very tight system of knots; at best all of it has been done in a most difficult, high strange, and in an unusual way!

Some many, most every horse plaited thus far, has somehow managed to have its natural Shorter mane, made through plaiting to look been done almost by magic to now be sometimes twice as long ("Much elongated!"), most often one or two times its original length! How this can be possible remains a very big question? Later in the story, after nine years of pondering all of this and its mystery, Phil Jenson, by his genius perception cleverly discovered one of the indisputable answers! This same strange sort of mane extension example has occurred repetitious times over many, many centuries, and has been documented all over the world! Race Track Jockey, Carol Harris, advised me once that it had happened every so often on horses tethered where he worked during the 1960 – 70's, as a Jockey at the Del Mar, California Race Track. "Can't say, he said, that I ever saw this happen myself, but I sure as heck seen the results! It had always much confused all of us! How many times did I see it? Well, I don't know, but it was several! We had no idea how it was done!"

Well, I know Harris, and his reliance, and believe that all of that probably happened! The question remains, Del Mar Race Track is located in a highly populated area! How, unless having had access via the near by ocean beach front that extends for miles along there, could anyone or anything as strange as a pseudo wild hominid other wise think to approach any large city? However I remember once taking a deposition that was documented in my first book, "Sasquatch 2001," that maverick Bigfoot researcher friend, Stanley Luzak, then a resident of Tonapah, Nevada, "explained how he with a partner once tracked a larger strange biped for several miles across the California desert to where its tracks finally became lost just outside of the outskirts of a city park near Los Angeles!" I don't know, but here is one last thought... Many times all up and down the west coast, from Mexico, to Seattle, and far far beyond, all of the way into Alaska there have been countless reports of Sasquatch types of humanoids known to wander there sometimes described as, Hairy Man, and other names O'course are ascribed to the continuing belief of an aquatic type hominid creature roaming the tide-out ocean beaches and river water ways! Anything it seems is thought possible? The totem depiction/effigies and clever carvings of Sasquatch, Otter man, etc., all of the way into Alaska/Siberia etc., are all a definite belief source if not a belief artifact fact and adherence to something thought still alive and very real, or was here long ago!"

"No infatuation with imagination or fantasy writes this manuscript!"

Hardly is this treatise a compromise of wild ideas, as the book comprises nine plus years and ongoing of difficult study and arduous observation of wild and domestic horses in the field, and it explains in some important proven part, some explanations of the high strange plaiting anomaly that have now actually been solved; some explanations now are completely founded to denote founded reasons in some cases why the uncanny braiding continues being done by various world collected artifacts, depositions, photographs, and ever it has been more accomplished by investigative common sense and on location applications via much Montana bob-cat and horse sense logic, as the book ever opts to explain some of the UN-canny nature of various other wild and domestic animals caught in the wake of the mystery, ever inclusive are the hard facts now conclusive in long existing plaster castings and other important artifacts unto viable explanations had from relative discoveries that evidence an existing real life feral wild man humanity of an Idaho cave vicinity numbering close at a dozen or more. Knowing that these creatures actually do exist, it is not all that hard for the author to continue to ascribe to this exploration while at the same time ever accessing all obvious now believed cause and effect of the monthly full moon phase upon these obscure relict's, as well as continue to document the full moons influence (All moon phase!) on feral man, and we current day Homo sapiens! Wild man explained here is simply a feral wild human that has remained that way by wanting description almost since man's most ancient of ancient origin, and as said they still are here with us at obscure places of the world living in parallel right along side of modern humanity! I have actually been most fortunate to have seen these wild forest people myself, and each time had with me one or more credible witness; I have encountered these wild hominids on three separate occasions, happening uncanny each time, near not even close in time or proximity to the other over more than fifty plus years of arduous exploration.

What will be especially considered in this, manuscript are the many various antiquated moon phase inspirations, customs, and abstract and UN-orthodox adherence, and possible idolatrous worship anomalies probable that are/could be a probable cause and effect, etc., to need warrant wild populations to continue for hundreds of years to want/think be needing to be plaiting the mane of any horse? Cited ahead are some of the obvious reasons of/for the possible worry effect that may at least explain on part of the strange anomaly? The full moon definitely and obviously has its known and un-suspected effects on feral wild hominids exactly or similar as it has on modern man! As unorthodox as all of this may sound to some it will be much much more {However difficult!} explained ahead.

At least for now in the author's opinion, the strange almost to be appearing as if magical; all of this looks to me as if to be a required carry-over thought dutiful obligation, had most hard to accomplish, all of it believed to be the difficult braiding the wanton workings ("Whatever the reasons?") of feral hominids! This is not your ordinary Saturday night read to be explained by the mentality of a critic as might be Bart Simpson... If anyone reading thus far remains in doubt of the book's validity, "them perhaps much self-adorned in some dubious, moot, narcissistic, "Been there and Done that, Non-thinking Attitude;" and actually by that ignorant denotation has done next to nothing at all, well, not for your sake, but for another, "toss the book that, that another may find it... as this mystery has continued unexplained for countless hundreds of years, and what is even more uncanny, "it has been done each and every single month to a close date and time of the year regardless of hell or high water, weather conditions, etc., and now it has been discovered that for some reasons it has continually been accomplished at or very close or a much similar night visit seemingly required at the time sequence of a definable full moon....!"

What anyone will believe true or not of this high strange anomaly, somehow to fact over the past eighteen months running under tight scrutinize, it has re-occur on a regular basses each month of the year, during each and every full moon phase as nearly as the author and at least a mega number of other people can discover on a norm! As said, this has occurred almost since man's first attachment to horses! What actual physical entity if not a wild human.. ("As the book goes on to well explain the plausible answers?") ..could be doing this? The quest to explain this mysterious anomaly is hardly over! This particular book research will end midnight, December (21 – 28), 2012! Its final pertaining entry to discovery will be added upon by the author sometime mid February 2013. Because of all new possible discoveries being investigated even as I write, there may need follow a sequel?

"Chung He Fat Choy, Little Mouse,
And A Very Happy Chinese New Year!

Hawaiian Island horses will continue to be evaluated on the Big Island of Hawaii,
possibly at the, Parker Ranch, as of April-May, 2013. Aloha, one and all!"

x

AUTHOR'S NOTE

Today is February 20th, 2013. Over the week ahead by the 28th, I will have required of myself to had completely re-written this nine years long study manuscript, as my final intentions will have needed to eradicate well over half of its now existing 750 pages! That done, all necessity of further edit for it to make any sense for publication. The pity, as all more of the abstract book data had much interesting importance, however for time, space, and all creature expectations, there is no other recourse but to continue this treatise by allowing myself one per cent writers license, and another one percent of fantasized projection in order to logically complete the complicated story to be interesting, as it believe me was a very, very, difficult paper to write, "especially when considering that I do not apologize for what cannot be avoided in the book's rough-shod delivery, as admittedly from here forward the manuscript did need however painful to be re-written; now its unavoidably, completely backwards, upside down, much jumbled, and when first read by anyone, will all need be done out of the purpose of its necessity, as it is not intended to be a definitive academic comparative paper nor is it a moot debate, and to some many initially the story might be at first thought; {"in particular persuasive excerpts"}, to have been written perhaps much too repetitious, however done that way in order to wander its true course "somewhat awry" until anyone finally becomes able to get the complete gist and message, and/or by then be able to fully appreciate the true crux of the complete adventure abrupt its pseudo complicated presentation, had much difficult for time and space to have completed it in slated time! There was far enough of that problem especially if/when one needs to be 24/07 physically active in the field as a decisive vagabond, cave explorer, and avid wild hominid investigator, and now over this sojourn to be further, "horsing around with horses," even that was done to my wandering disadvantage, as there continues but little time and space, or even a compatible place to opt to write my memories, and SO, often as not in all actuality, out of dire necessity, some of my best kept and important notes went down first time roughly scribbled on a handy slice of a cardboard box, or its equivalent on a collected tree leaf, chunk of bark, or even sometimes on a discarded gum wrapper!"

"No man is an Island:
however I have continued life long to pretend so!"

Well, readers, with that said, provided any wish to continue reading from here; over these ship-wrecked pages ahead, you will read exactly what truth of the plaiting has been discovered by who, how, where, and when, and all of the while be needful to allow that the author is ever first, last, and continues to be an investigative field explorer or of the unexplained and unknown, and I only become a writer out of the dire necessity want'n to get'er all down in manuscript before I myself become but another forgotten memory known to only to wolves and bears; as it is the fact that "the wild fascination Tiger," that guards the many, many, remaining unsolved mysteries of the past and present to include plaiting has for many years thrust its long sharp claws deep into my curiosity admission!

I cannot easily seem to break free of all exhilaration yet to be had from all new and exciting important discoveries still possible! My only true adversary is myself, when realizing my failing physical abilities, that of late continue to be taking there toll abrupt all latent, and current scars had of the obvious injuries of life's ardent requirement, "simply explained that way for the lack of a better, or more true explanation? All need ever be aware of what ever you dream for, and consider your particular age restriction, as all true exploration has an unavoidable price to one day need pay the very last debtor/fiddler, and much more perhaps in physical degeneration if any are particularly active and continue moot in painful and/or physical mishap abrupt all seasonal out-door rough-shod exposure!

"There still are a few holes in the canyon wall, where a wild man can crawl, as yet the government hasn't got them all! Some many people drink to sorrow, some few others drink like there is no tomorrow, or some lucky to the good times; but I pose my passion toast to the fascination of a new and better year, to especially to all of those truly exciting people, truly able to ignore all boring moot critic; the ones among us still able to hear the magic call of all truly UN-hampered excitement, and appreciate the wonder of all unfathomed adventure! Some many, of many, who have traveled and explored along side me write with me in fact and spirit by proxy and are a real living working part of this manuscript. Without their unconditional support, dedication, and equally stubborn patience, all passé important research would have likely gone a-miss! We had all often agreed, that some things are best left un-divulged! In case that I had never told you, enough or any of you during those bad, hard, and good times; it is so, because I still receive your phone calls...

"We had ever unconditionally bonded, as if all rascal were a true family, and I darn well will forever love you all! After all said, eternity is in the mind! Friendship and love are all another voyage into living fact, had within all fantasy of vast Exunda, that is the place of lost sundowns, inviolate memories, and where ever one gets lost in fond retrospect...

"It is better to have gone there, than not have done that!"

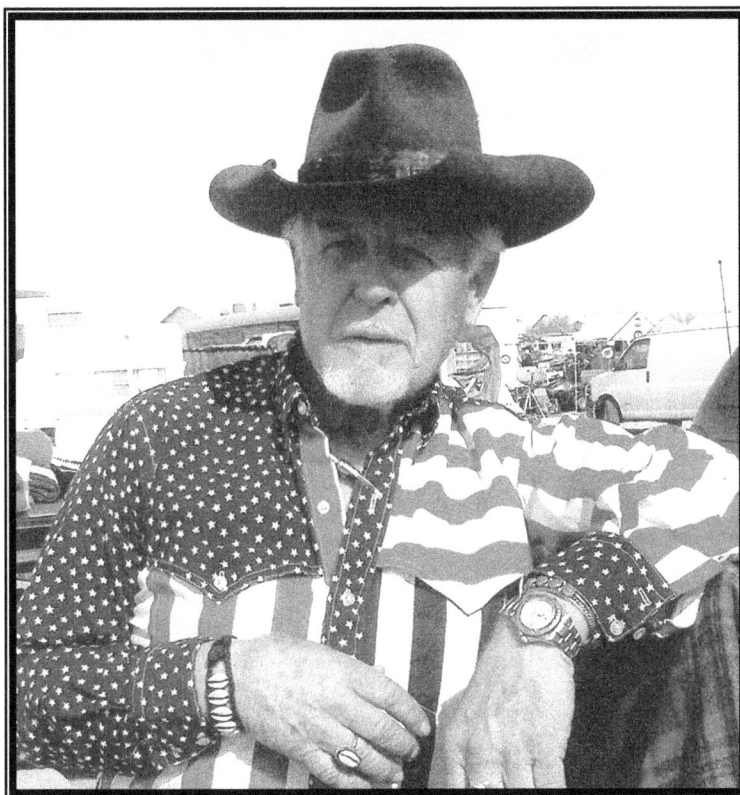

Donald L. Monroe

For correspondence, send a self-addressed, stamped envelope, to:

Donald L. Monroe, P. O. Box 18, Lima MT. 59739.

Will answer all serious mail.

Understand that with busy schedule it takes about four weeks for reply.

THE BRAIDED HORSES ARE COMING

Figure 1. Strands of the mane are twisted together and knotted at the bottom, forming a loop. In this knot, the hair appears to be doubled back on itself. We should ask whether this all could be formed by the forces of wind and weather or it would require a willful and skillful agent to create it.

PART ONE

PLAITING

"From America, Russia, China, and all lands beyond!"

"A Sasquatch Trilogy Book"

Plaiting

"What are the reasons for the high strange braids known as plaiting being left on world horses? This has continued being done unexplained for hundreds of years over America, Russia, China, Eurasia, and many lands beyond! The book explains the belief in a strange unknown feral wild hominid population likely to be responsible for the plaiting!"

Figure 2. Inspecting the tightly formed loop in a feral horse's mane.

Photo T. Mauney, June 7, 2011.

"Why, Really, Are These Strange Braids Being Left On Any Horse?"

This book explains the actual existence of a high strange and unexpected wild hominid humanity, that is believed roaming over North America and similar in other places of the world. It describes the next to impossible high strange elongated plaiting believed being left behind by these wild people on wild desert mustang and domestic horses. As said, this uncanny anomaly has gone on unexplained for hundreds of years. The book is written without chapters, as all facts of it are down verbatim with very little corrective editing just exactly how, when, and where happened. "This was the most difficult book that I never had expected to need to write. The book if want can begin confused on any opened page, as its on location dyslexic message and mixed bag adventure will begin! This discovery and all elaborate full moon theory has proved able to partly explain it! The nine year long difficult adventure now re-evaluated completely reopens Pandora's Box!"

Figure 3. An apparently feral horse encountered near the Salmon River in the Klamath Mountains of Northern California with a tightly twisted or braided loop in his mane. Notice how smooth and straight the rest of its mane lies. If this were wind tangled, wouldn't the rest of the mane show it?   Photo T. Mauney, June 7, 2011.

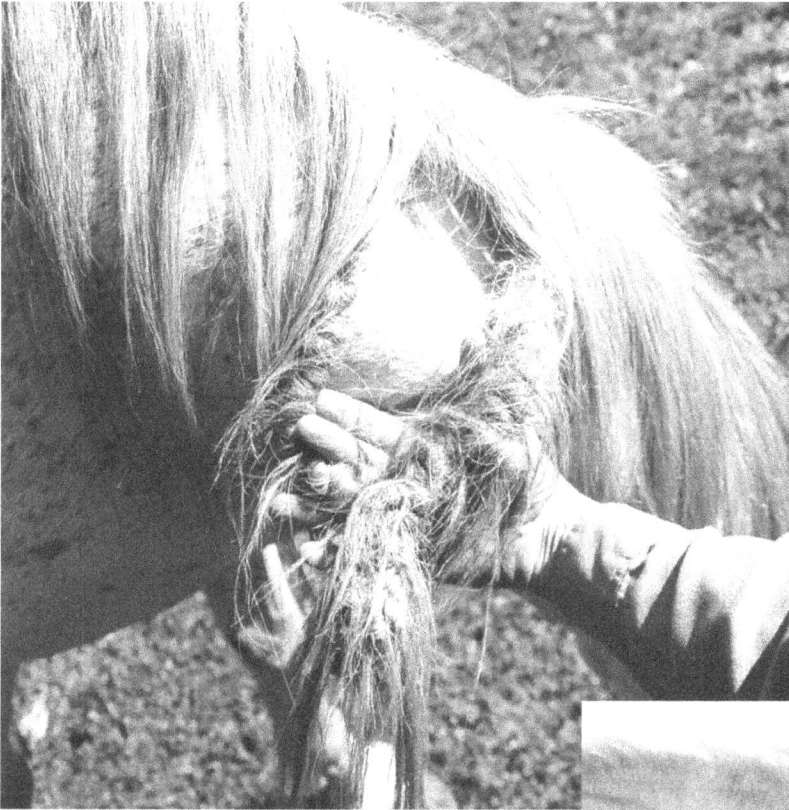

Figure 4. This loop is so tightly braided that it feels quite strong, although the tufts sticking out make it appear a bit fuzzy in photographs. This location is roughly 40 miles south of the famous part of Bluff Creek in Northern California. Photo by T. Mauney, June 2011.

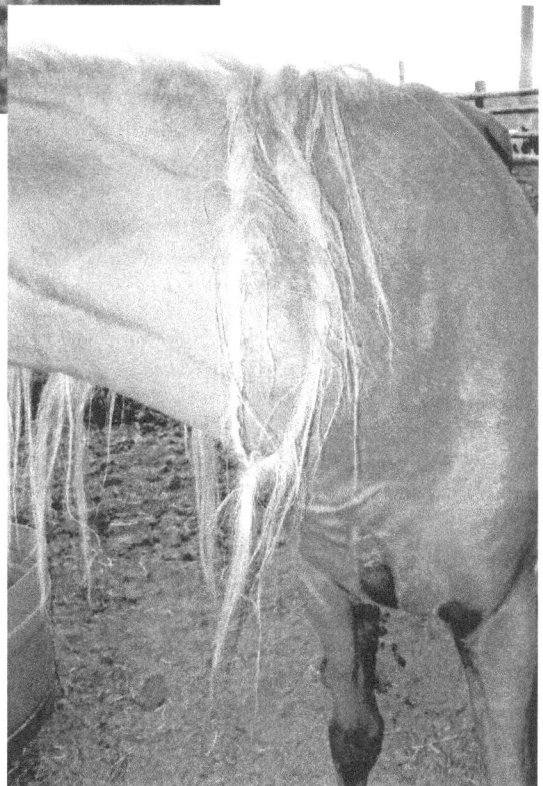

Figure 5. A long loop twisted into the mane. Strange? Is it just a wind tangle, or is it intentional? Notice that the strands appear to twist in opposite directions (outward).

3

Log: "Saddle up!"

"Next we are looking for wild horses with, Kathy Seavey, and wild Nevada Opal Joe Stromer!"("Tonight we are at Soldier Meadows, Black Rock Desert, Nevada.") "Hey Stromer! Hey guys...! Kathy, look! Look over there! (Pointing!) Do you see them? Do you see those running mustangs? Those wild horses are coming hard and fast towards us on the run! And, what is it that we are see hanging down from off them? "Something looks amiss, and far out of place? What are we seeing? What the heck is that long scraggly hair stuff hanging down, and flitting wild and free on the wind along side of them? Those manes look much too ragged! They are way, way, too long and gruff to be possible? Some of those horses with their loose manes look almost air-born as if flying on the wind! Hell Joe, do you see that? Hell, some of those manes appear to have been braided; or somehow they have been elongated? How is that possible? And what in the name of discovery are all of those strange wild devilish looking things riding on their back? What the hell are those guys? Kathy, are they man or beast? Wow princess... Look behind them, there looks to be a mounted Vaquero riding after them fast and furious, as if he is wanting to catch them? "Don, Kathy said, did you hear what he was saying as he passed by? Well, to me it sounded just as if he were calling out, or shouting something having to do with some woman named,*

Figure 6. "Behind them there looks to be a mounted vaquero...."

Art by Phil Jenson.

"LA LLORONA!"

"Hey wild Joe, have you ever heard of her? He said that he hadn't! And next he smiled as if all knowing! Joe just like the plaiting, was ever a paradox! Anyway, he said, look, more horses are coming! Perhaps watch for her?"

What, really, To Say Of Plaiting? Why Do IT?

Another time said, to have plaited a horse's mane, is to have cleverly braided it, as perhaps done with the intention and purpose of parading the animal public? Horse hair being as it is very coarse, at best it is difficult to manage, and especially hard to braid, and if it need be tied-off at its long ends, or into a tight square knot it is very difficult. The high strange anomaly of night braiding of mains and all its unexplained reasons has been deemed another wonder of the world, and as of the result of this long research probe it may prove to be the One, and only One, highly plausible projection ever to surface, and in time may prove to open the long closed doors of this almost mythological if it not found to be another magical UN-explained mystery, even if not here and now been included what more strange anomaly probability that we now are aware of that is also being more considered that has thus far been omitted... Nevertheless what is here down for the record may prove to be the only true important and a very first stepping stone into all future plaiting discovery that will completely jam wide open the long locked doors of Pandora's mysterious Box?

"These Many, Many, Plaited Horses Are Very Strange Indeed!"

... and this plaiting has continued regardless of all far off ranch and/or urban location all over western America; it has been done in all weather, conditions, season, etc., with not one single clue ever as yet to explain one real small bit part of it! If not what follows it is but very close to the first beginning?

(The Full Moon Of December, 2011!)

Log: Deposition: Jenson Ranch Property

Owyhee River, OR., with Phil Jenson.

Author: This next is a two years running combined interview had of wrangler Phil Jenson, then with me at his ranch location at Owyhee River Oregon, deposition first time taken was, December 13th, 2011 – and the second time, one year in time exactly synonymous to the exact same calendar dates of both years running each abrupt a full moon phase plaiting re-concurring again on, December 29th, 2012! Better said, following is a combined deposition, taken deliberately exactly one year apart from the first deposition date and time, each plaiting date confirming with the second, as witnessed by Phil Jenson!

Phil's candid response to all questioning is much typical of most all persons questioned over the past nine years! ..."Well Unk, he said, I know that you are onto something, but I just don't know what more to say about all of this? I have never seen anything quite like any of this strange stuff ...? No, I have no idea how our horses get strangely braided, and especially elongated many times, again, and again, year after year this has

Figure 7. Even as a boy, Phil was a natural horseman.

5

happened, without anyone ever having one valid clue! Especially the plaits have re-occurred on our Blazer mare, "Hink," and as you know, it has been again in several new braids only last night! This has been done at times on our other horses too... Well, the white mare died about one year ago. Back then, both of them we would always know would get it done to them on a very same night! This stuff is much more than just strange?Sometimes it takes several nights to completely happen! (Be Completed!) We just can't believe any of it... But as you well know, all of this is for real! "It definitely is not being done by the wind either! The wind sure as heck can't braid, or can it be tying every time the exact same looking knots all done in a same tight row!

Just look closely at all of these tightly done hard tied knots! Every one of them is repetitious, and it's very difficult to try to untangle each knot! Some of them seem to have been done for some reason as if in a purposeful long row? I myself am well adapt to braid just about any material known to a ranch, and to try to plait horse hair would be about the most difficult, as it is very course and tough! To think to be braiding something like that in the cold wind and rain of any season, and to do it at late night, would be you'd think.... It would be about the most diffi-

Figure 8. Phil Jenson's white mare with several loops plaited in her mane, Oregon, 2011.

cult thing ever, that anyone would want to try to handle! And besides, even if the wind could account for any of this ... and it doesn't! Well hell, there has been no significant wind around here for a very long time! Maybe a lot of weeks! This sort of braiding stuff is very difficult to do! And just look at it again, all of these knots, are all of them almost the exact same sort of knots...! Every one of them has been tied off the same at their long extreme end, and each is done in a very much a same way? It just makes no sense Don? It makes one wonder (Tongue in cheek?), well, just exactly... Just as if it all of it hasn't been done exactly in the way that it looks... "You know, it looks very much like as if it were done by something human?

Well I'd say, if you ask me, it much looks just as if all has been done by some sort of an obscure magic ritual, or maybe something much similar to anyone's abstract imagination? A lot of strange stuff that few people realize goes on in today's world! That magic stuff idea really makes no sense either? As, all of us around here including Marvin and Diane Hollens, and that other guy down there at the lower ranch that owns the place... Well, none of them, or any of us have any idea how its been done! Marvin sometimes feeds our horses... When he's around, he keeps a close watch! Marv is sharp... he's not seen nothing! Mom, me, you, John and Sheri, them, that guy, and all of the many more that have seen these braids... Well, none of them has one more idea of how to explain it either? Yeah, by now we all agree," this all seems to happening at a very close same date and time of each month of a new full moon! What more have you found out to explain any of this?" (Sheri Jenson's, much, much, more than an uncanny and incredible experience/story is written somewhere ahead!)

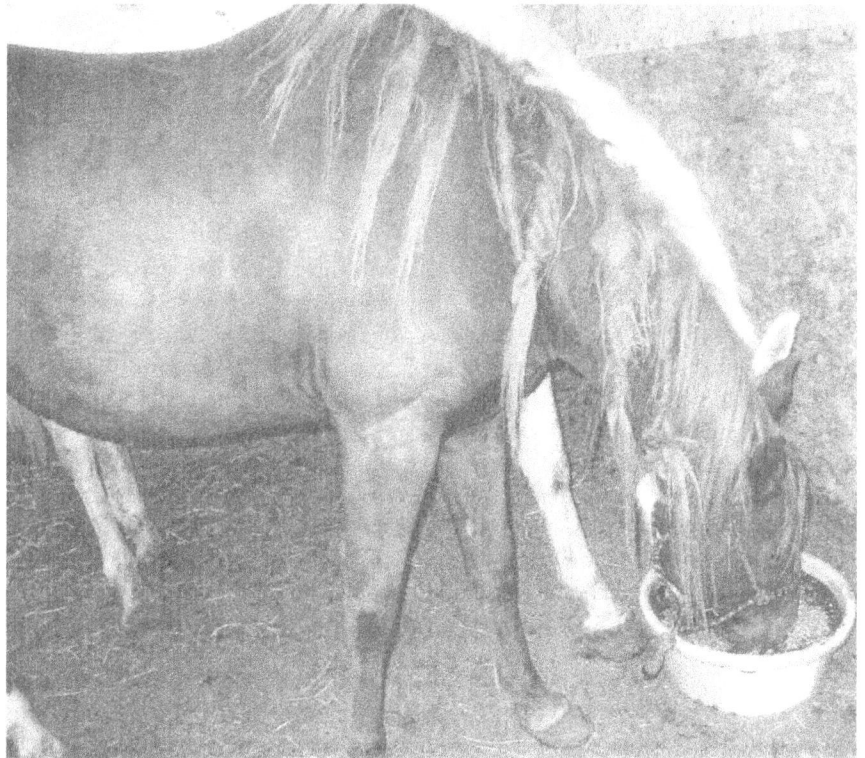

Figure 9. Hink on Dec 13, 2011, with three loops braided in her mane on the right side, feeding, with the white mare behind her.

The Full Moon!

As you will read, after all arduous research done over the past 9 years in regard to plaiting, and especially now over the past 13 months running Now 17!), ... the strange plaiting has continued each and every late night on one or more particular horses every new full moon phase over a vast portion of the far west where I have also been keeping close contact over several distant apart ranch lands of Idaho, Montana, Oregon, etc. This strange anomaly has continued to happen eve-

7

rywhere without fail! If not it done each and every time exactly on time and on a exact same horse, then it's done on another. However on all ranch-lands including the Jenson property, once in a while due to a particular calendar moon phase missed monthly running; due to the calendar

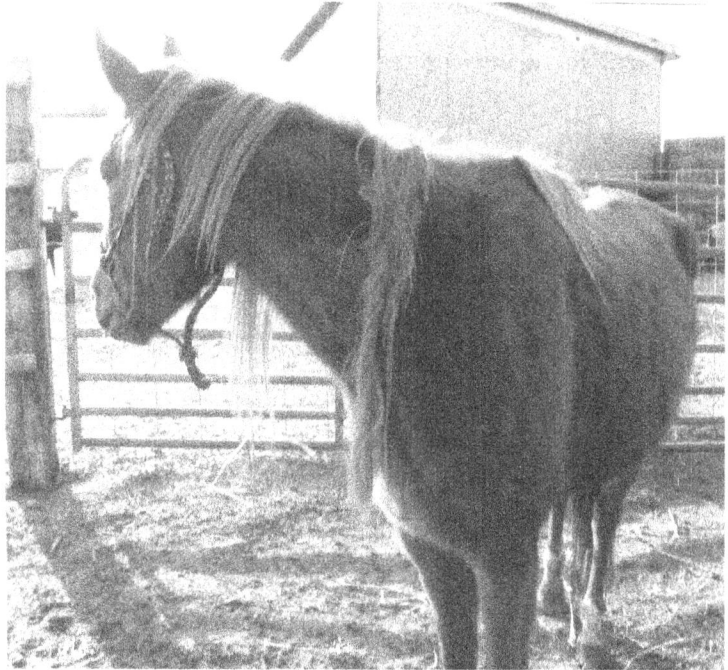

Figure 10. Hink with renewed braids a month later, and now on the left side, Jan 13, 2012.

overlap of logged time variations of numbered days in a month; after say in just a few days either way to reasoning, it all happens all over again regardless! During some months of the calendar year there includes an additional full moon phase. Most new moons happens every 28 days. Considering leap year, many centuries, times and calendar dates that over lap, the change pace of the moon can be determined if watched close... It is to remembered that mankind invented a need for a calendar to calculate time! Before that what, really, was time to anyone? With particular indigenous peoples of South America, time has no measure, and so in that way time with them stands still. This time conjecture, space timing of plaiting, wild man, and witch-women peculiarity, and much more beyond actually having to with Moon phase to explain the plaiting is still under study. What now may be found incredible in time may rock the foundation of cryptic hominid study? If fully understanding the difficulty of plaiting, nothing seems impossible!"

Most manes measure at 9 – 14 inches, some longer, hardly shorter. If a mane has been brushed out just prior to a full moon it is all the more likely that the plaiting will re-occur almost at once or very soon after. Sometimes for what ever the reason some persons charged with watching a horse become incompetent, and so after a week or two, it becomes very easy to miss the fact that the previously plaits have in any way changed, been re-braided, etc. Sometimes it is hard to detect that they have been only very slightly messed with, and in that way all has gone completely unnoticed by a lackadaisical attitude. Ranchers have limited time to be inspecting each and every horse on the property, especially if not all that interested or been convinced. Unless anyone has actually tried to call the attention of any busy rancher, or even think to easily gain his permission to wander their ranch lands, or convince them of your project importance, you have no idea of the extreme difficulty! An impatient rascal might even decide to break out his shotgun!"

The Lunar Theory, and Other Beliefs!

If this effort will not prove to substantiate at least a part of my ongoing Lunar theory, or establish a reasonable assumption of the true existence of feral hominids, it will not the matter, as by the very nature of what has already been discovered true it will have been very close. After the book's final computation January 1, 2013, I plan to continue only candid research similar, as other dissimilar interests need take priority, however my extended curiosity leaves many unanswered questions. If this plaiting is not truly being done by these smaller relict hominids as described, then it might be being accomplished by an even much smaller unrealized facet of humanity, that is completely unsuspected, as for most people today little people are thought to be completely moot and impossible, especially this is the case over most all of North America. Does anyone remember the small people known as the Flores ions, now extinct from memory since about the latter part of the 17th Century, that livid and survived right along side of the dread Komodo Dragons on the South Pacific Island of Flores? Well, according to particular Native American opinion, they well know, believe, and even sometimes fear a much similar humanity? And there are beliefs within the stories of the peoples living on the slopes of Mt. Shasta, Adams, Rainier, Hood, and others as are the Idaho Black Foot Indians that also attest of there existence, including the Nevada Paiute at Pyramid Lake, the Lumi of Washington, and many others. How many people today that have rural or wilderness property; how often do you actually see any real number of the white tail deer population that daily leave the many thousands of tracks over your lawn, garden, and/or drive way? Who reading has ever seen a true set of house mouse tracks, or found the remaining bones of a bear, Mt. Lion, etc? What, really, describes elusive, blind, irregular, impossible, unless it is people themselves. Later you will read of the documented case of a true relict feral hominid when we slightly touch upon the discovery of the Wisconsin Ice Man!" (Doctor Isaac Sanderson, 1967!)

"Pandora's Box"

"Perhaps This Manuscript Truly Is, And Perhaps Not, The One And Only Logical Key That Will Finally Prove To Open Pandora's Locked Box Of Questions Able to Answer or Explain Plaiting?"

If So, or Not, Let's Go There!

Log: Suzette Brantley, June, 2011, Klamath Mountains, California.

Thad and I had several days of unallocated time on a business trip to Tacoma, WA. Since we were planning an excursion with Don Monroe in the Klamath Mountains of Northern California, we decided to adventure on to scout it out. Some of the roads were still snowed over up high, so we couldn't access our original destination. We found ourselves at Nordenhiemer Campground near the village Forks of the Salmon. It was early evening, early June, and it was pouring rain. We got set up and had intention of making a fire, but

Figure 11. Suzette quickly has the feral horses eating out of her hand.
Photo T. Mauney.

9

the kids at the neighboring camp saw us coming and rounded up all the firewood from all the empty sites. A little peeved , tired, and insistent that I must have a fire, I set out to the campground attendant's abode to beg for firewood. There was a fence of steel re-bar and nylon rope around his little yard. I stalled at his barricade and called to see if anyone was there. The campground host came out explaining that he had to rope off his space because of the feral horses would come through and wreck his vehicle and yard.

How EXCITING! Wild horses! A fairy's dream! So I immediately started sending them "messages" to come visit. Day 1, it was late and wet, Day 2 was sleeping late, a romp in the forest, collecting rocks & panning gold, and an ice cold bath in the river. Day 3 we wake early, Thad unzips the tent and peeks out. "Guess what is outside" he said. My eyes widened as I knew what he was saying but in disbelief I had to see for myself, so I peeped out to see what filled my eyes with tears of joy that they had come.

I skipped the coffee and cigarette, grabbed a bag of carrots and went off to introduce myself.

Greeted by the largest stallion, we friended up quickly as the carrots were good currency. Soon I was surrounded by horses. They were very sweet, and soon we had my hair brush out and were having a lovely experience with these beautiful creatures.

Then we found a braid on the white one!

Figure 12. Examining the braid in this white horse's mane.   Photo T. Mauney.

Log: Thad Mauney, June 7, 2011

The nights had been very wet and chilly. It was early summer but in the drizzle it didn't feel like it. The nights were very dark, just after new moon with heavy clouds to block the starlight. When the rain finally quit and the morning light on the tent hinted of actual sunshine, I opened the fly and peered out. I knew Suzette would be delighted that the horses had come. So very quietly I let her peek out, and you should have seen the smile: "Horsies!!!" It didn't take but a couple of minutes for her to have them eating out of her hand. Before long they were happy to have both of us brushing them down with her hairbrush (it will wash). Obviously they were familiar and comfortable with humans, loafing in the campground and munching the spring grass like it was

Figure 13. Carrots and grooming, won them over, or was it just Suzette's love?   Photos T. Mauney.

11

their own meadow. As the campground host said, they seem to be feral, meandering up and down several miles of the Salmon River valley here.

Of the dozen or so horses in this herd, one lightly dappled white one had a strong loop twisted into his mane. Amazing! This looked very well crafted. The loop was attached partway up the neck, lay on the right side, and hung down a bit longer than the rest of the mane. The two attachment points were 2-3" apart, and the opening of the loop was 9-10". The forward strand of the loop was about twice as thick as the rearward strand, and the two combined at the bottom to form a cylindrical portion about 3" long and 1¼" to 1½" in diameter with feathery tufts hanging below. The entire structure was quite firm to the hand, but the tufts of loose hair sticking out make it look fuzzy in the photos. In the hand it wasn't mushy at all; the strands were tightly wound so that it made a double twist (spiraling on itself like a telephone handset cord). The forward strand appeared to be made from two twists, the rearward of just one, and at the bottom of course all three came together with the end wrapped back into the coil to finish it. There may also have been a knot, but I did not attempt to unravel this structure, so I cannot say whether there was knotwork in addition to twisting. (Compare this structure to the illustration from Russia in a later section.

The form of this loop did not appear to involve any right-left overlaying like the three-strand braid we humans use to make pigtails or a queue, nor the four-strand plait used to make lanyards. Nonetheless, it appeared to have been purposely and skillfully done, so I have no objection to using the terms braiding or plaiting for this structure. I cannot imagine how wind or running through brush could have created such a structure. In fact, going through brush would more likely undo a loop than form it. As the photos show, there were no other significant tangles in this horse's mane; his hair is wiry enough to lie flat.

If someone wanted to use a loop like this as a lead or halter for riding, grasping the thick forward part in the palm would let the smaller back part lie across the back of

Figure 14. This loop is quite strong. The front strand is about twice as thick as the back strand, and even the bottom could be a good handhold.

Photo by T. Mauney, June 7, 2011.

the hand. One could also grab the cylindrical part at the bottom, which is readily accessible while standing on the ground.

As I walked around petting, brushing, and photographing this horse, I contemplated this structure. It could not be formed at that length from the mane hair alone. The extra length had to come from somewhere. I couldn't see any chopped down parts of the mane, yet it was all of the same color, so it might be from the horse's own tail. Close inspection of some photos shows a small tuft of short hair at the top of the tail, but whether that is due to clipping or due to natural growth and breakage patterns is yet to be determined.

Because women often braid "inserts" into their hair to make their hairdo longer, It is easy to imagine that the maker of the loop might twist up a piece of tail hair, cut it off, then twist it into the mane to get the desired length of loop. What to cut it with is open to question, but broken glass or flaked rock cutting tools could easily do it, and even certain plant leaves have sufficiently sharp edges to saw hair.

As soon as we got back into cell phone range (no reception out there) I phoned Don to report the observation. He was excited, of course, that we had seen this in person. When I brought up the "Tail Hair Insertion Hypothesis" he got even more excited! "Yes!" Suddenly a lot more things fit. Long braided loops were found all over but how they could be made so large was unexplained. Adding tail hair makes sense of it.

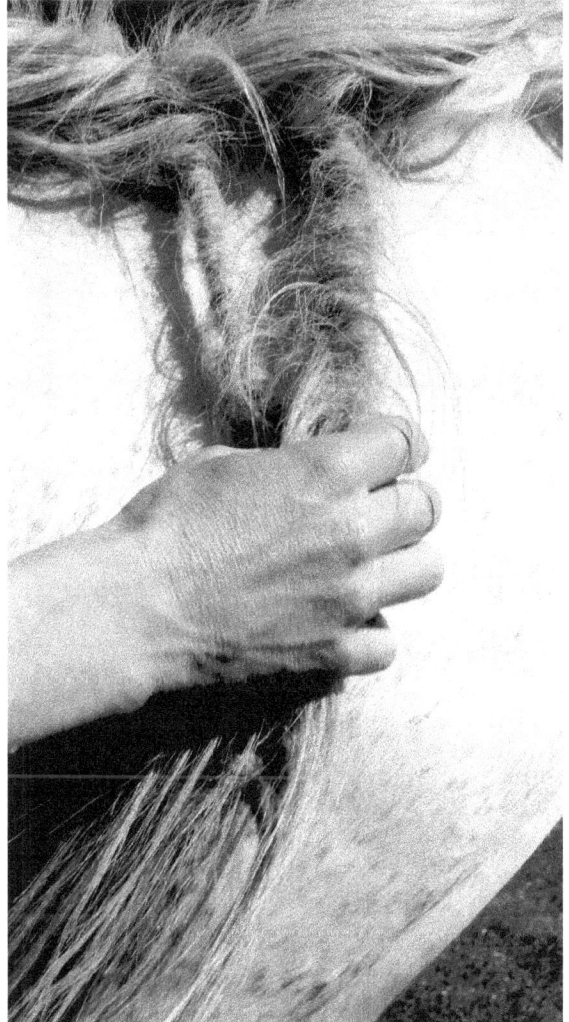

Figure 15. The thick cylindrical part at the bottom could also be used as a handhold.
Photo T. Mauney.

13

Log: Thad Mauney, Carbon County, Montana, August 8, 2011

On the road west from Bridger, Montana, toward the Pryor Mountains we came over a small rise and spotted three horses loafing alongside the road, so of course we slowed up to greet them. As before, Suzette had befriended them within minutes. I quietly got out of the car and joined them. Sure enough, one had a nice braid in its mane. He was big bay with a nice black mane. As we ambled around with them we were able to inspect it closely. As we stayed with them, more showed up on the other side of the road. All were branded, but they were far from any ranch house. We were at a watering hole out on the range, and we had chanced upon it just when these horses were making their visit. The more we looked, the more braids we saw. In total there were nine horses in the herd, of which five had braids! Some really liked human attention, others were offish, but none ran from us. Eventually the cattle started coming in for water and the horses wandered away.

Figure 16. In the valley of Clark's Fork of the Yellowstone River, Carbon County, Montana, we met a small herd of horses with five of the nine carrying loops braided into their manes. These are not as tight as on the white horse we met in California. Notice that the two sides of the loop seem to be twisted in opposite directions (outward from center) then joined at the bottom.

Photos T. Mauney.

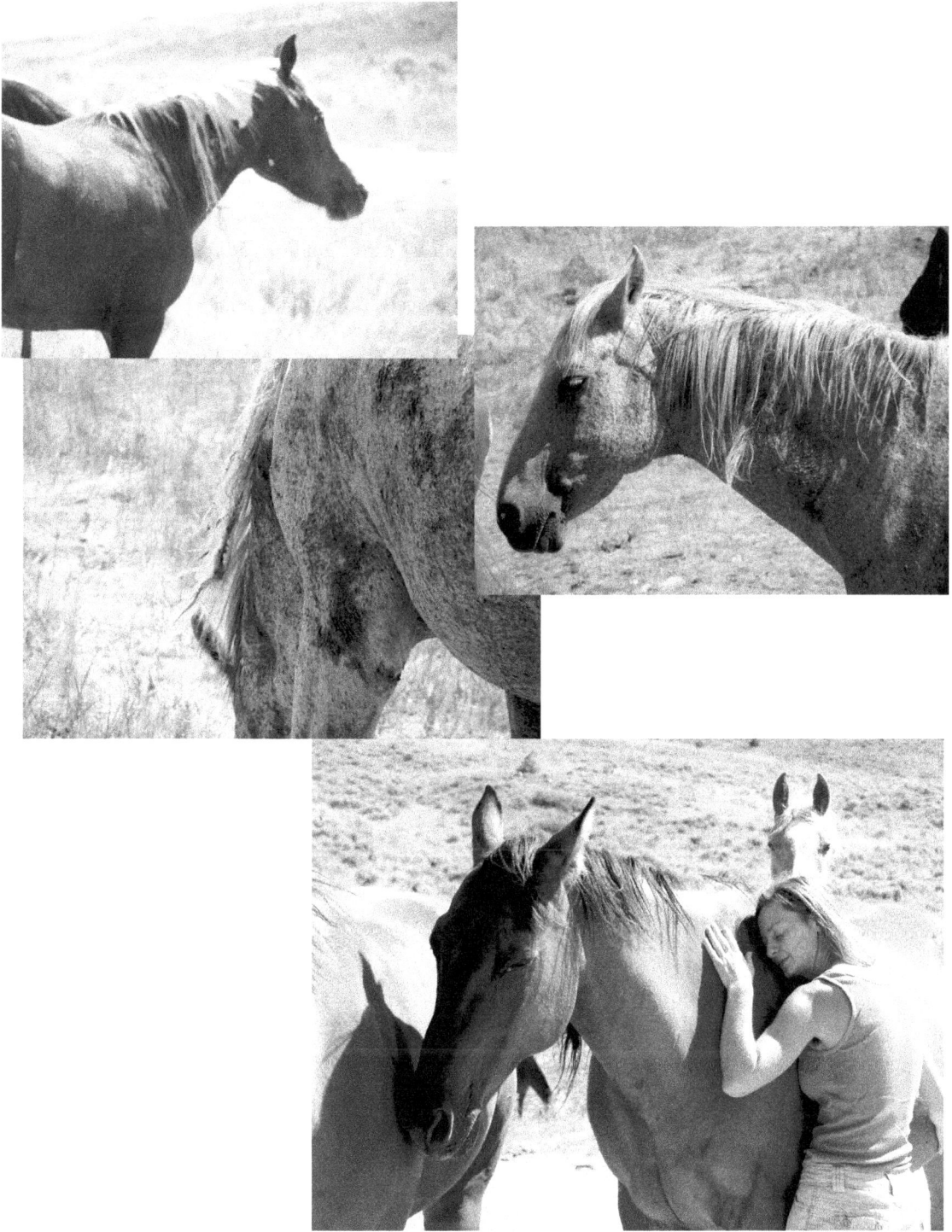

Figure 17. Five of the nine horses in this herd had braided manes. Notice the long thin loop on the paint in the top picture.   Photos T. Mauney.

Log: Candid deposition comments of Kathy-Jo Seavey

Sweet Home, Oregon.
December 6, 2012
Kathy Seavey

"Don, I am surprised that in such a short time as you were gone tonight that I have actually managed to read over the first twenty four pages of your manuscript. I had never heard of such a thing as plaiting! This moon theory really has aroused my attention! I was amazed at how much I read in 20 minutes! Hardly do I read most stuff half that long before falling asleep! This horse stuff really has me fascinated! What came to my mind was... well, I had a horse once myself, and when it laid on the ground, and roll-kicked around, its mane often got all tangled, very dirty, completely unmanageable, and extremely hard to comb out, etc! However those tangles never once looked anything like all of those cut samples that you have in that case. Don, did you notice, not one of those mane samples is one bit at dirty! How many did you say you have? Show me them again! You will see that every single one of them is almost as clean and shiny as my own hair! Wow, even it were half true that a horse's mane can get braided while its tossing around in the dirt, well as you can see, not one of them is one bit even dusty; and there is no dirty stuff as would be leaves, sticks, straw, and even much worse that is found in a barn yard would be on them! There is no chance that the wind and hanging brush has anything to do with this! This is the first I have heard or seen of this, and that is completely obvious!"

Yes Kathy, thanks I said, you are right! All of that you said hadn't yet occurred to me in quite that order, but what you have just noticed becomes very important and much meaningful to my theory, and would be to any intelligent public, as there are well near or over fifty count various cut mane samples in that box, and not one of them is anything but just short of being immaculate! Thanks sooo much for what you have just observed!

Its people like you that really matter in discovery…. "Next Kathy asked … What more all relative topics to plaiting and horses have been written in all of this story? There are a lot of pages! And you mentioned horse milk? What, really, do you think is doing all of this stuff? Do you really think it is being done by wild hominids? What actually is a hominid? Are there any around here?" Well Kathy, yes, and yes again, as a wilder hominid might include a similar sort as me! We humans are Homo sapiens! You and me, we are both a hominid, we are a people! Yeah, that's all, a feral wild man hominid amounts to a feral existing human sort population of a much mixed gene pool origins of wild people still living in parallel with us today! Perhaps they would be better understood, as you think of them as an obscure unknown relict human race, that is perhaps an extension of mixed yesteryear gene pools with current day DNA etc!

All humans are hominids, however a humanoid is completely different and can perhaps be best explained in simple terms; they are slightly, or even very much different in looks from a human in all obvious sexual dimorphism, as includes similar facial comparisons as has any of the great apes as are Orangutans, Chimps, or especially the Gorilla, etc! A humanoid is anything resembling the looks of a human, or it can be said humongous; even a filthy rich mentally disturbed lawyer, looking liken-to a big dumb ass monkey wearing a necktie and a grimace-smirk on his face behind a 20 dollar cigar, could easily pass for an ugly ape-looking humanoid: especially this so when the ugly troglodyte attorney insists to be defending the ugly-coward bastard humanoid that is now hand-cuffed down at the city jail, that just broke some old woman's nose while stealing her purse! Anything and everything Kathy, that might look to us as if it were one bit less adapt than has today's fast being lost mentality that is not all that much different as was considered the Chimpanzee, Oliver? Oliver remember was the unexplained human looking chimp that aired mid year, 2001, and prior some say, on the television show, Unsolved Mysteries! Oliver was discovered sometime during the later 19th Century, etc! He has quite a long story history, you should have a look!"

Kathy looked back at me laughing in innocent woman surprise while asking…"Well Don, what more wild discoveries do you think will be made in your future that will more explain all of this strange plaiting anomaly?" I don't know I told her, as its a long hard road! But no doubt if anything significant is found in future it will have started with this manuscript, as it is the first of its kind with this theory, and follows closely about everything that has never before been realized, or even considered as comes from Montana bob cat, and fur trapper opposed logic, cougar cave existence, and later in the manuscript is the humorous side of all story, with considerable California beach-bunny mermaid type compassion and humor, had via much Onya Tiger Cat opinion/reaction, and female displayed tenacity done in hard evidence of claw scratches, soft and hard bites, frost bit fingers, and a small bit of South Pacific Theater Cannibalism, and Australian Native Aboriginal Southern Cross belief, and ever one of my favorite interests inclusive of all legionary and true facts had of Native American and late neophyte and mythological Chinese wrote history, and any number of other wanton relative sort type topics to be reconsidered of anything else that anyone opts to bring on-board the good ship, "Far Off The Wall USA?"

That said, this is a true book of out of the box experience via slight Montana pride, world accredited academic cooperation/non-cooperation abrupt maverick exploration/adventure, and particular cowboy discoveries, inclusive of much far sighted, back seat, and back fence, and wood pile logistics, and all notable horse happenings, had when venturing Montana to Mississippi and Florida, to include a short important and colorful sojourn had with re-capped Mexican bandits, while ever in search of more and better answers to plaiting, 2009 - 2010. And ever Kathy, the story continues in logical cow puncher, swamp rat opinion, and unless I opt to change my mind, "I will reluctantly share in its place, an all true, incredible high strange romantic love story adventure of sorts, had desperate of Onya when she subterranean and miserable, that is almost beyond descriptive exhilaration that will probably be little understood by anyone who has never ventured underground ecstatic while experiencing claustrophobic repercussions, and frightened enough in the wake of the threat of marauding mountain lions!

The question now posed, is how could anyone at all be happy while at a same moment unhappy, however with all of that strange and infatuated exhilaration; all fast changing flashlight wall shadows that were following along with her in an all true discovery mystery, had within all bleak, damp, and extremity dismal dark surroundings of a stark abyss-recesses of a little realized beautiful but also dangerous unstable Idaho mountain cavern, winter/fall, 2009 – 2010! And if time, space allowing, there may be included much more? If not there is enough here to fully explain all of what's pertinent to all theory. "Don, Kathy said, did you mention Mermaids?" Yeah, I did, but its used here only as an expression! You know, surfer-girls, beach-bunnies, mermaids, etc! "Don, that sounds like awesome fun, but really what was all of that trying to say written above that you just read me? What exactly did you say? If it will be of any help, I will let you use my 28 foot out-board/in-board boat? It easily sleeps six! Maybe you with your nautical friend, AZ., Gene Sheller, might even be able to discover a real mermaid? Some people out here in Oregon/Washington, Scotland/Ireland, Norway/Lapland, etc., actually do *believe that they very likely exist! What do you think?" (I don't!) "Well, babe, I said, I really don't know? But from cave evidence projections done in much pictographic art known of in places of Egypt, anyone would truly begin to need to wonder? This book is not the place for any further thought on that! But perhaps, and just perhaps? Kathy, have you ever heard of the beautiful ghost women La llorona?" ("Of course she hadn't!")*

Log: The gift given Tonia Two Feathers by the New Mexico Diablo, Fall, 2009 -

The Anasazi pottery sherd, plaiting, and the high influence of Tonia Brown upon Jim and Ellie Martinson, the Diablo, and our two new bandit friends, Poncho and Lefty, when at Deming, & Socorro, New Mexico -
&
"LA LLORONA,"

"After you told me about her, and her name, Tonia said, she was even a well known personage among the two Vaquero Mexican Bandit Owners of the little visited, Eli-Ranch' O, Diablo of Socorro! And Don, they said this Devil Women is as real as the old fable ghost story! I don't be-lieve that, but a lot of strange things do happen! Somehow long ago, she got separated from her handsome Conquistador lover, and so now she wanders forever as if a lost soul out on the far desert lands North of the wild Señora! This beautiful Devilish ghost women is ever in search of him! Often she is said to be riding hard bent to find him whenever she can catch a desert mustang! She has been said to have been seen many times on this ranch land! And so it has been named,

"The Eli Ranch' O Diablo!"

"That night at the bunk house the two colorful retired banditos told us more stories of the Diablo Women, and how we would become their first to witness the plaiting being done to their horses, and of course they told us all that they could about the Wind Devil, "or they said that it is a Wind Devil, or some kind of a Diablo sort of a wild man, or something strange that comes sometimes often to braid our horse? We do not know what it is?"

(Story Continued!)

"Jim & Ellie Martinson, Tonia, and the strange gift exchange!"

"'Plaiting Evidence Had Among The Bad Boys, And High Strange Unknown Feral Beings?" This is a most fortunate treasured gift story and discovery, as I still have its reward in safe keeping as the undeniable gift proof of this story in my collection! Our story continues concerning a very strange horse plaiting experience, happening late fall 2009, near the small berg cow town of So-corro New Mexico. Jim and Ellie Martinson whom had been my good friends of countless years, over breakfast at their home; Jim finally said, Don, this plaiting mystery truly is interesting and

Figure 18. Tonia, Wild Two Feathers Onya, Brown.   Photo by Author.

crazy stuff! I know of place where it is re-occurring repetitiously about every few weeks! This has been discovered again, and again, on a desert ranch just a bit east of here! Well, anyway we should go there, it is close by and near to Socorro! I know these two great guys... They actually are a couple of ex-Mexican Bandits, that got up here some way on the lam many years ago from Old Mexico! I am sure that they would love to meet Tonia.. They would love you for your knowledge of old guns and the Mexican West! We should take you guys out there and have a look! These guys are really great people! Just don't act like you might be a federal agent or some damn thing of a Federal lie, or these guys will have us all for supper, and feed you to their ducks! I've known them for a long time! These guys are right out of the rascally sorts of bandits as were Poncho Villa, & Viva Zappa! They will really love Tonia! She will need take care of herself! By now Don, with her traveling with you, I am sure she can well do it! Ellie thinks the world of them, and one of them speaks a little of her German! Guess you know that Maximilian of long ago left quite an impression on all southern Mexico?" This colorful story could write a complete novel! Well, first off we met the two ex-wild boy Mexicans, both of them we found out were once well respected caballeros! They left Mexico just shortly after the Mexican Revolution after taking part in raid on the US Army then in-camped at Douglas AZ. In 1911, and next, after that fiasco, rode north, went straight, and finally wound up on the lamb in New Mexico!

"Viva La Bandit o's!"

"On each of the two rascals weathered heads were proudly displayed a genuine American made Bailey straw hat, and each of them toted a small caliber semiautomatic pistol tucked in to the back waist back drop of their pants! They at once took us out to the holding corral where this strange stuff they said was being done... "by none other Amigo, than a very wild sneaky creature Diablo ("Devil")!" One of them explained in broken Spanish/English... "This you see, for sure, has been happening for a very long time! We do not know too, much, or how it is done, but hardly do they leave any tracks, more than just to disturbed the dust, as the wind blows hard a lot... and this Diablo mostly he comes to braid the horses exactly when it is very dark and the wind is very strong! They know how to avoid amigo! Yeah, they do it that way every time...! That direction over there, (Pointing!) is the way from where it comes and goes! It, is very much like a very smart wild hombre! But we are not afraid of hem, as they never stay, or do any one of us harm! But Amigo, it sometimes wants to steels from us our American tools! This one is a very bad hombre to do that! Yeah, he likes our hammers, and his crow bar? Sometimes we bring them food, and they are grateful? Anyway, best thing, they like our cornmeal pan cakes, and the, "muy e calianti Baja

Californian-havanyera hot sauce, even if it is much-o calianti and it burns them! And he eats every time just like a very hungry Desert Mountain Lion! Nothing is left!"

Log: At Eli Ranch O' Diablo!

Verbatim notes slightly edited, taken while on location where staying three nights at the, Eli' Ranch O' Socorro, close near by to, Socorro New Mexico, "with the two original prototypes, from the song, Poncho and Lefty!" We are here looking for plausible answers that might help explain this wild plaiting! Last night after hearing all of the most recent wild stories had from the two colorful amigos, insistent on their Tequila, and expensive Stella Artois beer, that for them was a mild chaser, along with all peppermint snoops that was offered Tonia, "while me offered that strong black gringo coffee amigo, or you can have much' O Coca Cola, that is the very finest thing for the strong evidence of Montezuma's Revenge Senior, if that is what has caught you?" After Jim had lost to them at Poker, Tonia and Ellie were instructed how to go carefully out to the horses, "and they left the Diablo much food from the box, and some of her trinkets from her purse to see what is happening in the morning? "Just as Jim had predicted, the demanding bandits out of kindness I suppose, "and a particular liking and appreciation for this red-headed gringo women right here, as they called her!" When speaking to me, one finally said... Amigo Don, we really do like this skinny women Onya... Only we do think that she is a part of an Indian like us! We have some many of these green eyed half Indian Ones like her down in Chihuahua too! They are very popular, and we spoil them... But this one I think is not too spoiled, and so we could keep her here for you... She has a very quiet and nice voice! Can she sing? We would let her talk and do that... Here amigo, take this banana out to her, maybe she is hungry?"

Log: The Next Morning!

It was most fortunate that we had arrived at the ranch during a full moon phase, as early this morning before anyone was awake, Tonia left the shack to discover that in exchange for the food, etc., she had received a treasure trove offering of a sizable piece of Anasazi pottery, that was a potsherd of high value, as pieces of very ancient fired clay vessels are very rare! The Anasazi race long pre-date most all known Native American Indian mixed gene-pool associations, as can be exemplified by the many Shoshone Tribal Nations that originated from memory in the Idaho/Montana regions from obscurity somewhere dated well into the last Ice Age on paper of what was the Pleistocene said lasted about 10,000 years, etc., but in spite

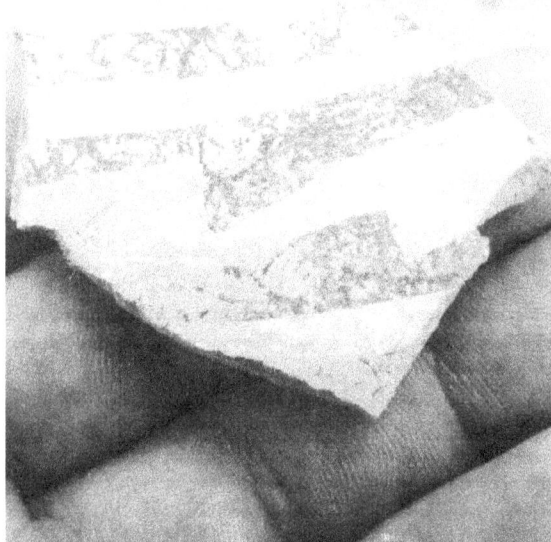

Figure 19. Anasazi, etc.! The potsherd Tonia found where the food and other gifts had been left.   Photo by Author.

of their antiquity they still are more recent to native American history than is the extremely an-cient Mme-bra culture that far precedes the Anasazi. Indeed she had been lucky! The pottery sherd can be seen pictured here. On our return trip back from Florida via M.K. Davis at Missis-sippi, we stopped again to visit Poncho and Lefty to re-discover that the same horse had been re-plaited again! Needless to say by then we had all become treasured friends, as each of us much the same well understood their own separate regional bobcat logic, differing only slightly from the in diversity abrupt south west cowboy rational, comparable via the time proven Ida-ho/Montana mountain cat, coyote, mink/muskrat trap-line, California beach ball tiger cat fe-ver, via proven values of common sense, etc. Well, we just all four of us had liked the guys!

Before driving off for a last time, Tonia gave the two rascals a last hug and a small box token gift left in ones hand! I never was able to learn exactly what the gift had been, but knowing her nature it had been something special! Early in my days, I had acquired a needful respect, love, and passion for particular places of Old Mexico while hitch-hiking miserable with Ed Neese across its vast Sonoran Desert form, Tijuana to Juarez, after having had a disappointing bull fighting miss-adventure with an irritated picador! I had explained some of this hair raising stuff to the aging bandits as we left, and they were still laughing when I told them that I was still a sick gringo from Montezuma's Revenge acquired all the way back to year 1992, when first time traveling with my late wife Marion over the High Sierra Madre Mountains. Marion at the time being Chinese, passed off convincingly (To some many marauding Yaqui caballeros!) as a highly important and beautiful Chinese Phoenix Bird Princess that she was! Every caballero, federal-lie, and potential Mexican bandit on the Easter Train Running then towards Los Mochis, was instantly captivated and in love with her! She was indeed a very pretty women, however she had only needed to put down One obnoxious admirer, "one and only time," with her con-vincing battery radio! All of that is another story, of another incredible life and great times! Marion when necessary could hard swing, and throw a mean rocking chair! So be it!"

"Tonia's last Tortillas!"

More Story: Upon our return arrival back to the bad land bandit boys; as said the same horse had been re-plaited, and almost at once they handed her two new cut off braid samples, had re-cently taken from their horse! It was obvious that they both had her respectfully wrapped around their lonely hearts, "as since having been raised in Southern California and many Mexicans, she could easily heart talk there separate innate totem ethnic language, and much understood their distant idiosyncrasies, learned of early life when she herself had sometimes been lonely and alone on the stark beach fronts in and around Pismo Beach, where she had acquired an obvious compas-sion and understandings for the hard working Mexican people;. She well knew their trauma, hard-ship, romance, good and bad karma, and all mischief had from all local pirate and Spanish -Indian fishermen beginnings had at Cannery Row; and had acquired considerable Chumash Native Indian lore, and somewhat understood all vast potential of the upper Sonoran and Southern Baja Califor-nia Desert premise. Before leaving the boys handed Tonia an arm load of flower tacos as we con-tinued swapping more yarns with the colorful rascals..."

At age 16, when I had aspired to a low rating of a wanna-be, failed gringo, Tijuana Picador, before being almost maimed by a training bull, and later need fend off a barrel full of bar-room hipped-up monkey eager, wild women, ever after my money belt, if not my very life, I next ran faster than Speedy Gonzales, just one short ahead length faster then an entire tough lot of a damn well seasoned street wise Mariachi Band, numbering six; "one of them from over my shoulder harbored an antiquated probably empty revolver (?), as I never once remember it fired? Well, their sense of humor, if could call it that, was just short of Pan 'co Villa's toward all gringo-neophytes had before, during, and forgotten after the Mexican Revelation... ("As most all American white Europeans it were shot on sight!), ...when General Pershing was at the same time hot in his pursuit of Mack The Knife, who was also busy in Chicago chasing after the Junk-yard dog! Every one of that Mexican band/troupe was a tough bastard right out of the original prototype New York City, Am Boy Duke's! The two cowboys boys laughed hearing all that comical account, and so next I showed them my scars of battle, and where I had needed sixteen stitches done to my lower lip, after a short sip and the taste of a fly floating in my Tequila that I had spat a short distance past my broken nose and one suffering black eye, looking concerned down to a gaping stab hole had in my limb from a broken bottle, that had been wildly thrust by some women into my right arm! It was not exactly in a happy Saturday night mood while groping in the dark for my lost pesos and drivers license to be saying anything similar as, Viva LA Mexico!"

Log: "Plaiting Evidence Found In Mountain Caves?"

("Nah, & Perhaps!")

"Dexterous hand work done with feathers in caves! All of it found was done with similar requirements to those needed for hair braids! All of what we found today was accomplished by use of an opposed finger and thumb, like those of humans. Such hand structure is a necessity to completely hand pluck bird feathers from off a kill, and opposed fingers are also needed to do plaiting! Apes and monkeys, I remind you, had not been awarded this obvious convenience!

Wild man as a hominid definitely also has them! They are us, and we are them! Ahead is a slight briefing on plaiting, caving, and its most uncanny relativity considering all collective wild man handy work ability having been already earlier discovered, and gone unknowingly unrealized by the author some years prior to a time ahead, to explain the time when I would eventually become first time aware of this strange braiding anomaly fall, year, 2004. As said, various clues back in year 2000 – 2004, as yet UN-realized to explain plaiting were/may still be found within of all places... Found even still today in the highly unlikely dark chambers of particular habituated high desert Idaho mountain caves! Often as not, when re-interning some of these little known questionable grottos, if not at times unstable and dangerous caverns; we are ever in search of further evidence that would suggest/prove that wild hominids were at least part time inhabitants of some of them during winter? It is often so true, that the bull headed foolish often rush in where angles fear to tread; however at all times of subterranean exploration, we strictly enforce a tight tradition/requirement of one and all's personal safety considered, as it is our solemn rule that if at any time anyone feels to be in imminent danger, or dire uncomfortable, extremely claustrophobic, stalked by a dangerous animal, etc., we have agreed to abort the project at once and get back into the sun light and fresh air at first opportunity, etc., as over competent people rarely live to write their own memories,

I definitely have been most fortunate!"

"Bob Cat Logic, Virus Hazards?"

To decide to participate in high risk adventures, O'course one needs to follow their innate decision to follow one's intuition. Experienced group discernments are always of a great importance, and if over looked, and if for example one suddenly finding oneself in the presence of any unwanted large animal, etc., this can be turned to an advantage if it can be seen continuing ahead as a departing shadow, or the same applies whenever made a new discovery of a fresh mountain lion track, etc., as all of this adds much credence to safety projections, especially when first time crawling into any thought impossible or unstable surrounding, as when first time crawling into any thought impossible or unstable surrounding, as when making a fresh track discovery (Perhaps first thought unwanted!) it becomes exactly important, as are also any recent evidence of rattle snakes, wild pigeon, hawk, or eagle nest, etc., as this hard evidence instantly attests a safety flag importance pseudo cave stability, and or the ever dangerous presence and real threat of dread radon gas, and much more that could be explained ever essential to true wild cat discernment much similar of basic human-wild man intelligent conjecture as wild animals as mentioned will not survive or remain where there is an acute danger from an imminent cave in, radon gas, poison water, other chemicals, etc. All such mentioned, or any real part is easily to be found ahead of ones flash light enough to indicate living animals if no more than the disgusting evidence of cave rats!"

"What do most know of Bats?"

There has been a lot of flack recently concerning caves and bats and their safety and reproduction habitats. Environmentalists would have us convinced that bats are found in all caves, and that their extinction is eminent. It is a fact that bats in significant numbers are found in very few! We have explored many caves and not once have we encountered bats! Bats require a much special, peculiar, and a highly intensive cave atmosphere in order to multiply and survive. This becomes important to understand concerning the natural history of cave bats for anyone in future being able to intelligently debate all pseudo dictate out of sink protesting authoritative environmentalist blindly in favor of vast regional cave closures intended to void all public entry! There those selfish among us who would continue to take away many more of our Constitutional and natural God given rights! This is not the place to flaunt politics, but a bit more on this will need be said ahead when we update on the present day efforts to close all caves within Idaho state and just possibly via the domino effect in all fifty states? The Dangers of Radon Gas are a real threat, however feral hominids do not frequent just any and all caves either. If for example there were found dangerous radon in any cave, none of these wild animals or humans could survive, as even snakes when choosing a winter den are also very particular of what sort of an atmosphere they will tolerate, as ventilation, mean-temperature, etc., as all highly sensitive animals most always well know the all obvious dangers of nature and deal with them on their own terms, and so most do not go further under ground than can tolerable. It is a complete falsity that wintering bears go past the sight of light past a cave entrance to den for winter! I am always reassured whenever in a cave when discover an obvious place as a ledge where mountain cats have recently slept. Most always cougars just as domestic alley cats, wild Lynx, and Bob Cats, etc., prefer a founded back door exit, however this is not always the case with them, or either where feral humans are encountered.

At a minimal cost there are various reliable radon gas detectors on the market. I highly recommend all serious about cave exploration should get one and a needed spare first chance. Much caution should also be taken in regard of "flame lit lanterns" as are Colemans, etc. "Better said, "unless there is a damn good reason, just stay the hell out of most all unknown unstable caves period … unless of course you have a reason to be thinking yourself to be on an early death wish, however with caution, most caves when using common sense are admissible... Of course if caution is tossed to the wind, any number of even a very slight mistake can become your last wish and testimony, and you may prematurely discover the open door to hells gate! Later in the story, Tonia when explaining a personal experience when confused under ground introduces all reading into all hells close proximity!

"Why, Kathy asked, was all of that above said necessary, if we are just looking for plaited horses?" Well I told her, I am ever hopeful to be able to incite ("Not Insist!") to the reader viable enough evidence to convince them that wild hominids actually exist. It is all necessary to explain to them at least some of wild man's true and absolute human relativity in physical tributes for him to at all be able to plait, and next explained ahead is more of what truth of them has been discovered more able to validate all thought to be relative to plaiting that has taken place in caves. Long ago before having had any knowledge of plaiting, quite by chance and now by coincidence, I have now realized that back then, when considering comparative handy work, I had already discovered particular hand-work anomalies more able to validate particulars of may present day moon theory! This Kathy is a very difficult sojourn to explain! It would have been easier and more direct to had been satisfied to opt to have used the original dire-dry boring manuscript that this one will now replace, as I could had just condensed down the original into five or six pages for the record and let it go at that! But if that done, just think of all of the excitement we would have not recounted! Who wants to read through the pages of an outdated foreign telephone book written in the unlikely runic or hob-gosh alphabet? Without the rush of new discovery and a little human frailty lets opt to buy each other a fish bowel!"

WILD NEVADA CHIEF SMOKY

"One Humorous Pongoniff Satire?"

Log: Author: Ely Nevada, Xmas week, 2004 –

The Paiute Indian Reservation, five day camp out Xmas Party!

We done this with Chief Smoky and company, where we now have camped the first miserable night to awaken to a bright sun lit frozen Pongoniff Xmas Day! Wow, but these Indians are tough! I just fell over the end of my dragging blanket, and my frozen ass just got bad scorched by the fire! "Don, Smoky said, if we were cannibals I guess we would start with you! Some of them I think would like their hams cooked slightly rare? And my brother, you are very rare! I am glad that you have agreed to cook our food! You white men eat about the darnedest awful stuff that many years ago some of it had began to kill off many of us Paiute! We brought the right things with us! Look into that burnt box and see what is not ruined or is now frozen? We should have a good Xmas dinner out of that box? Ferlinghetti here, "our some one part or something Italian Indian brother, came back this morning with this ugly fox! He told me that in Italy they us-to have a fox! Each year everyone cleaned their rifle and all went out to hunt the rabbit, but no one had ever saw it! I think we will cook this one ....? It looks like it is healthy! What do you mean asking me what is a Pongoniff? We Indians don't know either... We just like its sparkle color! Sometimes though when it comes we can't find our white horse! Our horse I think is much the same as that Italy fox? Stand here Don, and tell me more about this plaiting... I think we have some of that around here too, as I have seen it! Do you have a story?"

"The Indian Pongoniff,
And The Stark Bright Nature Of Her Day!"

"If a winter Pongoniff was truly a women, she would be a beautiful white haired albino, a temptress, beyond all stark white descriptions of all various snow; and her cold heart as dread determined as the least smallest of the weasels as is the shrew. She is a definite wilderness temptress leading to disaster if anyone miss-understand her purpose! She has been thought of as a weathered ship, lost frozen fast in winter deserted out on the wild desert sage brush sea! Sometimes she is a danger to the careless or unwitting vagabond! I have slept in her wake, and have experienced the concern frost-bit hands and feet...

Photo T. Mauney

Ah, but what, really, is more beautiful than the Pongoniff and the Siberian tiger?"

(Written on location at 7,000 ft.. Winter Xmas Party, Ely Nevada, 2004.)

Log: Horse Plaiting, and, humorous Chief Smoky Satire continued:

"A Pongoniff Christmas spent with Chief Smokey, Xmas Week 2004, at Ely Nevada, Paiute Indian Reservation - Ahead, is where the humorous Chief Smoky, explains more on the Pongoniff, and Horse Plaiting well known among his people!

"Smoky speaks ahead, slightly paraphrased for dialect content!"

"Don, where we are going tonight it is very cold at 7,000 ft., and we will experience a very frozen time with cold beer and the blessings of legendary wild white Indian women known as the bitch lady, Pongoniff! She lives during winter everywhere on a the high desert wind blown frost covered mountains and deserts, and only comes out after the coldest of nights!"

But that is but only one description, as she can be just as beautiful as she is miserable, or be as deceptive and uncanny as can be any sudden early frost or plight, and as bad as a devastating plague of locus or the Mormon Crickets that sometimes comes now and then to destroy the crops ahead of the gulls that swoop down to devour them!"

25

The Mountain Top

"Further evidence that Chief Smoky definitely had long ago visited East Chicago!"

"Don, he said, this white bitch Pongo-Pongo woman is truly very tempting in her white snow dress, and when she is all sun lit-up, she sings her sweet wind-swept voice as ever persuasive as was any 1950's siren lament, sang long ago by, East-side Chicago's much pampered, Sandra Sexton, or was more appreciated than the undeniable, invincible, Tempest Storm, who also is revealed in legend, story, and song, as a desirable in womanly fact, "not fiction," as is still remembered, Hilo Hattie, or Molly B' Damn, and Mamie Stover, the South Pacific prototype of, Lady Godiva, in some many wild particulars all of them are to probably be considered by some reading who can still well remember them in retrospect? Foolish men have loved much less than the beauty of the Pongoniff or Molly, Sandra, or Tempest Storm, etc., but all of it I can tell you Don my friend... All of it was ever done in vain!" Smoky, I told him back..."Truly, if it could be said, that anyone has actually ever been every where and done it all, well it's gotta be you!"

Photo T. Mauney

The Mountain Top Cave!

"Don, Smoky said, tonight we will view the wonders of the Pongoniff from the mouth of that dark cave I told you about where sometimes wild people have been seen? We will go up on the highest mountain that's just behind the town! There sometimes are horses up there... but I don't think that at this time of the year, anyone would want to braided them for Xmas? What do you really think does this?"

(Plaiting story to be continued!)

"ALL Of This Don, Is Truly A
Great Northern Mystery!"

All Exunda Lies Ahead!

Tonia Brown, as, Wild Onya, On The Road!

"Don, she said, ever the search for plaiting had at once since the very first day began as a great adventure! I just can't hardly wait to be on the road again! There is so very much to see and learn!"

"True Wild Bob Cat Logic!"

"What you are about to read is a sophisticated/conglomeration of enough off the wall speculation and hard true Bob Cat Logic as ever was had from any one small group of people as now by proxy writes with me in this book from shared journal notes; each of them were/are of a somewhat of a wild and wooly nature, in order for them to have ever accomplished particular hard pressed facets of this ongoing ten year plus and continuing horse plaiting sojourn!"

Our Journey!

In this manuscript where explaining Tonia's part, we will be going just about every where that hell hadn't already frozen over during her last hard winter season of a time when there was a highly beautiful and sometimes dangerous Pongoniff' weather conditions scattered over the vast Northern areas of the New Mexico and Nevada deserts. More will be said of this ahead. There are still to be found if look, a few wild mustang horses wandering some of the high country of the remaining far and middle west. During winter to locate them is hardy a record heat wave! When last time in New Mexico it had been the coldest winter season on record in many years. We returned back from that portion of the remaining wild west via the far west coast of Oregon abrupt famed Heavens Gate, or what has been named, "The Bridge Of The Gods," that spans the Columbia River high above the spawning salmon that return in thousands each fall up that magnificent water way. While there we made a stop where I had friends then at the, Celilo Indian Reservation, located on the Oregon side south of Washington on the shore side shore of the Columbia river to learn if could all of what was new there that had recently been discovered to do with plaiting, and learn more in-put to the wild tribe Sasquatch, as the Celilo had once called them when we had conferred back in 2004! My native friend Jim had since sadly departed this life. "About two years ago Don, one morning he finally just went his way! Jim died with many secrets! He even seemed to know of the Water Babies believed in by the Pyramid lakefront Nevada Paiute, and the west coast Native belief in the Smoke people, and the Stick Indians of the Spokane and Colville Indians, called by them, S'cen'ey'ti! We had many conversations. Jim will be long missed. Especially I was

27

interested in what he knew of the ancient Nevada people of the reeds, or the, Sit-ti-Cah that I have long been in pursuit. Jim's wife had also left the area, she was another to draw to that I was anxious to introduce to Two Feathers!"

"The Celilo Indians"

We were invited to stay the night, and so became re-acquainted with some of the Elder men and women that I had only slightly encountered years back when I had known Jim! That evening at the yard camp fire a colorful Indian man who wanted to be left anonymous, after a few inquiries of him began telling us more about his belief in wild human peoples! "Don, These are a People Of The Cat Tail! Because They eat and use them many ways!" Don, as you know, the white man does not know that those wild human people wander far and wide, and very much of a distance on the windy days when there are high waves along the river shores, or when the blowing dust storm makes the shy colored yellow, causing all of the smaller game to hold-up and be easy to catch, and especially this is easy with the game birds and ducks! In this high wind it becomes almost impossible to see these people, or either to track them that would be dangerous! The wind quickly destroys all of their tracks! None of us wander then either!

We don't tell what we know to the white man, because of his of his THIN shared whiskey habit: and his fat mouth of laughter that is really not from his heart! I know that the heart of this girl with you understands our fishing ways, and some of our other ways, as I can observe that she is some kind of a part Indian herself! Here, have this larger salmon to take with you, as it was caught fresh only today! Perhaps this skinny, shy, red headed, little half-breed Indian woman with you will cook him? At hearing that, Onya wanted to know how the man knew that the salmon was a boy? What do you mean he ask her: how do I know that this fish is a him? That is easy! Just look at that sly fishy face smirk where his mouth is open! This is spawning season, and all of the males at this time have that smirk! Have you not ever seen the salmon dance beneath the water in our river? They dance a lot here in September!"

Later, Tonia cooked the salmon without salt and impressed them, as I had told her of the custom! Before leaving, in appreciation for all of them, and all hospitality, she loved them back by cleaning out her purse of any and all useful items another time since her earlier experience with the New Mexican bandits; ate with them their unsalted fish, and had unknown to me already bonded in compassion with, "some many ugly of those poor little cat fish Don …Just look at them, all of them are trapped in that wooden barrel! Why are these people keeping them in there, and for what reason? Are they bait?" Yep they were! So, we left! "One aging women over-heard her comments and question, and so walked over and politely told Two Feathers while scratching at her chin… Don't you know young lady, that all of our fishermen and us women have forever been cannibals, and so are those damn cat fish! Sometimes we come back the next day and everyone of the smaller ones are gone! These fish in my opinion would be better called pig fish, because all of them can really make a pig of themselves!"

"I don't believe you, Tonia said … Most of those fish are much too big to eat the other!" The old women told her back… "That is because the other ones are all full of the rest of them! All of there tummies are full of everyone!" Two Feathers also loved their fishing boats, by explaining how as a child she had almost needed "Sea-Legs," since her California Chumash Indian relatives living then at Pismo Beach had been fishermen even before the first white men came and first time

28

tried to put clothes on them... And then next, after an out numbered and desperate defeat, "via peonage, that is very close to slavery, the whites had forced them to their dismay, to become the Mission Indians!" To this day that unwanted denotation is completely UN-appreciated by the Chumash! I ever have sided for the most part with the native peoples whenever among them. Anyone further interested in the invincible Chumash Tribes, should plan to attend their annual Pow-Wow, held each year (Free camp, first come, first served!, during the first week end of September! (Become a true part of your California Chumash history! Many a white-eye's wannabe Indian attend in support! See you there?")

"No Salt!"

The Celilo also explained to Onya, how they smoked their fish without using salt, while she in turn surprised them at the late night fire under the stars, of a bit of French Indian acute astrology knowledge of what sounded much like their own rote-history! They and I were both astonished of how much relative was their wisdom and her own latent native traditions. Many, many, of these Native American traditions are not a few of them very much similar as are the Hawaiian and lower South Pacific Islanders... "Don, one old rascally man said, we like this wise starving red haired women! You can let her stay so we can feed her more fish! Or she can bring you back to get her when your not ready, but do not ever come back without her, unless you bring some more skinny others like her! As we know that she will keep our secrets, and you have not told us one damn important one of yours! Where did you snag this wild Tonia? Maybe we are fishing for the wrong thing?" Upon leaving, they gave Onya a golden colored feather, and she treasured it to her last day, as they told her last thing words to the effect, ...you girl are much more than an interesting mixture of French/Indian and colorful humanity. Come back and stay with us! Your home will be with us anytime you may need... "They were a beautiful people!" You will meet much more of Onya later when she writes while miserable from where tent camp in the off season in the wilds of winter time Arizona, New Mexico, Cal/Neva, and every where between visiting Marlin Keith Davis at Mississippi, and experiencing the trying miss-adventures while with wild cab-driver explorer, Ron Roseman, was then addressed, "at the water front, somewhere mid-Florida?" Before her demise she enjoyed her last fond memories of her mother, re-uniting with her on the desert winds of all Sedona! "If anyone wonder why I write so much of Tonia; I had promised her at her passing, that I would write some of her adventure sojourn for her children and close friends so that they would forever better know her. Onya was a very private person; there was very much unrealized of her humanitarian potential. Kids all, your mother loved life and you! We all will love her memory! Heaven forbid anyone ever write of me! So be it!"

The Adventure Continues with a small bit of sentimental appreciation.

"Time Out for Angelo, Josh, and Amy Stanzeonie."

Well, we found horse plaiting as far east as Tex/Ark/Kan, and as far South to the Mexican Border below Tucson, and North as far as Soho-low AZ, and later I saw one single horse with a plaited mane pastured near Monroe Utah! There is no doubt about the diversity of regions where this is going on. Never again do I expect to put so much effort into such an unappreciated and dubious project. Today's humanity as we are becoming are much a programmed people having little interest it seems in unfathomed anomalies. Guys like me just never really happened. Onya helped much in her short sojourn, her undying spirit undeniably writes with me in this book. She wrote last words in her journal promising that she would forever think of me and all of her loved ones at a same designated time each day!

I do not apologize for any thing in life that I could not have changed or avoided! As it is all so very true, that you can pick your friends, make your own mistakes and decisions, but you can't pick your family, dictate to them, or change anyone's moot or disrespectful judgmental opinion of yourself regardless, unless of course, Bob Smallsbach, that you pick a good ship, have a mug of grog with it's worthy crew if have, and next choose a friendly star to sail her by while meandering with me in fantasy towards all many still hidden wonders of unrealized Exunda! Next Gene Scheller, you and I may need return back to sea, as I have an educated good hunch that what you had purposed some years ago having to do with the Norse Selchie may indeed have credence! Perhaps along side wild man and that mystery, we should also look also others unfamiliar within the worlds oceans?"

"Are We Looking For True Wild Man Or What? Yeah, mostly what?"

(Warning: You may need read this next difficult explanation several times, or not at all

(?), down to as far below as is the word, "End"... Either way it will not matter! If confused just skip on down to the next topic and proceed to, Full Moon Theory Defined?)

"Everything Includes Awesome!"

Yes! Mostly What! This Book Runs Deep! Plaiting truly is awesome, and is much more than astonishing! What more is written ahead might be to some thinking, at best a highly misunderstood, unrelated confusion in wanting mixed gender humor, inclusive of horse and bob-cat mixed logic expression, that eventually (As said!) will include a short treatise of slight human passion, and high emotion explained, had abrupt all things of a serious nature while one thought themselves to be trapped underground! Cause and effect having to do with ones high stress, had from much miserable, and continuing unfamiliar travel, lack of sleep and creature comforts, while ever requiring as it had been, ever necessary and constant ongoing difficult plaiting investigation; all new and questionable difficult cave exploration, etc., and next all of this attempted to be reiterated intelligently abrupt an uncanny second hand best expressed story, "as I can only hope to relate all of it at best slightly paraphrased, and in that way be hopeful to be able to explain another's true story that is next to horrendous! All is a subterranean much high strange love, miss-adventure experience? And after that, ever the book continues in all its first interest hopeful to more explain all wanted answers more able to solve the mystery of the strange plaiting being done on American horses; and all more necessary moon theory as pertains, and its noted effects had upon wild hominid, and horse plaiting associations! "All of that message, if and when anyone fully realizes all of its purposeful conjecture, by then they will eventually becomes fully aware also of its all obvious ramifications and urgent understandings of mixed emotions had of one in particular person, a very delicate and highly sensitive dedicated person in mind; Tonia Brown helped to write this book unsolicited (Me unknowing!) far beyond her call to voluntary travel and re-discover with me over a very difficult, long, miserable, and uncomplaining, physical and mental sojourn! Onya without president, or re-quirement, researched so much/many of the accredited logistics, histories, and interesting informa-tion, that was all necessary to have accomplished any real part of such a difficult, and much dubi-ous manifest as this! The book in all truth amounts to a much collective account of a pseudo or-thodox/unorthodox treatise probe, based entirely upon ("base") Christian religion, witch-craft, paganism, full moon adoration, and includes comments on animistic/ritualism, Idolatry, etc., and it contains enough side track blather and hooch, as has ever been expounded prior by myself, or by my near silent partner, Mr. Johnny Foxx at any time! This book is but the very first stepping stone, that is in my opinion a land mark document. "It is the first ever written theory thinking to be able to explain some many unexpected truths of horse plaiting!"

"A Full Moon Theory"

What is it?

"Perhaps this next is the Main Event?"

(Before you read further, understand that what ever anyone make of this theory, or do not agree, it is a true fact, that over the past 18 months running that we... {"Five persons on the Jenson property, plus various numbers of ranch horse owners, etc!"} ...have been keeping close tally on various plaiting that is constantly reoccurring during, shortly before, or shortly after each full moon phase monthly, "that this high strange plaiting had also prevailed well known to the author how-ever was only observed, "hit and missed," over the entire time of the past 10 years since first be-came aware of all plaiting fall year 2004! Finally came my close observation of plaiting dates and times.. Thus began my theory research! This strange anomaly has definite and decisive reasons and answers to explain it. Written ahead throughout the book are some of the reasons, cause, and ef-fect. It is only a matter of time until we will have a lot more to write conclusive. My personal un-derstandings are actually just beginning, changing, and currently being much re-evaluated. There is much, much, more to be realized to explain the story than is here, but this may in fact be one true clue to an important part!)

"Begin"

From here we are going about every where and back again looking for plausible answers to solve this strange anomaly. My theory has to do with the most ancient of peoples, dating back in time beyond what is commonly accepted today, back to a time when men and horses were about the full extent of a wilderness civilization. It was a time like so many others similar that would come after: fear prevailed everywhere! Fear of any, and all things new and/or unknown, not un-derstood, etc., including the peculiarities and customs, or lack of them, of all other obscure humans living close or far circle with them in parallel.

Everything was foreign to everyone. There were many misunderstandings among them. Lan-guage was not even as yet well established or at all defined, and the separate cultures that would one day surface had not yet had a real beginning... Horses and dogs had been somewhat been befriended and tamed; and beyond a few personal effects, ones horse, or the number of horses that he had control over became his wealth and respected status. If having no horses, one was eventually doomed expectant to become as if enslaved, made to provide for himself by serving out a hard and simple life of dread peonage or worse under a powerful master. Eventually there would be envy, greed, thievery, blood shed and warring among neighbors, and or small clans/bands of joint horse ownership, etc. Horse adornment lorded over the times... Men began to idolize them, "and finally much like is written the classic Biblical story taken from the Christian Scriptures, explaining the idolatrous adoration of "The Golden Calf," ancient man much similar, first had began to worship particular sky, land, sea namesakes, inclusive of noted horse effigies, and obscure animal Gods, and eventually the stars, sun, and moon were included in the over all picture, until finally a human side of adornment identity began to prevail, effigy identities were slightly, or much changed, or re-named, as for example the crescent shaped moon phase became, The Moon Goddess Diana, Ishtar was born, Odin was revered, etc. Nevertheless, extensive fear of all unknowns continued in all corners of the ancient world... There was little or no comradely, plagues and the Dark Ages, the Crusades, the Inquisition, etc., happened, every thing, nothing, and anything not understood, denoted witch hunts and much superstition, and at times blood sacrifice, the Roman Colosseum lasted its entirety for all of 900 years, etc...There is existing documentation telling of butchering any number of wild feral people in the Roman Arena! Because of confusing times, much idolatry, witch craft, etc., prevailed! The common man that lived among the horse task-masters, much as if himself a true wild beast; that had not already long before escaped with the others into the mountain forests, where they out of situation and necessity became out as a feral hominid... (As almost forever written in all world histories of any day, there is reference to wild people, and/or wild man has been included, explained in pseudo research, etc.),

... those poor souls that were left behind as desperate slaves were worse off in many respects than what had already became the wild feral people that to this very day continue to survive in limited, or very mixed gene pools, as covert feral humanity, sometimes called Sasquatch, or by what ever other pseudo identity wanted. Those poor souls left behind in squalor to exist under dire task-masters long had became required to adhere to adversities, "for one," likely required forever to think to need to continue to plait (Braid!) the manes of their masters horses if only as an abstract protocol (Call it a religious involvement, etc?) adoration to the moon or similar as man, idols, effigies, etc., required done regardless of weather conditions at each new full moon phase (About 28 days apart, or close!) to eventually include the Crescent Moon Goddess Diana in adoration, or also she is known as the Goddess of all thieves, bandits, pirates, etc., and was considered by the old day and current known Gypsies. under the reference name of, The Goddess Diana, or, The All Seeing Eye Of The night, etc! Under her Sliver Moon (The crescent moon!), the dim light much opposed to the bright light of the full moon, is considered most ideal to accomplish any and all negative mischief, thus, The Thieves Moon! What better moon phase would be also best for any masquerading bandit, or covert wandering wild hominid to have his way? This plaiting tradition/custom/contest/fear factor/art-form, what ever, remains prevalent today with at least a real working part of a much scattered little realized wild feral population that to this very day is evidenced just about every where that ancient man had made exploration contact! Wild man disbursement had occurred over all of the ancient world; had arrived via capture to be used as forced labor working slaves, coming very early to the Americas with the most early and still obscure Chinese base ancient mariners! Most all of them came from vast Eurasia!

Think about it, it is not all that hard to contemplate. Ancient man, wild man, today's populations, then, now, and forever, we are required to make decisions to continue to sustain life as can and we require it.. Feral humans are to this day likely still impressed with horrid ramifications of very distant ancient beginnings, had to this day abrupt a continuing real, and/or dire latent fear of a sudden mass subjection, or perhaps even a sudden horrid death if they do not continue to participate in horse adoration through plaiting or similar? All moot projections had of them of the various good and difficult seasons, growth, weather, rivers, animals, Ice flow, cloud formations, all list endless of long ago still unexplained to them dire phenomenon, that today through pseudo civilization have long taken much for granted, as are full understandings of the universe, astrology, moon madness, the seasonal awe and constant change of the mid-night night stars; all moon curiosity, etc., that in due time had finally been required of humans, plaiting if involved in any sort fear factor abrupt all of this still an unexplained mystery to wild man; all of this plaiting is/could be a very real or imagined required worship adherence, thought needed/convinced to be forever accomplished in order to be able to deal with all possible moon phase change, life and death outcomes, etc., based upon a needful reliance upon all moon light; real fear of its impending dark side, and/or sliver moon phase (Diana!) resulting in many directional confusions, dictations of moot theory, the moons definite observed changing sky positions, its various color moods of change, its recognized influence upon the tides, the varying times of the day a well as the night that it would appear in the day and evening sky, its definite influence upon reproduction, attitudes, child birth, resistless, and even its high aphrodisiac influence leading to birth control cause and effect, customs that are still recognized today by the Northern Mandarin Chinese, and others similar, that will more explained somewhere ahead in its place.

The moon became to earliest man as an object of fear and hope, an awareness of evil or wanting all knowing, all seeing eye, that in some many unorthodox beliefs became a very real all seeing high expectorate Moon Goddess, possibly even cruel in required sacrifice, etc., or even an unnamed as yet to be named Man-God as became Zeus, much feared, loved/hated, and/or adorned by any number of worshiped names and wanted/unwanted expectations, as for example as is the highly revered, The Rabbit of the Moon allowed of the Chinese, etc! Even the pseudo savage peoples of Africa, as today still exist almost unnoticed as are the mysterious Dogon, and others similar, and many distant obscure tribal peoples, some many even today still less than understood, remaining a much, much, misunderstood, improperly written, unsung of lament almost enough to be considered a cursed attitude towards them by many; the many peoples of South East Asia, Eurasia, The Far South Pacific, as Australia, New Guinea, etc., still even now many put much high superstitious requirements upon the populace, and require displayed body adornments respectful of good, bad, and evil/ever fearful and often having much to do with moon adoration! All of this is to be remembered/understood had began many eons earlier than finally came the earliest calendars, as are today represented by the Chinese, Jewish, Egyptian, Etruscan, Aztec, and Mayan Calendars to name just a few!

The world concern experience that took place happened only a few short two weeks ago on, December 21st, 2012, was the proscribed date and time when many of the above calendars would end and all concerns had a definite warranted/unwarranted ramification effect upon even some many Orthodox Christian concerns, not as yet even once referenced here the endless sun worship and its relativity dating in mystic belief as far back in time as Atlantis and its prior supposed civilization the land of Moo! Do most reading have any idea what expectations were said had of the populations of Moo to moon phase? Wow, all of that must be examined in another book? Not this Indian gonna do it! No thank you, but it might also have some best answers?"

Wow, that said, the plaiting requirement I believe had began in very ancient times. Probably back in time to when first happened the opportune domestication of the smallest ever known example of a wild horse that were no doubt used as food before trained to carry baggage, children, etc., and so plaiting/braiding of the manes and tails had first began by tying packs, etc., onto the horses by using the elongated long hair mane! Even if that so, how please explain to me how in the world a horses rather short mane measuring at best at perhaps 15 inches long, can be measured on some many plaited manes to extend all of 26 – 38 inches long? Is that plausible magic or what? Well, it isn't done by magic, and there is an answer ahead that took the author with the help of Phil Jenson, all of nine long years to comprehend! "The most exciting message of this book is to realize that there actually are unknown intelligent personages out there still wandering unrealized in our managed world!"

"Time Out!"

As this theory for now is way short of what more is now under study, but far close enough for the moment to suffice as, just exactly as it now stands, entire volumes could be written concerning the moons influence on animals and humanity; astrophysical phenomena, Lycanthropy, and its proven psychiatric influence, etc., as in my present belief a real important part of it is an all confused probably unwanted feral wild human adherence thought to be all necessary to continue to accomplish plaiting until death or similar, done to appease the Moon Goddess, Diana, or what ever idolatry; to ever be done at each and every seasonal and or monthly full moon phase... This physical and mental torment has to becomes in time a notable hindrance/obligation even in regard of the strongest of their kind on any terms, for what ever the reasons, that were set apart as almost an expectant cursed activity eons back in time to be accomplished forever to the sad drumming of a madding and much latent Lycanthropy type belief and adoration exemplified by the real life or imagined fear of a dread were creature similar of a vampire, succubus, were wolf, were tiger, bear, or what ever dread serpent adoration as had Atlantis, etc, or what is still today well established in psychotherapy as Lycanthropy Moon Madness, that was instituted by a harsh unethical requirement many aeons ago; done to control or even punish all wild savage strands of a very possible vast unwanted outcast society of its far day! Every dispensation of time has had them! Many thousands of innocent thought savage wild populations were brutalized/but chard and worse over the near 800 plus years blood-let of the Roman Empire Arena alone! Think about it, there still exists very wild and highly mixed intelligent underground population! Where do anyone think they would have ran to in ancient times if all realized all pending fate! What are you going to do when they come for you? Yeah, what?" If by now anyone is still unable to believe or consider the true existence of feral wild man hominids you just as well chuck the book, as some many lost souls wandering under the night sky are not all that lost! This treatise is much more than just an idol-wild sorry confusing DE-notion of moot belief, as I myself on three separate occasions have seen different unknown types however similar of these hominids. That stark awareness has much changed my life understandings! On two of the three occasions I had another person as with me as witness to include my late wife Marion on the first to confide her creditability that had always been a beautiful rose in an onion patch! On the other brief encounter my trail mate was occupied otherwise?"

Log: The General Plaiting Theory!

"Theory is hardly superstition, however superstition in this case has much to do with the plaiting, and very likely because of all evidence now had there is in my opinion a definite full moon

adherence done to lunar totem Gods, Goddess, or a lesser effigy as might be considered, the fascinating sliver crescent moon that always occurs slightly after and before each new moon long known since the most ancient of times as, "the all seeing eye of Diana," or perhaps some other little known powerful effigy of Idolatry, fetishism, secret societies, and/or the controversial unorthodox adoration of particular hypocritical pseudo Christian false profits of deceptive belief as have surfaced countless nameless money mongers; any and all sorts of obscure, seldom realized botanical worship as even might include particular trees, plants, hand woven basketry, or even sacred medicinal plants, forested tree and brush avenues leading into sacred mountains, canyons, caves and the hidden grottoes of beach fronts, and difficult hidden pathways into seldom visited places, and definitely not to over look all popular wanting studied chronicles of Sirius, Medusa, Isis, Kali, the I-Ching, Hanuman, Brahmanism's adoration of the seven headed serpent, and many other differing interpretative effigies and lost and found influential manuscripts somewhat unknown to most persons, and to be also considered are particular natural stones, stone and wooden totem idols, and all supposed magical crystal type effigies, and said haunted glass, silver, and brass mirrors; East Indian adhered fall-ace adoration, pig, cow, monkey/ape, shark, serpent/reptilian, worship, etc., and the long recognized artistically embellished nautical portrayals of fearsome sea-serpents, mermaids, etc., as were much adorned by the far Voyaging Vikings of old, or were ever to be encountered and needed to be dealt with in many early human exploring campaigns sometimes hampered or discouraged by abstract beliefs and unethical superstition all relative or much similar had during the countless epic sea voyages accomplished of the Invincible most ancient Chinese Mariners, ever intent as they were, to completely circumvent the earth and colonize the unknown world, as they actually did in part even along many sea coasts of the world including North America; they done this long, long, before the disbanding of the Chinese Navy, and the final destruction of all ships by the Mandarin Chinese during and after the after-math at the beginning of the Ming Dynasty in, 1405 - 1407; the most ancient of the ancient seafarers were ethnically most often of an established Oriental base culture with the exception of the Greeks and some few other now realized navigators long written out of history by the bloody English! These early Chinese were invincible map makers, most all of them had with them feared warriors who explored with them the worlds vast oceans and inland forests far beyond most neophyte persons tolerant imagination up to the time of the return of the last naval expedition believed to had been back to the Forbidden City, around 1421 fifteen years or so after the disbanding of the Chinese Navy as said, by the Mandarins by the year 1407, when was instituted the beginning of The Ming Dynasty. Why all of this Kathy, because during these epic voyages many captured feral people as Almasty, Yeron, Yeti, etc., and the long known wild human snow men of the Himalayas.. (Not either were these last mentioned the coined example of the Abominable Snow Man!) ..had sailed with these them as working slave laborers doing all menial and difficult jobs like manning the oars, mining, logging, etc.. and very likely for any number of misadventures some of them had escaped or were left behind during the long sojourn and their remnants are still with us today alleged as Sasquatch, Bigfoot, etc. Not to forget to include all general realized evidence of wild man existence had recorded in far west travel journals during the America's Wild West, claiming many sightings wild-man encounters had at places where wild populations are surprisingly still to be to found in many of the same unlikely locations in spite of all BLM and Government efforts cooperative of nameless amalgamated with private enterprise annoyances aimed for selfish and monetary reasons of control to void all public from entry to our National Forests! (All at once, what nation?) In spite of efforts to completely eradicate them, there are still a few remnant wild horses to be found in the far places of the, Cal/Neva/Or-Ida Far West, where it is still possible (If white man will listen?) to understand much of importance to be had from all native American cultures customs and mythological rote history, where the legendary witch y women Disonga exists; Disonga by explanation has yet to be introduced, as she is the miserable equivalent of a Shape Shifting ugly effigy denotation of the Arizona Chiricahua Apache known as the blue women, and/or is somewhat much similar to particular disruptive beliefs had regarding The Down Under Australian legends relative of Southern Cross, and the belief of two separate kinds of Yowie creatures much similar of our Sasquatch, and all other thought strange adherence of the remaining Australian aborigines, to name only a few of the need be understood comparisons to be made to further ahead to more substantiate all logical conjecture had of a few thought Unexceptionable Maverick Renegades as Myself, that proudly officiates this book and speaks for them by this book as, "Laugh at nothing Don, least you be cursed among the laughing dead, damned, or disabled! And ever Kathy be much aware of the big Kahuna, and all old and new legends of the very possible to be existing Mermaids, and especially be aware of the dread White Mono Shark, as believe in them or not, there are obvious shark type fins to be seen on the naked backs of some many young people caught off guard of far off Oceania that opt to rise ones eye brow as if to think that indeed there were some truth to the obscure belief that they be born sharks...? If not they were born of sharks Kathy, then where from did the fins come, and how did they get them, and, of course none of that is possible, but nevertheless indeed this is a very wild, and continuing strange world, and in some respects it is still completely unknown or identified! Definitely babe, according to Johnny Foxx, there is something very fishy about all of this crocodile sacrifice, and that went on for aeons of time in places as ancient Egypt! Look at some of the unwanted pictographs to be seen in some of those far off now desert regions and some many of you would be shocked past another cup of tea at mid day old chap! Yeah shocked! Kathy, lets go down on the Oregon beach and have a look at what all new to admittance might be found there...? Ever since the fall of 2004, and all of the mega numbers of land-fall beached whales found washed-up and bleeding on the Washington Coast, "I have really been most curious of exactly what the world Navies might be actually hiding in fear from the public, as before the present day and before the twentieth century. as far as I can determine, there was No Known Record Kept of mega numbers of beached whales, dolphin, propose, etc., anywhere known in the world! I suddenly wonder with you Captain Gene Scheller, if the alleged Mermaids of the North and South Pacific Ocean actually plait their hair as they look on the advertised tin-can of King Oscar fish cuisine? Remember readers, there are also validated sea-horses! Not the same Kathy... Stop laughing! Well babe, the Mermaids in Hawaii wear the Mu-Mus, and there is no telling what, really, are some of them? But Yeah, why not, Mermaids just might exist? If not, I love the thought! A lot of people live in a human fish bowel don't you know?" As said, the book has been much revised, as in first efforts I had written it without particular human character, humor, etc., and however good it many have been in sound research, I realized that it was hollow, shallow, and without any real story, as I had just opt to leave Sooo much thought unimportant out! The book at best amounted to a long drawn out boring paper, all necessary as it was however to flaunt all theory, as I ever new that this high strange braiding of the shaggy manes of horses had to have some founded reason, and I was determined to find out at least one v viable good answer?" The first effort had nothing to keep the attention of the reader as at the time of its long and ongoing research then only five years (2004 - 2009), I had then written only and serious of my wild theories, with all self-viable reasons to believe them, and so now I am accomplishing the manuscript a last and final time with all of the rest of the needed story slated completed hell or high water by the first stroke of midnight, New Years Eve, 2012, that hour will have been inclusive of the last date and time of the last full moon phase numbering 13... {"As I continue to write Feb. 18th, 2013, the count will soon be, 18 full moons of continued plaiting! Or, 5 more!"}... running since December, 2011 – December 31st, 2012! A complete 2013 update documentation far in time ahead and beyond what is here with ever pertaining research proves difficult however I will keeping notes! document! I am at the moment re-writing the original 2009 manuscript as a stepping stone to hope to help further educate all future understandings of my discovery, as by the summer of 2009, Onya joined my efforts, and since her the manuscript discovery I now will includes some of her interesting manifests of humorous and serious humanity, as the first book had none of that and so was written shallow and without character.... All story now also includes animals, and explanations of animalistic humanity ... Actually we humans, truth realized, are all very much just like the higher animals, be them tigers, polar bears, or an obvious couch potato boring fat bore! Not to be so negative-opinionated of slow locomotion-motivation people, but they seem to be on the increase, and nothing gets done many times any more unless you are the one!" The Sasquatch Trilogy in a future may include to update the further discoveries pertaining to Plaiting, AND, the book further explained is inclusive of an uncanny preview of many sorted well kept covert notes now intended shared to be able to complete all future slated books that will, "God Willing, finally comprise the collective Trilogy! Those books are of a first importance to further understand this manuscript as well that now comprises of nine years of hard travel and research. Many pertaining excerpts from my present field journals, and short story revisions, to include all and current updates or changes to all data of this manuscript will become important. "After reading this book, and especially the complete Trilogy, the mountains that you wander under the mid-night moon and stars will never be the same! All of The Trilogy manuscripts will ever need be written backwards, up-side down, hither, and yon, come what may, and then, Back-Ass-Wards Again in a special nonconforming sojourn with one percent of literary license, as they will not be easily to write or be forgotten! When and if reading through all of them, many of you, in projected comparisons, are likely with us somewhat in the books? Our world is truly a fascinating and unforgettable adventure!"

Log: "Lets go there left handed?"

You and your favorite horse may identify with this manuscript, as perhaps you have had a much similar experience? Never again after reading this account will it be possible to pass by and not want to examine every unattended horse! There are many varied and distorted opinions want to explain plaiting, but none to date as I am aware have noted the fact that predominately almost every sing time the plaiting as done by a magical equation as it ever results in a left-handed twisted braid or what ever outcome; the braiding each time begins with a left handed twisted/spiral twill, and then next it is intractably braided or worked into all knots, etc., left-handed, and when finished all project is left dangling precariously of the mane in a very odd looking useless type entanglement of an elongated mane, or better explained, hair described is often to be seen flitting down from off the horses neck when it runs or plays in an uncanny elongation of sometimes 28 or more inches! What is doing this and some of the reasons why, believe them or not, are partly explained ahead completely plausible! O'course, to some conjecture there may be another better answer, as this book is but the first beginning of the end to a great unsolved mystery. I sincerely do believe that this revelation however primitive and/or ragged and confusing, or demanding in its presentation, in time if not already it will have a land mark importance! Some of this logic was derived from pure unadulterated bob cat knowledge as if intended for the wild cat to ever evade the trapper using its ever watchful eyes. Like these elusive cats, what you see, and what you get, as a result of the authors endless wandering spree, "as this research does not insist it's opinion," rather it is an uncanny insight into the fact of existing feral hominids computed from much experience via constructive Bob Cat Logic and common sense, and ever includes "a far-side, or a wild-side" assessment of various interesting facts seldom considered except by the wild desert mountain lion, mustang, or horse! Read the book complete if for no other reason than your opt opinion of its message pro-con, that when decided either way, ("Neg-Pa,") will not have proven one thing to change one single word of this truth! Thanks to all of the many persons that have contributed to this unforgettable memory as for me it has been one hell of a journey and Our Discoveries Are Hardly Over! At the conclusion of this uncanny sage brush voyage, some of you will have already opt to pack your bags to join us in the search; if so, bring your courage, much patience, a few bucks, and a little humor definitely will help, as for me laughter is meaningful and I have learned not to laugh at the most random of questions and opinions, "as sometimes the smallest undetected/misunderstood clue excites all new awaited answers the becomes the new age of education... ever wonder for example what, really, is/night be the true reason why so many, many, many strange numbers of adult whales, porpoise, and dolphins, continue to choose to come ashore on many world beaches to die? Or, why for a second opinion do these wild elusive hominids for what ever the reason, choose to be predominantly to be plaiting only the female horses? For some reason it is true, that most often the plaits seen to occur on the fillies that are about to drop their new born colt! What do any of you think is the logical reason for any of this? When first explained the plaiting, you will probably have a hard time to believe it! In the case of the aquatic creatures, as far as I can discover this high strange beaching had not been recorded in times prior to the later twentieth century?

Log: Tonia Note –

Onya once said, (Paraphrased!) "...and next Don need be written a few lines of question and comment made to the less than intelligent "been there and done that childish critics ever insistent that the plaiting is being done by no other than the wind, dust, pixies, fairies, goblins, ghosts, or what have you;" and even if the wind and say the blowing dust could do any notion of that, "then how could it also intricately twill, cleverly braid, tie exact same knots in a long row, do all of this at times peace-meal over a few days, and over an extended times shortly before, during, or after a full moon phase, and after all of this said and done be able to have managed to elongate its mane, ever to be leaving its long hair squeaky clean, resulting in the mane being twice its normal length? And why if this is the wind and the dust, then how and why has it not been ALSO done hardly ever to the studs? Its the wind selective, prejudiced or what?" Just like you always said babe, "many a wantin' unexplained question still needs be answered, numbering into more than one hundred thousand million surprises!" Well, to some of the above, we now have some plausible answers, as it is true, that for some unsuspected reason most of the braiding has been done each and every time most often on the pregnant fillies, with an occasional exception done on a wet-mare. ("Wet mare, a horse still with milk, and her aging colt still suckling, etc.") "Somewhere ahead, one good reason for this will be explained! Wait for the surprise!"

Log: *"Doctor Issac Sanderson, on, FERAL HUMANS, and the Roger Patterson film!"*

(Uncanny consecutive indisputable evidence found years, 1967 -1968!)
"We need to further understand and identify them, in order to fully understand plaiting!"

"Where, Really, Does Anyone Think This Book Is Taking Us!" The next hominid proof all taken from documentation is much more than logical conjecture! Yeah, I agree, what, really, can be said in simple terms, that would best explain the many differing origins of world wide feral hominids, ever wanting as it seems at least over North America to be called Sasquatch, Bigfoot, etc? Following is one best logical and true answers, as to fact we already have some answers and should know or at least suspect as we have long had the undeniable evidence to some-what identify them in for the 1967 movie footage alleged taken by single handed by Roger Patterson that indisputably through the genius film enlargements (Film enhancements done 2001-2013 by MK Davis, and others!) now accepted that completely exposes Patty Sasquatch, filmed one and only time, at Bluff Creek, California and not seen again since, to had been ex-actly was she was, "a true flesh and blood, living, breathing, walking example of a wild feral wild women, and there is some additional opinion that she may have been protesting herself being discovered and filmed by talking on the one minute footage, as her lips and mouth on the footage seem to be moving constantly a mile a minute (!),"and in addition all of that and her, "we need remember the high strange male body identified by none other than Doctor Is-sac Sanderson; in his assessment of the male body then enclosed in a block of ice, Sanderson claimed that the body was for real, was definitely some sort of a relict hominid (Hardly any ape!), and more likely a wild hominid juvenile or child than an adult... (An Ice Child? Wow! This body to all belief for reasons unknown had at once been covertly hidden/stashed from the public at the time shortly after Sanderson's appraisal early year 1968 {stolen, by who? Went where? }, ...and very likely to all speculation the body to this day probably still exists some w hare hidden convenient for what ever reason in of all places, Canada? Perhaps Canada's pseu-do Bigfoot/Sasquatch guru, John Green, has further knowledge of this?), in other words, some w hare in North America remains the hidden bloody gun shot body of the controversial Wis-consin Ice Child, that so much in fact actually resembles what female hominid it was that Roger Patterson had filmed and discovered at Bluff Creek remembered as Patty Sasquatch in, 1967! The Wisconsin Ice Man, 1967-68, and Patty from all photographic evidence, so much did the two look the same; in my opinion, as I have so many times wondered, "could they just perhaps somehow have surfaced at a much similar same time up from a very same family tie, or a much similar gene pool? Its my opinion/belief that Patty's, if not also the Ice Man's genetic connec-tions still may be wandering in North America."

Oregon's Passé Genius, Emory Strong.

**"Emory was man apart from his times!
I wish that I could have known him."**

Recently I sent a rare book from my collection titled: "Stone Age In The Great Basin," written by, Emory Strong for his comments to M.K. Davis, at Yazoo City, Mississippi, to see what if any-thing more than interesting he could make of a particular photograph in it taken passé in, 1871, or

1872, by maverick photographer adventurer, German born, John Heller. Heller was one of the accredited, "Long-Boat Coxswains," that had accompanied Civil War, Capt., Powell ... (Today AZ's Lake Powell is named after him!) ... on at least one of his expeditions down the Colorado River! Heller had intended that the rare photograph be re-published by Powell, then having much to do with The British Born, Smithsonian Institution, that at that time was much under the influence, if not the direction of the same famed, Capt. Powell himself!" The revered, war hero, Capt. Powell, finally lost his boat with others when it jibbed in rapids and continued cascading down through the mist and wild rapids of deep the great gorge of what is called today, The Grand Canyon, later turned into The National Park that divides Utah from Arizona. Powell before becoming directly engrossed and much powerful and influential within the Smithsonian, had spent several years living with his rescuing Indian tribe, after was explained; having lost his boat, these kind and naive Indians of his attitudes towards them had saved him on what is today the Utah side on the river. As notable as he was, there is very much more unheard of, and possibly unwanted known of him to realize of his Smithsonian power sojourn, having directly to do with particular future irregular Indian affairs abrupt his developed controversial attitudes toward the American Indian and their ethnic back grounds! Well, the photograph wanted published by John Heller never happened! The Smithsonian refused to publish it for several obvious reasons, that now as of close considerations of all exposed controversial photographic evidence the history of particular Native American peoples would need be re-written! That seems more than interesting and strange, as cameras back in the year 1867-69 was it (?), were not all that common, and because of the tight comradely associations of Powell and Heller it becomes obvious that Powell was uncomfortable? There is much, much, in ramifications to the story, not the place here to write it. For further understandings of some probable reasons all of this photo. was wanted disregarded, read on the Net and have an educated guess, listed under "The Great Smithsonian Cover-up!" You don't have to be a rocket scientist to reason the more than likely reasons the photo never surfaced! There is much more story here to be understood between the lines!"

Note: It is not to be forgotten and to be highly considered, how gifted/adapt were many, many, passé Indian Tribes. Clever plaiting was naturally learned, past on, and has been around almost since the earliest dawn of humankind.

Log: John Heller.

Slightly having to do with what is written above explaining John Heller!
Do some of your own informative home work!
There is much hidden over North America!
Why Not They Publish All That Is Now Known,
Or Was Passé Known, Of Wild Man In North America?"

Well anyway, Davis and myself, MK helping me here through film enhancements: "as best that we can decide to explain it; well, the photo was way, way, way to much revealing of a much separate, and all much different looking, obscure hairy type of a little known Native American people, probably not at all wanted known to the public, being them very controversial and wild looking, however also very much a docile and no threatening complacent desert people, completely non-typical in the photograph of all wanting Smithsonian acceptance and allowed expectations of the day. However now through the genus film enhancement ability of MK. Davis, it is very easily to denote by anyone that the pseudo Indians pictured are very much other wise far much different to descriptions than are most all other wanton prototype believed of Native American High Desert Indian Tribes, as can be exemplified by the typical people as, Ute, Paiute, Shoshone, Yakima, Black Foot, etc., and this photograph by n little stretch of the much imagination may have something unwanted to do inclusive of the highly incredible and growing controversial alleged discovery and description wantin' of ISHI, who was said of in 1911, to have just all at once walked out to the world to claim that he was the very last example of a forgotten Stone Age people. And according to pseudo records kept, he had exclaimed: " I am Ishi! I am a Ya-hi, Yana. Or Yana, Ya-hi! According to record, if that was said verbatim, everything to come next, and ever Since, has became conveniently confused, as in truth he was saying that he was one of the last examples of his then nearly extinct passé, California Ya-hi, Indian Tribe, and exactly he also told them, that there were a few others!

"I am Ishi, Ya-Hi, Yana!" That was exactly what was told to Doctor and Mrs. Kroger who be-friended and attended him till his death! "ISHI," translated says... "I am, Ishi, meaning, I am a man!" Ishi, was not to be implied was to be his name!" And, "Ya-Hi," to mean, that he was from the "Ya-hi Indian Tribe," and the word, "Yana," depicts a particular wilderness river drainage located in Western Russia, easily found on current day, and old maps!"(Year 2008, MK and I closely explored all little know history and bogus artifacts had in the Berkeley California Museum, and the window display is completely wrong and bogus when compared to still existing original film footage now in safe keeping! Wow how we have been deceived! "Lawyers are mavericks compared to governments!"

At the 1917 Worlds Fair ISHI was denoted by all attending Native Americans Tribes present to be a completely UN-orthodox Indian! Many important Indian elders acknowledged this! There is much more to write of Ishi as an UN-sung and invincible man. Believe me, ISHI was far from being only a hold-over UN-educated Stone Age relict! He was definitely very far from being a true example of most all Native American peoples. It is more than interesting and little known that ISHI could speak fluent Chinese and very easily learned English! For some reason his true history is wanted left covert! Much time and money books and a movies was spent to cover up his true identity. Perhaps there needs be written another book? Perhaps we should ask, Emory Strong? "What, really, Emory, is all that much different in John Heller's Indian Photograph from all others? It is beyond historically important that Strong had realized something very unusual in the snap shot and had bothered to record it for all time in his book, as the photograph fully attests that these particular wild people unlike most other Native Americans definitely had very much facial hair as they wore long full beards, had thick leg hair almost to be suspect of fur; supported dirty looking elongated dreadlocks almost suggestive of African, had peculiar colored blondish red hair mixed with the dark; a skull type that was definitely not similar and completely non-typical of what is thought prototype American Indians ...Some had on their hands and feet to re-place of gloves or shoes, what were wrappings of some sort of possibly skins, or obscure cloth as would be much as if a protective bandage; moccasins were scarce, and all were beadles; had an irregular slender half starved body type, and of much of importance, each adult men had with them a much unfamiliar type of a hunting bow and arrow that was hardly to any imagination the expected prototype usually observed over the Americas; it was a more typical bow of what looked Asian origins that was far ahead of the times as would have been a much familiar type of a re curve-bow, that was definitely suspect of being a very close or was an exact copy of early Eurasian steppe horsemen bows that are far more powerful and proficient than is a typical Western American Indian, short bow!

What else had also gone completely UN-noticed until were done film enhancements? "Well, on the leg of one of the men was a definite tattoo of a large bird resembling a raven or a crow! The adults also evidenced elongated skulls, of a sort known in South America and Ancient Egypt, etc., that can only be accomplished by wrapping the head from birth! As said, this practice is not un-known, but looks completely out of place here! Another man pictured has much thick and heavy chest hair, and a curious tattoo done on one body part of the same obscure bird! All pictured look ragged, unheralded as if all were of an out cast people of sort exiting in complete desperation, that to all considerations of today's comparisons not to be derogatory, but much as would look un-kempt in anyone's opinion eventually happens with street people and/or beggars, swag-men of any dispensation of time... and they were even much different in descriptions from early 19th Century diary-logged California' O savages, that were ever early-on shot on sight by all comers, and especially this done by other Indians; as they were said to be debase, naked, homeless, a non-tribal people, useless, without tribe or a leader, etc! These people lived very close to what might be considered true wild hominids as were also described completely impossible by none other than our own, Samuel Clemens, or "Mark Twain," as he was all during his wandering mid century sojourn had before, during, and after the California Gold Rush of 1849! There is much to speculate here from about all directions. Read, "Life Among The Paiutes," by Mary Winnemucca Hopkins?"

Log: Comment ... "From Then To Now?" - Author

Even these people are different from the little re-conned with, impossible to approach, be-friend, or civilize, preach to of God, or much of what was said was not understood, much just the same as were the early California' o, Go-Shut' e' peoples, living hand to mouth where ever possible, where is today, north and south, over and far beyond the vast reaches of all of the Baja, California Peninsula, and all of the wild down to and to include the Sea of Cortez, where there are other distant tribes some similar, and others UN-familiar! Nevertheless these obscure people to the over all physical lean body proportions, and very long extended fingers, and are of a long toe description; this peculiarity was also had by the now believed, to have long been extinct "Fuegian Yámana," who were a very ever little visited, confused, and a forlorn, and almost unknown people, living on the frozen shores off the tip of South America at the Land of Fire, that is today on world maps as, Tara Del Fuego, described by Charles Darwin while on his epic, 1840's Voyage of the Ship, HMS Beagle, was it? Any way, there is a definite Asian/Eurasian anomaly connection here pictured in John Heller's single photo shot. We have him and Emery Strong to thank for the preservation of true hover obscure history! Much more will likely be God willing be written about these, or much similar western nomads in an up coming manuscript still in its infancy within the authors slated Sasquatch Trilogy collection.

Log: "The Siwash Indians!"

{"A far North West Indian term for one kind of a renegade!"}
{"A self-decided, or wanted cast out from a society, for what ever the reason, an outcast!"}
The Nomadic Tribe-less! The Obscure!
Idaho Chief Nampa, Was One Very Infamous!

It is true, as I have had them tell me themselves, "that the Native American peoples of yester-year, and still today, wanted nothing what so ever to do with many of these several still to be realized obscure peoples often called: The Other Tribe, almost to need be considered human-oids of a strange type - up from wild hominids;" some of them still thought even in my opinion, to be non but a relict hold-over from population an obscure Eurasian beginning of base Asiatic humanity as still are considered the wild snow-men of the Himalayas, ("Not to be confused of the legendary Yeti!") that still just might be found existing today, somewhere hidden in small bands as modern day troglodytes beyond the regularly visited Idaho/Montana desert moun-tains far over some distant horizon, best described from my vista as a much mixed and a varied people, a mix-mash of sorted active gene-pools as possible, existing in parallel almost unknown to the other over all of the immense extension of 46,separate or more wild desert/mountain river ecosystems, that comprise today what is called, "The Great Basin America Wilderness?" ("If further interested take the time to see what more can be realized/learned of the 17ᵗʰ - 16ᵗʰ Century Hidatsa Indian peoples that existed in caves for thousands of years until came the neo-phytes and traded them their first Tipis!")

Figure 20. A 1905 stereoscopic image from of a "Siwash Indian Shack" from the Library of Congress collection. You may be able to merge the 3D effect by viewing at 5-6" from the page; (reading glasses may help.)

Log: "SIWASH"

Captain Fremont wrote considerable of them when exploring far into The Lands Of Great Northern Mysteries!

"They are an outcast population! The Eskimo, the wolves, the Elk, feral man, and even you may become one, or even now be one? I am probably one? Donald Massey, of Butte Montana met his first and last one for real we that we ever after referenced "Rascal" as we continued for several seasons to find, and sometimes cast his separate tracks! Don Massey met his match, in

*Zakynerous Cave, Idaho, April 2003! If he had dare tell his story public back then when hap-
pened, he would had become another one! It was agreed that we not tell his adventure until
long after his death that would I write it! That part story is first time told in part somewhere below? Its been Ten years Donald... I kept the word!" If for any reason not sanctioned, that any
person of the tribe had mixed blood, it was for them thought UN-tailorable, or it was considered by them as a disgrace, at best, completely UN-wanted, debase, etc; if they had no one, or
no known relative that offered to care for them, then they sometimes thought themselves
needed to become a cursed outcast, etc." Many of these unknowns when realized were killed
on sight! This is not the place for any more part of that rote history... but during the early days
of all far Western American exploration's; famed explorers/wanderers/adventurers as was the
far spread Caption Fremont, Walker, Payette, Finan McDonald, and countless other notable
and little-sung great western pioneer's; many of them to our advantage also wrote somewhat,
or slightly of what took place, when first, or only time when confronting some of these sometimes described, "dastardly, pitiful, human wretches, etc!"*

*"Out of compassion, when finding unknown human evidence in caves and mountains, I have
felt true pity for them, because of still not knowing completely what, really, are all of these
wild people still alive in small numbers today wanted called Sasquatch, Bigfoot, or call them by
what ever as I believe that not a few of them are all of an exactly very same singular gene-pool
birth right, as from what we have discovered evidence of living in Idaho/Montana caves of late
over the past fifteen years running; when considering all mixed variations of physical body
parts witnessed in plaster castings, etc, all may indeed have something dire, and very directly to
do with all of this described pre-history/history conjecture of wild feral man beginnings, as well
as with the first true originations of Americas wild desert mustang horse populations, and as described all continuing moon adoration, hair plaiting, etc., via the allowance of the all seeing
eye of the Moon Goddess, Diana, or similar, and very much more! Just wait for all surprises
when we get into the varied reasons yet to be explained ahead having to do with, "Kumiss," or
what to fact is mare's milk, or horse milk! Wow, the absolute discovery of that evidence that
has been mixed into some of the long hair of the saved artifacts; it was my solemn promise to
Onya Two Feathers that I would not let her down, and would one day document our plaiting
discoveries! That promise had completely turned the tide of my avid determination to accomplish this manuscript come hell or high water, and so far it's one hell of a very hard job! So be
it, we are gonna get'er all down!"*

The Descent of Ancient Humanity!

The Unwanted? All world populations anciently had little if any real knowledge of the other,
and very early man became easily estranged, persuaded, and confused of his times sometimes in
strange response to his environment, etc. As the populations dispersed into all possibility, ethnically
we finally aspired to what we now have become today; as every single one of us are now an extremely mixed people that amounts to what is a true Mestizos, or a product of a much mixed
base/confused blood line; as for example, Pottawatomie with French, African with Dutch, and German with Shoshoni, Polish with Latvian, Spanish with Italian, Conquistador with Spanish Indian,
Navaho, and Aztec, Norwegian with Scott, Chinese with mega North American Indian and mega
Russian types of neophyte with Eskimo, etc., and so on, and on... Volumes could be written, and
still the list would not be complete able to completely describe Feral People! Where really is all of
this going? Well, since as far back in time to the present day all societies have had their unwanted,

as for example had became the East Indian Untouchables, similar demonized renegades as became the SIWASH, the colorful and disgusting pirates, many out casts as outlaws, the homeless, and the beggar, the undesired cursed Leper, any number of reasons for particular eccentrics, or thought peculiar people of many, many unattached human origins! Well really, where do you think all of them went when down trodden and perused? Wild man populations have existed living in parallel since the dawn of UN-recorder history! There is mention of them in most all important world documentation. I have a much similar, however separate opinion that would perhaps even more explain at least a real part of the mixed blood lines of the feral generation that now exists in particular Idaho/Montana mountain caves! What do most reading actually know of the ancient Hidatsa Native Americans, or the Sit-ti-ca, etc? The passionate mixing of blood lines is ever all obvious in all modern day ethnographic comparisons. "Yeah, what really are you, and who am I? What is anybody?"

Log: TRASHED COMPASSION! "Perhaps The Roman Colosseum!"

The story belief in wild man begins and perhaps ends in the sacrifice of human comfort, wanting compassion, and ever the mixed emotions of the human heart, abrupt the clash of cultures, much UN-wanted betrayal, and unnecessary blood shed, the furious wrath of forced religion, etc., to be reconciled and well understood within pre-history and continuing Western European, and Asiatic conquest. Humanity has only survived his violence as a result of the tender exchange reserved in the act of love … We are much more a part of a wild animal than most want to admit! Unknown, unwanted, and unspeakable wild populations were ever captured for hundreds of years from all Eurasian forests mountain ranges, to be brought back to, "The Colosseum," were they were predestined cursed/doomed, to be horrifically and mercilessly slaughtered numbering into the many, Many, thousands, as this still can be read today as recorded in existing collected journals as for one is, THE MARTYRS! These important historical accounts fully describe the unwanted history that became the heartless blood-let of the mighty, Roman Colosseum Arena, that to fact had gone onto human derogation for more than 750 years, plus another 150 years underground! Man is truly as brutal as he is also wonderful!"

What, really, Have We To Say Of The Full Moon?

In a last and final explanation, it seems to me that perhaps one abstract, or even the complete reason for the plaiting might be unexplainable, as some sort of a very real concern had of a particular antiquated, if not extremely relict, feral wild population, all latent fears had irrational, and ever required almost painfully demanding and stressful during all Full Moon Phase and abnormal conditions; that is to say, that these pitiful hominids exist in a "Definite Carry Over Tradition/Requirement," still much having to do with a very ancient and possibly a, "Cultist Type Society," as there apparently exists something extrinsic to the collective group experience, that seemingly exerts a controlling, unusual, and an Overriding Influence, resulting as an unwanted pursuit, done dutiful of terror, fired by a very real dread judgment concern of their acts, as might be further explained when we soon access, "The All Seeing Eye of the Crescent Moon Goddess, Diana," as there seems to be a common mechanisms of group influence in these various plaiting examples, different from what would be suspected their personal needs to insure survival! Something unmistakably is at work in the seemingly demanding and strange nature of a very real compulsion to plait the horses much the same or similar as the others! That in itself is a recognized cognitive basis for a conformity in a shared belief wanting to remain in harmony with the many? That is a definitely a conformity to some sort, of one or another, very ancient charismatic and ever demanding cultist adherence, much similar of the unsuspected influence of the unexceptionable demands of The Unification Church, had of, The Moonies, and some others!"

"AGAIN!"

The horses are coming and what does anyone think might be chasing them? Wolves, coyotes, Mt. lions, dogs, wild hominids, cowboys, or what, and why? This story truly big! Its explanations will set an uncanny president of curiosity resulting in more discovery. The book reads methodical and informative, and when considered from all base facts, it is as logical in presentation as it is completely true! We are now the ninth year of its arduous research. All conjecture and facts sighted here remain at the mercy of all future plaiting discoveries. This out of the box message equation insures a long season of continuing investigation and further needed common sense logistics. Surely other books will follow in its wake, as in every case scenario this book cannot possibly resolve every new and exciting question, or new idea posed. Everything here is first time conjectured, "just as if during all investigation, it were inspired to be coming straight out from the legendary, Pandora's Box, perhaps to be thought all relative of everything anywhere or at any time to had been highly mysterious, confusing, and/or perhaps magical historically; at least its content accesses some small facets of the worlds unrealized, unknown, unexpected, and even perhaps thought bazaar, or high strange and/or unethical and unorthodox traditions/customs and facts! Some of them as pacifying as they are a dire danger and demanding to the player even if a cultist, and every bit miserable during all seasons of cold and/or hot weather.

Each new full moon phase considered is a separate insight into the real world of ancient passé, and pseudo wanton current high strange, unorthodox, and barbaric queasy and orthodox Christian humanity. This is especially SO where humans have opt to associate themselves with all higher animals as are horses, cattle, goats, fowl, etc., to any particular lunar moon phase adherence, superstition, etc. This book is not intended for the lazy of mind! It is a far voyage across all of Western America's Last Remaining Sage Brush Desert Sea! Be ready for an extraordinary ocean depth rewarding, non-deceptive voyage into the truly unrealized, "Wild Neither World," of already proven living wild man entity, as can further realized/exemplified by the 1968 discovery of the shot twice and killed body of, "The Wisconsin Ice Man," and only one year earlier, was discovered and filmed, "Patty Sasquatch," at Bluff Creek California, year 1967, "now I ask anyone, weren't those two separate events highly coincidental? Within the wilds of all North and South America, in fact the whole world at large, there are perhaps several possible separate identities to be had if known, to denote wild man hominid types as yet completely UN-realized, that are popularly accepted in today's academic/maverick, Mad-Rush for an affirmed name to account for American Sasquatch, ridiculously called, Bigfoot, when there was ever the all true wild man hominid identity of, Bluff Creek Patty, and, The Wisconsin Ice man!"

(See all true story, Doctor Isaac Sanderson's, Ice Man probe-report as written in, ARGOSY Magazine, spring issue, 1968!)

Log: December 13, 2012

Today I am again at the Oregon residence of, Bob and Patty Reinhold. Exactly two days earlier, one year ago, I left Sweet Home and drove six hundred miles directly to the Jenson Ranch property along the Owyhee River, to observe the historical full moon eclipse evolving on the 11th of December, 2011, to see first-hand, what if anything would occur having to do with all new and ongoing plaiting being done on their mare, Hink? "Much Did Happen! The next, and very last December 2012, Full Moon Phase, will occur on, December 28th, three days past Christmas, I will be somewhere to update for a last time any and all conclusions to this manuscript! Patty Reinhold, while reading over my shoulder tells me, "Don, this book reads much like a confusing mystery novel! I can't wait to read it!" Thanks Patty, that is encouraging! At least you got the mystery part right! Lets Next Send In The Educator Critics, For Their Separate Opinion?"

The Horses Are Coming!

"Edgar Allen Poe could have dreamt this story up!"

"Vincent van Gogh could have best illustrated it!"

"Max Brand would have completely exhilarated its content!"

"And, Sir Author Conan Doyle, under the guise of, Sherlock Holmes would have solved its mystery!" And, that said, I have been inspired, and had also promised Tonia Brown, that we would one day share some of its incredible mysteries, and hidden secrets! As you well know babe, all of its explanations are not everyone conclusive, but for the moment there are no better answers? If so, lets hear them? And for the moment in time, lets opt to ring the bell for an abstract recess, "had outside of all highly judgmental, and ever programmed class room dictation that is had of many of today's illogical instructors!" Decide for yourself what is, or is not written here easily noticeable between the lines of all story that is not intended to further persuade or convince anyone of anything other than the stark fact/truth of a definite known to be existing little realized Neither World of plaited horses, and further update them perhaps a little-bit abstract, of the true facts of a less than known wild humanity, that if anyone are wantin' of them or not, they are still much a real part of today's humanity! Wild man exists, and I am here to write it!"

Generally Speaking... What Are We All But A Natural Man or Women? Like it or not, you might be a biting, scratching animal yourself! Watch all full moon phase peculiarities, its many effects on wild life and humans; their interesting reproduction go gestation, all seasons of the spawning fish, the migrations of wild ducks and geese, in fact all animals and birds, and in time each of us will perhaps realize, wantin' within our latent fantasies, is a covert desire at times to be returning back to all of the basics of what we once were, "a wild searching hominid, ever lost in a mixed adventure of mixed gender solicitation, and abandon exhilaration, no longer acceptable, that that modern society has allowed forgotten. All humans, after all, are an ancient breed. Our difference from the lesser animals is our blessing, or is it a curse to be able to become bias, prejudiced, obnoxious, and unfounded in many a questionable and reasonable opinion. Blathering/jabbering speech is only understood between monkeys, apes, and particular wanna-be king of the mountains!"

EXUNDA

The Answer To Explain The Plaiting Anomaly Is Hidden In Exunda! Academics and moot critics, not any of them name mentioned here, that insist a non-truth seeking past an opinion of a ridicules Gigantic-Ape enough to be anyone's monkeys uncle, or relative of mine, thank you! "We evolved naturally from humankind! Wild man has always been with us if nothing but an out-cast! We should not fear what we can't understand; we need to just ignore it! Nothing is written here that cannot be changed, proven, or added upon! This treatise is but the first beginning step taken down a long road of future discovery. The journey ahead will be very difficult to write, however it will also read much exhilarating. The world deserves to know these highly mysterious truths! After all is said, there remains very much more of this anomaly as yet to be unraveled! My efforts are but the beginning of many more relative discoveries to continue in another future book, "as this book, abrupt all continuing priorities, is intended to be my first, and last written word on the subject?" Decide for yourself what more to all satisfaction will need be revealed when we finally reach down deep into the little known abyss that is the almost magical far off place that the author is eager to explore! In that exciting place of the exciting and mysterious, and exhilarating the slated Sasquatch Trilogy, ever describing all of the improbable, will be a very mixed bag of research had from Exunda, the fantasy description place that suffices all mystery short of deception! "If a thing is not the obvious, then Doctor Watson, it is the reverse!" - Sherlock Holmes.

My Apology?

To all readers that may continue thus far somewhat confused, as I just tonight for another time read through some many pages of its passé and continuing material, and well realize the possible confusions of its extremity mixed bag jargon had abrupt all of its foreign to most, Bob Cat Logic! That last said, because over the past nine years of chasing plaited horses, I had continued to write the book as if most of it were intended only for myself, ever earnest to be including in my log many a side trip into the various far corners of about every where, no-where, and back again, in order to exonerate various admired people. and to be able to site much needed comparative experience that still continues to further validate this difficult research! The wanton need to appreciate public various persons has much inspired this book, as to fact it is just as if all of them were still along side myself in a separate d-j-Va u inspiration, dedication, and unconditional support as their separate effort was ever a definite labor of love to had explored all project outcomes, etc! Much need be said in the horse manuscript of Tonia Brown, as she wrote extensively of our research covert until was discovered in her left behind treasures of gender insights to our adventures! So much so did she write, that the book at places as we will see, could have been written as hers! I am writing dutiful to include her insights into a manageable story! Onya Wild in action was an adventuress extraordinaire-icon. Truly I do miss her unheralded idiosyncrasies, that said, the manuscript can be best explained, as a literal informative description of plaited wild and domestic horses, ever exposing possible pertaining suspect cultist information, while wanting to be accessing ancient passé culture, virus contemporary pseudo Christian humanity and all mixed and hidden idiosyncrasy, and various introductions (where fit!) into the wild world of high desert-mountain cave exploration, ever accomplished in this manuscript, for the dire sake of discovering if possible even more existing wild hominid evidence further siting the plausible reasons why if for any explicit reasons we have continued to explore further into these caves; all reasons having to do directly, because it is in these remote caves and grottoes where exactly we have continued to discover much credence to further validate all further high plausibility of belief in wild hominids being five fingered opposed thumb and index, adapt in that necessary way to be able for what good reasons to be able to manage the high strange plaiting done on American horses! Because of the book's many variations, and for time, "it remains almost impossible for the author to further edit any real part of this revelation, as even as I write I have now only 12 short broken four hour days until the 28th of December, 2012, ("The final date of the last Full Moon!") to complete this book and its research!

"2013?"

As said, I am wanting to publish this manuscript by the early months of 2013! What is down for the record will surely raise the eyebrows of many a sorry "short beaked," long winded, extremely desperate wanna-be self-praising narcissistic, Johanna type, sink the ship critic! Yeah rascals, the plaited horses have arrived, and what more intelligent have any of you to say what did it other than pixies, fairies, goblins, ghosts, etc? That's completely idiotic B. S.! No we have Not left the light on for any one who would think at any time to opt to purposely shoot, harm, or unnecessarily capture a wild hominid, Sasquatch, miserable, pixie, fairy, goblin, or especially Molly b Damn, etc. As I well know from personal sightings, that there are at least three, if not actually six wild hominids already known to exist, and still be roaming over the far places of Idaho/Montana, and beyond that to fact are very much of a humanistic characterize! The book's true message, however confusing to anyone was well worth the effort for the author, as the many self-explanatory photographs included, along with the extensive research done abrupt all the mixed camaraderie of exploring more than wrote this jargon!"

Log: Gin Davis, Dillon Montana, October 23, 2012

A true deposition of a particular importance!
The candid happenstance deposition taken of, Gin Davis,
Whitehall, & Dillon Montana.

"An incredible recent per-chance discovery of many more unexpected plaited horses! "Gin said, that just possibly there are more of them still running in, The Crazy Mountains!"

Lunar Magic?

By now it is surmised that the bulk of all readers have well thumbed through the many pictures of the book, and have a reasonable curiosity if not a good idea of where we are going with this almost unbelievable adventure? If not, please pause and have another long educated good look, as the full moon phase of Halloween is only one week away, and its full lunar importance will be fully explained. Gin's Deposition:

Gin Davis, resident of Whitehall, & Dillon, Montana. "This is a deposition of great comparative passé, and current, artifact importance!" Note: It was first intended that Gin's story be related at the beginning of the book, as all of the facts of her timely message is very far ahead and very important to the relativity of the manuscripts intentions, and her short story is also much of a local importance to aid the author and others to continue in the time taking and growing expensive plaiting study! However said, this sort of pertaining research will continue to surface up to very last hour of its intended end, at the last stroke of midnight, New Years Eve, 2012, before we shoot our revolvers into the night sky of year 2013! The reader need remember this particular story for its uncanny importance. As all happened candid, and it was impossible to take a written deposition, and so out of necessity it is written here from memory only slightly paraphrased.

Log: Gin Davis, the moment in time, now at Dillon Montana.

"Gin, quite by chance, while busy at work, unexpectedly ambled on to me with her incredible story of plaited horses, that still overwhelms my imagination! Every small bit word of her impromptu-information blurted out of her mouth, with recognized facts without her at all being aware that she was explaining to me much that I was long aware of and of much importance, if not a God-Send oral artifact of comparative information to further validate my on-going nine years of high strange plaiting research!" As said, our meeting was most uncanny, exactly as would be her story! It was all just as if it would seem that all of it was destined to happen on that day? Later in the book, the reader will fully appreciate all of her true story worth. Perhaps in future I will need ask if her if she will opt to include more details in writing, as her deposition seems to had been an uncanny example of mental synchronicity? Some things thought to had been only coincidental, are not necessary just that at all? "I have the darnedest ability to ever be discovering, or attracting a tougher man, women, or beast, that I have to eventually fend off in order that "they" be able to fight someone else on another day! Yesterday while walking down the street, I was attacked without provocation by a sizable yellow dog! "His color was indicative of his cowardly character, and we told him so, as the women with me threw the, "idiot cur-twit," back over his garden fence! Pirates and cowboys just don't belong in town!"

Log: Author! "With The Rest of Gin's Story!"

This afternoon I ambled into the Print Shop at Dillon Montana to have some photocopies made of some many of the photographs intended to be used in this book. By now as already said, most readers if still with me, have already thumbed through the book's photographs and are still ever in wonder, if not completely in awe of what exactly can all of this plaiting mean? I can't as yet give you all of the detailed answers in one sudden burst, but trust me, in due time, there sure as hell will be many a pseudo, "Been There, And Done That, know it all critic that will opt to flaunt their arrogant ignorance! Perhaps Ronda, we should send in that yellow hound?" "

Gin's Deposition Story Continued: From where I was waiting and standing at the counter, my turn next obvious, "I handed Gin my stack of photos intending for her to make copy! Out of habit, before doing any printing, she quickly flipped through all loose pile exposing it's many pictured content! "Wow, she said, boy have I seen a lot of this sort of stuff in my time! Why in the heck would anyone want pictures of anything as puzzling and strange as this ugly stuff?" "Needless to say, I was overwhelmed at Gin's response!" Flabbergasted, is a better word... It was almost enough that I have stammered and fell back ward, as I asked her... "Exactly what is it that you are telling me? Are you saying that you have seen this sort of elongated plaited confusion before? If so, where? When? And how many times? Please be specific, and tell me what you know?" The busy girl had no Idea of her importance! "Yeah, she said, I got a minute, I can tell you! What is this all about? For years I had to untangle that stuff! I was always the one!

None other would do it!" "Thirty Five or more Plaited Horses! Wow!" "Heck yes, Gin said... We just recently sold all of our horses! Most all of them had left on them those sort of braids! All of them looked very much like this! I was always the one over the years that had to be picking them apart! Man, some of them were more than impossible! It was a lot of hard work! No, I had no idea at all what was doing it... but it just kept happening over and over? I never really gave it much thought... But I can assure you, that it wasn't done by any wind, or by the heavy brush either! Every time the horses went up to the Crazy Mountains North of Whitehall, many of them came back with all of that sort of incredible looking tangled long strange hanging plaiting! Some of it really looked impossible to had even been done at all... Some of them were really strange! Well, back then, we ran a lot of horses... We kept a large string for the hunting season.... Maybe at least a good 30 – 35, or more, or less, all of them were Quarter Horses! The strange thing was, that every time it happened, it was only done on the mares... The females were the only ones that had that stuff done to them! Not once do I remember any of the studs (Male horses!), having had the braids!" No I don't know what caused it? All of us at the ranch along with my father, thought it was probably being done by the strange vibrations of the quaking land? What she asked, what more can you tell me about this?

Do you have any more idea of what is doing this?"
(Q's, that were asked of Gin!)

"Were any of the braids at any time ever left hanging down from off the horses neck, that looked to be, or actually were without a doubt much longer than the length of the original mane? Were any of them say …. "to be looking to even be twice or more elongated than the natural mane? If so, how would any of that even be at all possible? How could any horse's mane be made to be longer after it was braided, than it was shorter before it had been messed with?" "I don't know, she said! That's a good question?" Gin: "There were a lot of wild horses up there in those mountains, and perhaps there still are some? All of us would go together and round them up, and next sell them for mink ranch pet food, etc!

Nearly everyone of those horses always had many, many, wild and very strange plaits on them! We caught a lot of them! No, I have no idea how anyone, or anything as you say could think to bond with a wild horse, and no idea either of how they could make the mane even longer? That's all pretty spooky stuff! You got me really thinking! "Well, what really do you think done it?" I made no further suggestions, or told her any more of the known particulars of my theory, or how long I had known and believed the strange curiosities, and/or wild stories ever explained to me by the local Mexican wranglers; there are many wild tales still today coming out of the Crazy Mountain Range! The entire region had long been known by the ancient Hidatsa, and many current Indian Tribes; it was well known to be an almost forbidden place, "a place of hallowed ground if you will, ever it is still considered to be a sacred place of spirits, mischief, mystery, etc., it was a traditional region to be highly avoided! People were not encouraged to traverse the land without good reason? One look at those mountains even from a distance to this day one can well understand why on all current road maps those mountains are still referenced as, "The Crazy Mountains....!" As even the mountain foot-hill hillocks run confusing, irregular, and most all of them are completely catty-wompus to the other! If on foot say, or on horse back during a, Montana White-Out Blizzard, it would be very easy to become temporary lost! There are many a strange story long time coming from there?" I promised Gin I'd be back to talk to her when she had more time? "She agreed to add her name to this deposition, in order that the book would have further credence?" Thanks Gin, without my having al-

ready had much of that same separate knowledge as related in her deposition, who if anyone would opt to believe her? "Realize it or not, if you have a story similar it is more than important to all continuing research!" "This is truly an undeniable all true Montana story, and, Gin Davis is definitely another invincible first prize, Montana Women!"

"As I departed the door, I asked Gin a final question! Gin, what do you know about wild horse mares milk, clabbered milk, and/or Asian type primitive yogurt? Have you ever heard of Kumiss, or ever notice anything strange white colored, or a glue like white sticky mess stuff mixed in, or fasted and dried into the braids?" It was ironic, never once had I mentioned my belief in wild man, or offered any further explanation, for the reasons of those last questions. When I left Gin was looking back over her shoulder, as if as much curious and perplexed as myself! What was she thinking, or remembering? What else did she forget, or even know that had been told me? Our per-chance acquaintance O'course was much interrupted by the business crowd... "I have actually gone back twice since, to no avail, to ask her more about her experience, but couldn't catch her, as she works a broken shift! In time there will be another opportunity? I will try one more time before publishing to contact her in case she has something new to update?"

"Good night Marion!"

{Time Out For Me!}

I know that you are still with me, and just as you always knew and told me so, "that one day Don, we will need to write our adventures if for no other reason than for the entertainment of our grand children! Other wise, I am sure that they will never know us, and especially you, or realize the love that we had for each other or for them! We were forever off wandering into somewhere, or coming back from no-where? Don't give up in what you are doing Don! We both know the importance of our discoveries! Don't be to sad too long when I am gone, and never forget what it is like to be poor! Finish this cabin house, that you will have a place to come back to when you are old! I darn well know because of your acute independence that you one day will be a very lonely man! You are sort of like the mountain lion on the mountain ridge! Nothing, not even I could tame you!"

Well Smoochy, I have begun to write a part of our sojourn! And I am sure that you, like me you will never forget the, "Giant King Bear," up on Honey Jones Ridge, or the, "high strange Ones," that we left behind each fall with the Black Bears at "Happy Creek," deep in the St. Joe forest to the ever ponder, and/or worry wonder all future bias critic imagination if ever any read my manuscript? And just as you were always the catalyst, and bright candle light of every inspiration, that guided our early, and all late night discoveries, you also knew that one day I alone would probably need to write of your discovered fascinations! As no matter come what may, you are ever with me on every far flung impossible trail! There will be no beautiful sun down anywhere that will not exhibit your remembered supportive spirit. Even during our times of nothing to do, we did it all most willingly! We shared many a wild dream, and much, much, more, that was ever to be another almost impossible adventure!" We both forever will remember every single black bear and frozen candle light night! "As you often said, that you would wait for me at sun set, at the place on the mountain where the King Bear, Grizzly, and friendly grouse would return back to ponder you ahead of the long shadows just before dark at the far corner of our favorite wild berry patch! The bears were ever there with you harmless, to feast on the moon light ripened berries by the time that your signal candle flickered its lighted message from way down off in the that lonely canyon. I always knew, that you knew, that I had ever watched back to you, for your safety, from every rock strewn mountain, timbered ridge, or cliff. Our separate confidence in the other was ever your true protection. Your bear collection adventures I promise will be been written in a separate manuscript journal. Perhaps one day our grand children will visit me to read all Original Grand-Ma wild bear enticement? "Just as you always said, Don, don't, I won't hold my breath till any of them come, and don't look back to far in retrospect, as all things of an importance are ever to be relived if only happen in the fantasy of another dream! I will never completely leave this house! Be sure that you clear its title just as soon as you can! There is something very wrong with the way this property is being handled!" "In my garden are things wonderful, things exciting, things exhilarating, things very special as were each of my children! Come here when you can to visit? I will always be here in spirit to comfort you! Remember Don, that life goes on! Don't be sad too long! I also learned to love the mountains as much as the sea! But we loved each other beyond expression!" So Be It Ah-Lun, So Be It! All Children And I, Continue To Love You Inviolate!,

A SHORT INFORMATIVE PRELUDE:

(For Phil Jenson!)
"Written in horse whisper, to all of those curious that still hear the call!"
"The Far Nevada Sage Brush Sea!"

"In the Land of Northern Mysteries, where remains The Sage Brush Sea, the wild plaited horses are coming on the wind; all excitement of their running play and frenzy, will be gone by dark up towards the evening star; where the wild ducks, geese, and swan in flight, look down at the wandering bear... By the dark of the moon on the Wild Owyhee Range, the North Star hides itself within all drifting clouds of night and the climate change.. The welcome smell of rain and something very odd and strange is with it on the wind..? From somewhere far off distant, comes the unwitting wily coyote rally, of barks, calls, yelps, wines, and gnashing teeth; all of this is far beyond the comradely and safety of my sage brush fire, that reflects its dancing comfort shadow back from the unknown petroglyphs stone, where something, or someone, "sure as hell," just cast its ghost like imagine telling me that it is has hidden itself behind that rock! "I only fear what is frightening... but at the moment with my hand on my ax, my coffee cup and pistol, I feel no ill, or do I really? Another long look, and what ever was there I ponder has gone its way?"

Upon morning, once again mounted on my horse, I quickly un-lash my rifle from its boot, as I pause to ponder an uneasy sound? What the heck? "I discover again that my horse's mane has been braided another time, in a very same strange and precarious way?" Now I am off my horse, by a moon lit sky, apprehensive of the bright lightening flash, I curiously examine another time the much elongated plaited mane...? All of this is truly more than strange! How really Old Floss, what done this to you, and why? All looks impossible! "The horse was tethered every time, not all that far, if not very close by the fire! I continue to ponder the unknown problem and its ever improbable cause? There had been no wind at all, nor had the horse done its dusty roll-kick! What the heck? What or who was there on that late night in the dark shadows of that fire lit petroglyphs stone? It was also odd, that Floss had not once floundered, bucked, bolted, or ran, as for much lesser reasons she sometimes had? Horses, women, card games, and now high this strange plaiting, and those odd sounds...? None of this makes any sense! "I gave my horse my last jelly beans, before used my knife to cut loose the long tangled hanging mess, and next tossed the braid into the fire pit with my cold sage brush tea before on my way ... "Old horse I said, you got a problem, but who in the hell would ever believe the details? What done it girl?" When I awoke at sun rise, I'd checked my gear for tools, and every tool was gone? What ever had managed the plaits has now became a thief!" Lets ride to Paradise girl and take the problem to, I.W. Harper, Jim Beam, or perhaps Old Crow, we will get us what ever they charge the least? Perhaps one well known king of wandering fools seated at the bar will have an idea of fact to appease my curiosity?"

Log: Halloween, 2012 -

"What is Really Different and special In The Blood Lines of a Blazer Horse from any other?" No doubt about it, the plaiting continues even as I write! As the full moon of October 31st, Halloween, is only a few days away...! The horses on the fringe area of the Oregon Owyhee Desert every full moon phase, according to the options all considered of a bright night opposed to overcast weather, for some obvious reason the latter seems most likely. "There definitely is a high intellect involved in all of this!"

Log: "More Strange Plaited Manes Unk!"

Norma, and Phil Jenson,
Owyhee River Ranch, Oregon,
October 6, 7, 8, 2012.

Assuming that every one has already read the strange plaiting account related of Gin Davis telling of the Montana Crazy Mountains, and read the short ode to The Sage Brush Sea, etc., it seems permissible.... "in spite of being way, way, far ahead of all story facts needed that are necessary to really be able to understand any real part of this uncanny extraordinaire adventure;" it suddenly seems important that I opt to update this uncanny message regardless, with a most interesting high strange true life plaiting event, that took place and had occurred only recently on the Jenson Ranch Property! A phone call came to me from Norma Jenson explaining that the high strange plaiting was done another time on the Blazer blood-line mare named, Hink! "This happened Don, about 96 hours ago! The message was right on schedule, as two full moon phases over lapped into the Month of October 2012. I had somehow forgotten to stay in close touch! The collective research becomes very difficult to administer. Input to the manuscript seems to continue almost night and day, every day, even as I sleep! The book to anyone's best advantage needs to be written backwards! All need continue patient with my sorted descriptions! I only have became a pseudo writer out of dire necessity because these truths badly need be revealed. Trust me, other better writers will come after me!"

"FOUR FIG BARS!"

< Another Full Moon Phase! >

Norma Jenson

Paraphrased next is that exact story, word for word, as best I can relate; "exactly as was told me by Norma, while visiting her sister Shirley Chandler at Pocatello, Idaho, October, 10, 2012[t]! "Hink" (A pseudo explanation much short of all needed facts needed to further explain the plaiting been done last week on Hink, as was related in the short account above! It is often most difficult to get all of the pertaining facts from anyone to account for all of the rest of the story importance!) "I had instructed my sister Norma to opt to leave a considerable amount of fig bar cookies … ("I had suggested that she leave five pounds! There is a definite reason, and meaningful intention to had opt such a large amount, as the possible extreme importance of the Halloween Full Moon phase, an eclipse of the moon, etc., anything at all to do with possible Lunar Adherence, in this case scenario becomes paramount to outcomes! I just know that without a doubt for some reason that the Unknown creatures were staying somewhere close by to the horses, just as I also knew from many previous experiments, that the wild creatures love them! Norma said, "Well at first I was reluctant to leave that many cookies out there! But I did exactly as you said! I left "4" fig bars close by to the horse! Two were on the ground.. Another one into the feed pan, and the other one I left on the window ledge of the stable. Marvin Hollens came over and brushed out Hink's elongated, tangled and braided mane, that had been left that way just as you had suggested from last month! Well, when Phil and I returned back the next morning, the mane had been completely re-plaited, and the four bars were gone? Everyone was completely shocked! This stuff just doesn't happen! There was no wind... Nothing at all to more explain any of it! It is all just strange... It just keeps happening over and over! "What I can't understand is, so far, not once has it happened to the other horse with it! Now explain that?" ("Can't yet, however, both of them are mares! Only suggestion has to do with the Blazer blood line … As ahead will be explained, that Brenda Hinck and I, several years earlier, took a careful one day long head count, of 135, "Neil Hinck, ranch breed , Blazer Blood horses, "and the tally then was, an incredible, 40% of them had been plaited, and 99% of them were pregnant fillies, opposed to mares! Only two studs of the fast dwindling herd, had at all been messed with and those manes were done but insignificant, as if perhaps something was wanting to practice? That last said is not necessary so, as I have since been developing a more substantial theory to explain it?"

Update: Log – October 25, 2012

"I got to admit it! The temptation to keep writing ahead of all story and pertaining information, is overwhelming! Bob Smallsbach, if by now you or anyone is already completely confused or bored, throw the book, or jump ahead a few pages, and you will quickly catch up and return back to nowhere? Actually I will be complimented if you ever admit that you read the complete manuscript! Anyway Bob, Old Pal …! Be in touch, as the much awaited Halloween Full Moon is pending in just six days on, October 31, and only last night Norma and Phil agreed to leave a considerable stack of UN-opened, one pound heavy packaged fig bars (I had Suggested four lb packages!), close-by to the brushed out horses, where all of the treats would be ever obvious, etc! ("Leaving the cookies unopened on this possible special night, might be much appreciated, and in a much personal way the offering also speaks of friendly associations if any are to be had future; as much has happened that will be more explained in its place, this was an important experiment and was far, far, from the first time done by the author!"

"PLAITING, & HALLOWEEN?"

"Indian say, many white people, women and man, plenty head strong, little cooperation, much stubborn! Their children laughing at them! It is spooky how they waste pumpkin, and money to make Jack O' Lantern! The European brought this strange custom to our land! It was never our custom! Perhaps there is a warning in the grimace carved face on the squash? We like the pie! We let them have their way! Save me the seeds please! Our people like to eat them!" - The late, "Chief Smoky," Paiute Indian Reservation, Ely Nevada, fall, 2006. Stubbornness as a tradition, must run in many families blood!

"All Hallows Eve! I have never liked Halloween! Never! What, really, Are The Little Known Traditions of Halloween, Unless As It Is The Obvious, It Must Be Fear? How did this strange adherence abrupt all Lycanthropy of the October Full Moon begin? And how long, how long indeed, do we humans need to submit? It is definitely a controlling factor of little or no choice! "No choice is of a diabolical nature ... I'd rather be fishing!" - J. Foxx

Traditions

Plaiting, History, Obscure Humanity, The Ocean,

Stars, Sky, and the New Moon!

"We Are definitely Connected! Historically speaking, ancient European, and particular Eurasian Halloween Traditions and abstract adherence, were all much un-similar, and yet similar to some extent of what is still observed today "On, All Hollows Eve," in North America! However on that night, far across the Sea of Bake I, to include all of the wild wind swept mountain desert steppe vastness of all upper European-Asia (Not to include all of Eurasia!), and in many far distant neophyte cities, beyond the southern borders of countries such as, Mongolia, Tibet, China, Bhutan, India, all wild countries of the Himalayas, to as far East, and West, of them to as far as you want to go with your imagination; you will not find Halloween observed even today in many places, as the natural horrors of all the frozen lands of all high steppe, desert forest, and mountain of most lower Eurasia, had already far enough off the diabolical to combat with before the undeniable plague came by the white community! Early Vikings very early had sailed up the all main inland navigable rivers to trade and plunder as far as what now is Russia, and places beyond of upper China! Others followed after them as is exemplified by the sojourns of Marco Polo, "and so came with them, the unheralded rush of the UN-wanted neophyte Halloween, "that was a true witch's celebrated UN-holy day of sacrificial adherence," that history is little realized for its hideous ramifications of harm and misery, especially this is so in North America! South America does not all traditions of Halloween quiet the same. During the Dark Ages, The Crusades, the Campaigns of Charlemagne, The Roman Games, Genghis Khan, Attila the Hun, all endless pillage of man and beast, human terror, torment, sacrifice, etc; "during all of that dark now wanted forgotten history," horses then were much, much, in use! Tonia researched a lot of this alone for her own knowledge and education, "ever telling me excited as she was, of the many, many, ancient and per-history uses of horses, including food, etc. "Everything back then, was ever tied to them, by what ever the means, including their manes and tails! The plaiting of horses is not at all new thing! It was a useful practice done of long, long, ago...

Log: Needed Humor

"On the fun side Kathy, to answer your question as to what are wild hominids opposed to wild Homo-sapiens? Well we humans are hominids, much just like wild them! But wild them as hominid-humans, thought to be a true humanoid, are not us either, or is a wild those, or any thing exactly like them either, or are they one of us, unless you insist to be a monkeys uncle! Feral hominids as wild man have always been with us <u>voluntary</u> or unwanted as an outcast of orthodox society, and/or will remain little realized to be living in parallel with us as long as Homo sapiens continue to exist with them as voluntary, or an unwanted outcast of any society!" "Thanks Don, she said that's just exactly the way everyone should write it down to memorize it?"

"Important!"

Log: A True Assessment

Early wild people as had passé Russian, had well documented a wild woman called, Zanna, who was captured and taught to do useful labor during the latter 19th Century, she became a valuable commodity. Persons similar as her as slaves, would be able to perform all improbable labor not wanted of humans! If my theory is correct, and I firmly do believe that it is, wild hominids as are, Almasty, Yeti, Yeron, etc., that today are wanted called Sasquatch in America, etc., are of a very mixed blood line extension of any mega number of obscure mixed gene-pools, blood lines, regional home range, etc., and in addition they comprise much of a mixed DNA appropriations had from all world populations of today! It has been proven through exhumed DNA, that Zanna had born three or four human children as a result of several unfortunate circumstances! What tells us that? ("Zanna's history and sad plight, is well documented, and can be read on the net. Her son, Kuwitt who has been since his death exhumed, married into the passé twentieth century society, became a farmer, and left behind children! Wild man, wanting of rejecting his existence or not, to name a just a few, includes all of similarity gene-pools of the relict anomalies as are named above; there blood lines extended into the Americas, via any and all pre-history navigation efforts, as are the incredible noted Sea Voyages accomplished by the Chinese, prior to the invasion of the Forbidden City by the Northern Mandarins, who instituted the beginning of the Ming-Dynasty in, 1404 – 1407. Eurasian, Greek, Roman, Arabian, etc., also sailed far to plunder and explore in close alliance with many an early Northern European Voyager, some of them arrived to the Americas even before finally came the Norse Vi-kings! Obscure Eurasian, and even some South Pacific Islanders, by what ever the means also were brought here, as their blood lines are also much evidenced among the native peoples of Canada-America! At least twenty two separate American Indian tribes, "for one the Navajo," evidence high count Chinese, and various Asian DNA! As early year as, 500 B. C., the UN-known mariner/explorer, "Zakynerous," carved his last message to the world in basalt on the, "New Mexico Signature Stone," located in close proximity to the small berg town of, Socorro! History as we most think to know it, is hardly taught properly. The Chinese even mapped a great portion of South Pacific, and Antarctica, long before the destruction of the disc Forbidden City in 1405 ... Where really does that put Columbus? Some scholars today now realize that the Chinese had very likely circumvented all of the Northern Territories of far Siberian Russia, by following as closely as possible, the yearly, short seasonal Ice Melt, separat-

ing the land from all Ice-pack had along the shores of all Northern Siberia! They accomplished this by sailing from East to West, after sailing North past Kamchatka via the waters of Alaska; by sailing East from there they had finally arrived to, Rain Bow's End, or to the vast frozen proximity of what today is Icelandic, Lap-Land, Norway, etc!" Wow what a trip! I would liked to had been with them! Very Ancient Beginnings! It is ever obvious that some many obscure combinations of early, and late coming mariners, had actually arrived to many, many, an un-realized land fall, probably much earlier than what is wanted realized in pseudo English world history (!), "and ever sailing with them, were some many feral wild hominid populations that could be considered today, to had been the true founders of all, Hairy & The Henderson, ri-diculous/misleading, Bigfoot Mythology," and All True living wild man fact! These pathetic creatures - ("Call them that?) - were captured/solicited, and maintained for the specific inten-tion that they would be manning the oars, scraping off the sea-moss and barnacles from the ships hull, and they were ever intended to be taken any where needed/wanted as forced slave laborers, "at best said, were treated... if by the imagination comparisons-exemplified, by the less than compassionate treatment had, and the horrendous true history known of Zanna; all of these hominids were brought to do all difficult mining, logging, and what ever? Some many of these, "Untouchables," were loosed to the wilderness by various circumstance, and obviously knew very well how to do braiding, as plaiting, and how to interact with horses! Combine any part of what is written above, to include all possibly unwanted-demanding, and even some-times horrendous full moon phase adherence, and its possible ramifications that have not been explained thus far that requires covert mischief done within all understandings ever harsh and difficult are the demands of a very real, or a vivid imagined fear factor, as has are enlisted the slightest requirement of witch craft participation, and as will be mentioned many more times ahead, fetishism, idolatry, lunar, and aquatic deity belief much the same or similar, to include the misunderstandings, fears, and sometimes real horror factor abrupt all world wide reenact-ments of the debase being done on each and every Halloween eve, that have been forever practiced five stars in all country theater of the North Western Europe, etc! The true witch hunt has just began in America, and cultists are on the increase! Considering all of this, and much more to come... how difficult really, is it for anyone "not" to be able to imagine the full magni-tude of unheralded diabolical power, obligation, and negative sway, that could be easily dealt from any satanic deceptive point of impatient control, "moot of, apathy, mercy, compassion, etc., and the obvious misunderstandings ever continuing in blind participation had of the play-ers on the opposite side of a two headed coin and serpent; so completely confused are the lat-ter so as not to able to identify exactly what it would take in price or blood-let to admit one al-ready living in wrath and fear, any reasonable assurance of continuing free life unto beyond hand to mouth survival; all of that indeed would be a big concern of anyone that did not comply unconditionally without question, and be ever repetitive of any negative attitude to-ward any already blind sighted commitment/allegiance completely predicated upon ones ad-herence to a questionable duty fear of the unknown, or even a sacrificial requirement directed towards some obscure moon goddess, or possible animism that might even include a horse fet-ish idolatry? The Lunar Goddess, Diana, was long adorned in some way or another, almost since the dawn of time when considering her, "All Seeing Eye," that becomes ever obvious more than a week or so before and after each new full moon phase; "first appearing as a the moon dwindles as a sliver Crescent Moon until if finally graduates in size to becomes the ever popular, "Omnipotent Crescent Moon," that without fail follows prior too, and after every New Moon phase!"

SIRIUS

And there is much, much more, as what if little does most anyone think to know of the mega influence allowed world over of the passé alien Sky Goddess, SIRIUS, that over the centuries has been credited to be even more influential than most all other many unorthodox deities similar as those already mentioned with the premise, and allowed pretense of being, or becoming a Savior, God, Goddess, etc? All of this is very easily acceptable to the savage and/or pseudo uncivilized pagan mind! Almost anything among the true barbarians of yesteryear believed to had been a controlling factor of man, his mind, body, and emotions, all higher animals and nature, might easily become the Moon Queen effigy explained, along side the Women Phoenix Bird of the Chinese, "Ware-Creatures," and all horrible more possible to the UN-wary as is ever explained in the book of the, "I-Ching," the Moon Rabbit depiction during moon phase; any and all directors of the darkness and daylight, etc., and if nothing else, be allowed to become a definite missile of an uncontrollable Damnation via self-sacrificial misery unto mass hysteria, and death, or much similar of what actually happened only a few decades ago, via charismatic deception of the infamous sucidal ceremony at the Peoples Temple, under the sway of, "Jim Jones," Jones Town, Guyana, South America. All of that genocide was contingent upon a very real, and/or imagined mind-set fear, founded upon one's unstable life and believed consequence, done explicit of all irrational until dust becomes dust; much similar of this might include all ancient wanton unorthodox moon phase adoration, or a much similar requirement? In Lew of deviant behavior, we must ever be very careful what we accept as gospel, in blind charismatic sway, and reliance, that in time may come back to haunt us as a deceptive form of, "Covert Cultism; as can be exemplified even when considering all wanting adherence done/expected of the pseudo offerings respectfully required, of strange humanistic fire, and brimstone entities, as are believed can become if wantin' of "Kali, Madam Pele, etc.," and, the unlikely North Pole, subterranean living, Ghastly Beautiful Witch if ever there could be one (?), "SHE," written of in entertaining mythological comparisons of fact, through fiction by author, H. Rider Haggard, in the invincible 19ᵗʰ Century Classics!

Continuing Folly!

Other obscure effigy deities, and horrors, to consider-research, if interested include, "Medusa, Es'tar, Fatima, Isis, Madam Pele, Odin, King Neptune, etc., and the ever popular extended writings of, Omar K yam, who seven hundred years ago or so, wrote:

"The Night Has A Thousand Eyes!
The moon struck, Diana, has only one all seeing eye!"

The Jack O' Lantern in use today on Halloween, and used historically every where over Europe and the British Isles, etc., was mega flaunted every ware in clever examples of intricately carved, or roughly done, deplorable leering, if not hideously represented, were the facial depictions of much impossible dimorphism on, pumpkins, Squash, Turnips, Gourds, Potatoes, Beets, carrots, etc., and to this day it has continued past Cro-Magnon Man, "who thousands of years prior, painted effigies of true art form much depicting the, Crescent Moon, etc., as a highly revered adorned anomaly in indisputable proof in petroglyphic witness, over the large rock walls of particular deep subterranean caves within France, etc! Back from the dark ages of those times; from all abstract adherence, worship, adorations, etc., wild man of those beginnings may still to this today well understands their influential indications, and incantations! The hideous Halloween effigies were to avoided if not feared! American wild people possibly still have a vivid, if not an innate deep memory base fastened within all latent fears, that includes the earliest adherence to Goddess, witchery, moon phase, and later Halloween, and they are ever to be distrustful and reminded of it, "each and every, "All Hallows Eve," under the naive guise of humor, compliance, as if had an undeniable belief in Old King Lunar, Neptune, Goblins, Spooks, etc., each October 31st! There is much, much, more real horror of Lunar Adherence to avoid! Perhaps we should do a little more research? It remains difficult and always will be hard to insight all of one's self-felt enthusiasm abrupt all others for wanted results! Not intended derogatory, but until another has been long enough into the effort all of this stuff to most sounds completely bonkers, etc. Out of the box rational mostly has to learned by considerable trial and error experience, and then often we seem to have gotten to nowhere(?) … and then all at once things begin to happen… and wow when they do, "boy, oh, boy do they sometimes happen!" I also suggested for reasons of my own, "that Phil carve out a Halloween Jack O Lantern, using a turnip, sugar-beet, cantaloupe, etc., instead of the prototype pumpkin! We will update this experiment with much more needed explanations, early week November 2012! Wait for!"

Halloween Update?

What happened on October 31st?
To my surprise nothing as yet!

November first, 2012, I spoke with Norma Jenson asking about the happenings of the past night? "Well, she said, just as you said to do, we left candy (Tootsie Rolls! Not fig bars as directed?), in place with Hink, and with them was included a carved eight inch in diameter sugar beet Jack o' Lantern with a frowning face, but this morning the candy and all stuff was still there. Yes, last night was a fairly clear night. Not as clear as the last, but yes, the weather is changing and it is clouding up! I will keep you informed!" Update: On Halloween night, NOT EVE! All happened to Hoyle, as the moon was not all that bright compared to the prior, and as I have said the plaiting always somewhat irregular to the phase up to 4 days or so prior and or after each full moon somewhat contingent upon the moons brightness? Anyway all happened, and the candy vanished! It is reasonable to assume that the creatures cannot actually count accurately the days between each new full moon phase and plaiting is determined accordingly to each new weather pattern situation.

It is to be remembered and understood that it was man that invented the need for time, as time in truth could have begun at any place of the seasons according to who first decided what, how, when, etc! Wild man I doubt have a calendar or a wrist watch, etc., but who knows? The full moon phase for them is probably completely visual?"

"High Strange Indeed!"

"Plaiting-braiding; bonding; interacting, etc., and the most difficult part to understand, is that "IT" has actually been documented as an unexplained anomaly world over for many hundreds of years! Here we go explaining far ahead in so many descriptive words and mixed conjecture had over many pages, and more pages on and on, are some of the authors viable and adamant reasons for all of the unexplained high strange plaiting anomalies that are still being left behind on many domestic and wild desert mustang horses over all vast western America. All story reads a logical, plausible, and clearly opts in its message to be an easily understood theory (?), able in its sway with-out tongue in cheek to likely explain what surprise entity is accomplishing the uncanny braiding, via, logical conclusions long had from the authors varied experience; endless pertaining research, discovered and collected artifacts, etc., abrupt much viable witness far ahead in exasperations than are even all much appreciated haphazard depositions! Thanks All! Ranchers the world over have long been astonished by this unexplained anomaly. Nothing like what is here has ever been considered to contemplate it! No one except perhaps the Russians, and Chinese have anything more concrete to say about it. The mystery of the plaiting continues over most of vast Eurasia and Siberia. All this confusing story is truly one of fascination! Its unsolved mystery reads truly into an unexpected Twilight Zone!" What ever your opinion, I have discovered enough truth doing this research to satisfy my personal need to know a thing of importance and obvious truth. Until a better, or a much more conclusive answer comes along, this opinion need suffice. This manuscript, I well realized is not the last and final word to explain the anomaly, but it is very close, and in time perhaps there will need be written a sequel? I really do hope that another will opt to do it! This journey was difficult! "Q - What, really, Don, do you think are the true reasons for all of the braided manes of American horses? All or most of this seems to be been done by the light of a full moon! What is doing it, and why? So Much, So Much More, To Know! To some things there will never be answers? But there is ever a reason for everything illogical, or logical to cause and effect! Raise your glasses high if you will, and drink to the fellows and gals that hear the true call of the unknown, and your telephone won't ring off the cabin wall! As some few of us still well understand that there are still a few holes in the canyon wall where a wild man can crawl, as yet the moot critics haven't discouraged them all! Never give up a just cause simply because someone opts that it is time to for you to stop, or that what you are doing is foolish, as your wanted priority in time may become an absolute world mentor! Never give up a just cause!

ALOHA!

"A Plea For Additional Hawaiian Input
To Further Explain Plaiting?"

The next efforts to this project will be attempted another time on the Big Island of Hawaii, sometime during the month of April, 2013, as to date since 2004, I have not found one bit of evidence to substantiate plaiting been done to any horse there? If not again found this time, I believe to have a logical theory to explain at least some of the reasons why not! Any Island Paniolo, having any information to share would be greatly appreciated, as my investigations till now have mostly been done but on Oahu, and to fact it is very unlikely in my opinion that Sasquatch exists any where over the Island chain, I am very adamant of that decision for viable reasons – as prototype Sasquatch/Bigfoot are not found there now, or had they ever been long deplored there passé. If indeed per-chance they had been many hundreds of years ago, for good reasons they would have long been completely annihilated by the locals. Never once, even back when in friendship with the late Honolulu professor of anthropology, Glen Grant, prior to his mysterious death in 2003, had he believed that I was wrong, or had either of us ever been told differently. If they were anywhere on the Islands, Glen surely would had heard about them.

"THE HAUNT BOOK STORE!"

< Glen Grant & Jill >

Many an Islander, I am sure, will remember, Glen Grant's extremely haunting, informing, and mega entertaining radio show, done weekly, and/or monthly from, The Haunt Book Store? Glen was truly and exciting person, great story teller, and writer. His off the wall knowledge of Hawaiian spooky stuff stories, all local "Huna-Mystic Talk Story" was next to none! Glen's complete investigative sojourn adventure is all a much fascinating true story for another time, just to explain how he had accomplished his talent would be a great education! Lets just say that he would have said it himself, or fully agreed... "That the collective Seven Island World of Hawaii that is the Island Chain, is truly a magical and wonderful however is also a very strange and mysterious place! "Don, he once told me, there is still so much left unknown for us yet to discover within these Islands of true mystery and diversity had from all mixed ethnic peoples, complex and mixed superstitious and unorthodox belief; I find this magnitude of mixed spooky stuff happenings similar in very few places of the world! Perhaps by accident, in spite of being extremely cautious of my investigation probe, very possibly I have explored to far? Some things here are best left alone! Glen untimely passed this life early year 2003."

Big Island Hawaii!

Some real part in the abstract of Glen's investigate interests are here! Islanders, please have a good educated look at every thing around you, and especially at your horses if plaited? This book is but a small slice of the human/horse, Far Side, of a horse sense experience, that somewhat compares/akin to some of what has already been experienced before, of all high strange activities that forever have been known to take place in such far strange places as, Hawaii's famous/infamous, KAU, Desert! If when there next again, and if there is horse plaiting to be discovered, this time I hope to find it! Aloha Jill!"

"Timely Retrospect For The Good Times In Hawaii!"

Memories of my wife Ah- Lun and I,
as I pause again a last time at Sacred Island!

"Aloha again little Island flower! We really did about do it all! From taking pork up the Old Pele Pass, to visiting Madam Pele in her fiery mood, before buying Dad his freshest shrimps, and his bock-coy bundle in old China Town, where the memory of our first hello will only be stifled at the passing of my last sun down? Babe, I will reminisce of you another time when I return there soon in all fond memories of you, Tammy Yee, and your beloved Brother Clifford!"

"Plaiting Critics and Their Ridiculous Nonsense!"

No matter what is all mixed opinion of what is plaiting the horses, the truth of everything ever writes its own destiny! No, now don't tell me another time that you have been there and done that ... as anyone claiming such moot blather thinking that statement will explain anything is more full of foul wind than is the Wicked Wind Witch that some critics actually denote is doing some of the plaiting! Can anyone actually imagine some serious suggestions had of arm chair critic insistence; some many persons over the UN-Thinking, "Think Tank Net, have the audacity to promote the idea that the plaiting has been done by none other than, pixies, fairies, goblins, ghosts, restless spirits, aliens, etc! Give us a break! And, happy, happy, Halloween grimace from Disonga, Diana, and myself you idiots! Come on critics, can't we do better than that? Give human intelligence a just cause and effect! Go back to your mundane Monday night football, beer and potato chips, and you will need Good Luck?"

Explanatory Candid Deposition?

Citizen Cowboy!

Log: Plaiting! October 4ᵗʰ, 2012

While sitting down with Jim Roper for breakfast at a restaurant in Pocatello, Idaho, I was introduced to his wrangler friend recently back from the borders of the Ore/Idaho/Neva desert. After Jim casually mentioned my theory, and we showed him a photograph, he next explained how he had many times captured, broke, and tamed, a considerable number of desert mustangs... When I ask him about the braids, he simply said, we saw a lot of that messed up stuff ... What's it all about? None of us ever thought one more damn bit about it!" After that naive answer, he went right on blathering lingo about what I can't even remember! Some many persons have no real idea of what, or why, they have such a shallow interest in so many, many, interesting things? For lack of a mutual interest, the rest of our inquisitive conversation went completely over his head!" After Jim's friend left, Jim said ... "You know Don, it really is difficult at times, to even hope that some people would respond better than that; or even need to be almost forced to become aware of some may things! At least you'd think in that guy's case, that he would realize, or question back, to want a better explanation?" "I told Jim, that I well knew cowboys, their attitudes, etc., and his deposition comments however obscure, had a valid ring of humor, and an undeniable truth to them! His comments and demeanor were much typical of myself, before I had been made aware of such strange plaiting; or even before I had given much real thought to the strange and natural ability of anything unknown, or anyone for that matter, being able to intricately braid, and next leave hanging down in mega inches thought to be and impossible length of elongated hair of a horse!" Well, I said, just like so many others, myself, you, and your friend, until of late I had no idea of the importance of this strange stuff, or could I think to need/want to explain any real part of it? And So, much just like your friend, mister, no-name, Wrangler, Nevada, had told us! "Well, we all just passed it off as unexplainable, however strange, and crazy braided and tangled it was... as we had no time for more questions, or to wonder more of it, and so we just letter-go!" Winter/fall, year 2004, after first becoming aware of this strange anomaly, I was already impossibly hooked to try to discover plausible answers able to explain it! But I never in my wildest dreams expected to discover any possible answers! All further surprise story ahead in its place. "Wait for!"

Comparative High Strange Idaho Lions!

These big cats roam the entire desert plaiting Vista!
Jim was never known to be a liar!

Two extremely Strange American Lions
spotted in the Idaho mountain wilds!?

Hardly is this story about plaiting, and perhaps in truth it is just a little out of place, but to my thinking it is not, as it takes place in an Idaho region where happens plaiting, and still continues many strange discoverers and happenings. One might almost say, it takes place almost the same as once happened with an odd large wolf that had once come into my yard and mysteriously vanished! The man Jim Wilson next to be telling the story is as creditable as anyone realizing that Capt. Cook truly wasn't the very first navigator to have ever discovered the Sandwich Islands!" {"Hawaii!"} Meet Jim Wilson! By having read this book you have voluntary entered into a high strange world of wild horses, wild man, and what ever comes next, after this short yarn ahead that explains two very unusual large, dark chocolate colored, completely out of sink strange Idaho lions, that also includes another comical part jargon story telling of One fast flying Mexican lizard? "Come on Don, Jim said, we both know that armadillos and reptiles don't eat garbanzo bean salad, drink tequila, or can run faster than a bear or a Quarter Horse!" Jim had just cut me short of my humorous story explaining to him about the time when Marion and I were broke down and desperate in desert Mexico, and had stopped for lunch at Donaldo's Canteena north of Durango, where a very "macho-buracho hombre," was stumbling on to us while chasing his sombrero through the wind and cacti, while busy chasing one very small fast running anxious lizard!

Log: The Wilson Lions? First Deposition: Jim Wilson, Spencer Idaho

"No Don, Jim said, not yet …. Never once have I seen a damn wild man, nor do I expect to! But, I have seen some damn strange huge, big, lion looking cat-animals, up on the top of Idaho Creek, just about where it breaks over into Montana! These were damn strange lions too for any place around here! But not yet have I ever got to see a true wild man except probably you, and the other skinny guy that sometimes walks early morning past our mail box …? But I don't doubt either, that somehow they exist, or that we have them around here? I have read both your books, and heard a bit more about the possibilities? Ask my neighbor next door… he's got some sort of a strange story, or something he knows about them? Ever since he read your first book back in 2001, he's been on the watch in all of those Idaho places that you described! Especially he watches hard whenever driving past the Craters of the Moon… He remembers that you had explored some of that area one winter! Man that area really is a crazy place! I don't doubt what you say is possible there during winter either! Yeah, I know too about the wintering rattle snakes that hold up in the big balls up in Medicine Lodge! There are many more of them up at Warm Springs too…. I'm really surprised that you know of them too! I guess that you know that I us-to own that hot springs didn't You? Well any way, Mary us-to cook up there at ….

64

Log: Whiskey Jim Wilson, on tape recording, Spencer Idaho, August 2004.

A wild tale of, large lions, horses, lizards, and just perhaps a bit more? Jim was always, The True Life Article Idaho Rascal, well known to have no reason to want to exaggerate. His adventures were a lot of things interesting, but he was not known for intentional deception. Word for word next, you get his story just exactly as all was told me on tape recording, by my old pal, "Whiskey Jim," then a long time resident/neighbor of colorful passé Spencer Idaho. "Don, Jim said, these truly were very big strange looking cats! There were two of them! They were just too strange of a mountain lion type for this part of North America! Yeah ... and they were not all that far from here either... I could take you there, but no one would probably ever believe it? In my opinion, they were much similar as what looks African lions! Only these looked to dark for them, and even were a bit larger? Yeah, no kidding ... this happened about ten years ago, where I was hunting up on the west side top part of the mountain, close near where Idaho Creek runs on down towards the Montana border onto the highway...! Oh, then, you know the place...? Well, it was there, where I saw the lions chasing after some ranch horses down into a brushy box canyon some several miles distant from off the road. "As I said, these cats looked just too much darker in color to have been any of our local mountain lions! And both of them were considerably larger than the Africans! One looked to be a male, and its mate... but neither of them had that ruffey looking long hair mane stuff that you would expect? Never before had I seen such big cats like that! They were out of rifle range... I watched them for a long time through my field glasses.. Finally I fired a wild shot down onto them with my pistol, and after that they run out of sight! I have seen plenty of mountain lions in my time, and these were more of a deep chocolate brown looking things and sure as hell weren't them!" I only include that last story as many strange things are sometimes seen in the Idaho-Montana wilds.

Log: Bag-Dad Arizona, January, 1999 ... "A small Flying Lizard?"

("Story for, Gene Scheller, Lake Havasue City, AZ.")

Prospector: Humor - From tape recording... "No, damn it, he said, that blasted lizard wasn't no baby Tetrahedron, or any Dinosaurs either! The darn thing landed hard into my garbanzo salad, just as sure as hell that both, K-Mart and Wall-Mart, look just about as boring and both the same! Well, it flew across the bar room in a hurry, when an Indian/Mex, threw it hard at an Arachnophobia, or a kuzacatoid drunken Mexican amigo....! That's when I first noticed that the darn long thing looking hombre had no wings! The damn bastard was a lizard lair...! What I wondered was it doing in a bar anyway? later, we caught the ugly wretch, and we shot it along with its two already sun burnt Gila-monster cousins with our .44-40! We had no choice but to put it out of its misery, as the flying rascal had injured its neck in my garbanzo... and the others watching back had a darn bad attitude ....and besides, the local vultures were grateful for the tucker! In Australia they got bigger ones, some they eat that are big enough to cast a foot high shadow! Believe any of this stranger and you are as crazy as us?"

"Marion laughed as I told her that maybe she should tell him about our battle with the Mexican Yaqui Indian, or about her less than famous Kit Fox Supper, eating roast fox, had with, Maria, Socorro, and Lolita, and all of the rest of there per chance wild troupe?"

More from the Zakynerous file?

Regarding the obscure sailor Zakynerous, his continuing history here perhaps remains insignificant except that his land fall is just more evidence of all passé knowledge of ancient marination expeditions now known to have come very early to the Americas, inclusive of ancient Montana/Idaho regional petrologyphists and others in Washington State known to the author that fully attest that there were ships likely wild horses running along side UN-sung bipeds that had been loosed onto the continent possibly even before 500 B.C. And the advent of Zakyneros.

("Q") "General, for Bob Smallsbach!"

"Are there biblical references to wild man? Who knows were the wild goose goes ... is man a beast, or is the beast a man? What, really, is anyone? Women snap commands or fingers at their husbands, and wimp men perhaps go drown there stress with another beer or six down at the local water hole? The Gideon Bible, King James Version, at one place in the Old Testament is an interesting reference ("Don, find the biblical reference before publication?") to man beasts said (Paraphrased!) to be actually riding off into the sun-down on horse back! And there continues several more interesting concepts mentioned to be considered... why I have wondered were not these references to wild people not also edited completely out of the Bible, "as about every thing else not wanted passed on by the pseudo Christians of the day or agreed with was!" That becomes really not all that hard to explain, "as apparently at least some passé biblical scholars of the day and time had well realized them!" Anything more having to do with horses, plaiting, man beasts, etc., or civilized man as we think our self-superior or what; there all confused and obvious begins the joint horse/Sasquatch theory and story anomaly to further explain how much animal actually are we in fair environmental comparisons? How much animalistic do you think you are, or are not? What, really, is all that much different in the collective cleverness between man and beast? Perhaps the answer resides within our latent fears, God given talents and natural ability, and/or our recognized/unrecognized abilities?"

The Desiderata Should Be Our Mentor?

"That last written can't quite be enough answer to explain all of the differences, but I am most certain that within each mentality and our separate allowance, all fully understands and finally will go to their grave with a much similar outrage of irrational misunderstandings, as I don't cut grass, and I do not shovel snow, does that fairly conclude that I am uncivilized, impossible, undependable, or simply completely undomesticatable? Either way, many persons not concerned with the wisdom afforded similar of, The Desiderata, they deserve more hard-ship than even the wild animals rate in their wilderness, as man-kind is completely obnoxious, vindictive, improbable, and impossible, much far ahead of horses, dogs, cats, bears, etc., as most animals are more reserved and dependable!" (Tonia Brown, is paraphrased above in of that last incite!)

"The Book Is A Complete Paradox"

The Book Is Irregular
And Completely Awesome And Confusing Out of Necessity!

Because of the book's irregularity, the book's true introduction was omitted, and has now become re-evaluated, re-written, and condensed for space and time complete into Chapter One, that ever explains in more detail much more than what was first intended; amounting to an all new updated first chapter preview assessment, allowing more true facts divulged now known of the author that continue to explained in some varied viable detail and logic, and some real working part of a completely unrealized/unknown true life style facts had to explain feral hominids taken from much experience and nevertheless is still much highly indisputable conjecture, etc; that was ever acknowledged during all collective wild man exploration that fully attests without a doubt, the absolute validity of existing wild man remnants found over North America today are likely the last existing feral hominid populations, or what ever other identity anyone may want call them, if not Sasquatch (?), that are in my opinion, an unsuspected, irregular feral hominid population, existing over the Inter Mountain West as a much unrealized, very real, active, extremity cautious, and much curious, at times playful, ever of a precarious of nature, being much covert out of necessity, highly varied to prototype descriptions in a completely varied much mixed/matched blood line case scenario, all relative however unto all obvious sexual dimorphism notable in all males; some monstrosities in outcomes among them, as opposed/suspected in limited gene pool mutations, resulting from the understood expectations of consanguinity, etc. All of them within their own kind and allowance, remaining a wandering, undetected, undetermined numberless, body count, existing as, best can be said; housed during coldest winter (at least part time), after October – April, as now has been discovered ever happens since fall/winter, year, 2001! All survivors amazingly adaptable, out of strict requirement (Self exiled, winter months, fast/safe, within a literal ever dark, dank, miserable, subterranean, Cave/Surface, Nether World!), existence best said: Living in a dismal cave, where need share all out of necessity; a much scattered hectic community existence at best; consisting where possible, many a small band, or tribe; that are to descriptions perhaps each member somewhat different in stature and anatomical allowance different than what anyone might opt to expect of any sort of a high strange and while y humanistic wild hominid, just as if all of that collectively said is not truly everyone of possibly differing? Perhaps them even more best explained to be of a surprisingly highly intelligent wilderness savvy mentality, a mixed hominid extension of all pa say humanity. that because of a much wanton base pseudo academic prototype description had, some of it far beyond conclusive fact and/or all believed and/or accepted descriptions allowed one's imagination within today's populations. Wild man in particular cases is often, just as said, very much hairy, and some in fact evidence little if few hair; this is also evidence with both genders, however each gender seems to much emulate a much noticeable muscular example of a much mixed powerful breed of world-wide orthodox humanity. Concerning basic survival, as it is ever necessary that all man, wild man included, opts/insists in future to continue to survive that he opts to be living side by side at peace and in a relative parallel existence of adaptability first and last, and forever! Last, but not least in-able to truly survive, then all will have needed out of dire necessity to have been completely convinced of adaptability by others or another, more experienced than the last! As it is now obvious, that most truth that once was accepted, today is much distorted in the context, and opts in future to become completely worthless, if not already has been realized to had been awesome and invincible alongside the ever all new scientific discoveries being accomplished, best explained the all new, intrinsic and incredible, if not said better to fact... "The survival of all continuing human race in future history, is much contingent upon man understanding all of the miraculous confusions, and all new had truths ever pending into our tomorrows! Mankind has become almost an evolving Out Dated, out of control, evolutionary misfit of eminent complete self-destruction! Homo sapiens, sapiens, and all relict hominids as wild man, etc., and you and I alike; it is ever all necessary for everyone of us to have opt to understand the other harmoniously, or all will parish! So be it, & God help us everyone!"

IN THIS MANUSCRIPT

is the

Need to Understand All Humanity, and especially

Wild man, as has already partly been explained? In order to fully understand all manuscripts projections, it is to be understood that wild man as a counter part of humanity and is more similar to us than most first want surmise. For all of those still completely convinced that such a statement is an Outrage/Sacrilege or an abnormality, I am not here to try to convince you differently, but I can sincerely attest in all earnest confidence, to say in no unadulterated terms, that wild hominids actually do exist! Read on if will, and if need, do it for no more good reason than to had been an educated entertainment that may prove to have appeased your dismay! As in time future when all the books of the Trilogy have been intelligently conjectured through reason, all of what will be written will one day help to have proven true wild-man for what he is! Any one of you still of a negative mind, will by then have opt to wave our flag! Welcome aboard Ship Mates! Ever the Captain of, Conclusive Decision, sails into all worlds of mystery and adventure well satisfied with the ships company armed in indisputable proof!"

Is it all over?

Are there no more tomorrows ahead in free-lance hominid exploration?

What, really, does anyone expect that governments do not want us to know?

"Tonight I lament all of the adventures of yore, as time is fast running out for me or anyone to more convince all world community of the all true existence evidence already found to attest their awareness of all wilderness brothers and sisters! Yeah, Var Harris, we should have handed each and all of them at least one carrot! In salutations, retrospect, and fond reflections of all our combined efforts and mixed gender crew's discoveries; weather any of you are still aware of me or not, It sure as hell had been one hell of a magical trip! "And just as many of you will perhaps remember I am sure; in the very beginning of your exploring sojourn, when you first time entered The Dark Abyss That Amounts To The Valley Of the Pits, .it is too revealing that not just a few of you had at once insisted was the literal open door way into the, Literal. Subterranean, Valley, of the Shadow of Death! (?), well, many of you that would aspire to became the very best, and highly acclaimed, invincible, and most valuable trail mates, "had many of you first time when had entered the caving project, had arrived at best, "tongue in cheek," and eventually each and everyone of you early disbelievers, had in time needed to swallow your gum, or chuck your big chaw of, disgusting tobacco in order to want to ask all continuing questions when underground in an obvious quiet whisper! What, really, do you continue to think even now just I am like you in retrospect, still wondering back into those exhilarating times, what all more was impossible to comprehend or understand was actually often ahead and looking back in the pitch dark ever possibly, ever curious, to be wanting to learn your intevntions behind the carrot? Wow, the memories! Remember the muted sounds of the unexplained, the garbled gobblings, and continuing subdued mews, and undetermined sounds, and more to questions, heard short distance ahead of mixed distorted sounds, etc. All of this had as witness in dank dark cave surroundings to this day especially during the dark of moon lit night, has well been remembered by this aging historical derelict much the same as you! Perhaps one day you will chose to write with me that yes, Paul Wright, and partner, Lewis Chandler, that indeed, and, "Yeah, I heard the undetermined sounds.. but no matter the denial, as I well realized all that first moment that you so early-on in the game, really shouldn't have! We all bonded unconditional in those wild sojourns...! Sometimes exploring much determined, chance taking, foolish cavers, opt to unknowingly experience an accelerated sort of a temporary claustrophobic death, ever unaware and all unknowing of their blood rush desperation/perspiration had from enduring high confined stress until much later! Wow, how I miss the stark excitements of continuing unrealized discovery! Be seeing you again in another miss-hap caving-in paranoiac lost forever night mare! We did it all... "But none of us can really say we have been there and done that! Done a lot, yea! But in truth, nodda, actually! ... Loved you everyone!"

"More adventure Begins!"

Log, update: Cataloged far ahead of all story!

October 4th, 2012

Phil Jenson, Nyssia Oregon ranch property, has only recently of late, during the remaining Full Moon Phase, ending October 5th, discovered that in addition to the lost green colored hatchet taken from the horse pen location some months ago ("That complete story already written-up far ahead!), now he has discovered that two small sledge-hammers are also missing from the same location near where they were left in close proximity to the horse named, Hink! The same horse that will be much more introduced through out the book, as I link is the very same horse that has been repetitiously plaited many times included messed with again this very week! What continues to take these useful tools, becomes an additional ongoing mystery? It is hardly the first account of tool collecting reported having been believed to had to do with wild hominids? The Halloween Full Moon of October 31st. is next! After its final accelerations, the full moons of November and December in that last needed sequence of study, will have finally concluded our Closed Case scenario in the pseudo belief that indeed we have somewhat accomplished to have explained the plaiting? If anyone were able to actually look straight into the dimorphism content had within the night eyes of wild man, perhaps then and only then would all humanity fully opt to understand that there are some things best not to know! "Trust me, you can fully trust that last said, as the author already in his sojourn of discovery experienced a very strange near Last Will, and last Testimony, ordeal! Enough said that! Nodda! Zilch? Tilt! And Wow!"

It was good, that the Introduction had by proxy become book content, as in retrospect it actually has somewhat prepared the reader to better understand most all reasons for the author's absolute and insistent belief in North American wild man. "If not this book becomes an accurate assumption of the unexplained, and extremely strange; to denote at least some of the pseudo ploy intentions of wild hominids and horse interaction, etc., if you will; if it not becomes at least an important part an ever necessary plaiting explanation, that through-out sites man and horse-animal interaction done between them, or becomes an able jargon that continues to further help all persons to better understand the full importance of all slated books of the Trilogy, then, "it," and I, collectively were a failure, and we have explored all, Exunda in vain into vast lost nowhere!"

"The Trilogy Manuscripts. And The Full Moon!

Study them, and Be Hooked!

The Sasquatch and plaiting world is truly all around us!

The collective Trilogy Manuscripts each in their separate approach, fully attest present evidence had of the author needed to further document viable hominid discovery, and in abstract, as even as I write, all of those books via strange content continues to inspire even a more all pseudo theory than is ahead presented here inclusive of the last Calendar Date and time of a Full Moon Phase that had began, December 13th, 2011, inclusive of ending with the final Full Moon Phase observed to the last day of year 2012. The story pertaining to all many horses being observed afield over a sojourn period of 13 months running on a same calendar year up to the date and time of the last Full Moon noted of, January 2013.

This high strange plaiting continues without a doubt as one of the greatest unexplained animal mysteries of all time! No one has ever solved the mystery, and the question remains, "if all is not done by mankind as we think ourselves, then what pray tell sort of unexplained strange biped entity is actually accomplishing the braiding being done to all world horses? When and if this book's continuing conjecture is completely understood; perhaps one or more readers will recognize having made a much similar discovery that would be more able to add more credence to the book's facts than has the author. Perhaps as said, in time we will need to write a sequel? This long year probe of horse plaiting history being done over the vast reaches of Western America in all seasons of weather, travel conditions, distance, etc., was very difficult to accomplish! Especially this so, whenever being hard pressed all necessary to be writing it all to the separate needs of persons both young, and old, hopeful that all will be able to fully comprehend the many unexpected strange anomalies ahead? Yeah Charley, sure enough, indeed! Wow! I really got a bad head ache from attempting this one, as the manuscript has suffered an ongoing sojourn of confusions, since March 2012, at the unexpected event of the author being laid-up with an extremely painful "snake bite!" Even as write, I am somewhat stalemated by the handicap, unable as I am to easily continue to explore all wanted inclusive, and all necessary to my research. "However, in spite of what ever the intrusion including the snake, this book will be accomplished as planned by the eve of January 1st., 2013!

Happy New Year!

"Research History, and Sage Humor!"

... and discovery had before Tonia's plight; all of it is a continued story intended to be added to the book's dedication platform that reads above. Tonia ever had an acute love of all horses. And even more meaningful to me, was her unconditional devotion, and constant insistence that I promised at her passing that no matter what, I would complete this uncanny project! The difficulty to write it meaningful overwhelms my first intentions!

Tonia wrote: "What is here Don, is important! No one has ever done anything like this! Tell it all just like it is! I will always be with you! As astonishing as all story sounds, the moon theory makes much sense!" True, or not babe, more will be said of you in its place, as you were was very important to the book's research, and your needed worth and humor need revealed while exploring cold winter in high country Arizona, New Mexico, and all more vastness of the South West that continues when all readers first meet, "Viking Jim, and, German-Indian-real sweet heart, Ellie Martenson."Ellie remember Ton, ever required of me fresh socks, under-ware, and a shower, or its equivalent daily, "No matter Jim, she said, that we have no real shower, hot tub, or water, or that all of us are living frozen on this devastated dust swept property! You and Don heat the tub and bath every day, or there will be no dinner! Tonia here looks just like she's a fresh flower right out of the bud vase! Wash your damn selves up right now or go eat down at McDonald's!"

Next... After that said, Jim the Viking wondered what's down at Micky D's tonight on special? "Hell man he announced, we got enough gas to get us all there? Lets Go! I got this friend east of town of Socorro that has lots of semi-tame and wild horses! He said to bring you over! Wants to meet you, and hear your stories! The guy is a bandit Don, but he's honest! Bring your rifle, and especially get Tonia there... He likes women, and really likes to shoot off his pistols!"

Yeah Ellie said... "The Dumb-Cough makes his own beer and wine! He is a Crazy like is Yam for jam, and Yelly for jelly in Norwegian...! Don't you dare drink with him, or we will never get home! He once shot his five dogs for arguing with him! Second thought leave your rifle in the corner, and bring your knife! No one ever thinks that a gringo can use one? I have seen you and Ellie chopping up carrots and onions in Los Angeles and know you are good for something? "

Sadly both Jim and Ellie both passed away shortly after all of the above humor. A very important story-incident will continue in its place, sighting both Tonia and Ellie that both together had become the crux of all that incredible experiment outcome! Wow, high strange things do happen! Many of them can never be explained or understood. "If we hadn't visited Jim Martenson and his Out-Law friends, some of the book's high importance would had never have occurred!"

"That all high strange happening will perhaps not be believed Don, but who cares? The photographed proof is shown in Figure 22, Ellie and Tonia's incredible Anasazi Pottery sherd! It just so happens that the best Western Native American Museums in America that is authoritative on Indian pottery is located at Deming, New Mexico. At another place of the book we will go there!

(To be continued!)

Log: November 1st, 2012.

As said, in some respects this manuscript needed to be written backwards, as new input to all recent discovery continues almost daily. For sure there has needed been a constant Update abrupt every full moon over-lapping the calendar date since December 2011. That's now eight months time since the first documentation of the strange plaiting was done last December. It is now November 2012, and we are approaching the final eight weeks study for credence that will opt to end this documentation New Years Eve. All next to be written explaining research difficulties is far, far, ahead of all planned story explanations! Unless you are there and serious...? With us to actually investigate! Have been there and believe there is a reason to return? Opt to go there open minded, etc! Well, we do the best that we can during arduous research to continue not to confuse the issue! Pseudo know it all cattle men, nosy cowboys, poorly trained investigating twits, good looking, and cattle ugly ornery babes, all of that, and much more, can ever can get in the way of instinctive discovery and keen observation! Competition between pseudo knowledgeable wanna-Bees, men and women alike, and corralled animals can be as alarming and distasteful as it is also wonderful! Every contact becomes a separate opinionated education. Most would rather fight than switch convictions! "To even be able to approach some ranchers' intending to do research is like fighting the Alamo!" "Well Don, she said... that is not so! How come whenever we go to visit these far off ranches and wild places, every time there is usually also a beautiful women looking back? It is just as if some of them were expecting you!" "Well Tonia, lots of pretty ranch women suffer base paranoiac reclusive symptoms. Some of them are not even sure that they are attractive? And some many of them just like some men, look a lot like their horses too! Actually the pretty ones, "truth known," are all just much similar as another wilderness stubborn horse, but of a human color! Some of them are like Pintos, some many resemble Strawberry Roans, some even look the high tones of a Honey Bay, and that one over there by the fence, looks especially to be a fair complexioned black haired green eyed beauty! "But none of them babe, has your incredibly beautiful fiery red hair, or your distinctive personality! Before you walk away would you please hand me over that cell phone camera? Various Plaiting Experiments! During the first New Moon Phase of October 4th, 2012, I have proposed to the Jensons that they tack (Using Scotch Tape!) several candy bars lightly set onto the sway back, or within the brushed out hair manes of the horses including Hink, in order for them to see for themselves exactly what happens when and if all horse plaiting continues over the pending moon phase? If so or not, trust me (Things did happen!), this manuscript continues as an all true high strange American wild and domestic horse investigation adventure. Story criteria now running eight years since the date of my late wife's birthday, October 4, 2004, inclusive, December 31, 2012, conclusive and over as of, January 1, 2013.

Log: Pit Stops!

This is perhaps where the adventure truly begins, as this is indeed a wild manuscript amounting to a training ground for something? I'm sure that I have already managed to confuse some of the readers. Particular ranch lands, etc., are at best difficult to continue to update/investigate as often as wanted over such an extended period comprisimg13 months up to year 2013! Enough time in my estimation to have well established by now a logical assessment of at least some of a high strange activity as perhaps has ever happened to animals? How ever this book is accepted, truth or not, perhaps as said, "it is actually the One and Only possible true answer ever ap-

proached, wantin' to think to explain any small part of the mysterious plaiting (The mechanics yet to be explained, etc!) of what I adamantly do believed are the workings of high strange human looking like creatures, able and capable as they continue, to completely baffle all world horse community... Nothing else but anything man or beast having opposed fingers to thumbs could manage such an anomaly! In my estimation, for any one in future to be able to repeat any real working part of this difficult and extensive field effort, would be highly unlikely, as the time and travel expense is all of a separate matter! To had accomplished this documentation for a spance of nine years almost overwhelms human tenacity. It was most ironic, and extremely lucky, and most fortunate (As will be much more explained ahead!) that some eight years ago, year 2004, "that I was able to accidentally stumble onto The Neil Hinck Horse Ranch, be introduced and be-friend, and next discover quite per-chance an incredible research opportunity of a life time! All of this had enabled me to exclusively investigate any mega number of recently, and ongoing plaited horses! At the time of first permission, the numbering horse stock was in access of approximately 150 head! From the first date of that surprise beginning; at the conclusion of this writing we actually have some definitive answers if anyone is wanting to believe it or not. The pity is that by the mid month of August summer 2012, the Neil & Norma Hinck Ranch no longer exists! Since Neil's recent demise the horses have all been sold! "There are no more famous, Hinck Blazer Horses! Not one of these magnificent horses any longer wanders that beautiful ranch that today and forever more, has been turned into a silage corn, and wild weed patch! How timely really, was my uncanny and separate opportunity to opt to be able to explain another facet of the truly unknown? The first step was to recognize and seize the moment! So be it Neil Hinck! Perhaps this book will appease your anger? And, Yeah, Phil Jenson, by now 2013, you and I actually do have some of the answers to all of this strange plaiting! Tonia anticipated what Phil would next make the discovery, and all future advanced logistics and high plausible conjecture afterwards is fast falling into place! Finally with everyone's unconditional help, the author has managed "however awkwardly" to accomplished this confusing documentation! Sorry Charley, pixies, goblins, ghosts, the North and South Wind, and definitely not the swiping willows, had nodda to do with any of it! I have seen much workings of the wind on horses and none of this has been remotely similar! Anyone further claiming that nonsense should definitely toss this manuscript before the wind throws you overboard beyond The Sage Brush Sea!"

Log: Phil Jenson's Story!

Early summer 2012, Phil Jenson was the first to notice the strange anomaly of a messed with horse tail still attached to a horse! I said still attached, as far ahead in this treatise, we will opt to explain an even more high strange happenings! "Look Phil said, look hard at the top most part of that horse's upper rump at its tail! Do you notice anything odd? Wow! Well yes, after the trite autosuggestion, almost at once I did! It was very plain to see after his guiding comment, exactly what he was suggesting!" That's pure genius Phil, I said! Darn smart too! Gotta give you the credit man, you have got us on the right track! Wow you...! Phil, that long tail stuff was all cut off with something very sharp, something other than a common knife, and definitely not scissors! Next it was braided into the horse's mane to elongate it to more than twice its length! What do you think? "Phil well, me too, Yeah, I think that's right! It was probably done just as you say, by someone, or something, that had to have used something like a piece of broken glass like is a beer bottle, or something just as sharp like obsidian, or maybe an arrow head chip? There is some of all of that broken stuff scattered about around here! What

73

ever done it, was much too smart to use a common knife! "Using a knife would be obvious, and would definitely give them away! These guys Phil, are away out front! Just as you say, they very, very, carefully, "close cropped," or carefully shaved off that upper rump long tail hair from the place where it starts from the ass, and then next just exactly as you are now showing me, had opt to be braiding the cut long tail hairs cleverly back into what are the hanging confines of the mane in order to have much elongated the effort! Wow! Who in the hell would ever have thought of that? And who, and why, would anyone ever go to all of the trouble? And what more is all incredible asked next; what, really, can be the good reason? Wow! Holy smoke Phil... all of this is just very hard to believe? You know darn well know that the creatures well realize that us humans would long be wondering why they constantly insist to do it!" "Yeah Don he said, and last time here they took away my green handled hatchet! These guys are also thieves!" Continually over many years, even before my becoming aware of horse plaits, there had been mega reports from many places of the Far West of them pilfering various useful tools! Makes One wonder what other useful skills beyond primitive that "they" may have accomplished? Collecting the hatchet spring 2012, and only recently again two hammers late summer, has to be all more than an obvious clue to something very interesting? Sorry Charley, no ghosts or goblins here either! Of course, there are still many unanswered questions! However now since we can at least somewhat explain the shaved horse tails, we know how partly how the manes are elongated, but for what useful purpose is this done? Why they choose to work so very hard at a difficult accomplishment has to have some adherent cause and effect? For example, how can anyone explain otherwise how it is possible for a typical 14 inch long mane to be intricately braided to it's max, and then next be left to hang down as much as twice as long to an extended length of all of 28 or more inches, that's twice as long as its original length! Surely everyone is fully aware that when anything is braided, out of proportional necessity it naturally becomes much shorter! The necessary answer to explain all of this took wrangler Phil Jenson all of six years to explain it! Wild hominids seem to be incredibly ingenious. I very much doubt that in my remaining life time one will ever be captured? I have definite theories to how this could be done, but to accomplish it in my opinion probably borders on criminal. As it is my belief that these wily creatures are far from being monsters. The happy savage in myth, fantasy, and reality, in some respects is to be envied? "The only real monsters that I can prove that are out there in our world, are those persons narcissistic of their ignorance, prejudiced, self-glorification, and small mindedness!"

**Read: "Monsters Myths and Me!" Author, Robert Schmalzbach,
(ISBN 978-1442125469)**

Log: Norma Jenson !

Nyssia, Oregon Ranch, September 2, 2012.

Her Deposition: "Don, I am flabbergasted! How in the world this strange braiding is continuing being done monthly right here on our property before our very nose each Full Moon Phase since all long years ago before we began documenting them December 2011, seems completely impossible! It truly does seem to be happening most often during the time of each new full moon! The plaiting, and the fact of something stealing our tools, to me is one of the greatest mysteries of all mysteries? Phil and I just can't believe that all of this strange stuff is actually happening! Darn well as you say, the wind is not doing any part of it either! There hasn't been any significant wind down here for many weeks! And even if it blows, it couldn't possibly braid those tight manes!" Yeah, how indeed? Norma I told her, the strength and dexterity alone needed to tightly knot-tie, and hold down, one or more knots at a time, and to do it one after another; some of them were also tied twice, and three times again, and all done on the top of another! These braids are done so tight as to be next to impossible to pick apart! All of these to be seen knotted on the table were intended to be plaited right along side the last in a row along the horses neck; they are done so tightly intricately braided as look completely impossible? All moot attempts to unravel them have failed! Certainly all of this attests to a most stubborn and tenacious type a creature ever, and it more than proves to stark logic that no wind of any kind could have done this! Even if that were probable, a strong wind would need to funnel down so to speak... need to attack the horse's mane in a singular and fin-ate portion, and then continue to wind-work for a long time until all repetitious plaits and hard knots were satisfactory completed! And just as all of us well know, every one of these strange anomalies upon completion had been tightly tied off for a most part in a definite "Square Knot" at each of their separate ends! All was done just as cleverly and skillfully as can be accomplished by any proficient sea going boatswain mate sailor! Smoke that in Popeye's Pipe critics!"

Log: Everything Relative?

Are Their Actually Several Variations of Wild Hominids?

"In my opinion yes!" There are possibly several separate variations of wild hominids allowed as Sasquatch roaming over wilderness America, and just possibly other variable gene pool blood lines of them originating in all vast Eurasia, and some differing somewhat in places of Russian/Siberia, Australia, etc., where there they are also elusive beyond even what has been proven are the Ice Tiger (The Siberian Tiger!) and is the very small Alaskan Blue Bear. The reasons for this belief has been calculated from actual sightings, three inclusive of the author. The collective content of the slated Trilogy Manuscripts, in time will surely have proven to rock all pseudo authoritative, Big Foot in Mouth Community, and likely as not will opt to spill their coffee cups, if not sink most all the Wanna-be Foot Club Captain's Unstable Boats! Since as, far back and long ago as year 2003, the late famous Washington State Anthropologist, Grover Krantz, who by acquaintance also became a con-firing friend that referenced me kindly as a Crypto pirate, had expressed his interest to further explore with me into some of my high desert mountain caves and voice his opinion public to substantiate if indeed I had discovered pro-con any true living wild man evidence. Had he lived through my exploring sojourn; his hobnobbing with me if in agreement or not, by now surely would have written a meaningful book, and perhaps the supposed moot claims of particular Argonaut academics insisting that Sasquatch are no more than a simpleton gargantuan prototype great ape, no different to speculation then is supposed a Gigantopithecus, long calculated its giant size from an obscure handful of approximately five teeth; from that allowance calculated that Giganto would have weighed in at approximately 1200 lb., "no problem with that notion," but by the very fact that wild man can easily approach unfamiliar horses, accomplish bonding, befriend and intricately plait and braid their manes, possibly be riding or walking them around the pasture ("Riding and/or walking them first time mentioned! Just wait, many more surprises ahead!") speaks unequivocal of a stark animistic controlling high intelligence far distant from all giant apes, if not

75

*also enough to eliminate most humans! Just anyone try it! Probably try it is all that you will ac-
complish! "Horses have been shot for lack of human patience during a difficult capture chase!
Arizona Bob Krebs, Larry Meredith and I all together have seen this happen! Bob, do you remember Old Idaho Black Jack, and your trusty .30/30?"*

Log: "Things Happen!"

Are There Really Needed Gene Pool Abductions!

*This book, and all its pseudo enlightenment, or even perhaps thought fascinating explanations
will have not touched the surface of extensive wild hominid ability and possibility. And because
of the extreme irregularity of a firm belief in relict hominids, to opt to continue to include all
following content of the book, and all subject matter ahead, this manuscript and all Other Trilogy Books continue as needed to ponder/wander freely in exploration reminisce experience
over the remainder of this, and all following chapters in order to "somewhat continue to explain the many more varied reasons for all the book's abstract conjecture, and all stark conclusions that continue to attest that without any doubt unsuspected wild bipeds of some kind are
indeed plaiting the manes of horses. Please continue reading in the needed patience to hear me
out, "as it may surprise you how many of you completely unknowingly may already be identi-
fying with particular facets of this wild jargon, perhaps first thought by some many, to had
been just too much of an abstract narrative to at all be real, and/or a viable approach for profound answers; many more to described ahead that are a continuing testimonial interesting trip
to attest that there actually does exist a much unrealized highly intelligent wild man Nether
World, consisting of much mixed/varied humanistic wild hominid humanity of separate gene
pools amounting to an extensive world-wide feral community having absolutely has no need
what so ever for human fraternization, "except in all probability, to think to need at times, to
need/want; to think it all necessary if wanting to continue their ethnography, to commandeer
an occasional needed "either gender" gene pool extension! Anyone doubtful of that possibility
should read books One & Two, written by David Paulides, titled: "Missing 411! Things do happen! Proof, and more proof? No, its just all the stark truth, as when in caves, forest, where
ever, be careful where you hang your coat, vest, purse, tools, car keys, and especially your rifle
and camera? Things happen and sometimes disappear when in wilderness, and are not all of
them taken by prototype thugs, as you will read somewhere ahead that when things vanish
sometimes things are returned back as obscure gifts in trade!"*

Log: The plaiting predominates on female horses, as are fillies, or mares!

*Introduced next, are some many more of the difficult facts surrounding the late night visitors
doing the plaits cast from viable high strange track-way hand and foot artifacts, and much
more that well validates that there actually exists an unrealized wanted unknown world-wide
colony of bipedal creatures; indisputable evidence of strange nocturnal activities going on
among them passé and current that definitely opt that Sasquatch (Wild Man!) have a high interest directly to do especially with female horses, including some of the unrealized reasons for
it as a high priority as they continue to wander the earth. Ninety nine percent of all plaited
horses examined have been fillies or mares in that order. Only rarely has been discovered studs
or Geldings. The reasons for this will be completely explained. While making gender comparisons, it is also a fact that when many horses are running together in a mixed gender herd*

untethered and free, almost true to the very last plaited horse ("Hard winds, dust blowing, thick brush, and more!") only the females evidence the strange plaiting! That so, doesn't it seem strange that indeed if the wind/brush ad anything to do with it that it would not also include the males? No Charley, not fairies, goblins, trolls, leprechauns, ghosts, or butterflies either! Them or the wind has nothing to do with it!"

Log: A cave is at best a miserable existence during cold winter!

Feral hominids are very capable of Plaiting! The following is validated from many undeniable discoveries made in creature cave habitat evidencing broken, twisted, distorted, and even at times absent foot and finger bone parts, as toes, etc., frozen fingers, one missing lower wrist bone, etc., as is much evidenced in the authors more than one hundred count plaster cast collection. It is at once obvious that these wily creatures survive harsh winter often completely miserable when subterranean in particular Idaho/Montana desert mountain and forest caves along to be found along the far reaches of The Continental Divide, etc. In some respects I have begun to wonder if cave exploration as we have known it is over, as recently, Sept 7, 2012, over Idaho news radio came a short distressing announcement insisting by pseudo local government policy that the Idaho public no longer has free licensee to visit, and/or explore Idaho caves, except for the exception of three chosen lava tube cave examples being allowed entry located within the confined boundaries of the famed Craters of The Moon National Park. The reason cited had something ridiculous said, having to do with people in future disturbing cave bats? Truth known, most caves, grottoes, etc., not all of them merit the natural and ideal habitat place of mega cave bat reproduction, etc! Special conditions need be innate within wanton said bat habitation all necessary as it is during certain seasons of the year for them to even want to re-produce. An easy bat study to appease the doubtful all authoritative mind, can be had if contacting the authorities at Karchner Cave, New Mexico, and /or, the long documented famous bat reproduction locations at where is, The Carlsbad Caverns, Mammoth Cave, etc. Bats are hardly at risk in Idaho caves. In the first place few persons ever find these caves, and most that stumble onto them have little or no desire to enter beyond the opening! In the authors opinion such unwarranted cave control is but Another Bogus Federal Slated Control Program, aimed to further eradicate all passé American public freedoms had prior on inherent National Forest lands, that were, truth over looked, initially originated as, Public Domain! My current exploring partner MK Davis had this to say: "Don, I would gladly go to bat anytime for anyone who would go to bat for bats! But legislature like that wanting above evidences that some many federal and local government agencies have nothing more than bats loose in their bell-free! Bats are fussy where they defecate and copulate! Perhaps we should set aside a place in Washington D.C. where they can join the party of their own free will and choice? Batting average at the White House has less recently to offer than appreciated! Next thing we know there will be legislation against the legality of plaiting wild desert horses! This is the election year, who really do you think we should go to bat for? It is most fortunate that the author during all recent and past sojourns had managed to explore many a mountain and desert cave, as many as 15 years or more prior to the ridiculous above notice. Not here the space or place to elaborate upon moot government controls, but when indeed will all unheralded government controls be reconciled with for what they are; the public need soon awake to realize the current negative sway and heavy toll already opting to further destroy our already slanted media controlling opinionated Liberty Bell? This book is timely! Even as I write there are mega unfathomable bills before congress threatening to stop most all public foot travel over our remain-

ing national forest wilderness lands outside of pseudo projected government allowance! Next thing we know we may find ourselves dangling upside down like a bat, lashed fast onto some remote government cave bat perch! God help us! It is damn well time don't you think, that a few good men & women actually come to the aid of our waning country before it is much too late! "Yeah, really, what are you going to do when they come for you?" "Yeah, really, what? If they manage to confiscate our guns, perhaps we can use a bat?"

Previews!

The further slated books of, The Trilogy, promise to share many more astonishing hominid insights taken from recent and past discoveries, some may even be disturbing to some many compassionate persons? Actually, under present day conditions, attitudes, policies, etc., there is next to nothing that we can do to help them subside. Many relatively unknown and secret places remain hidden in all Idaho/Montana regional terrain mountain forest lands comprising the Continental Divide. Most part, where strange humanoid anomalies are actually known to government agencies as the BLM, etc., they cleverly squelch all knowledge and/or rumors of wild populations as fast as they can, easily exemplified by what all more secret antiquated human remains remain hidden from the public in private basement lock-up in places such as Barclay California, The Smithsonian, etc! Pseudo critics as include accredited academics, etc., can not hope to contest contrary anything considered truly viable revealed by maverick discovery that will be exemplified within The Trilogy for the obvious reasons of ever encouraging public exposure! Extreme knowledge can be highly important, and even at time dangerous to all higher Arianism! There still remains very much untold in more starling evidence unshared within existing/waiting photographs, plaster casts, etc., anxious to be shared public to substantiate all now hidden truths awaiting The Trilogy Exploration Exposures, that ever manifest the true existence of a wild and free feral humanity. The great North American topographic wilderness ever is inclusive of the endless adjacent mountain vastness as exists the well known, Great Basin Wilderness, extending up from, The Mexican Sonoran Desert, to the North Far-Side of little known and less than completely explored Northern most Borders of all Wilderness Canada and Siberia!"

Log: Unreasonable Reasons

Why really do anyone think that the government wants cave and mountain exploration over in many places of the far west as is Idaho? Idaho will likely not be the last vista to set the non-sensical president of extensive land closures'! By writing these books it is my intention to at least get a small part of all this important wild man documentation down on paper before I myself become history; and do it much far ahead of all of the continuing moot policies of obnoxious State and Federal Government ploys. What indeed may be the highly covert reasons for all of the sudden public land closures over vast America may come back to haunt our grand children and theirs! When and if all Trilogy material is closely studied, even the most arrogant-ignorant air-head critic will have understood some of its obvious logistics of the absolute plausibility and importance of a working knowledge of wild hominids. Nothing to date in theory presentation or other wise is more conclusive, or is better written than what is here presented that could better explain the strange plaiting or its many manifestations. There has not been anything researched better able to explain any part of it. None at all! Oriental and European researchers as will be further explained, have for many years professed some plausible answers similar of what is here but not nearly as elaborate. Why, I wonder, are we Americans so pompous-quick to constantly conclude everything not fully understood in moot negativism, or in meaningless statements such as, been there and done that, etc!"

Log: A Candid Deposition:

Unnamed citizen, per-chance meeting while seated and pondering a pseudo wild hominid photograph in the Idaho Falls, Idaho, Public Library, late afternoon, October 5, 2012. Question asked of me... "Hey man, what you got there? Is that a picture of a Sasquatch or what?" Ever heard of a wild man, I asked the Twit? "Hell No, Man! what are you asking? O'course not! There ain't no such thing as A damn Stupid wild people! Besides brooow, all of that strange stuff believed in like Bigfoot, etc., that stuff just can't happen! Hell Man... Just look at the truth! We got forest maps! Internet! In-fired cameras! All of that good stuff, and more! Lets talk football, etc., or discuss something that we all understand? Them Bigfoot Guys out there by now sure as all hell would have caught all of them anyway!" To What guys are you referring, I ask him, and by the way, what month do you remember happens an all new Halloween?"

Citizen: "Hell Man, I don't know? What does Halloween got to do with it? Hell man, all that I know is, Halloween, and all of that spooky stuff, just all happens when it gets cold! See you on the Net! Heck man, you need to learn to adapt! This is year 2010! What world are you living in anyway? Who are you man! Think I have seen you someplace?" All of that last said above made perfect sense! Adaptability is what future survival is all about! The kid wasn't completely misinformed, just didn't believe in Bigfoot? In particular incidences neither do I! That said by the twit was true survival via couch potato logistics!

However, all such base-blind-bias, couch potato attitudes are all a part of wanton programmed insanity! Especially if similar of that above is said within the pseudo authoritative Bigfoot community that at times proves to confuse most all new discovered truths uncovered in earnest wild hominid research, and such attitudes are ever prevalent within all far differing "Bigfoot Think Tank logistics!" The last ones standing in any case scenario, will be those intelligent few persons ever able to be constantly adjusting their moot opinions updated to the extreme changes of all new future proven discovery of what ever regardless! It will not be the strong, the obnoxious, or the able bodied educated entertaining, the tough-stubborn, or even the beautiful ranchers daughter, or especially the popular often windy wanna-be academic, including the informed unsung maverick explorer, etc. that will survive, "but it will be those few smart, unbendable persons that well realize the full importance to be able to adapt to any and all new/true changes within discovery! Adaptability it should be understood, takes many hats, and it does not mean to surrender, be compliant, less than compassionate, or opt not to want to join the choosers! "Show me the scars of the warrior! In their painful scars, blood loss, misery, and mixed compassion had for all those fallen, lies the true untold complete story of the battle! Much similar could be said of true exploration."

Log: Deposition: Honolulu Hawaii, 2009

China born, Naturalized US Citizen
"Don, why do so many Americans squander their time looking for wild man? In China we know all about them! I could take you to many places where they have been encountered!

China has long known something important about them, and has even written some of their ancient history... Yes, I know too that some of them also live in your caves. They live in them too in China! You cannot catch them, as they are too wild, and very smart, just exactly like the wise Hawaiian cheeee-ken hens and roosters! They are much too fast and clever!

"Don, Idaho and Montana are just too cold! Just like in China, wild people need go into caves to keep warm. Some of them live along the high mountain river waterways, in places found as caves the canyon walls... There is plenty food, where ever are found fish, and small animals! Some believe that these wild people can swim, and some they say have with them trained wild animals as pets?"

"Thanks, you were ever an inspiration!"

Log: The Rabbit?

First Off, what has been overlooked? Consider Halloween? All Lunar Eclipse! Or, every 28 Days there begins a New Full Moon! In China it is called, The Rabbit Moon!" What does anyone ponder/realize important of the moon that we may have over looked? For One Thing, "any thing that can opt to braid a horse's mane would be clever enough (If wanted?) to sleep on woven mat, be able to manufacture primitive foot wear, plaited clothing, construct primitive temporary stick, pole, corn stalk, reed, and/or willow woven lodging, etc! Think about what an acute plaiting ability indicates! "That considered, the case is closed, as wild man living on the fringe of humanity has in the ways above described the edge on civilized man, as to fact he lives an unspoiled less than dictated existence; the life if you will, of a classic, happy savage! Hardly is he ignorant, or at all stupid! Stupid would be however, if humans remain insistent that all wild doors to further understanding of their life mission is shut! What, really, might be their destiny in league with all passé and future humanity? What more not yet considered can be learned from them? From where, and when did "they" arrive to America? Yes, I am suggesting that some of these intelligent creatures especially where found within some particular gene pools may in some respects measure up to believable expectations of humans, and by the same token are the same are gifted ones that for what ever more reasons than will be explained ahead are continuing to be plaiting the manes." Read on, even if you only do it tongue in cheek, and give sway to digest all you can from this hairy man and horse stuff chronicle. Highly consider all of what has been written, and especially pay close attention to all of what more will be said, as it may surprise even the most biased self-centered critic twit of you, to well realize who is not, or what exactly may be actually looking stark straight back at you on any given dark frozen night, by the dim light of a full moon? God bless all, and good luck "Charley Tuna!" As on Halloween in places of the far Islands of the South Pacific, or anywhere river if you dare swim under the full moon, all may need it, as just perhaps and perhaps not Sasquatch can swim, as the author has high reasons for the belief that they can!"

Log: What's New Under the Stars?

And all of the above is especially so, if anyone dare have the courage to take an even more educated look deep down into a dark candle lit cavern, or any large Cave Hole in the ground leading into a place where few men have dare to tread before! Just possibly if you dare, you will have a hair raising experience extraordinaire, abrupt the howling wind, and/or the unex-

pected confused Winnie of a surprised horse, or an actual wild man, or any number of as yet unknown high strange creatures that have avoided detection? See you somewhere ahead in another grotto for strange trick, or treat? Either way, you have been warned! Wild unexplained entities indeed do wander under The Milky Way!"

Log: October 6, 2012. Norma Jenson.

An important Update!

I write excited... Moments ago Norma Jenson reported that only last night for a second time in recent weeks the strange plaiting had happened again on Hink! Ironically, the mane had been braided in a very same precarious way as was done on at the beginning take of this book's research on, December 11, 2011! This particular type of a similar plait had not occurred again since that date all of ten months ago during a historical documented rare eclipse of the moon! The photograph section will evidence two separate but much similar circular plaits that are extremely important to the book's ongoing theory research. At the above date and time, exactly as happened last night, the same type of a "carefully fine tuned round braid of a rather medium sized measured as best can to be exactly a round circle formed as if one were to close ones index finger held to thumb forming a small circle somewhat smaller however than was the first one plaited last December 11, 2011 similar; however both much resembles the other in a Full Moon look-alike facsimile, much resembling the December 11th. Full Eclipse of the Moon to be round as all would appear to the eye! Wow! The plait done last night looks very much the same! A very same creature, or what ever has done it, did it each time by the full moon phase! Exciting photographs have arrived! This exciting information writes way far ahead our intended story, as much more will be written to more explain all continuing theory and possible ramifications! Wait for! I am anxious to re-visit the Jenson's, definitely a same creature had to have repetitiously plaited the exact same horse with the exact same sort of a plait! Diane Hollins, who one mile distance from where the horses are corralled, reported again that on the same eve her two dogs again were much reluctant to leave her front door! "Something on those nights she said, highly spooks them! Don, do you remember "back when," when those dogs were all strangely chewed up and bad bit by something? And you well know that Norma and I have both at times heard those very strange sounds... Well, my dogs are staying in the house until the moon phase is over!"

Log: A Needed Hink Explanation?

The horse named "Hink" is a true blood bred famous "Neil Hinck" "Blazer horse," and is the main event of current interest, as she year long will continue to be well brushed out monthly, mane ready, for any new wild man or like type trick or treat plaiting mischief? Much more on Neil will be written in its places.

Log: October 1, 2012.

A Full Moon, and, Plaiting Update:

Tonight I am writing from Pocatello Idaho, where on my way to the Salt Lake City, Utah, Veterans Hospital for a follow-up on my ongoing painful snake bite mishap that occurred six months ago on, March 28th, 2012! I am very anxious to recover, and very grateful to be alive! God has been good to me another time on no separate terms! The inconvenience has been a great detriment to the manuscript research. Some of my original intentions will need be temporary aborted. Summer months 2013, if able, I will resume plait explorations beyond this tries. Weather or not I will write more of it I am not sure?"

Concerning all horses, and plaiting to date! Without exception, on each and every full moon phase segment it has happened over and again, and again, to every single one of our candidate mares! Every month strange plaiting has happened each 28 days running... (At least happens at some point of time on the particular darkest night of the five day phase! Darkest overcast night, still under close observation, etc?)... each month ever since I began the first recent moon probe, December 11, 2011, now all ten months time as of October 11, 2012. It has been extremely difficult for me single handed in snake bite condition to properly access all far distant locations where has been found continuing plaits. "As said, I write dutiful," as never again will I ever have the opportunity to had observed and worked one on one with all of this wild stuff over the last eight years on the incredible passé Neil Hinck Ranch... So be it Old Friend, I'm sure we miss the others wicked self?"

Priorities? "Hink, and all others are now being closely watched, and the very same thing is taking place far and wide over the study area of parts of vast Montana – Idaho, and has been somewhat steadily reported far beyond! As said, all final plaiting results from recent observations will be concluded as of the final date of the last pending December full moon, by January first 2013! All story research intended for this manuscript will be over, as by late February or March, "God Willing," I plan to return back short term, for a week at Honolulu, on my way to "Big Island Hawaii" at Kona, via Hilo, where lives my half Mermaid and fish fond daughter, Lawrie Provost, owner operator of two separate, "Dive Stores" located at both of the Island towns mentioned! After January 2013, a continuing observation and documentation will continue concerning all horses, and especially "Hink" will be of note during my absence, as all research need hardly be over, as the excitement of it all has got me scientifically curious, if not completely hooked!

Log: A Big Project!

Universally speaking, this is a very big highly interesting story! In time it may prove to have an incredible over-all ratification, very much of a historical importance when/if actually concerning all world wide distribution of relict wild man type hominids! Not the space here for all of that nautical history conjecture, but there definitely is a fin ate connection in them reminiscent of all vast Eurasia! "Another book perhaps? And another life?" As said, December 11, 2011, to, December 31st, thirteen plus months running taking evidence should satisfy anyone's needs to know and consider a thing of truth? But when realizing all stark after-shocks and confusions had from much pseudo discovery, and still being unable to explain all of these distant horses as much as I'd like, "as said, many of them have been monthly plaited and messed with much similar as Hink, etc., has me needing to continue a separate research 2013; as some of it is intended, however, to be much relevant; having even more to do with plaiting conjecture and may prove equally as/or more important to ancient navigation and humanity settlement, than has till now been only relative to Hink and interesting others of her kind, and is even far beyond the importance of all of what will be completely defined over the following chapters! Possibly during my visit to Hawaii, "as I am hopeful," I will be able to investigate places far places of the Island as, "Parker Ranch, etc.," and if lucky discover (If anything of significance?)

any continuing evidence of plaiting there? Wow, if indeed it is, that fact alone will more than slightly change some of the mi-nut e important logistics of this paper! As for now in passé times (As will be more explained), I have not once found one single bit of evidence of plaiting having been done anywhere over the Hawaiian Island Chain? This peculiarity of high interest carries over in ramifications into all ever high strange almost to be magical little known 19th, & 20th, Century discoveries had in Nevada! Research the Owyhee Desert to realize the origination of the name! Much interesting and highly peculiar remains hidden in passé Cal/Neva/Ida! One day in a future I also hope to return back to visit bloody David Jennings, at Warwick Australia, to con fire, throw darts, and have a much better hard educated look at all of his, "Good-On Ya, Mates, fine horses!" What further interests me is, that it is just possible that any number of Neil Hinck Ranch Horses were shipped there in past times, and if so, in any remote way would it be possible that any of them might be having their manes plaited in much a same way as in America? A considerable number of "Hinck Horses" were sent all over the world to discriminating owners for over forty years prior to as recently as five years ago! "Neil Hinck, was much more than a famous, Wrangler Hombre! Many persons I am sure to this day still do miss his rascal self and extreme ability! Perhaps one day there will need be written an all true surprise Australian/Hawaiian extension-sequel that will further explain this documentation? However as said, another will need to do it, as to had accomplished such a difficult study as this, requires much time, determination, travel, uncanny patience, much discomfort, and ever an assured ongoing financial difficulty!"

Log: From a Distance!

Actually, all of the high strange anomaly of multiple plaiting being done in many distant localities of the world at exact same dates and times, becomes more than an incredible, and a worthy mystery of note in itself! Enjoy all story ahead! Believe any of it, or nothing? It matters not to me! I have for considerable years kept a close net collection of cut off horse hair plait artifacts, and now have in access of fifty/sixty count of the braided mane samples taken from various area horses! "The truth ever writes its own adherence!" All at once I am more than anxious to continue to share what I have discovered! It is my belief that there actually are a few valid answers to ponder ahead! Anyone out there reading having had a similar adventure, please fell free to contact the author. We defiantly do need all help to further explain this collective high strange Twilight Zone Anomaly! "Remember, no one has truly been any where and done enough! Not you, not me, not nodda amigo! Pirates Maybe?"

"Ishmahachi!"

Or,

Much thanks to all readers if still with me!

The meaningful word above is taken and paraphrased from the Ancient, Hidatsa Indian language, best known today as the Montana Crow, interrupted here to be a friendly variation best explained similar as "Aloha" is allowed used in Hawaii, or best said...

"Best wishes from all, Idaho/Montana Territory, the author, all extended crew, and all remaining seldom wandered, high desert-wild mountain cave lands, that are the place of the part time

"Pongoniff," better know as the cold winter white frost abode of a notorious, controversial, somewhat much smaller type of high desert wild hominid, purposed to be in fact of a much variable mixed/matched gene-pool origination, consisting of both smaller, and some very much large Sasquatch living along side the other in parallel harmony (Hardly Bliss!) as elusive to discovery beyond what are the legendary mountain lion, and especially the little known highly aggressive Onza! All that another story!"

Log: 2012 - From Theory to Reality!

So be it so!
"A side trip into Lion Cave Idaho!"

"Believe it or not, the Mountain Lion, and the relict Hominid, hunt together somewhat apprehensive, and at best pseudo cooperative! As only recently is proof; during mid October, I trailed a wandering desert cougar to the place of his den, where found at the end of the fresh blood trail stashed into his cave, a dead pronghorn antelope half eaten and temporary abandoned at my intrusion. "In the beam of my flash light for the taking if wanted was enough red meat to have fed you and I for several weeks! Proof enough for me that animals and humans if understand the other, could easily survive without harm to the other in parallel unalterably! Why not Sasquatch the same? All American large wild cats when aware instantly abhor and avoid bipeds! It is written in their eyes, latent fears, and, DNA!"

("Ask and you will receive! Watch and investigate what you will hunt, and you will eat!")

"The Notable High Intellect Of Horses and Lions!"

("Need wild man have any less?")

Var Harris first time Visits Lion Cave!

"Ok Var Harris, Lion Cave, may be the only place where you may actually be able to hand a wild hominid or mountain lion your scrunched hot dog or carrot? I will watch from outside? Got your .44 handy? If you don't carry a gun in today's wilderness you are completely nuts! "Once inside Lion, Var's eyes opened wide at his first sight of the many, many, strewn animal bones on the cave floor scattered just about everywhere numbering easily fifty to one hundred visible in the beam of our flash light, almost to be a solid mass over the cave were the rib remains and various leg bones and spine extensions of antelope, deer, elk, etc! Var was mesmerized! "Wow Don, he said, I never expected to ever see anything like this! Do the lions stay here?" Yeah, Var, they do! Once outside again in the sun light, not all that far from where we stood, at perhaps only a short rifle shot distance away, roamed a small herd of local ranch stock horses left to wander the open range till fall. "Through field glass Var, it looks like some of those horses have been messed with! They may have even been plaited? Can't be certain, as we can't approach them up-close either, so of course its all a wanton guess? But from here it does look like some are braided?"

"Yeah, Var said, even if they are Don, how in the heck does anything bond with them, etc? You know, even the wily Mountain Lions have a hard time catching deer and especially horses!

How in the heck do you your wild men as you call them do the plaiting? I've chased horses all of my life, and they are impossible critters! That's one of the reasons for my bad back! Cowboys finish last, when it comes to horses! Lots of them have even been killed by the bastards! Lets say for example that we caught one of the rascals... How and why after all of that effort would we want to plait its mane? That couldn't be done even if wanted under the best circumstances! Maybe we should hand them horseduvore's wandering over there one of my carrots? They look fat enough to even eat!" Var was always a Hoot! I have missed his tall seven foot impossible self! I once asked that he write with me in a book? Later in the story we discover that his very own pet horse gets plaited right under his ugly mustached nose! The horse at that time and probably still is was almost directly under his bed room window! Var remains unconvinced of the importance of plaiting! Not that unusual even among the anointed! Today's people for a most part are afraid of what they cannot explain or understand! Once convinced however Var would be ahead of most others in discovery! "In earnest, it is very, very, difficult to find true adventurist persons." Many profess interest, and many more re-regurgitate what ever they could have digested from opportunity! "The proof is in the pudding, and some many refuse to enjoy the meal!" Only a chosen few recognize true adventure for what it is and reap its benefits! "Matters not, as that is the way that it has always been, and is the crux of much academic confusion, and lay public support! "Sometimes the truth eats its witness, and the world is never the wiser!"

Var again! "Don, about them bones in the cave...? What the hell done all that really? I have never seen anything like it?" Well, Var, that is one of the best kept secrets of one of the intelligent hunting methods of hominids! Few persons would believe it, or put it all together. But as you well know, these Lions are constantly tracking us as we explore these caves. "They are tracking us out of pure curiosity!" And in our separate way, we are also keeping close track of them! "The lions do the same thing with the Sasquatch!" They are constantly watching each others back side, whenever possible! And when a mountain lion makes a kill, and next opts to drag it into a cave, etc., "well, the smart bipeds give them enough time to lick their chops in a short fiasco, before next showing up on the scene, and at their leisure making off with a free meal! Its all just as confusing and simple as that! These wild guys are super smart! All American wild cats, most of them are very afraid of man! Its no real problem if cautious to snatch an animal from them!" There is so much to know and to understand in the animal world! So much to investigate! So much important instruction needed of the naive reader if he is actually well able to fully understand all coming chapters, conjecture, and explanations. True wilderness savvy takes a life time of experience and unadulterated evaluation and still most bias humans are no where! Ever all separate chapters of the book are needful to continue with more sample excerpts taken from all related manuscripts of the Trilogy, that collectively well preview some of the valid reasons for the authors discovery and theory rational beyond the best kept secrets of this book. I am not the last word in true wild Bob Cat Logic, "but don't try to track me down to catch me without notice! Believe me, any wild man, or strange entity, that has the ability to plait the manes of wild horses, etc., "definitely has several viable reasons to be continuing to do it! We are about to enter the world of much further explanations!"

Doctor Watson I presume...

To quote, Sherlock Holmes ("Sir Arthur Conan Doyle!") slightly paraphrased: "My dear Doctor Watson, all of this stuff is of course superficial! Actually, if a thing is not of the Obvious, then of course it is of the Contrary!"

Cowboy Egotism, etc.

"Cowboy Negativism is Nuts, and borders on Narcissism!"

"Well, Var said that, and in particular cases it is so often true, and it is ever viable, and comparable with most wilderness illogical conjecture, unfounded logic, etc., if had from only around the camp fire! As all true important exploration discovery consists of close observation, much tenacious determination from experience, and ever an endless stubborn tenacity of purpose, maintaining all expectations positive, and when not, accepting moot negativisms had from pseudo authoritative opinion voiced contrary to all extraordinary and much varied wild experienced studies already had in Crypt 'o investigations, etc!"

"Var had passé, served as a local County Sheriff, and knew exactly what I was all projecting! "Next he said, Well Don, we both know the we both are all of that! And you at times are also a horses detriment! Well, in spite of all that said, I still want to hand one of them big ugly two footed creatures one of these carrots!" Lets go get em Var, all of you Idaho Cow-boys are completely Nuts! That's why we don't let you live in Montana! Insanity and crazy are not quite the same thing! Up there we got The Crazy Mountains... You are going there next? Var and I, will continue ahead, to further educate all interested readers using more needed examples of what will probably at first read to many thought to be Completely Out of the Box Logistics, "all necessary however to understand/consider if anyone is expected to believe any more of this jargon in intelligent terms? Many of these all relatively well kept secrets being shared have directly to do with the ever uncanny, highly intelligent, intricate, and obvious high strange, and ever awesome ability definitely needed had all necessary for anyone, or anything thought humanistic, or other wise intelligent to be able, or even be wanting to plait the manes of horses for what ever the reasons, let alone be able to further stretch the imagination of even the wild magician depicted in the movie titled: The Lord of The Rings, or be compared to the merciless, "Hounds Of The Baskervilles! Do you think... Should all of the unexplained mysteries of the world need be solved? If so, perhaps Sherlock Holmes should be Our Mentor? Are we by now somewhat slightly understanding wildman projections? All study ahead is much predicated upon wanting to understand their talents, uncanny ability, and tenacious determination! "Without a reason and a rather definite determination there would be no plaiting! Please dear Watson, UN-case my violin, and re-load my .32 revolver!"

"Wild Bob Cat Logic!"

Wild Man Could Have Taught Them!

There is a reason for all seasons, and always a logical reason to highly ponder all Bob Cat Logic had them by the light of the any moon phase! Cat eyes at night (In dark!) likely see similar in proficiency as are an eagles by day, and to further validate this, we have often found Bob Cat, and Mountain lion tracks deep inside mountain caverns where few canines would dare to tread. Bears I am sorry for similar reasons do not sleep deep in caves either. In one incident explained in another Trilogy book was found solid evidence to suggest that wild man may indeed train wild cats as pets and hunting companions. What better animal is better suited to a dark cavern world than a cat? Do we think that all wild creatures are cautious only had from supposed instinct alone, or could it include latent intuitions had from consigned DNA and all learned/realized fears experienced abrupt many recalled vistas of high danger early life taught all surviving kittens by the adults of the pride? Often three mountain lion kittens out of four born parish in the wild before maturity for any number of expected reasons. Instinct alone will not every time save them. They need to have a mental capacity abrupt an acute ability to learn and to teach one another.

Cat People?

There Are Many Tales!

"See her eyes so red! They are redder than a Jungle fire! To catch her would be like putting out a fire with gasoline! To keep her would be impossible, unless she volunteered!" Concerning cats eyes, some many of the South West Indians, because of wild man's realized ability to easily see so well in the dark, have dub them the Night People, or, Cat Men! This is an interesting scenario, as countless times all crew have been astonished of all cave inhabitants undeniable uncanny ability to perform so well in completely pitch dark surroundings. Definitely all cats and the higher animals can reason danger. Any one that has ever been a fur trapper well knows the proficiency of a shadow cougar, that is very much like the wolf, and wolverine that are almost next to impossible to see, catch in a trap, or in a snare. Much more is said to explain all of this ahead in manuscript titled, "The Cavern of Zakyneros!" Back track when you will any wild or domestic cat, and well learn the great wisdom of covert stealth! The Ancient Egyptians highly revered and considered all of the believed magical abilities of one origin an-creation of all cats as, DE-notes Baste t, held second to none along side all cat mysteries and ancient traditions practiced under the guise of the Full Moon! The Abyssinian Cats of Persia, and many others that could be named have a definite roll model place in all Cat Adornment History! "What ever the wild creature, many of them are highly intelligent, and can reason safety, etc., weather anyone want to understand it or not! "Contest that last said illogical to the book's theoretical conjecture, and we have arrived exactly to nowhere!" Chuck the book, and choose to be on your way to perhaps visit "Chuck y Cheese!" In all probability, "if can," please read well between all lines, on all of the pages of the manuscript, and well ponder all separate stories, and just likely some answers here yet to explained will begin to make sense in the wake of all diversity regardless of however abstract, or was at first thought this book perhaps ridiculous, "as for sure, probably you yourself, in a very short time if were with us in the exploring field, would likely sooner or later come to all much similar projected erratic if not eccentric conclusions! Eccentricity invents genius, as many a known genus is highly eccentric! Who really other than the obvious generic person wants to be thought to be that way? All intelligent persons traveling on differing roads, eventually arrive at like destinations, abrupt all necessary abstract adaptability had from both Bob Cat Logic, and purposeful human thinking that is reasoning; especially this be so, if it were ever possible for one to relate as far back in time (If could?) to ones unrecognized awareness in early child hood, and be able to access all their separate morbid, and/or latent fears, inclusive of all hidden fantasies, etc! That if possible, would be the best kept secret of all time of how to open all of the now closed doors of the pseudo metaphysical interactions thought highly improbable between man and beast! Beasts can often well realize all human intentions! Man falters in this ability! "I only write that last, as some many of The Twilight Zone Chapters, mostly strange cave experiences lightly introduced ahead; "not one single one of them to this day leave one logical answered question beyond probably being moot speculative! No real closure ever for most, "except to say, there are no ends to all stories! Or better said, other wise, don't go, stay out!" Charley will we be having roast beast for supper, or, will it be that the beast will roast us first? Either way, "the truth ever writes its own destiny!" What's for dinner may well be, Chicken

Little, or a little chicken will be serving us for supper! "With wild man and horses, its ever who's on first, and what's on second?"

Plaiting?

"It is to be understood, that I am not the last word, or a conclusive authority either on the plaiting, or of any supposed unobtainable horse magic considered beyond this manuscript, but the fact remains that because of all separate efforts, and all that has been discovered, and as a result all many high strange animal associations through experiments, etc., certainly by now via endless Bob Cat Logic Considerations, forest detective magic inclusive, much human/animalistic logical considerations, etc., "definitely I have founded opinions believed well able to probably even more explain at least a logical working part of all remaining unexplained anomalies not already addressed in this book?"

Log: Author's note

After having just completed a re-evaluation of this windy treatise, all at once in my opinion, suddenly all of this strange plaiting when documented on paper in the abstract, begins to make sense! As by this place in the book, by now it should be obvious that wild man in general seem to experience an definite infinity if not a needful comradely towards horses. Perhaps it is highly logical that countless eons ago, Wild Bipeds coming to The Americas from perhaps all Vast Eurasia, Tibet, Cathay, etc., ("All of them brought/captured wanted for hard labor, conquest, etc!")... it is logical that the ancients brought with them many, "Steppe horses," as the Mongolians had ever highly treasured them, and done this if for no other intention than, ("If needed?) to opt to Conquer all New Frontiers of discovery! Wild man came with them along side many, many a horse! Horses in fact of a much mixed, and varied early blood lines; that to this day, some many pseudo historians refuse to allow that they ever existed! "As said, many horses long, long, ago came to the all of the Americas, as well as many other far regions of the world, along side UN-sung adventurous Asiatic, and fearless Euro-

Figure 21. The author, Billings, Montana 2009. Photo T. Mauney.

pean Voyagers? Even the legendary, Norse Vikings highly revered their horses almost above their women! Can anyone imagine? "There is now much documented evidence coming to front to attest that wild horses were roaming the Americas for many hundreds, if not a thousand years before the arrival Columbus, or much later when the Spanish Conquistadors first had introduced their heavy unfamiliar war horses into The South West! It took a very large and *strong horse to be able to cart around an armor clad, heavily armed to the teeth, Conquistador! Long prior to even the earliest Viking invasions, much smaller Asiatic Steppe horses and Chinese base ponies roamed North Western America all of the way into places of what is today Canada.. To prove this, one need only to confirm with the Ancient Hidatsa Blood Line Native Montana Americans to realize all ancient territory that had once comprised the long known Wild Horse Prairie! Get a map, have a look!" (Beaver Head Mountains, Montana. Summer 2010.) Local Proof of smaller horses ancient in North America! Today Darrel Miller, Lima Montana, guided me to an unsuspected high mountain cave, located well above 6,000 ft! In the small enclave was a mixed/varied animal depiction in petroglyphs. Definitely there was solid evidence that anciently horses of a much smaller sort were brought to America and were running wild over the high desert landscape long before the arrival of the Spanish. These petroglyphs drawing of small ponies was proof enough for me that wild horses of their kind still found today in small numbers in Montana were right along side the elk, deer, antelope, bear, etc., The cave depiction definitely references smaller horses as are the many typical examples of Asian Steppe ponies rather than prototype huge war horses that had been brought to Meso-America in the late history, 15th Century, etc. The Spanish horses were a much different animal all together than were the fast sleek smaller Asian ponies. These had to have been what was later called the Indian Ponies that were long known for hundreds of years to have roamed the open range of what is today as the far western corner of Montana, where in Horse Prairie, etc. Aeons, ago, Horse Prairie by name was well established by the native Indian peoples, set aside to be forever a peaceful gathering place where any and all cooperative tribe's warring or not would be able to solicit horses as needed while in an agreement that rather than kill the other; instead, it became the custom of all warrior's to "opt to Touch Coo instead as each tribe well realized the others obvious necessity of maintaining an active gene pool of male warriors if for no other reason than the very survival of their race! Had the Indian Tribes early-on to been able to unite as a fighting force, North America today would likely fly quite another Standard-Bearer rather than what we have! I have life-long opt to side with most all Native American peoples and have had considerable friendships among them. Their ancient logic and wisdom if can be deciphered is some of it written in stone concerning their reverence to the moon, stars, and especially the Sun that is well realized for its warmth and extreme importance to life and happiness! Some many of our white community are shallow of mind, and so opt to run quickly a 'muck by their own folly never to fully realize the magical shadow world of their native brothers! The Native American Indians know much of unfathomed, fascinating, and ever incredible rote history lore! I am most fortunate that some of it had rubbed off on me early in my sojourn, much similar as had also happened later as a result of living in Hawaii, where I also experienced many new and unsolved mysteries found only in those fascinating Islands! It was from the Indians and in the Hawaiian Islands when met Glen Grant that I well learned that some things are best left untouched, untold, and unwritten! Like Glen, I have ever life long been respectful and cautious when on sacred ground. Horse Prairie, for specific identification can still be found on some out dated maps. It is a fact that a definite pseudo Asian association can easily be contested in a definitive language similarity had between the Ancient Hidatsa Crow Peoples who frequented there and the language of some present day Mongolian Tribes, as when compared there is only slight dialect difference in both languages! Aside from the realization that smaller horses were early to the area, it is also interesting that up to fairly recent times some many of the ancient blood line peoples chose to reside in mountain caves rather than what seems the norm to white man thinking that all Indians preferred tents? In my opinion, anciently along with the Asian type steppe horses that were there brought by the early navigators, probably roaming with them were mixed examples of Eurasian wild man; probably* *these miss-fits of the day also roamed other wide regions of North America long prior... or most probably were already here at least far into the later dispensation of recognized Paleolithic times... (The last Ice Age on paper!)... as documented evidence found in Wilson Butte Cave Idaho, proves that ancient unidentified man according to left behind artifacts people occupied the cave as long ago as 20,000 – 15,000 years ago, and the Shoshone base western American Indian tribes did not form/begin until just about the later date dispensation. I have found human worked bone artifacts myself that were carbon dated at 14,000 years ago. Ruth Gruhn writes in her 1961 book, Man To The New World, that people were first to the Americas 35,000 years ago. All of this conjecture is well evidenced for my personal needs to know when/if considering all existing petroglyphic art, much more of it still to be re-discovered over the remote far places of all, Montana, California, Utah, Nevada, Washington, Idaho, Oregon, and who knows where next? I write this last, since during July of 2012, I with Dan Petebar for a witness, discovered in the remnant mountain extensions of the horse prairie what are more possible petroglyphical proof than what is already written? Summer 2013, I intend to much further search the area for viable Petra-artifacts, etc. Obscure tribes of humanity long ago lived extensively over the regional mountains, and in the desert caves! Horses we well knew for a very long time ran the land! Makes sense to me that early plaiting of horses may have been included? If I could somehow find viable plaiting evidence in say valid petroglyphic art well, there will definitely be written an addendum!"*

"Donald Massey's Greatest Adventure"

A Side Trip Reprieve Into A Horse Prairie Proximity Desert Mountain Cavern!

("Beuta Superba Salt 'tau!")

"Everything impossible, improbable, or unlikely?"

A slight candid preview to wild man,

&

"THE CAVERN OF ZAKYNEROS!"

All reference hither and Yon explaining Idaho/Montana cave exploration, took place prior to September first, 2012.

< "If ever a sojourn became impossible, it was this!" >

"Zakyneros"

The incredible cave was named for an unheralded explorer, one man named, Zakyneros, "who was an obscure sailor having arrived most likely to far desert North America on foot from where today remains, The Gulf of Mexico!"

One year prior to his death, etched evidence in stone, "dating 500 BC", had been found in 1849, near where today is the small berg town of Los Lunas, New Mexico. Before passing, "Zak" carved his final message on what today is known as, "The New Mexico Mystery Stone! "His last words ever leave high suspect that he may have perished at the hands of unknown wild bipeds in pursuit? If so, "left to conjecture, they were much similar in descriptions as are the living wild ho-minids of today, that in my opinion are the very same wild man examples of what is wanted called Sasquatch, etc., that continue to plait the manes of American horses? In Zak's last message, he wrote a much meaningful testimony possibly long overlooked in all current linguist testimonial clarification .... ("Q") "I, Zakyneros am about to die! I am but the hair of a rabbit, starving, and much afraid! The others died a timely death one year ago! I am now out of touch with mortal man!"("Mortal Man?") In those last words there is much left to ponder... "Out of Touch With Mortal Man?" O'course Zak well realized that wild Indians of the day were also mortal man! Who then, or what to fact running on two legs, had actually managed to chase and kill him? It becomes more than interesting that they had allowed him enough time to chisel out his last words in hard basalt lava? And what tool did he need use to manage the effort unless it was his sword or similar? To had destroyed the sword doing carving would have been to forfeit his life! Lions, wolves, bears, etc., are ruled out, as to have killed any one of them they would have served as food, and certainly by then he had encountered many! To have explored alone in-land from the sea, 12,00 miles abrupt all of the obvious dangers of the sojourn, he most certainly at times would have needed to survive in a much similar cave as Donald Massey and I that day were about to enter!"

"FIRST DISCOVERY"

(Excerpts taken from book, The Cavern of Zakynerous!)

All Rights Reserved. Library Of Congress Number TX-553-708.

Written and edited by, Donald L. Monroe.

"Dedicated to the extreme bravery of, Donald Massey/and friend Tonia F. Brown, both dared with me to explorer the dank dread dark abyss that ever supposes the high strange and unexpected,

"The True Nether World of Zak and Sister Caves!"

Donald Massey!

"Sassy Massey," as we often called him, dare enter first and only time into the unexpected confines of a large Idaho cave, that we latter dubbed, The Cavern of Zakynerous.

Don was ever the bravest man to enter the cave that I would ever know, void of all future crew that would return back many times after him to more experience the more than highly unusual, and most extraordinary adventure. Much extended mystery that was found in the cave to this very day remains almost as if an unrealized latent phantom within a haunting memory. The conditions around Massey's horrendous experience, could best be said slightly paraphrased taken from his own words from off tape recordings... "Well Don, It had been an extremity wild, hair-raising, and was a completely unsuspected nightmare, it was as horrible an experience as anything that I could imagine could be enough to stop one's heart?" Don was adamant ever after his experience that this part deposition story to follow not be revealed until after his untimely death occurring fall, 2008. He was life long a true adventure.. everyone is not! I damn well do miss him, long before and especially after his horrendous experience he was completely convinced of wild hominid existence. Sometimes it seems as if he is still looking back to me from his walled photograph taken when exiting the cave where I somehow can still hear him saying... "Monroe, I'm going to shoot you at least twice or three times if we ever get out of this cave! The devil himself could be following out right behind us... I don't dare to even look back over my shoulder to see if that big ugly bastard is still after us?"

More of Massey's experience as was appreciated through the understanding eyes of his new found friend, Tonia Brown! Perhaps just a bit confusing to the present story for the moment, but Massey's account continues in more detail slightly after this next brief mention/comparison also had similar of Tonia Brown, as mentioned earlier, this next short excerpt is added here to further compliment her gender, as she was a prime example by her extreme courage, ever supportive to her end, faithful in unconditional dedication, even when in questionable exploration surroundings as when the two times that she also had ventured into Zak Cave, and experienced much questionable exhilaration and fears as had aging Donald Massey his horrendous day in the cave. Her high women's intuition ever excited her passions even when in the face of all pending cave danger abrupt the unknown! Her first and second Zak cave experience ever met its zenith much similar of Don Massey, as will be read at the book's excerpt place where later to come she shares feelings very much the same of Massey's unwanted, horrendous, unwarranted feelings had when without a warning he had encountered what he next describes as ... "That big ugly thing standing there was the dread ugliest awful looking, Big Bastard, red-eyed, Son O' a Bitch-en, Ugliest ever cave hominid in the world that was, or it was a Sasquatch something or other, of an humanoid, or a definite sort of a who knows what in the hell it was... I don't know? Or it was something much like that... And well, Don! Wow, well hell, and after that the big ugly Son O' bitch-en Os-spring of Hell, came right up close to my eyes and face, and next thing he was face to face with me! About then and the next thing... Well honest, my heart was about to be already stopped! I swore at him in every rotten words of bad language and better that I know'd! I cussed him in Japanese, Chinese, Spanish, German, Northern, and Southern, Indian, and English, and probably Siamese dog... and I know'd darn well it all went right over his leering head! And after that, I probably cussed him some more, in Canadian French, Polish, and some of that Vox Russian, I can't remember it all? But no matter what, the big ugly brute just would not go away! Sure as hell, if I Could Have seen his Face close up, I'd had surely died already? I Never saw his Eyes though... but darn well they were Red!"

("Never saw his eyes though? Wait for that importance, and all of rest of the incredible story in a slated Trilogy Manuscript opt for year, 2014.")

Things Happen!

The Rest Of The Donald Massey Story!

"Massey The Brave, and Important Others!"

"Don, out of necessity had been abandoned alone in Zak, for a long 45 minute plus sojourn. His single handed extreme courage, and near hazardous lone adventure on that day became the meaningful inspiration that would eventually prove to spark the need to opt to write The Collective Trilogy Manuscripts! There is so, so, much to tell I will never get'er all down! Don, to no ones stretch of a minute exaggeration, was the real article Montana proud male toughie, best described as one hell of an educated, heroic mentor, and about as exciting a man that few men live to be at his young age then of 86, or for that matter of any age could have endured what he had needed to experience on that day and few others would have lived to swear to it's truth! Don's story when completely read ahead will prove to accentuate Tonia's much similar arduous candle light vigilance; her separate adventures, and ever controlled excitements, that did much to aid/abet my ongoing efforts and further encouraged me to re-explore further into all hidden corners of sister caves in the vicinity and far removed from Zak, etc. Once convinced of wild man, the adventure , however risky, Tonia could not get enough underground exhilaration! "Don, she said, don't you dare tell Sherrie or Van, or any of my kids about what we are doing in these caves, but lets go do it again! All of this wild and weird stuff is something else!" When it comes to women, in a general non-senses I gotta take third place to some many of them and obvious bravery and indisputable tenacity! However, I will never figure any One of them out, or, especially any Two of them at a time especially when/if under full sail a-head! Women definitely, just exactly true, as my Daughter Lawrie Provost says, "Dad, women are in a league of their own!" What's heavenly, foolish, devilish... what ever powers that be that opts to ever protect them from harm is definitely up for quite another hidden book of meaningful chapters of unsolved mysteries! "Lawrie Provost is my half-fish Co-operative daughter that jointly owner/manages two separate, "Sun & Sea Dive Shops," located one in Hilo, and another in, Kona, HI. ... She sometimes opts to dive off the Kona Side Shore of Big Island Hawaii with the hammer head Monos and Moray eels, while my daughter Tatiana Harrison, ops for harassment for chasing questionable black & white cat looking skunks deep into the dark corners of Idaho forests, while Tammy Yee, daily patiently contends with the confused tourists, ever lost as the are just past Hotel Street in China Town, and the Ala canal at Old Honolulu! And, Holly Mulvaney, well, she is in my opinion at least one might say, The Ninth Great Wonder Of All Seattle, and all far regional vista! David does everything his way, while Mark remains ever covert and blissful, and Dad here, was always too late, to little to soon!"

"Respectful Of Ryanne Ke' Alohilani Haligan"

Wow! Love them all, but Bob Schmalzbach reminds me that, "are we drifting slightly off course or what?" Well what the heck Bob, its my book, and it's most ironic that even as I write there comes a new family baby picture and message from my daughter Lawrie telling me proud, that today, Oct. 16th, she has just become the Auntie of a new Island baby girl, one little pink looking shrimp named, "Ryanne Ke' Alohilani Haligan," born to my grand-daughter, Crystal Haligan, daughter of Tatiana, who also just confirmed the birth of her first grand child by saying, "Dad, would you believe it, my baby is having another baby!" Well gang, if your mother could be with us now, she would be Island Proud...

Loving you all was always enough for her...
So be it! We will always remember the way it was! X

"MY SPACE!"

< A NECESSARY AND, RESPECTFUL REPRIVE! >

"Down a Relative Memory Lane!"

"A necessary side trip into the unforgettable world of wonderful Friends, Family, and More! Anyone reading not wanting to include this sentiment as a real part of the manuscript need skip the moment and flip ahead a few pages? Writing from winter time Montana Siberia in this cold wood stove cabin without but ice frozen water, the wind for a maid, and a stray cat at my door has me in solemn reminisce! Too much wind and not enough whiskey! Flowers for the good times, and booze for the bad!"

Yeah Marion, after all considered, I guess I was a part human after all?

You told me not to look back!"

"Sasquatch Hunters, Almost Every One and All?"

Some of Tonia's comments abrupt exploration, heart felt feelings and humor, will be included in her meaningful insights somewhere ahead in the book; "short demotions of serious and calculating wit, that others of her gender especially would appreciate," as I am sure exemplified in place would be her gender crew mentor, "Red" from Montana, Tammy Brown, and my improbable much loved daughter, Hollace Mistletoe Mulvaney, for whom, "Mistletoe Cave Idaho" was named, and my green eyed innocent "(?)" grand daughter, Candace Blackman who bivouacked with me during cold winter 2003, unknowingly naive into the then harms way of, "Mysterious Mistletoe!" And without president mention again my ever unforgettable late wife "Marion Ah-Lun, Mark Monroe," forever is to be lamented, and continues to be a life long mentor of Chase Character example; Love lost; and always she was my friend! Marion was ever all of that! That said, to name a few, all of them are but "an example crux" of all the many persons that I will never forget... "Not however to mention another competitive impossibly wild and restless talented tigress adventuress, wanted left unnamed, that we need just call , "Sara-Sara," as she about did it all beyond catastrophic, advice, permission, and dire warnings unto an almost timely death! Lessons are learned, or are they really? Our sons, Mark, and David, each in a separate spectrum had also dare opt their separate adventure. Courage is the name of the game!"

"So be it Ah-lun, your children every one had loved you!"

Log: Hawaiian Island Ways! January 1, 2003.

"Marion Ah-Lun Mark, Monroe"

Her last time to be seated on Island beach sand was that unforgettable New Years Day, "Talking Story," as was myself with her brother Clifford, while enjoying much Island, "KAU KAU," that was on first, an old faithful tradition, "LAU LAU," and Clifford's ever favorite calabash food, "POKY!" All of us on that afternoon were as if three beach bums, opting to be Making House at Oahu's, Queen Surf Hotel beach front, at Honolulu!"

"Marion said! Ay Clifford... B-rudder! Go over tell Don, "The White Alu-ha," how to use the, Wi-li Wi-li Leaf, and put-em ova him nose when he go swim!"(Those explicit directions someplace? Wait for?

"Marion seldom spoke in Island Pigeon English as, she when wanted spoke perfect Parochial School Bostonian English, and had always been the literal Captain Mentor in good example at all times whenever anywhere in notable compassion, love, humor, respect for God and Country, etc., and especially this so in all extended family devotion! She ever had a special place in her heart for all of her children to the most difficult of the most rebellious! Each one of them had also loved her back for her magical self, and being much more than expected than in all toleration of strained idiosyncrasies, etc! She was never known to an necessary gossip, or be a judgmental hypocrite. Any personal heart ache was ever kept to herself! What more than love and high esteem from children could anyone wish? We get what we denote! The word meaning of, "consequence" had long ago had to have a tragic cause and effect! Marion also loved horses, as she had spent much time with one in particular crippled one during early childhood when housed with her grandfather on a horse ranch on the Windward Side of Oahu! Her uncle, "dubbed to be one of the most famous Island Paniolo cowboys of all time, had many times been exonerated on the front cover page of the irreplaceable National Geographic Magazine! Clifford too, had several times been photographed and portrayed in a much same way; thinking him to had been the typical Island prototype of all yesteryear all but forgotten, colorful, "Throw Net," Hawaiian Beach Boys! Clifford, on the beach at Magic Island, or siting casual/precarious anywhere with his back against a palm tree: looking Island tough/smart, and much capable with his home-made Hawaiian Sling Spear Gun, Unukalhai, al of the while smoking his habitual black Tipi-reel-o Cigarillo; ever wearing his palm hat and with his fish-net he looked the movie classical part, and so lived it well for so many years that he actually was! Clifford was also pseudo convinced of mixed types of wild ethnic Island peoples, including main land Sasquatch! There was never a better Island brother! I miss the Poky? Yeah, and just maybe the Pepper Hot! Had anyone really known Marion and her extraordinary and almost magical perceptive idiosyncrasies, there was everything about her to opt to envy in natural and uncanny ability, beauty of spirit, soul, and a healthy body, not to mention admirable courage, and an extended non demanding ever sharing natural family spirit of good will offered in kindness and friendship to most all mankind. Most of the collective Island Mark Family were much of the same intention. Nothing in my life prior to coming to Hawaii had ever been important until I had thought to had been accepted in that calabash family!"

PART ONE

Marion's Part Deposition!

Sasquatch?

"It Was A Thing, Don, and that is all that there is to say about it!

I have never seen a Sasquatch, so I don't know exactly how one looks? Yes, you can write in your books that I saw a human looking "Thing!" That was exactly what it was!"

After Marion's first wild man surprise experience when with me on Mt. Index Washington, fall/year, 1982, and having finally experienced the exhilaration of sighting close encounter; "close-up, and walking tall one hundred yards or so above us on the rock slide, was a gangly tough looking Wild Man!" Never again would she doubt the existence of, "One of Them," as she forever more had insisted to call it, or what ever sort of a wild "THING" hominid that we encountered on that day that definitely "to true identity had been a Sasquatch! For 20 plus years prior Marion had wandered about everywhere with me looking for viable evidence of them. This is not her biography, but if it were, her credits and deposition would ever be as true and fresh as would be a ever a sweet smelling Rose in an Onion Patch, when and if compared to all lesser humanity! "With her there were no lesser humanity, unless O'course they required it of themselves, and fear was not in her character if anyone were to test her patience; once in Hono, I'd need run with her as she chased a voyeur many city blocks until our bare feet saved his two cherries and a stem from much worse than Bob-it! No one messes with the best, and Marion was the mentor!"

If huckleberries were spilled from her apron it would require a bushel basket to pick up her spilled treasure intended to be turned into pan cake syrup to go with her jerked venison and home canned everything that she had prepared for the coming winter. Out of sheer determination and the necessity of the moment and requirement she could accomplish almost the thought impossible in record time! Truly there have been few women born that would be anything like her. Her natural ability as an artist was next to none; there seemed nothing that she could not create or accomplish... It has been now ten years since her timely demise, and I can still hear her saying to me... "Don, for goodness sake! Get our rifle and the shot gun! Heck it's a beautiful fall day, and I am sure your heart is not in painting that stupid porch? Bring the fishing pole too, we might get near a stream?" We left that day with the cloths on our back, and were gone without looking back for all of 28 months! After returning, left again shortly after towards Canada and the Pacific for another 18!

"Yeah kids, your mother was a true adventuress if ever there was born another! As said, Marion was a true adventuress, she had braved the unknown with me several times from, Mexico, and back, to almost everywhere USA and back, as well as into much of the Canadian Outback wilderness by canoe, foot, and auto, often as not wandering on our way via far off vistas of the Pacific Sea, past the far place from Idaho to where were her native roots in Honolulu. Often she was far ahead of me in meaningful encouragements, as, "Don she said, listen to me! No matter what others may say about your exploring and belief in wild man, etc., don't ever give up what you are doing! It is important! Some day you will be appreciated! Wild man as we both know exists, we both have seen One! And that is all there is to say about it! For goodness sake, go feed those poor cave creatures something nourishing! They are probably laughing at all of you, and all of that crazy experiment food and strange stuff that you are giving them? And take them some warm blankets... The poor "things" are probably freezing to death!"

That day on Mt. Index had much changed both our lives! Within all slated books of the Trilogy, women as will be noted are by no means considered by me as, "Second Fiddle," and definitely just as Lawrie said, "the unlikely female gender is completely in a league of their own," especially this so when it comes to special innate discovery, important intuition, and sage advice! I do not pretend to fully understand any real part of woman-hood logistics, there personalities, or most anything otherwise that they aspire to, or require important, however I ever appreciate and encourage them to be in company whenever permissible, and without asking most always depend on them to be in charge? As pirate tough as most opt to think I am, I most always am on the woman's side of reason. Marion was not at all uninformed of horses as she had grew up on an Island horse ranch! Her stories of sharing black strap molasses with Old Swayback are a classic event right out antiquated movie titled, "The Yearling!" Had she lived, "We," not just "I," would have been documenting this book together! In my separate efforts stashed somewhere in the wreck of a cabin hidden for safe keeping, until a time when I have a better opportunity to fine tune her meaningful manuscript; somewhere lost in time within my memories exists, "Marion's Bear Collection," that without a doubt is one truly wild sojourn of humor, Ice, Snow, dust, and mega true love, courage, and adventure! She was truly in a great many ways beyond invincible!"

Another Incredible Journey!

"Tonia, It Is Going To Be An Adventure Towards Bimini Island, Discovering Plaited Horses, And petroglyphs Along The Way From Montana, To Florida, Or Bust! We Did It All And More Too! She Was Never Domesticate able Again! Wow what a voyage! Tonia in her own way was somewhat of a much similar of an adventures nature as was Marion, as for two years running she had unconditionally braved the unknown in much a same way, and was ever as much in awe after having once realized the importance of all unlikely research. Especially this so, when making all new re-evaluations in Zak, and other regional caves, 2009, when we first time returned back into some of those caves since discovery years 2001 – 2006!

We did this evaluation short term, before wandering to Florida with designs on reaching Bimini Island by late December 2009, planning to return by April 2010, to re-explore recently discovered plaited horses, new found petroglyphs, and much more over the far-vast frozen desert reaches of New Mexico/Arizona, Mississippi, etc.

During the sojourn in January to visit M.K. Davis in Mississippi, with him as guide we explored locally, and discovered exceptional definitive artifacts and lost Spanish brick work architecture able to well attest that white explorers as was Ponce De Leon and Hernando Desoto during the 15th Century had reached the confluence of the, Ya-Zoo, and, Sunflower Rivers!

"Important Notes On The, 1967, Roger Patterson Film!"

In this book segment, MK Davis surfaces indisputable film evidence to validate that wild man actually can manage plaiting!"

"Yeah, and wow, M.K., what next?"

"Yeah Don, I assure you that it is true! On the original Roger Patterson Film Footage, Patty Sasquatch can actually be seen "without a doubt" to have "braided hair," and, much, much more!"

Bluff Creek California, 2003 – 2012!

MK Davis and I have long explored the mountain regions of what Bluff Creek, California drainage many times arriving to the very spot where relict hominid Patty Sasquatch was one and only time ever filmed! We first time reached the scene on October 20th, 2005.

Our infatuation began September 26, 2003, ever hopeful as we have been to discover more living evidence of Patty or her relatives?

"CAVE LIFE IS THE EQUIVALENT OF EXISTENCE!"

"Winter refuge in caves is all necessary to sustain life!" "Here mention, all high desert, and our fast dwindling Sage Brush Sea; Strange America horse plaiting; the necessity of protean in diet, opposed fingers and thumbs, and much, much, more!"

"Caving definitely is not for everyone!"

The discoveries made under ground having to do with feral hominids has much relative importance to all explanations ahead able as they are to help explain plaiting in the undeniable truth had from many cast artifacts that attest a definite and obvious use of human like opposed fingers and thumbs! as well as the fact that all wild man dire need continuing nourishing animal fat and protein type foods, especially this is so during all extreme cold weather seasons where ever they exist. More will be said on needed protein where are included further up-coming explanations ever needful of the reader to better understand the extremes of the difficult life of wild hominids when confined long term during harsh winter, not to mention the fast dwindling mountain desert regions of North America that once comprised all of the incredible vast Sage Brush Sea that is now only a mere 10 percent at best of what it once was in historic times. 90 percent of our deserts are now under cultivated agriculture. "Sage brush UN-sung in its natural state is excellent protein food to be had for at least 30 separate large and small warm blooded mammals, and some 200 separate bird species, small and larger game type fouls are found over the Inter-mountain western deserts directly or unilaterally depend upon it. It can also be used as a valuable starch food source for humans if know how during hard times, and yes of O'course it can, and is, consumed out of habit and necessity by wild hominids! Only one heaping handful of dry sage brush leaves eaten directly with or without foods weekly insures even the undernourished vagabond safe against scurvy! Mt. Ash berries, and Sliced raw potatoes soaked in apple cider vinegar do the same."

Log: November 4, 2012.

"A Credible Professional Opinion Attesting Chinese Wild Man!

Of Women, large and smaller big wild cats, mixed gender paranoia when in caves, extreme caution thrown to the winds of time, another recent Sasquatch sighting, I think I want out of here, and caving is not for everyone, etc!" "Next, We Need To Explain Just One More Part Story, To Explain All Mixed Gender Tiger Explorers When All Pitted Together In A Cave! Things Can Get Interesting!"

But First,

"An Unexpected Interruption!"

Ironic as it sounds, as I began to continue writing this sage bit of promised blather, "the phone rang with Van Stallman, Wise River, Montana, telling me that just today, November 4, 2012, over the Internet news, "Grind Blog (?)," came a story telling ("paraphrased O' course,") that a recent close encounter at fifty feet distance, evidencing an unknown wild hominid of some kind was just confronted by a considerable number of credible witness somewhere in, Provo Canyon, Utah, believed by all present to had been a valid Sasquatch, described dark black in color, hairy, and likely best described, "had been human like when standing up-right," calculated to all imagination to had been perhaps up to 8 or more foot tall! After realizing that the creature was not a bear... the witness group fled back to where they were camped, and next opt to vacated the area, but not before a man named, "Beard Card," had managed to take a single clear photo of the creature, "that Van Stallman adamantly attests... "Don, without a doubt, that one single the non-deceptive photo to me looks to be truly valid! As far as I remember, a Local Utah Channel 4, Television interviewer, by the name of, "Max Roth," opt to take, "Beard Cards, deposition!"

(Thanks Van! Perhaps an update in time?)

Cats in Caves!

"The following is written as if all were being seen through the ever revealing, stressed and nervous eyes of a watchful cat? Cats are the literal epitome of paranoia! What sees better, unless its an eagle?"

What sort of a cat?

"If You Are Still Reading, Well Then, You Are Also Hooked Beyond The Dangers Of Paranoia! That's Long Been My Problem Too!"

"Misery Loves Company, And Most Cats Love People!"

However, some many cats, tame and wild, under the right conditions will opt to eat you!"

"Its darn true gang, caving and strange location exploring is not for everyone. Glen Grant while manning his Haunt Book Store once warned and assured me... "Don he said, in these mosquito infested Oahu woods, things, and pigs, and strange dogs, and weird cats, and many projected things actually can go bump in the night! Compared to all of that, your main-land wild man is more of a kitten!" For those reading, perhaps some many will remember Professor Glen Grant, his wild radio show, and his famous Honolulu Halloween Haunt Walks... I first met Glen, after the fact, during, and weeks continuing beyond one of his fearless fantasies! He was truly a man apart! Glen passed the same season of year 2003 as had Marion. She like him, but hadn't at all liked being in his store! That wild tale is all another hair rising story for a one day intended book titled: "Poky Why?"

Tonia's Chapter Eleven!

"Was She A Green Eyed Cat or What?"

I Never Did Know?

"Next, everyone is invited to spend a day deep in a mountain cave!

This is a collective true experience combined from mega the authors log notes! "Never look for adventure... Life itself is the ultimate adventure, and few persons are completely prepared for the experience. For example, never try to convince anyone to just put off what they are doing and opt go blindly explore a dark unknown cave.. That sort of an attitude can easily get you killed!"

"Don, Is This Cave Even Pseudo Safe Or How?"

Well Maybe!
Some Never say Never,
and Sometimes Some Many should have!"

Upon entry, always look for big cat tracks, they know every safe way in and out, how far to go, and where, and when to stop! Where there are lions devastating radon cave gas is not in question! But then all remember, cats are feline, and feline has its by-line of high paranoiac limitations! Be Safe, listen to all gut feelings! Even soft footed lions can be misleading! What constitutes unstable surroundings may differ. Too Late to back out without going completely over someone's head and shoulders!

< Sometimes There Is A Great Beauty In Hesitation! >

"Tigers, every one, there absolutely is no other way out of this cave! Yeah really, there is no other way out of here! This stuff does happen... and you are all mine, and I am all yours, and there is no way out except to start digging! Turn off all flashlights except mine! Lets do it now, and stay breath shallow!"

"Crawl Slow And Be Safe! And Occasionally, Do Look Back,
As Doors Can And Do Close Behind You!"

Life Is Also Much Like That!

Story

My curiosity on that day was much like many others, when similarly miserable, thinking themselves destined to be death trapped beyond irritated regardless of all acute emotions aroused and semi fearful each time prior and future ahead if/when can continue to be slowly belly crawling face down caught fast and breathing in questionable filthy fine powdered cave dust or much worse, while ever somewhat fearful to admit all concern while mega ever aware as we all are, "that at any moment without warning, all persons ahead and behind could suddenly be hopelessly trapped, crushed, suffocated, and/or be left completely helpless subterranean; and who knows what the hell else just might happen next of no further concern really... And about that time Tonia, or someone else or others at a time would ask.. "Who's anywhere? Who even remotely knows where the heck we are at? Who would be able to rescue us in this caves if...?

Next thing, Paul Wright's voice breaks the silence in a sorted subtle sullen voice exclaiming/alarming everyone... "What in the name of hell, prey till, is that "Strange Cat Looking Thing that I think I can see looking straight back to us in the beam of this light? Hell Don, what is in this cave with us?

With that stammered said, all were stalemated, numb-brained, with all eyes staring useless ahead in the pitch dark that was behind and ahead of each-ones dragging back packs not having another single clue able anyone able to understand what if anything horrible Paul may have been describing (?), "as for the moment everyone feels ever more concerned in tight confines where all wait impatient toe to toe behind and ahead another like a long human slow snaking pack train definitely bound for nowhere with on-going horrendous thoughts of actually being lost forever in a stupid desert lava tube!"

Paul again: "Don, are we all crazy or what! That big cat could easily have chewed off an ear! Looks to me like its a damn dumb big one too? Are we sure we can't shot off a gun in here?" Nodda I answered! Nodda! Never! Not even in Scandinavia, Mexico, or Alaska... "What the heck has all of that got to do with anything Paul said!" All high stress of that last said, big cat, had some many of us undecided and the entire "human snake chain" wantin' of a nervous laugh, or a shouted shudder... Mentioning Scandinavia and Mexico, for a moment gets the mind off the problem... People naturally are curious... "Well, Paul said, if we can't use these damn pistols, then why are we carrying them? And what in the heck is in these heavy packs anyway...? I can hardly tote mine much further?"

Rocks Paul, silver and gold painted rocks! Lots of rocks! And did you notice the small five fingered hand impression lift in the soft cave dust ahead of you? Its fresh too, and it sure as heck is not one of us! "What kind of a cat Paul, someone ask?" No one ever knew, as for the reason that what it was that had been staring back from the dark had opt to vacate the moment! "Paul Explained! Well, it's just gone! But it had big eyes though..! Starting to laugh as he spoke saying..., "it looked a little bit like a green eyed girl that I use-to know named Ronda, that wanted me to call her bright eyes! Truth is, I never called her anything at all, or planned to call her at any time! Maybe that was her? Her eyes were always big like that in the dark! She said that she could always see right through my intentions!"

All were relieved at Paul's humor, and especially me, knowing the actual color of the eyes, as in the worst scenario green eyes in cave dark are usually no more than just a young confused mountain lion cub, or it's departing mother, as we later found two fresh sets of departing pugs, one large, and another smaller that weren't at the cave entrance when came in! If had eyes yellow or described red, we would be in big trouble! My biggest concern of the was encountering hibernating snakes and there none were here? Unwanted snakes shake most everyone's reason except Ron Roseman that at the moment wasn't with us! Probably that was a good thing! While being ever cautious of dangers and on the alert for any recent sign of even one small hand spray painted gold sliver red and black rocks, we next came onto one of the most incredible discoveries that I or anyone could ever make; I was leading the crawling, and when had reached a most difficult tight place overhead location of the lava-tube channel where it was impossible to hardly even be able to raise ones head up at all without twisting ones neck, "right there before my very nose at perhaps 6 inches distance ahead of my walking hands was one single very tiny baby wild man hand print" measuring perhaps 2 1/2 inches or so in length! The print was so fresh that there had not even been time for the cave mice to had walked into/over it, and so the print was completely barren of vermin tracks or a disturbance of any kind. We have the proof of this print on film. The attempt to take cast was impossible because of the difficult position and location. The attempt was fruitless. I could not do it without destroying the evidence. Creatures from birth teach their children to walk, crawl, travel at all times when possible on solid turf in order to avoid detection. This crawling child had, had no choice at the spot, as exactly where it had needed to place its hand, all area was only but fine powered cave dust. What a break! As Lewis Chandler and I entered a close by cave chamber at the distance of two yards, we at once came onto what we still believe were to had been the large foot tracks of two separate left feet! We cast both these left feet! Both left feet are much similar and yet far different from the other in over all descriptions. Read all Trilogy for continuation. Wait for. "Everyone got water? Stress always makes you thirsty! Later that same late night after our exiting the cave, some many persons were contemplating visiting Burger King, Captain Morgan, and/or Jim Beam, and French fried potatoes, ahead of another beer or soda? All by then firmly agree that caving isn't for everyone!

"Your Mom, Tonia, Was Ever A Tigress!"

A short tribute: For Josh , Angelo, and Amy Stanzeonie.

"Your mom Tonia forever told you.. I will forever be with you!"

"Once out of the cave, and none any longer desperate for solace as when temporary stalemated claustrophobic and perhaps gone half mad when thinking that likely one is truly trapped forever destined to die in pitch-dark, questionable, dank, dirty, and breathless surroundings, your mother like all others was quickly able to overcome her anxieties. Best said, the high stress had of desperation during anyone's mix-matched passion's that unquestionably have been strangely exhilarated, or thwarted, abrupt continuing excessive admissions, as are all strange, sorted, hollow looking shadowy wall surroundings, experienced via only the ever questionable queer dying illumination dealt every where ahead of a tight fist grasping onto a dull flashlight, not to mention an acute awareness of all very real, stark, and undetermined strange vocalizations, that keep coming back to your ear from somewhere just ahead; not to mention all mixed wild variations of aroused curiosity, passions, and perhaps continuing wild thoughts of how in the hell if need-be would I or anyone opt to compromise all possible pending wild animal dangers, as are snakes, cave rats, and/or, what ever similar slimy-creepy crawly awful thing comes next after the last Bob Cat that just jumped/flew over one's shoulder (?), and especially what the heck would I do if all at once I come-up Face to Face with an unexpected anything looking human that really wasn't? If indeed that would happen, my heart would surely stop!"

"Brave Isn't The Word For Your Mom!"

At a time like this your mother was likely pondering:

"What next Don, what for hell sakes, could be more uncomfortable, dangerous, hair rising, and be an equally miserable experience had for the Simple Stupid Sake of wanted discovered some miserable living hairy, or hairless hominid! What indeed more horrible will I need to be experiencing next even more awful before I cash in my chips?"

"Yeah, she was truly a Tigress!"

... as well as realized all of this to probably be her last year, and that she was adventuring on borrowed time.... Tonia coveted that what ever the cost, to mount a last wild adventure with a purpose for gusto and of a last hurrahs! Your mother truly exemplified a brave, extraordinary, and a courageous women... She braved her last sojourns unconditionally, and uncomplaining, while ever enduring excruciating pain! She was as improbable as she was wonderful. It could be said that her persona emulated a magical example of true-grit, and all independent women hood! So be it babe, you are never forgotten, and will be forever cherished by all of the honorable enduring warriors, and each of brave maidens of Valhalla! We sailed on familiar ships! You always kept your sword in hand to protect your cherished Biblical wisdom, and did it with your back up brave against the stone against all comers! Tiger, none was ever quite the same as you, or ever did it all better! You were always secretive and tenacious of your intuitions, and had an acute determination to write for me, and others interested, in a separate account of our wild times had into all Vast Exunda; and there was more written that you wanted said to your children before your sad passing from dread cancer.... Much compassion, lust for life, extreme love, and unconditional devotion to all was expressed in that short compassionate little green book message, all intended as it was, that in future I somehow find a way to share its impartial instruction with your family, friends, and especially your children. Perhaps this record will do that, as your last heart felt prayers and humor were left behind in that heart-felt treasured little note book journal that you had refereed as, Your Secret Little Green Book.. Lets go there!"

"Tonia's Green Book Writes of Plaited Horses, Cave Wisdom, Gender Humor, etc!"

Tonia loved animals. We continued investigating plaited horses on our to and from Florida between time spent searching for petroglyphs, etc. Some of her journal logic and importance to the mechanics and humor of exploration are shared ahead, as without a doubt by that time she had learned much of the wild-side and misery of extended exploration equivalent of all experienced crew!

"The Valley Of Pitts!"

"Of it, she wrote in her journal...

"Don, it is true, your caves as you call them, amount to what you said was a bottomless pit! They really are to fact a hidden miserable neither world of unfathomed experience leading into no where! To explore them is an exhilarating and exciting adventure with enough awaking danger abrupt the unknown as ever could be found anywhere in any Far-Side reach of a mountain range. Definitely this sort of exploration is not for everyone! In spite of all obvious pit-falls I can't wait to do it all again! Lets go do it all!"

Why explore caves?

I continue to explore particular caves because there is where is found the best on-going evidence to validate hominid existence! Throughout history caves or similar have ever resulted in the most productive humongous discoveries of ancient man and animals. Survival requires food, shelter, and seclusion, and mountain caves during winter meet most of that requirement. When underground, Tonia's native spirit sparked her uncanny intuitive ability to recognized an innate incommonness with the ancients and all probable current cave habitation. She was ever invincible in all her separate observations. She was ever akin to the collective Trilogy Adventure, much exactly the same in influential inspiration, humor, and encouragement as had been Donald Massey. Each of them had exemplified the collective high spirit and camaraderie that could be expressed similarly of every single one of my passé exploring mates down to the last most difficult person! The collective Trilogy Adventure continues to include each of them even as I write, as in order to rate eccentric you need be somewhat difficult if not completely impossible Holly Mulvaney, and each sole mate among them could be said to be at least an unlikely prodigy; everyone of them well able with imagination enough to be able to think completely out of the box! Strangers to any community of all programmed thinking are never easily accepted or popular to couch potato logic that is actually nothing!

"A Toast"

"We should drink to the Ones that hear the call, be them academic, maverick, or small... There are still a few places in the canyon wall, where a wild man or women can crawl, they haven't yet found them all!" No one has really been anywhere and done anything quite enough! "Odd to all past adventure, future experience, and the now of the all continuing uncanny happenings of the moment, as while thinking how best to be able to more credit all crew, memorable indulgence, discoveries, etc., all persons passé more than continue invincible to all project success. As it is suddenly uncanny even as I write; just as if it were, that somehow all mixed gender trail mates evidenced explained as was Tonia, and Donald Massey, are still much able to inspire their separate importance to the manuscript! It is just as if at this very moment that each of them were a combined friendly shadowy dictatative spirit prompting their undivided support while looking down from over my shoulder!

The body, spirit, and soul, can separately be injured, crippled, and broken, but there are some things unwritten within all bonding hearts that are timeless, and cannot be measured or destroyed.

All of these unforgettable people that have inspired the Trilogy effort, as was Don Sassy Massey, and Tonia Brown, who also wanted be called by her nick-name as, "Tonia Wild Two Feathers, Onya," and all of the many, many, admittedly comical, courageous, and intelligent others that had much bonded with all efforts over the years, opting as they had done, satisfied to further explore "free license (Voluntary UN-funded, etc!)," all fascinating, unknown Exunda! To the last and final person, in spite of our many differences of expression etc., we were ever on a separate but a much relative plane! It was always a wild and incredible adventure! Sincerely I thank you; many I will never see again. We accomplished a lot, if not at times the thought impossible, but still, not one damn One of Us need to the covert person need ever to say that we have been there and done that! Long ago I had run out of compassion for such statements as that insistence above, had the majority of it said by the feeble minded, the jealous, the incapable, the unlearned tenderfoot, the unimaginative, the dull witted, and ignorant critic wannabe, and at times the pseudo bias educated accredited! None of all crew were ever that! All of them were ever able to adhere to the wild call through intuition into a reasonable interruption of ancient man, his society, his pitiful and horrendous existence, etc. Never again the twin shall meet, and that is the our great reward of progress? Actually all of you, through out your combined ongoing support; desire to voluntary explore and experience all trials and tribulations required of the caving sojourn, not one of you at any time had one-small-bit choice in the matter, as it is true that every wild thing eventually recognizes all kindred spirits, and eventually all sail on a similar ship! Aces, Jokers, Kings and Queens, Cowboys, Pirates, Ship Mates, Sweet Hearts, and all More Unwanted Unforgettable, truly all of them are the unlikely hero/hero-wen Wild Cards and Sportive Tigers of Every Important Game! So be it!"

"A Short Zak Cave History!"

@

I am writing from the year 2012...

"I am seated on a boulder at the rock strewn cave entrance of Zakynerous Cave! There are still any number of summer range horses within eye sight awaiting the fall round-up. Beyond me yonder blows a windy sky. I wonder when the creatures will be wanting to returning back into the cave for their winter season? I ponder the by-gone days and all adventures had with, Tania, John Doitch, Paul Wright, Tammy Brown, Var Harris, Bear Iddins, "Red", Lewis Chandler, and Ron Roseman, to name just a few. It is highly improbable that we will ever again repeat that sojourn. As this particular slice of once Open Range land where includes this cave; this particular land section, now has a new owner... And Zak Cave by now has probably been well realized for its next to covert grandeur, and as a result it has been fenced off to the public with an insistence signs posted reading... "No Trespassing, Beware Of Dogs! "The pity... It was inedible, the new owners have not one single clue of the hominids, or of the caves ancient traditions. The signs, the dogs, the dreams of mice and men... no amount of unwanted cave intrusion will keep the creatures out! All future discovery here is over? (?) "I would not be surprised if at least one or more of the cave family can not somewhat by deductive reasoning be able to understand the full intentions of the postings? As I am quite sure that may have experienced them any number of times quite similar before and are rejoicing in their way of their good fortune to privacy?"

"Nothing is Over Till it's Over!"

I am still seated at the entrance into the cave.

What follows is only a small part of the many strange happenings that had occurred here years, 2001 – 2006, which includes numerous caves spread out south/east of here over a 90 mile radius inclusive of Two Feathers and I exploring Zak fall, 2009, spring, 2010.

It was while we were continuing to be exploring these caves back in 2005 – 2007, that my suspicions were first aroused in some uncertain way that the cave population might be in some way interacting physically with the range horses and cattle? As every year any number of ranch stock for plausible reasons are expected to come up missing during each and every round-up! For example, on October 20, 2012, I was told by Mrs. Stanchfield, life long accredited rancher of Wise River, Montana, "that already this season she said, for some odd reason this year after our round-up tally, we counted at least, 20 pair of cattle missing …. !" Now that's, 40 head, when assuming that "Pairs missing" in this case indicates, "sets of two cows," being an adult cow and her calf! Now Mrs. Stanchfield had volunteered all of this without being in any way aware of my suspicions and/or theory, so upon hearing this, my suspicions became even more founded? I ask her next if she thought perhaps the area deer and elk hunters with their rifle blasts had opt to scatter the heard far and wide in all timber? "No, Don, that was not likely, as the hunting season has only opened up in this part of Montana as of today! We counted all of our cattle long before that!" I failed to remember the remaining head count of her cattle, but it was considerable. Wow, with that said, and all reference to pairs missing. and no particular mention of steers, I am suddenly all at once even more excited to in future be further investigating more of my on-going theories and suspicions? O' course we have many coyotes, wolves, bears, etc., in this region of Montana/Idaho, and so with a mega new number of wolves running brought into the area recently by the government, that ever explains a possible and reasonable part of the mystery (?), however in another book/story within the Trilogy Collection, we will more to be said in regard of missing cattle, etc., including one fairly recent very strange cattle mutilization found fall 2011, on the muddy north bank of the Carbon River, when exploring with, Becky Butello, of Auburn, WA!" Initially, as said, Zak Cave was a happen stance, per-chance discovery, some months later called that respectful of the namesake of an unknown ancient mariner, "Zakyneros," documented by his name carved in basalt lava stone on the surface of the New Mexico Mystery Stone, ever proving that he had explore inland probably up from the Gulf of Mexico, to as far as where today is New Mexico prior to year 500 B. C. "The mystique of that courageous adventurer in my opinion, deserved further recognition, thus, we named Zak Cave! The account of Zakyneros can be further read in the first chapter of the book, "The Best of The West," by Tony Hillerman.v

"Wow!"

"More blood and guts, more strewn feathers, and Zak Cavern!"

Discovered on my first minute of discovery, that had occurred via dead reckoning, when trying to track-down a large unknown biped, my efforts finally took me directly to the surprise entry of Zak Cave! Only an hour earlier, having just stumbled onto a first bloody pile evidencing a fresh bird kill, when I had next stumbled onto the entrance to Zak Cavern, there was another!" "Yeah, right there laying in front of my snooping nose, was a second pile of wet fresh blood, more strewn feathers, and bird internals!"

("Total count in time tallied is, 13!") Because of the uncanny circumstances surrounding the cave discovery, "all first impressions of the cavern and a possible large creature present to contend with was suddenly of a slight concern!" Especially this was so, after having for a second time on the same day, and only one hour apart, having just found what were the bloody bone, guts, and feather remains of the first one and number two of what later became 13 separate in count, recently plucked, and on the spot devoured game birds! Each evidence pile of remains every time has been exactly done in same way, as all was first found out side of each cave, dropped precariously outside of the entrance, or just slightly inside! All of this bloody mess found on that very first day of discovery, both done only one short mile distance apart, "and because of these fresh kills, and all track-way evidence telling of an unknown heavy large creature, as said, I was admittedly somewhat reluctant to proceed into the dim lit abyss, as I only had with me a very small dim-lit dying battery type pen light, held outstretched as it was in a hand far ahead of my courage, and somewhat just along side, and ahead of my revolver!"

Today's contemporary Wild-West Montana/Idaho still has its bad-lands, bad boys, and human hazards abrupt wild animals, and its ever ongoing 21st Century unsolved mysteries and problems, "and there ever is no telling what exactly or if anything anyone is in for to face next? I had long learned not to toss all caution to the wind! Any number of times over the years I have been Damn well Glad that I carried a fire arm! Not the space here for examples, but believe me, the Second Amendment of Our Constitution, "God Willing," will never be breached! ("?") Mountain lions can often frequent these caves, and knowing that, each time I thought that it was also strange, that something or other hungry, had not bothered to eat the bloody remains? In two hours time I knew that it would be dark.... To be able to return back to my rig would require most all of that time. I stopped to think clearly before climbing down blindly into that cave! The devoured birds had both been left in an almost mastered, if not a preferred piled bloody mess? A definite intellect had done this! As said, both times then, and every time again found in a future would all be the same! Finally I climbed cautiously, all distance of perhaps most of sixty feet dim-beam light in hand down into the caves bottom as my thoughts kept going back again, and again to those bloody bird kills, all of the while feeling much aware that something, or someone, needing two legs, opposed fingers and thumbs; and in that way I very well realized, that what ever it was down there with me had to very much human like have managed to feather pluck those birds, and what really bothered me was to further realize that it had eaten them raw!" Wow, who, or what, was that hungry to opt to eat raw birds? And especially, who would chance to devourer feral wild pigeons? And how had they been caught without shooting them with something, as upon first discovery wild pigeons are almost as paranoid and would fly as compares an alley cat! At both locations of the birds found, all plucked feather remains were wide circular scattered, and at once it was ever also obvious to even an untrained eye; at each location was to be found, a primitive rock-seat of sorts, as would best serve a flat boulder, as easily becomes a perfect primitive chair! ("13 separate times, as said, I have found all of the exact same evidence!") Both two first birds found had been very carefully plucked, having all feathers removed, and after perniciously strewn around the circumference of the rock-seat in every direction. It becomes important to note, that each and every time found, there was also left a precarious pile of red blood dripped on top of them; the carefully eaten undamaged, skeletal remains of the bird, left just a foot, or so, ahead of the front most place of what would have been the rock-seat, looking down from there to where the blood while eating would have been dropped from the birds, And Ones Mouth; the blood would have drained straight down onto the top of the piled remains! "Yeah, wow, Someone, or Something, very Human Reassembling, had sat down right there each time and enjoyed another game bird meal!" "This next becomes more than extremely curious and important!" Each and every time, on everyone of the 13 birds, a left wing was always left attached to the bone skeleton remains! Every one of them thus far, has ever evidenced an intentionally left in place, "fully feathered and UN-plucked left wing, that from experience and necessity, looks to me just as if all of them were fully intended to have served each time, as a clever primitive "hand-hold of sorts," that to all common-sense, and reasonable logic, would make eating any blood-slippery all that much, much, easier to control if one feathered wing could be hand-held when eating of anything blood slippery! Especially this would be the case, with any freshly plucked wild fowl as small if not dainty is a delicate wild pigeon! I have one of these skeletal artifacts saved, and kept completely intact under glass in my artifact collection. As said, I have found more than a dozen (Possibly 20!) of these same descriptive bird kills, and without exception every time there had been left attached one fully feathered "Left-Wing," wanton in opinion to had served as a do-able hand-hold whenever eating!" You Decide? All crew of 2003 – 2006, more than a dozen creditable persons, all of them had fully agreed, when considering all obvious evidence had of all probable, "left-handedness being indisputable," in time as is right now being explained, I would also one day future ("Now!"), become completely aware of its similar indications being of a much similar importance, when wanting to be further explain any and all predominant left handed plaiting, now being evidenced to date, now December 21st, 2012; it is a true fact that there is an all much similarity, as astonishing as it sounds, "had from all collective photographic, and collected cut physical evidence in plaits, when very close examined in various opinion, and all of what more ahead will be explained that has now been found mixed in with some of the Filly horse plaits, it looks like the braids much just the same as were the birds, in every case scenario on each of the pigeons was ever found left one single left side feathered wing, and just exactly the same has been found predominate of left-handed being accomplished with the plaits! Every single one of them numbering over fifty, when closely examined evidences they had been done left handed! However in some few of the plaits they have been twisted/twilled (Twirled!) in both directions, right and left before being braided, indicating perhaps that someone, or something, is ambidextrous? That in itself is not all that hard to believe either! The proof of all of this is in the collected artifacts, and we have the artifacts! Educated university studies having to do with left handedness, reveal a much interesting media-physical ramification that suggests that in some cases this might indicate a higher scale of adaptability and intellect than usual! If so, what's discovering who?"

The Cave!

Needless to say, when first time I skittered carefully down into Zak Cavern, I was complete overwhelmed by what I would find next! Being somewhat concerned and apprehensive as I continued, I called out in aloud in a strong voice to be announcing meaningfully "that I was damn well coming in, was armed, meant no harm, and wanted no problem!" I did that regardless if, or not, anything or any one could hear, or understand any part of it, as it mattered not, as at that point there was no further decision; I had not then at the moment had one small bit choice in the matter, as my curiosity was beyond aroused, and everything from there became do or die!" My egotistic and slightly eccentric nature, has every so often resulted in foolish, if not too daring a decision, and believe me I have often need pay the price for disregard of personal safety! I have often done thing solo that I would never expect of others... Who I was thinking would ever believe any of this? My futuristic intentions that instant were already planning to be back in a future with a full regatta of lanterns, miscellaneous paraphernalia, casting material, etc., if/when that would be, if when I was able to find a reliable and secretive partner? The last explained was the most difficult anomaly of all future intentions, "as people like to talk," and I could see at one the full wild potential of the dark grotto, and Zak Cave was mine to explore without conditions or restrictions? As said, I would need be very careful whom I would include to share its secrets!"

I was perplexed of the difficult timing of the discovery ....

as Marion and I were scheduled to be flying out to see doctors at Honolulu in just four days, and it was already five degrees below zero on the first frozen day of December, and without care full preparation and a trusty partner to rely on there was to little time to schedule but a hurried expedition... All future discovery would need wait till spring, as we would not be returning back to Idaho for another eight weeks; that would put me still excited late January 2002!

In retrospect 2001, I left the cave exhilarated, confused, and more than concerned, and still much curious of what actually had been in the cave with me and staring from the dark? I would not find out until the following April 20th, at the complete near heart attack dismay of, "Donald Massey The Brave!" His near horrific and/or fatal experience had resulted in my final decision to attempt to write all further books of the Sasquatch Trilogy including this if for nothing else than their message, in belief that one day perhaps someone serious will have appreciated them? Trust me, I'd rather be on a beach somewhere if could with a flock of wild game birds!"

Don's story is a classic example of what all less than imaginable critics will opt to think next that was impossible and not want to believe! Not a concern, as moot airheads in time decay and dwindle away like an old man's failing bank roll ... Thank God, and Johnny Foxx, that we still have freight trains running every four hours to warmer regions out of Lima-Siberia, Montana during winter!"

"Left Handedness, and the opinion of, Becky Butello!"

More to know of left handedness, that may have much to do with plaiting? Certainly some many will say something like that has no credence or real importance to anything?"

Once inside the cave, I was at once overwhelmed by all first antiquated animal bone and current foot and hand cast evidence still to be found to attest probable recent wild hominid occupation, and am still in awe of what we were able documented in video films, photographs, credible witness, etc., that further attests relict humans of some unknown kind are living in parallel right along side in rural Idaho/Montana America! The total equation of all of this discovery has much change my life and times as I will continue to explain over the pages ahead. I still have the bone skeletal remains one or more of the devoured birds found in my cast and artifact collection, and again remind you that every one of them evidenced a left behind feathered left wing! Why I write so much of this uncanny left handed anomaly, is for the benefit of the reader, so he can fully understand all of what is needed to know that will further help explain all intricate, strange, and dexterous, thought ever purposeful plaiting comparisons ahead, when we closely examine all cut-off extracted plaiting in question, and read the verbatim and candid deposition of professional show horse, parade qualified horse mane and tail plait-er, Becky Butello, opting to validate all 50 suspect or more, cut-samples; "and I for one was not astounded, when her opinion without Auto Suggestion Attests that, "each and every one of them, predominately evidences all been done obvious of left handed twisting, twilling, braiding, etc!" "Wow, thanks Becky!" And she went on to say, "Don, there is much, much, more that you can probably write in future that I have not taken the time yet to completely consider?" Thanks Becky!"

Government Controls!

All the sister caves to Zak, are much difficult to locate within all high elevation mountain terran comprising The Continental Divide of Idaho/Montana, that plummets up at places to more than 8,000 feet. It is the pity that free spirit cave exploration in the Idaho region is wanted over beginning year 2013, and likely will come next much pseudo National Forest Land within Idaho, and endless other places of western America as said will likely soon wanted be over? Not the place here for politics, but what further unethical government controls are pending, to include beginning serious gun legislation efforts that are being media announced negative even as I write, December 21, 2012, that further opt to completely abort our freedoms does not look pretty!"

@

Message:

"No Questions! Just Don't Trespass! Ka-Pu, Br-udder!"
No Fish! No Net! No Poky! No Beach Mat! No Crab!
No Hunt! No Sleep! No Pork on Pal i!
No Kidding, No Reason!"

"What, really, Was Intended To Denote Public Access?"

("This Land was your land! ... Or, This Land is my land?)

"Wanted! An unquestioning, uninformed, Dumb-ed Down, public!"

What ever happened to Burt Lancaster, and, John Wayne?

"WAS BIG BIRD ONE OF OUR SUNG HEROES OF YEAR 2012?"

That said, thank you all for your educated patience while reading through this book. "As it may not be long until government controls may omit anyone via confiscation from reading all books similar of this and all others now slated that will finally comprise, The Sasquatch Trilogy, as for the covert reasons of the government is not wanting public domain to remain public! It is obvious that this is not wanted explained public, or at all over the media, or other wise, as not yet even once has been given one single logical reason of good reasons, WHY! All public land truth known, is suddenly wanted eradicated, entry prohibited, over the U.S.A., beyond all continuing and prior efforts to continue to honor our Constitutional Rights!"

You Tell Me?

Particular federal, and state agencies do not want the public to be at all aware of the reality of feral wild man probability! For the reader to be first time aware of that opinion of fact, "if that is the case?" All book, etc., ahead, and continuing from here should now read much better when considering all more that has now been understood to more explain the fact and belief of existing feral hominids, named by what ever wild name is insisted of the public? Definitely Sasquatch of several obscure identities do roam freely over many a world far-place, and many more exist than I have stumbled upon yet to be explained that continue to be wandering under the light of the Chinese Rabbit Moon!"

@

Introduction to: "Mistletoe Cave, and

the, "High Strange Twilight Zone Chapters,"

Of The Sasquatch Trilogy!"

{"This stuff just doesn't happen Don, but it did!"}

"It is paramount that we include with this a short introduction to another extremely important difficult to be written manuscript that will be akin to plaiting, wild man, and the Cavern of Zakyneros, that is the uncanny discovery of, "Mistletoe Cave, year, 2004, by my daughter, Hollace Mulvaney!"

Log: Holly...

"Dad, she said, the Cave is Awesome ... Come quickly, before I forget where I found it! Get the light, your rope, and our candle, and our pistol, and I will show you where it is! You will need to duck your head! The way it looks to me, I feel that there might even be some sort of creatures in there!"

The Twilight Zone of course, indicates a far-side trip, into about everything, and every where beyond anyone's wildest imagination! In short, it also explains much, much, more of the high strange, uncompromisable, and on-going completely unexplainable, happenings similar of what were first encountered in Mistletoe, and are also likely much similar still, 2012, in cave places as Zak, and likely continues even now as I write as bazaar however un-similar in adjacent arias of Montana, some fifty miles or more distant? The Twilight Zone extensions in Montana are highly uncanny, and to some thinking would be thought literally impossible? Much of what was first wanted explained in Zakyneros, needed be over looked, as it read far beyond early belief to further understand or validate wild man intelligence, "unless that is that anyone had first read and

111

fully understood the book titled: "The Twilight Zone Chapters," that explains all further high strangeness that went on much at the very same time as all continued being experienced in Zak, Mistletoe, and other caves in close proximity years, 2003 – 2010! Most of everything to be explained in The Twilight Zone has even one remote answer to validate most anything! "All continues to this day to remain as much a mystery as it all was when first discovered! Perhaps this can be best explained to emulate a much similar anomaly comparison to what was finally found to be the true riddle able to explain, and comprehend the occurrence, The Northern Lights? Often it is Sooo true, that if a thing is not the obvious, then it must be the contrary!"

"All Is Almost As If Everything Uncanny Were Metaphysical?"

Well, believe me, to all interest of the unexplained, The Twilight Zone truly writes the everything completely contrary! All of the book's wild considerations, conjecture, and logical projections are extremely extraordinary, and some of them in future will likely prove important to more explain, or even possibly confuse, true hominid mental intellect ratings, reasoning capacity, common sense rational, and their extraordinary and much unlikely ability! Things took place in those caves that are far beyond even an irrational comprehension to think to explain them!

"If indeed critics, fairy pixies, ugly goblins and spooks, ancient haunting ghosts, unexplained cold and hot geological change takes place, strange flowers and artifacts re-occur, and any number of, etc's., made any sense; any or all of this be at all possible, then in the places to be described in book, "The Twilight Zone Chapters," would be one place! All reasoning done during, and written from this exciting sojourn of exploration, thought/believed in any way to be able to make future comparisons to further discoveries of intelligent wild man prototypes, are completely based upon the undetermined expounds and opinions of all much varied experience had from all many valid crew members and their experiences. Our kept collection of undeniable artifacts well continue to validate credible witness to actual hominid existence, etc. All attempts to more explained them to the public and piers has resulted in the authors current unpopular status had among some many pseudo Bigfoot investigating know-it-alls, that includes one in particular unimaginative highly influential associate academic that has long proclaimed himself to be the literal one and only, "Ge-rue Demi-God Prototype, Of A Wanton Narcissistic, God Father Image," to be highly revered of all many similar current day confused Bigfoot Think Tank Community, "many of them also much in agreement with his moot opinion, that Sasquatch in reality is no more to fact, than being a reminiscent hold over example, of the once supposed to had existed relict; the long believed to have been extent, humanoid looking, much humanistic appearing, supposed was the passé great ape, academically accepted as, gigantopithicus! If any of that were at all true ... if it were true that gigantopithicus was our boy of renown, then likely not one of the happenings explained in The Trilogy would at all be probable, as every strange occurrence in that manuscript collection, had ever required extreme mental ability of creature, a very high mental capacity well able of all uncanny interaction, that was ever completed between all crew, myself, and themselves, "and so, just exactly as all now stands, the very intellect comparisons now realized of all creatures; by that well founded anomaly alone, all, or most cave creatures, are obviously far, far, much superior of intellect, than would ever be a Supposed Stupid Giant Ape, posing as a Monkey's Uncle? Sorry Charley, Gigantopithecus does not rate Sasquatch, or be any candidate either, to explain a true wild Almasty, Yeti, Yeron, Yowie, or what ever else wanted.... As he is just too stupendous a creature to fit the pattern!"

Var Harris

"Var Harris, Idaho Falls Idaho."

The aging ex-sheriff was separate lucky great discovery
to my efforts in himself!

"Var spoke, making comment... Don, he said, have people today lost both their courage and imagination, or what? And if so, what are the reasons? Since exploring with you, skeptics have said to me ... Var, that sort of stuff that you are telling me that you are doing just doesn't happen! Come on man, you just know that all of that is complete blather, as it is just is not possible! Anyone, and even you if believing that sort of nonsense, needs to be locked in a straight-jacket, etc! Darn well Don, we both know from what we have experienced, that wild man of some sort does exist! After just what we have seen today there is absolutely no doubt about it! I'd really like in time, to have the opportunity to be able to hand one a carrot! Heck man, these guys are much like us!" Well Var, I said, maybe they are a bit like you, but not like me ... That sort of negative critic logic as explained above, "follows an acute lack of imagination, experience, common sense, rational justification, and becomes very curious of the proficiency had among all persons who proclaim intellect! Much just exactly like your critic piers, never once have we ever encountered one single one of them, or any wanna-be similar computer scientist exploring along side us involved in any sort of field research, and yet many have the audacity to think they have all of the answers? Best logic abrupt couch potatoes is to boil them in their own negative stew!" Yeah, Var answered ... "Never as yet, have I ever seen an angle-worm catch a robin, or a mouse catch a cat!" Next Var Goes Head Over Heals Against A Rock Wall To Uncover Undeniable Evidence Of Existing Sasquatch in Lion Cave, Idaho!"

Log: Var Harris

Var Harris, with me today for a second time 2005, discovered a sizable clump of unknown head hair from off the over head ceiling of a cave roof that later evidenced unknown biped, The hair left there where something else had also bumped its head on the very same rock out crop where Var then stood in his boots right at seven foot tall that is even higher than the overhead ceiling. The hair was promptly sent to Henner Farenbach at the Oregon State Primate Research Center vIa Ray Crowe then president of the Western Bigfoot Society at Hillsboro, OR., Farenbach was very excited, when he finally answered back via e-mail to Ray he said, "Well, it looks like a winner for Sasquatch! Of course human hair cannot be ruled out because for the reasons of ???... yada-yada-yada, etc? All of that was said in good stead, while at the same time explaining all the good reasons in the E-mail why it probably actually was a indeed a Sasquatch, etc! Henner asked first to Ray with intentions for me; he asked back to me the question...? "Where ever in the world did Monroe get this evidence? We definitely do need more of the same if it can be had?" I did not receive word back from Ray for many months explaining the answer... I had no idea! If had known of the early importance of the message... Well, perhaps, and perhaps not, we could have accelerated our efforts and may have actually hottrailed the creature, in further pursuit, as the bounds of the fall hunting ground then had been defined...Had we known in time who knows? "Second and third hand communication for me has always resulted in a complete unconcerned disaster!" The reason that Henner had been so adamant in his personal assessment, enough to have included the word description, "Also Hu-

man;" is in my opinion, "that whenever it will eventually be found what in truth Sasquatch are, they will be found to be a true hominid! ("Human!") Or, said another way, "a wild man," in the true sense of feral wild hominid, no different at all, or much similar as what was the humanoid looking creature that had been documented of the, Wisconsin Ice Man in, 1968, and allowed of Patty Sasquatch, discovered and filmed in, 1967, "and truth known in my belief, had Var and I known soon enough of Henner's urgent message sent to Ray, way back when the hair was first discovered, there may have been other hard evidence just waiting to be found and annualized?" The most unusual part of the Henner Farenbach's message analysis, was that most likely for the very first time ever, Henner had allowed used the word WINNER when he explained: "Well boys, it looks like a winner for Sasquatch!"(Note: all of this was some years ago.. To date 2013, I have much more reason to understand the many, many, covert attitudes held inside, and outside, of the "diligent" hominid investigative community; "opinions aside" from what is the wanton prototype Bigfoot message and identity? The public has a right to know the truth of feral hominids, perhaps they never will? However, they still are with us in several separate identities! "I may never live to realize all proof, but I have during my long sojourn discovered enough hard evidence to know and believe a thing of true importance. Henner, the word, "winner" was most convincing, however considered the discovery of, "The Hand Of Unknown Origin," had convinced important others, and the many, many, other discoveries that are now slated to be further divulged in the, "Sasquatch Trilogy Manuscripts" now await my time of priority. ")

"Winner meaning exactly what?"

Doesn't the word, winner, especially in this as yet undetermined case scenario, cause one wonder, "if not somewhere, hidden much covert, however well known to some many scientists or who-ever; it is my firm belief that somewhere there actually exists one, or more, un-divulged Sasquatch bodies ..., or at least one highly interesting, yet also to be further identified, relict hominid carcass; or perhaps it may be instead, "the long awaited further explained, extremely controversial, all strange disappearing, "still hard frozen, Wisconsin Ice Man," or better said by Doctor I. Sanderson in year 1968, when him still investigating on the identification site: he had said words to the effect, "that instead of this being and adult wild hominid, by my professional assessment, and opinion, the unexplained hominid frozen before me, instead of being a true adult, it instead from all appearances, looks to be just possibly a juvenile hominid child? After Sanderson's appraisal, the Ice Child body, all at once without one further clue disappeared to what looks forever into controlled Canadian Obscurity?" Before Henner's reply I had never once read or heard the words used to credit unknown hair as, "Looks Like A Winner for Sasquatch!" Most all hair evidence sent to him many times prior was ever demonized to had been simply said, unidentified carnivore hair, etc? With all of today's new possibilities in forensic... "I really do wonder... What for a real answer had ever be-come of all of the many, many, many, unknown human hair samples that were sent for appraisal to the Oregon Primate Lab? It would be very interesting to find out? The Twilight Zone Manuscript compromises current mystery with passé conjecture and confusions to the year 2013. Many an abnormal strange occurrence that took place in Mistletoe Cave and Zak, 2001 – 2006, and all sister cave extensions up to the time of the final page documentation and publication of that slated manuscripts. "Truly, if I had not experienced all of these strange anomalies myself, along side many an able witness to attest all validity, I would never have attempted to write any part of its story preview in the Trilogy, or hardly would I find much of any of it believable if written second hand by another! Mistletoe Cave as said, was first discovered by my daughter, Holly Mistletoe

Mulvaney, then residing, year 2003, at Seattle WA. Being a city girl, all of this was much foreign to her, but like many able women she is ever well able to adapt."

"Mistletoe Cave Idaho"

"Holly's discovering this fantastic cave was hardly to become her folly! However to this very day ten years later she has yet to realize the caves ongoing mystery and true importance. "Dad," she said, in her outspoken, fun loving teasing, ever striking effeminate way, "I am without a doubt a true example of an ignominious-ette extraordinaire ... Without me today, all that you would had accomplished would have been to be flitting around on this sage brush mountain eating that apple, and tossing that dried out dead-dying cheese sandwich out for bird-treats! This cave was crazy! Wow, is it ever spooky in there!

If I believed in ghosts, probably they are in there with all of those bones! What are they?"

Indeed rascal you are a wonderful paradox! Later in the story I had to take her to a local chiropractor to straighten out her back, neck, and impossible stubborn self; Hollace had received a dislocated neck, and slight back injury when her 110 lb. self, kept insisting to be trying to chop her way threw more than 18 inches of the hardest possible arctic type "blue ice" that covered over much of the cave floor, exposing beneath it what were hundreds or more of high suspect, still undetermined large, and much smaller bones, that proved to almost captive Ones imagination, "just as if it were, to be looking through thick dismal glass! ... Mistletoe Cave remains next to impossible to completely explain! "Read one or another of the slated Trilogy Books to discover all of one part of the more than incredible strange bones story, and how soon after first discovery were all mysteriously lost forever to obscurity! The UN-solved "exhilaration" that is word perfect to describe Mistletoe Cave, almost supersedes anyone's high expectations of what is truly startling, hi-strange and ever almost unbelievable! It is almost as if all of it was to had been a multiply witnessed all true and viable ghost story? "All anyone needs do to be further convinced, is to ask,

Var Harris, and Paul Wright!" It has now been ten years since Hollace first discovered Mistletoe Cave, and when last asked she was as perplexed and excited as when she had first stumbled on to it! The cave continues to this day each time there to be a different, however all relative, unexplained adventure. Scheduled ahead to re-value it, will likely include, MK Davis, and George Seboldt, and Darrel Miller. The Cave continues uncanny, strange, and ever is a mind devastating event as anyone could imagine! My grand daughter Candace Blackman, Spokane, WA., with me, Thanks Giving Day 2004, "after diner and a movie," experienced one short-long-miserable frozen day of its rapture! Tonia Brown made her determined visit to the cave with me, fall 2009, and her comments were extraordinary having to do with interesting pseudo suspect Native American indications. Twice during the fall of, 2011, with George Seboldt, of Lima Montana I have revisited the cave.... Up to the last times there with George; since two years prior, since there before with Tonia, the cave was intentionally left untouched, until a time future when it would again merit an evaluation; when George and I returned, and what was found next, still remains an awesome mystery ever to think to be able to completely describe it let alone explain it? George remains as mind boggled! It was Tonia who said without prompting or prior notice of the caves high strange... "Don, what ever has been done here and done all of this...

Well, I just know, I can just feel, that something undecided is right now watching us from somewhere, and we should just leave, and let the best of the worst alone!"

**("All future story of Mistletoe Cave, slated for,
The Twilight Zone Chapters!")**

Figure 22. Donald Monroe and George Seboldt in Mistletoe cave.

Log: George Seboldt

"George is reliable in particular intestinal fortitude; methodical in bob-cat logic; honest/sober; and is as intuitive and sensitive as he is curious and tough, hardly he exaggerates past an appreciated jest, and neither is he gullible either! He is as colorful as he is a creditable rascal of a quiet character, and ever of intent of a good-will toward proper humanity! He is ever aware in today's world of mixed confusions, as was ever any passé urgent yesteryear proud Montana, or Hawaiian Paniolo Cowboy!

His separate imagination still cannot even slightly fathom the depths of all plausibility for viable answers that would explain any real part of what he had experienced on his first day, and second trip back into Mistletoe Cave. George is a separate gold mine in local lore of passé Montana Western history! However with Mistletoe, it looks he has met his match in the gray matter and the multiple confusions of the unknown. I look forward to George and his comments when we explore one in particular facet of Indian mythology portrayed, strangely carved in stone, in an Idaho canyon. "George looks back hooked as any fish?"

116

Log: George speaks little, but here he says much!

"Holly Mistletoe Cave Definitely Exists In The Twilight Zone! Fresh Wild Flowers Found Left In A Sealed Cave?

Come on Don, what other B.S. Are you promoting next? (It just was not possible, but next thing we knew, we were there taking pictures!) What the hell Don, what in the world are fresh wild flowers doing in a place like this? There is no other way in here, or either out! Who ever left them there, had to have come into this cave exactly the same way as we did, "past all of those many stinging nettle thorns, that you just hacked down! What kind of flowers are those any-way?" Yeah, I'm wondering too? Really, what kind are they, and how in the heck long ago were they left here... And why? Wild flowers wilt almost as fast as picked! These look as fresh as very recent!" {The answer remains with the provider!}

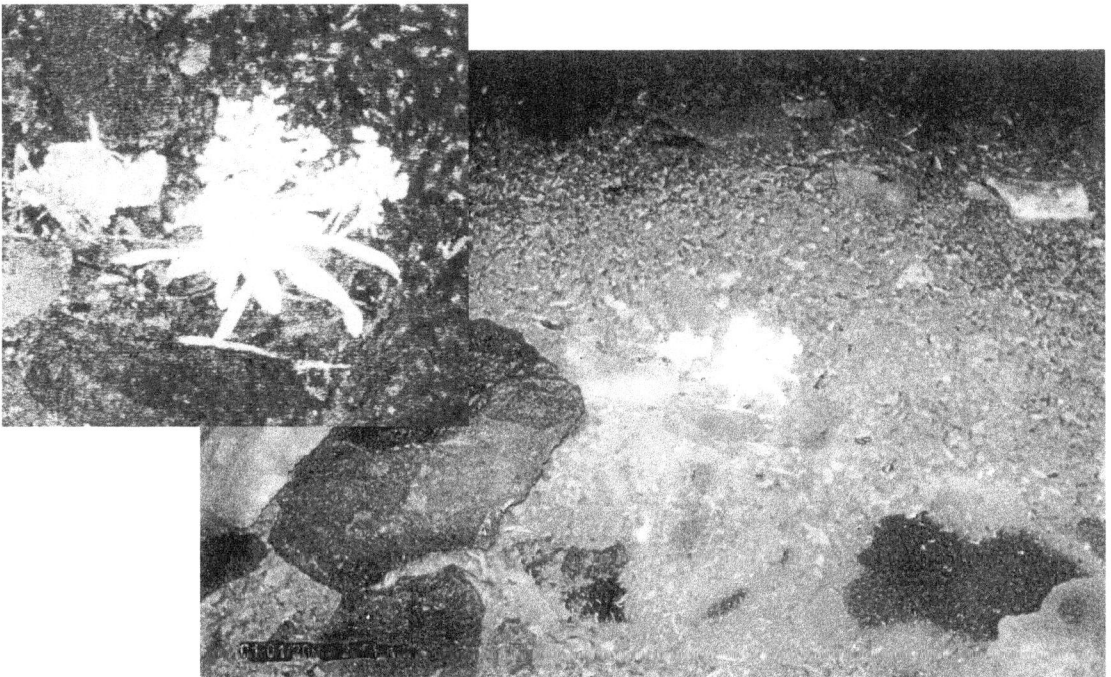

Figure 23. Array of un-wilted flowers where found on the cave floor.
What brought them here?   Photo Author.

Considering the flowers found that day, and two other separate discoveries made much similar of them at other times; the first year 2005, being a typical primitive type of a bundle of freshly harvested wild Bunch Grass, left behind as if ceremoniously wrapped... ("Ron Roseman, John Doitch, Carlos the brave, and myself as witness!")... and second time exactly the same left at the cave entrance 2007... ("Var Harris, and Paul Wright, with me!")... and now these strange flowers, 2011, for what ever the reasons, these offerings had actually been left where they were after being precisely placed much similar just exactly as were found these flowers flaunted on the top of four recently placed rocks on the cave floor? "The others with me, first time, had no way of knowing that I was pondering over all Cave Passé Unexplained Missing Bones!"

"Lets Ask. Onya Wild Two Feathers Brown?"

"This stuff is really wild Don ... Its just a bit spooky too!"

"You say that you once found many, many, bones in this cave, right? Well, this cave is really not all that huge... Its big enough, but ... Yes, well, when/if considering all of that big spacious room up there over our heads past that do-nut shaped gaping hole... where you say that you and Holly had first found all of those many, many, half decayed animal bones, this however is all very strange and seems most incredible if not impossible! How many others did you say have seen this cave; and what you think all of those undetermined bones need indicate?" "Well, like you say, this cave is well hidden, and much difficult to even imagine that it is here! Well perhaps... Well, I really do think it may have been, and still might be somehow even today, a very special, if not be still considered as a much sacred place? You and Holly, were probably the first ones ever to find it that recognized its importance! This cave very easily may have been an ancient burial chamber of the ancients, much like what's today a mausoleum, etc? Did you ever extract even one single bone artifact from under that ice? No! Well, I'm glad of that! No telling what actually was there, and the probable reasons for them? Show me those pictures again, I really need to see them!

What more do you know about pre-history burial grounds and various customs? You say you found one single animal horn left behind from was a long extinct Bison-Antiquus ... Well, if those missing bones under that ice were only the remains of four legged animals like one of those.... Well then, no one, or anything, would have any good reason not to want to just leave them exactly where they had been for a very long time! That vanishing ice is all another matter? Do you realize how long it takes for ice to turn to a blue color? I really wish that I could have actually seen all of that! And, you know Don, it really is odd too, that all of the other bones that you have discovered in many caves have all of them stayed exactly put, exactly where first found! All of this strange missing bone stuff really makes one wonder?" Naw, its really not all that hard babe,, as I think I have a good idea of why, if it not the one true answer?

One bone resembling a human knee cap that was (The Patella!) found on the mud floor of this cave, was sent via Ray Crowe, next to be sent for research to Doctor Orr, of Oregon State University... Orr later related back to Ray, claiming that the bone was "carbon dated" at close to being 11,000 years old! Onya, that makes the bone date back into fit the latter part of the Ana-thermal Period, to a time when the planet was experiencing a continuous 2,500 years long drought! (It was the planets most devastating hot time, said to date at 7,000 – 10,150 years, so that would include the mammoth, and of all larger animals similar here then as existed the, Bison-Antiquus, just short of the Cave Bears, and another ferocious bear; what is still believed to exist today in the Russian Wilds of Kamchatka, what is, "Ousts-Sims," that actually in truth is a more than huge long legged, shorter haired carnivore bear, different in several obvious ways from the true grizzlies that are instead, Horrible's!

This huge bear easily dwarfs the Grizzly, and the Polar, in much mega proportions, reaching much larger and taller in documented descriptions, that can be seen if wanted on the Inter-Net, ("Wrongly cataloged!") under, the worlds Largest Grizzly Bear! This is the first and only example of this bear photographed of record? This massive animal was killed within the close borders of Alaska, fall, year 2004, almost exactly three years to the day of the date of its now documented descriptions that were written more than just similar by me in my first book, "Sasquatch 2001!" Also is explained in that book is the adamant and adornment belief of the Native Koriak Russians, descriptive of what they call the, The God Bear, {Ousts-Sims} as was once told me in earnest...

118

"This bear is huge, and it is beyond very, very, dangerous! And, it is still to be found roaming in some of the far places of the Kamchatka Peninsula!" As said, that interesting story was first written to the last minute detail... (just repeated!)... of the bears description by the author three years prior to when This One was finally killed, and by its very size it is now proven that such huge bears actually do exist!"

"Onya, I Told Her,
I'm Pretty Darn Good, At Being Pretty Damn Suspicious!"

< A Johnny Foxx Chronicle! >

"Sometimes stubborn bound is the mother of discovery!"

Bias Opinion Often Chokes All Smoke Before The Fire Has Even Been Lit!

Onya was once fascinated of the new world that she had discovered in mine! In her journal she wrote words to the effect to explain: "Pretty good, Don, is still only second best when contesting any first place winner of anything important! Second best if anyone is that is still only being the very first looser ... Being a maverick, an academic, a critic, what are we really that matters in all new discovery allowance? What ever is, was passé, or has been recently considered will prove Mistletoe Cave, is definitely by now a prime example of an over looked important piece of long forgotten humanity history! What is interesting is that have photographic witness of all strange fact as evidenced to prove all strange happenings explained as has been the ceremonial type grass bundles of grass, etc., and now again 2011, there were found these strange unidentified flowers, etc! Well how hard is it to anyone's imagination to realize that someone, or something with at least a primitive hominid mentality of some sort of a reference adherence is still wanting to visit this particular mountain desert cave! My ongoing researched suspicions may somewhat be able to explain a real part of this incredible plaiting anomaly that will more than likely go unsung for wanton doubt of accredited academic belief! But what ever anyone believe anything or not, trust me babe, wild people of several different sorts of possible descriptions, most stemming from a much similar original ancient gene-pool blood line (DNA!) actually do exist, if they only be to fact you and wild me, and don't forget for a moment wanting to realize it or not, I have witnessed them on three separate occasions, even if ever our twain shall never meet, because believe me no-one wants a true wild man for more than another free drink! And know this Johnny Foxx, if you want to become great at anything and know that you are pretty good, that is not enough! Because pretty good is still only pretty bad in the real world of becoming great!

"Candace In Mistletoe Cave!"

Some of that above said was paraphrased from Onya's writings of something like written in her journal taken from the invincible "Osgood Files," and it is damn well the truth too!

My beloved green eyed grand daughter Candace Blackman who made it possible for me to make a significant discovery winter November 24, 2004, by her stubborn insistence after dinner and a comical movie; on Thanksgiving Day, Candace begged me until I was convinced that she was serious wanting that we re-explore the incredible cave that she had heard about discovered by her daring and impossible aunt Holly Mistletoe Mulvaney... "And more, she said, well grand-pa, I know that darn well that you shoot your pistol pretty darn good, and we would be safe from anything that might be in there... But how come she went on to say... How come I seem to be able to beat you at shooting cans most every time we practice?" Now I said, with that particular case scenario, that is a great thing to realize, but you Candace as I write will never realize how very much indeed you had experienced of a possible impending danger on that frozen day so long ago in Mistletoe Cave! "If it wasn't for her youth, ever insistent excitement, and my understanding of her inherit ant blood, I would have not gone there on that twenty degrees below zero winter day and made another significant and extremely important discovery still proven in an incredible casting more able to further validate wild hominids!" For all of the rest of the story, please read the slated 2014 book titled, "Twilight Zone Chapters!"

Log: 2012- Mistletoe... The Rock? 2012 -

When re-counting the cave and especially the flowers left near where the alter stone had once been, all of a sudden all was a completely out of place, or was it? The bouquet was left almost exactly where had been the Ice and many bones. It was as if the flowers had been brought as some sort of a reverence to someone or perhaps a memory, etc: as when thought more about, the many bones actually had looked possibly to be human remains; and now these flowers, and next finding single strange potato shaped round river rock (A stone) still unaccounted for as to how and why it was placed so deliberately on the cave wall shelf... and especially still remains the mystery question of the reasons for fresh flower bouquet, and this river rock, and how exactly each got placed at the strange places were each were left? That high mystery to this day continues to need be explained... as Tarah Redfield of Dillon Montana, working in a local Green House 2012, since last September has now opt to be working on the horticultural identity of the strange flowers, that as yet are unidentified from any book of horticulture or anywhere including anywhere Idaho or Montana. There are no answers for any of these discovered extremes, as even the potato looking stone was a rock similar of anything to be found over the vast sage brush desert closer than several miles, and there is written very, very, much more high strange of Mistletoe Cave in the Twilight Zone! Wait for all complete story 2014.

Log: Mistletoe Cave, 2009 -

The cave needs closer evaluation however unless it includes members of the early crew no one would truly understand or suspect all changes of importance that have taken place without had been there. The cave still remains completely unfathomed to understand its true mystery and worth. Who knows what else over the eons of time has taken place in this cave. To any unsuspecting visitor it remains almost as pristine, barren, and base hollow and empty as if had never been discovered, or any of its past secrets had already been revealed. There is not one single clue left to validate its countless bone artifacts now vanished without one clue how that were once easily to be seen below the frozen ice. What remains the next wonder is what had ever happened to the two hundred pound heavy stone strange shamanistic rock slab and its artifact display of various ancient bones, animal parts, and who knows what that were very possibly all an important part of ceremonial and/or sacrificial teachings, etc., "high suspect to had taken place right along side the now vanished ice that had been there likely for hundreds of years where weeks ago were the countless unidentified bones?" Of course there is no way to prove any of this now, but my strong gut feelings have me wondering; especially when considering all of the recent and passé strange flower, and grass bundle offerings left, etc., that were found, and the recent sudden and highly mysterious unexplained disappearance of the many bones *and all traces of the ice that once covered a large area of the floor; and now the obvious hand worked horn ceremonial cup found that has since vanished; and the several times in the cave when all crew had precariously/accidentally and quite unknowing haphazardly random camera flashed strange Orbs floating around us over head in the pitch black dark! The failure of video cameras to want/function in the cave, the upstairs strange cave extension chamber where Holly and I first explored and found undeniable evidence of passé humanity, and many, many animal bones; none of this is any longer possible to appreciate since the sudden high strange caving-in of the chambers overhead roof falling in and covering everything in several feet of rock that will forever cover everything! Almost it would seem that I could write an endless list of strange happenings that have taken place in the cave, but for now.. just understand with me that eons ago the cave had to have been much used, at a high suspect of far distant UN-written pre-history dating back possibly in time before all regional Shoshone base Indian tribes had written their identity in petroglyphic artifact?*

What all more was there or had been discovered by another, or what ever or who ever continues to visit there before Holly stumbled on to the cave will remain UN-written, lost, and perhaps much more is still hidden there that will never be discovered? All true explorers inclusive of the author for reasons obvious will go to their grave with kept secrets? Maverick and academic misunderstandings of discovery often writes a false value and story impression leaving many an unanswered question any first time heard. Actually the truth of anything relies entirely upon who anyone will choose to trust, and/or what you will allow yourself to believe; and more important, "when in doubt, we must learn to trust our own intuition. All through the slated books of the Trilogy many things explained have no absolute, logical, obvious, or even a contrary answer... There has never been anything written to compare to these revelations unless it is written in the incredible book titled, "In Search Of The Skin Walkers," that has much, much, interesting reading and in some respects a comparison to what I have at times need experienced. The exact location confidentially of Zak Cavern, and all sister caves, and where, how, and when, feral hominids live in them part time during winter needs be understood, as there are just possibly a great many more un-divulged little explained secrets to be known of them world wide? Wild hominid man exists... To hell with what the non-believing critics, or anyone says contrary!"

Part One Of Donald Massey's Horrid Cave Deposition!

(More able to explain the experience will follow in its place!)

Deposition exerts taken from Chapter Nine of the manuscript now in progress titled: The Cavern Of Zakynerous! We just had to include more part of his story! Don was one of the most remarkable, intelligent, and one of the bravest men that I have ever known. "He would not have given one hot damn twit concern of anyone who would not have believed the following story, as he had once also said to me... Why bother to tell anyone anything Don? Most persons are so set in their opinionated that they can't even hold an intelligent conversation! I'm not all that smart myself... Or especially as smart as some many smart assess actually think that they are ... but I will listen, and when I am wrong... Well, to hell with them!"

**"Aging Donald begins his incredible revelation
deposition of creature discovery!"**

"The Monster of Zak Cave?"

"Monroe, he said, I will never again be the same! I think now I hate you!"

Deposition of: Donald Massey – Age 86, year 2001. Don's remarkable story begins in slightly paraphrased excerpts taken directly from his own words down on tape recordings:

"Deep Inside The Cave"

(Miscellaneous message blather!)

Donald Massey!

"You know Monroe, any improper loud or Unnecessary noise made an unstable cave such as this could easily get us caved-in on, and crushed us kilt-d...! Killed another time that is, if that big Son O' bitch-en Bastard Creature back there that I saw hasn't already killed us first before those unstable boulders up-over head don't crush down on us next! Remember I have been a miner for many years, and to even think for anyone to have entered such an unstable cave as this is a complete disaster! And, kilt-d, is killed dead no matter what! My sur-name is Massey, and yours is Monroe, and that's another problem... Both being Scotch, perhaps we should just drink a bit of that filtered stuff rather than be One? Right now I could use a drink!"

(Log Continued:)

"Said to me slightly ahead, and after the fact of Don's horrid creature misadventure discovery story to follow; all excitedly expounded paraphrased close-case from memory, as we were then together under high stress and in a great hurry while still careful and trying to quickly depart the cave! It was indeed a trying and exciting long moment in time!"

Massey

"Monroe, after what I have just experienced today; all I want right now is to be out of here as fast as we can! The Devil himself could be following right behind us? I don't dare to even look back over my shoulder! When we get's out outside into the day light, I am gonna shoot you at least twice for getting me into this unholy wild man mess! I am not even sure that the big ugly devil back there wasn't actually old Satin himself? No one will ever believe this story either... And so, you need promise me that you will never tell it till I am gone! I don't need to be arguing with critic idiots about what I just saw for the rest of my life!"

("I kept my promise!")

(Massey Continued)

"Don's initial experience had definitely inspired the writing of

The Trilogy Manuscripts!"... After we escaped the cave he never asked again to enter another. As said, his short horrid sojourn became the most decisive reason for the writing of the Trilogy, as his true story becomes of witness importance to further validate wild hominid existence. Don's short story is somewhat humorous, as he himself was a natural comical wit; what next is only partly explained is much more than horrific and was no laughing matter that few men (especially of his age!) would have probably endured! Massey's stubborn self and dry-wit humor had lifelong helped him to survive all various mixed adventures, and especially this one, and his difficult rigors, trials, and sad heart ache experiences had during World War Two serving in war-torn France!" Don had ever been a life long natural unsung unconditional hero much enduring far life beyond the expectations of what might be thought all of the normality and necessity needed be endured of what ever it actually is to fact that can explain to me or anyone what would be in truth an ordinary man? Don was extraordinary! Ordinary in his case would read he was ever beyond the call of human duty... His extraordinary life and times could easily write an interesting and informative volume of new encyclopedia whoa and whit!"

For space and time his story needs written in a next book. Just know that Donald becomes the catalyst of The Trilogy!

To Crew?

Are the cave dangers and fears of wild hominids when housed in caves much similar of humans do any think? From evidence found in precautionary determinations via animal signs found, etc., they are. The high strange events of cave exploration explained ahead in separate experiences unravel one's latent fears, imagination, and real life understandings of what at first may be thought improbable and ever accentuates the explicit truth that relict wild man exists, and of their obvious concern and high fear while subterranean of the acute possibility that without warning one could suddenly become burred alive! If that alone in all probability is not one good reason to torture any one's reasoning enough to thwart or discourage their desire to explore every where underground much closer to home, then nothing other would? The adventure of your life, or a horrible and unsuspected demise, had during a daring adventure, regardless of all caution taken any where might be waiting right out side your own back yard fence, or on some distant mountain vista.

All pent up unrealized emotions and fears come much alive when cave exploring, especially this is so to those already much aware of true wild man existence, and especially while one is crawling stark-uneasy underground completely unprepared regardless of all understandings of what danger might/could come next, and that said perhaps it will even be better understood by anyone of a much similar pirate and devil may care nature as has the author; them perhaps reading intently, and ever interested and in further discoveries of the unknown and so could be already fantasized to some extreme, and/or may even be wanting to one day be exploring with all future crew completely lost in a close fantasized proximity of another future Zak Cave Adventure or similar regardless of all of the moot policies now being set down even as we read by cooperative governments 2013, and/or after, as sure as hell regardless of any of that, "in all near futures sanctioned or not, there will be additional important and meaningful visits back into all of the wild unexplored cave places of Western American Exunda, as when finally all of this now pending political gray matter is resolved through intelligence beyond the current non-thinking Abomination Round Table where all of one's logistics need be ever exclude to include most every pseudo critical negative opinion had imagined; or when once again we dare explore even if somewhat concertinaed and confused of all regimented men in black, surroundings, and/or are thirsty subterranean, before having had a need for at least three more shots of, Russian Vox, since of late I have included that sort rush to need be included (?) as a dire reminder necessary to have soothed all cave stress and anxiety, ever since was recently thrown at me a small toy Russian gift Bear named Koshbeare-nough, that is now dancing and watching into the far horizon from off the widow-dash of my car... and if indeed the Russian Vox were as excitable and beautiful/dangerous as are some particular Russian women, all of us by now would be more than scared to half to death of something, as there is definite wild madness in Vox Vodka, and especially in any distressed women more than there is of any danger of caves! "However what ever the scenario I cannot fairly say that men are any better at exploring or anything than women, or to have them in company during any hair raising experience, but they certainly are not any worse!"

I have not as yet left the horse plaiting creatures whiskey or similar, but in future may consider? Cooperation among all participants remains the problem? I have discovered however that the Zak Cave creatures will consume beer! Wow what more I probably need write? However never think to include alcohol, or anyone in use of it or similar, in order to accomplish any serious adventure at any time and especially where or when anyone's life may be at risk! True field discovery includes hazardous risks! Taking unnecessary risks is hardly adventure! We once left particular cave inhabitants Vox Vodka, etc., ... and the wild ramifications beyond comical need be written in a pending Trilogy book to be titled: The Twilight Zone Chapters!"

Log: Plaiting

Viable explanations are sometimes difficult to explain, and so in time messes-up what ever opinion was concluded. To some things there are no answers. What ever actually are the many strange powers that be, at least those found within the pitch-dark Niter-World of caves, and the ever improbability of plaiting have to do with them and his manuscript at first may read as improbable as it is true, exhilarating, and preposterous; even I suppose when all unforeseen happenstance at times may even become somewhat frightening the book in its collective message must also read as enlightening as it is an educational account of western America wild hominid and horse plaiting relative activity. Sometimes when we confront the eminent danger and high fear of being buried alive, etc., there is no turning back when four or more persons are crawling ever forward threw a lava tunnel in line where all are head cramped and pondering in a questionable lava tube tunnel death with no remote possibility of ever turning around no matter what, and everyone may be thinking we will soon all become buried history? Fortunately thus far, not one person has ever been injured during our expeditions beyond a broken rib, bumped heads, or a minor forehead cut, etc. What becomes more than of a concern is the anomaly of what real horror of antiquity such as discovered human bone evidence had from a past mishap could suddenly surface discovered right before ones very eyes. Would this ever happen remains the question of what to do about it? Some many unexpected discoveries I suppose are best left found exactly as they are! In a recent 2013 book published of Ray Crowe, the first of three slated for year 2013, titled: "Big Foot Behavior," are included but one photograph of several more than interesting unknown animistic creature skeletal remains discovered by the author found in Idaho/Montana caves. The Trilogy Manuscripts collection untangles the rele-

vance of a much mixed bag of high adventure and mysterious discovery that amounts to the hard fact of a sometimes dangerous real life multiple lived experience had by many! The credit of perhaps several never to be written books writes the unsung adventures of many of our past crew ... I would only hope that another of them one day will write their exciting memories. The Trilogy Books including Zakynerous writes a discovery adventure quite unlike any other that you will ever read to experience... An indisputable insight to living wild man existence and interaction in today's world of submissive doubt and confusion, with enough insights to a much better understanding of wild man's most obvious miserable and difficult life! I would hope in my future not to need to repeat all of the complete experience again; however much of it may need re-evaluation if anyone actually expects to ever find more important answers. Anyone interested in current writings and menial descriptions of hominid artifacts found in this cave and several others of the area need read author Ray Crowe, "Bigfoot Behavior," the Anecdotal Evidence Volume One, ISBN 9781475171468 90000 9 781475 171464. Crowe, retired director of the Western Bigfoot Society sights in this book much importance to further substantiate current day and past existence of relict humans and/or Sasquatch/Bigfoot. The undeniable exhilaration of discovery, and the beckoning call of the unknown and uncanny continues to haunt the ongoing excitement evident of all current dedicated crew! Each of them remain separately cautious, and understandably reluctant to continue the effort for the reasons of current day volcanic activity, however we are all anxious to be going back to the excitements! Once you have discovered the stark truth of relict living feral hominids, seen them, interacted, etc., well, by then you have became less concerned that in due time you may need to abide by the negative equation of discovery, and so for reasons undecided you have relented come what may to opt to suffer the dire consequences! The choice is not always easily written; as there sometimes becomes no decision at all to be made by the extreme curiosity factor had of human interaction with the unknown... Often I myself have dared particular foolish exploration because the obvious rare opportunity that would likely never be had again, alone at the time with none other than myself to need consider their safety; have done this when if had another been along would have probably often as not likely aborted the objection? Age and experience are suppose to render one the wiser, rather than the highly venerable as becomes the dumb beast! Thoughts to the perilous of this devil may care attitude anomaly has always left me misunderstanding and wordless to better explain what it is that really continues to temp humanity sometimes into early retirement to the bone yard?

We Are All Hominids One And All...

Only pseudo tame man ever discovers relict man, but wild man has always known that civilized man was a real part of his concern to be out whited and avoided, and so wild humans have always had the upper-hand to better understands civilized humanity than the contrary! All of that is as if a bit comical, but it also is true, and sufficient to say, that the unknown has always included all mankind including the lesser animals thank goodness that had never opt to concern it either! Never once during the sometimes high adventure of exploring has any sole mate even one time doubted his latent fears and objections! I do wonder however, if wild man truly may also experience fear in an all much similar recall? I really doubt it, as in my opinion he exists mentally in a world almost similar of suspended-animation in particular progressive outcomes; pseudo subdued in a controlled existence much different than civilized man, as ever their concern is mostly for food, sanctuary, and shelter!

Log: Zakyneros Cave, December 1, 2001 – 2013.

What, really, have I discovered? Who do I dare solicit to share in this obviously important discovery revelation? With who other than my intelligent wife Marion do I dare share my new found secrets? It would take me all of six months time until I could finally be self-satisfied to trust/divulge Zak Cave to anyone or to explain rationally what were to become my high suspicions of the all new found truth of living feral wild man discovered to be inhabiting during cold winter particular high desert mountain caves. Even as I write and/or continue to explore in future past year 2014, I remain somewhat apprehensive to continue to confide every all new discovery to the bulk of new twenty first century pseudo intellect of any recommended academic for reasons of past lost trust of some of them in all maverick research sojourn, the world sudden think-tank expectations of today seem ever wanting of anything new discovered outside of the box too; the sudden irrational display of everything and anything in a sudden rush of accomplishment hardly seems to have in mind the true end result of UN-bias truth...! The priority of accredited Crypto studies seems to require non-but the badge of irresponsibility and narcissism! The good old boys seem to be as much historical as the saber-toothed tiger and the cave bear! Day One At Zak. The temperature out side the cave today was minus five degrees. To have made its discovery I need almost fall into its hidden chamber. I was completely overwhelmed to the very last discovered freshly killed wild pigeon, ever evidencing a red-wet bloody trail of hand plucked feathers up to the last foot distance of its rocky entrance. Upon entry of the cave at once I had definitely felt watched. "Now writing twelve years after the fact of the caves discovery in retrospect my life, times, and beliefs, have much changed as the result. What I will write in future to further explain Zak and all sister caves to some will proves almost beyond their imagination. Not my concern, not my worry, as every bit of it will be written the truth. Truly with Zak Cave the Adventure had began! "Zak Cave, Two years later, continued: 2003 - To date we have found much evidence of some sort of a wild humanity, but as yet we do not know exactly what they are? We have made many plaster castings of strange bipeds running over this vast 90 mile plus square desert that includes Zak, most all of them evidence a same small population of perhaps a dozen or so. All of this discovery has cost all crew sleepless nights. Regardless of all recent derogatory academic opinion had of associate professor of anthropology Jeffery Meldrum, ISU, Pocatello, Idaho, telling me blatantly "that these castings Don do not match the prototype of Sasquatch, because they are much too human looking, etc!" That said was exactly true, and exactly what I wanted to confirm, as I have found in my sojourn more than what I need to know to satisfy my curiosity that there are at least four variations of physical descriptions of living wild man hominids able to partly explain all strange varieties of sexual dimorphism to identify the supposed descriptions of wild hominids! What Meldrum has told me on similar various occasions as slanted negativism/ridicule was unknown to him at the time that latter by year 2013 now ten years later my castings would finally match all new found accredited academic opinion, but for that moment in time and all years after he and his pier critics continued laughing my efforts enough to had convinced important others that my efforts were bogus/moot; the damage done to further credit to my exploring crew had finally discouraged much sincere interest to continue wild hominid investigations. "If the academics would not rally around us then sure as hell the public would never learn the truth! Since Meldrum's sway at best I have been able to only temporarily re-kindle interest in Idaho cave exploration and for a most part have needed to go it alone. Having myself seen three separate examples of these Wiley creatures 1982 – 2006, in three states Washington, Texas, Idaho, had close encounters with them during late night hours in Minnesotan, Washington/Oregon, California, Nevada, etc., by now there is nothing more new needed for me to be completely con-

vinced of their varied existence! Disbelief in anything does not disprove an existence!" What we have discovered in relict hominid actuality and crew interaction to date to fact are not necessarily Sasquatch/Bigfoot creatures, or are they either in any remote way any stupendous giant great ape as Meldrum back then insisted was Gigantopithecus... "However strange he and/or any other bias critic may have thought my plaster foot, body, and hand castings irregular to prototype Bigfoot, every single one of the hand casts evidences an obvious opposed finger to thumb absolute!" Perhaps in a near future through new approaches to DNA, etc., we can somehow finally establish an all true identity? For now in my continuing opinion these creatures are; "they are to be considered as hold over examples of a very ancient and completely unknown relict mankind variation, that is much less changed from his species of origin than are we Homo-sapiens of today also much, much, irregular one from the other. There are notable variations in many of the higher animals, and wild man because of his continuing difficult life style is much less unchanged than modern man because of his required unchanged hunter-gather physical existence resulting in a acute exactness of brawn, stealth, strength similar in every way less removed from his origin from man as we know ourselves since his most ancient beginnings; especially this so in the physical sense, when considering to include his simple needs, and so to all logical reason his brain is likely also much unchanged as well, as much perhaps the same as his entire physical being is unchanged, much less at least than we humans have become over the recent centuries anxious at best said, ever wanting to trade off our physical brawn and dwindling natural ability for pseudo intellect resulting in a supposed humanity improvement (?) of creativity and inventive ability, etc. "At the end of this long tunnel of comparison conjecture, when considering all world wide wild humanity virus we Homo-sapiens much differing as we surely are; if for example at the end of times ("Worlds End?"), if indeed any sort of a standing erect hominid remains (?), then likely for the reasons of its brawn, simplicity, and definite adaptability, all bipedal creatures still existing as said Sasquatch/wild man, etc; all of them in their separate example will need be protective strong when standing along side the wolf sniffing at the blowing dust and ash remains of we milk/wimp-weak soon to be forgotten historical Homo-sapiens, the Polar bear will also to be seen walking right along side the clever coyote, snake, and disgusting cockroach! This incredible Sasquatch Trilogy jargon needs be shared! There has never been anything like it written! There is very much to swallow in this collective jumbled ship-wreck book collection! All of it is truly mind-boggling, informative, and was often a high adventure. I know no chains, bounds, or programmed ethics! To hell with the babbling, idiotic critics... Most of them are less than completely alive! For anyone to had missed reading this crux manuscript of horse plaiting and wild man descriptions, or to have put it aside thinking it perhaps to unorthodox, etc., they would have missed an enlightenment marvel that is still much of a hot candle burning message taken from life! Plaiting as we have discovered it has definite reason for happening! Exunda may be thought to be just another wild place of fantasy and imagination, "but in reality, for any of those that will truly continue to explore every remote possibility of every where, and all strange hidden anomalies, oh what an exciting world is still out there left to wander! The wonder of it all is how few of us today continue to explore. Perhaps it is the reason of our much programmed education? What ever... Get out there and prove me wrong!"

Log: "Halloween 2012, November Full Moon Update!"

Not to my surprise the plaiting on the Jenson ranch property has continued on the horse named Hink each and every full moon phase segment running for all of the past 12th months *consecutive! However on July 4ᵗʰ the hominids had refused to take away or eat the tightly paper wrapped Tootsie Roll candies offered/left for them by Norma Jenson? More of the plausible reason for this denial will be further explained in its place. All of this plaiting sojourn is more than exciting!*

"LONG STORY VERY SHORT!"

FINAL YEAR 2013, LOG UPDATE:

"Done For Bob Smallsbach, Happy Camp, California!"

(What's for Dinner Bob besides raisins?)

Way, way, far ahead of the book's final message and conclusions; written over the next few long paragraphs down as far as mid page 2017. if anyone can be read to decipher it, will be found all current moon phase conclusions in a short manuscript update intended to further explain all research now completed done since December 11, of 2011 – inclusive of December New Years Eve, 2012 – and to date January 26ᵗʰ, 2013.

Realizing the readers' position, Bob's time to read, his and everyone's seemingly hurry world, etc., "I thought it most appropriate to get'er all down and said for the record ahead of anyone needing a reprieve from all of this confusion; as need be said another time, this manuscript jargon was very difficult to realize and explore to write.. and even much harder to attempt to conclude, as its incredible journey continues to hold me spell bound for any new and continuing better answers! Thanks for all reader patience! Mine too has needed become the first considered priority of this restless soul!

OK then, Ray Crowe, this short verse is also written for you! Lets get there and do it all again! Kathy Seavey I will be there with you and Katherine at Hillsboro by tomorrow January 27ᵗʰ, 2013. "By the way Ray, I just finished reading Volume One of your new book for 2012 titled: Bigfoot Behavior! "Looks like a definite winner for the purchase of new SKEPTICALS in order to read it! The book is great Ray …! Give my best regards to Mullis Rhettman Jr… Remember old buddy, I named a very special hidden Idaho Cavern Grotto located within the incredible Valley of Pits for your Theata. Ron Roseman and John Doitch exploring with me there caught and salvaged a wild dying raven! We named the bird Theata! I raised her six months with my 28 magpies till late that November when I taught her to fly, and now she is in flight somewhere over all Montana Blue Sky as your patron Almakoa! So be it."

Log continued: January 27, 2013 – Sweet Home, Oregon.

This next explained will perhaps be a bit confusing: But tonight is a last full moon phase to be mentioned in this manuscript, as all horse plaiting intended for the book to its completion was wanted to be over as of New Years Eve, 2012. As already explained I was guest located here at Sweet Home Oregon during the beginning of the last historical new moon eclipse phase of December 11, 2011, to date considered, that tally is 14 new moon phases ago passé, so to date, tonight, when I will again make a last contact by telephone to the Jenson horse property to discover what if anything more has taken place of plaiting with Hink, or any other of their horses this segment of the all research continuation is complete?"

(Continued:)

Inclusive report concerning all passé 13 full moon phases had of The One Long Year In Time Plus Experiment just over that had began with the noted historical moon eclipse of, December 2011 explained above – Then next after came 2012, and the new year beginning with the full moon display of January, Feb, March, April, May, June, July, August, September, October, and now we are writing with the splendor of November's full moon that will end in the result of 12 months research running to the moon phase of December just ahead for a last full moon/horse plaiting observation. Book research was wantin' conclusion as of Jan. first, 2013, however I am still writing from an on location update:

2013 Full Moon Phase Projection!

Now with all past 13 month of moon phase concerning horse plaiting completed, it is most astonishing to write that the mysterious plaiting had occurred in sequence on all domestic and wild horses' manes observed, and continues being done exactly on schedule on time or about the same all during or at the beginning, or near the end of each particular new crescent moon four day moon phase. For the most part the study was done and reported on a very same Oregon Ranch horse known as Hink, however others horses over Idaho/Montana/Washington, etc. as can were also being observed on four other scattered ranch setting at a same time. All of this variation of extended territory adds definite month by month credence to all updates of my wild moon theory! Yes, I am excited with the incredible results, as if it hadn't happened on Hink ("However each month it had!"), then it had happened on another, horse, ("Did!") however no horse as yet observed monthly after been brushed out has failed to be plaited much relatively close in time as could be observed! For some unexplained reason during the last October full moon phase of Halloween 2012, the plaits on Hink and some other horses didn't happen either until the 4th night? It seems that a severe overcast cloud condition may have something to do with it? Probably all of that has to do with moon light elimination, or lack of it? Incredible photos taken of this last Halloween and all continuing plaits through December 2012 are included where marked in the photographs. Needless to say as can easily be observed in the photos, never once on any horse month after month, was the plaiting ever done in the exactly same way, except it is ever obvious on "Hink" that at least one regular visitor continues all project in a much similar way. Definitely all critics must realize, that the wind and brush have not been the result of one single part of this! For anyone to think to continue to insist that the wind or whatever is doing the plaiting is to recount anyone's more than obvious stupidity and ignorance!

("Most Important!")

LAST ENTRY?

Plaiting!

Log: Continued update of Full Moon Phase Horse Plaiting Research Being Completed As of December 28th, 2012 – December 11th, 2011

On the above date of 2012, the author journeyed bad weather weary to the Jenson ranch property just prior to New Year's Eve in order to be physically on location during the final full moon phase of year 2012 and was especially interested to observe if anything as new plaiting would happen on Hink? Well, it darn well did ... What is more than amazing are the comparative photos of both December moon seasons included in the photos to compare all of this, as when the new plaiting was done at the Jensons' on that final moon phase, the plaiting was accomplished almost exactly to the last strand of hair and in the very same way as it had been done just exactly the same ONE YEAR earlier on the very same horse, on the very same date of both separate moon phase month dates, set exactly in line with one another exactly one year apart and now more than all obvious and conclusion indisputable... "Anyone at all to see the photograph; anyone would be convinced, no one would be able to deny that both plaited mane examples are not almost identical in all total braided outcomes. Each had been accomplished by a very same creature effort, done exactly one year apart... and I was most fortunate to had been there on location and been a very first witness to the magic? Nothing is written that cannot be erased, changed, or added upon... "Get out there Var Harris and have a good look! Spring begins another season of adventure in the wild horse prairie proximity of the Salmon River Idaho mountains... Bring that rangy black dog that understands Sasquatch! They are great roasted, backed, fried or boiled! Remember we once opt to one day be eating crow!"

Log Note: Various unknown hominids and the reasons for plaiting?

We have much far out of the box research accomplished in this manuscript, and I am writing ever dutiful desperate to get'er all down before I myself self-destruct, as it is high time that the pseudo educated world of couch potato critics opt to sort out all of the probabilities of this more than high strange plaiting anomaly and closely examine all further probabilities of cryptic wild man truth beyond bind bias spookulation! Spookulation extraordinaire, as wild hominids are hardly actual monsters regardless of them in some world regions considered to be monstrosities, bogyman, etc., however very possibly some many of them are cannibalistic just as some very ancient societies became head hunters among themselves and they may as some many researchers believe at times even eat their decaying dead. More on this will be written of in viable belief in the Trilogy Twilight Zone Chapters. Wait for!

Perhaps one day I or someone as enthusiastic may sail again to recount the exciting places of the world as Asia, Indonesia, Australia, Thailand, etc., to further investigate all various wild entities still said to be wandering there under the guise of the full moon. On their way they need opt to visit all new contemporary and side track traditional Old-Day Cathay-Chinese traditions via The Han Tortoise on the mountain road to, Tibet, Bhutan, Mongolia, etc., in order to further assess all ancient/current new found Zen Buddhist belief still had there in Tibet of various types of wild-men being anciently tamed as were said to had been separate kinds of Yeti, and the little known and forbidden to contact, Wild Snow Men ("Not considered in any way to be Yeti or remotely the same!"), them written of in the secret chronicles of the ancient Dalai-Lama, as Almasty, Megar, etc., including the legendary little understood "Tulpa" ("Or incredible Mind Creatures!") well known mostly to the mind-powers of the mysterious and legendary Bhutanese Dubtu Monks, etc?

Of course when considering all of that future fantasized travel plan as above considering all questionable gun happy insurgents, desperado types of world bandits, etc., negative policies and moot governments laws to contend with, etc., any significant new discovery it seems needs be made by another much younger misfit expert seeking the ultimate unfathomed adventure? However the wind on the sun down will forever call my name each and every time that the horses are coming home I still can catch them? My father's favorite horse was Old Floss, and together they experienced many memories... Miss you Dad, you were a tough act to follow!

Log: "New Plaiting Has Began!" July 5th, 2012 -

I had a phone call from Phil Jenson today informing me that July 4th 2012, by the full moon for the eight time monthly since December 2011 new plaiting had started for another time on Hink! This time it was first noticed by Marvin Hollen who sometimes feeds the horses. The uncanny braiding was accomplished exactly as predicted on the late night eve of the forth on the very exact same night after Cheri Jenson that afternoon had brushed out the previous months plaits. This time at my directions several pink and green colored ribbons were left tied onto the horses back in close proximity to the manes to see if anything at all would be done of them, as I was in hope that by the simple manifestation that the creatures might opt to somehow braid them into the main exactly as I had seen it done in photographs had from Russian experiments where colorful ribbons were left plaited after on horses!

Cheri this time was visiting again from Guam and some may remember she was the same person that had experienced strange and incredible over night plaiting outcomes on Ukelele, and now for a second time she had brushed out both of these horses. Sometimes the plaiting begins part done on one night and ends completed over several extended efforts done in part over several consecutive nights.

This last incident of July 4th was done exactly to all expectations of full moon phase, etc., and what might have significant cause and effect here is that a very same person each time had only recently brushed out all there next to impossible braided knots before Hink and Ukelele had been re-braided.

The first time that Cheri had brushed out Ukelele nothing to do with the plaiting anomaly was told her, she was completely unaware that I had requested that the plaits be left on the horse all long summer season to observe the outcome. Out of compassion for the horse she brushed out the mane without another thought! After the plaiting done in July, and the years earlier having to do with Cheri, I was beginning to consider that what ever, or who ever was braiding the manes just might by some stretch of the imagination be choosing to re-plait the manes each time immediately after brushed clean just as if it all were perhaps somehow intended to be an abstract creature to human bonding being done through the horse via Cheri; perhaps mani-

fested through her obvious womanly odor or left behind hand perspiration, perfume, or whatever anyone wants to think similar, etc., as it is a well known fact that fish and animals respond much similar to cigarettes, food, perfume, sweat, etc. In regard to the colored ribbons, instead of leaving them as said, Phil decided to slightly tie them into long hair of the manes, and after that the ribbons were still all in place when last seen only a few days ago since the last April full moon. To everyone it seemed that nothing of had occurred, "but indeed it had," as I suddenly realized by this and said so, "that by the very fact that nothing had changed, much actually had, as the ribbons had all been left in place exactly as they were, since when the creatures had first seen them, intelligent as they are, they were at once reluctant to do anything more to manes until they had been brushed out again exactly as they had been that eve of July 4th !

After again brushed, they dare again to re-plait the manes! For the creatures to have remove the ribbons after all such recent unexpected activity had from humans; in all probability the creatures likely became awestruck, if not also became somewhat fearful of their initial discovery, further realizing they would need time to sort things out before resuming there braiding tradition etc.

Figure 24. Ribbons. "Cheri took the braids out the night of the full moon, nothing that night, or next—big bright nights; she brushed and combed hair everyday. The second night it was overcast and the next morning these braids were started—even Cheri said that wouldn't happen by itself—no wind that night—horse is separated from others. Muddy corral—no rolling. She took them out that day—nothing since—pink ribbon has disappeared." Photo P. Jenson.

Phil had also noticed that after the ribbons had been removed and put to one side, that all of the several green colored ribbons had vanished after the new plaiting! This next said is of course for now unfounded, but considering dolphins, chimps, sharks, various animals of several kinds, etc., it is my extended theory that now after all of that conjecture, that just perhaps a real part of what is happening considering all plaiting etc., via human interpretation/interaction and so forth; is it at all possible for the creatures to be able in some way to want to realize further communicate with humankind, as without a language there has not been any way till now as is being done through ongoing experiments; there has been no other real way for these pathetic wild people to actually communicate with humanity! Notes written to help describe more of the facts of the forth of July incident had been requested of all persons present that day on the property, however there had been no response. However before and after photographs were taken by Phil Jenson to validate the story that can be seen with many others in the photos.

Log: *Doing Regional Research Very Difficult!*

Of course it is impossible for me, or anyone to constantly be able to travel to all horse plaiting observation locations at once and do it all on a same day after moon phase, but if it could be done, after each and every new plaiting accomplished; for any reasonable time if was allowed, I would opt to stay on a few days or nights, and immediately brush out the new braids each time and wait hopeful as long as could, until it all was another occurrence , and do it all over again, and again, in a same way until who knows what might actually happen to be much better written up in a book sequel, as a reasonable and definite pattern of activity, cause and effect, and possible multiple purpose are much under new and continuing considerations beyond this manuscript. Sometimes the simplest things thought not important and yet tell-tell, are completely over looked. However this book in its complete revelation will definitely prove to incite others into further investigation and insight. Nevertheless, it will take a much imaginative/investigative horse rancher with much purpose, curiosity, and sacrificed time to want solve the plaiting mystery. Without constant horse to human contact, being ever at the right place and time, realized active creature interaction in any given area, much patience, compassion, etc., this book will remain non but just another curiosity for most! The time needed to had researched this journal was difficult and done almost daily. To write all of its real adventure anomaly and sorted curiosities, would take anyone many years. Thanks to all of those unmentioned non-helpful who have given me alkali water, bad or no directions, and or have insisted of us the bums-rush, and not much help after or before having had an argumentative bad time extraordinaire! "Some many been there and done that people actually give nothing, and take all!" Not necessary that the case with all people really, as there are many wonderful, "but believe me there are those of that particular ilk and beyond interesting deception! People that claim to love horses do not all love people! Probably being long out to sea and out of sight of land is where is true Shang-grala?"

"THE MOST DIFFICULT OF ALL!"

Perhaps the most difficult part of doing research

(Any research!) is to be able to inspire enthusiasm in anyone unless they already have an active imagination and are able themselves to think separately out of the box for answers. How to cope with this peculiarity and not be insulting another's intellect is a very great disappointment and unanswered dilemma. During experiments, after a time it becomes obvious that the wild hominids or what ever they are, soon realize that certain persons mean them no harm and so some of us become almost as if a recognized friend, and very slowly through mutual discernment all players begin to comply, wanting communication through useful artifacts, food, blankets, etc. No doubt over the long sojourn of western pioneer settlement, passé railroad efforts, ranching, logging, mining, desperate human intervention in obvious atrocities early on done towards Indians; and any and all struggling humanity as were the ethnic pioneer peoples, and especially all cruel treatments as were afforded the invincible Chinese, via slavery, peon-ism, etc., and if the creatures today be thinking much like them have good reason to be living in dire fear of discovery, etc; that said they have long been aware of human degradation, genocide, etc., and so as a result out of the necessity for survival have became even beyond elusive as once were the legendary Oriental base assassin Japanese Ninja, etc! And if any of that just said be at all understood, then why is it so hard for today's American humanity to accept the fact that there still exists various types of feral wild people? In most all Europe and Eurasia, Australia, Indonesia, all across the India-China Himalayan riff mountains, South America, etc., almost everywhere but North America the possibility of living wild populations are accepted; in spite of all wonderful technology, smart pones, etc., today, and all almost far beyond magical communication, etc., it is almost true that particular knowledge of the wild sort as is realized common sense, examved best by practiced old fashioned bob cat logic or similar, has all but gone by the way side. Wanted or not, computers, robots, moot government project policies, etc., as yet for now have not yet been able to completely dictate our thinking, or do any one either yet consider that probably they actually have! Perhaps wild man for his adaptability and human evasion at the end of humanity and times will be the last man standing! Then what?"

STORY

Log: Socorro New Mexico, fall 2009.

Jim and Ellie Martinson; Mexican Bandits; Anasazi pottery.

Don, everyone said, this is another one of the best adventures had possible! As candid, complicated, ragged, and desperate research as is written here has to be a true labor of love! Regardless through out the book the horse plaiting stories keep coming, and what by now do anyone accept might be actually chasing them?"

On The Road Toward Bandit Exunda!

"Dusty road rage conversation, and true travel comradely!"

Beyond her acute love and understanding of particular problem people, family, and horses, Tonia before reaching the remote ranch house east of Socorro belonging to the Mexican bandits, Lefty and Poncho, had said to me, and next was agreed the reply by Jim and Ellie, who each next in their separate way implied words to the effect that... "Don, you are driving much too fast on this UN-maintained dirt road, and with all of this dust and heat the air in this car is stagnant, hot, and filthy, and all of that trailing dirt and sticky dust blowing back into the car from behind is every where over our hair and cloths! We all look almost like a bunch of discarded human sweating chocolate chip cookies, and Jim's new sun glasses are lost somewhere over the back seat floor! You and your damn careless attitude are completely improbable, impossible, and unlikely, and even if we all hate to admit it, you are hardly ever wrong about what is never very important, or what was a good idea, and/or are always correct about condemning all things moot that you shouldn't have done, and you do nothing to correct all of the impossible that becomes your habit! We just missed the right turn in the road when you turned left back there! We are now going the North, instead of East; and you'd better stop the car before those milk cows up ahead come flying through our windshield, before its to late to stop and solve our water problem! Let me out of this car!"

MORE STORY

"Well, next before getting underway again into the right direction, I found Jim's smashed glasses under his foot and said, after all of this chocolate dust stuff, I suppose you girls could use a hot shower, and at least a cool drink of undeniable New Mexico alkali water! This wilderness exploration has extended us into various big cities, caves, rivers, mountains, etc., and when considering all of the dust had on just this day, this horse thing has got us into one hell of an impossible dirty mess!"

Somewhere above we began this saga with all of us on our way to where ever it would be that we had been invited to a visit a Mexican bandit sort of a horse ranch hold-over setting, located near/far away from the small berg city limits of Socorro, New Mexico, where we would be the first ever allowed to investigate particular ongoing strange horse plaiting long occurring on their mare ranch horses.

"Out of kindness I suppose...

Upon first arrival, at once all became somewhat awkward, as the host troupe of four staggering caballeros had already been drinking Tequila since morning, so as best possible we politely communicated and fraternized in accordance with wild Jim's direction for unfamiliar gringos, that had for the moment seemed to appease his pseudo wild bunch bandit friends, who we next dubbed out of kindness I suppose; from their appearance and character, we honored them with the names of Lefty and Poncho, and other was Carlos and Mathew.

(To be continued!)

Log: NEW PLAITING!

Update – Feb 2, 1013. Jenson Ranch property, Owyhee River Or.

On January 26, 2013, I was at Sweet Home Oregon, some 600 plus miles away from the the Jenson Ranch property. This research being over since January first 2013 (?); "well, I just had to know if the plaiting was continuing as it all had been so astonishing over the past15 months that I had no choice but to return back there another time to have a look. Feb 2nd, I arrived to the ranch setting to discover that the plaiting had indeed happened again over the past few days since the 26th and all photographs to prove it are now included in the figures here." Phil had been trucking, and so had been gone over the past week till last night, and so until this very A.M.. Feb 3, we could not take new pictures. "Phil said, you know, it seems from what all has been done here and on most all of the other horses and on the wild mustangs that you ("I") have described, what ever is doing this has a definite preference to the smaller horses as would have been the hold over Indian ponies and/or the smaller Asian Steppe horses like the ones that were used over Mongolia, etc. Hearing this I was elevated in my assumptions, and in Phil's blind statements my theory had all that much more pseudo validation. Phil has promised to have a close watch monthly on his horses during year 2013. I will try to arrange this in oth-er Montana/Idaho locations as well. I am overwhelmed just as are some many others at the strange plaiting... "It is just all so highly incredible! Unless anyone were closely on top of all of this stuff with me, indeed it would be hard for most to believe. I remind all reading that for over 30 years all of the Neil Hinck ranch family had no particular interest in the plaiting that was going on unexplained right under their very nose! When Brenda and I had finally tallied all the head count of 135 Blazer horses, forty percent had been over and over repetitiously plaited! And as noted, 99 percent of them had been phi-lies or mares. This indeed is a book need be written without chapters... At the moment I am attempting to finish this manuscript if can by Feb. 21st? My efforts considering all travel, exploring, etc., seem impossible.

(Continued from above.)

"Poncho & Lefty!"

Socorro New Mexico

As said, we began our introduction most awkward as all of the four ranch hands were deci-sive mucho-burracho (Drunk!), and one handsome caballero in particular took an instant liking to Tonia's dusty red hair, etc., and without further incident more than a gringo eye to eye hard look we instantly agreed on the matter of who was belonging to who! After that all American border, and bad had Alamo memories were never the better! With limited Spanish, I next asked the ranch foreman about the plaiting, and all that Carlos could say was... "Well, it all was being done on each horse several days apart by the Ghost Diablo... We not have any too much wind here now for a lotta days, and so it is not the wind can be doing this...! And if you look closely, the mains are all left to much too long for its beginning! I will brush out one mane, and every time in a short time it happen again? We know that this has to be being done by the Diablo, because he leaves us no tracks! What can leave no tracks? "Before coming to the ranch o, Carlos had agreed over the

136

phone to brush out the manes, had invited that we could stay for a few days, but to call first, as we were staying then with Jim and Ellie for at least five more days. Believe me, the evenings spent at the ranch were eventful, and true to his word on Monday two days later the phone rang tell Tonia that all her experiment food, the copper bracket, the gum-drops, etc., that she had left for the Diablo with the horses was all gone, and in return she had been left a tiny gift of a broken pottery sherd! Excited we all drove out to meet the ranch bandits, and at once were more than amazed at the age of the rare pottery! Later that same day at the Deming New Mexico Indian Museum we closely examined and compared the sherd, and sure enough as I had surmised it turned out to be of ancient Anasazi! The prize is shown in Figure 18. Anasazi artifacts of any kind are extremely rare. Tonia left her prized treasure and her little green book for me at her demise. Jim, a life long writer and western historian was overwhelmed at all that happened, as he had researched much of the Anasazi. On our return trip back through Deming six weeks later Jim had passed his time, had saddled his last horse, had seen his last sun down! With in four months Ellie had also opt to pine away somewhere in Canada? That said, Carlos appreciated the bottle of Bimini Island Rum brought from there, and handed us over his collection of recent photos of plaiting been taken faithfully each and every time that the Diablo had returned and had plaited the horses! The photos numbered four! Heavy rain coming down in torrents into our tents where camped North West of the Carl's Bad Caverns, N.M., much destroyed the small photos that today exist nevertheless most as a water logged important part of an all but forgotten fond memory. The loss of Jim Martenson and his life long unpublished historical probe manuscripts of sixty plus years in there writing has been another naive tragedy done of all new age youth ignorance. The pile of important exploration documents could have inspired published material that would amount to at least a yard high pile! My efforts to rescue them were fruitless! Jim, was long considered by his family as an outlaw, and by knowing this I had long grieved the tragedy of the lost manuscripts long before his passing. Jim had orally willed the manuscripts to my dictations as I had helped with small parts of there discovery data, "but things within families continue to happen and so I was overlooked. On the phone before Ellie's Exodus back to Canada, she told me that on my way back from Florida that I was to go into her locked house and take the pile of books, but somehow she forgot to mention this to any one, or to leave the key!" We never saw her again. But before hanging up the phone that last time Ellie asked to talk to Tonia... "Hey, she said... Tonia, that cow boy guy Carlos, you know, the Mexican guy out at the horse ranch... Well he said that he believed that the green eyed skinny gringo Indian women (Her!) carried with her the blessings and good luck of the famed Virgins, Tommarra Korenna, or Mamie Stover who ever they were? I remember now that the two women had laughed back and forth, as Tonia had wanted to know from Ellie if Carlos had truly ever actually saw one? "Ellie answered... saw one what?"

Log Note:

Respectful of Jim & Ellie Martenson and their life long adventurous spirit... That short clip above was but one small true life adventure to more explain Ellie and Jim and others similar as Tonia yet to be met with in the Trilogy Material taken from the author's private library, ever exemplifying in all but forgotten names, faces, and places, and events much much uncanny and high strange enough of unexplained happenings that some of them are far beyond just exciting, improbable and all true Twilight Zone Manuscript conjecture that are even more suspenseful of true life than most persons likely cannot imagine! Again it must be said meaningfully, that in my opinion no one has really ever been anywhere, and surely not everywhere, or done everything at all, as there is ever a new horizon of chance discovery, or a new mystery, and/or a new adventure that will prove to re-write many a dusty book! Only a fortunate few recognize all true adventure, or even sometimes appreciate the message of an artifact, or any person enough to fully realize all discovered treasure! When this happens another night star may suddenly be discovered, or may fall from the moon lit sky! Let no one dictate another's future or criticize what is not of their mind to understand. Few probably even realize The North West Passage actually exists at particular seasons of the year!"

Log: 2009, New Mexico Desert At Sun Down!

"Never Doubt The High Intellect Of These Wild Hominids!"

What, really, was the full meaning of the broken Anasazi pottery sherd given in return for Tonia's token gifts?

"You can only hope to write a story such as this, and hope that in time a significant number of its readers can finally relate to appreciate it, and/or will somehow be able to compare it to one or more of their own high strange experiences. However abstract, or unfamiliar all events of their own may had been, or what all may or may not compare to all of what's written ahead that may seem at first undefinable, strange, and/or not fully understood? With that thought, you may want to compare your own particular sojourn adventures that may prove to have been every bit as exhilarating as any thing written here thus far, or any of that ahead that will prove almost unbelievable! In my opinion our world is far from being completely explored. So much moot world policy of late controls all people so much that ones high intellect has little to do with new discovery as much as rebellion often does as far as for example dare to sometimes go under the wire... Programmed intellect is not all that smart until smart taxes intelligent decision... Indeed where is the beef! Don't look, don't eat! There are still a few holes in the wall where a wild man can crawl, they haven't yet closed them all, but that is coming!" What? Yeah, what, really, Kathy Seavey do you think by now is chasing the horses want'n to plait them? The horses are coming and what do you think may be actually running along side, or may be even riding on top them? Read on and discover for what good reason anything, something, or anyone is wanting to be repetitiously braiding the long flowing manes of world horses? The following projection is perhaps the one and only plausible theory/answer to be realized through collective logic, conjecture, common sense, and hard reasoning, etc., had from much historical fact, various world customs inclusive of all passé and current humanity, abrupt all now recently studied nine years of full moon phase abrupt all many various peculiarities that when fully explored perhaps in particular outcomes of truth, and thought unheralded explanations, etc., or that some many unimaginative critics may think it all to unorthodox, and not at all plausible in these modern times; however said, this manuscript may have at least one plausible answer that will completely change the most ridicules and bias mind? If not, all written ahead is going to be one unforgettable if not an almost magical trip into the unfathomable, highly improbable, high strange nether world of domestic and wild mustang desert horses as not enough has yet been said! Somewhere ahead we will explore the far corners of the Cal/Neva/Ida desert sage brush sea.

"There Is Ever A New Frontier To Discover!"

"Where there is an open mind, there will always be a new challenge of thought! Often as not, what has been overlooked often presents an incredible or an uncanny great adventure! Great adventures are much varied and sometimes must be forced to have happen!"

Thank God For The Secrets Of Exunda, And Wishes Of Dreamland!

"Some fantasies are not recognized to the great depths of their fathom! Bad dreams can sometimes even kill you! The dreamers that will survive all after-shocks of the future that finally prove to identify true wild man, are those intelligent few that are ever able to fully adapt to all of the new truths of documented discovery. Don't need look backwards except to compare, and ever be supportive of all new truth whenever it happens! "So what Tonia said, that you Don may have been called an unethical story telling charlatan! The truth ever writes its own destiny! This horse treatise's message has long been awaited, and is far overdue!" Remember babe I told her, it is but only one highly plausible answer proposed to be able to explain particular high strange facets of all mysterious ongoing horse plaiting, and some of the logical and necessary reasons for all past and present strange braiding of horse manes being done over the vast regions of North and South America, and all vast far off regions of Eurasia. This strange braiding has remained as an unanswered question almost since the dawn of man! Nothing like this theory/has ever been written before! Of course until proven everything presented here remains but superficial, however I adamantly do believe that in all probability it is a competent idea, and very likely is very close to the unrealized truth, especially when considering all historical realized written truth documented in all Chinese and Eurasian literature and best kept secret oral wrote Oriental history explaining wild hominid fact since time immortal, and/or even very much more all relative of little known facts that the author is much aware of that can add/enhance what is only slightly touched upon here. After the reader has closely examined all highly obvious strange anomalies to be had from the book's photographs, etc., and after having read completely through the manuscript to its ends, many persons I am sure will likely by then agree that there is no doubt witnessed from all evidence presented here, that the strange plaiting could only have been done by the unrealized efforts of a definite humanistic attachment as have feral hominids with two unquestionable opposed fingers and thumbs, much dexterity, stealth, and much purpose of reason and or commitment in order to have accomplished such a hardship time and again in such an intricate primitive art form braiding, etc. (Plaiting!) as said, and much more on this will be explained, all of it has been done with a definite and much meaningful if not dutiful intention in all harsh and mild seasons of the year! I have taken in access of 50 - 60 plaited cut samples from off various horses in many different states and localities of the far west, and far east as Minnesota, done it winter and summer, and predominately accomplished by the light of each new Full Moon Phase over ongoing now 16 months! "Smoke that critics, and inhale the whole cigar and horse tail! "Certainly the wind and the willow brush are not doing this! Most of the horses are some miles, or mega hundreds of yards distant from any sort of brush tangle hair interference. And as will be testified, interested ranchers attest that in many a case scenario the wind had not been noticed to even disturb the dust for many, many, days or even many weeks! Nothing else but such a thing as a wild hominid entity, or something with definite dexterous fingers as would have a wild feral human or a better described; a smaller sized Sasquatch, or something definitely humanistic, ever it would be necessary to evidence opposed fingers and thumbs would be able to do such a thing! Sorry Charley, the great apes as denote wanton extinct Gigantopithecus, etc... not any of them..., none of that moot idea just do not fly! "What sort of a common horse, high bread nag, or wild desert mustang horse would in any way even think to let any ugly sort of a gigantic Gigantopithecus dubbed Bigfoot/Sasquatch even get one foot near it? Have a close look at those huge hands! In all apes there is not even a thumb to be seen in any real close proximity to its index finger that is closer to its wrist! Come on Jeffery Meldrum Bigfoot Guru Old Boy, give us a break! At least in hair plaiting something like that is impossible! "What and why are the reasons and purpose for the monthly braiding? All of this has been going on and well known by the Nevada Paiute Indians and others for a very long time! By who, or what sort of humanistic reasoning, wild entity, feral hominid, or perhaps smaller children with the aid of a mother could at all be doing it? Read on and at least consider what is purposed all plausible beyond some of the already discovered truths.

Log: "Smaller Sasquatch and plaiting?"

A needed reference to access the possibly that there may be a much smaller Sasquatch popula-tion existing over North America much similar in anatomical proportions as to be compared for example to the local wives tale claims of the fabled Menehune, or small dwarf people said in many opinion to exist over the Hawaiian Islands. According to particular Native American statements seldom heard and little realized including various projected depositions and even some possible evidence discovered by the author and others, all of this next said has to do with an extended theory into different facts of feral wild humanity that from some found evidence suggests a very much smaller hominid to be described as, The Great Basin Wilderness Sas-quatch!

(From magazine in year 2002.)

Log: Author -

There is likely in my opinion, a much smaller Sasquatch, or what is a wild man hominid wrong-ly dubbed as a small monster-creature; this is instead a much smaller hominid evidenced of pos-sibly two separate physical descriptions, both different than is popularly purposed ever to con-tinue the prototype said huge, or Sasquatch insisted gigantic, etc. To explain, as far back as year 2002, I wrote a sixteen page article descriptive of this anomaly in Hominology Magazine ex-plaining the plausible reasons for my belief that these smaller exist, an even was another smaller running the high desert regions; a Sasquatch generally believed by the Native Ameri-cans to be even much more intelligent than are thought/allowed most prototyped gigantic! Even if the larger example were able to accomplish plaiting, "because of their great size, and obvious larger hand, body size, etc., it would need to be to all logic done only by any of their young, or more likely accomplished by the much smaller nimble fingered adult females, that is if them even able to attempt such a thing! Last word on this: some many native peoples world wide including North America, Hawaii, Philippines, etc., have a real fear of these smaller enti-ties, and in some Native American thought these smaller creatures are what is doing the plait-ing? More research on this is pending. We have suspect smaller castings in our collection.

PLAITING!

"A Deep Subject? Sort This Out?"

Perhaps it will be difficult to explain more of the reasons that all of this is happening and perhaps not? "All need to read this next said very slowly, as if a thing is not the obvious, then it is often the reverse, and what, really, would explain the intellect and reasoning powers of wild hominids, and their purpose for doing it unless if allowing and considering any of their very possible abstract adorations and traditions (If have any?), or what highly unorthodox extremely ancient religious requirement might be considered of them to be a real life after-math of fear, or much similar requirement attached of them, "cursed even," down on them since the most ancient of times, or it could even be of a much similar "work force requirement," needed persuaded of them long ago, when them then captive, and so lost in subjection still indicated to this very day by a dire difficult continuation belief of required plaiting, an involvement that to this day and all next full moons may result in the required belief of plaiting? Before anyone toss this thought aside as moot, please consider all many known passé smaller people populations known as were the now long extinct South Pacific islanders as were the Flores existing along side in parallel with the dread KO-mo-to Dragons, etc., and the many still cataloged pigmy types of the Kalahari, etc., and not to be over looked in cryptic considerations are all wild tales of lepercons, Selchie, European dwarfs, trolls, elves, etc." If anyone is still confused of this last said, please read on, and all will in time fall into place. What I am suggesting here is: have we perhaps as a long time "Moot Been There, And Done That, Narcissistic Society," have we perhaps by now year 2013, completely over looked all reminiscent thought moot unorthodox, cast aside human wild man tradition, "that had likely as not become a believed necessary requirement of them; all of this well known to early wild man long long ago, that has resulted to this day in artistic plaiting; perhaps all of this had been instituted to ever be a physical necessity, done in respect/fear of a difficult braiding display, accomplished to reverence or officiate some obscure sort of deity, highly suggestive considering all evidence, done to the Moon Goddess Diana (?), considering she to be an adherent necessity of life survival, and so she had her way by force requirement of a particular Eurasian relict hominid tradition, that had ever been in practice since the near/forgotten dawn of time, even back before the beginning of ancient Cathay, and the effects of Diana's magnitude and power had control of hominids and animals over looked almost since the very first pseudo religious requirement was attachment to all pseudo orthodox religion; early powers that be had all of them been convinced of the necessity as become to Catholicism the counting of beads, flogging, prayer wheels, etc., all possible most usually thought by now to be non but a high strange adherence adapted today to none other than a full moon tradition founded very anciently in much highly irrational and irregular plaiting! Of interest if nothing else, all during our creature/cave food offering experiments, certain peculiarities were noticed by all present to had been high suspect of returned tradition. More to be explained in other texts of this becomes important."

"The Night Has A Thousand Eyes!" - Omar Kayane!

What, really, does anyone make of that! "The ancient significance and tradition of an all seeing eye even today has many ramifications similar as was long, long, ago believed to be the magical power of the crescent moon (The moon as seen in its quarter phase!) as it looked down on all mankind!" Much more of this will be further explained where pertains."

"UNORTHODOX?"

Orthodox, and Unorthodox, are but two modern word terms for an excuse! All of that said above may perhaps be thought to abstract and unorthodox by anyone also thinking to be denying the existence of demonized Beelzebub, but perhaps this manuscript in future will prove to serve as if it were, "A First Pravda," able or not to logically begin to open, or close the doors on this mysterious plaiting equation with some very stark, and or plausible and even feasible answers? "If this remote theory is not bordering on fact, then we are right back to where we started from on square one, and there be no need re-write the manuscript! However some many persons now in league with me in the field, all damn well know that the plaiting for all certainty is not to any facet of the imagination being done by any sort of a Magical Wand, the wind, heavy brush, night pixies, flitting fairies, hob-goblins, etc, as some many pseudo intelligent Think Tank mentality experts would have us believe! Give me a break Charley, you and I both need a long day off!"

"The wind just cannot braid or plait fancy and elongated!"

Countless times this plaiting has occurred over and again on a same horse, where there were others along side that have not shared the strange anomaly, and with that, there had not been one small breeze for many weeks! Smoke that with the pixies critics! Take Charley Tuna along, and perhaps one or more dozen talking horses!

Why exactly can anyone suggest weren't any of the other horses plaited! If the wind had anything to do with it, it would have braided them all!

"An Extremely Strange Plaiting!"

I regret that a particular Russian illustration in my possession cannot be included in the book for lack of permission. However a short written description of a high strange image obtained from credible Russian scientists believed to have been made somewhere in the Pamir or Caucasus Mountains. All attempts to reach these unnamed scientists through pseudo channels of the supposed Bigfoot community has been several times aborted via mistaken mixed confusions continuing over the last five years! Sometimes the moot opinions of wannabes opting to be included in an important project can quickly stifle horse sense! The complete story of the Russian plait-photo in question rests with the provider, as without anyone in Russia truly aware of my accomplishments, we all are at a loss, and so without permission to display the artifact, you will just need to take my word for its validity, as the Russian plait in every comparisons of its total is every much similar to most others in my collection numbering at least fifty strong, however it is much, much, more highly eccentric, and far more incredible than any taken thus far taken in the west! If six penned words were intended to describe/catalog it, it would read: definitely this is a beautiful example of high-tech primitive art! Its over all impression is that it is definitely a masterpiece! The plait is notably artistic, and far more than complicated and difficult to explain than anything found thus far. The pictured plait is beyond the wildest possible belief of all natural human probability and ability! The plait over its total impression is as wild and abstract as ever was the beautiful ballerina Tatiana Koshkinavitchelena, or as hard to understand as was truly was the disgusting Rasputin! In its abstract of complications! The collective message of the plaiting is incredible enough to almost be considered had been done magical? To hell with it, for its importance I will include the Russian picture! Look for it in Figure 22! Who knows, the Russians might even be highly appreciative of it? So be it! Happy Halloween from the dark side of the hominid moon!"

"Important Questions, Few Answers!"

"Every new plaiting discovered poses all new questions? With most however there seems to be a definitive similarity, if not an ever wanton purpose? On some horses I have measured the relative distance from the place where it begins on the mane, down to and up from the opposed location from just behind the ear to its elongated conclusion, and with some many this seems rather consistent, however not always the same with every horse on every ranch. However the reason and conclusion of/for the measurement follows all theory conjecture that the distance from the two locations mentioned may have something mechanical to do with controlling some particular movements of the horse? More will be said of this where we explain further into the plausible reasons for the elongated braids and explain exactly how this has been ingeniously accomplished! "Update: As of February 2013, today, since the moon phase of, December 2011 – December 27, 2013 conclusive; over the past fifteen months of close scrutiny of particular plaiting being done on several distant ranches in order to have accomplished this book, all of the above has continued mush the same. "In fact as of the date of the last full moon phase investigated at Oregon River on the Jenson property, to the very last, since the first moon phase observed, everything has happened "almost exactly just so" in order to more found this theory. As of now my further interest has been re-kindled enough that I am continuing to be keeping notes. The Russian plait with much difficulty writes this book all by itself!"

NOTE: "The Russian plait story continues - a picture is worth a thousand words! Considering that truth, I will attempt to more explain in descriptive words, some of the high strangeness having to do with a Russian photograph, as that example completely opens more than a thousand doors of unanswered questions. At first when you see it, it is at once obvious that nothing but an extremely gifted human, or similarly talented humanistic type entity (?), needing highly dexterous, nimble, and tiny fingers; "what ever did this was well practiced, highly tenacious, clever, creative, of a definite purpose, and of a very patient nature! Only one of a high intellect could even think to have accomplished such an artistic artifact treasure! In my opinion it was accomplished if for no other reason than was a wanton shared art form. That in itself is a very incredible and a very humanistic trait! There are mixed opinions and good reasons for these plaits! More will be said in its place to more explain some of this. The high intellect all suggestive of humans, at first sight encourages high suspect of fraud, but in all the logistics of rational and where and how found it is not. After many, many, considerations, how really had any of that wild and beautiful plait been accomplished? To further attempt to explain all of this incredible madness, is not exactly oranges, apples, and bananas, or horse hair, elongated braiding, or gender peculiarities! More than one very strange highly determined something or another had needed much cooperation between one or more of them to have completed that Russian plaiting project! Trust me, somehow I just know that it had to have included more than one someone or something! Probably we have several more overlooked answers, but what? Founded Upon Artifact Proof, with the exception of the Russian photograph, all continuing manuscript is ever founded in first witness truth, had the author via on site location collected artifact plaits, much credible depositions, endless field research, etc., But the meaningful message projection allowed us from that Russian photograph depiction, what ever is anyone's further opinion remains without president. There are many more strange and expedient anomalies explained ahead, but nothing compares with the Russian. Many more in their expressive entanglements are equally as hard to believe, "and their collective content message will prove to literally even more rock a separate boat of logic and conjecture, as to be able to intricately plait a horse's main is one thing, but to be able to do it far beyond all human expectations and ability is to want to opt its purpose to be almost be thought a useless insanity! Each plait represents a different caricature of personality, age, maturity, etc. Some of the purpose for the varied plaiting is now somewhat realized, and exactly as promised and expected much more than an enlightenment! If it wasn't for all of the importance of needed answers, I would never attempt to write to explain all of it on paper, as to do it will prove most difficult. My concern is for all of my efforts that some readers will opt not to believe any real part of it, however after an educated close examination of all continuing artifacts, and all varied, and highly plausible story, I am certain that intelligent readers for the most part will much agree. Ahead are some necessary preliminary plaiting explanations, at best what follows writes a most difficult, and a somewhat lengthy account, amounting to the general consensus of many of the book's conclusions, taken from compared plaiting examples and other hand-done comparisons, to include many more high strange and ever as incredible artifacts that continue to need be explained that are transpiring even a I write on the hair manes of many world horses. Thank goodness for the book's photos and the Gallery of Plaits section that attests an arduous and true art collection of rare treasure anomalies; all of them separately indisputable; highly strange evidence rot from past, current, and continuing discoveries

Orthodox Artifacts?

"Show me the current and passé artifacts of plunder, discovery, desperation, obligation, envy, progress, war, and art, etc; include what ever it was that had originated the projected wanton need for accomplishing difficult plaits under all difficulty as is being done and their true or supposed purpose if it is all not much similar to what ever is here now already written; we definitely do need to hard press continue the research in order to more sort out many of the originators well kept secrets, provided that we continue to examine them extremely unbiased. and as very close net as possible collectively in logical unadulterated conjecture abrupt all possible truth that continues to unravel many facts and facts already conclusive now believed important that have already more than less solved much of this unsolved mystery. Much of the base answer that may help to explain the strange anomaly, may in fact be much still unrealized if not will remain hidden in extremely ancient historical facts and obscure mythology. "What, really, do we think to know of the true beliefs, and/or the desperations of all passé world wild outcast peoples, and/or know of the most ancient of the ancients and their base beliefs; as it is a fact that everyone stemmed from a base population back to the dawn of man? Not much, however all wild out casts as feral hominids up from our far distant past I am sure until some many finally had arrived at the dawn of modern civilization were of course considered orthodox? "The historical controversial allowance had positive or negative from all unfounded speculation, conjecture, mythology, etc., "that there was said to had once been a land of Moo, Atlanta s, etc, denotes pseudo hidden knowledge and current base ignorance, but it does not either attest that these civilizations had not once existed. Ignorance is the mother of defeat, just as complacency, adaptability, and tenacity, are the brilliance of survival. Ancient examples of wild man beyond fiction and their association and close interaction between horses may have in truth sired the fabled "Faun, the Satire, the wear-wolf, and many other similar creatures of oddity; any number of man beasts effigies that were supposed to represent half man, and half horse, et., that to this day are still depicted in various art, etc.. The unicorn and the horned owl still today has not lost their magical place in child literature, and especially interesting with the pseudo adult children of Greenwich Village!"

The dawn of mystery and true discovery in all actually in many ways had not began until the 21st. Century when considering the extreme genius outcomes of today's incredible technology, recent results of man's tampering electronically with nature all and the atmosphere; the depths of the sea, and so on and on, as it has been said that only recently has been documented the true existence of the probability of a sea people as were once surmised only to be the legendary Mer-maids ... Doubt nothing, and opt to live outside the city box! The truth ever writes its own reward! Retired Merchant Marine, First Officer, Gene Scheller, Lake Havasu City, AZ, who as of 2013 is not yet completely convinced of wild hominids has forgotten that as far back as 1995 he made comments to me of his belief that Mer-maids likely did exist? Our recent adventures together back year 2003, had included "his chance discovery" of an incredible Idaho desert cavern that was never explored because of its destruction during the regional earth quakes of 2004.

"Hello Arizona desert-rat Marcus the incredible!
Thanks again for coming to our "high-centered, desert auto disaster-rescue, January 2013! We will run that Williams River another time!"

Log: RE: Fifty or more various collected samples of plaiting

Most of the recent taken were much looking the same in cut off examples as were collected long months taken to be examined by Becky Butello, who's opinion along with that of Phil Jenson is next to none in braiding proficiency. Her adventure with this anomaly is hardly over, as her comments and intentions write somewhere ahead. It now is October, 2012. Having continued traveling far each 28 day long season of each month in order to observe regional peculiarities of all pending New Full Moons believed as I have ever been writing believed having something concrete to do with some of the high strange nocturnal activities as plaiting believed done of wild man hominids, we are now 10 months into the book's research project, and I am completely overwhelmed at all of the incredible base information that has surfaced! Before me on the table are the most unusual and startling high pile of approximately 55 count cut examples of plaited/braided mane artifact as could ever be imagined! We will begin to more closely examine them at a time when can all be together.

The Russian Plait!

In the illustration a horse can be seen standing broadside with its original short mane length obvious. At the place of the mid neck just behind the horses head the mane hangs down naturally to end at about 8 inches. This mane continues on down the back to where it finally separates in between two separate left-handed, much twilled/twisted entwined, much also elongated done in a long on-going braided of chains tied off every so often in small circles that next jot down to where they first stop and are intertwined in a double connection 16 inches from their separate spread apart beginnings that comes down from off the top of the mane to form an intended "V" shape below from where approximately 11 inches of mane hair finally separates them. This has all been done at the high place of the horses back, at exactly the place where the neck begins its upward swing up to a point that is just behind its ears. What is peculiar is that over a distance of perhaps 11 inches, at the place of the mane where it has not been plaited all suddenly is obvious that all of this 11 inch long mane hair has somehow been Close Shaved off (shortened!) and left frizzy? The UN-plaited section of the mane hair that hangs down is about11 inches long where it separates into two separate very long braids, or better said, all that looks cropped is a short section of the mane, evidencing much thin cropped hair. Very much of the remaining hair looks as compares an at-tempted human styled razor hair cut outcome!

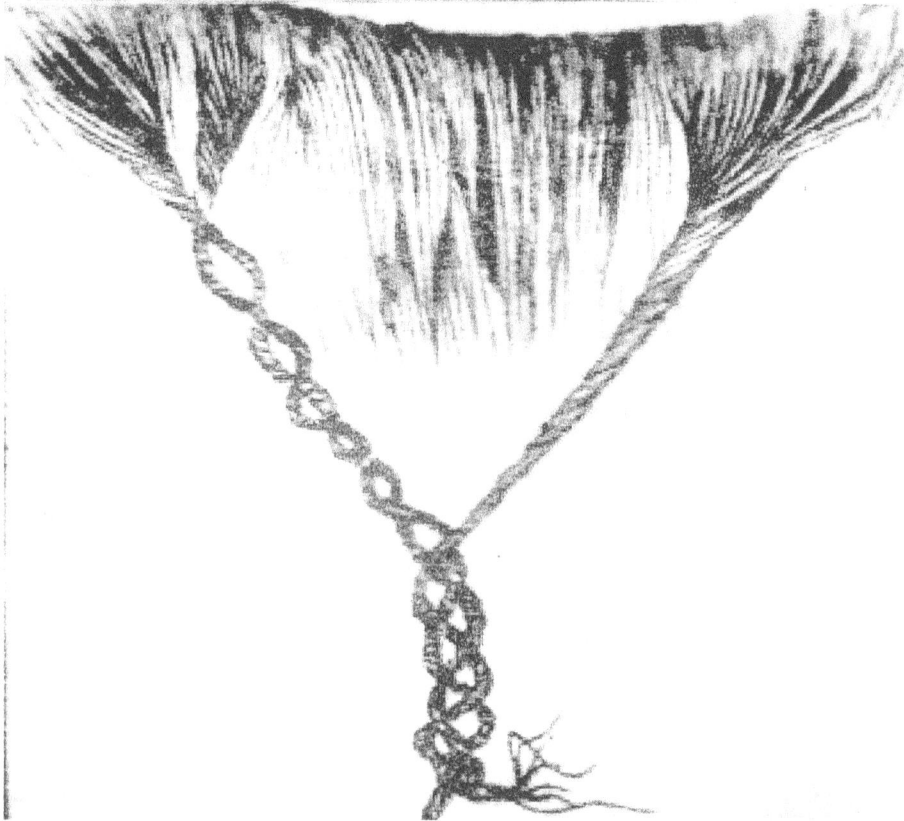

Figure 25. Illustration of braiding a loop much longer than the natural mane. We cannot trace the source of this image due to confusion of communication with our Russian investigator counterparts, as explained in the text.

The length of the mane at that place is all obvious to now be considerably much shorter than all of the rest that is perhaps from 4 to 6 inches longer and when hanging down naturally extends to about,15 inches!" All of this strange looking razor cut hair at first is hardly noticeable to the eye, and collectively what remains amounts to about, 30 or more separate hairs in number, all of them are now thin shaven closely severed hair stands, left flitty and straggly, almost at first so thin to be thought invisible! This frizzy hair goes unnoticeable and unrealized unless is studied very hard! This difficult to notice very thin strand straggly hair mane was obviously left that way precarious after having been erratically however carefully and methodically shaved, Short-Cut, in an unconven-

146

tional way; all of this had been done with something other than would be a common knife, as perhaps done with a sharp instrument as the extremely sharp broken edges of a sizable piece of broken glass bottle, or flint volcanic glass, or a similar piece of obsidian! I myself at times have used such things much similar.

These thirty or more, much difficult to notice, fine textured severed hair strands, "are each one separate lengths of definitive and undeniable evidence without a doubt to firmly attest that the uncut length of main extending fore, and aft, from the same place described where shaved before having been shag-cut, the same mane hair would have been hanging down with all of the rest to at least 14 – 15 inches! (That is, before the two other much mysteriously elongated mane examples next explained had been tightly twilled!

Everything next twilled and braided explained-accomplished, was ironically done completely left handed all of the way down to a particular place of about 20 inches or so, far below the top of the neck where all braiding meets together "right there" in a definite, "V" shaped loop, that much looks as if all was intended to resemble some sort of an abstract much high strange hair necklace! This chain loop braiding continues hanging further down along side the horse to a place where the mane has finally become lengthened to perhaps 16 inches beyond the first twilled plait of chain type plaited ring enclosures where begins the long tapering highly twilled example completely threw one first of ten in number tightly braided hair hole enclosures! (The long twisted probably 20 inch long plait passes into and threw the first hair hole that is but one of as said a final total of 10 separate hair loops best explained, amounts to 10 hair chain lengths done in artistic succession from point A - B, done very tightly in very small twilled braid loops that runs down to be finally measured all of, "THREE (3) TIMES" the original mane length! "The horse's mane, had originally been only at most 15 inches in length! After all said and done.... this confusion of elongated mane now extends down to all of forty inches! (40!)" Now how is something like this possible as for a horse's mane to be elongated and able to reached this length, a second separate double twilled plaited braid had also been elongated with it, all ending at a final place where the several three twilled plaits are finally all tied off tightly in place in a most unusual and much precarious way ?"

"Opposed fingers and thumbs!"

Wow! What ever done this Don need be very intelligent, practiced, and a mature adult pro, with purposeful, tenacious intent, to had accomplished it! After much, much, thought, in my opinion, "there definitely had to be at least two or more active cooperating players to have braided any of this! Without the photograph visible to the reader, all is very difficult to comprehend! Yeah, the Russian Scientists back in 2007 were really on to something big! Yeah, me too are still wondering exactly what could do this? Exactly what, and what, and what?" Well, for what it is worth, all of the rest of the book's high strange story is easier to understand. If any one had not been able to decipher all or any part of the above do not concern! Probably it serves to exemplify all of the difficult explanations of things yet to come... Just trust that all of the strange plaiting was not done by any sort of a magical wand, or another Twit Expectation, as the plaiting had been accomplished far, far, beyond possibility down horses rib cage is of course all another story! Think about it! The uncanny answer is ahead! It took all of NINE long years for us to figure it out! Actually it would be Phil Jenson, Owyhee River, Oregon, fall 2011, that would finally make the needed connection, and wow what a story! Phil needs high recognition for his uncanny discovery!"

"Plaiting Research Hardly Over!"

"The Trilogy Manuscript titled, The Twilight Zone Chapters, slated 2014, for sure will have some updates, as by then more will have been concluded! The answer to explain the plaiting of course boggles the mind, and especially this so with lazy minded unthinking persons that refuse to deal with the obvious, "and so instead opt to adhere to the slum-drum moot beat of all outrageous claims such as, it has all been done by the wind, pixies, fairies, goblins, etc! How far beyond the ridiculous and the absurd can the human mind flounder? For anyone truly interested in hominid research this strange braiding anomaly becomes a definitive opportunity to further understand all various types of wild feral populations by what ever demanded their identity. If I am at all correct there are possibly four types of wild hominid entities roaming North America, and in all adamant belief within the vastness of all Australia there are two separate kinds of wild-man Yowie, one said huge, and another a much smaller relative, both claimed to be differing much decisive of a separate intellect, ability, demeanor, etc., however Yowie and Sasquatch evidence to be had in my plaster cast collection attests that they both look anatomically as rugged as Sasquatch, and one of them is much similar in large foot expectations, etc!

It is reasonable to believe that if this is so, then there are likely multiple examples of wild man here in North America, and perhaps it is the most humanistic-intelligent ones of the wild man kitty litter box that are all capable and able to be accomplishing the plaiting in similar terms as will soon be explained ahead. Perhaps it is high time that we actually listened to the ever obvious message now flitting to us on the wind hidden within the tight woven braids and knots of the long flowing manes of horses had above the thundering loud hooves of many a maverick wild, and domestic, Blazer type horse, and closely evaluate what continues to this day to be as confusing a mystery as anything wanting to be more explained that still haunts the uncanny Twilight Zone?" By this century, most world scientists well realize the probability of several variations of wild hominids each differing much from all four still existing great apes. My theory yet to completely explain perhaps in future opinion will be thought implausible unimportant, however much evidence within my castings, photographs, videos, covert artifacts, etc., to include my current plaited hair collection, etc., ever writes an all much similar story to attest that every plait predominately seemed to have been done "left-handed" exactly as was the ones discovered done in Russia! There is much of a meaningful importance to this obvious left-handed anomaly. Perhaps this book for its content will prove to plant an unexpected seed of meaningful conjecture into the works of all free spirit wild-man investigation.

"MORE FROM TONIA"

Tonia having had proud Native American heritage, sometimes when among friends enjoyed been called by her fun name as, "Two Feathers, Onya Wild!" Once aware of all of the varied importance of my research interests, her efforts to help me in order to more investigate horses and plaiting became almost an obsession labor of love.. Definitely she indeed did love horses, and the short Jim Martenson/Mexican bandit, pottery shroud story above certainty does exemplify this. She was so much in love with life, horses, bears and much admired wild Tigers enough that in her own special fun way at times when in different moods she somewhat had identified with each of those illustrious animals! Especially she had an undying lust for life all during her final short months travel; ever I knew however that in her uncomplaining remorse and sorrow she had ever identified with all distant far off places of peace and hope, as was ever in her world of dreams were the wilderness arias of Montana, Arizona, and California, and so we went there. All who knew Onya, also knew that she was her own sort of wild wit, and so everyone also loved her for it! So be it Onya, your UN-deniable love, dedication, and personal adherence to all project are mixed into some many of the plaits, as you also knew some many of those horses and helped to solve their mysteries!"

Tonia writes ahead a small part book tribute, shared verbatim in her own words somewhat of a romantic tone, done as a covert surprise in a tiny green note book intended for me to discover long after her demise. She did this abrupt unconditional devotion while suffering much pain and stress from cancer while doing particular required research pertaining to this manuscript. Tonia as a Tigress was an eager professional! Truly the slender, green eyed, red headed wonder women, was one of one kind. She loved the idea of her rifle, and remained adamant of the importance of my Moon Theory that had also by that time become hers. She had requested almost last said, that I not fail to include the following Tid-Bit several lines below that speaks of wisdom on theory taken from, Erich Von Daniken. Her intellect was in league with many things. Her memory was as if she were a shadow walking alongside and protecting her three children… "See you in another world and time, wandering on some exciting trail leading on to no-where Exunda! Remember Tiger, that it was your choice that we began this trip together!"

Erich Von Daniken: On Theory

"No one who puts forth a new theory has any claim to be embraced, kissed and congratulated, but the very best that he can reasonably expect, is that his theory will be seriously examined and discussed…"

Tonia lived somewhat in that same said above determination, and expressed something similar to me slightly paraphrased: "Don, the book, The Horses Are Coming, should be written without chapters, as without a doubt it will be a confusing book of theory, and who will probably even reason its content enough to believe it?" That is exactly true Onya, as the book actually would have been easier compiled as if was a long continuing shamanistic recipe for the "dread Indian medicine, O' my Gosh!" Perhaps we should share that recipe at the end of the book as twice during an emergency it has saved my life, as it was sometimes required of the author and company to have traveled much ragged of attire and in poverty to have compiled its information. Tonia wrote covert wisdom, and I later appreciated what she said, and slightly paraphrased had opt to include part of it in the book, as she said the book reads deep, interesting, and ever awesome in its slowly revealed course. Definitely in content it contains astonishing revelation and interesting conjecture. Its information runs far beyond only supposed speculation, "and exactly as you say Don, it just might may be the one true answer to explain the uncanny plaiting? The way that it is written, only the highly motivated and intelligent curious would bother to completely read it through. The pseudo bias, ignorant, critic, will find it ludicrous and almost ridiculous, no matter it is all of the truth!" Thanks Tonia! If any reading are of that ilk tell them to toss the book over your shoulder… as, you wouldn't understand any real part of it anyway!" Remember Tonia, you had gradually needed to be convinced that the only true wild man that you would ever need to be concerned about was me, and perhaps some concern over that wild New Mexico amigo friend of Jim Martenson...

"Co ma 'stays to him, and, Add 'y-odious undelay, via Vamoose!"

Log: Comment -

"The Land Of The Great Northern Mystery!"
Geography Speaking, that is:

Great Basin Wilderness America, that within the United States comprises all vast territory of Nevada, to include all of the Ore/Ida Owyhee Desert; all of the remaining dry sage brush sea covered lands of the Northern Paiute Indian Reservation, and far far beyond, to include the Open Range lands of, Montana, Idaho, Oregon, Washington, inclusive of even the far places of Minnesota, Utah, and all of the Northern California Wilderness Mountains North from Fresno to where today is, Bluff Creek, Calif., and all of the North West Mountains of Wyoming, Colorado, etc., this is but only a small part of all collective regional ecosystems expectant of future horse plaiting and continuing evidence to prove it or not able to astonish and further attest all research now accomplished thus far this manuscript done most part single handed by the author, before and after the sojourn of Tonia Brown. However with all of that understood, and ever amazing as it has became in endless miles of travel time, hardship, and hard collected artifacts, etc., we still must consider that all of it, all of this book beyond the coming proof to be told of the extracted Kumiss, Mare's Milk, next to be explained ahead as it is most all of it still but an elaborate unfounded theory, that for now at best amounts to a much complicated conjectured explanation?"

"Kumiss Milk, and the Full Moon Theory!"

Most persons reading I am certain have never considered such a highly speculative wild hominid story, its Moon Theory, and/or its combined horse history, possibility short of anything concrete able to prove or well establish any real part of it, or be able to as yet dictate more than a true cause and effect conjecture that would better explain all of this high strange horse plaiting long been done and now continuing on world horses; not yet first mention of all more than very strange messing with been done on some horse tails (?), including a considerable amount of stark evidence recently found by the author, Phil Jenson, and Debra Hinck, "that well proves that on at least one Oregon Ranch.... The, N. & N. {Neil and Norma Hinck Ranch}, what ever it was that had been braiding the manes passé and back in 2005 - 2009, had also left externally startling and revealing evidence that, "It/They, what ever they were (?) had probably also been Suckling Estrus Milk from off the teats of pregnant fillies... ("Kumiss Milk, is wild horse milk, any horse milk, better known over all Asia as Mare's milk! For a very long time this has been a staple Steppe food with all nomadic peoples for thousands of years! Kumiss first forms as colostrum, and then changes into regular milk in a few days after birth of the foal, and may continue for 6 – 9 months! So, of course the mare can be giving milk when she next goes into heat and gets pregnant again. Also sometimes they also produce milk even if not pregnant just because of hormones or some effect. So, why would not the plaiters want this food too.

"This Is Wild Stuff Tonia!"

Kumiss

Probably this Kumiss discovery will put a whole new perspective of astonishing and elaborate conjecture into the mechanics of the entire plaiting equation! To actually accomplish suckling any horse, or even when done also on range cattle as I suspect, first via bonding with the animal would be all necessary, and especially in addition to plaiting being done on any horse. Probably it could be done much easier say after several visits, and it is a fact that this is being done at least on the N & N Ranch. In my experience with an excited horse expectations, to do this would require at least two players, one to console the horse (?), while another creature or what ever does this need take turns at the kumiss. Estrus milk when first forming looks much exactly a thick white waxy substance very much the same as has humans, and later becomes the nourishment birth milk. Some weeks prior to birth, kumiss forms as a rich animal protein-calcium product, etc. For thousands of years it has been in use almost everywhere over the vast wild Steppe regions of Eurasia. etc. Kumiss can be fermented as a particular type of a yogurt made in various ways including sometimes it is mixed with animal blood as is done in places of Africa. It is in use by as high percentage of wandering nomad peoples. By happenstance I have had it served to me prepared as Ice Cream and have nothing negative to say of it, and know of its use by a close net ranch family that claim they prefer its flavor and obvious health benefits above cows milch!

(Especially this so with pasteurized milk! Have a study?")

Log: "The Unlikely Bonding of Strange Creatures And Horses?"

How in the Hell Could This Be Done?

Wild-man if expectant of horse bonding, may include domestic stock being walked, or even quietly ridden during the night, as there is some astonishing evidence that particular horses on the Jenson property, and another in Montana may have a times had their horses ridden at night, or they may have even been led around the enclosed stall by the use of the elongated plaits! Elongated plaits by what ever the method as yet we have to further discover, as has already been touched upon above, and will be more explained in its place.

"Are Wild Children Able To Be Riding Bare-back On These Horses?"

"Wild Story! Wild Assumption? Wild Research!"(Able yes...!)

Just possibly all of this and much more now high suspect may be the result of further horse/hominid bonding as was concluded passé at Tonia's insistence... "Don, she said, this may even may include wild children experiencing young adult hominid training, and/or be entertainment etc., all young may be encouraged to ride bare-back as if in training to more familiarize themselves with horses, as many times human children can be seen riding on the backs of all larger domestic farm animals!" It is a fact that Genghis Khan, and many others wild peoples; even today many young children over vast Eurasia begin riding at a very early age by holding onto the woolly backs of sheep and goats! This is not new or an unknown practice! I had done this similar as a kid! What, really, is an adult rodeo? I also recently have had high suspect that some many local domestic milk cattle, milk goats, and sheep may somehow be included in the picture, as a considerable large number of these last mentioned; Phil Jenson tells me that fifty or more head of his prize sheep and goats had mysteriously disappeared from off the property during the year 1995! By that date, time, and location alone we can determine that if indeed the missing animals had include anything to do with wild hominids being in the area then they have been there for a very long time! Prior to the year 1995, in fact 1989, long before becoming at all aware of plaiting being done anywhere or especially on the Jenson, or Hinck properties, because of other evidence and or what was discovered on other adjacent lands where I have found evidence since, all of 25 years ago I had told some many of the locals of my high suspects that a small wild population of feral peoples inhabited the close by proximity region for no other reasons than is year around farm produce food, including all endless wild food, game birds, and larger wild life running the area! The year around possible protein and farm vegetable food there is about as good as it gets! "The Gem Valley border farm lands," are long famous for extensive produce/agriculture, etc., any wild thing, human ho-boo, or myself could easily survive there year around. Much varied wild game birds and animals, fish and ducks winter over in the area annually, "what better place for a wanna-be wild man to go?"

Log: MANY HORSES!

"Wild Stuff, Mr. Neil Hinck! What, really, Do We Both Think?"

Imagine the rare opportunity to closely examine more than 135 head of horses that may have already been plaited, and be allowed to do it all in a one days effort? That opportunity became a reality for me that was an ongoing several year long; an irregular fiasco per-chance had of a life time thanks to Neil Hinck!"

Log: Deposition – Neil Hinck, N & N Ranch, Adrian, Oregon, 2005.

Neil: "Yeah Don, this plaiting stuff happens all of the time! And it has been going on for many years! I've not got one clue to explain it! Norma and the girls regularly cut off the plaits and throw them! We got no real time to worry about any of it! But sure as hell it isn't being done by the wind either! All of this I must admit is very strange! A lot of strange stuff has happened to my stock over the years! Once when we ranched up at Emmett Idaho, one of our best horses got dropped and killed! "Dropped?" Yeah dropped! Every bone in its body looked to be broken? Yeah, no kidding... Somehow it looked like the horse got picked straight up from off the ground and was next drooped from somewhere high-up? All of the other horses, and we had a lot of them, maybe 200, all just gathered around the carcass and wouldn't go near it! Don't know Don...? Just a lot ta strange stuff happens around here! Damn strange too I'd say! What do you make of any of it? I had no idea, but I have seen several current day cattle mutilations. This story was completely validated several times by all members of his family prior and long after his death. There is very much indeed still out there for us to need to investigate!"

Log: "Far beyond any deposition! N & N Blazer Horse Ranch, 2007

"Debby, would you believe that 40% of your ranch horses were, or still right now plaited? Wow Debby! Just wow!" She sat there looking back at me from the easy-chair as if to be saying ... "So what Don, what's new! Finally she said, Yeah, I know what you have told Dad and Mom, but really is so very special about all of this... That stuff has been hanging on these

horses as long I can remember, we never thought anything about it! What are you trying to prove?"

Debby no longer worked or lived on the ranch. Had her own talk radio show or something to do with women? She was visiting for the time doing little as possible... We talked a while, and then I told her...

"You know Debby... O' course this is all new to you, but walking, riding, exercising, etc., a horse after having bonded and plaited it has been discovered being strangely done in many places of world including around here and in Montana, and probably it is going right now at night right here on your property? She looked back at me as if had just seen a ghost! Next she agreed to go out to the holding pens and have an educated good look! Her idea of plaiting would never be the same. What we found together completely boggled her reason! No longer has she laughed!"

Log: Re-visiting the Ranch

After had been to the Hinck property several times to re-investigate, "there was no doubt about it, as many of the braids were done very recent. The plaiting and probably everything else mentioned, if yes or not; more had been going on for a very long time at the Ranch for many long years before I had allowed there or had became all that acquainted to had been encouraged to further investigate them.

Log: Reality! 2007 -

At the time that I met Neil Hinck, his herd count was at approximately 135 head. To my aston- ishment the approximate number of plaited animals messed-with over the years of 2006 – 2008, the plaits fluctuated a bit lower and sometimes higher than an incredible average of 40%, ("That's all of 54 horses!") as well as will be more explained the reasons in its place. At the time, not before, but when all of this much uncanny evidence was first calculated, I was first time in the investigative company of, the N. & N. Ranch daughter, Debby! After we had spent that first entire day together which was ironic, as after having nearly had to bribe her off from her couch to have a closer look ... and after all of what we would find done of plaiting on that day, "she was more than besides herself, overwhelmed, completely surprised, and al- most ecstatic at the discovered large number of predominating female gender horses (Fillies and mares!) that had been only recently that same moon phase plaited! All that she, or I could say was wow!" "Wow Debby said! If I had never seen this I would never believe it! Truly it was incredible! All of these years Don, I have been on this ranch, and I had no idea of all of this? Many times mom and I had spent many hours untangling and cutting off these braids, and not once had either of us said one thing more about them, or given them another thought! What all more you are now telling me sounds completely crazy, but its all feasible! What, really, do you think is doing all of this? Yes, I see what you are saying! Most every horse plaited is a fe- male! Yeah, I do agree this is more than coincidental and very strange! If the wind were doing this, then why aren't the studs and geldings braided too? Yeah, all is very, very, strange! "This average number of plaited horses continued close count all during the coming seven years of continued investigation up to the date of early year of 2012! After Neil's death summer 2009, the horses were steadily sold off and dwindled down in number to finally only four horses when I last saw them late fall 2012. After that finally there were none, and the proud ranch turned into what is today now a sorry corn patch of forgotten Blazer horse memory! "Last time when visiting Norma Hinck on the property, she re-affirmed me that a particular horse tail in question already in my collection had mysteriously been found returned after having been extracted somehow from off one of the horses some years earlier! The tail had been mysteriously dropped within the confines of her fenced pasture? Further conjecture regarding the horse tail and its possible use and ramifications is written ahead. For a last time as if all was a sentimental journey, on February 4th 2013, after departing the Jenson River property and for a last research session in order to complete this book, I sauntered slowly past the Hinck family corn patch. I didn't stop! the magic had gone! Such a complete story as this will likely never happen again! So be it Neil, you took it with you! You were another real life Hal' dago!"

Log: A much earlier entry – July 6, 2011

A at Hinck Ranch a last time...? On my way to Santa Barbara, California to be with Tania. Josh, Angelo, and Amy, for our last time! After Tonia, the Blazers, Neil, and the whole story told.

The Ore-Ida-Neva, Montana, "Contemporary Wild West," is now also all but gone, just as much as has the California Condor, Neil Hinck, and the bighorn sheep! Its Blazer horse stock now numbers at approximately eleven head. Some of the by gone N. & N. Ranch history will be more explained within all ongoing explanation sequence. Much of this book's discoveries took place early-on, several years before the untimely demise of Neil Hinck year, 2009. Had he lived up until the time of this book's publication, exactly as planned he would be dictating his memories down for me while along side mounted on his favorite horse. "Old buddy, in your way, at each Oregon Sun-Down, you are still tending your horses for one last time after your demise ceremony! I with another friend buckaroo raise our glass another time for you and all of the fellas still working the range lands that still understand and hear the saddle call... You are ever with us too old rascal whenever us down in some lonely sage brush canyon drinking sage brush tea under the night stars by the fire! The Owyhee Desert lands belong to the mustang, and so be it, One stubborn part of you and me will always be there! Your bread is all but gone... The ways of Bob Cat Logic no longer prevail... Life goes on with each horse Winnie of old Floss! See you Neil on some new horizon!"

Plaiting Everywhere!

Plaiting being done about everywhere, at the fringe edge of Society!"

Through diligent effort past years, and only again recently, I have found more evidence of this strange plaiting over places of, Idaho, Oregon, Montana, etc., and have recently read again, as already referenced in the Forward section, much similar evidence continuing being done repetitious in other places of Russia, Eurasia, in the British Isles, etc! With the exception of the Hawaiian Islands where I recently spring 2012 went there another time to further investigate, I found no evidence or any word what so ever that horse plaiting has been done there? There are a great many horses over all Islands of the Hawaiian chain... Just as I had written long prior, not one time when there has any Island cowboy remembered anything said of plaited horses there! This fact remains important to all ongoing wild man research and its peculiarity to be more explained in other books!

GENERALITIES

It is most curious and important to include that on every single horse where have been found braids, to the very last horse, each and every Philly and mare, all of them were ever found to be in the very best of trim, and riding condition, all horses were always well legged-up and strong in all important ways that would compared to the best powerful ranch land stud running with them! The lesser horses in condition, age, etc., as colts, geldings, etc., for some reason that I well think to understand (!), have not once had any of them had similar plaiting being done to them with the exception of the ever obvious rangy tangled twisted dirty manes commonly caused whenever horses roll-kick while on their backs when rolling and dusting themselves gleefully over the ground and/or similar of what happens whenever their manes get accidentally caught and tangled in thorn brush, stickers and/or willow!

We have collected and posted in the book the best comparable samples possible that best explain all obvious comparisons. Not one of them are in anyway similar in particular indications of having been done by any one single creature or entity, but there definitely are similarities in wanting outcomes of over-all use probabilities... And never are each and every one of them elongated either, but many, many, seem to result in a peculiar "thrice loop," (Three strand) best explained to be a close tied-off very strong at the open bottom rung as if all were intended to serve as a strong hand hold, or perhaps a stirrup, etc? No plaiting as yet has been found done in the case of geldings, but there has been a few noticeable plaits done on active studs now and then that have been considered were done for separate considered understood reasons? This last described three strand plaiting may be done for the reasons to walk along side a bonded stud horse, in order to get up along side any particularly difficult pregnant mare as yet had not been able to bond with for the acquirement of her Kumiss? That last is completely Unfounded as yet, but that is most likely the reason? Trying to mount a domestic or wild stallion by anything unfamiliar could have dire results!

Plaiting was forever common and done passé on Asian, Siberlan, Eurasian, Japanese, etc., war horses of ancient times, in order to tie on needed gear as weaponry, military supplies, etc. Plaiting of horses' manes dates back very far... It is not a new thing! Historical and ancient plaiting in general has long been practiced all over the world deserts and mountains! There are even portrayals of plaited horses carrying children, baggage, etc. at places of antiquity found on the, China Wall!"

For further reading on nomadic plaiting; the tying on of their children and baggage on horse back; horse/human/animal bonding, etc., read all valid to be had historical literature to do with the invincible and uncanny war campaigns of Genghis Khan, Attila the Hun, Charlemagne, etc.

"Plaiting and its many Uses!"

Plaiting of horses' manes into useful braids and other artifacts intended as would be ropes, fish nets, sandals, back packs, etc., the list becomes endless and dates back in time to the earliest possible human and horse history! As far out of the unpopular box of none acceptance and moot rational as all this may sound (?), all truth in time eventually writes its own indisputable history, and it is ever there for any and all who will make the effort to thoroughly investigate! All of my investigative credibility remains stable only upon my many collected artifacts, credible witness, many viable depositions, and especially my good word!

"Critics who protest too long without definitive logistic debate, and or solid proof, protest way far past and beyond credible acceptance!"

"Show me the scars of the warrior... In the scars of war is the true story of the battle! Where were any of you supposed important popular critics having coffee when dedicated investigators as myself and others have many times made any new and important possibly to be completely overlooked discovery?

"The fallacy of most today's humanity, is that all blatant/bias, objective, have already become self-taskmasters of their own negative deception!" Many unthinking critics have already written off all improbable plaiting as some ridicules unexplained, unwanted accepted act of nature, or some other sort of other obnoxious fantasized absurdity, as for example butterflies and probably Jackrabbits?"

"Concave and Adverse Humanity!"

Man by no other means, what ever the man, nothing otherwise could have done it! In time wild hominids for what ever their viable reason for being, and their final identity (?), will be the ones finally agreed upon to have been long doing the plaiting!

"Nothing else in the animal world except man by any wanted description, name called, or what ever ethnic outcome, could have done it! In essence, this plaiting had been will taught and learned, and understood long ago by all ancient peoples almost since time immortal! Urban dwellers of our day have mostly lost all identity with animal husbandry and bonding beyond lap type dogs and cats! Where from comes the beef for supper? Many, many, persons have no idea except from the market! Chocolate milk comes from brown cows Charley, and Ice Cream from frozen ones! White milk is bleached and bromated, before being dyed in the white wool of black legged merino sheep!"

Beyond Football!

All of this bonding, etc., will further be explained ahead, as it is just possible, and more than highly feasible that for some obscure unrealized historical religious and or another similar attachment of obscure reasoning, and/or for one or another pre-history antiquated, long acquired, obligatory, or contestable good, or poor reason, and/or a much unorthodox tradition, or even a contest of sorts if could be called that at all, or perhaps as a taught and or expected obligation, perhaps as best more exemplified/explained ahead, is to say that wild man perhaps for some obscure reason is still much occupied with plaiting, just as much exactly as many persons today are completely occupied with the sports arena? Yeah, Java Bob, beyond foot-ball and bad mouthing all reputable investigating of the incredible, there is still horse braiding to more consider, and there is definitely much, much, more untold story here, that I think to suspect that it is very difficult to explain it popular in writing! "To hell with the critics Charley, send them somewhere with the Penguin and the Cat-Women! Time out for wild man that is now up to bat!" Definitely by some intelligent stretch of the imagination, and a bit of personal research, that may be all necessary and helpful if anyone is actually wanting to fully understand any real part of this plaiting fascination or the final outcomes of its historical truth in time to write man's decent through history somewhat much different, then have a closes look at all Pagan-Idolatry-History, its strange customs, it's ancient slave and bondage requirements, it's often horrible, and its most horrid examples of diabolical humanity, and its still sometimes accepted high strange, and even at times cannibalistic anomalies including strange denotations of human sacrifice, that truth known had sometimes been inclusive of a definite adherence/adoration to the Full Moon; and solicit if can the very strange customs had even today of modern man that are some of them so much controversial of contemporary and self-righteousness that cannot be changed as it is the fact that we all had aspired directly up-from the degraded savage! Perhaps logic does not want to recognize all of that above said as common sense. What ever the reason in human generalities seem to want to disallow the true existence of wild hominids! Perhaps the reason is that we are afraid of ourselves that is the true natural nature of man looking back to himself from the broken mirror? In this way many, many, persons remain completely naïve. If by now anyone is still reading as if completely lost into oblivion, well common sense to fact is a gift awarded from one's intellect, "and beyond any doubt wild feral humans world over possess an incredible unfathomed intellect, now in my opinion much obvious abrupt all peculiar and particular wild hominid ability that ever seems of late much more than admirable! "Not exactly what has done it Charley, rather, who, what, and why? Or, rather how in the name of Hell before the invention of wheel, pliers, and a wife, had any of it ever been done in the first place? And what exactly if anything already not mentioned, are some more of the possible, and if not that then highly plausible reasons why? Answer that Charley, and there will be one more good reason that you will not to be shipped straight back to the Tuna fish Cannery at Samoa!"

Obnoxious Opinions Are Sometimes Excusable!

Perhaps All Of This Next Could Be Considered To Be A Short Logistic Written To All Expedient Credible Night Stalkers, And/Or, All Wilder Cats Among Men?

Or,

all more needs be written to all tenacious night stalkers, avid critics, and to warn everyone that all things that go bump in the night, logical, or illogical assumptions, common sense and conjecture, exaggerated facts, true accounts, etc, that are next offered ahead; that are ever believed at best by some many, to be nothing more than a completely unproven opinion; that said I personally do accept this completed treatise to be true in some reasonable opinion objection, "as for now it is truth ahead that is at best an interesting conglomeration of unfounded outcome, but an all true adventure horse plaiting explanation; that with exception to date, however perhaps all of this jargon will prove possible to help explain at least some the probable plaiting theory, and other important projections that in due time will actually opt to eradicate all of the moot critic blather

157

now well known to be everything completely illogical? "Better said: This is the place where imagination and fact gather together to solve the implausibly of any particular mystery unsolved with unlikely answers, and the acute finesse of unfounded theory, reaching out far beyond all existing pseudo solutions of such things as/or ridiculous as wind creatures, fairies, pixies, ghosts, elves, etc!

Give me a break Charley Tuna... How really can anyone actually imagine to distorted all public belief of some many number of such obnoxious critic idiot reports out there flaunting sub-statements, even that dare put their name to something moot like "that" all over the distorted coffee-cup-dunk Think-Tank Inter-Net...

Yeah, how Charley, how indeed?"

Animals and Moon light!

Wow, yeah... What's new Pussy Cat indeed? Probably all night prowling cats as was our loyal Tom Cat friend "Jinx," the wild frisky cat that had long belonged to Tonia Brown; cats of the night probably have a pretty good idea of what was ever plaiting the horses' manes at the times when he wandered all of Montana mystified as he was eager beyond cat-nap action while under the bright light of the full moon! As said Java Bob, there is very much more here than you first expected needed be considered written in this manuscript concerning wild and domestic animals, human comparisons, wild man, horses, and much, much, more, including yourself that now is needing much further understanding and investigation, and even a more unfounded explanation to more confuse the issue that is not at all that easy to think to explain it all here! What other strange anomaly do anyone think by now has also been completely over looked here that may have better founded logistics pertaining that as yet has not been considered? Speak up as time is of essence to catch the nonsense boat! Plaiting continues happening!" Readers, give this some deep thought... There is strength in multiple numbers of logic, thought, and opinion, and most often much more wrong of the last consideration! So for now in yours, all that we have is my opinion until or when there actually is a much, much, much, better answer? It just may be truly possible that there may exist a very much smaller, much less inhibiting feral wild hominid to be considered of why as yet we have hardly! For any of the gargantuan type Bigfoot/Sasquatch actually having directly to do with plaiting is very unlikely." Good Luck Critics, and have a much better arduous hard look around you on particular Moon-Lit Nights, and especially ponder the moons definite effect on all humanity, and especially consider the dire plight of our miserable living wild hominids, and if actually do, you may be quite surprised at exactly what abstract reasoning may have well to do with the plaiting that may prove concern all of us? Perhaps if lucky, you may exactly just as I, also one day be much surprised of exactly what could be looking straight back to you and at your astute curiosity, and next opt to hard snap off your critical nose if not your nonsensical head! What ever any do, or don't find, "I badly do need even you to help solve this plaiting mystery! Please! No matter what is anyone's opinion, think hard about the options, and logically speculate everything here and much more, and intelligently consider and discuss openly all of this high strange unexplained explanation-continuation of plaiting ahead whenever with intelligent friends, and please for the sake of truth, and all humanity's importance, "do some of your own research, and get back to us with anything even if thought illogical, that is if all does not include butterflies, spooks, and what ever else unorthodox that you may have formed a moot opinion of that will not need mush more unintelligent consideration? And please remember to say anything about me that what you want, "but keep your opinion to yourself, as intelligent research-investigators do not have in lock-up reserve, "Only Smart-Phone, Think Tank Time For Remote Moot Bias Blather!" "Asses, Horses' Asses, and Real Men, and, Women! "The plaited horses are coming.... and some of the Horses Asses that are avid computer commentators abrupt all Bigfoot Community will be riding backwards (!), and some many may will soon be wanting off from this thought noxious midnight full-moon illogical merry-go-round ride as one of my close friends had disappointed me! After all is said and done, everyone still reading should be warned, that all continuing research and happenings ahead are going to be one heck of an original contrary theoretical off the wall trip!

"WILD KUMISS"

("Is Horse milk!")

&

The Logistics Of Plaiting?

("What, really, is this book?")

As Tonia implied, "Don, out of necessity this book needs been written without chapters," as she knew just as I that it would ever be necessary to re-new and update all such entries of dubious research. She knew to have written chapters would have required conclusions that by decree would have closed all doors of possible opportunity to re-evaluate additional discovery! We are soon going to be exploring some of the traditional and little known unorthodox effects of the Full Moon on man, animals, and auto suggestive requirements, and some of its possible ramifications having directly to do with this uncanny plaiting, "and to cite if can, viable explanations of humanistic wild hominid reactions unto moon glow, as it is of my opinion that some wild hominids encountered at times may be high suspect to be realized most desperate when in it if not dangerous, and in any unexpected particulars if felt provoked might even attack!" One physical example of questionable sexual dimorphism via a facial example evidencing a deplorable expression was on the face of the very last one of the three Sasquatch that I have actually encountered in my sojourn since year, 1982, last two sightings were both year, 2006, the last one of them seen in a Texas swamp, and the deplorable example mentioned happened in Idaho mid-month of July of that same year; to this day, since then, that separate sexual dimorphism experience has completely altered to the extreme all of my earlier projected prototype wild hominid considerations! Two of the three, the first and the last, were encountered during daylight, and the second was accomplished when with researcher, Don Sherman, a Native American Ojibway Indian home based in lake country Minnesota. "We encountered this tall creature when both together late night at two A.M., while casting earlier found Sasquatch tracks along a small river bank deep in the Texas Swamp lands near Paris Texas; Don first saw the creature by moon lit darkness at a distance of perhaps fifty feet! Together we watched in awe as it finally went its way! After, we managed to cast its 17 inch plaster foot example. No doubt about what we saw!"

"Just as the wind ever calls my name, God willing, I will one day write all of the above story message descriptive of that Ugly One that was last encounter of the three in stark detail as best can in a future manuscript? There is much, much, more than meets the eye to be well realized whenever one is close up and cozy with anything, "Belly to Belly, and, Eye to Eye," yes, with particular types of wild hominids, "trust my judgment," some many my indeed be extremely dangerous and highly unpredictable! Not wanting anyone to fear the unknown, but ever be able to quickly adapt response to any new uncanny discovery! "No one have been there and done it all! No one!"

Perhaps plaiting in this manuscript need be explained analytically, as it is ever analytical, or of an interpretive in nature, and is ever dealing with its subject matter from a limited and personal standpoint, that permits a considerable freedom of style and method, comprising all of ten or more on-going long arduous years of difficult research now compiled for publication here in just 13 short months, December 2011 – December 31, 2012. It has ever been a difficult manuscript all necessary to be written much happenstance, just exactly as if all were intended to had been a ships log, or perhaps a lengthy News Paper Article, as even as I write the telephone keeps ringing off the wall with all new and exciting research data, and impossible invitations for time set invitations to investigate up-coming unexpected fraternizations! I can't possibly check them all alone! The book was ever needed be written as if ever backwards of its constant and necessary update considerations. To think to have further edited this amassed confusion single handed from its original text, however is its presentation would have eluded most all of its important message. This truly is but the very first beginning compromise of an incredible ongoing highly unsolved mystery! Any further earnest conjecture, fact, or opinion, able to continue to overwhelm, over-ride the subject is ever welcome and appreciated, as this treatise is not the last conclusive word to be said on the subject. Perhaps via its comprehensive conjecture and educative auto suggestion it will spark a lighted candle of interest in plaiting, and acknowledge all beveled wild entities that in time will light the midnight new moon sky bright as day with many more realistic and/or conclusive answers to exactly what they are?

"To all things eventually there is an answer! However even with that said, how much indeed is very often completely overlooked via the unrealized fear of ridicule, apprehension, and the collective disruption prone of particular professional and lay ignorance?" Many people seem to remain ever self-satisfied to drown in their own unsavory illogical soup! Mankind has forever been annexed to animals even before having ever accomplished to tame them! Ancient art and religion had literally began with clever cave depiction pictographs, and uncanny petroglyphic art done of obscure animals and man, and much similar effigies continue to this day in all popular creative abstract and primitive art. One might realize that base art and animistic idolatry, unorthodox and orthodox customs and base and abstract religions all had directly or abstractly began with animism, and finally would surface in astrological moon magic as well. What do any think to know of the moon, or the, Southern Cross Beliefs and little understood traditions of the Australian Aborigines? It may surprise you what takes place by moon light that is ever possible when wandering the endless Islands of the South Pacific archipelago, and/or when close to home among the superstitious American and/or foreign Gypsies! Have you ever been bamboozled by a young pert and extremely beautiful to die for Gypsy fortune teller type women; or chased by her protector till both were out of breath and you have escaped on a box car? Or perhaps were hexed by gosh by golly by a Hawaiian Kahuna? Or escaped a carnival lizard man after having just snapped off his rubber skin shell from across his hairless back? "Actually no one has been anywhere and done much of anything have we?" Indeed this world is strange, and wild men do exist, and they are the reason for the strange plaiting! Lets have a closer look at the, French Revere 'a, and some of the wild happenings there?"

France, etc! Moon Magic, and Were-Wolves Ahead!

Within the Paleolithic era, high regard of animals remains evident ever petroglyphical over the walls of many world caves, well exemplified by, Lascuax Cave, France. Evidence left there if fully understood ton be symbolic symbols much evident of the early foundations of human belief. Man as akin to animals continues in a high regard kinship with them to this day in many high allowances, especially this is obvious within particular paradoxical beliefs of world native peoples in regard to the full moon. To them the higher animals when defined can and sometimes do became something more than animals as perhaps religious objects insistent of high symbols of image, myth, superstition, etc, as would in time become referenced as idolatry, fetishism, idol worship, exemplified as had became the Golden Calf, if allowed to be exaggerated, may lend logical ramifications leading into belief in witchcraft, Satanism, Shamanistic rituals, etc. In essence animals very early became the captured subject necessity of wild man's first scientific efforts. Without animal associations wild and domestic, all humanity by now including the wild hominid populations would have already self-destruct!

"Our most profound relationship to art

lies at the metaphysical level."

-Andre Malraux

"Hand Art, Basket Craft, Weaving, Etc!"

Plaiting, as weaving, leather braiding, hemp-art, etc., all relative of the other within the suggestive range of ramifications within this manuscript that leaves very much to contemplate. Some imagination will be necessary from here to fully understand any real part of its almost magical equation. What's new pussy cat (?) indeed, might be easily answered by any number of wild feral, or domesticated farm cats and pet animals, as next to humans all cats, and all house pets are the literal epitome of mid-night paranoia that wanders continually beneath their skin, especially when any cat, or small dog wanders anywhere under a full moon wanting ahead of the chase! As a cats overwhelming cry, definitely has something very strange to say about what ever has just walked out of no-where and had startled it from the urban wilderness brush pile, and next causes them to, "Fast-Ass climb up, under, or over, every picket fence, wall, and/or otherwise what ever is a possible obstacle! You might be surprised indeed if you knew exactly what wanders abrupt you almost within arms reach within your neighborhood woods on any given dark nights that is considered by some to be a wild man, or bogyman? Hardly do bogymen exist, but there actually are some many close seconds as much weary of you, as you are of them! The difference is, they know that you are there, but hardly do ever we actually suspect they are also?"

"Was It that Strange Wolf, or Was It Something Else?"

Perhaps it was a, "Der' Fencen Climben' Nighten En Yoweler,' or something much worse? I am still contemplating-confused to this day about what, really, was the true identity of the strange

161

wolf like creature killed here in Madison County Montana, year 1886, by Israel Ammon Hutchins, at a location once known as 'The Sun Ranch of Montana'? The ugly brown-black livestock menace measured all of 48 inches from rump to snout, called by some locals to be the, "Ringdocus, or Shunka," and stood 28 inches at the shoulder, ahead of several faint impressions of what much looked to be all dull tannish colored stripes. Ironically, having grown up in all Idaho/Montana, Nevada, I had first time encountered the strange wolfish like creature myself presented as a mounted specimen when still a boy of 12 years, while visiting Joe Sherwood's combination Store-Museum located back then on the shore line banks of Henry's Lake Idaho. Earlier that wind-blown day of July, the three of us fishing together, my father and first cousin Ronald, had nearly capsized our small row-boat mid-lake on Henry's high and dangerous waves! Why I cite the Wolfish Creature is to exemplify how really little anyone knows to describe what more high suspect, high strange creatures besides unknown wolf types, may still be chasing the elk and deer, 2013, under the bright moon lit stars of Montana? What's out there howling with the coyotes also strange to them may opt to surprise even the most pier-crazed pseudo authoritative lame-brained know it all critic? No on knows it all!"

Plaiting and the Moon!

In North America! What is doing the plaiting?

"Yeah, what, when, and how?"

What are the effects of a full moon on man and animals?

What, really, can be said of the unexplained intricate braiding now being accomplished on many North American horses? And more important, what, really, is the ever strange reason for messing with their manes, tails, and now teats to get at in Kumiss in the first place? Second place? Any place? By January 17th, 2012, the New Moon has now entered into its first crescent phase! The effects of the moon and lunar astrology leaves much to ponder! During all full moons aster effects are noted all over the world among inmates in correctional institutions, asylums, jails, etc! There are many unrealized moon theories. Domestic and public violence escalate! Amorous confusions, and even horrific homicide has been attributed to bright moon light! Crime rates of every kind seem to sore at each new full moon! Wild Monstrous tales of creature mischief including horror bed time, Were-wolf Legends, etc., and any number of pseudo true ghost and spook stories of sorted monstrosities are ever told legion and loosed during the lunar phase? Who reading has not heard of the legendary, "Wild Loup-garou!" Or the horrid Were-wolf of Gevauan, said to have terrorized endlessly over years, 1765 – 1767?" Fear had from old European, Oriental, Hawaiian, Native American, etc., "Wives Tales," ever reach their zenith during a Full Moon! The wild unorthodox said religious beliefs of the controversial Druids during all 13 full moons yearly literally boggles the mind, let alone the known escapades of the once covert still much miss-understood feared European Grogans, etc. The known moon phase effigies are many, many, however truth known, our strange day light world in some cases is even more than peculiar! The children of mysterious, Tibet and Bhutan, etc., by day light much fear the horror-worry bed time story told them of the dread fabled human faced, fire ash blackened, wild Snow Men, that wander under the sun and full moon light ever described to be a ferocious and of a much cannibalistic sort that are a known as an ancient human wild-man population hold over demented race, far apart and much separate in human description and orthodox origin than are believed the dread Abominable

162

Snowman, or Himalayan Yeti! Yeti are a much different humanistic entity all together! "Neither of them rate my invitation to a dinner of Yak meat, Ibex liver and butter, or anything else, unless it be the mountain river fish that exist in uncountable numbers having fed for thousands of years on the discarded dead bodies of all Poor Class Tibetans and all similar peoples of the Himalayas! Fish for that reason are not a w wanted cuisine of the highland populations."

Log: Comments to -

"The Chinese, and their highly revered, Love Moon, that is also known as The Rabbit Moon! The all seeing eye of the Goddess deity of the Crescent Moon. (That is the particular moon phase just after all full moons whenever it looks to be in the thin sliver mode!)"

"The Rabbit Moon"

The Chinese revere a much similar wild bipedal creature to the Yeti, known in its Northern Territories as the Yeron! However with that of more importance here is the favored, Rabbit on the Moon, or, The Chinese Rabbit Moon, that is considered a good thing, rather than what is misunderstood and is still underestimated is the moon's true rank of aphrodisiac importance world wide and the full influence of the Man in the Moon, compared to the Chinese Rabbit, if or when anyone reading was ever lost in a grave yard past midnight, wandered down Lovers Lane as it was once called in the West before all of our fences went up! Of Course all of this you say is most ridiculous, or is it really, as who among you opt to re-plant your garden crops yearly only if done by the phase of a New Moon, and then only via the guidance and interpretations traditionally accepted found within the Farmers Almanac? The ramifications of The excitement probability of the Chinese Moon remains my favorite! "Gotcha Charley Tuna, the fishing by moon light is good then too! Watch your fins! "As said the Chinese Rabbit Moon is said to have particular aphrodisiac ramifications far beyond the alleged expectations of renowned ginseng, ground animal claws, hooves, antlers, etc. Ancient tribes a-kin to present day holdover European and Native North American Native populations, in some reserve still today believe in the wearing of wild bear skins, or vests made of them, etc., as when engaged in battle or self-defense as they are in firm belief that through adhered Bear Clan association it renders them next to invincible and intolerable to injury. Even they dare fight if by the light of the full moon when under the guise of a wild bear in spite of what has forever been shared and well realized among all native peoples, "that night war-fare was ever a taboo, much foolish, and for superstitious traditions next to forbidden!" ("If further interested in bear, animal, moon fetish, etc., reference the, Native American California Chumash Indian culture, and the customs of the Canadian Black-feet Tribe, that includes the northern Montana based, Black-Feet Indians! (Separate they are from the Idaho the Blackfoot Indians!) And good luck, or, "Ishmahachie..." as is paraphrased said in an ancient Hidatsa-Crow, language! ("Good Luck, from the Northern lands of the Mt. Lion!")

Moon Light!

There is very much, much, to consider, as I am more than highly convinced by now that there is a definite full moon connection to horse plaiting, as the moon is much historically significant in

163

all passé mythological history. As said some many civilizations through out the ancients have long revered the moon along side animals as a religious anomaly and/or a fetish of a good or bad symbolism, much as is also well known to be in good and bad effigy in animal idolatry, black and white roosters and chickens in Voodoo rites, etc. The estranged anomaly goes on and on world wide! That moon in reality allowance is much pertaining to plaiting, and is but one of the important reasons for the crux this manuscript, as it is my high speculation that a much still unrealized and all unsuspected and ever a relative power of abstract control some has to do with a definite full moon phase connection through any number of misunderstood, misinterpreted, and very confused ancient traditions that may help to explain at least a large part of the extremely high strange humanistic physical ability needing be done via extremely nimble finger mechanics, much tenacity of purpose, and an all ever necessary intelligent imagination, and traditional of determination! The actual reason for the plaiting may also only be the best and safest avenue to animal protein nourishment! (The feat of braiding a horse's mane, or wanted called the strange plaiting now being accomplished world wide on the long shaggy neck manes of horses.) The artistic and intricate plaiting may also serve as an abstract payment or respect of sorts, expected paid as you go requirement for received Kumiss, animal kinship, etc?

Completely Unsuspected!

Another all separate high strange full moon kinship association and theory of the author not written here is under study/considerations of late, that if in future indeed has pseudo credence, all will be further explained in a future book of The Trilogy? Wild man however believed docile, passive, withdrawn, thought demented, etc., wanting explained simply as elusive, may at particular times of moon-phase, need actually exist completely out of caricature? Enough said with that to perhaps excite ones imagination …

(See you in another book?)

Log: Of late, summer, 2010 – 2011,

I have discovered that much the same plaiting is now also being done on the Indian Reservation Lands of the Nevada Desert to the wild mustang stock found roaming there on the open range, and only recently during the first week of April 2012, saw it done again on the necks of four of the remaining out of 11 head of Oregon Hinck Ranch horses! Definitely there is much more important to learn far beyond the study thus far of all of this high-strange anomaly than first probably meets anyone's curiosity! For a most part, many naive unconcerned persons much typical today of the Bart Simpson mind set are very quick to put aside all unexplained phenomena, in spite of all hard evidence found, and usually do it without even looking at any of it while saying with one short wave of a much doubtful hand... "Ah, but Don, that stuff is not true! Come on man, all of this stuff is all just being done by the wind, and the brush, and all like that! The horses are all just rolling around on there backs in the dust, or frolicking around in a brush pile and their hair just gets all tangled-up like that! Have a cold shower and a soda, and sit down there and watch the sun go down! Hell man, the foot ball game is about to start...! Lets take a break?" Give Me A Break" Yeah, I am thinking, I need a break! I will have more fun watching the moon in the midnight night sky waiting for the appearance of little green men than watching some mundane ball game and the funny thing is, I once loved to play the game! Regardless, it is true that horses' manes can get hopelessly twisted and tangled exactly like all of that projected negativism above, and because of the fact, and all much dis-

torted related belief, long go we purposely took very good photo samples of such wild assumptions, and not one time ever; not one single time has there been even an abstract similarity to had been a viable and all convincing comparison! Not once!"

Log: What Done it?

(Critics will love this!)

In my belief it is being done by the smallest Sasquatch of the clan, as would be perhaps the adult, or smaller children, and/or the effeminate women. Perhaps mothers etc., in that way are teaching their children games, tenacity, purpose, patience, dexterity, motor skills, and definitely useful plaiting, etc? All participating players what ever any think are ever in need of small, nimble, strong, and capable hands. Remembered that these wild entities are very much like us, but hardly are the larger one's prototyped gigantic if actually are, as they would not be able to accomplish plaiting after aspiring to an adult having by then massive bulk, large feet, big hands and thick fingers, etc. Obviously the larger are no longer capable of doing such intricate braiding! "Heck I even have a difficult time to open a bottle of prescription medicine, or anymore be able to tie a dry fly! Not even a Very Windy Critic could better explain the horse braiding! Show me?"

Log: What of Bigfoot?

Needed said: Bigfoot as a word term is ever a misleading descriptive term! Hardly does its auto-suggestive indication need necessary evidence huge! That description is not a definable reality! Most of them through out all stages of maturity when encountered are not every one gargantuan in every single case! True, some are described extremely large, and in some cases that may be the absolute, but Bigfoot as a definitive general description it is not remotely a conclusive determination of anything either. But of late when considering all recent discovered huge tracks, recent unknown creature viable photography, sorted depositions of credible witness, etc., "there definitely may be exceptions of up to 12 feet or more?"

I have one foot cast in particular in my cast collection of six found, measuring all of 24 plus inches long! M.K. Davis per-chance has obtained valid video footage of one very huge Texas swamp creature estimated when standing up-right to be likely in assess of that! On that lofty creature my 24 inch cast example would likely suffice? What, really, to fact might be the many unrealized large and smaller variations of up-right walking wild man-beasts? All of that last paragraph overwhelms the imagination. However in early last century newspapers there are still existing accounts of skeletal remains been unearthed to evidence humanity once that height. As said, the author has seen three examples of unknown bipeds, and the first and the tallest may have been eight feet. The second also in Texas was much huskier and looked to be about the same, however the third and last encountered within in a close proximity to a trailer-house screened window was at best no more than six feet tall, very powerfully built, extremely masculine, looked intelligent and adapt; the over all impression was he was not all that hairy, extremely capable, and if provoked could be beyond dangerous! Most difficult to describe were its eyes, somehow I have never quite found the words... but believe me they emulated a definitive statement of power and independence!" Certainly a gigantic creature described huge need evidence a Big Foot, but many adult castings in viable collections are much lesser in size than are usually prototyped massive, or wanted projected on display as the ultimate Prize winning Big Foot casting among all pseudo authoritative Big Foot community. Numerous castings from about every where measure @ approximately, 11" – 17, or 18 inches in length; larger are @ perhaps 18 – 20! "Most thought normal human feet measure very close to 12 inches, and then of course they are larger to the extreme of a size 12, or 16 shoe, and it is not all that uncommon that some rare persons require an even bigger size! "What Say More of Bigfoot tracks?

Excerpts taken from authors manuscript notes published in early books years, 2001-2003, describe various Sasquatch plaster foot castings made on location while exploring portions of the vast western desert mountain fringe areas of what is today known as,

"The Great Basin United States," that extends up from, The Mexican Sonoran Desert, and all the way to Canada! Over a period of fifty years, various body descriptions, including definable foot measurements had many times been taken, and as was written in book, Sasquatch 2001, "at a place of South Eastern Nevada near Railroad Pass, where is locally famous, Christmas Tree Pass towards the Colorado River, two separate adults were said to had been encountered at close range.... Track measurements taken when investigating the above! "I am writing from the Nevada high Desert, near by and above the distant City limits of Laughlin, Nevada ... Foot evidence taken today a-top Christmas Tree Pass, measured well within human expectations, and were at best at perhaps 11 - 12 inches, by, approximately, 4 inches wide at the heal! This inclusive when considering all hill slope angle, etc., as needed foot pressure had on the dust and sand covered slope. These two creatures were described rather short in stature compared to what was expected?

(What's actually thought to be short, in undetermined wild-man proportions? Short in most encounter estimations of wild man are less than six foot tall, or maybe just a bit shorter, as many times reported over Desert America, a considerable number of believed to had been adult Sasquatch were said to had been no taller than 5' 8 – 6', and in some extremes much shorter as perhaps under five foot!)

(?)

A Very Unlikely Discovery And Unique Story!

"Critics will love this one?"

Log: Wow!

In my cast collection is a very small foot casting taken June, 2008, at Bluff Creek Cal., when in company of, MK Davis and his son Brian who at the time was walking fast backwards for a considerable distance to prove to us how easily a clever Sasquatch or wild man could confuse the issue leaving foot tracks over the road dust! How little did we know that on that same expedition and on the very day we would experience small wild bipeds of some kind doing much similar! This smaller casting measures approximately 6 inches long, by three inches wide at the heel. The cast is only one of two separate small tracks taken in soft road dust where only moments before both creatures had been walking backwards while each were slowly backing off towards a steep road embankment close behind them all of the while facing toward us where

we were also walking fast pace toward them and only moments away as they quickly disap-
peared backwards over the bank, but not before each had carefully wiped away their obvious
foot tracks behind with the other foot before going off down into the forest brush in order to
evade us! To have had the basic reasoning to self-destruct a foot print in soft dust by the me-
thod described is definitely a humanistic anomaly. What had been there and just vacated the
scene as they had done was either children Sasquatch or two examples of the fabled Bluff Creek
little people. Either way the discovery was incredible, In my opinion I would opt for juvenile
Sasquatch as it was hardly the first sets of foot tracks that we had discovered within the area in
recent years. I cast both separate tracks; the second was just a bit larger than the other, measur-
ing at perhaps one inch longer than the smaller, however later that same day the larger was
accidentally destroyed in an uncanny mishap before it could be completely measured and ap-
preciated. This smaller casting was posted sometime year, 2010 over talk radio
www.artistfirst.com, and if any desire to see it up close in detail it likely still can be viewed by
accessing the program internet archives under the heading of, Bigfoot Central, via Don Mon-
roe, &, M.K. Davis. Update: The smaller foot cast is posted as of today, November 13th, 2012
on, U-Tube Net, M.K. Davis. Begin U-Tube search with...

"Don Monroe falls over a cliff at Bluff Creek Ca." Look next over parts, 1 -7, then go all mate-
rial posted on that blog by M.K. Davis. What is to be found there to include all sorts of topics
will more than surprise everyone. All new stuff will continue to be posted all future through
December 2013. Since all Update material posted on U-tube, we have now after four years
concluded that instead of Sasquatch children the tracks may have been made by something
hominid even more intriguing as was slightly mentioned above.

No comment possible as yet due to much needed further investigation. Just possibly and perhaps not we are returning back to the Bluff Creek area sometime 2013 to have a further look?
Massive Tracks explained huge big feet, etc., definitely do still exist made very fresh all through the
Bluff Creek drainage, and in many other far unrelated regions of the Western America, as during
the month of July, 2006, with credible witness besides myself, one being John Doitch ex cop, N.
Y., N.Y; and Ron Roseman, WA., State, together we discovered and made cast of an incredibly
huge and massive foot track measuring all of, 24 inches long, by 9 inches wide at the mid foot, by
5 inches plus wide the heal! This example of course is far beyond what anyone might consider to
be simply huge if perhaps it were only 17 or 18 inches long? Believe me our casting is truly huge!
The massive wild hominid track that we discovered was one of six found in running stream bed
soft sand bank beach location of a flowing desert stream within the South East Idaho Bad Land
extremes of high desert Idaho! Finding all of six definable tracks more than validated the discovery.

Ron Roseman with me that day said, in his usual/expected to be ever somewhat dry humorous day tone when thirsty expression, and ever obvious/special assumption done verbatim in his
particular UN-lovable demeanor; "what ever he said next was just as if he himself were to be the
very first informant and the last at all much aware of everything that probably as yet hadn't been
noticed that day by anyone that would alert all to the discovered anomaly; sure that he would be
the first if you will, ever to explain intelligently by saying, "Guys, do you know... Now that's a
very, very, Big Foot!" Well Yeah, well, we all had finally agreed! The cast remains as yet soon to be
viewed on the U-Tube, watch for?" "Thanks Ron, that is brilliant! "I do wonder Don, exactly what
made it? It is not a fake! Something like what made that track, needs to stand all of 15 foot tall? If
it was a made by a Who, or made by a What, we need ask Doctor Seuss! And if it's actually a
monster Don, well we need ask the Devil?" Well, Ron and all of us are still searching for more definable evidence of the monstrous creature, and just perhaps now since we have found some vi-

able clues from a much similar huge track way anomaly that has been left now for five years running exactly where it was first found at a new hand dug hole reaching three feet deep down to water in a hard-pan gravel stream bed in that same particular dry desert canyon located only eight miles distant away, and if anyone believe in huge monsters, or even large Sasquatch or not, "all much similar high strange stories, and much more will be written in all future slated books of The Sasquatch Trilogy!"

Wait for? Larger Tracks? "Yes, and some much, much, smaller!" I have been told of other alleged hominid foot tracks that have been found in places of South America, and others found on one particular Island of the South Pacific, that were claimed much larger (?), and one deposition

taken from memory written in my early book, "Sasquatch 2001," relates a considerable story account of many baby sized bare foot tracks being followed in snow on the high wind swept slopes of Mt. Shasta, Ca., and stories had from other difficult locations! The proof of course is always in the pudding, and even with some of my discoveries I can well understand how some many however true are likely hard to swallow for the average lay explorer, however that does not change anything... Deception ever writes its own demise! What actually can be said of something like huge 24 inch foot tracks, or others similar or even bigger discovered similar that have been found in wilderness locations such as, Northern California?

The invincible, UN-sung, lone wolf researcher, Rex Havashell, once told me of another large creature track that he had discovered late summer 2010, measuring all of 22 inches in length within the close proximity of Happy Camp California! Sadly that cast has now gravitated like so many other important artifacts into an impossible private collection. That gigantic Idaho foot track and the one found by Rex are proof enough for me that at least two very huge and extremely elusive something or other are likely still to wandering somewhere UN-noticed!

Figure 26. 'Red' holding a very large footprint cast, (but not the largest found). This is a replica of a cast made by the late anthropology professor Grover Krantz in eastern Washington State.
Iddins collection.

There Are Numerous Types Of Sasquatch?

"Yep!" Anyone Say Nope?" Well, numerous Sasquatch evidence encountered in my long experience indicate that there are likely at least three if not four probable varieties, and now suddenly for explicit reasons there are some suspects of six? Again said, I firmly do believe from much cast evidence taken and all personal encounters, etc., to have been able to identify at least twelve or more separate irregular descriptions of relict hominids; all of them far apart in descriptions from most wanted-realized huge prototype Sasquatch, as these three evidence separate variations of a somewhat smaller creature in stature according to all distant gene-pools, regions, etc., and who knows what more about them is not all that hard to discern? As we definitely have discovered much that needs be shared! "Why not multiple ancient hominid examples exactly as we have people and horses?"

Log: October 3, 2006, @ Monroe, Utah

Today while at Monroe Utah I had a hot soak in very ancient natural steam baths and hot pools said to had been formed there as distant in time as the Paleozoic. Located near them were some more than interesting pictographs done on the bare face of a fare sized boulder. A fellow from Switzerland shared with me a recent Salt Lake Tribune copy having an informative article written by Creg Lavine... The clip follows explaining a much similar wild hominid theory as my own that will be much more explained in other Trilogy books. Creg writes: "Doctor Jim Kirkland, Utah State Paleontologist attests that many hominid artifact found in Utah share an ancient connection to many China Pale o finds documented in books and journals, but the picture and diagrams fall short of seeing them on location, as seeing is believing! Recent discoveries of bird like feathered Dinosaur, Falcarius utahensis has direct relatives in China – Falcarius was there during the Cretaceous when 44 – 65 million years ago Western America and China were directly connected. This could add credence to the evolution and varied DNA found in Native Americans"... Why not wild hominids, and horses, and/or Patty Sasquatch, and The Wisconsin Ice Man both discovered in 1967 Perhaps their DNA might be found to indicate much the same? There is documentation written in particular religious beliefs that strange animals were seen in North America as late and early history as 458 B.C. ("Ho, Prester John, etc.?")

CHINA

"The Great Han Tortoise!"

(Han Dynasty)

Among the Liang artifact wild beast collection, there was only one gigantic carved stone turtle ever unearthed, located today and forever it has to be seen at the "Tomb of Hsiao Hsiu," A.D. 518. It is most interesting that to this day the turtle effigy is highly revered and wanted over many far locations of the main land and most of South Pacific Oceania.

I was once most fortunate while early-on exploring places of off limits Hong Kong, with ship mate Tom Shrusbury to witness countless very old hand carved fantasy animal effigies stored deep underground below the city side walks. A retired Mandarin Chinese historian then with us explained the intrinsic high worth of them to world museums. He also claimed that particulars of them were created in fairly recent times modeled from living examples? I noticed among them were various relict hominids, some depictions of them exhibiting possible cannibalism were almost alarming! The Chinese will forever harbor many well kept secrets... The Western world hardly realizes their sage history and/or potential. I for one well understand that! Much like the Native American wrote history much is misunderstood and so has been left overlooked. If it wasn't documented by the English, few understand to believe it!

Log: Happy Camp California, summer, 2012

*I am here with MK Davis, and Bear Ken Iddins ... B.S. Had, of everyone, and candid comment
had of the Author and forest detective, Wild Bob Sasquatch Smallsbach! His Logic? "Don, what,
really, has all of this stuff that you are writing have to do with plaiting anyway? Man you and I
should be up for grabs for the invading Martians! If captured us there would be nothing else
left to say that they would not at all want to know! "Well Java, it's having to do with trying to
explain all probable separate wild-man prototypes, their intelligence, their reasons for plaiting
that definitely much varies with them according to all natural birth-right idiosyncrasy and traditional belief variations had from ancient and current day human allowance, possible ancient
captivity requirements of man and beast, however all variations of wild hominids (Unless as
some insist that Sasquatch have alien connections?) they are all much relative to the other
through out all past historical acquired DNA gene pools, etc., in spite of some few that may
have aspired hideous as a direct abstract result of consanguinity/mutations or not? These few
unlikely 12 foot tall, uncanny, humanoid examples (?), or not some of them be more taller
even, or what really next is to be discovered of them, "some of them are probably not to be
thought as monstrous, hideous, etc. et al "I interpretive sexual dimorphism allowances (?), etc.,"
vand remain even as I write completely unrealized beyond further explanation; if indeed they
are not all, or everyone of them related of a wanted/unwanted prototype that would prove to
be a true wild man of a Sasquatch example found running loose over both North and South
America as they are, being highly claimed to be often encountered by the locals on Mt. Chim-
borazo or anywhere else! Each of them described above, Bob, are a plausible much separate
regional prototype result of many possibilities? Everyone of them thought of an unlikely sort
very may be still more uncommon in same gene pool to descriptions just as we humans; each
wild man hominid entity ever allowed from DNA, only according to all local gene pool sexual
active members, their DNA, and what ever that extended birthing might allow them, etc., that
perhaps is much exemplified in all separate comparisons of all much differing descriptions of
said Sasquatch as explained above, as myself, the three separate unknowns that I have seen
were much alike, and yet not alike either. Especially this so with the last one seen in Idaho
2006. Some few persons probably will not agree with some of this above conjecture, but actually what more concrete suggestion have any pier arm chair professional lay critic able to better explain any real part of this ongoing high strange anomaly and the obvious high intelligence ever necessary to be able to accomplish plaiting, as every single wild entity likely cannot
do it? What's on first, and who's on second matters not, "as most negative regard to the non-
relevance of Sasquatch/horse plaiting, etc, extends up from moot critic couch-potato, choco-
late-chip-bagged obnoxious indigestion, and/or all latent acquisitions of NFL beer can logic,
and/or what ever nonsense is still being argued boring again and again of all foot ball score
tallies as Joe Namath's, or I would hope, which Texas cheer leader has the most up-front influence? "Wow critics, it is time that we all get out into the field and have a good educated look
at all the real truth there is to be had of overlooked Sasquatch evidence abrupt all domestic
horses, and especially of all wild Nevada, and wild-mustang plaited evidence! Maters not to me
what others think! Don't think! Won't think! Don't allow, etc! As I truly have found over my
long sojourn what I have actually long needed to know to be able to fully realize what seems
mostly unrealized to many others... that indeed it is a fact that wild hominids are the only logical entities for what ever the true reasons that are doing the plaiting! I am here excited to continue to share some of that high plausibility no matter how much thought to be unorthodox,
and/or an unwanted truth! What truly matters is that we do not continue to over look or at
least consider all new and inventive opinions of others! This treatise is not, and will not be the*

last projected theory, and even I may need change my mind! But what ever if true or not what is now down here for the record may start a moon-rush of new and interesting explanations? There are countless viable plaster foot and hand castings that have been taken world wide, and much other valid hard evidence of high strange artifact examples similar as those of the author taken on likely and unlikely locations, including the many, many, undeniable photographs that will be shared in future manuscripts, hopefully ever inclusive of the many discriminating still shot photographs taken from never before visited to film cave cite locations; my long covert video footage collections, and particular artifacts that perhaps one day soon may needing be exposed? "Even as I write, M.K. Davis, of Yazoo City, Miss. is working overtime his separate indisputable film genus to more enhance them." (To enhance, is to enlarge!)

"Deliberate Hoaxers!"

"We Got Plenty!"

"The pity is how much harmful adversity and negativity has already been accomplished over the media and all moot think tank logic being flaunted over the private sector that has undeniably down played or has not already exasperated much naive and general disbelief in the existence of wild-man that in future effect earnest interest in horse ownership cooperation that could actually help solve the plaiting mystery? Ray Wallace, everyone remembers him and the year 2003.

Log: Ray Wallace:

"His disgrace[*] should by now be long forgotten, disallowed, or his bogus narcissistic deposition buried exactly separate from where was covert buried Patty Sasquatch! The negative ramifications of his ridicules ploy are no longer felt (?) by any and all who took the time to investigate the truth; but for a very long time, perhaps all of six months or more, the ones that didn't bother to investigate his exaggerations are the ones that remain disbelievers of Sasquatch existence to this very day? It is interesting that just about the time of the timely passing of credible anthropologist, Doctor Grover Krantz, (University of Washington), that Ray Wallace also passed, and next thing we knew with the help of the much slanted media his ridiculous story broke headlines and all his family stormed the Bigfoot palace! Hvowever for a very long time now he has been debunked! Nothing is worse than an out and out deceptive lie... Ray Wallace was all of that! His disgusting media success highly exemplifies what can transpire of all wannabe negative media support; deliberate hoaxers completely insistent via pseudo proclamations that he, and him alone was the only true opinion in the world. May he rest in peace. What, really, is there more to know of the late, Ray Wallace except that he was the all time King of the hoaxers in regard of Sasquatch-Bigfoot negative validity. All of that now a cold case bit of history Charley! Yeah, I agree, there definitely is something fishy to be said of all of that!"

---

[*] [ed.] See for example his obituaries: "Lovable trickster created a monster with Bigfoot hoax " Seattle Times, December 5, 2002, Retrieved March 17, 2013,
"Ray Wallace, 84; Took Bigfoot Secret to Grave -- Now His Kids Spill It", Los Angeles Times, December 6, 2002., Retrieved March 17, 2013, or
"Search for Bigfoot Outlives The Man Who Created Him" Timothy Egan, New York Times, January 3, 2003, Retrieved March 17, 2013.

PART ONE

M.K. Davis, and www.artistfirst.com. Talk Radio!

The genius of, M.K. Davis was much still unknown back then, but just a little later in that same year his indisputable film enhancements of the alleged taken 1967, Roger Paterson Bluff Creek California film began to make the difference and if watched has completely sank The Wallace Ship of Fools! Radio Show host Scott Zalasko with me however M.K. reluctant we nevertheless got him started broadcasting weekly along side the blather of the author on talk radio show, www.artisfirst.com.org. ten years later and the show has became very popular. Check out the incredible show archives. As of now the radio show airs monthly, yearly, heard, every first Tuesday night, @ eight P.M. Eastern time.

"The Roger Paterson film in its abstract has to do with plaiting? How and, what? Well, for one important reason, when all original film frames are enlarged it is very obvious that Patty has much similar black head hair as has Native American women, and it has definitely been definitely Braided!" ("Plaited, no kidding, take a very, very, close educated look! Copies of MK's work are available!") "I was one of the first persons in accordance with the films validity back year 1967, when then first time confirming with Doctor Grover Krantz ... (Then visiting at The University of Idaho, located at Coeur d'Alene where I was a resident then.) ... I was in full agreement with him and his earnest assumptions (That at once in my opinion are all ever all obvious to any seasoned hunters experience with wild game and animals!) ... of the films absolute validity! In those days many years prior and to this day I remain an avid bear hunter, and have served as a companion guide on many a large animal chase and catch, and well recognized at once along with my wife Marion, that Patty Sasquatch to be seen on the one minute film was not remotely wearing any sort of a man-made bogy-man suit!

"More Ray Wallace, Why More On Him! By Now All World Knows That He Was A Bogus Hoaxer! Well perhaps here is where I write his last necessity! Every dog has his day, and the cats rule the night under the influence of the moon!"

"Yeah, we need not concern more with his untimely deceptive exaggerations, as charlatans ever worry and earn their own doom! For what good reason if not for whom the bell tolls is finally written all truth! Incidentally, believe in the MK Davis film enhancements or not, "the Patty Sasquatch's, Fast Walk-By Segment; the short few seconds of it are done to be plainly viewed on a One Minute film definitely evidences long enough to well recognize the truth of her definite upswing styled braided hair, that amounts to what has been carefully done resulting in a definite Plaited Hair Due that can easily be seen if wanted in the available photo enhancements! This Plaited hair has been done in a much similar fashion and primitive style as was forever with world women, and is still much in use today! Mid way down from off the pushed back hair on top of Patty's head; this piled hair has long been mistaken for what was not, :as it was wrongly projected by even academics to had been the obvious effects of a possible slanting forward skull cap, much resembling the Male Gorillas well recognized saggital crest; in the first place, "And This Next Becomes Very Important," a saggital crest is not possible on Patty Sasquatch, as all even lay zoology students soon realize from animal anatomy studies that Only a MALE Gorilla has a saggital Crest! Even if Patty Sasquatch had been an obscure hold over large ape female; the famine gender in nature concerning the gorilla, never was quite that unlucky, because the crest top my opinion is definitely ugly! The saggital Crest, simply said, is sexual dimorphism; having directly to do with highly predominant, strong, and ever distressing male features being highly suggestive as they are, of a threatening danger from the creature if provoked! (RE: sexual dimorphism!) "Not the place here needed to continue further into all of that..., HOWEVER it has always be an important negative academic issue with me; as I have forever been "unable" to at all understand in the "absolute remote..." how in the hell pray tell me, can any supposed credible academic, ever not to be able after so many, many, years of pseudo said experience and voiced opinion, and high education, "have opt to over look public such an Obvious and Decisive analogy of Hard Fact, "as only the Male Gorillas at all evidence a noticeable saggital crest?" Yeah Charley, you are right... "Yeah, how in the hell could any supposed professional, or an associate anthropologist professor, Not Know via all present day unwanted/wanted need unsophisticated sophisticated smart phone narcissistic logic?"

Log: A bit more Ray Wallace?

Updates to, Year 2003!As said, the already established photography genius enhancements of MK Davis by the year 2003, had been stabilized in large part way long prior to all of the moot claims of Ray Wallace, and his highly bogus "Big Foot Exposé Misgivings," then being flaunted everywhere over the world media by supportive idiots, and their obnoxious insistence of the Ray Wallace family! "As said, it is much interesting that ALL of this bogus ploy had suddenly come front only but just shortly after the then recent 2003 demise of the renowned Doctor of Anthropology, Grover Krantz! It is now a well known fact that even way back then, that Wallace had been completely deceptive for many years in his many exaggerations of off the wall insistent s, and it was long known prior of all his latent Wanna-be Charlatanry Flaunted Testimony, as he was ever bogus in all his derogatory claims of himself, and most all others Pro of his Moot defense! Ever he expressed in a definite narcissistic obnoxious demeanor of an obvious Wanna-be Famous Bigfoot-er in ever Outlandish Decree, and he was ever Self-Convincing to himself, if NOT to all others, including my old buddy, "Ray Crowe," well known back then to be the active and highly credible president of the Western Bigfoot Society, then operating from, Hillsboro, Oregon. "Don, Ray told me several times... Well concerning Ray Wallace... Out of compassion is suppose...Well Don, for his nonsense, and himself already being a fast aging, and long-time member of the society, WE all allowed him... (Expecting no harm done in a future!)... to act out in his long exclusionary ploy of deceptions and fantasy, an so just expected that one day he would eventually go off on his own way?

Ray Wallace actually dared attest himself to be a meaningful and most important deceptive mentor in ever wanton desire of to be exploiting the many deceptions of all pro-Bigfoot community... by claiming to all the world that Patty Sasquatch, and the complete Roger Patterson, 1967, movie film was a complete hoax, and then next the much uncaring Naïve World at large Most Part all of a sudden opt to fully believed his decreeing and sad-sung unreasonable "blather" heard from the lofty roof tops!" (A small bit paraphrased, but that is exactly what Ray Crowe said! I just recently with Cathy Seavey, December 20013, visited Ray at his home at Hillsboro, and he sends his regards to all that had loved and admired him! "Just tell them all that I'm doing great Don... Well, he is! So know that!"

Log: 2003! Ray Wallace Speaks!

Quote: Written if for no other reason than for the record - "Ray Wallace, slightly paraphrased again as from above, however all content is very much verbatim!

"Yes he said, that is right! I am him! I was the only person in the whole world that had ever accomplished single handed; ever was able to be making bogus plaster casts, next thought always valid by all Bigfooters! I alone had been the Only One singular person in the world ever successful at the bogus deceptive ploy of flaunting Bigfoot invalid by using a casting! I was the very best cast maker extraordinaire, ever able through my superior expertise, to ever be able to completely fool all of the experts!"

"Wallace Was as A Complete Hoax!"

Ray Wallace had managed to hoax all of his castings with an obvious much bogus hand carved flat wooden board used to cast all foot tracks! It looked to be a ridiculous bogus poorly made at best wanton foot track nuisance! Best said again paraphrased slightly from Ray Crowe... "Well hell, Don, they... Well, it remained a well known fact, and a much obvious ploy, that the moot hand carved wooden planks were ever known exactly for what they were, and were throughout all opinions of the passé members of The Western Bigfoot Society, and the naive America public and the media fell for what Wallace came up with , Hook, Line, and, Sinker!"

Well Charley, it is now just past the election year of 2012. "Some of that Ray Wallace Ploy suddenly sounds a bit more than just slightly familiar in bogus ramifications! All of the bogus facts of his insecurity were completely over looked by the public and the media; just as if by self-determination Wallace well realized his deceptive day in the sun year 2003!

Close Encounters?

However as a result of Ray Wallace and his bogus self, even two of my own daughters back then had suddenly lost all interest in the plausibility of feral hominids in spite of all hard facts had to the contrary that included my own research... Much unspoken dismay has continued as a result of the Ray Wallace deception, and they both had spent much of their early life wandering and fishing with me into the darndest wild places, and at least one time or another, if knowing it or not, one of them that especially loved to sometimes wander off alone to color and paint had likely when very young looked at least One Sasquatch straight into its ever watchful-lustful eye? They were younger then, and perhaps after this long stress of hard effort, "if read it," and all reference to horses and plaiting; and further bother to examine my hominid, and mega-many unusual artifacts, etc., perhaps one or the other or both will have opted to change their mind? Without at least a slight bit of family support in such dubious efforts, "as my being a true forest detective in the wake/comparisons of, Charley Chan, The Shadow, and W. C, Fields, anyone remember them, as I have been roasted! That said, it has been gone down a long lonely road for an impossible aging vagabond! However, nevertheless, their own mother had much realized wild hominid truth, "especially after she herself had seen her first, and last, "THING," as she called it, high up on the top most wind swept summit slopes of all incredible rock-slide strewn Mt. Index Washington, fall 1982... "She never denied to her last day once what she had witnessed, and in some ways it had concerned her, as she said... "Don, no matter what others say or believe, never give up what you are doing! It is important! We both know the truth as we have seen it! One day you will make a difference! Sometimes I really wish that I had not seen what we did... But we did!" Well, Marion honey, all of us, every one, forever have missed you...

Log: *Continued from above*

A short preview into Marion's sighting, and all close family encounters! "Children by nature, and dead men never tell all of the rest of their untold story! I still have good reason to believe that at least one of my daughters, at one time or another when very young, may had seen some sort of a wild man when camped with their mother and I in true wilderness, as in those days, all of us were ever as if to be considered lost forever by everyone that knew us! Marion when constantly hunting and exploring with at all seasons of the year, had several times experienced the physical presence of wild hominids looking back to her/us from the smoke blind dark night vision beyond a thousand and one more wilderness camp fires, most often during late night or sundown, as was the one that she had actually encountered when with me as said, year 1982 at a-top most rock out-crop on Mt. Index, Washington. Her true story is told verbatim in a short deposition written in my first book now long out of print, "Sasquatch 2001," as she had long years endured many more high strange and unusual experiences, some of them are explained in Sasquatch 2003,. hopefully both books after being updated/revised will again be published by mid year 2014, intended re-titled as, "Wild Man!" God willing I will get'er all done before running my canoe aground on some forlorn wild western river!"

Marion's very name mentioned by anyone, was indisputable proof of her true word, as she was a respected mentor with most everyone in ever positive approach to life and compassion; by her womanly example plain spoken honesty, honor and respect for God and country, she was ever as if a fresh rose in an onion patch! No one had ever known her to exaggerate a truth, or especially expose a secret! She truly had seen a wild man, and she had described it as a, "Thing," and that was all that there was to know about it!"

Don, she said... "I do not know if or not it was a true wild man, as I have never seen one! I just know that it was not one of us, and so it was a, Thing!"

"Pseudo Big Foot Clubs?
Some believe that Bigfoot sometimes carries one?"

"Harry & The Hendersons!" The meaning of pseudo is to would-be, as would-be is to unlikely! Who is believed, and who is almost magical, at times is to be almost disgusting within all negative wanna-be pier persuasion and self-adoration had within much of the pseudo Bigfoot community; some many if realized are much less than creditable than was passé Doctor Seuss, who in all extended probability was far ahead in abstract and comparative plausibility than many of today's unreliable self-righteous politicians professors, mighty local mice police, and perhaps particular academic critics as are Doctors Speculate and outdated Spock (?), and especially to be had of all negative sway in negative ramifications of the illogical character-age Hollywood Movie titled: "Harry & the Hendersons!" About the movie, as entertaining as perhaps the movie was, for most part its negative ramifications flaunted much sway and unneeded persuasion to an already much stifled, naive, and if not already, at yet to be more confused public; ever completely lost if not already also bias and/or in much doubt that Sasquatch, Wild Man, Bigfoot, called them what ever need wanted (?), that any of it at all was at true probability, especially if by then the public were not already lost to the mercy of media and critic auto-suggestion beyond the reality of artifact and maverick-academic proof; as many doubters still today seem to lean towards the movie, that in my opinion, "beyond all humor," "was non but a wasteful sham, of purposeful if not motivated and intentional hysterical laughter, abrupt a highly slanted critic media, wanting of further attempts to more convince the public at large, ever already most of them negative of all further true wild man associations already believed to had been moot back then ever since the moot wanna-be claims of the late Ray Wallace! To view the movie; for any serious professional or maverick forest detective... (As I do not personally consider myself as a true Bigfooter!), ...was almost to be looking through a much opinionated dim-lit kaleidoscope of unwanted hallucinations, at best to be seen under the dwindling dawn misinterpretations of an over rated Coleman lantern, etc., ever disassociated as it was, of any new and exciting truth or passé discovery, for example as was the original Sasquatch movie footage alleged taken single handed by Roger Patterson October 20, 1967: all of that collective photographic material now continuing being closely examined and completely enhanced by the extraordinary expertise of, MK Davis, one day, if already hasn't, may soon really surprise you! Within his work are always found new hidden and revealing anomalies as ever had surfaced almost by magic... There is always something unwanted, or wanted over looked, for its extreme importance that may sway all prototype/popular thinking, etc., something new and revealing seems to ever surface in almost every small bit flicker enlightenment of his enlargement ability! There is so much more of the film to date, and even more being revealed future through close study of enlargements, that in a near future all persons will much further understand all of the complete true and horrendous story!"

Smaller Hominids?

"Really, we should perhaps ask Paul Wright, Rexburg, Idaho??"

During the year 2002 as already mentioned I wrote an article published in the Spring edition number two of Homology Magazine, titled: The Great Basin Wilderness Sasquatch, written from endless descriptive depositions had while on various desert locations where ever was described to me a much smaller Sasquatch best described here as the Great Basin Wilderness wild man often encountered if wandering under the moon in the far places of the Inter Mountain West of Nevada, Utah, Idaho, Montana, Oregon, and parts of Southern California, Eastern Washington, etc., all of that article shared the opinion that there truly is a much smaller wild man hominid running over all far high mountain desert North America! Of course if so, and I fully do believe that there is, then it is also to be realized that these smaller hominids regardless of size had all derived directly from an ancient basic same gene-pool blood line as ever were any others encountered described huge, gigantic, much larger, etc., unless (?) of course all smaller hominid differences have occurred according to any one separate foreign gene pool DNA carry over mutation, etc., that is not all far-fetched or impossible either, as wild hominids over all vast Eurasia and even Australia very considerably in different types and descriptions. All of this is easily explained if anyone at all understands all mega number of different existing ecosystems and vast regions of the Great Basin desert comprising the many separate American high desert mountain ranges that to all probability all separate congenial gene pools as they are, are the result of the fact of much similar understood human consanguinity, marfanism, etc. and genetics *per se* that is here not the space/or place for all of that explanation beyond the happy exchange of the sexual active gene pool partners had during the season of the Chinese Rabbit Moon, or love moon of reproduction, that by simple reasoning and all logical understanding had resulted in the massive hand and body proportions as would surely have any true huge described forest giant Sasquatch that would make it unlikely that as huge, anything of that sort would at all be able to accomplish such fine artistic plaiting as is continuing being found done on high desert and world horses!

It is easy to reason even in the vaguest of abstract cases, that much smaller hands are ever needed in close conjunction to braiding to have at all accomplished all such fine intricate handy work that is much more difficult to have accomplished on a living animal than ever it is done on willow and/or cattail basketry! "Sorry Charley Old Tuna, Harry of the Hendersons, is just ludicrous short of being a prototype hairy depiction other than the a hair example of Sasquatch und Der Frankenstein? However of late, demonic subjects, witch craft covens, and disgusting blood cults, have become more than been popular world over! What we shudder in fear of when in fright, might be just outside our window at late night?"

The Unwanted Truth Often Emerges! "Be Ready!" The illogical truth experienced through happenstance beyond conjecture often becomes the unwanted truth, far beyond man's fantasy, and all exhilaration had through exciting influence, infatuation, and/or wishful thinking. Mythological heroes are sometimes the only real answer to all logistics. The pastime adventure, and realized fantasies of sea pirates had to have been measured in dreams of things to come far from way beyond the next horizon. "Plaiting, and wild tales of Sasquatch and similar stories of mermaids seem to relate! What I do wonder is, if indeed any of this wild jargon of horse plaiting adventure writes anything related of them? Where do we go from here? There are recent claims that merman has actually been discovered? According to Hawaiian mythology and current testimonies as recent as 2003, sea-people of some sort have many times been seen walking atop the stone jetties and rock walls just off shore Waikiki? Darned if about anything doesn't sound possible? Perhaps, and perhaps not something a bit fishy is strolling wiki-wiki under the full moon light near Queen Surf Beach? Wild man as I think to know them, are not coming to dinner especially if you opt to serve them Idaho potatoes! That's all a well realized experienced fact that will be exciting reading ahead within the slated pages of the book titled: The Twilight Zone Chapters!

Sexual Dimorphism!

"No Charley, not more of the Chinese Rabbit Moon please! "Sexual dimorphism here relates to male gender head, face, and over all muscular body shape if have it noticeable or not, and/or at best recognizes a much varied gruff male gender facial expression as would be thought to be a horrid countenance, etc! Actually in the male gorilla only can be realized a natural built into actual protruding facial bone structure of the skull, or what is a protruding saggital forehead crest that easily identifies the dominant male gender. It may be true, as I further believe that some Sasquatch often referenced as Bigfoot in general descriptions as huge, ugly, beautiful, etc., and/or much smaller, very small, or even claimed to evidence no more than three foot tall (?), some many, many, adult identities are claimed in various sizes, weight, height, and sexual dimorphism variations of differing facial proportions, etc., (Apparently much like us they exist in many varying descriptions?). Often some are said much smaller than what exactly constitutes larger, uglier, or what is really a pleasant countenance, etc., and logically by this particular dispensation in time, some many may of them may have even needed to re-surface evolutionary/naturally, or abstractly be changed with all separate environments as needed to easily blend back into their separate type of humanity in multiple origins, and/or result in a definite and separate body exaggerations, etc. Even if this be so within all known close net regional gene pools, there very easily could be this definite noticeable difference among all individuals, especially if any of them are not born of an absolute first birth generation, exemplified by, Say, some small number of them long, long, ago had stemmed from a much already antiquated and separate gene-pool blood-line, as is highly probable that some of them had possibly several times of aeons of time mutated? Sasquatch types of wild man are every bit an ancient a bread apart as we humans. Doubt that and doubt your owe existence! As with some logical assumptions, anything said contrary to large as perhaps smaller in some regional case scenarios as the norm to encounter them seems not improbable, as for any wanton reason all descriptions of feral humans could wander at will into any and all ecosystems! Of course hominid size could easily vary as often happens even in human families, as there can be, and there often are astonishing exceptions! "However Charley, alligators never are to become crocodiles!" Anything thought to be less then that, is complete unadulterated B.S.! Perhaps peculiar to the each sorted wild hominid example encountered, are multiple, complex, and/or a collage of much mixed recent origins, if that makes any sense? Simply said, by the rational of all obvious cause and effect, relative of any natural active gene-pool, to be had over any vast extended region, environmental conditions, etc., as such, almost anything becomes likely and possible! The Great Basin Wilderness alone comprises from memory close to 148 separate wilderness river drainage ecosystems! "Many ancient prehistory clans, tribes, and when later came the warring nations had no, or very little prior working knowledge of the others similar existence!"

Log: Have The Huge Sasquatch Of The Clan Become The Investigative Protectors?

"Probably So, unless they have been expelled from the band?" That said, I have a separate theory to creature usefulness, especially in regard of these much larger members of the Wild-Clan so to speak, not the space here for all of that projected importance, but the larger examples definitely have a useful purpose as to size, and the cause and effect of bodily dimorphism; a logical fear effect upon all others of a foreign tribe, and/or their own (!), and if when for no other reason than their massive size, strength, and ability, and obvious sexual dimorphism denoting fear, any thing supposed to be a Giant Anything on Two Legs, able when/if needed to become without question the natural guardian, or expectant bully-protector of all lesser creatures than he; or if for example the large one became much, to much, self-determined and it become most obvious that he was much too aged and apart from the others to expect to compete against all other impending younger male prototype bullies, etc., and so in that way, the creature has purpose and was not over the hill, and so regardless of being thought by the others as a useless menace instead has an abstract alliance with the tribe; however when forced it can be logically rationalized that all tribe is suddenly wanting him to become an out cast renegade, etc., and for what ever the reason, all others smaller may have also found it suddenly obvious to all members to grant him stay ever to be avoided as a desperado, or perhaps even a natural enemy to be avoided in any cold case cause scenario, etc? (In a future manuscript I will explain the complete story of one such true case of an unknown huge creature already touched upon now called Rascal, first met when earlier explaining the horrifying true life adventure of Donald Massey promised somewhere ahead? All cave crew during years, 2002 - 2006, continued dubbed the cave creature as Rascal that had lived up to his name!"

Log: Monsters?

All Nature Sooner Or Later Solves Its Own Problems!

"Study an ant pile, the elk, deer, brat-children, rogue bears, humans, any number of the larger, wilder, hostile animals, as lions, elephants, hippopotamus, crocodiles, Tigers, etc., all of them have a legion of unmanageable problems to be solved within their confusing, cruel and hostel world of survival! We humans are no different from them in many ways, as we actually do have comparable problems and aspirations toward dangerous animals, and them to us! There eventually becomes in all nature an explicit confusion that finally becomes a definable relativity much the same with wild hominid Sasquatch, etc., and if indeed the later perhaps be suddenly thought to be monstrous by humans, or by their hominid-feral-brothers more docile or vicious, then in physical requirements of self-preservation they are not all that much removed from we Homo-sapiens as we ever think to know our selves and understand our separate peculiarities. Surprisingly many humans are at their very best or worse when wandering for what ever the reason in wilderness and/or at will, as when completely away from creature comforts and rec-ognized popular statuesque, when suddenly alone in a sudden reality-world, at a time when true human equality requires of oneself and all surviving with him, to all at once out of neces-sity become compassionate and tolerant of the other, the latent animal instinct often dormant within man becomes dominant, and he becomes creative, his senses begin to supersede his un-realized idiosyncrasies, he realizes his real worth, strengths, weakness, and becomes efferent; some many persons after a pleasant or difficult sojourn away from main stream society, when return completely re-adjust their life back onto the exciting side of nature to forever after relate to the happy savage. Nevertheless when we are compared to feral humanity, they are only much similar in survival logic as are we humans, as no matter what we are the least efficient on the scale... We are wimps compared! Our pseudo superiority is our educated brain, however I am not all that sure that we are actually (in so many ways) all that much smarter! What is alarming is all blind sight accepted moot science, as there are current think-tank theories flaunted of late that want-suggested that humans today may need to be realized to actually ex-ist as quite something else, far and apart from what we have already allowed ourselves to be-come? Wow, humans compared to exactly what else can we be? "What absurd, unrealistic, ab-stract, moot improbability won't wanna-be realized next? We humans are our own worst en-emy! For the sake of another dollar more, we toss out the baby with the bath water! What, really, have today's pseudo educators taught our children or us? Sometimes I wonder if we don't need to completely re-educate our natural ability, common sense, and logistics, in order to be able to re-learn what time has allowed forgotten? Have we all completely lost our cour-age and separate imagination to dream, ponder, wander, and to intelligently separate the Wheat from the Chaff by sharing in writing all of our new discoveries or what? Even if a thing is true, because of adverse opinion, ridicule, and pier pressure; fear of hostility, honesty, etc,. many persons choose to stalemate? Science hasn't got all of the answers, however human brain control has already entered its mid-life! Next thing we know we will be married to a Caddy Kathy Doll!"

Log: "Courage from Onya's note book, 2010 - ?"

"Tonia's night, sleeping out alone on canvas beneath the full moon! Writing during a cold night while pondering its inspiration?" "What, really, is to be said of exploration she wrote? Where do we go next when the sun turns off? Where is the beef and cheese? Where are my

179

kids? Where does human curiosity end? Where to go from here? What day is tomorrow, and what will be its purpose? Where are we now? Who was I, when I was who, when I was young, and who am I now? Where in the heck are these damn horses taking us? Why am I doing this at all? The night is very cold! Don is completely impossible! He is determined! I am committed, and I am going to stick it out!"

"The invisible Maverick in Room, # 126!"

"Ninja Research"

Ask M.K. Davis, as he well knows that room #126 is ever open to the weary-dismal, the defeated, the exonerated, and all first and last hungry comer! It is the most unlikely resting place of blistered feet, blood shot eyes and hammered nerves, where the wind is your butler; and the only all seeing eye is Diana, with her cold hung jury of bright night stars allowed to look down on you judgmental, "and if you lucky, by the mid day shadow, there will be more water, or perhaps you will opt to eat your last apple? The wood pecker has become my alarm clock! When marooned thus under the moon, there is ever the need for good tucker... (Nourishment!) As/if without it, One opts next to chew on a tough weed for moisture, and sometimes continues to enjoy it by the view of the Evening Star, before re-tightening Ones belt after another day of being way to thirsty! Too much wind, and not enough whiskey, or enough wood to start a fire! It is times like this when you better understand the feral hominid, the wild mustang, the confused domestic horse tethered imprisoned in some miserable holding pen! I won't be hobbled or caged! I don't shovel snow or cut grass or be domesticated! Hey, lets go have another look at those plaited horses!" MK, all that above if were written on paper would eventually become the folded sole mate note carried in the top pocket shirt of all true wandering researcher adventurer, as when money becomes short nothing is always easy in one's lone sojourn, and especially this is so with extended exploration! "Better said, nothing in discovery ever becomes certain until it is academically accepted, and then there is very little, or even a very slim chance of any monetary reimbursement. You are alone with hungry the wolves of no mercy! Writing a dubious manuscript is much the same! "The reward of the season was ever understood to had been the discovered truth, wasn't it? What, really, is more magical than all fond and precious memories? I will dream again of you tonight and you will be waiting! The night truly has one thousand eyes, and I know that you will be looking down to me without judgments! Belief in anything, or anyone, depends entirely upon who, and what we will allow ourselves to want to believe, and believe me, "there should be written a respectful over-due ode to wild man, the maverick horse, and the explorer, and to man's base survival, his acute intelligence, wild tensity, and his ever needed bob cat logic!

Log: *"Wild cats don't cut grass or shovel snow, and neither do I!"*

Imagine what it really means to be able to exist as a feral human, and in addition be required to be constantly finding food, shelter, and ever needful of unselfish compassion from all tribe to hope to raise your covert children; and all of the while be strangely wanting for what ever the reason to monthly comply to the demand of each full moon, "for what ever for hell sakes is the unnamed calling answered," and opt to be able in all seasons to accomplish horse unreasonable plaiting? What, really, comprises the stark influence of this most difficult to explain or un-

derstand anomaly? For just one time, over just one month of 28 days, anyone try it? Humans as we think we are today most competent; none could hardly think to do it on a nervous horse! You'd need prove it to me!" What, really, is to be said of these wily crafty hominid brothers and their ability to plait? Their Obvious Intellect Seems To Stay Their Provider? "They are as invincible as they are elusive! Perhaps we should more closely study the "Way" of them and the Invisible Ninja? For over thirty years I have written much adamant of my belief in feral hominids, wild-man, etc., well realizing that in due time the last laugh would finally be on a particular accredited air-head academic, ever insisting until of late slightly the adverse para-phrased: "that all Sasquatch running over North America are nothing more than a holdover example of a long thought extinct order of great apes, abrupt the had theory taken from a mere few-five or so in number decaying crumbling as we read antiquated bone fragments found of something walking bipedal, accepted by science to be the wanted remains of a par-ticular kind great ape in anatomical proportions, etc., as is supposed to had been Gigantopith-ecus? Even if that last said were true, the lack of general mentality; the duped posture of giant; all existing examples of the four larger apes, renders them unintelligent, and it is no wonder that eventually they would have become extent, "as if say any of them were loosened any where near where runs today's highway traffic, etc., no simple ape would be smart enough to avoid all of Americas road-rage prototype nation wide Los Angles type freeways! Think about it! Giganto even if he had survived into modern times, by now would have already at best long ago become a documented highway road-kill fatality! Wild man intellect when compared to an ape has no continuity!" "Highly Questionable? "I have heard of late that particular profes-sionals abrupt piers, are now thinking covert out of convenience, as some many are now changing their opinion of Sasquatch being instead a hominid rather than being a simple Gigan-topithecus, and so in time beyond objections some many may dare opt to re-write all pseudo descriptions of early man as is still insisted within many outdated academic books? Could it be that at last "the no-nothing maverick investigators among us are making a significant differ-ence to prove living hominid discovery? Early Man? Why for example would it be necessary for all early hominids as were Neanderthals and Cro-Magnon man to have needed to walk stooped-shouldered forward? That clumsy depiction would have made them extinct even much earlier than considered! I very much doubt that early man looked every bit as demented as is often depicted! Even our big boy Sasquatch if was also around back then in all probability never did either walk stooped-shouldered ahead more than modern man? Where is the actual proof? No ethnic passé race that were considered savages of any day performed other than highly agile, capable, and athletic! And to fact some of the wild peoples of Africa, as the Zulu and Watusi Nations; these athletic people have even been bored from particular Olympic Game competition because of their extraordinary ability to jump from off the bare ground head high, and their natural ability to heft a javelin further than any other people would even dare dream! The intricate plaiting of horses speaks obvious of wild-man's anatomical profi-ciency! Ever have I been self-encouraged of my personal hominid-Sasquatch prophecy of them being obscure human via reasons of endless field study, obvious common sense, and the many collected cast artifacts that I now have in my collection inclusive of posterior body parts, many hands and feet.

My firm belief of them being of an obscure human origin had always been true; as their close net human decent now has been once and for all time absolutely proven and accepted by the undeniable definitive photographic proof enhancements done by, M.K. Davis; everything to date possible has now been enhanced, (Enlarged!), all was taken only from off the original 1967 Roger Patterson movie footage copies, alleged taken at the time of the discovery of Patty

Sasquatch, October 20th, 1967! It is more than interesting that during the enhancement updates, all has now become clear the Patty Sasquatch has plaited hair! Yes, her hair can now be seen to evidence braids!"

Log: "Other Drummers! You Decide?"

Much other wild hominid evidence exists, most of it is kept covert, for the irrational fact that for many years many dedicated persons important within their own discovery abrupt hominid exploration, have been so unnecessarily roasted, ridiculed, and/or refused due credit, or any public recognition beyond all separate opinions of what's academically allowed popular, etc., "and so with that known, much unwarranted harm has often been done to credible reputations." Many a maverick and professional investigator within all private and academic exploration sectors, abrupt having had a separate genius within his own right has been treated ludicrous; as some many UN-deserving researchers have been as if "drawn and quartered," and left hung out to dry, resulting much discouraged of all efforts, abrupt pseudo piers, "who often as not out of narcissistic jealousy have collectively chose to bury their work conveniently under some obviously envious academic, or persuasive popular lay critic rug!"

"No Kidding!"

Never once to my knowledge has any professional abrupt all applauded much bias critic adoration, ever given anyone lay, even post-humus credit for their hard efforts? Particular academics seem to have already logged exactly what others besides themselves will be allowed to discover, and under what circumstance permitted by who, etc! "What have we become in this supposed magic Twenty First Century, that we have allowed our selves to have been so much self-betrayed by moot tradition, bias policy, etc., resulting self-captured if that be possible, in much latent academic opinion and obvious denial? Has all humanity suddenly ordained only what is thought to be orthodox computer logic to became our literal, "Lord of what Flies," ever wantin' of a smart phone opinion of what is allowed gospel according to who, when, and where, or what number of persons will decide exactly what will be accepted conclusive in all new hominid discovery or what? The truth allowed public of most all things important passé and of late 2013, seems only viable via the slanted media that is most of the time completely decisive of what, who, or if anyone otherwise will opt to believe them!"

More on Plaiting!

"From Ancient And Recent Mongolia!"

"Ishmahachi!"

("From the land of the Mt. lion!")

"Show me the scars of battle...! The scars of our warriors are definitely written in blood, and so are the true records of vigilance, compassion, and bravery! There is no second chance if your sword has been discarded, or confiscated! Hang on to your standard bearer, as the horses with the enemy are coming, and many, many, without saddles have plaited themselves to their horse by the long braids from their mane to hold them fast on their backs... Most important than your sword will be our rifles, be certain that the ammo stays dry! We have wax and honey to protect all from rust... What is foremost will be our courage! The adversary is very united! There is no second chance in battle! You can visit my Yurt when you choose, but I will decide when you leave! Da-gon Temenah, or better said, you are forever in my heart and on my lips!"

"Patterns Of Braided Hair!"

"Plaiting Been Done Almost Since The Beginning Of Humankind!"

"Steppe Horses Long Ago Were In The Americas!"

("The following is only but a short outline of all of the rest of the much probable story of North American Horses! There really needs be written another manuscript. The Steppe type horses have almost forever been in the Americas. The war horse of the Spanish Conquistadors hardly measures up to true Montana Indian Horse Prairie History. It is extremely interesting that I have discovered that the very same sort of smaller Steppe horse of a much similar type as was/is still used in Mongolia and many places of adjacent China, are much similar in type as are the long been in use American Indian ponies, that in true fact are most of them not all that un-similar to the horses of ancient China, and very much the same size as are the Neil Hinck Blazer horses. It is also the fact that where ever I can find the Blazer horses, the strange plaiting seems to dominate. Smaller animals for some reason seem to be predominate choice of what ever entity is actually doing the plaiting. In future I am hopeful to run down if can actual sale locations where many, many, of these Blazer horses were sold? It might be possible? The continuing research to this effort since all new and recent discovery has actually just began. I have no choice but to leave the reader from here with just exactly what information has already been written. Not all that long ago during this research sojourn, I was guided to a little visited high mountain Montana cave by Darrel Miller where he showed to me a very rare pictograph evidencing very ancient Indian Steppe type horses. Mixed in the treasure were animals dating back to include the Pleistocene. I know this possible dating due to artifacts passé turned in for carbon dating, etc. Updates to all of this will be written if ever I find the time to continue the priority? Suddenly I am excited to search for the actual extended whereabouts of passé purchased Blazer horses!"

Log: "Critic Note: Respectful Credit!"

("This Isn't The hot Pits, or The Cold Hammers of Hell either!")

In spite of all supposed ridicule and roasting of academics and critics here, this treatise wants no further part of all these misunderstandings; as perhaps all of what was thought derogatory, debase, judgmental, misleading, was written in good stead to enlighten all public appreciation of all hard working fellows, academic and lay maverick alike! Most academics are far and above and well beyond unrealized unsung creditability! Believing in them, me, or anyone or not, wild feral populations as hominid-Sasquatch, or name them what you have existed in parallel right along side of all pseudo civilized humanity since the very most ancient of ancient dispensations of humankind, and has managed a close net restrictive survival pattern along side, and has ever endured all human encroachment since our earliest beginnings! Just as surely as there is the wind, a sun, and ever a bright full moon, each month hominid Sasquatch or something realized as wild-man truly plaits the long manes of horses, and I very well know it and am damn well here to write about it. Again said, I have encountered wild hominids on three separate occasions and know without a doubt that some many of them of one obscure sort or another are the only ones likely that can be doing the plaiting! Doubt that, and everyone without further founded conjecture to a logical debate becomes an ignorant bias critic! Blind ignorance, bias opinion, unfounded moot and harmful blather, arrogant air-heads, etc., are the prototype of narcissism, jealousy, and selfish inapt-sterile inability! Persons such are completely incompetent of mind, unethical, uninteresting, and a devastation to all true scientific discovery, and a real and honest threat to all Boniface Good Intention. There is no place in hominid discovery for the narrow minded Gold-Fish Sooth-Sayers of any ilk that opt to selfishly thwart newly discovered importance! It is to be strongly emphasized that all truly intelligent, credible, compassionate, and highly dedicated critics, and accredited academics are not remotely of that particular above described, "cold school of no-class spineless week-fish! If I am describing you, well, you know damn well exactly who you are! Your illogical harm done to many a diligent productive fellow will one day prove to bite you on your improbable coffee cup shaped fat ass!"

Log: Animals and the Moon!

"The Moon's Strange Effects On Men And Animals Are Many!"

Moon phase undoubtedly effects civilized man and wild populations much the same, as any wild entity existing today thought to be even half as intelligent as Homo-sapiens would need react much similar in behavior? It is well founded that the moon effects the ocean tides, calms the wild wolves and coyotes, as by moon light all animals are more able to see to hunt at night, etc. The badger is highly nocturnal. His dependence of substance is when wandering beneath the moon. If one wants to see one of these magnificent brothers of the night, such as a gray fox, bob cat, etc., keep a sharp eye-out for them most often on moon lit nights, as then is when they wander most amiss! The Native Americans much revere badgers as very important to their understandings of life and all nature logistics, even to include lessons in child care, birthing ability, re-production, etc! Knowing that the moon highly effects the higher animals, ocean tides, etc., and considering that the human body is comprised of approximately 75% parts water, isn't it also likely that the moon may also somehow directly effect some of our chemical and emotional make-up outcomes of the human body and the brain and body structure of wild-man as well, and especially this much SO of all we pseudo civilized night people! Definitely there is something within that reasoning within the wanton magic of the city lights, and bright rabbit moon light to consider!"

Log: Unorthodox or Acceptable Conjecture?

You Decide! I well realize much of: Full Moon Totems, orthodox and unorthodox mythological worship, etc! Worshiped initiates as were often highly revered in ancient times were of many, many, variations of known, and little realized descriptive idolatry, and many of the long de-stroyed endless non-descriptive mythological totems still to be realized in museum basements, etc., date beyond understood antiquity and conclusive origin, and were well known and in use over most all of the early European and Asiatic Nations, and this adherence had included many a previously worshiped or highly reverenced, Moon Goddess or God, as was the renowned the popular, Selene, Hectate, Neptune, and one more simple example that still with much with us today as is, The Lunar Crescent Moon Goddess of the Gypsies, "the all seeing eye of, Diana, etc!" Many such though unorthodox effigies Idols, etc., still exist in obscure adoration. Truth known, even the innocent Kachina Dolls, Worry Dolls, and the shark God Mono, and the re-lated, Kahuna, from the practice of Huna, and the dread Voodoo belief, etc, all of this and much more to be said still are able to weave their magic spell and abstract messaging of con-trol within the adoration of considerable numbers of today's world populations, including all high strange cultist, full moon adherence, etc., as is referenced of a respectful mention of to-day's hold over ancient Druids, that long ago beginning about the 17th Century many of them settled their resident beliefs within the coastal villas of much of all Northern California above where is today Fort Ord; after landing here from The British Islands, many Druids settled over the Northern coast of California, etc. There is just too much here to think to hope to explain, and far not enough book space and time here this manuscript to think that this is the place to attempt to cover all known abstracts adherence of the full moon and all of its effects on man, but if completely understood, what if anything does any one make of the influence still to be recognized of the cleverly hand carved, meaningful totem-pole effigies, still to be had that are highly revered of many a North West Coast Indian tribes and beyond, where there are beauti-ful wood sculptured depictions of totem animals including Pacific Ocean Salmon, Beavers, Bears, Man-bears, Otter-men, eagles, definite retrospect identities of Sasquatch, etc? The Scott-Irish identification with the legendary, Sea Selchie is much similar of the legendary Otter Man, and the many, many, tons heavy, hand hue n, very ancient stone Idle effigy depiction of ,"The Great Han Tortoise of China," already mentioned is another magnificent, if not it the eighth wonder of the ancient world (?), and in places of the Eurasian Steppes, there are other astonish-ing horse effigies suggestive of idolater to compare to the documentation of the long sung Tro-jan Horse! Magnificent Asian and Oriental animal effigy examples are done in endless hand carved beautiful stones, Jade, and incredible jewelry representations of human/animal com-bined effigies dating back as far as the writing of "The I-Ching!" The possibilities of abstract probabilities of Sasquatch and similar representation as wild-man is still much in adherence through my horse plaiting theory, and perhaps some of the plaiting requirement if not all of it is accomplished of a long forgotten Idolatrous worship carryover expectant custom, up from all varied influence and habitual adherence to a particular moon goddess as suggested, etc., and just possibly all of this is a latent result of the understood mega concerns for safety and life continuance its itself that even today through habit and toil remains as if required unwanted burden that threw fear or similar none dare not adhere? Just because someone insists/demands that only pseudo Orthodox Christian Worship be allowed/opposed to all other abstract tradi-tions respectful, etc., perhaps if any considered highly Unorthodox, and/or much moot in opin-ion, to be a release of unwanted Pagan religious practices, beliefs/customs, etc., this does not grantee in the least way, "that in all stark fact and reality, that Very Ancient Deity Outcomes, and all wanton influence had among ancient and current semi-demonic adhering wild popula-

tions are not still being carried out, and much practiced covert in some particular part through plaiting wanting be accomplished via the light of each bright or sud-dude full moon! For example, Witch-Craft, at the present time like it or not is ever popular all over North America; in fact even as I write, it is now ramped and on much on the increase, and yet few persons will admit to participating in the practice regardless of being an active member of a coven! What more need be said? Wild-Man in all true innocence, may be completely unrealized himself of/or by all his miss-identified humanity to need to continue to exist very much just the same as if he were forever to remain as if forever was cursed to be a more than miserable highly tormented sole (?), completely self-captured and ever lost and confused and much in awe of an ongoing mixed confusion of physical and mental requirements that has literally become an extremely ancient tradition (Over-kill!) of sorted misunderstood requirements ever resulting in a habitual need to be participating in required plaiting? This at best is a classic example of a highly deceptive and very cruel self-damnation, completely unrealized and unmeasurable that as it seems will ever end? If any of this is true, the poor self-condemned souls may think themselves forever cursed to damnation and per-destined if you will to forever need endure a life abrupt all human rejection and to eek out their time in complete misery of the elements! Whoa, what a thought! Not that is is conclusive, but many persons that have been completely unknown to the other over many years apart in deposition testimony, etc; upon hearing first time (Any time!) the forlorn hellish sometimes almost pitiful wale of an alleged Sasquatch has often voiced similar auto-suggestion that the poor creature sounds just like they were calling up to us from Hell!"

Log: "Sasquatch Vocalization!"

Titan River Washington, April 15th, 2002.
"Excerpt from book, Sasquatch 2001!"

"I have long wondered at the implications of the loud, and ever seemingly miserable cry of a forlorn Sasquatch, that my late wife Marion with me when together had heard more than several times! The undeniable miserable cry has often as not been described as if something were very forlorn, forbidding, and completely miserable, and/or was in dire need of human compassion, understanding, etc? (?) "Or perhaps Don, Marion said, something is out there very miserable and highly uncomfortable, and is in need to be crying out in distress just as if it were right now perhaps having a baby!" Wow Marion, I had told her, what a thought! The high pitched and variable sound truly is forbidding enough to be considered by some many to be almost beyond frightening!"

Log: A Friendly Plea To Intelligent Critics,
and Accredited Academics!
Absolutely we do need varied opinions, and mixed

comparative logic to solve mysteries and problems? However false profits are unwanted! My space, your space, and every opinion considered; and, perhaps you have noticed that in this book we have given critics and professionals a lot of space, and that's much consideration in my opinion for them to have aired all basic idiosyncrasies! The reason for that is that the author well realizes the general populace naive mind-set, and many a negative attitude pertaining of some critics, and a few of today's misguided, uninformed, misinformed, lay and professional

186

pseudo hominid investigators, etc. Many a truth searching critic are not all of them particularly bogus! I am ever of a high respect and regard of honest hopeful research expectations. Truth known, less than bias, open minded critics, often do become wonderful contributors of the truth, ever able to aid all general and abstract knowledge of about everything possible! Many of my best commandeered exploring crew had often as not first time approached me inquisitive in a much critical, negative, and sometimes even an obnoxious demeanor! Some many since have became almost as if family! We do need to ask each other questions, and collectively most everyone wants help solve answers! It is sad that many critics do not adhere to that equation!

Sometimes it is the pity, myself included, that many a pseudo informed professional and/or critic, often as not, if only by his very inquisitive and impulsive nature is unable to respond satisfactory spontaneously to all questions posed to everyone's satisfaction, and at a same time be convincing to himself and all lay spontaneous pier critic roasting and questioning thought unsatisfactorily when/if any thing was answered only in comparative logic, conjecture, etc., and so, often an academic, or any defensive/informative thought moot of response, results only in an obvious and dubious mode of spontaneous irritation to all audience already bordering prior on complete disbelief, without the person in question having had a full opportunity to better explain all rational intelligently; to explain it more intelligently than was perhaps first presented satisfactory to all illogical know it all been there and done that doldrum objectionaries, smattered with no further logical or conjunctive thought than has an angle worm! Sometimes a speakers instinctive answers to quasi-questioning is offered way far and ahead of too much wind coming from an audience of to much pier whiskey! "Flowers for the good times and booze for the bad! Other Vistas! Sir Francis Drake during his early Pirate and exploring sojourn, when sailing off the coast of South America, discovered what he described was an extremely tall unlikely, said to be a very savage and cannibalistic example of wild man who called themselves the Ona! They were found in a coastal river mountain region of lower wild South America not far from what is today the State of Santa Cruse. It seems that wild man are found about everywhere! It is possible that the Ona, and the obscure, high strange, and wild, Fueagian Yámana people of frozen Terra del Fuego, described mid 19th Century by Charles Darwin, (Now nearly extinct?), because of anatomical similarities to much Sasquatch evidence found in castings, exemplified by the particular peculiarity of extremely long fingers, toes, etc; from compared foot and hand casts taken by the author much far North of the Border in Idaho/Montana, all of this may indicate that at least some Sasquatch may have been at one time all relive to some of our South American wild people, as some of their strange habits are also much similar in vocalizations and all obvious interest in astrology as moon phase, etc? This observation in time may have further ramifications to plaiting? There is a much more high strange story most untold of the Yámana! I have thought to go to there frozen land to investigate their passé existence, as there still are founded reasons to suspect that the wild Ona Tribe as well as some remnant Yámana may still exist? It is to be remembered that South America is the land of the long hired Lama, and Alpaca. As yet I have had no opportunity to investigate further suspect of plaiting also being done to them or by the Indians when in use as working pack animals? It is likely this could also be being done, as it has been the custom since time immortal for owners of pack animals to want/need to plait the handy useful long hair of about everything."

"Christianity (?) and Wild Man?"

PLAITING!

"Are there Biblical references to wild man? Well, yes indeed there are, but they are not referenced Sasquatch, and this is not the place here to air all of that sometimes unwanted argued projection, but whether anyone is interested in the scriptures or not they should have a close educated look, as there are several places in the King James Version where wild man is referenced! The Adam and Eve avenue of approach in Genesis, thought to best be able to explain all mankind and his reasons seems to be the only safe Christian path to attest man's origin. Truth known, as far as scriptorium goes, there is still much, much, more to be understood of man's early beginning and all of its many ramifications ("If accepted?"), that might even more help to explain exactly what else unexpected my have been allowed to be wandering with them out of The Garden of Eden?"

(For further stark evidence of wild man beginnings, and historical reference, "read," the historic Jewish manuscript titled: The Book of Jasher," and "Mother India!" Actually in many ways Christian religion and its theologies are uncomprehending differently than are most all other non ascribing religions, as this slightly naïve attitude touched upon above, is prevalent with almost every new idea, Pro-Christian or otherwise, that might have been first thought by anyone critical of the subject to had been too far outside of Christian ethics for serious considerations, or to had been to far off the wall to be considered to be more than a completely unorthodox topic, subject, or an improbable all new theory, idea, etc., especially if it hadn't already been decided in the first place that everything debated there was illogical, and/or derogatory, much slanted, bias, and so, on and on goes the story, even sometimes argued suggestive of diabolical, etc., but regardless, ever resulting in them critical or not, for the most part most Christian subscribers are still congenial enough in spite of what ever their opinion may be, or not be, they are ever firm of convictions, and still most all of them prevail in their own way, unrealized hypocritical of any new opinion viruses wild hominid entities, etc., even if it had been admitted that they believe in a thing or not! However on the other hand, some many Christian persons as I know them, also remain open minded and some many are of a much sorted opinion, and are ever in high support of Sasquatch being only one of a kind of a pseudo wild man probability highly suggestive that to fact of their opinion he is satanic! However for some people to even think it possible that a very ancient moon phase adherence could have carried on to this day past the Inquisition and Dark Ages, and still have an influence on humanity; even if it were true that wild man was only an army of one, "it still is unacceptable that he be anything but devilish," and for most the further explanation him being a true hominid actually is probable via much historical fact and reasoning, as to be able to explain plaiting is completely unthinkable without something having an opposed finger and thumb! Religion, fiction, fantasy, and reality, are tough! For Orthodox Christians the contest is harder! For them no opinion beyond Biblical connections, pro/con, are ever enough! Church, and State, determines all wild man, and human fate!" Brother Wild, perhaps projects that all man's doom is to be finally swept away by, Some morbid hell fire wind, that comes from somewhere off the dark side of the moon? (The moon again?) At some obscure beginning it is true, that we all were created much, much, similar... but in my opinion hardly are we equal in intellect, and that makes all of the difference! At least as far as the astute ability to plait, wild man is much our superior!"

The Wisconsin Ice Man!

"Ice Child Anyone?"

"Some of you will likely remember him, and if not then by 2014?"

Undeniable, definitive, proof of wild hominid existence does exist!

Not all that long after the discovery and filming of Bluff Creek Patty Sasquatch in 1967; shortly after during that same year but not to come front until early 1968, the horrendously murdered bloody body of a dubbed valid hairy wild man hominid was found shot dead with the back of its head blown away! The pitiful creature had also been shot another time threw the chest with a heavy rifle where still can be seen ("In existing photographs), what is the huge gaping hole! The obscure entity mysteriously turned up with much high suspect of a fraud, moot, and a more than bogus story attached to it, "and next thing we knew, very shortly after its discovery it had completely vanished into oblivion; to this very day there is not one small clue to when, how, where, or who got it (?), never once to any ones satisfaction has anyone been able to realized all of the rest of the Ice Man story?"

"Well, just perhaps there are some small clues? Where is the Ice Man today? And why has he been hidden? The complete true story to this day remains beyond extraordinary and highly controversial to his whereabouts? Where really do anyone dare think beyond all reason that the Ice Man may be in fact on ice in Canada? And for what important possible political involvement good reason has the Wisconsin Ice Man been stashed? It has now been all of 46 years since his disappearance, and since the alleged discovery of Patty Sasquatch in 1967! It has its good reasons that no one after her initial discovery has ever seen Patty since...! And what actually has happened by now to the documented body of the Wisconsin Ice Man? And who, why, etc., was he taken? Definitely that story continues to this day as, Another On-Going, Great Northern Mystery? Perhaps all must read after March 2013, the next slated book that may partly explain it, titled: "

Memories of Discovery, co-authored by, myself, and MK Davis!"

Log: Notes on "Patty Sasquatch, and, The Wisconsin Ice Man"

Excerpt From My Old Log Book:
Journal, June 19th, 1997.

Whether anyone believes in Sasquatch or not, there is definitive proof of them in the discovery of, "Bluff Creek, Patty," alleged filmed single handed by Roger Patterson, thirty years ago, October 20, 1967, and shortly after during the year of 1968, was made a positive identification of a male wild entity that turned out to be a murdered, shot and killed believed in 1967, and said/believed to had been a juvenile hominid ("Likely Was A Child?"), wrongly dubbed adult, or, "The Wisconsin Ice Man," because he was first seen hard frozen within the confines of a large block of clear ice! The murdered juvenile from photographs in very many ways much resembles "Bluff Creek Patty," and it hardly seems plausible or completely believable that two separate much similar hominids would turn only a few months apart? Something is not right? A positive evaluation was done on the, "Ice Man," by, Doctor, Issac Sanderson, and the conclusion stands to this day as said next in his exact same words, ("Doctor Issac Sanderson!"..."the hairy carcass remains were definitely of human descent, best explained it was an obscure wild hominid!") All of the rest of the known facts of that pathetic story well attest/confirm its truth as well as continues to rises high suspicious that the unexplained reasons for the sudden disappearance of the carcass in time will horrify the world when all finally realize his true origin, if not further distress us all when we learn why, how, and who, for what wanted reason the Wisconsin Ice Man remains hidden to this day, and the considerable many high political persons that may have been involved."

Log: "Don, that above somewhere in our manuscript, as in my opinion it much pertains to the 1967 discovery of Patty Sasquatch, and is of considerable importance!" - Tonia!

"A Completely Unsolved Cold Case Mystery?"

"Patty, discovered and filmed, 1967; the, Ice Man, discovered, shot and killed, year, 1967! Ice Man brought public early year 1968? One wild women discovered, & and one Ice child! Both very much similar dates and time? Now isn't that extremely Interesting? As said, both dates are very close! Wow, what am I thinking? A Sasquatch Child indeed! Anyone further interested in this high strange anomaly, should get a valid documented copy of Issac Sanderson's 1968 deposition report, and next read it methodically between the lines in order to fully realize what else informative its actually exposed in the presentation that remains to this day highly important that most persons going on fifty years probably haven't one clue? Obviously in Sanderson's professional opinion, he provided definitive proof of wild hominid existence, and professionally verified to his satisfaction that the Ice Man was indeed instead a child, and that it/he had been definitely been twice shot and killed! Everything about the discovery of Patty Sasquatch and the Ice Man seems odd? Well, yeah, be sure to get a copy of the slated book for 2013 titled, "Memories Of Discovery," for all of the rest of the horrendous story!"

Protective Politics?

What is also interesting and ever obvious to many that has long kept silent remains the fact that even now perhaps for some highhanded International political reason that to this day has long been wanted overlooked and not empathized, "was the ever obvious, and stark much kinlikeness comparatives of both of the separate creatures, that today becomes even more than obvious when closely examining done the ever incredible M.K. Davis film enhancements! With these film enlargements, there is an undeniable high suspect probability of them each being of a same close net family type, of a much similar tribal resemblance! This is at least for now, but all of it at best hypothetical evidence, that can be easily determined at least to be circumstantial within all photographic enhancement comparisons, as BOTH of these wild entities each provide astonishingly similarities, and probably speak for undetermined clandestine reasons for all of it wanted remain unnoticed? In my high suspicions, both alleged dates of discovery are very much almost to close together to be at all coincidental, and may in time have much overlooked significance? What ever is finally found to be the complete truth of the Ice Man disappearance, "it was I remind you, the profound opinion of Isaac Sanderson, paraphrased as follows, best can be said word perfect from memory... "Of the Ice Man he said... Well, the creature here before me is very young, and definitely as all obvious is an immature male! Perhaps instead of, "Ice Man," we should call him,

"Ice Child!" As of record, all stark murdered physical evidence of the Ice Man quickly disappeared shortly after Issac Sanderson's testimony, and the creature remains are now believed by the author, and important others to be somewhere kept covert in Canada? Anyone dare have more information? Please contact the author.

"M.K., dare we tell it all?"

"1967, &, 1967?"

(?)

All considering the Patterson/Gimlin 1967 discovery of, Patty, and soon after the appearance of the, "Ice Man," in 1968, is that an interesting date similarity or what? What more say anyone? Not here the place for an elaborate debate, but wouldn't it be wonderful if at the present time we still had The Ice Man Carcass; or had available a valid hominid field journal reference book explaining every ethnographic possibility of everything hominid of everyone via DNA, etc., that would fully explain/describe all wild-man Sasquatch, Bigfoot, ethnology, etc! Perhaps in time that will come, but for now we have only the unfounded blathering of all persons lay, or, maverick/professional similar of me! We all in my opinion have one hell of a lot more yet to learn before wasting time to throwing moot rockets and fire crackers at Sasquatch; wasting time doing more ridiculous as continued banging on forest trees, etc! (Tree knocking, etc., all of that, after enjoyed making possible contact, the continued effort is complete nonsense! Sasquatch as I have thought to hear them answer probably responds, but after that first attempt is actually laughing at the Naivtè of all mankind for good reason! Of course some say it works.... However Sasquatch when/if answers back, is ever in complete control... Probably him saying in reply... "Man, you are stupid, we are not coming out to visit, etc!"

Sasquatch have no use for mankind! They well know that we well realize their existence! Not in my life time, but perhaps in a future of yours, they will come forward, but I much doubt it! The full reasons for that belief in my opinion is still being conjured.... Sasquatch are likely a much more important, completely unrealized hominid extension of human and historical religious history, etc., than probably most persons realize! "Indeed, the truth makes us free, and Sasquatch sure the heck are!"

Log: Chief Smoky.

Northern Paiute Indian Reservation, Ely Nevada, talking Sasquatch logic, horse plaiting, strange aquatic creatures, and tribal rote history, Christmas week, 2004 - "Chief Smoky, speaking in a somber but humorous jest finally said... "what is it with you whites anyway? We Indians have long knoticed that when Sasquatch inters your thoughts many of you without enough whiskey thinks of them too much and some seems to looses his sanity! But our local Sasquatch sometimes come to our caves and brings us pinion nuts and then stays a while to enjoy our hospitality, fry-bread, berry pie, and sometimes even try to be off with our women! All of them are not the same... Some not so friendly? Chief, I asked him... What more can you tell me about the strange braiding done on your horses? And you say that you have seen the Sasquatch? Heck yes he answered! Do you think I am nuts, or what? Heck, we Paiute have seen them lots of times! I hope that you well realize that there is not just one? One of our local Indi-

ans named Gary, just last fall he... well, it was very funny too! We were all down fishing at the lake, and we came onto this crazy looking braided horse... Gary went over and grabbed onto one of the long dangling braids, and next thing we knew the horse ran off with Gary hanging on for dear life along side it, trying to run and keep from being drug or killed over all of those big rocks and brush! Finally he let go when landing in a thick clump of sage brush and boulders! We all ran over to pick him up, and he was crazy angry at all of us for not that trying to stop the horse sooner! To say the least, Garry's understandings of horses was much enhanced! Indeed, I was thinking, this definitely was going to be a much candid record of a wild Christmas Surprise Party, Chief Smokey, horse plaiting, Sasquatch, Sea-monsters, deer and bear hunting, and white man's good, and bad food, and way too much Indian whiskey! We all however had the Christmas Spirits, and so none were much on the war path!

Continued:

The five day extended Christmas Week Party spent at Ely Nevada!

"Part time (One long day until late evening!), we spent time in a local Mt. cave at 7,000 foot elevation. The cave after would never be the same!"

The Chief Tells it all?

All following paraphrased from the partly recorded wisdom of my good friend, Chief Smoky Frederickson, Paiute Reservation, Ely Nevada, when many gathered together at the improbable Indian/white man, Christmas Pow-Wow, held beginning December 23rd – 28th, 2004 - "I still keep a treasured feather!"

"Don, Smoky began: like I told you, the white man goes home and thinks too long, and way too much about Sasquatch, and goes crazy, and then drinks his whiskey! We Indians consume our whiskey first, and think nothing about them after! The Sasquatch are unlucky, they have no whiskey, and we actually want nothing at all to do with them! Sometimes like I said they come! We have learned some of their ways and get along! Those who understand this wild tribe cannot tell the white man as he does not want to hear it. Why do you think that white man cares so damn much about Sasquatch, when sure as hell Sasquatch do not care about him, us, or much even about themselves? For some unexplainable reason white man seems to have a need for a monstrous bogyman-wild man in their life? As for the messing with the horses, I have no idea? But they just do it every so often? Some of the wild ones sometimes look like a lot of loose scraggly hanging baggage! The desert mustang are very hard to catch! Yes, its hard to understand? Some think they may be braided for hand holds... Don't know Don? What you think? And guess what? We got some kind of an unknown sea creature or something swimming in one of our warm thermal lakes! Yes, some of tribe would take you there... Come back when you can and we will go !"

Gene Scheller and Ron Roseman, you are invited with M.K. Davis, Johnny Foxx, and myself! Perhaps we can do it spring/summer, 2014? Bring along your knife, Rye Crackers, Cheese, & Spam!"

Log: November 23, 2012

Java Bob Schmalzbach's Radio Show!
"A needed aftermath reprieve!"

Well Java, after last nights show, in order to truly answer your pointed question of who am I (?), "back to you I ask the same question, who really are you?" For another time I have appraised your slanted opinion, and you are still much criticizing some of my predicted confusions, all of the while me still somewhat compassionate of your misunderstandings when you said that my books wander way to much far ahead, and are always way to far behind, and still they are ever close ahead at the same time, and they are definitely full of wind; they are as difficult to understand, as they are impossible to compromise. You jump from one thing to another almost as fast as you can think and sometimes talk!" {"Well Bob, just as I said last night, I need to get this all down having to do with horse plaiting as fast as can, as this manuscript might be but close to my demise as a last hurrahs! Time is fast running out for free spirit exploration. Man-kind has become influence by unimaginable machines! I am struggling to write this expo say as fast as I can for time without any further edit, ever hopeful to be making logical sense enough for others reading to be able to decipher all of what is not said here pertaining important had between all story line. I can actually rationalize, if not fully agree with some many of your wandering thoughts, as I remember you said .... "as perhaps Don, I do fully agree that there is a critical need for intelligent rational in order to fully understand your theory leading up to the plaiting; and it is most important also to be openly conjecturing most all mixed and varied opinions of others thinking themselves better able to explain the braids beyond some flaunted wanton insane gobbledygook nonsense claiming that it was done by pixies, ghosts, etc, and what the hell really other high strange sort of an unknown entity some many might claim may be doing it?"

If by now some many of you reading are still without a general conviction; "have not arrived at a decisive able to even pseudo explain what wild Sasquatch might be, then by all of my hard efforts we have arrived to exactly nowhere, and may as well settle for Bart Simpson and/or Big Bird importance had along side Monday night Football? What more completely off the wall conjuncture do I dare next? "Ok, what, really, do anyone think to believe of the likely probability had of some belief to attest the true existence of a sizable world population of aquatic Mermaids? Yeah, really, there is some highly persuasive thought on this!"

Log: Donald L. Monroe, "MOON PHASE"

"After much study I have concluded that "moon madness," sometimes called that, said occurring during the bright-lit "mesmerizing full moon," when considering all hard life necessities, and possible lunar beliefs had of passé and current day feral populations that has been partly explained may actually have something direct to do with plaiting? If that true, then what and why is the high motivation controlling factors if not for abstract submissive reasons? Ancient man remains with us today as if a relict hominid bogyman in part if only in our latent fears, anxieties, fantasy. and him wanting forgotten within dis rot of disagreements disgusting of particular queasy religious practices of idolatry adorations, etc., including some many metaphysical adherence of uncanny influence and unexplained/unexpected human desires, emotions, peculiarities, requirements, etc., best said, that in ever so many base ways common man still re-

PART ONE

mains interconnected of all "natural man," and natural man as recognized in a particular as-cribed Biblical Quote said next (slightly paraphrased) is: "Natural man is the enemy of God," and if that so then man as a Christians accepts himself and others only if them up to orthodox beliefs from unorthodox superstition and the unwanted influence of witch craft type associa-tions or similar, and everything related of it still practiced that to fact is on the increase in America as are realized viper snake adoration, vampire cultists, grave-side ceremonies, and other covert types of strange covens and cultist associations similar as is the "Bohemian Grove," etc., as for example what do we accept are the basic effects of idolatry, paganism, highly re-vered effigies, statuary, etc., and its effects upon participating humans to include wild man an-xiety via full moon adherence and culture?

Perhaps some many of you have journeyed to the far South Pacific Islands as are the 7,000 Is-lands of the Philippines, or Indonesia, Borneo, Australia, New Genie, etc., and if so, or not, if you were ever in the least bit interested in different ethnic cultures, customs, etc., and/or realized all many unorthodox paginate adherence to serpents, monkeys, nautical adoration, etc., obscure sto-ries of man like wild bipeds, and the unprecedented rational thought all necessary be any part of it abrupt all similar full moon adoration, then you at least somewhat realize the many unorthodox manifestations and the strange magnetism that continues to effect the animistic mind evidenced perhaps in wild orgies of disdain and even sacrifice had of many still existing considered savage and debase cultures. "The sliver moon phase," known as the "Crescent Moon," is said to be the ever judgmental-decisive look down effigy upon all mankind via a lunar depiction of the Moon Goddess Diana, that ever follows the night stars to first shrink and then evolve soon after into a full bloom moon again after each and every full moon phase; Diana appears and re-appears on both sides of the full moon equation in order to observe what ever took place good or bad during darkness in the after math of all past lingering light of full moon phase. Keep Diana in mind, just as if she would forever be expectant of all mankind and in judgment of his accomplishments, customs and traditions as all becomes of a mixed important to the crux of the authors theory as what if ... as will be further conjectured, "what if indeed the Goddess Diana besides having a definite adher-ence importance to wild-man, gypsies, thieves, etc., likely her alleged powers (where ever al-lowed?), have also influenced some of their beliefs concerning life and death requirements of some many indigenous peoples, including birth and reproduction practices/customs, marriage, etc? Likely early man's fears, anxieties, fascinations, as well as him being forced through bondage after capture (If he was?), has resulted in the ever strange plaiting thought to be done according to the moon, etc. , and so to this day all of the strange anomaly continues as a required tradition at the mercy of an obscure effigies such as Diana, Ishtar, Isis, etc?

In all probability most all of what is conjectured above will be said by the bulk of the been there and done that western neophyte community to had been nothing more than wanton unor-thodox improbable haberdasher-hash beliefs of many a far-lung distant considered savage nation to be experienced if ever anyone visits any of the exciting extensions of Oceania as are, China, In-dia, Sri Lanka, Thailand, etc., and all extended mixed Oriental, and Russian middle eastern/Eurasian unnamed lands that were once the passé, and some still predominate in Neophyte habitation (Neophyte meaning the white race), inclusive of all mixed-ethnic settlements found within all fro-zen land borders of mixed nation Siberia, Eskimo and Indian Alaskan peoples along its coast, etc., Lap, and Finnish-Icelanders, etc! The Eskimo for example unrelated to passé Orthodox Christianity, or idolatry etc., nevertheless adhere to superstition still much alive today in remote villages, as the Eskimo for example dread/fear the tenacious powers of the tiniest shrew.. ("Or what is the least

194

weasel, the smallest member connected to the ermine.") ... in the dire belief that if/when it wants, it can burrow through a man's chest during sleep to his heart and kill him! With that said, what many, many, other high strange customs still prevail among us that we have not even began to contemplate or never will that are far too obscure and difficult to explain, and much too long winded to want to realize here for time and space; in spite of all next said, I only know but very little of mega diverse customs, but enough to fully relate to what is ever possible within human morbid fears that had sparked this moon theory! What if indeed there is a meaningful allegiance, a special wild-primitive alliance, a realized acceptance of perhaps Diana and the moon or some other; just as if all plaiting were a for-born requirement to be learned and mastered on horses? A required physical indulgence expressed wanting to participate or not judgmental through plaiting (?), just as if perhaps all can be defined to be an intricate and most difficult accomplishment, or could be instead, a definitive reverence payment thought all necessary to signify some unknown long forgotten (?), or even perhaps an expressive physical respect, via hand dexterity through much difficulty, indulgence/endurance, ever required to be done of those capable/dedicated, ever to be accomplished in a vague, almost unfounded/fearful latent/recall, had conjured-up from deep within the memory data-bank of particular alleget wild hominid entities; it even may be an un-wanted custom if you will, a confused conglomeration of unexplained long forgotten reasons to want/need to comply in physical and difficult hardship/appurtenance at moon phase (?), a drudg-ery in fact if done by adverse weather conditions; an unheralded and highly irritating nuisance at times, just as if it were a cursed harassing obligation dating very far back to the very beginning of the dawn of man? Wow! Unthinkable? Well maybe, and perhaps may be not!"

Log: Close Encounters!

"Q"

"Does particular high mountain desert topography geography, longitude, and latitude, have anything definite to do with wild man sightings and plaiting? Well it some cases it may, as it depends on what sort of wild hominid we are trying to define, and it just might be in part be possible, as, as far back to the early 1990s I had already began to notice from endless deposi-tions taken over regions adjacent to the Great Basin desert wilderness that comprises much of Nevada, Utah, Idaho, etc., that predominately wild hominid close encounters had over that part of North America seemed to come from particular much relative high altitudes similar in elevation. These sister regions seemed more than coincidental. To date, beginning 2004; as of fall 2013 I have been documenting horse plaiting all of nine years and continue even as I write, and plan in a very new future to further investigate particular ranch places of Big Island Ha-waii that is the only state where to my knowledge feral wild relict hominids have never been documented, and to my excitement new horizons of probability suddenly have caught my at-tention there and on the main land, as will be further explained, my most recent and two past hominid encounters predominated at higher elevations, and the several do seem to rather co-incide!

Higher and low land geography of course very, as there are lowland regions in the highest of places as Hunza/Tibet, where the lowest elevation is 10,000 ft., and in low desert Arizona there are high places south of Kingman, etc., and every where very low where AZ. borders California, and of course Death Valley is a literal paradox of incredible topography in itself. Cal/Neva, and Idaho/Montana can be significantly lower at particular locations, and still anyone would think themselves to be standing on the top of the world all most any where. Now where in the lower

United States are the elevations higher than are the vast Himalayan mountain ranges reaching all the way into and beyond the middle east. The Washington Olympic Peninsula Cascades plummet up from the ocean floor at much lesser altitudes than some places of western Colorado, and still the peaks of the Olympics and the awesome Cascades are very high in spite of there near ocean side vista locations. Many Sasquatch reports come from all western coastal mountains north from Mt. Shasta California inclusive of Randal B. C., and far beyond toward the Alaskan Brooks Range. Sasquatch reports continue in all of these locations however most in the far west seem to evidence most from four to 6,000 ft., and that elevation predominates the largest populations of domestic and wild mustangs, and it is interesting that over much of Eurasia where wild man and wild horses are noted much is the same. In far west America geographically where are Idaho/Montana, Nevada/Utah/Colorado, etc., all surrounding regions of high desert mountains running into Wyoming near Jackson Hole, as are the Wind River and Bridger Mountains, and others adjacent into Idaho 5000 – 13,000 feet, however most high desert America elevations realistically are variable inside these limitations compromising an elevation of perhaps four to seven thousand feet. It is to be realized important that California topography alone has 110 count high mountain peaks over its entirety ranging in elevation in access of 10,000 or more feet! Mt. Yosemite CA., where the snow never melts at the higher elevations is the lowest of the California high peaks @ around 10, 023 ft. Mt. Shasta CA., the last Northern most Cal. Mt., is the first inclusive of the vast Washington Cascades. Indeed there is much high country left almost untouched year long through out much, much, of Western North America, and to fact all of incredible Eurasia north into Europe and past Mongolia into Siberia is much the same and even more remote and little visited by outsiders. Sasquatch, Yeti, feral wild man populations, etc., indeed have a vast habit world of their own and no need what so ever for human intervention.

"The Truth Of Wild Horses Brought To America!"

Little considered by contemporary American historians, and probably little realized if at all taught in school (?), is the fact that much smaller, faster, able and agile wild horses were long centuries wandering over all of the North Western Americas long before the eventual conquest and horrific devastation done to the Central and South American native peoples by the relentless blood-let conquest of the legendary Conquistadors, etc., that plundered here all during the 15th - 16th Centuries, "and where do anyone think that the very earliest of the early horses to America came from that were brought here countless eons before the Spanish had arrived and they finally had loosed into the South West the huge heavy work horse type war mounts that had been necessary to carry them and their armor that have long been misrepresented to had been the very first horses ever to arrive in the Americas (Not So!), and the truth known, the much smaller and agile multicolored Eurasian Steppe horse variations as still roam parts of Upper China/Mongolia/Butan, etc., for the most part were loosened/traded to the West Coast Native Americans by the earliest realized Oriental Voyagers. These same smaller mixed bread ponies became the earliest of the true far west examples of wild horses, released how ever happened right along side the possible escape and/or out of desperation release of wild relict hominids that were also brought here to aid in heavy logging, exploration, mine gold, silver, copper, etc., and work the land. Steppe type horses came with them, and were well established long before the Spanish had arrived! World-history as all is now being more and more understood today is beyond incredible and is truly fascinating. Why are children are not taught newly realized history is another wild misnomer! As already mentioned, Darrel Miller of Lima Montana, recently guided me to relatively covert very old seldom re-

196

discovered Montana petroglyphs undeniably evidencing depictions of Asian pony type much smaller horses that are still to be found in use over places of the Eurasian steppe deserts. This petrographic illustration possibly pre-dates or is very close to anything wanting dated inside of the last Ice Age or Plasticine on accredited academic paper! The Ice Age to fact in some many high-riff North and South American high mountain ranges is hardly over, as/when if considering all of the permanent glacial examples still remaining over the lofty 110 highest mountains of California, not to forget the vast snow fields of the Cascade and Olympic Mountain Ranges of Washington State, and the Canadian Rockies running all in various directions all of the way into Alaska! "Yeah, Java Bob Smallsbach, to have experience the long walk of the Contented Divide Canada-Mexico, is less than an unimportant side trip into vast wild man territory! No, I will not further spare you! Actually your dire-negative encouragements, comments, and opinions are much appreciated and very often have much merit… However you have made me aware of nothing new that was not already ever obvious! On my windy side, I can't wait to drink your latest bad and stale coffee! Love you brother, and you are invited with your wife to join us during mid August on the far shores of Ross Lake, WA! Call me for dates and conditions?"

Log: Wild Horses, Plaiting, & Feral Hominid Habitat!

A hard look at high mountain desert elevations of 4,000 to 6,000 feet, inclusive of particular comparisons of extended world longitude, and high desert mountain latitude, various mountain elevations of the North West Seashore, and high savanna Plateau and lowland variations, sub elevations as are high desert lake sinks and all deep river canyons as has Nevada's Owyhee River tributaries, etc., and all general high mountain topography, etc., as Western high desert mountain ranges above 4,000 feet, is perhaps where is best thought to have possible unrealized moon phase and plaiting ramifications having to do with current day horses, and/or a special application having to do with relict wild man habitat, especially so when considering that seemingly all first preference of relict man home ground habitat is much found where there are still to be found wild and domestic horses. Please look over all vast of mountain ranges on a world map, while at the same time considering all factors of high and low topography as are mentioned above in order to be able to fully understand and to/if will agree with what more of that obvious truth wants imply!

More conclusions to more explain horse plaiting?

It has been most ironic that the bulk of accredited wild man sightings and discovery, especially where all is wanton relative of plaiting, that most all of it has much occurred predominately in a much same pattern of high world longitude and latitude as exists in all high desert terran, and/or in all far places of Western America where ever the higher land mass elevations seem to run together much similar, "as for example, where ever all high desert mountains reach 4,000 – 6,000 feet, etc. This seems so where ever are found much similar world mountain ranges as has most, Eurasia, Russia, China, North America, Siberia, etc! This geographic topic could easily write another complete long manuscript of far more than interesting wild animal comparisons! One example would include the ever evident comparison of all continuing plentiful large and smaller game animal populations also wanting to range in these higher regions. What's for dinner has for a very long time included many variations of roast beast!"

Log: "Wild Animal, and Horse Bonding, is Difficult!"

"What is to be said of man to horse animal bonding, any animal?" What really do most persons know? Bonding with anything, even humans can sometimes be very difficult! Random plaiting done on anything one would think would be impossible, or at best improbable for just anything or anyone to all at once walk up and bond and next plait?"

As projected, could plaiting be an ancient wanton requirement; an expected offering somehow thought needed accomplished under the guise of the all seeing eye of moon goddess Diana, or a much similar strange anomaly that might include pseudo meaningful primitive applications in order to accomplish much difficult horse plaiting? And if so, then to all reasoning, "animal bonding must be first and foremost done to accomplish the equation in all regard of horse/human fetish associations. Nothing usually can just walk up casually close by to any horse, and next proceed to easily braid its mane in any number of tight, twisted, elongated, and ever clever hard tied knots, and then continue to plait its mane at another, or several more neck locations, and has somehow managed the finished all plaits to be in fact; some of them are more than twice the original hair length, and to have done this without some sort of a special bonding could not be done!"

Bonding?

For those reading who perhaps have no idea of bonding, there are more than several ways this is done. Even when however believed this has been accomplished, with horses there is no grantee that all of your attempts to approach the same horse in a future will be any better than the last! Horses are completely unpredictable, and can even result as highly dangerous! One seasoned cowboy member of my family was killed by one, and I myself have had several close calls to during an unexpected misadventure unto a untimely demise! Horses bite, kick, and when with their ears back, they can run amuck at the damnedest times, and into the damnedest places, and you damn well at times consider to shoot them?"

To bond with a horse; when allowed to approach, one can blow ones breath softly into their nostrils, or it sometimes it helps to shove its wet nose up under an arm pit and hold it there long enough that it will know and remember your scent! Feeding it apples, carrots, sugar lumps, etc., can be helpful... Always watch the horses ears!

If held back, he is not comfortable with you or the moment! If forward, realize the positive reasons and continue. Never approach a horse from its rear, or either on its right flank if know it to have been trained to expect your approach from the left. Horses can fully read your intentions, any apprehension on your part will be completely realized! There is much more to know, but that gives some idea of the potential difficulty! And remember that anything or anyone that by the light of the moon, and all diverse seasons of the year that can accomplish this strange plaiting must be some kind of a magic something or other! Plaiting is truly a great northern mystery! Perhaps to further understand it Bob Smallsbach, we should try adding tea leaves and whiskey to your coffee and look after at the grounds for answers!

"Why Not?"

"Saltu, and, Kung He Fat Choy!"

("Saltu, a multidimensional word said in Chinese chosen to express the difficulty of plaiting to be much more confusing than it is comprehendable, and, Kung He Fat Choy, here to express Happy Chinese New Year, love and good fortune, and happy Valentines Day to whom ever anyone remember, and a special Happy Birth Day to Shirley Chandler, who has much endured some of the difficulty had while me documenting while exiled in her some of this impossible sojourn, etc! However by now February 14, 2013, some small bit part of the mystery is somewhat solved?")

Or at least a small part of it is definitely much more than just high suspect, if not some of it definitive and completely conclusive especially after having just spent the past sixteen months doing its very difficult research beginning or near the end of each new full moon phase re-occurring every 28 days while extending our efforts over a vast all much similar high mountain ranch type terran encumbering the several states of Ore/Ida, Cal/Neva, and Montana! However in the case of the Jenson property, all of this is taking place at a slightly lower farm crop elevation.

Log: February 14, 2013 - "New Beginnings!"

All next said somewhat explains metaphysical thinking of the book?

"This last bit of important manuscript research had begin after all considerations had, at the first beginning of 13 successive full moons as of December 2011 – December 2012! And now has continued into late February of 2013!

In this complete case scenario, if the moon actually has merit to explain any part of it, "and it certainly appears to be the affirmative" (!), then perhaps as conjectured, this unknown creature/hominid, horse/animal worship, or better said, it is well founded world wide as a direct moon fetish adoration, worship, allegiance, that could amount much similar to what is accepted/expected of ones personal fetish adoration, or to be an animism associate, or what is considered in Hawaii to be ones "Almakoa," or what ever good-luck piece keep-sake, neck carving or what ever may suffice, as might be a treasured fisherman's hook, turtle, or sea shell, a shark tooth, or wild boar tusk, etc., as in Hawaii, etc., all much similar items afforded the Almakoa allowance, "might almost be considered to be abstractly or similarly amalgamated to the wanton alliance of the difficult braiding requirement, or be in part a wanton reverent accomplishment much similar in tradition as is an offering of Tea Leaves, whiskey, flowers, etc., what ever is given as an expected and much encouraged offering intended to highly honor, appease, recognize, the revered Hawaiian Volcano Goddess, "Madam Pele," (?) or could it be that plaiting in its difficult way be also compared to the arduous Islamic Pilgrimage that is making the fabled long trek to Mecca?"

Bob, did you know that Sir Richard Burton, ("In spite of his English title, hardly at heart was he a true Englishman!") who indeed was a very wild natured, and a brave man apart, and far ahead of his times, Burton was the first neophyte ever having been accredited to have been the very first European able to complete on foot the highly difficult trek to Mecca done at the risk of his life in order to witness the sacred ceremonies of ancient Mecca! He accomplished this incognito posing as a Hindu, dressed completely in their costume after having cleverly stained his skin and facial features, and somehow had managed to mask the color of his light green or blue eyes? "Indeed The Bastard Blackard Burton, as he was sometimes called, was one very brave 19th Century adventurer/explorer, and Bob, you really should read further into the life of this invincible man, as his world wide accomplishments remain as much a marvel as in his day!

Plaiting perhaps has other mentors of comparison similar as Burton's exodus to Mecca, as much similar although hardly the same requirement needs be done by all males of the East Indian Ghurka tribe, as if any of them has reached adult status having survived the difficult requirement of life unto manhood... The authoritative tribunal would only grant them manhood when/if proven worthy; as they can only aspire to that acceptance provided they have managed to completely sever off an adult water buffalo's head with one single slice blow of their special curved Ghurka knife! The head when cut off, must fall completely from off the carcass! As said, this must be done with Just one quick sweep of a time tested, highly sharp specially designed protection knife that has long been famous as the efficient Khyber Pass Ghurka Knife! All this ceremony is necessary before any young adult male coming of age is allowed/permitted to manage his own affairs, take a wife, grow a respectful beard, etc. If he fails, he need re-apply one year apart.

"The Crux of Fear, Acceptance, And Failure!"

Could something much like these above requirements be inclusive with similar high implications as plaiting if indeed thought needed be endlessly accomplished by the feral population living in dread fear of ancient condemnation if not comply? Think about it! None of this is all that far removed from what is practiced/expected of today's elite military special forces as proudly evidence for one are The U. S. Navy Seals, etc., or what for example does anyone think to realize of the truly difficult and demanding requirements had of the ancient fabled invincible armor clad Chinese horsemen warriors, or the adapt ancient Japanese Ninja, etc?

Many a wild indulgent thought to be an irrational custom of the Far East and ever mysterious Orient are still much prevalent in high attitudes of proud esteem already founded in the extraordinary accomplishments of many Asian and Middle Eastern peoples much realized for their astute proficiency, invincible high mountain monastery monks that have never set foot out of their district, and yet claim by accurate descriptions to have walked the streets of some many world cities, etc. Not the place to get into all of that, but in my opinion there are definitely unrealized strange things that go bump in night that we are better off staying away from! Not to suggest either that plaiting is anything that far off the wall, but even Charley Tuna well knows that feral wild man exist, "and some many E-Mail, Think Tank, pseudo intelligent air-head critics, wantin' of the opinion that the plaiting is being done by ghosts, goblins, garden fairies, and pixies; critics it seems with hardly enough historical education to opt to chase The Golden Fleece, or The Trojan Horse, but for sure they ever remain true to the ridiculous dictates of Bart Simpson, Ronald Rocket, and today's demented heroes as was the late Green hero Shrink or what ever that was (?), founded by Mac Donald's? Wow Critics, accomplishing difficult plaiting done on any horse, under the obvious stress and duress of possibly being discovered just might have some requirements ever necessary pertaining in comparisons to uncanny unorthodox religions as customs of self-abuse as through flogging, etc., and/or what might be even more considered moot, unfounded, or thought to be even much more eccentric and off the carpet in similar unspeakable beliefs! Plaiting may also have something to do in part as if being an abstract contest having to do with the humanistic challenge of the norm to see who or what may indeed have the ability to have done most often and/or the best, etc? These wild guys have their own natural ability and intellect! If in case any of my daughters are reading, "disbelief of anything does not constitute that everything and anything disagreed with by anyone render it to be absolutely untrue, or either impossible or improbable! No matter anyone's opinion strange things will and do still happen regardless!"

What Say Anyone Of Very Ancient Humanity!

"Could they braid?

Probably, as it really is quite simple!"

Log: "How Plaiting May Have Begun?"

To all humans that were alive in that first quarter of life's game of "till death do you part," to them then it had to have been a very real mis-adventure of extremely undetermined highly dangerous and, an ever evolving much changing wandering endeavor, and ever the world then was an endless unknown ecosystem of encroaching water-ways teaming of natural and much hideous evolutionary land and aquatic animals had abrupt all high strange and questionable land fauna and flora that some of it may have been dangerous...! Everything and everywhere was a daily survival challenge! It was far beyond being a much dangerous and simple world; there was constantly any legion number of fearful, forbidden, and impending involvements! All world then was an uninhibited existence of a much realized and real fear of the unknown, that is much still with us today in our present day latent inhibitions and fears. ("That last said is one reason for some many persons of today ever fearful to admit/acknowledge to themselves or anyone that in all logical probability wild-man may still exist, and they just do not want to deal with it!")

All of this as described above and much more was had abrupt the ever expected known anomaly of an ever varying moon phase that sometimes dim lit the night sky, much opposed short of the wanton brightness and warmth of the mid day sun; however, whenever under each of them it made no difference, as every where possible at any extreme it was of a first importance to sustain life all night and day, as every vista was literally teeming with highly dangerous animals, serpents, and small UN-determined hominid populations living together in parallel however apart right along side the other in unknown facets of wild men and some of them of a debased humanity!

"Said as if all were up from a voice from our human dust ...!"

... it was ever possible, and we knew it, that some of the others living around us were ever to be feared; them to possibly be one or some several types of sub-humans and be highly dangerous and cannibalistic?"

Indeed very much as yet is not fully understood of all ancient life styles of man. Much historical fact still remains in spite of discoveries much is conjectured, and much is left unexplained. Humans then, beyond later Biblical comparisons within Genesis, if So, certainly must have had a very short life span, and if nothing else, had much been killed through all high ongoing stress of constant danger and endless exposure to the elements?

Cave Populations – Wild Hominids

Wild man today in many ways has it much easier, with the exception of the constant fear via necessary submission as is required any regulated existence abrupt modern technology, machinery, intervention, and human urban encroachment, as it has become almost impossible even for us pseudo civilized enthusiasts to go, or be anywhere anymore entirely alone! Wild man actually has to be highly intelligent to have submitted and survived as well as he has to the drum beat of subjection and humanity realizing it or not! We are them, and they are us!"

The Fear Factor!

"It is very real!"

Fear in ancient man became beyond fantasized, and mega superstition prevailed decisive... The world then without question was an almost Topical Nether World, over flowing with the unexplained and the ever unknown and unwanted! To the intellect understandings of earliest man (wild man!), even perhaps the shadows of mid-day moving caused by the shifting earth, sun, moon, and wind may have resulted in legions of supposed fears and superstitions, and out of the high fear of safety, all of the above mentioned may even have been worshiped beyond the imagination, in unholy fetish sacrifice or worse, or referenced holy, unfathomable, and dread sacrifice of may hundreds of thousands of people is well documented by today's ongoing discovery of ancient antiquity! After such blood let, ramped cannibalism as I suspect may have even entered the picture, etc! Admit it or not, there is no race of man that has not at some historical time or another not been involved in cannibalism!

Any sudden thunder clap, rain or wind storm, or flash of lightening, perhaps any and all new moon phase first time noticed would opt to further influence everything unpredictable, as would be any thing as rare as a Blue Moon phase, or a sudden unexpected Moon Eclipse, sudden stark dark black moonless nights, and all possible similar ramifications of much more than uncertain, was certainly a stark, and real-world of wonder and fascination, fear, mystery, and high superstition, let alone high adventure if could be called that? Perhaps all of this here explained/unexplained, and long feared, had/has became their mentor Goddess Of The Moon, or something similar? Thus such uncanny belief and conditions had resulted long, long, ago in wanton Moon Worship, etc?

Plaiting!

Plaiting in my assumptions was well realized in the most ancient of times as, to this day in every major swamp land of the world including all Southern most States of North American is to be found many examples of entwined vines and tree roots, twisted and otherwise fascinating entanglements of different combinations of small tree and brush trunks, all of this at once is highly auto suggestive and easy to emulate and copy and put to use for all enduring strength, etc. Wild man well realized this and much more in nature. Plaiting became a natural and ever enduring practice! Why couldn't plaiting have been included on horses? Well it did! In our up coming book slated for 2013, titled: "Memories of Discovery," undeniable plaiting will be described and pictured contrary to current belief (?), as it is thus far little known that it is pictured found photographed on the original 1967 Roger Patterson film footage that through the uncanny genius film enhancements of M.K. Davis, this can easily be realized as is to be seen; there are definite braids of the female hair due sort on the top most head part of Patty's head!" Idolatry

"Fetish Adornment, etc., and Idol Worship! The Golden Calf if you will, and … And more adherence similar plaiting! Moon Gods, Moon Goddess, lesser Gods, Animal Depictions, Aphrodite, statuary of ever sort, and kind, were many, etc., and when recognized, accepted or not, statuary became ever a continual, play-toy very likely every new moon phase, seasonal, or monthly, climaxed in physical participation, adoration, sacrifice, and self-penitence done via the light of the stark dark, or new full moon! (Perhaps sacrificial in comparison to a much primitive manifestation of penitence, as could be, would be, as when doing required plaiting, etc? The harshness of all raw nature unleashed during these times was hardly an entertainment, or was it a wanted curiosity to the ancients. The awe of the bright night stars, or the Full Moon, must have left them emotionally beyond awe stricken with a desperate yearning for many wanted/needed plausible answers! The Mesopotamians believed that the stars, moon, and particular stones were all citizens of a cosmic state! Ordinary kitchen salt was to them an inanimate substance, a mineral at best; to them salt became a fellow-being, whose chemical help might be sought for in time of need! Example; salt to become a real aid especially if perhaps one had fallen victim to sorcery, or witchcraft, etc? To Salt he would cry… "Oh Salt, break my enchantment… Loose my spell from bewitchment! And as my Invincible Creator I shall extol thee!" Wow! That example alone speaks its own course throughout the history of witchcraft and sorcery…

Note: In the reference to Salt - Thee and Thou are recognized as if required rather than, "it"! Definitely that is a humanistic personalization view, an inextractable confusion in which wild beasts, plants, stones, stars, moons, etc., are all of them recognized to be on a, "One on One, humanistic level of personality, and with that considered to be locked in an animated existence."

(That above "Note" is only a partly much paraphrased added upon excerpt, taken from the writings of the author in slated book:

"The Twilight Zone Chapters," and was much influenced by the writings of the late, Andrew Lang's book "The Intellectual Adventure of Ancient Man!" page 130, ISBN 0-226-26008-9. You should read it!)

"Full Moon History"

(Lycanthropy!)

"We humans today are still as much lost in all astrophysical matters, just as much ever were the Ancients confused? However we much more rational and civilized some say? But I very much doubt it!"

"A Brief Plaited History Of Steppe Horses"

What do any of most people think to know of the war campaign histories, religious customs, witchcraft fantasies and fact, horse adornment, star craft, and animal-man fetish attachments, etc., say of, Attila The Hun, (434 – 443 B.C.), Genghis Khan, The Great Emir ("Tamerlane"), or, the strange customs of the invincible, Scythians, "the fearsome red headed green eyed horse mounted bowmen, (Scyths, 700 B.C.), finally to be defeated by the, Sarmatians, known for their stealth Stirrup (Horse) Strength, or the, Ancient mounted Mongols, long known for the acute clever ability to be able to tie themselves onto their running horse facing backwards whenever in wild retreat doing this by using only the various plaited long main-hair of their well adapt Steppe horses to hold them on ever steady, while continuing to be shooting back arrows to evade the advancing enemy as they precariously rode for endless leagues over the far vast Steppe Regions still to be identified on the Old World Maps?

"Plaiting, Kumiss Milk, And Blood!"

(Brenda, we are going far beyond the discoveries found on your father's Oregon Hinck Ranch, fall, 2007!)

The Mongolians highly considered the importance and accomplished statements of pride, and status quote, when their mounted warriors had completed the intricate task of decorative plaiting done to their horse manes, or had cleverly short cropped all long hairs of their war-mounts neck, tails, etc. so as to more easily shoot arrows proficiently in all directions from over their horse, etc.

All of these peoples had much need to sustain themselves of nourishment by existing much on, "kumiss," best explained, horse milk, still much in use today, that in past times as then was sometimes mixed for added protean with horse blood leached/taken directly by mouth from out the tourniquet swollen veins of a mounted horse as they rode!

The China Wall, "2,500 miles of recorded human misery," (221 – 224 B.C.), built by "Emperor, Sheh Huan Ti," (214 – 221 B.C.),

"Ti," also associated similar unknown ancient wild green eyed red-headed horsemen... (Probably they were a mixed blood Tarter-Russian, Mongolian?)... that long pillaged Northern China, around year, 1,000 B.C. These Wild Invaders, also were known to had sustained themselves on similar horse kumiss. All of this was wild warfare stuff to be sure, however all ever clever, logical, and ingenious! Just perhaps with wild man some much of these ancient customs prevail relative of very ancient abstract plaiting custom requirements to this very day, as it will be slightly explained the belief-fact that at times captured wild populations fought by force right along side these and similar ancient armies, and in logical conjecture as will be explained they were also made working slaves. ("Horse plaiting amounts to much, much more?") What think? Write us!

Extended Theory?

Yeti are but one separate entity of different types wild man!

What is written here is but a smattering of all of the authors extended theory to help explain many little considered perhaps long over looked ramifications of existing wild man hominids that may indeed be a direct carry-over from very ancient nomadic voyages to the Americas by the invincible, now much realized, Oriental Chinese Navigators and Company, up until approximate the mid years of the 1400s, abrupt the approximate fall of the, Ming Dynasty and the abandonment of the Chinese Maritime after the Mandarin Invasions, 1405 – 1406, etc. Short case history, the Tibetan monks have recorded in ancient text that long ago they were able after many years (Twenty two or more years!) able to teach the captive wild man Yeti of their day, the Chinese language! As a result these Yeti became a political threat and had refused to fight willingly in their military, and so many were annihilated… Do your research, there still is very much more to be discovered!

"I have long believed, and written myself that particular Chinese Voyagers had likely brought exotic hominids with them to all landings of world discovery, from Australia south, to about everywhere northward including America where had landed over endless voyaging years, long before the advent of any and all known neophyte (The Occidental Races!) populations including the favored, Norse Vikings, Columbus, etc! Not the place here to elaborate, but the ancient Chinese even had covert settlements within the confines of, "The Grand Canyon of the Colorado," and had actually discovered a still much covert, or at least little realized, "North West Passage," via the extreme coastal reaches of Northern Russia Siberia via all of the way to Finland! To my knowledge Charley Tuna, this fact is not recorded in pseudo English history? You will need ask the North Land Selchie off the Shetland Islands that are likely closely related to the legionary mythological Mermaids?"

"Following Is A Short Ode Continuation To Onya Wild!"

Tonia F. Brown

("Taken From My Space, that here is her space!")

"This short excerpt of reminisce is to further honor the book's unforgettable, highly dedicated, Sweet Heart Researcher, Tonia, or, Wild, Two Feathers, Onya!"

Onya, from above became Tonia's self-acclaimed fun name! As she had explained it to me and anyone asking… "Don, Onya tells you and every one else that I am ever On to You and all of your nonsense!" Thanks Onya, so very much for all of your treasured, Eurasian-Asian Steppe Mongolian-Tibetan, historical horseman research, etc! "You babe, are still just exactly as you always hoped to be; you are very much a real part of all of the Trilogy books!" All passé Asian, Russian, and further Eurasian-Siberian research to follow is much accredited to her guiding efforts!"

205

END OF PART ONE

A Gallery of Plaits, Braids, or Tangles.

All images are of specimens in the author's collection, and were made on the spur of the moment of heat to get this book finished by self-imposed deadlines, warming his hands by the cold light of a copy machine on a Montana winter day.

The images were made by placing the specimens on the copier glass, and trying various settings. Most of these are displayed here at 38% of life size. Some are better than others. This is the beginning, not the end.

What is the cause of these? What do they all mean?

Figure 27. Plaits.

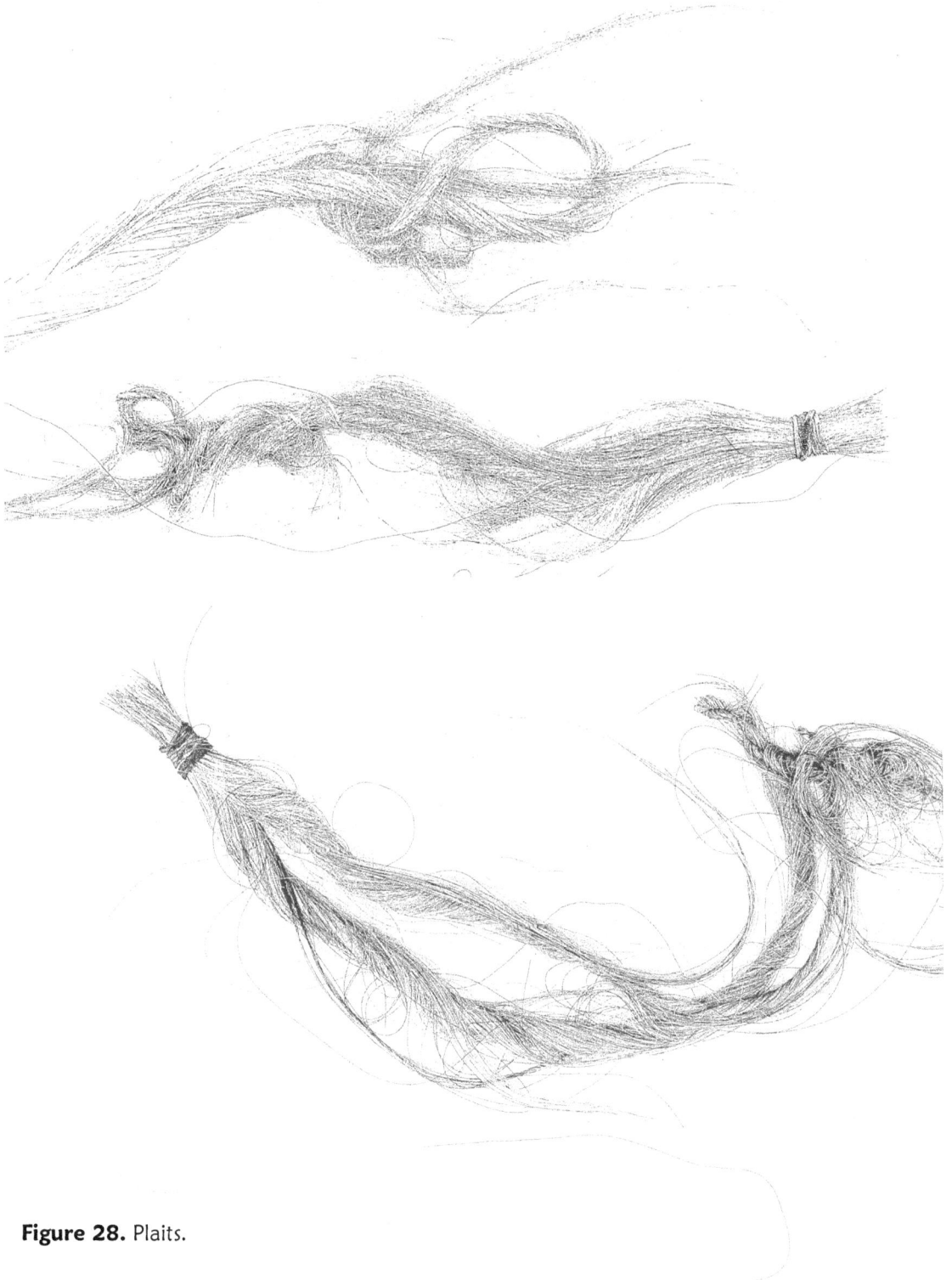

Figure 28. Plaits.

Figure 29. Plaits.

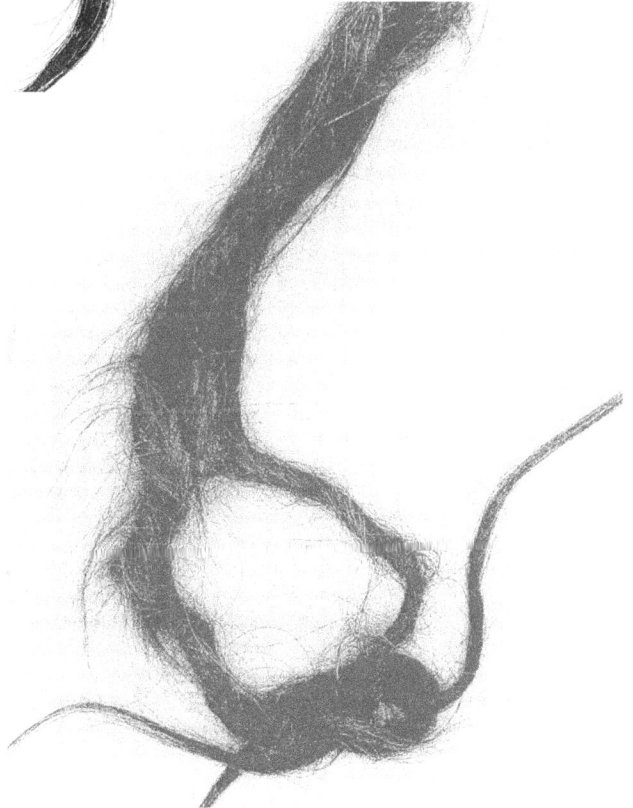

Figure 30. Plaits.

Figure 31. Plaits.

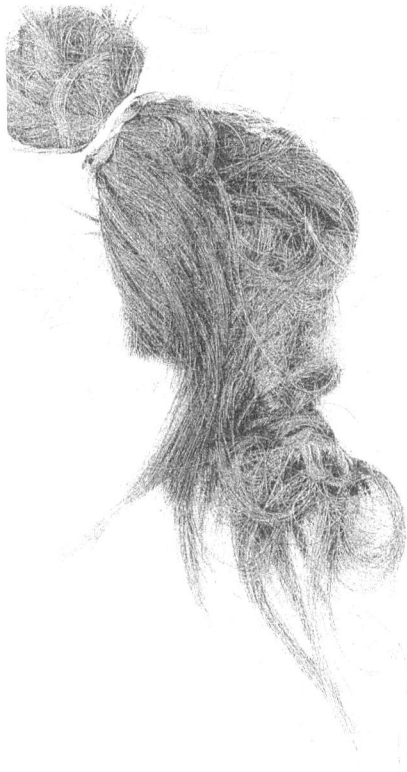

Figure 32. Plaits.

Figure 33. Plaits.

Figure 34. Plaits.

Figure 35. Plaits.

Figure 36. Plaits.

Figure 37. Plaits.

Figure 38. Plaits.

219

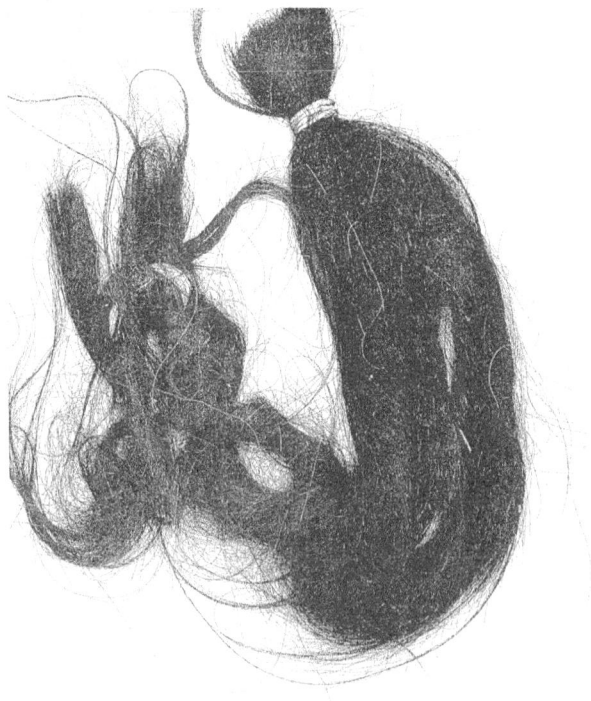

Figure 39. Plaits.

Figure 40. Plaits.

221

Figure 41. Plaits.

Figure 42. Plaits.

Figure 43. Plaits.

Figure 44. Plaits.

225

Figure 45. Plaits.

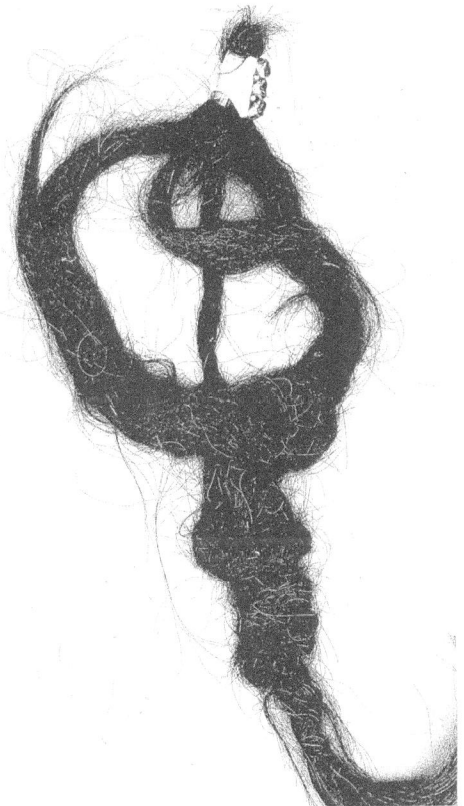

Figure 46. Plaits.

Figure 47. Plaits in mane hair collected by Var Harris.

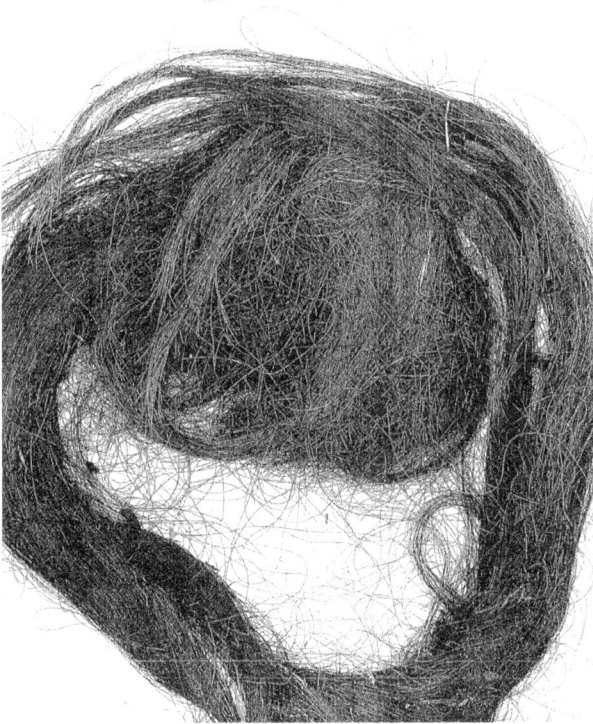

This part of a tail was found by Thad Mauney near Two Medicine, in northwestern Montana. It appeared that a horse had died in the forest and the carcass had been eaten and dragged apart by animals, leaving just the bones and hair. Essentially all the residual flesh had rotted off the bones over winter, leaving them bare. Of interest are the flecks of white material remaining in the tail hair after all this. (See sections on Kumiss.) This tail hair was not plaited appears but seems twisted a little. It was coiled up merely for transportation, but was extended when found.

Figure 48. Other specemins.

This ball of horsehair and dry plant matter (such as straw) is of unknown purpose and origin. It was discovered and collected by the author near to horses that also had plaiting in their manes. (It is not related to the above specemin.)

Figure 49. Other specemins.

PART TWO

"THE HORSES AND HUMOR ARE COMING!"

Donald L. Monroe

WILD MAN INDEED!

The Empty Quarter beyond Arabia is actually, Here, There, and, Every where!

Mustangs!

Horses, plaiting, wild-man!

"What do I know about horse braids?"

"Don, you got to be kidding!"

Hell, we don't even know our selves?

Who are You? Who is me? What truly is the definition of human? And what other than humans, or humanoid types of wild hominid as you say are doing all of the plaiting?

Is modern man actually smarter than the Yowie, the Yeti, and/or the feral wild man?

"Makes One Wonder?"

Mavericks!

Circumstances Decisive?

In a true wild-man environment, civilized man is ever at a disadvantage, as even if we were invited by them to visit temporally in order to more understand them, most wouldn't, and most would rather fight than switch places even for a day! For any real length of time beyond a few days we wouldn't be able to continue to exist as they do! None reading could even come close to plaiting a mane on any horse even if it were tethered in a coral! If any say that you can... "Well, it's Dinner, a Movie, and a Motel on me, and an unforgettable canoe trip down some wild western river of near inhospitably! If anyone or the wind or goblins can satisfactory plait a horse's mane in a like fashion to anything similar of what is in this book's photos, well, you gotta prove it

231

to me, and especially also to, Becky Butello of Puyallup Washington! She couldn't do it after many weeks of effort, and she is a professional parade animal plaiter extraordinaire! Her verbatim deposition to explain all of her efforts is somewhere ahead! Wait for!

More on the Minnesota Iceman!

Remember we are continuing to explore the unfathomed, unknown, unrealized (?), unexplained, and perhaps the not wanted believed? However wild man however named no longer remains an issue with certain government and private concerns, that don't even want any new truth of them publicized. Remember the high strange disappearance of the Minnesota Ice Man, mentioned above in part one dated, 1968? "Well, that story is hardly over, and one day there may be another book explaining who was who, and who is what," as it is my firm contention that the Ice Man still exists in good condition behind closed doors.

In future I plan to attempt compiling additional research to it that effect, to continue what amazing that Tonia had already started by year, 2010! Perhaps that paradox via her magic wand of interest will surface as an important part story within another one or more of The Trilogy Manuscripts? For now just everyone all need to realize that the powers that be within the North American, and Canadian Bigfoot Community; all controlled politics had covert, had also began and will one day end at the far reaches, high mountains, and deep canyons of "Bluff Creek California, starting with the one and only filmed discovery of Patty Sasquatch, year 1997 and her complete disappearance after! "Read Memories of Discovery," by the author and MK Davis, slated early year 2013. The Patterson film will never again send anyone the same message! What is there is the awaited truth and a complete historical revelation! afterwords, which leads us to believe that the US government is not the place where we will hear of an official proclamation that Hairy Man exists. Spik TV (Channel 38) is now offering $10 million to anyone of presenting irrefutable evidence that Bigfoot exists. Well, whether or not they will be declared a real animal or human is up in the air.

Think about Patty Sasquatch, after discovery she was never to be seen again, and there was considerable hard efforts made to make her re-discovery! There is a lot of undeniable deception to be had beyond all pseudo-critic think-tank self-genius, descriptive and photographic argument in firm hard film evidence to further attest the high similarity of Patty Sasquatch and the physical anatomy of the Minnesota Ice Man ethnography, but for now we must stick to the plaiting of horses! Wait to read much more on this in the up-coming book, "Memories Of Discovery!"

Log: "See, Hairy Man, Gabriel Fox, Kwethluk, AK., 1960."

Update: From – Ken Bear Iddins, MT./AK., Feb., 14, 2013.
"Interesting, Important, Pertaining! Thanks Ken!"

The following excerpts were taken from a recent publication dated: January 30, 2013.. Volume 15, Issue 5, published by, "Delta Discovery, Bethel AK., @deltadiscovery.com. "Got a sighting, let us know if you want to remain anonymous in your story. We reserve the right to publish any account sent to us, in order to try and weed out those that seem untrue or written in jest.

"Hairy Man in the Y – K Delta!"

Gabriel Fox is a story of a young boy who ran away from the Children's Home near Kwethluk AK., and survived in wilderness by turning into a hairy creature that lived in the extreme wild? Was it really Gabriel Fox, and not a starving young Bigfoot that was raiding fish camps for food when he was caught? Why did the military and/or the US government say nothing about him after they took him away? And most importantly, why didn't they return him home? O'course such a transformation from human-to-Hairy Man in such a short time is physiologically impossible. Of the humans that are reported to have become feral, the only hair that grows long is on their heads or faces while other parts of their bodies remain hairless. (See Mowgli, @ R, Kipling's India!)

What are these creatures? Some say they are adapted to all kinds of weather just like moose and caribou are adapted. Some that want more proof need a body of a Bigfoot ("Patty Sasquatch, and The Wisconsin Ice Man!"), yet around 30 known Bigfoot kills have been recorded in US history, several here in Alaska. Several were reportedly found dead during the big clean after the massive 1980 eruption of Mount St. Helens in Washington State. They even got a live one from right here in Bethel AK., but every time the US government obtains a body, nothing else is heard about it (Credits: "Bear Ken Iddins is also an adventuring man, another of the sort of a credible past history of doing every thing exactly as impossible as he is himself. He has been with us on numerous important discoveries. M.K. Davis and others of our explorations have every confidence in his opinion. He was with Ron Roseman and I to Idaho summer 2006, when we discovered and took a plaster casting of one of six massive biped tracks found. Believe it or not, it measured all of 24 inches! Richard Grover of Randal WA. says, "Don, now that is a big cast!" Open the door Richard, Ron is returning back to see if your up again for hunting more of those impossible AZ. Desert Scorpions?"

The Empty Quarter of 19th Century Arabia!

"Just like all of remaining wild China/Mongolia, and all lands adjacent into Siberia, it is forever going to be an old and a new Frontier, as to date no one has really been there and finished exploring all of that vast Arabian desert even as I write year 2013!"

"Richard Pillgraves"

Plaiting Extensions, and a short side trip, and a comment excerpt had from the desert sands of all wilderness Arabia, said by the 1840's mentor explorer, Richard Pillgraves as he viewed the vast unexplored Arabian desert vista before him! "How much he said, how much indeed is there yet to be discovered?" That was said when first time him attempting to explore the unfathomed 19th Century Empty Quarter Wilderness of all vast Arabian Desert. The words were written in his journal as he paused to assesses all vast hidden treasures said to exist within the legendary territory? Arabia is still producing incredible archeological discoveries. Everyone who loves adventure need read, Pillgraves, and all books denoting, The Blackard, Richard Burton, who also dare research and write, the controversial Comasutra during his mega high adventurous sojourn, and when had also discovered the Rosetta Stone, next using it he sorted out what truth that has since been much edited out of today's existing Arabian Knights, and much, much, more. Burton also believed in wild hominids with claims to have encountered them when exploring in South America.

"Horse and Man Anciently almost lived as brothers!"

For further insights into horse and human nonsense, and probably plaiting, read Burton's "Book of the Sword," and by all means the true anthropologists Bible if ever was, "The Golden Bough," by the 19th Century pier of Anthropology, "Frazier," you will be educated almost endless in completely true, hidden, and much little known abstract and wanton knowledge! You will be busy reading these good old boys of yesteryear at least for a fort night! "Doctor Watson! It will be a complete lesson in critical anthropological discovery, and an extraordinary education in legendary detective logic! These good old guys are all but long forgotten... We really, really, do need to revive others of them as was India's legendary tiger hunter, Col., Jim Corbet! They were, if ever there was any, the real article no nonsense man's, man, pier!"

Log: Hope & Whoop!

"Protest Anyone, What You Obviously Had Never Understood, and after that, understand much less than you probably never could?"

Whether true, or false, all pseudo explanations here able to explain, or not, this strange plaiting alleged to had been inspired done by an ongoing high strange moon light adherence is in essence important, as by its delivery I have planted a new seed of rational consideration for any after me to ponder that fully adheres to the plaiting anomaly, and/or the all wild man probability! I fully do agree, that serious criticism is meaningful and healthy, as of this manuscript an all new harvest of much less than pier criticism lies ahead, and I can't wait to hear all of the pseudo opinions, hoop-la blather, and whoop, that is all much less than hope had under a dim-wit muse of perhaps Coleman lantern enlightenment, and all further expounds of similar of Doctor Seldoms, and all piers of the unthinking think tank critics; please hear me out to the last page of the book's conjecture, as summer is yonder, and it is near time to explore much, much, more of wild horse probability, and Get'er All Down before the Ides of my final winter season halts my efforts, "and if at all possible please everyone do a little of your own research in addition to what is here, in order that everyone to be able to intelligently debate all wild man's stark ability pro-con to exist and be capable of plaiting horses?" Protest what you will, or opt to think moot of anything that will be written ahead, but it may surprise you that in the end exactly how much of this discourse is very highly plausible (?), and especially how very much, much, more we all may need to highly re-consider of all true human nature, logically, and illogical conjecture concerning the true existence of all remaining wild hominid populations! If for no other reason than a further entertainment of many expounded all new ideas able to further reserve a place and needed space for all future wild man populations now existing within our confused and bias world, read the book tongue in cheek, and/or other wise reconsider to believe everything, or nothing in wanton unadulterated support! No matter to me Sherlock, it won't change one bit of the truth, as I am ever ready at any point after having likely completed this elaborate nine years and 17 months of close net Tid-Bit study of mixed horse research; if necessary for better answers found to put this extensive essay of theory to rest, and if they right, I will spring for bed, a breakfast of steak and eggs, one a loaf of home-made bread, and the best coffee today made at the restaurant of your choice, "Dell Montana's, Yesterday School House Cafe, or Jan's Cafe located right here at Lima Montana," will loan you a leaky tent, a patched canoe, and for the discriminating fishermen, a split bamboo fishing rod with a broken tip, and one rusty gold pan with an incredible exciting history, one pound of Jack cheese, an ample supply of raisins, and enough oat-meal each morning for a week! All of this is yours regardless of all your new abstract, derogatory, and/or moot opinions, etc., that you may opt to flounder truth or consequences, as Montana is close to being the shoot the coyotes and rapids first capitol of the west." Be my guest, no matter your gender, or what ever you are not, or what you are satisfied to be, as I give credit and support, and an appreciated reward to anyone that can discover more viable answers of what the heck more than is written here man, women, or beast, at all capable to be doing any of this high strange plaiting that truly is but just one more very big unsolved great northern mystery! I really do need all help pro-con to think to ever completely solve this one, however all of it can eventually be solved, but it won't be easy! Thanks for reading all serious blather and needed humor ahead!"

Log: "Onya Wild Says,

Don, there needs be here a little bit more written of true life humor! Let me explain a few ex-cerpts from my journal of what is a woman's true opinion of exactly what winter exploring is really like!" No Charley, Onya hasn't been there either, nor done it all, or will anyone ever! Ac-tually no-one will fence the night stars, or find all hidden caves in a canyon wall! If any dis-agree, I insist that you toss the book, as you really don't need to enjoy any more part of it's fur-ther fun. Onya was her own sort of a covert genus!"

Log: Book—Exploring

"EXPLORING!"

"Humor according to Tonia!"

(Slightly paraphrased for content from her covert journal!)

"It could have been February 9th, 2011 – Montana! Or, may have been, Feb.. 13th, 2009, or, perhaps January, 2010, when winter camped in New Mexico? Or, may have been when shiver-ing together in the wilds of all high Desert sage brush sea, that is almost all of Nevada year, 2011, or where we had camped beyond the known out-of bounds region of all Paiute Indian Reservation open desert close near by to, The Nevada Paiute Indian Potato Patch where lives Gordon's grand-parents, or ever in plain sight of the outskirts of Paradise Town Village Ne-vada? Or it could have been some place somewhere way out on the Idaho high mountain de-sert, or on the Mt. foot hills at the winter elevation and season of all local wintering elk and deer herds? All dates trust me would amply apply, me feet are very cold!"

"Exploring Dithers!"

235

"Even My Laundry Is Frozen Don!"

"Tonia, Four Plaited Horses, And, I'm One Frozen Hard Ass!"

Onya

"What do you mean saying, we are playing a game of chance? What, really, is that silly game called four horses anyway? If you ask me, we have no chance at all! Hey, that's my clean laundry that you are throwing into that ice bucket!" The object of the game Onya, is to see who can Slam Dunk four piles of laundry (basket balls?) through the hoop (bucket!) first, or into the can before your competitor can beat you at it. The loser buys the lunch!

"Throwing that laundry on top of that ice makes no sense! And besides my hair, my ass, and that laundry are all frozen in any direction, and no part of me will ever be the same? If Van Stallman, or Sherie could see us now, you would be dead history! What, really, are we doing out here in this frozen waste for any reason? And what, really, have we left to eat?

I see that you already ate the last whole candy bar and your last raisins! If that truck will start, I am packing my bags and driving out of here, and am leaving you behind to chase and cook your own rabbit! I will miss you down at Carl's Junior over a Star Burger! You just as well come along though! Those four horses are so spooked that you will never get any closer! Your staying? So long then, I'm gone... We are history!" Perhaps exploration with a purpose is a little like that? The stakes run high when you are down to your last three bucks, and your last change for a clean shirt, and have nothing to show for anything much more than the North Wind for a maid, and the Moon for a butler!

I watched the snowball flit for a third time into the bucket on top of Onya's laundry where it was propped-up against the Quaking Aspen Tree where had been the Owl, as she tried again to start the truck...? "That's it Tonia said... You continue this nonsense expedition by yourself! I am tired of winning at loosing, and you and always seem to win! Now the truck won't even start! Wow, this is really great fun! Put me down for next year! If you can start the truck, we can buy us both breakfast, as you said that you got three bucks? Well, I have three too, and that's six, and so its just enough for two sausage biscuits, me coffee, and if we lucky, a free cup of hot water for you? Anyway, which ever way we turn Don, you loose and we end up broke! And besides, we only got enough quarters left in the ash-try for one more short load of laundry! What do you mean you have spent two million dollars several times staying poor? Yeah sure, you got class! Right? Yeah, we can melt snow water in the can, and both be drink hot jello and sage brush together long into the frozen night with your wore frost? What flavor is the stuff anyway? I hope it is green, you hate green jello!"

Finally seeing the humor of the moment, Onya laughed, sort-of, while making a fist! "Yeah she said, you're a sailor alright! What is all of this about a sage brush sea... Yeah, its all sails up for a miss-fit, and his for-fit little chicken! I'm Chicken All Right, just as you say, all of this at best has become a complete misconception, and loss of sanity. So tell me for true, after today's last can of roast beast, what, really, pray tell, do we expect to eat tomorrow? And what do you mean you have a big surprise for me... Nothing we do ever surprises anyone! I was warned not to join this expedition! I wish every one of them were here right now to realize that they were right!" Well Tonia I Said, today you are really a Wild Onya Ruffled Feathers over everything, everyplace, me!

What did I ever do to deserve all of this luck? What surprise? Oh that! Well babe, I found our missing five dollars in my top shirt pocket, and so now we got eleven bucks! Eleven is a lucky number in Vegas! And besides, according to the map, the nearest "Carl's Junior" is another 100 hundred miles away towards Lovelock, provided they got one?!

("Continued from above! Again slightly paraphrased almost exactly said as was taken from Onya's journal! She was a real sport.")

("?")

"Where ever it was that we were camped last night, it was another miserable hard frozen night. Don said we remained self-exiled for a purpose? What purpose? Don says we are camped under a pending new full moon phase! I'm not impressed! In just one more day, "Old Lu-nus as he calls his Moon, will be bright enough to travel at night on snow shoes! Don doesn't know it, but trust me, he will be going alone!"

Log: Frozen Desert, anywhere USA!

"Tonight the moon looms over the sage brush almost as if it were magical! The moon-lit desert sky, abrupt all high bright stars and the white mist haze that is now cast down upon us; and over all white snow covered sage brush to be seen far in all directions every where over the vast sage brush and lava rock expanse is beyond said awesome! The night is truly frozen! "I feel sorry for what I am putting Onya through!" The weather has turned record cold, we had no way to know! We huddled closer near to our humble fire coals... Hot weather enters the conversation... Tomorrow we will be going to find it!"

Photo T. Mauney

This could have been anywhere high desert, where ever we cold and miserable when camped beneath the bright night stars of all blue sky Montana, wild New Mexico, vast Utah, Idaho, and Nevada, and any where between that we explored in the search for plaited horses? This has not been an easy sojourn! "I must get Onya out of here!"

The effects of this sort of existence is much just as if one were a prisoner, ever snow-bound and frozen-depressed during a long Montana Siberian sort winter, as the cold wind and blizzards seem to want to follow us about every where that we wander! I told Onya about the many years that my late wife Marion had adventured with me Canada to Mexico, and New York to Calif: in every state we went like two lost gypsies with a purpose... "In fact for the last twenty some odd years of her life of adventure travel, she treasured self-adorned pet title name of Gypsy!" "We did it all, I told Onya Wild Two Feathers, you would have liked her! I'm really sorry that you are so cold! As you know I can be difficult! We are heading for Sedona and Tyson Wells in the morning!"

"Your wife, Tonia said, must have been some kind of a special lady!"

("Yeah, she was babe, and so were you!")

Log: "Trail Weary, of Pongoniff Surroundings!"

"Poor Tonia shivers tonight like a cold, miserable, and hungry dog! Any smile from her becomes almost a degradation of classic misery! I feel guilty for being where we are... Out of necessity we are on our way to Arizona and the Vets Hospital. Onya compassion is next to none other! My back pain is beyond explanation? If I could cry I would! If that were only possible... I don't need her to know had much I hurt... Sit in the car Onya and turn on the heater, we have plenty of gas to get to Alamogordo!" "Thanks pirate, I will! What time comes morning? I think that I will hate you the most by then? Come closer, so I can slap you, before I cant stop hugging you to keep warm! Its so cold that my blouse and everything else under and over it has crawled up into my arm pit heat to keep warm! Boy is it all going to be disappointed! My arm pits right now are as cold as my heart!"

Hot Water?

There you see babe, melted snow isn't really all that bad... Especially its better when added a small pinch of sage brush for flavor? Day break will definitely be here soon with the hoarfrost Pongoniff... "We need not let our fire burn out, as it will be very hard to re-start!

"To heck with you Don, I'm going looking for more brush and fire wood. I will be right back...? And besides, sage brush makes that awful snow water even more bitter!"

(?)

"Don, what are you saying, are you kidding, what is a Pongoniff? Is it something alive, dangerous, or what? Every thing out here in this white snow world wilderness seems to bite, burn, scratch, cut my finger, and it has already frozen my everythings to worthless and irritated my skin... And you should know Don, at this moment you and this stubborn truck are up for grabs!"

"An Indian Pongoniff I told her, is the white hoarfrost epitome of the Indian mythological blue skinned witch women called Disonga, or on the other hand, she is everywhere to be seen on the desert as a beautiful glistening snow white ice color over everything; as highly dangerous and a dire beautiful as any blond witch to die for known in Russian legends, or as dangerous as are the Siberian daughters of the winter witch, DeOnlyelitaVoskena BitchVotkaVoxa, or, the Lo-let-ta Lollobrigida between us everywhere!"

("Lollobrigida Onya, means irregular rolling Terran!")

238

"We Were Deep In It!"

Many an old timer of yesteryear, when traveling alone on foot during winter, had perished in its beauty! Yes, a pongoniff sometimes is as dangerous, as if all caution been thrown to the wind, as it is very easy to get turned around and lost on the winter desert.

Hoarfrost

Pongoniff is one Indian word for hoarfrost, as its sparkling with thin ice melts very quickly during direct sun light, and sometimes the water dropping from it quickly destroys ones foot tracks. During Pongoniff, all desert life and its vegetation seems to become as if to a complete stand-still! It is just as everything has suddenly been quick-frozen in time, as even the wind does not want flicker or much move the desert trees and brush. Everything in all directions has turned stark snow white with a heavy ice moisture that shines bright and sparkling in the morning sun just as if all was done instantly by some sort of a magic! Everything in all directions becomes stark white and glistening beyond descriptions of beautiful! \Best said, it is the unprecedented time of all natures stark, and sometimes unrealized dangerous white frozen wonder world! "Wore frost, as the white man calls it, is said by the Indians to be the giver, and one taker of life! This anomaly is especially dangerous for anyone short of a decisive purpose, that dare wander unprepared under its spell on any white-ice frost covered night; it is easy to be lost to its fascination by only the light of moon! Romantic poetry has been written to it!"

Log: Author - November 2010.

**Camped out on Idaho's Sage Brush Sea,
close near by to what is known today as,
The Craters of The Moon National Monument!
Retrospect**

"Tonight all of the others are warm by the fire - Every thing around us is stark white with frost... Almost it would seem, that all were a moon-light delusion of frozen sage brush, willow, and tree! We are here another time to investigate recently discovered semi-wild domestic horses that have been another time plaited near Cary, Idaho.... How I ask, can plaiting be done during such bitter cold season, and do it in dire winter frozen conditions?

How really could anyone, or anything submit to repetitiously be doing such a thing as difficult as braiding the mane on any questionable horse using only fingers? All of this discovery continues almost beyond sound reasoning? Tonight again the wind calls my name, as there no longer is the heated magic of the fire pit, coffee, and hot food! I truly concern tonight within, as I wonder the whereabouts of my several scattered children; about the time they all got interesting, everyone left! This truly is but another important discovery night abrupt an undeniable high strange Great Northern Mystery, and to think that this time during wore frost it was done on a difficult to locate white horse!"

"This Is A Miserable,

And Sometimes Humorous Exposé!"

With all of that above said, perhaps I should title the rest of this short story to read... "This definitely is an undeniable extended frost bitten misery exposé, had abrupt many a mixed exhilaration, strained emotion, difficulty, hardship, and much bad weather and dire disappointments!: At the times of wore frost Pongoniff there are no lawn chairs, condiments, or deserts, nothing but sometimes the loud breaking noise of ice dividing and opening wide over river water, and then returns the silence, or off in the distant comes the whales, and high pitched yelps of young coyote pups calling on the wind for their mother; all of this heard beyond the soft hoot of a treed Horned-Owl, coming to the ear with the feather muffed projections of all wild creature objections! It's warning is familiar, as if to be saying to the world, that all things much similar and miserable are all ahead again tomorrow!"

"FROZEN NIGHTS!"

"More Story Line; Slightly Paraphrased For Content, Taken From Onya's, Left Behind Little Green Note Book Journal!"

Perhaps this next best be said, reiterated much closely,

and just exactly, as she had written it, now titled:

"A Bit Of Humor, Had

"One Very Windy, Wild, Cold, And

Hard Frozen, Winter Vista!

I Hate it!"

Onya!

"It was so cold last night that I couldn't even braid my frozen hair! Makes One wonder exactly how anything can easily plait a horse's mane under the best of conditions; as their hair is much heavier, and more coarse, and it is very difficult to tie it off! Don seems to be almost obsessed to find the answers! I never knew anyone so stubborn, determined, or set in his fantasy! No one is ever going to believe one word of our book, or any of this anyway! Wow I am sooo miserable, sometimes I almost love to hate him! I actually thought he was going to feed us that big hooting tree Owl last week!"

Log: *"Exploring Necessities!"*

"Adventure consumes misery, just as misery and pleasure consummates bonding... Trail mates earn their separate appreciation, as an understood labor of love for the other via hardship, sac-

rifice, endurance, and an innate stubborn camaraderie that is next to none during unexpected excitement! It is not always easy, or especially a fun trail for anyone, as any new-blood human accusation to the project of either gender, unaccustomed to hardships, and all of the needed conditioning necessary of the trying ways of a dubious exploring ho-BO pirate as myself!"

"Creature comforts you say? What, really, are creature comforts anyway? Probably, I told Var Harris, Paul Wright, Lewis Chandler, M.K. Davis, and Tonia Two Feathers, and others: Creature comforts are likely when a mother badger or wolf whines her whelps or pups, and she is up for grabs again with all of the wilder district weasels!"

"Good Night Onya Wild!"

From Her Journal!

"Hey babe, it is time to sleep, and remember if you can, to dream of the warmth of all things South Pacific! What say you and all staggering gang to that? Lets all go there next!"

Hey Two Feathers, are you awake or what? You need to know before you sleep that your wet leather shoe soles smolder by the fire just as if they were made of hot steam!

Hey! Get out of that snow in your bare feet! I've already rescued the boots! Your tent candles are lit, and those wild flames will flicker-light your way toward morning, warm your gloves, hat, scarf, and bag, and heat up your everything else on you that you say is completely frozen?

Here wild-cat! Here is another cup of that famous, Or/Ida/Neva hot sage brush tea, just taken fresh up from the fire pit with the burnt hot dogs, where your melted cheese sandwich has just fallen off the balanced rock into the fire coals! Here! Have another bite of this dark chocolate bar before bed... The sugar before sleep sometimes helps to warm-up your misery? Heck, right now you look to be about everything miserable? "You want me bring you your peppermint what? And your warm what? I can't! All of it is every bit as frozen as you! Maybe by morning it will thaw, and we all can appreciate it?"

"Do Wild Owls Eat Chocolate?"

"The Night Owl prolongs its hoot from its perch on the leaf naked tree, as another muffled the scorched bread that we burnt on the fire?"

"Yeah, sure... Hello!"

cranky question flits out from the dark abyss of Onya's propped and leaning tent!"

(?)

"What do you mean, I can even eat this great dark chocolate bar? It's so hard frozen that I can't even dent it with the pocket knife! How dare do you say that it might be in some way, some

thing that will help me out? How in the heck could any stale candy bar like that help keep any ones misery warm?"

"YOU are my misery! Probably eating chocolate at this late night will give us both indigestion, and me granted no sleep, and I would just bet, that, that damn miserable hooting big bird out there can easily see all of me shivering uglier right now! I feel captured sleeping in this awful mummy bag under a caved in tent! Give the Owl that damn chocolate! I am angry too at my pajamas... They are way to thin and cold bunched up in my wrong place! They keep climbing up my legs where I really don't want them? I suppose next you will want me to toss you out this frozen charred deer meat and "I just can't wait to go out there and throw something final and dangerous at all of you! This is not exactly a T-shirt, Neck Tie, or Magical Chocolate, Tea - Cup Party, Trip to Hawaii either! Which way do you remember is it to that frigging hi -way anyway? I think I needed to be out of here like yesterday! What part of all Exunda is this supposed to be? All I can see is rocks and sage brush!"

"Next we stick-tossed, and/or prodded along the burnt offerings up from off the fire coals amid the floating ash and smoke towards the Owl still softly hooting, where busy pecking away at Onya's chocolate!

"Yep, I said, them Old Hooters are really the very best ever of the wisest of the Old-Chicks! Looks like they get hungry too!"

"Two Feathers Speaks!"

"You know Don, such a frozen adventure as this should be everyone first and last choice? It's definitely might become anyone's last chance for life and a bad time! This miserable trip was really worth all of the trouble too! My lips are cracked, and I have burnt my fingers, but not before scorching my buns last night by the light of the fire flames; lost my socks, and now I can't even find that stupid darn flash light or my shoe? I also must tell you that I dropped a piece of that sad crumbling, smashed, and sun faded stale, dilapidated looking chocolate bar into the bottom of my sleeping bag, where it will probably melt forever embarrassing? And I really must say, that it is also a rather obvious, that I came here with you so not to forget to remember to never to come back again?"

"Ta-Ta, Don!"

"I'm going! I will miss all of you guys, and that stupid irritating Owl when in warm in Arizona! All at once I hate peppermint chocolate! I'm going to Tucson to visit Stelly and Lela Greener, at least unlike the rest of you they are completely human, civilized, and neither of them snore?"

"Here, you can have what remains of the rest of that stupid feather covered chocolate bar, finally out form the duck down sleeping bag! Probably one of you or that stupid Owl will eat it?" Good Sports Are Sometimes A Forced Issue!

"Tonia Was The Best!"

242

"MONSTERS AND PLAITING?"

This Plaiting Adventure is Everyone's?

"Critics don't mess up a good theory with illogical roasting and/or uncouth disillusionary associations as to insist that the plaiting is being by trolls, ghosts, elves, lepercons, magical enhancement, Girl Scouts, or the spirit of the republic, etc! No problem with that concept if you are talking to a fence post or a think tank puppet, as truth ever write its own destiny!"

Yours truly, - Disonga!" Disonga? Who in the heck is Disonga, and why bother with her? Disonga, is an American Apache Indian Namesake association for a terrible entity, far beyond horrible, and all typical prototypes of any considered disgusting of any sort of a which y women long believed to be a close or much similar neophyte association of what might compare to Hawaii's IL-famed Madam Pelee, or any typical moon goddesses, etc., as Es-tar, Diana, Isis, unnamed legend legendary Sea-hags, and the undetermined examples said to exist as humanoid mixtures among seals, dolphins, and propose, and especially the legendary Norse and Scott-Irish Sea Selchie, and the ever believed in and highly popular thought probable to exist that are the Mere-people, or what is the classical case scenario of the Mermaid, or England's unwanted swamp creatures, exemplifies by the horrible Banshee, and the ever classic Northern witch SHE, born of the 19th Century writer, H. Rider Haggard, and all extended horror examples created by H.G. Wells, as were the factious creatures of, The Island of Doctor Morrow! Why I even bother to write all of that is to exemplify how actually gullible humanity is. Man kink for some reasons seems to want to encourage some sort of a monster belief in his re-call! The best white man interpretation of Disonga might read: "She is ever an ugly threatening terrible appearing, however at times appealing, cunning and deceptive, blue hue-skinned looking horrible Hag that is the literal epitome of a worst women ever up to our world from Hell; as bad as anything ever thought to be a hideous, ghostly, or be an evil human looking spirit that could be imagined to look like! Disonga is as threatening and deceptive an ogre, as anyone cannot even imagine! She can if wants, Shape Shift into anything desired at will; change herself into as many good, bad, and beautiful deceptions as wants, as for example into a voluptuous and desirable women, just as easily as she can at once regress again beyond a horrible stark ugly hag, and be extremely hideous even beyond the classic comparison of the fabled women of serpents that is Medusa! She is the evil compromise between Hawaii's much diversified spooky stuff "Talk Story," and as said, she is much similar of the legendary Madam Pele, and is the equivalent of the wicked old witch depiction as is ever wanton portrayed on Halloween, and/or the fabled fairyland wicked old witch women of, Hansel & Gretel! She is ever as horrible as was ever depicted the Goddess of death, Kali, with all of the negative attributes of the Hindustan's Shiva!" Why we need understand Disonga is because she is the epitome of deception, native fear, and horrific outcomes, and you will hear more of her pseudo exploits refereed to in other Slated Trilogy Manuscripts. Actually she is one prime example of abstract, and sometimes the direct result of wanton practice of idolatry, fetishism, witch craft, and moot-real creature worship in the extreme, as it is believed that she can also turn herself into various types of a Cannibalistic Ware-Creature, a Vampire, etc?"

243

Plaiting!

"Why All Of This Long Explanation Of Disonga?"

Because she also resides in the authors high suspect to be one more of the plausible feared entity reasons for the abstract requirements supposed has been revered since ancient times by what ever wild and very strange unclear notions are still harbored today if any, by what ever thinks the wild hominid? What ever drives feral man to react as they do, has to have a very powerful beginning, and be much of a strenuous influence from something revered much similar or perhaps is feared for their very life disastrous, other wise since long, long, ago? Disonga (Dzunukwa, Tsono-qua) by any number of various names and effigy depictions, can be easily conjured-up to further deceptions even today with most all indigenous peoples that reckon with her deceptions as far south as, Terra Del ' Fuego, South America, and north as far as the rain deer people of Lap-Land, and most all wild extended regions of far off Eastern and Western Siberia, as close to the Atlantic Ocean as is Russia's Ya-nah River. Otherwise, She is well known as a classic Bogy-women impersonation by what ever name wanted, or consideration allowed all over the world, inclusive of Australia in aboriginal comparisons down from the Southern Cross! It is also interesting that much of the same can be said similar of the far world wide distribution of typical Chinese type chickens, rosters, ducks, geese, horses, basketry, plaiting, etc! How otherwise does any one further explain all of those mentioned being there? Surely when all considered our entire world is ever obvious in mega number of discovered artifacts to well attest of ancient mariner contact. Indecently, many of these referenced lands named claim much similar strange anomalies of Plaited horses!"

KAPU!

"Hey B'rudder, and, Sis-ta, Don't Mess Wit this, PE-low Stuff!"

Speaking of the obvious, even Ron Roseman, "the passé champion serpent/scorpion expert of Aberdeen WA., well realizes that Disonga and Madam Pele are not exactly all man's best friend!" Don't mess with that Hawaiian Sister Kine Pele, Ron, as DAT spooky women has variable dark-sides and possible Huna associations all much similar of all powers mentioned any where above in donated whiskey out comes, concerning wanton or unrealized hexed Calabash Cousins, etc., and tea leaf mysticism much similar as South American Soul-Vine, and the strange powers of red-stones had of all black Kahunas of the far South Pacific similar in influence even much more unexplained than has any wicked witch passion realized past Disonga, or probably any had on some of Ron's Wildest Taxi-Cab experiences, exemplified of all impossible accounts told me that are impossible to accurately repeat written, or in rote expression that would further evaluate, or explain further, any single one of Crazy Eddie's magic wrist watch Time Telling escapades, happening anywhere beyond sunny shores of Florida, as Ron had likely as not, at one time or another, had more than several times needed cart both himself and loving Eddie and his phoney Rolex Wrist Watch to or from some questionable obscure ever dark dungeon like rendezvous held by moon light featuring famous fighting roosters as were, Gal-Del-Cairo, loosing his last great fight by the black influence of Haitian-Voodoo? ... As one time while experiencing all adversity and disgusting animal evidence left behind that Ron and I were crawling over and through at the moment in the dark cramped high strange reaches of a filthy cave, "for some reason Ron suddenly said to me, Don, you remember Eddie the time clock don't you? Well, somehow, for some odd reason, this terrible Chickasourous Cave as you call it makes me think of Eddie? ("Yeah Java Bob, the cave has directly to do with this book, as it is located in the heart land of many an unrealized recently plaited Idaho horse! All that had also happened twice during each separate four days of full moon phase, winter-fall months of, October and November, 2012!") Still I wonder Ron, what about the unlikely cave made you think of Eddie? Probably Ron, I said, Eddie rarely changed his shirt and socks? There has got to be a definite nasty nasal reason for that close comparison-association when realizing exactly what it is that we are crawling through right now to well justify the reason! That long time putre-fied "big boid" that probably flew into Idaho from somewhere foreign like Brooklyn, New York City, that I promised to show you is just ahead! In retrospect to all of that far beyond strange 'Chickasoures Sojourn, Ron, Eddie, and the long Putrefied huge unknown very strange foul smell-ing fowl that still to this day remains completely unexplained, did look when first considered to be abstractly just a small bit similar in perched position as Old Unreliable crazy wrist watch Eddie! What ever Ron Roseman in fact is, or is not, he definitely is the real article something or other sail-ing on a separate canoe from me towards a similar dream! As yet, plaiting horses have not entered his agenda. However his wild scorpion and professional snake hunting adventures of 2012 had with Richard Grover, Randal Washington, could write a whole new Scorpion Dictionary 2013 on how not to do it! "Ka-Pu, B'rudder! we got them in Hawaii too!"

Under the guise of animosity, and all of ones realized fears of dastardly fetishism, and all cov-ert self-realized attitudes short of partisanship idolatry as might be exemplified in regard of Ameri-can Indian Kachina Dolls, non related of Voodoo, and because of all true latent fears that may have long surfaced; any number of particular unreasonable demands might be less that a wanton satisfaction to the distressed dismay and degradation of any number of unwary players long much weary of the horrendous demands.

("Just Stay Away!")

Strange Entities, Their Possible Adverse Results And Plaiting!

The cause and effect via the controlling factors of such supposed diabolical entities as Disonga, and others similar denoted, need be fully understood as they can be real in all various concerning Native American fetish concepts, as truth known all such similar fetish and superstitious adornment falls only slightly short of being a true worship within a set religion, "just as much as the warming sun be much a misunderstood anomaly in most all general neophyte misconceptions of native peoples and their true reference to the universe as can be highly exemplified by extremely high regard and respect in adornment recognition of Sun as when the blowing the smoke from the sa-cred peace-pipe smoke wanton ceremoniously to had been favorably accomplished blending har-moniously into the four directions; and perhaps much rather similar are the expedient expectant duties surmised by the author ever realized to be a real part Cause and Effect of moon upon horse plaiting (?) as has been explained all through out this manuscript. All of this is even now more high suspect of being true after all endless research done of the author. I am now much more than con-vinced until can be proven wrong that indeed a very strange contrived and much powerful con-trolling comparative factor is with the life requirements of these unknown pathetic relic popula-tions that somehow stem handed down to them from a very, very, ancient origin! As for example, if this is SO, then what other un-similar reaction can be expected of any similar human or wild hominid interaction; or any other intense likely confused intelligent entity? How really would they think to deal otherwise with such a belief-adherence if truly believed in anything as humanistic, ghostly, and was a high controlling anomaly as would need be allowed a horrid Disonga, etc? That concept alone when separately considered is beyond frightening, and if indeed she were truly believed in, her effigy even if portrayed only petroglyphically would be as much feared pictured as in a real-life impression! Horrid outcomes beyond dream fantasy had in particular participant misunderstandings unto vivid dread nightmarish demands can be had during ones sleep even leading perhaps towards a horrendous heart stopping death? Believe me, such an occurrence is ever possible… or might it even be that when one was quite awake this could be influenced via all uncontrollable negative outcomes of ones latent and/or real fears of fetish adoration, etc! One could eventually become self-determined to end ones life in suicide as direct result of recognized unwanted evil controlling factors had within idolatry, witch craft, pagan rites, etc.

"Wild Man May Be Ever Existing As If At Death's Door?"

Excessive human fear, abrupt all mixed ramifications of loneliness had of separate thinking, possibly believed unorthodox among tribal piers, when burdened with unwanted obscure duties, etc; especially if/when constantly in the controlled demands had among ones own kind ever in a much similar and a firm belief of horrendous outcomes of expectations regarding personal degradation if not adhered to faithfully…Such a defeatist feeling as that had within ones self, if only considered in metaphysical self-punishment terms alone, could at times have resulted in particular cases of a much self-determined death wish? (Everyone should read the early travels of Mark Twin, had adjacent to the bawdy, rough and ready times of the 1849 California Gold Rush, to see what he has to say/describe of the many strange unknown mountain desert hominids of the times, "their lack of customs, etc., "…they live in almost less than a humankind of existence! ….their vocal death throws, descriptions, etc., much described in his vivid accounts, much rings a similar bell to some of what the author has believed of late to have discovered in Idaho/Nevada/Montana mountain caves! "I cannot help but wonder on a human scale of true compassion if the degradation of cave life if realized in modern comparisons of close cohabitation with modern society, is not enough at times to enact even in a feral hominid a personal celibate rebellion? Mental and/or physical suicide of anyone, or anything for any reason, needs be a terrible thing! Any adverse outcomes abrupt plaiting, as the shadow of doubt if any were evidenced by nonparticipating/nonconforming might become a predetermined expectant of self-destruction?"

"Plaiting Truly Is Weird Stuff!"

(See: African Zulu/Watusi, far Northern Alaskan Eskimo, and especially Hawaiian Huna-Mystic belief, and all much similar practices in, Australia, Indonesia, Tibet, Thailand, India, China, Bhutan, and the oral and written Japanese Obakie Ghost mythology, etc., abrupt all bogyman fear as has resulted in much more true happenings than what most people would easily want understand. Plaiting may have much similar and all true metaphysical ramifications having to do with reactionary horse plaiting via animal bonding, as more of bonding will be explained in all separate examples. Plaiting referenced here is not to be directly associated with Disonga, or either the high influence of all the lesser believed in unorthodox Gods of today, but her comparison might have particular logistics of human to creature moon fetish associations abrupt on-going Lunar worship practiced from the most primitive of man's beginnings.

246

Log: 2012 Expedition.

The June 9th, 2012 – Bluff Creek California. All members of the expedition as, MK Davis, Bear Ken Iddins, and myself much miserable while slowly recovering from a recent snake bite happening two months ago, March 28, 2012 are for the moment housed at Happy Camp California, at the home of our good friend and critic, Java Bob Smallsbach. We are here for a short reprieve by request and a short visit before mounting another time upon an expedition in the Bluff Creek Region of California. Our intention this time is to further recount all passé high strange expectations and wild occurrences had happened there prior, in regard of possibly rediscovering the plausible living posterity of Roger Patterson's Patty Sasquatch, alleged discovered in 1967. Year 2008, while camped at Bluff Creek, Louse Camp, we heard first time ever what were extremely unfamiliar non typical vocalizations believed to had been Sasquatch! On the trip in we cast two separate juvenile foot tracks found together left behind in soft trail dust. We are ever hopeful of more similar, or even better discoveries? This morning Java Bob announced to all Hey everyone, except you Don, the Sasquatch coffee is waiting with the eggs and bacon! I am ever your host, when visiting at Happy Camp, California …While hearing that, I was thinking at that moment of our recent telephone conversation had before arriving, when "Java" had asked me saying … "Well, yeah, hello Don, yeah, it's me, Java Bob! Hey, hello? Well, how in the hell, and what are we both doing anyway? How are you coming along with that wild horse manuscript?" (Bob recently has published his own book titled: "Monsters, Myths, And Me," and so knows very well of all impending difficulty!)... "I have just read over all of the few pages of the trailer you sent, and its all more than just incredible, as everything written there is a first time original, but... What do you think, are you are getting in too deep! Heck Don, no-body wants to think to need to read all that hard! Yeah, for sure, I do need to fully agree with some many of your particular issues, "but you skip around so damn much, and write everything just so much exactly as you talk, that thus far I can't yet easily get the complete jest of the message? However all of this stuff is really wild theory, and all your ideas are more than awesome! "Weather you are right, or wrong, its really going to get people to thinking!" Bob I told him back, "the book really opens and closes all doors! And realize that trailer was only the first incompetent rough outline! But the meat is right there in the sandwich! When I see you, the burgers are on MK Davis!"

Bob dislikes my writing, for its lack of uncommon solidarity and continuity, and beyond all first supposed confusions he finds it most difficult while reading, not to want to fall asleep while trying hard to mentally digest my stuff? At least in some of these relative founded anomalies we have a much similar intuitive common sense, as I also opt when late night trying to write it to want to capsize myself! Hey Bob, first time while reading some of the first several pages of your last book, I fell Port Side too, right off from my chair onto the deck to where I bludgeoned my fore head on a canine tooth projecting out from my bear skin rug! "Starving authors Bob, and starving writers, but all that you had written was the truth, "except what was said about me? Be in touch, and thanks much for all future manuscript support over your radio show!" Every writer Bob, becomes somewhat handy-capped in having no real way to accurately access his readers interests or support. But believe me, if anyone truly bother to hard study all little known moon phase anomalies, the truly complexed fascination of it all will prove to unravel a great many UN-realized ramifications of new interest. There is definitely a hidden magic ebbing down to us from the moon, just as much as there is a much similar anomaly had from the bright flicker of a camp fire!

This Next Said Will Likely Not Be Believed?

But, when speaking of fire, from various cave experiments the author has good reason to realize that Sasquatch as feral hominids, actually do know to understand some important aspects of fire making, and well understand how to hide its detection when and if needed under severe conditions as perhaps on the coldest of nights of winter I have several credible witness to attest all of what has been said above, and anywhere shared between the lines of all story, and when or if necessary, I am well prepared to provide viable photographs of burnt artifacts, etc., more able to prove it! Wait for the slated Trilogy books titled: The Twilight Zone Chapters, and, The Cavern Of Zakynerous, both will more explain it!"

Log: Hink! Phil Jenson - April 29th, 2012

"Hey, no fooling, we got all new plaiting done again just last night... No, no, I really don't know, but it looks like they took away some of the green ribbons that we left them... But they left the pink ones behind! They also took my green handled hatchet! (?)" - Green colored hatchet... I was thinking, what color blends the best to go unnoticed in the brush, or anywhere out of doors... Twice to date hatchets would be stolen from the same property!

What was happening on the Jenson property was all much similar as was to be seen in photographs sent to MK Davis 2007 from somewhere in Russia with several comparison examples of colorful pink and blue ribbons somehow braided into a horse's mane? Seeing the pictures had given me the idea to leave the ribbons. So Phil complied that he would see what he could do...?"

Log: May, 2012 - Phone rings... 10:30 P.M.

Its Phil's mother, Norma Jenson, with a proxy message from him, "wanting to informed me... that as of today they had just completed in-twining pink and green colored ribbons into the remaining braids that had been left on Hink, that were there since the last full moon phase of, April sixth, 2012. The ribbons were done very much in a same exact manner as were depicted in the photos sent from Russia, that are best described; there were several multicolored ribbons plaited precariously into a horse's mane... Exactly why, how, or by who this was done we did not know, as there was nothing more written with the photos, and so not knowing the complete story... Well, by auto assumptions, and the suggestion, I thought to try doing similar via the efforts of Phil, in order to see what if anything new would happen, during the next May fifth full moon phase? "Hink," remember is the name given to that particular Blazer horse that was also purchased from the same ranch, then located some fifteen miles East from the Jenson property on the Idaho side of the Snake River, within the three miles of Adrian, Oregon. Last time past the Hinck property fall 2012, several horses on another ranch in a close proximity to Hinck's had also been plaited! However not knowing the owners, and having little time to linger, I was only able to validate them by the use of field glasses... Feb., 20, 2013 – Comment: "My days of doing Hinck Ranch investigations are over, as the ranch as of fall 2012 exists no more! Realizing this, and being more than very up-set, Neil would shoot his way back to glory from his casket if he could do it in any remote way, and return back to his now long sold and forgotten dream ... Well Neil, old buddy! Abstractly your genius efforts somewhat live on in this manuscript account ... "Hink. and many other horses of your herd to the last stud, are still out there in the world being appreciated! Your legend continues!"

On The Jenson Property

Over the next few days of moon phase, Hink would be closely watched to see if, or when, anything new happens? The ribbon outcome and complete story results from Russia, are as yet still unknown, and sadly with that, I have no real permission to share the ribbon 'd photographs in the book! "The reason lies with me; by allowing another "trusted person" within the Bigfoot Community to contact the Russian scientists for me? That mistake resulted in a complete misrepresentation of my good intentions via much bias, wrongly directed, much moot parlay confusion of opinions and intentions! "When will I for hell sakes ever learn to keep doing my own walking through the Yellow Pages of all wide world pseudo Bigfoot community? Perhaps this manifest presented with, or without permission to show those pictures will make some difference with the anxious Russians, and in time they will submit? If not, all can still read if any can find, Dmitri Bayanov's exciting book that is an astonishing collection of wild man's beginnings and end as was ever early written, titled, "On the trail of the Russian Snowman!" "Sorry fellas, but you really should make the effort to confer with me on the plaiting topic, as there is very much more ahead to share? Perhaps write to: Donald L. Monroe - P.O. Box 18, Lima, Montana 50739!") "What are Maverick Investigators Besides being a field Work Horse?"

"The author is a maverick! Ray Crowe, passé president of The Western Bigfoot Society is another! Heaven forbid, the list gets mega long! Bob and Patty Reinholdt, for sure are avid barn yard curators of the innocent moon light rest stop, as they are ever supportive of about everyone been neglected including any number of the popular and dis-rot Bigfoot community wanna-Bees. Ridiculously gifted people as is Ron Roseman is another born improbable maverick magic something or another, but like all of them he is very self-convincing, I even have a hidden confidence in his ridicule! There are many others among us of both genders that are better, worse, and/or are just as

unlikely as myself to not succeed to impress even themselves, or they are very much similar of the expertise that is denoted MK Davis, him unlike almost everyone else mentioned, self-thinking themselves to be of a specialized expertise of little or nothing, not at all likely now, prior, or future or able to update influence the pseudo invincible passé, Four Horsemen, who's opinionated influence of Yore by this date and time, "in all due respect," are all but forgotten history, as in many ways they have long been superseded by many a new thin-haired investigative maverick prototype of them that by now have lost their curls!

Mavericks of note are mostly thought bogus, and most are non-supportive of the slanted media, etc., as they ever dare to explore and expound all of what needs be known

Figure 50. Hink with other horses loafing at the ranch; notice the apparent braids. Photo Jensons.

public "Out of The Box material", and do not necessarily ascribe to all wanton regimented think-ing! Academics when compared, are most of them captured within their own pier allowance and mixed collegiate status-quo! Without mavericks, what, really, would particular seldom exemplary doctorate academics, or any wanton Associate Doctor Seldom Professor of Anthropology or any-thing especially need next conjured up within his/her imagination to further roast-butcher particu-lar credible mavericks until well done on continuous fired opinionated, grueling expounds, ever oblivious to maverick objection, dejection, and rejection? When pray-tell, is enough protest of anything enough? By now it is obvious that I have a heated disregard for all over-rated, outdated, Bigfoot hearsay sway! Again said, when is enough protest of anything enough?" Moot opinions can and often have resulted much harm beyond preposterous and unacceptable! Seemingly some many moot opinions remain confused beyond the rescue of ones self-approval and obvious narcis-sistic adoration!" Red Headed Giants, referenced unofficially by the local Paiute Nation as the an-cient cannibalistic, Si-ti-caw Giants, or the Sa' il, People of the reeds! These obscure people also left behind many various artifacts of basketry and cat-tail reeds that well attest that they were capable of braiding.

"Don, Stay in touch with Ray Crowe!"

"Ray Crowe Well Knows All Story Above! So be it... he would say!" And, if ever there were anyone that has been there, and done that... our good old buddy Ray Crowe is the one! At least Ray, in some manor of lay blather and opinion we finally do agree on something! Hopefully by today you are feeling much better? Hope to see you next June at Sweet Home, Oregon, as I espe-cially needed to spend some time with you and confer with Tom Powell on some particulars, as I am most certain, "him aware of it or not," that we are on some similar facets of the hominid dis-cover beyond what for now is wanted public. Ray! for the record, my abstract moon plaiting the-ory, and your much similar moon phase Sasquatch encounter data, done via all Lunar research ac-complished year, 2005, etc., well, both our research without the plaiting mentioned is much rela-tive, and yours for anyone interested was written-up in segments of the Track Record Magazine, differing from mine that will likely in time, be hammered shut, "case-closed," never to be reconsid-ered much the same as some other important unpublished lay manuscripts, ever wanted left via shallow opinion undiscovered much just the same as are all the many, many, huge obscure skeletal remains long hidden covert in academic lock up basements as, Barclay California, the favored Smithsonian, and the long overlooked small collection of four obscure antiquated skulls still on the basement shelves of The Humboldt County Museum, at Winnemucca, Nevada! (These skulls have only recently been reevaluated for their questionable historical importance and are now to be seen on video footage offered by "ANCIENT ALIENS!") If haven't yet been commandeered into obscu-rity, to see them, ask for Museum Curator, Pansy Lee Larson, and if she still there ask her to show you the forgotten skulls of the human hair thatched to it as shoulder-slung, now replaced by the exchange of long Horse tail strands! Another example in my opinion of, hiding historical truths from the public! What have we become most part, but an anxious, money mongering, deceptive society?) they were well adapt at similar as plaiting! Furthermore, there is much more hard evi-dence of this incredibly ancient basketry to be found much over looked locked within the glass display that is little known to be the only one of its kind! It is an extremely rare water-basket jar! In forty years of searching over all museums of America, never have I found one similar! Look for it, right side glass case, second floor turn right, go next, outside window to your left hand facing East!

Good luck critics, what came first, me, you, or the dripping egg yolk that is now smeared all over your ever captive programmed bias face?

(The ancient especially worked basket jug is more than interestingly, as it has many long strands of pseudo human hair at-hatched to it as shoulder-slung, now replaced by the exchange of long Horse tail strands! Another example in my opinion of, hiding historical truths from the public! What have we become most part, but an anxious, money mongering, deceptive society?) Darn but I do wish at this moment that my, Nevada Paiute Indian buddy, Gordon Davis, or Frog were still alive! He, MK Davis, Ken Bear Iddins, Tonia Brown, my late wife, Marion, Var Harris, Paul Wright, "Red", and myself to name a few, well know that some things discovered on the Nevada desert not written in any manuscript cannot be written public at all, let alone be explained! Absolutely, the barbed wire fences are up abrupt many of our past, and now suddenly lamented lost freedoms of expression, as the future of every free spirit adventurer and true environmental conscious outdoors man is being as if mocked at almost every desert crossing, water hole, and at every recent forest stop sign now being placed by your amazing, BLM, and US Forest Service, and all pseudo wanton Government controlled informative wild desert canyon road sign! "Exactly when, "Opal Joe Stormer," do you think that enough protest will be done enough to completely thwart all present allowed desert travel had across the wondrous still completely little known, explored, or realized, vast, Reese River/Owyhee/Cal/Neva/Ore/Ida, and Black Rock, and/or Smoke Creek Deserts? "Opal Joe," as he is called, has become a desert legend in his own time... "Hey Joe, if you are still out there at Soldier Meadows, you owe me another twenty bucks, as your copy of this book is waiting for you with your dusty mail at Gerlach, Nevada! Your thirteen decaying wild mustang skulls, are still safe in my keep! Come and get the rascals before you and I and they all soon will self-distruct! SO, with that said Joe, lets sing, and drink, just one more shot of peach soda, and one more glass of sage and brush tea, to all of the wild fellas and wilder gals that can still remember you or me, and revive the high spirit of the beckon of the wilderness call, as there still are a few caves in the desert walls. where you and I can still crawl! As yet you say that the government hasn't closed them all?"

Letter sent? May 25th, 2012

RE: Letter to Ray Crowe, Hillsboro, OR.

"Ray, good to have seen you recently, miss our old friend Fred though...Your home seems bare without him! He always settled our differences with the exception of Ron Roseman! By the way Ron said hello! Don't know what he is up to these days unless he is out catching more scorpions in AZ. with Richard Grover?

Here next Ray we have a close hypothetical look at how and why plaiting long ago may have resulted in the ongoing strange participation that it is, if allowing that is, that the moon Goddess Diana be used for a prototype scapegoat? As you well know, women always have a way with everything! You asked me recently to tell you some part of my moon theory... Well, it is to be remembered that in the most ancient of prehistoric times where humans existed, the world at best then was a literal natural Nether World of horrid things and danger! What I have wondered Ray is, if the Bible can be referenced here, exactly what sort of mixed humanity and or beasts.. ("If indeed any others were included?").. had also been cast out from the Garden of Eden with Adam and Eve?"

"Lab scientist, Yvette, somewhere in France? Is There a, "Y" Creature?"

"Rumors have it that very soon a special academic report will surface to the world from California with claims that particular DNA absolutely proves without any doubt that Sasquatch are born of a human Mother of Middle Eastern Ethnic Origins, and the Father remains unknown?" This is no real surprise to me, as year 2004 or 2005 was it, through pseudo academic contacts had of Ray Crowe (All story not complete!), I sent high suspect DNA samples to a noted research lab in France, and the returned message sent back with the conclusions in an E-mail to Ray said... (Paraphrased from memory, as I still have the original copy!) ...She wrote: "We have concluded our study, and what ever has been found has never been seen in this laboratory before! "It is high strange, and appears to be a male, as it is only evidencing a "Y" chromosome indication? (This is next to impossible?) Whatever Monroe has found in Idaho caves; definitely he needs send us more evidence? ... Yours truly - "Yvette"

"The Hand Of Unknown Origin!"

Hell yes, and, Hell No!

"Offered help is sometimes a disastrous hindrance!"

"Dare we, can we, by our own self-esteem and logic, opt to remain an incorrigible maverick similar as was all yesteryear free trappers, that dare catch and sell their own beaver where ever wanted, discover Sasquatch on our own terms, and prove that we can catch mink or a wolf in a feasible trap! Learn to sew their own britches, tattered-coat, and tend our own wounds without the UN-wanted programmed opinions of the company store? Most important is to be on good terms with yourself, and be able to wear all unadulterated flack and roasting ploy, come hell or high water into hell and back, or to anywhere wanted that you had opt to share your good will, time, and flesh and blood!"

"The Montana Strange Creature Hand Of Unknown Origin!"

"Fires burn and so do people... I for some reason never to this day have understood why back in year 2005, that I had not received back in time to have responded different the meaningful and important message sent to Ray Crowe from France and Yvette? I did not hear one word back for almost a year! The complete incompetence, and all later realized ramifications of the sad account still angers my reason! By the time I learned of the report it became next to impossible to duplicate the discovery! I do mot think to this day that Ray had realized the importance of my efforts in the field, or either of the "Y" Creature report, or he may be innocent in having been human and completely over-looked or forgotten that he had not sent it?

A totally separate DNA investigation leading Where?

Similar of this had happened again year 2006, when first time ever I brought from Montana what is still referred to as, "The Strange flesh and blood Hand Of unknown Origin!" All of that loss, however un-similar in circumstances, is still nevertheless much similar in outcomes of the "Y" creature example, and it is still extremely controversial as to how to explain all high suspect reasons in simple terms of where the flesh and bone hand has probably vanished today, who exactly has it, and what are the now almost criminal intended reasons that the long awaited hand Has Not been long ago Returned Back To Me? Well, as it now stands, it is high suspect that all of the lost hand mystery has now been reasoned; that passé, several years ago, the hand was cleverly commandeered for further covert study, having directly to do with the alleged maverick-academic report believed now all able to at least identify some important logistics and hard found facts of wild man Sasquatch DNA? This real or part true story of to fact; this story is long, complicated, and hardly over? The announcement aired first time only recently over COAST TO COAST radio hosting one maverick women, Melba Ketchum!* As far as I have been able to find out of late, The Strange Montana Hand of Unknown Origin belonging to me on contract year 2006 between myself and Tom Biscardi, went first time to him for further scientific investigation, "and now this last time, somehow still confusing; "last known the hand exchanged from Tom, to the animal laboratory of veterinarian Melba Ketchum, who was then somewhat covertly rumored to be in future directly involved in the alleged up-coming Big Foot DNA report message to all world academics...* Well as explained her report aired via Coast to Coast AM only recently in late December, 2012?" "Any one still confused or fail to understand exactly why, what, and how are the reasons for the authors rebellion concerning integrity, honesty, academics, and all mavericks of good intentions should now understand, "and that is whole truth as I think to know all confusion, so help me God!" All that last said abrupt all real, and unrealistic characters completely lost to narcissism, wanton to remain confused within and out of the pseudo Bigfoot community? I really doubt that the good guys wear white hats little Mouse, as so do a lot of Lawyers wear them! Keep that in mind, as in a future I may need to see some many people before a judge late year 2013, I hope not?"

More on Plaiting!

"To think to more explain living hominids and plaiting, we must need discover (If already haven't?), another more wild hominids in the flesh to better understand all possible reasons for plaiting, hatchet/hammer appropriation, etc., however much of this has already been reasoned, but we don't as yet beyond this manuscript understand the mechanics of how bonding with the horses and the plaiting reasons done? It seems that the bulk of current day subscribing prototype Bigfooters, "if indeed there is such a thing as a lay prototype, or a professional anything or similar among them (?)," and if so, most have already dictated among all piers exactly what if anything beyond their applaud, will be allowed flaunted to further explain their separate protocol of any wild entity or anything!

How farfetched, deep, into sour attitudes is such a blatant, obnoxious, insanity, going to take us backwards before the world will finally realize to accept credible maverick or professional discovery? Do anyone suppose that, Marco Polo, or many other eccentrics like him were anything other than an adventurous soul, and often much of a restless maverick nomad? I'd liked to had explored with him... How far can such bias out dated negative thinking take us anywhere new into

---

* Coast to Coast AM, on shows aired August 29, 2010, December 23, 2012 and February 17, 2013, hosted by George Knapp. See also

* See press release http://www.dnadiagnostics.com/press.html dated November 24, 2012, Dallas.

this supposed New Age of Aquarius and miracles? It looks to me that if anyone wants to break the power siege of all those long considered to be accredited members of the accepted miraculous Big-foot, Rat Pack so to speak, "one need be prepared to become one of the above described highly obnoxious truth eradicating ilk, as I have come to believe that a large percentage of so called Big-footers, actually do not seem to want Sasquatch actually discovered and explained as simple as I have written it here, in some cases for the reasons of further popular pier associations, and/or all future monetary gain had from popular book sales, media opinion and pseudo entertainment? Not to insist however, that there are not many credible hominid researchers out there, because there are many, many, "but trust me," have an educated hard look at particular wanna-be people within the Bigfoot community, and you will no longer doubt that we disparately do need to pay more attention to all valid new discoveries made by anyone, and especially for now be closely con-cerned of all incredible valid film enlargements had available of others similar of all of the many, many, many, original film enhancements now continuing being done as I write intended to further expose the Roger Patterson/Bob Gimlin film for what it was, and wasn't, and several others now relative films that are now surfacing being evaluated! We must learn if want the truth of wild hu-manity to accept what becomes the proven obvious, "and stop being so moot damn smart and bias critical of all new founded reasonable logic and reasoning, as reasoning denotes truth, and truth is often found just exactly where it was completely overlooked! Dare trust your own self-esteem, and be a maverick free trapper! "To hell with the controlling Canadians they would say at the free rendezvouses.... To hell with The Hudson Bay Fur Company and Canada! Let them catch their own beaver, Sasquatch, mink, or their own ass in same, or a forgotten trap! Let them also sew their own company issue winter leggings, and tattered jacket! Be them always be on good terms with themselves, and be able to wear all unadulterated flack had form us and anybody into hell and back, or back to anywhere that they desire to return from if rejected! Comb your mangy hair boy! Put on your best knife and smile if have nothing else? And dare if necessary or want to shock the world in your birthday suit... Nothing isn't nothing but its free ... What ever, be damn sure that continuing exploration and discovery not be forgotten; it is the duty of the trapper to discover more territory! Prod every bush and mountain for Whom The Bell Tolls, and many new and excit-ing answers to explain wild man will be found! And for sure, aspire to Go to any Damn place an-ywhere that you want? I have also promised to go there! And don't apologize to anyone for what could not have been avoided! See you on some western trail? Why does the horse that you are riding have that braided mane? What done that? The horse looks haunted!"

Valid Film Enhancement?

(Enlargements!)

"Yeah, it is true, all real article educators, academics, Sasquatch, mavericks, and especially wild high-tone, and high maintenance beautiful women, should ever remain free in spirit, and thought, and be able to do just exactly what they want, and not be subjected to become some sorry cap-tured egoist, or be down trod, and discouraged of all separate opinion etc!"

In time if alert there can be found answers to solve the wild man anomaly, plaiting, and even your firm belief in the world wide distribution (If have one?) of existing mermaids, as in a close if not to distant a future, one or more surprise identities of wild man or even them will be found! Sasquatch in my opinion are much more human than supposed! Var Harris, where ever you are, I hope that you and I can be on location together whenever they are accepted human, and you just as always wanted, be able to hand the oldest wild man look-alike of yourself a fresh carrot! Perhaps Var, we are all looking for the wrong thing? In my life long reasoning, had some of it from all mixed Hawaiian calabash family Talk Story, wives' tales, local mythology, etc., I have never completely disdained a mermaids existence? Maybe we should have a better educated look? According to some belief, what lives on the land once lived in the sea? Perhaps to some imagination, some of them had returned?"

Critics sometimes have valid answers!

Critics may agree? Horse plaiting is not being done world wide by civilized man every single time in a same way! To understand plaiting, first we need agree and understand that no matter what else is written, wild-man if be allowed called that, Sasquatch do exist, and it is a fact that they are just to much wilderness smart, and that way beyond elusive for most of us to think to truly rediscover them, and they have not one good reason other than food appropriation other than an occasional needed human abduction of either gender to sustain their limited gene pool, otherwise they are completely uninterested to collaborate other than possibly in a far abstract consideration, "be tongue in cheek and enjoying the caused concern at their humor, by continuing to be plaiting horses, etc! And that said, for even harder to explain reasons here for time and space not the place to attempt it; after long years of observation through food and use full artifact experiment, "it is ever probable that feral humans as wild man, just may posses a limited sort of a primitive humor relative of all humankind when realizing our obvious inability not to be able to discover them, etc?"

Figure 51. Dr. Todd Reese and his secretary Tina displaying plaster casts of various tracks.

255

"Sasquatch are More than One Identity! I Sincerely do Believe it!"

However to date, considering all artifacts found and casts taken in all far places as the American South West, to include Minnesota, many more southern states; all of the way far distant as are the northern Outback Territories of north eastern Australia, it is further obvious that relict human type hominids of various kinds are still much alive and are well able to exist just about anywhere in today's much bias blind, and contrary to truth society. John Green, wild feral hominids are not even remotely any sort of a suggested Gigantopithecus or any similar ape like creature! Why a man of your experience and back ground chooses to insist that true, is more than an interesting reason to wonder? I look forward to reading through the new slated book that I have been told that you are writing..? If that not so, I apologize for any inconvenience, and wrong auto-suggestion. What they will finally will turn out to be via DNA, in my opinion will be beyond astonishing in varied ethnic human and animalistic outcomes, as they to fact are as far apart form orangutan apes, and mandrills, as the desert tortoise, is from the Jack rabbits! In one photograph included, is a graphic picture of Doctor Todd Reese seated with his secretary Tina, in his Idaho Falls, office, holding in plain view three separate monstrous plaster hand castings, taken from a very same cave area location of Idaho, and not one of them very obvious to define, are all that much similar! What tells us is that; at once it becomes extremely obvious to anyone of the uncanny abstract variations to indicate more than one possibility, unless it a case of dastardly mutations had from continuing incest relations resulting in consanguinity, etc? Astonishing outcomes of identity are somewhat explained ahead. There is nothing more about the true facts of hominid identity that academics can continue to deny! We are ourselves hominids! Sasquatch are much like us, and we are truly not quite like them! But out of human compassion and all good reason, unless it need be in self-defense, we for no reason should ever think to harm them!

END OF PART TWO

PART THREE

The Horses Are Coming!

Babe, where are you now? This is your part of the book!

"Written in part, in high regard, and fond memory of, Little Wild Tonia, Two Feathers, Onya Brown! She Was Very Much Less Than Naive! Her sister Sherie Stallman, of Wise River, Montana, once had told me with tears in her eyes at the time of her death, that Tonia she said, was smarter and probably better, and more honest than are any twenty five other people! With you Don, she had found a new beginning and an end to adventure! Had she lived, there would had been written another book! Please for me write something about her, that her kids everyone would further know her!" Tonia truly was every one's sweet heart! "Well Sherie it is written, and you will receive your desired copy of her proxy book! Her love of horses definitely helped to write it!.

"Onya Wild,
And Her Highly Treasured, Little Green Note Book!"

All New Memories And Beginnings....

"Don, she asked, where were you wandering when I was born?"

For Angelo, Josh, Amy, and, Jinx the cat!

"Perhaps this is where the book's story should have actually began?"

As before her death Tonia had much edited this particular section of my notes. I had no idea that she had worked so hard! Some excerpts explaining her earned credits and comical experiences while of exploring are written here. What is not, becomes painful between the lines."

I submit this last part of the book for its importance to understand the exhilaration of many others similar in regard to wild hominid populations, plaiting, horses, UN-president ed travel, and all new discovery. What Tonia had discovered on the road was a new and a definite lust for life and freedom.

"Take away freedom Don, and we have nothing! Nothing really at all …! And remember, that I am going with you, and there is nothing that you can do about it! Can I bring my gun?" Yeah, you better have that with me too! You never know what anyone, or especially any of them strange southern creatures you are going to meet are up to? Remember we are on our way to visit Ron Roseman... Yea! He's still driving Taxi-Cabs in Florida! Wait till you met his boss, Eddie... He is a cross between a rubber duck, and a sandwich! What kind? I don't know, probably a meat head?"

Onya's Story!

"Her Story, much more explains all further horse and plaiting theory; particular difficult efforts made to assess plaiting; pert feminine winter travel hints; various horse logic; wild destinies of fantasy; Lycanthropy in part; further Bob Cat Logic, to include some of the authors noted egocentricity, and impossible self! A there is written much more girls that you will appreciate! You all should have all been with us?"

"The Little Green Almost Magical Note Book"

Thanks Sooo much for it!

I needed make only a few changes in necessary edit from what Tonia had originally written, as well as I had needed to add a few all necessary updates. I have only slightly paraphrased for content some of her personal data. Otherwise all humor and compassion was much done verbatim as taken from out of her left behind,

"Little Green Journal,

that writes some of it, much compassionate of all family, now well realized wanton of a much personal message. Tonia wrote much intuitive of all worthy humanity, and especially of her family; probably ever self-realized of her surprising self, if not perhaps somewhat also overwhelmed that she had been so very much human, unselfish, and caring, as she sometimes tried hard to hide behind her obvious soft shell of the devil may care...

Wild Man, & Sasquatch!

My first introduction of Sasquatch belief and caves to her "she said had change her life!" In due time and in un-similar ways, "she also had much changed mine..." Honesty and kindness today are a rarity in humanity, and, "Tonia Two Feathers Brown, Onya Wild, as she sometimes opt to call herself, was ever an honest, kind, prideful, and of a very gentle, and a sweet heart type of a cute petite, "to skinny she said," little Indian girl!" One of her obvious passions was mystery, and astrology, and wanton knowledge of all higher type wild life and animals, and especially sea life, mustang horses, and not to forget to include most anything denoting hi-adventure! Most of all import was her obvious appreciation for Native American Traditions, and all life itself! Her first and foremost concern was for the love and concern of her three children.

"Yeah Babe, as she liked to be called that... this book when completed will have been a true revelation, as where ever "Onya" writes ahead in "this revelation," as she had ever called it that on page One of her journal! "It was ever important she wrote, for her to be continuing research having to do with this book..." Her rascally self had much inspired its spirit and enthusiasm, and all good humor! Her separate discoveries are written!"

"Don she said, don't take life so serious, as darn well we both know that it really is! Lets go down on the beach tonight, watch the moon come up, and discover all of the rest of the hidden places along the shore... and write our own wild story before someone destroys more of the best!"

258

Tonia was always exciting … All who had failed to know her, would have forever loved her! Her excitement included all fantasy and bright night stars, and the full moon past mid-night! She was one heck of a giant of a women of small stature …!

"See you later Tiger... We will continue to burn a candle for you! So you were loved!"

"All New Plaiting!"

Babe, it's Another Full Moon, and you are remembered!

Log: May 6th, 2012 – "The Snake Bite!"

("I'm writing five weeks into a Montana Spring, after having just experienced a terrible Brown Snake bite, happened, March 28th! It damn well nearly put me down too! "Never say never! Wow!" Update: It's now Feb. 25th, 2013, and I expect if lucky by late March, "exactly one years time," to finally have survived the problem! "I only include this last lament, as much of the important lunar research of 18 months running was accomplished to my dismay over the time of recovery, and when/as the book was also being written!

The commitment to the project, the hardship, and a definite lust for life God willing, had continued my sojourn. This was my most difficult problem to survive! Needless to write, I really do hate snakes!")

Log: Veterans Hospital, Salt Lake City, Utah

"Tonight I am waiting in anticipation of any new word to come of repetitious horse plaiting again, if and when being done or not on the Jenson property located along the east side banks of Oregon's, wild Owyhee River. It's another full moon phase! As explained in Part One, and Two, Phil Jenson has agreed to begin a new experiment, using colorful ribbons that have by now been tied fast onto/into Hink's brushed out hanging mane. All of five witness are there anxious to see if anything new happens or at all becomes changed on Hink's mane? All of this is truly another Wild Great Northern Mystery indeed! I am still in awe and in high respect for what ever intelligence is accomplishing the difficult plaiting? Everything that has been done so far, or has photographic artifact proof, has gone far beyond my comprehension. Can I truly be correct in all of my assumptions... Well, its all been happening pretty much to all expectations! Wow for now is all that I can say.....!"

Log: Phil Jenson: Colored Ribbons?

(Continued from above.)

Concerning the green and pink ribbons, as said in part one, "we had the idea that if the colored ribbons similar as the Russian examples, were next woven into the horse's mane, it might spark a response? If anything were to happen or not, the braiding efforts would be noticed!

That fact alone may be more importance to all future associations than realized, as if nothing at all has changed on the horses after doing that, "well something actually had," as if there is all at once no further interaction as plaiting, "then it is not to be over looked that probably the creatures for the moment were spellbound. and became a bit apprehensive that such a strange offering as colored ribbons had actually happened?"

Phil and I had agreed, "if a thing is not the obvious, then often it needs be the reverse?" What try next? It is to be remembered however that the green colored ribbons did vanish, and the pink ones were left behind! At least we now know that they are not color blind. More of similar experiments need be tried. Will update as continue?

(Update, below!)

"Wild Man!"

Slated for Year, 2014!

A Slight Introduction.

"By Onya leaving behind her covert journal, she actually had written much of Part Three, and to my surprise with all hard efforts she had also done much unknown edit on what I had told would eventually be an all new abridged Trilogy Manuscript for year, 2014, titled, "WILD MAN," by re-writing another time both of my earlier books combined and updated into one, and I had discovered that she had also written an intended part introduction for that project! Onya was amazing! How she found the energy and time to had done all of this still boggles my mind! As said, she was life long interested in astrology/astronomy, which out of natural interest will eventually include the pseudo effects of Lycanthropy on man and animals, and in that way she was ever excited to aid me in any way to help to re-construct my moon theory, do research to its interest, and covertly reconstruct Wild Man! Ahead where fits, all readers will surely re-educate themselves abrupt Onya's invincible Moon phase, and separate horse plaiting observations, and much more! I am forever grateful to had known this wonderful intelligent resourceful women, she was a real credit to her gender. To my thinking, Tonia well understood some of the intended applications of what were implied meaningful of the poet of old, Omar K yam, when he first time recited to the ancient world that ... "The Night Has A Thousand Eyes!" Using that for a spring board inspiration, she educated me to the moon adherence of the moon goddess of the night, "Diana," said in ancient belief and mythology, "to be the all seeing eye, ever watching down on all mankind! Eventually Dina as has been explained began to fit into the possible scenario, and on and on write I ..."

"Onya's, all tell-tell tiger cat French-Indian green eyes were ever hungry for additional knowledge, excitement and continuing lust for life while enduring her malignant misery, that for me became another pier example of unprecedented tenacity and purpose! I had seen similar of this in the non-complaining hardships and cancer trials had of my late wife Marion who endured unfathomed discomfort for all of nine years. It is not to be said that women are not as tough as they can be wonderful... The endurance and self-sacrifice example such as this I believe has helped to save my own life on several occasions to include my most recent mentioned hardship of snake bite. I can still remember hearing Onya exclaim when I told her I was leaving on Friday for adventures in Florida, and would see her in six or eight months.... "The heck you are! Its gonna be me with you... Its Florida or bust! You love boats, and I think me, and I you, so what's left? I am going! It will be Ships if you want, and horses for me! That should satisfy us both!"

Babe, I said, I was also planning to be going to Bimini Island?

"What did you say? What do you mean... From Miami we are going to Bimini Island? Where, and what is that? Are there horses on Bimini? "If not I'm going into my tent and diving I'm under the covers, but your not going alone!" Well, yeah, you got your own tent, own mind and free will ... I will try to find out about more horses? Yeah Babe, the old guy on the phone at the shop on Collins Ave, Miami said yes! They have horses there for hire! Maybe we will find some pirate gold? Ever heard of Mel Fisher? I 'm a friend of his sister Judy Staffen ... She to me ...

"Part Three Continued!"

(Tonia, 2009 - 2011)

Log: Onya writes

Ahead only slightly paraphrased, however still much unchanged in content just exactly as al was said when taken from her left behind Little Green Journal

"What do I know of Horses?

Well Don, I have always loved horses! For me the horses were always coming, or I would be wanting one! When I was a girl at Pismo Beach, California, I had always watched the sea, and the moon, and had always longed to have my own horse! I have to agree with you, all human type creatures probably do watch the moon a lot, and the stars! Each of them are a natural curiosity! Yeah, you might say ... just like I told you before, when I was young I must have been some sort of an impossible Beach Bunny I guess? Yeah, I really did spend most of my time at the ocean... I really did love to swim and surf ... but I also loved the mountains, and all of the wild horses just as much! And I had ever longed to one day have my own ranch, and have a safe place for a horse, as I had ever planned that one day I'd live Idaho or Montana! I know that you think of yourself as if to be some obscure pirate on horse back... well then, lets do it all again! Lets go down on the beach tonight and be wild pirates together looking for buried treasure, and ride on horses back from top to bottom all of the way down Florida to Miami! Its going to be just you, the adventure, and Onya!"

She was always anxious, and wild excited for most all new adventure! It seemed she couldn't get enough! Never once did her quiet self back down from any new challenge of the unknown.

Several times she told me that she had always yearned to write a novel, "it probably would have been a block buster," as her varied experiences from life were all very much a real part of most all of us in trite comparison and honest mistakes. Her early life had been difficult... "well, she said, the most difficult challenge will be understanding you, that will never be over... I can't wait until we are out of here and our books are published! They all should at least make a lot of people realize that there is much more than they think yet to be discovered, and many, many, over looked possibilities to be had of the full moon theory! I am looking at the moon right now... and yes, it is effecting me! Most people never actually want to think all that hard about the moon, or really much about anything! All of our research might actually be true, and prove to startle a lot of people? Some of it we already know actually is happening!"

Every time Onya talked in length of her early days in California, it reminded me of the early writings of John Steinbeck! Onya could have at any time been explaining her life right out of the book, East of Eden, Cannery Rowe, and/or, Tobacco Road! She came from similar times, and same experience, and was just exactly as colorful in her way as was her favorite auntie, Ravishing Ruby, who in part had raised her... "Tonia, Ruby said, was always very easy to want to love, and appreciate... She had, had, a hard life! All of these years I have missed her so very much! She was always good to me, and every one! Oh, thank you for bringing her back to see me!"

Plaiting!

"Don, she said, I guess you know plaiting on long haired animals was done very, very, anciently! Early smaller horses before larger were developed were used to carry baggage, children, and were used for food! Your moon theory is very possible, as ancient humans were always very, very, superstitious and worshiped about everything from stones and animals to the fabled witch Isis! People have been on the planet for more than 20,000 years. I have long studied astrology, and what you had conjectured of moon phase and its adherence by early humanity makes a lot of sense. I never had realized beyond fantasy the hidden truth of wild man until I met you! I was warned that you were highly eccentric, wild natured, and of a very woodsy type savvy nature, highly unpredictable, entertaining, full of B. S. but honest, and was not to put too much credence in your influence... And just as you say, "you do not cut grass, or shovel snow... you just kick your way out, over, and through all its obstacles?" I really do think that you are a little bit like that! Well... Actually, I am also glad that I did not listen to anyone! What people don't know or understand about anything, or anyone, they are afraid of! Actually you are somewhat of unpredictable ... Well, the challenge of understanding you will never be over! I can't wait until our books are published! They all should at least make a lot of people realize that there a lot more to discover, and many, many, over looked possibilities to be had of the full moon! I am looking at the moon right now! Most people never actually want to think all that much about anything! All of what actually may be true is here in our research ... some of it may prove to startle a lot of people? When can we be on our way for our adventure to Florida? Just having some of what you know has changed my life! I no longer think of myself as being a boring and doubting women! Somehow I have bonded with you Don! Some of your ideas of excitement are even exciting and completely unheard of! How you travel and when..., and especially when and what you eat seems impossible! However I never saw anyone cook almost everything so well on a cloths iron propped up side down between books either! You eat almost everything cold! We, for heck sakes; even you said will need to eat raw wheat and a hand full of raisins? What's next? I really don't want an answer?

My children say that they can even see a big change in me! They probably can! You are much more of a rascal and a problem than all of them put together... or probably for that matter, more than anyone could imagine? My bags are packed ... Come hell or high water, I am going with you, even if you don't want me to go, or agree! Here hold my purse while I count our money! I'm getting into the car, and I'm driving first and there is no turning back, and there is nothing you can say, or do about it! Its going to be us now or never Don, and never for me is a very long road! Can we take my gun? This is going to be awesome! And remember, my money is our money, and our car is still all mine too... Your piece of junk would never make the trip! You can buy the first, and the last gas? You've got me for competition, and I am one tough cookie!" After Florida my way I told her, neither of us will ever be the same?"

"Well, Two Feathers, Our Trip Really Was a Hoot Too!"

She took her gun... She only used it once on a coiled rattle snake in Oklahoma.. Onya could shoot! "Don she said, this is the place where my great, great grand father, John Ross came from before he went West back in the 1860s!" She was proud of her family ties... "You should read more of your American history ...Actually he wasn't an Indian!"

"Moon Theory, and Lycanthropy in humans!"

From here forward I intend to include various outcomes of comparative lycanthropic theory, having to do with human adherence to the full moon; enough humanistic proof of wild man's ability to satisfy the imagination of the most difficult disbeliever; all of the wile hopeful if can to be able to more explain the difficult mechanics all necessary to be able to plait the mane on any horse, loosed anywhere first thought when reading to be the scribblings of a wanton doodle that had likely occurred while her falling asleep when working over time covert late night on one or another of my books, if interested perhaps an all new two book combined abridged version to be titled, Wild Man! Wild man will surface as can sometime late year 2014The proof of what I write O'course is short of definitive no matter how accepted it becomes, it is but one more dark corner projection of all plausible moon magic had from theory via much logical speculation! All more unexpected proof of this manifest in time I believe will surface important, as it is high time in my anxious opinion that everyone had a harder and better look at all of what we now have available artifacts that is ever meaningful exemplified next within the short comment and personal deposition of Tonia F. Brown that follows, as in time any manuscript naturally portrays a very real if not a living part of ones life, times, and character! Some of what was already shared above in the book that was reiterated from Onya's little green volume was never intended by her to be printed public, however of late I have been strangely inspired to now share it parameterized and much just exactly as all was taken in my separate judgment out from Onya's private book!

Log: Year 2009 – 2010.

"This Manuscript, combined with the new volume of Wild Man?"

Tonia's continued her efforts to abridge "wild man" I have surmised on our way to and back from Florida, while ever busy as we were making any and all new discoveries possible pertain-

ing to the general and abstract importance of moon phase and plaiting documentation while, before, and after having explored all new areas too me and of course her of Mississippi, New Mexico, AZ, Texas, etc., especially we were interested in little realized and over looked petroglyphs that when found were some of them next to impossible to believe were more than graffito of the times, as Onya said ... "Much of it if you asked me looks like lots of the ancient Indians of yore, much just like and the drunken Montana Cow Boys, all had a great thirst and no purpose to leave a decipherable message, and less than fifty cents on a Saturday night? She had accomplished all of this covert editing abrupt documenting all old and new interesting true life depositions in regard to plaiting where ever we could find it! She had done all of this in spite of her difficult and much painful "red-flag" cancer plight that needed in part be shared here explaining her difficulty that can be remembered stoic and uncomplaining. Onya loved all wild animals, and especially horses and dolphins, and so it was inevitable that she would easily gravitate towards wild man logistics and have compassion for there obvious difficult and miserable existence, as she was ever adamant of them as myself after having experienced particular exhilarating sojourn of desperation in an Idaho cave. She told me in jest, that in all probability I was likely much akin to these wild wretches myself, as how I looked at times from all lack of creature comforts I couldn't look much different? That denotation understanding and allowance in time ever became two sided, as for our short sojourn of two years together we became almost inseparable. Tonia much as myself had forever been able to hear "the call of the wild everything out there beckoning on the wind," and had managed to have loved her way with compassion for most all worthy humanity over most every and all difficult obstacle! She could have single-handed founded an all new

One Women Salvation Army! Anyone aware of its passé history has them in adherent support... As once long ago as a kid on the road somewhere in Kansas, I enjoyed an appreciated bowl of soup! An interesting chapter of a much similar wild natured spirit as had Onya, and an awareness reminisce of human bonding of a much separate adventure probe, was left behind for me to ponder written respectfully to my future as if a New Year Toast within her little green note book! "Onya Wild," was rightly named "that," and was "ever far beyond awesome as a women and far ahead of her times!" Don, she once asked me ... "I have heard you mention her more than once when discussing Idaho history... But really, who in the heck was Molly B ' Damn?" Well I told her back ...On one July or another, on a day in a future, we will go to Burk, Idaho, and enjoy her yearly celebration... "She was nothing like you, but had a similar good will to all attitude!"

"There, Josh, Angelo, and Amy Stanzeonie, all of that above reads just a we-bit more Hoyle, positive, and truly exciting of your mother, as she and you, did probably neither realize! What for all cat's sake, ever became of Jinx?"

"The Book, Wild Man, And Its Importance!"

"As said, Tonia, without prompting became the covert proficient labor of love editor, arranger, of my up-coming revised wild man edition manuscript, and she even insisted that new title! The two early manuscripts that will finally comprise it, were first published as, "Sasquatch 2001, and, 2003," however most all copies since then for monetary reasons, time, priority, and procrastination, a re-print has been long over looked! The last copy found, "was still in its original wrapper, and had been thrown into a Montana County Dump! The book's revision is being brought back for its update importance …as Onya had encouraged the re-write of the obscurity by telling me... "Hey Don, stop snapping that stupid mink trap, and listen to me? Those books were good! Everyone left year 2001, in the Honolulu, Haunt Book Store, sold out almost immediately, except for the two copies that need rescued that were precariously tossed hidden and a messed that way on the top most part of a book shelf! Just about everything written in those books is now true, or has been re-discovered valid! I especially like the story that explains the huge carnivorous bears long known covert that still roam parts of Russian, Kamchatka, and ever loved the account of the two separate snow-shoe rabbits that were left as gifts (?) twice at the front entrance of your wife's tent door! And especially funny was when you were camped in the Idaho St. Joe forest, and you and Ted Henderson, from Coeur d'Alene had experienced two Sasquatch making noise just outside your tent, and they both at a same time were loudly answering back and forth to one another... Wow, now that is awesome! And you well know too, that back in 2004, about three years after your first book came out describing that huge unknown Koriak bear, revered there you said as the sacred, "God Bear," and next you said that they finally managed to kill a huge bear in Alaska 2003 just like it in a very much similar description, but not before it had killed two men! We really do need to bring those books back! They were so interesting! Why are you so naive? Take some time out to write! Perhaps you should revise them? Just what we have already done together is unbelievable! People need to know this stuff! No matter people don't believe you, tell them!" Onya, truly was a true women adventurer! She ever braved her untimely demise that happened, September 4th, 2011, in dire desperation and much heart ache... Old Jinx, her favored Tom Cat buddy, was ever in uncanny dedicate support of her to the very end! All of that high interesting cat story is definitely another far into human and animal bonding! Well Tonia, your kids still have the snapshot collection taken when you with Angelo paid your last respects to your late mother in Arizona when I was there with you, and you had softly whispered her name and said... "Don I know that mom is at rest, and that she is looking down on us from all of these wind swept vistas over-looking Sedona … I just know somehow that she can see us!"

Log: Plaiting - Late August, 2011!

A few last thoughts of wisdom and logic on plaiting, had from Onya, said just a few days prior to her demise September 4th. Posthumous credits respectful of her efforts, as she really had done it all! "Don she said, the wind didn't do any of this plaiting, and here is another good reason why not! Perhaps you have thought of this already, and maybe not? But any way, read carefully through my Green Book! I know that you will find it one day, and some things written in it may help you... Sometimes I was just to sick and tired to remember to tell you all that I wanted to say, but this is just a little bit more common sense to consider having to do with plaiting! "Oh," and just one more thing… In their own way some many hypercritical critics tell on themselves, as they sometimes must believe much contrary to what they argue, and actually believe positive in wild hominids, and/or anything having to say of it had been done on wild horses, or anything semi-tame similar as are examples as Mules, Jack Asses, Donkeys, or any of the smaller Burros, in fact any of the long haired four legged creatures! Heck I guess if wanted they would even do it on cow tails, on some goats, and long haired sheep, but they don't! And even if it were true that any wind had anything to do with it...Why do they try so darn hard to prove that wild man don't exist! I think they actually do believe in them and just like to blow their own horn!"

"Pure Genius!" I could have hugged her, shook her hand, and kissed her for writing that, including all of what comes next, but she had already long gone somewhere up on a wind swept Montana ridge, or to a Sedona vista to sort out all of her memories. High intellect makes hard demands. Considering her amazing knowledge of astrology/astronomy, she could have been a mentor student of Isis, or the revered alien Egyptian goddess Sirius of old. Onya even knew to my surprise, some of the importance of the Southern Cross Belief had of the Australian aborigines. She learned new horizons from me, and I learned from her how much more there was to know! What a meaningful revelation from had the dust!

Tonia had discovered independently with no prior knowledge from me, that plaiting has been found done predominately on female horses! "... and mostly Don she had said, this is done on the ones that are pregnant, and very close to dropping their colts! Most of the time only the fillies and not the mares seem to get the plaits? And you know it is highly peculiar that after all of this time, and so much flack given you intended to down play all of your theory and evidence found to validate the plaiting, that not one single time, not even once, has anyone as yet commented on why this crazy stuff hasn't been done to Zebras, and all other long haired animals of the world that surely could be braided if wanted to! And you'd think too, that all much similar, or much the same would also happen exactly to them as has been done on those desert horses; and just as you say even the Nevada Indians well know that it sometimes happens the same on the wild mustang fillies." I had actually given some thought to some of that, but not either all that much! She had been right on target!

Good questions, why not we consider a bit more of your obvious wisdom taken from the green book... Sherlock Holmes, or Samuel Clemens, could only had sired such a wild and woolly, smart red headed Indian, sage brush desert wise daughter as was Onya! On the final page of the green journal was her last entry ... "Don, she wrote, I am really on to something that you would really love to know ... Together we are darn well going to solve our mystery ... I never learned what it was that she had to say?"

Truly she was ever her own genius, compromise, and was an unforgettable wild desert rose! I smiled as I read over the many comical passages of her journal where was included one of her last wishes... One year dated before her final storm, it seemed she had written endless exhilarations from her memories of life, family, and high adventure, as said, ever the later was expressed "in a rather personal letter to me of a somewhat romantic note," left behind to one day be discovered where it had laid UN-noticed tucked up-under her little green diary, and abandoned personal effects without me knowing. The letter and the diary had been there for at least 18 months prior and not found until after her untimely demise in 2011.

Her final message and last wishes read right out of her impending desperation, and evidenced a much depressed, and a saddened heart full of hidden tears, and ever an obvious love of life, and family. She had a very special way of loving through her writing, and included in that letter to me particular interesting comments to exploration, fear, happiness, exasperation, and her excitements of endearment, and of her strange intuitive love of experiencing the unknown and unexpected abrupt an uncanny lust had from a latent passion for romantic exhilaration? All of that can be realized ahead, and appreciated second person by her obvious gender excitements when will be explained in its place what only a few fortunate persons ever admit, of appreciating the uncanny bonding of oneself with another, their wild nature, or admit/submit to all of the difficulty and challenge of field discovery while miserable! Tonia well understood all of this as much as myself, and in her own way without at all being aware, "she was a absolute daughter of all worthy humanity and human nature! Every one is special I guess, and some of us are extraordinary! Her solemn word ever denoted herself worth, and spoke of her high personal respect. She was ever a chase women, and was ever a real man's sweet heart in every important womanly effort. Everything she wrote pertaining to plaiting, cave exploration, expressive passion during new discovery, love, mixed emotions, etc., are ever repeated verbatim as possible just exactly as all had been hand written and scribbled down a last time in her little green diary!

"For Her Children"

The letter mentioned left for me was also in my opinion for her children, as for now no real matter Tonia, that the journal letter was all intended private and just for me, as for all of its life message and true worth, I am sure that by now you would agree that I would share if for no other reason than for the sake of your children, as you had ever expressed a need for all of them to one day more understand, and know you! Everyone needs that! It is not fair that anyone end their life and times without anyone having shed one tear or sorrow; had a dog, or cat to be looking for their shadow, or a least a rangy coyote, horse, or an owl to hoot and howl over their loss!" Had your mother lived, guys, she would be writing with me in this treatise, ever enthusiastic and excited, as any passé Bohemian ever had it much the same in shadow memory of Greenwich Village! She would have re-captured much of the humor, and worthy rupture and adventure had in retrospect, now lost forever to the winds of time; but within her journal of last words are personal exhilarations, and passions enough, had abrupt her separate intuitive, bob cat logic, and her ever impressive horse-sense research, as she indeed did love horses, excitement, and ever stood for honesty, sincerity, and unconditional truth, and shared her love and limited time more than generously with all of everyone that she had adored. Her solemn word of commitment ever denoted herself worth, high esteem, and self-respect. And as said, she was ever a one man's women in every important effort ... "I use to tell her, don't be too hard on yourself, every one else will do it for you!"

Tiger Cat! That was what we sometimes I called her, as she was dire in love with Jinx, "the two thousand, forty six dollar cat," that also stole my kippered herrings, or it might have been something else of a higher suspect angelic nature? Not the worry Jinx, you were ever a good luck omen for me ...?" Once in jest, Onya Wild said to me ... "You know Don, to think about it? Actually only a truly wild man, could ever appreciate an even truly wilder women! I never told any of my kids some of the stress they were, because they were half Italian... I never related to the three little rascals that they were ever my impossible three wild little Indians! Where the heck were you wandering Don, when I was non but that pert, lonely, and, highly bashful, moon and horse dreaming, skinny little beach bunny?"

Well, Tiger, I don't know? But I was ever aware of black eyes, claws and bites, sea snakes, wild cats, Chinese, Hawaiian, and Mexican food, and every kind of a scratch had from even a chop stick, soft tomato, an/or any two legged idiot land snake, or soldier on leave to Old Honolulu from Christmas Island; and learned the big difference between having prawns, and the lowly shrimps offered on the barbie (Barbecue grill!), whenever I had gone down under to Australia!"

"Yeah Bob Smallsbach, this next has not really to do with plaiting but Onya and Patty Rein-holdt, were destined to one day meet, had much in common, Patty was also a direct blood line descendant of a questionable land-mark historic eccentric passé celebrity similar of, John Ross, as was the controversial, Pirate Captain/Governor, Sir Francis Drake, who also explored if truth known, much of the wild coastal vistas and important river ways of all eastern shore, South America, where he also paused to write interestingly in his log book, "of having discovered a very wild, huge, tall, and a ferocious cannibalistic people, that had from all description a lack of, or none but an obscure language, non custom, and ran completely naked! They were much the same to the all expectations of other obscure early Deep Southern, and Southern California wild peoples that had completely disappeared with the natural encroachment of the Europeans and other far distant humanity, from what then was a much less than an explored North America, all of them having much the same denotations of some many varied and mixed opinions of today, had them wanton called Sasquatch! Doctor Ed Fusch of Washington state who wrote an interesting book describing, The Stick People known of the Spokane Indians believe different of them, and some others of a mixed humanity to have possibly survived similar of what was Russian Zanna?"

Mark Twain, Captain Fremont, Brigham Young, Captain Walker, and several notable others also wrote much similar of other tribes of wild peoples, as includes as will be more explained in a separate book of the Trilogy, that very possibly obscure remnants of the relict Nevada Red Headed Giants may also be somewhere found in our mystery world? MK Davis, myself, and Onya each had learned the reasons that the possible blood lines of some of these obscurities, may still be had abrupt all unknown high strange enduring plaiting hominids, if indeed they are what is doing it; if not them, then perhaps some non descriptive beyond fantasized/real effigy descendent, written of in the chronicles of the goddess "Sirius" that are completely Alien, and if that not even permissible, then all may still include some many of the long thought extinct far wild ancient peoples of North and South American as were/are still (?) some left, as perhaps still today are the wild Ono, and the unfathomed, long forgotten Yámana, or perhaps even the legendary cannibalistic Texas swamp tribes, as were until the 17th Century, the unusually tall, ferocious, and also completely naked, Kuranks, and the seafaring fearsome child eating Caribs, etc? There is so much to speculate, and so little time to stop to write! To think oneself to be a writer is one thing, and to keep being in the field as an explorer is quite another. There is no real way to ever thank all of the many persons involved in my discovery sojourn, but some many were ever also much appreciated similar as was Onya. However her energy abrupt dread cancer to her last holds her in the highest esteem as a mentor. I long realized that was in a class bonded of desperation abrupt a lust for life, and there will likely never surface again a person of a more high determination to want to live than you! Thank you again posthumous again for all of your help with all of the above mixed jargon informative exposé research! Indeed Tonia we both had lived a much charmed, interesting, challenged and sometimes strange life, and babe, I am sure that you would had found it more than highly coincidental and uncanny, and also most ironic, that at the very moment happened only a minute ago, when I just had completed writing all of above paragraph wanton next to explain that we sometimes insisted that you were a true cat yourself, that a soft fluffy looking wild feral cat jumped fast high up from out of somewhere and landed onto the metal motor top of Bob Reinhold's parked truck sitting just out side the door! Lets not even go there with any sort of an abstract explanation, until perhaps and just perhaps, we can find much similar happenings in the Twilight Zone Chapters of the Trilogy?

"Tonia Wild Two Feathers Onya, as explained, was an intended fun name that she had self-penned herself, as among her prides and passions for all extended family, she was also a 19th Century, 1860s, relative, John Ross that was to fact less than a full blooded Cherokee Indian Chief. To-gether fall, 2010 with her cousin Peggy Oden of Pismo Beach, we attended the California Chumash Indian Nation Pow-Wow, as Onya ever cherished all native family sacred artifacts and traditions. She was the true prototype romantic, and left for me as by now is treasured, her last wishes writ-ten in her diary. You don't easily over look the devotion as was had from someone like Tonia. Slightly ahead in where explains "The Cave" we share for a last time a bit of her last words and sentiment. For some reading perhaps they are restless for me to get on with the story and be done with my reverie, but Onya and her efforts actually finalized this research and inspired it docu-mented. Indeed with her the horses were responsive. Like my aging old buddy Nevada Desert Opal Joe Stromer us to say... "Don, wild horses are good for much out here, as they are hard to catch. But they darn well eat good though! I like them baked, boiled, fried, or roasted, I like em most any way... even they are good with a little salt on a stick over the fire. I ate a bad acting mus-tang once...! Yea! He was bad! Before I shot him he bit me twice, and tried to kick the living hell out of all of us! Some of those difficult guys that got after me with their rifles up there at the Duck Valley Indian Reservation try to eat them too, but they prefer my wild pigs! Some of them since back in the old days have a lot of Hawaiian blood! The BLM seems to hate the wild horses! But to me they are the desert children... Anything that survive out here in this wilderness deserves to be left alone! Why in the hell don't today's city people just mind their own damn business and leave all of us desert folks alone?" Yeah Joe, why?

"Book Winding Down!"

Log: October 31st, 2012, "All Hallows Eve," inclusive of, – Feb 26th, 2013

Last Update:

Tonight O'course, is another full moon... It will be the last full moon phase that will be ob-served intended to have been inclusive of the final horses plaiting message of this book.

I have just got off the phone for a last time with Norma Jenson, where she is watching her horses on the Owyhee Oregon River ranch property where pastured is their horse "Hink" and others expectant tonight, prior yesterday may have already happened (?), or will again occur over the close-net days of the moon phase of Diana ahead? It is beyond incredible that I can write true, that over the past 15 months running since the date of the documented Full Moon Eclipse of December 2011 – Feb 2013 (Tonight!) that plaiting has occurred without question each and every time without fail... This is mind boggling for any persons now aware since my research who are also watching this high strange anomaly!... ("If no more is to be said, (?) at least for now this manuscript: there definitely is something very strange and very obvious oc-curring on these plaited horses that had directly to do with the Full Moon Phase! Whether I wrong or correct, much more in future definitely needs be done to further this uncanny re-search! Anyone out there further interested in all of what is written here wanting my further help to solve this high strange, please feel free to make contact at.. P.O. Box 18, Lima Mon-tana, 59739.") ... Considering all of the above, I am now anxiously waiting for further word from the Oregon Jenson/Hinck horses property in order to further evaluate and fully update the manuscript... More will be written to follow as can find out? "This remains an open book mystery! What much more that we need to learn we need to know! While waiting I will re-

sume where Left Off? I forever have endeared the full moon phase and been inspired under its spell, and now because of all of this high strange mystery will need consider even more…..?"

"I have always endeared the moon and pondered under its spell!"

"THE CAVE!"

< Last Words From Onya's Little Green Diary! >

A mixed Bag Of Personal Sentiment; More Disonga; On Shape Shifting; The Blue Moon; Exunda; Last Vista Of Horses; and next, The Cave!

First off: "I write much reluctant … following are some of her last words written to me taken from the private letter! I am reluctant to share it but for its content?

Sherie and Van Stallman will understand and appreciate what was written… perhaps it is for those exceptional friends that I had relented to share what is not my nature. The human animal is indeed a complexed mechanism … We can only pretend to understand them?"

"Excerpts From Onya's Love Letter....

Don, you are missed!

I dared to love you sooo much… I had never dared before to love so hard, or think to keep a diary that would be also a kept record of ill fiat, disdain, and tragedy! The pain by now I would think would have surely put me asunder? I know that you will miss me too! Each night at seven, I will be with you, as seven remains our connected number! Don't you dare to forget anything, nothing that I told you or that we did … as, nothing with me is truly over as we will always share the starlight, the moon, and the connection of our wildest dreams…

I was in love with you before our first dance. Pick any star and I will be there… I am only one heart beat, and one deep breath away! With you I was always breathless…"

"It was the cave! Yes it was us going into those crazy wild caves that got you me! Some day you will find this message and know how much I really did love you! I have to admit Don, that you and I, well … after all of that horse and the caving adventures and every thing that we did … Well, just being with you, and realizing my feelings, and after that, we could go about every where, and we did it all too…! Hey, I knew one day that you'd find my book and this letter and read it …and when you read it I will be as if again in your arms… please, please, never, never, forget me! You were my wilder tiger that could ever imagine would come true! Thanks for all of the incredible memories, and especially for knowing you! My kids I think had even began to like you? After all of that wild

270

Cave Stuff, and all of that we did together, and all of the things that were all new to me, I just already knew that my life would never be the same! One can't exactly say that they actually love something as crazy or as dangerous as a cave ...or any place like that, or anything that is as intangible, but that is just exactly as were beginning to be the feelings that came over me most of the time when I was with you and you took such good care of me... I just loved you so, Sooo much in when we were in those crazy caves ... and all that crazy stuff.... just being with you and having you care for me was enough, I never had that before! And then there was that sort of a strange love that came over me for the caves... Especially the big one, with all of the colors... some of them I just loved, they were so awesome... and you Don were so awesome! Getting scared in those caves, and then being happy again when outside... well, all of that and having you to guide and help me almost became the best feeling for anything that I ever had...I was really happy! I just loved you sooo much... and then for some reason I could never do enough for you... I just loved you Don, and wanted to spoil the heck out of you! There really was something wild and crazy about us being in those caves, "and I must tell you, that there was also something sometimes with is in them besides you and me! But I also knew that you would always take care of me no matter what!" No, no, that wasn't really it either... rather it seemed that there was always something alive, or very strange, or a sort of wild, and maybe even an awful feeling following along with us that had already accepted you....? "I am glad that what ever it was, wasn't jealous of me, or had came after me, and that I never saw what exactly it was? I guess a lot of the time I really was very scared... but I just knew that there really was something sometimes watching us! It was Sooo so very dark in there... even the shadows from our flash-lights were at times frightening! I would never have believed that anything could be so scary, or be so miserable, or at a same time be so dammed thrilling and exciting, fun, and fulfilling... it was always awesome and so crazy... and I am sure that after that I was even more wild, brave, hard to handle and more difficult? I just know that I was probably almost way too, to much more than you could handle? With all of my mixed emotions, and me a lot of the time almost wanting to be climbing all over up on your back and shoulders! Wow, I must have been almost to much to handle! Wow those caves were awesome... Especially I liked that big one! I wonder how many people even would believe that it exists? Well anyway I am sure you will well remember how sorted were all of my emotions, especially when going down into all of that darkness! Going into that black abyss, well, sometimes sorta hard to explain, as frightened as I was, I was sometimes also next to happy, scared, excited, and overwhelmed all at a same time! "And you ... well, wow Don, you just well darn well knew exactly how darn well too, how wild and worked up I would get when being finally claustrophobic in those caves! It was sorta crazy too, for me to expect you to be able to more than be able to handle me down there... and still you took me every where all of the time... and I was really scareder than hell! And, well wow, I guess really I sorta loved every bit of it too I guess? I really can't explain it, except that it was sort of like wanting not to do it, and then wanting to do it all at the very same time! I swore after that first time that I would never go back, but I did, and I couldn't somehow after that ever get enough of being scared and excited! How was something like that possible? I just couldn't wait for us to do everything all over again! Well, my nerves were shot and much unsettled, and you were just exactly as some said; you are somewhat hard to understand, but for me it was always easy, and at times I guess you were just a little bit distant... but each time with you anywhere I was safe, and was my happiest whenever I could make come alive and be comfortable with you! Its been an unbelievable adventure Don! Now I really know why no one in these times understands you very much.... you are, well, I will forever miss you when I'm gone! I love you so much that I just can't stop writing this letter... I vowed that I would not to let you, or anyone read it until if found after my time.... Don, I know and I am sad that my time is short, but I will be anything for you that you may want until its over! I already miss you and what we were sooo very much! Take good care Don, as really, there will come a time when all of those unbelieving professionals that have put aside your manuscripts and opinions may need to re-count them, as most all of what you have taught me in these few short months is more than incredi-ble! I truly now do believe that there are some very strange and the wildest sort of people ever imagined existing in some of those caves! And, now since knowing all of that and having you, my self-worth has been revealed and I have completely revised my life priorities, realize my passions, and now all that I want to do till my end is to be with you! There is so very much that I suddenly really want to do and tell you... and there are many things that I want to do for you, but I have sooo very much little time left to do it! And there is so much more yet that I want to learn!

I have just one last request... "Please Don, no matter what ever you say, don't you ever dare tell any of my kids, or even Sherrie or Van, that I went down with you into all of those dark unsta-ble, miserable, and dangerous, and crazy caves! If any of them knew that, and especially Amy, they would freak out and want to kill you!"

P. S.

"I will never forget you Don, somehow we had bonded in those awesome caves! Maybe that was why I sorta loved them? All of it now realized was my wildest dream come true!

I really did love you ... and please never, never, forget anything that we did, or me, that was the wildest bad-good little Indian girl that will forever will be more than crazy for you! You were ... Well you know, some kind of an impossible dream with me! Good-by until we meet again in an-other unbelievable crazy fantasy world, "where you say exists Exunda, somewhere located in the the wildest, UN-explored recess/region of anyone's imagination! Exunda! Where ever the heck that is, I will be waiting for you! I really did love you tiger... Loved you sooo very much! Remember our lucky number will always be seven....

X x x x x x, see you at seven! Love you, your way, any way, every way, my way, always and forever, your Tigress ...Onya Wild Tonia Two Feathers Francis Brown..."

P. S. "Don, I just wanted you to know, that perhaps the reason why I was not so awful afraid more than I was when we were in those caves, was because back then I knew that I was dying, and it as all just a matter of time? Like you always said ... "I had to get'er all done, and do it all, before I would soon self-destruct! It just doesn't seem fair because I loved you Sooo very much!"

"I owe you babe! You were priceless! There is all at once something watering in both of my eyes! Well, now, there you have it ... So be it ...."

"Onya's adventures had also became yours, without one short sad song of shared complaint! "Indeed life is not always fair!" But, however it need be said, "I have ever been most fortunate to have known the true love and compassion of more than one unforgettable women!"

"I don't know if it can be said, that women are any greater than men, but they certainly are not less! I read that somewhere, at some time, and had fully agreed ...! However I also denote that some many of them are just probably a wee bit better, and far harder to understand? Being alone is hell, if that is all that you have to look forward to! Just one bear needs dig up my bones, and they will be paid back! Sorrow is sorrow, and that's all!"

"Indeed Two Feathers, you were the real article man's women! Just knowing that you wrote all that passé, 2009, long prior to our returning back from Florida to Montana, spring 2010, after having explored about everything possible together having to do with horses, plaiting, Indian petroglyphs, swamps, mountains, and frozen deserts, bandits, and Ron Roseman short of Bimini Island, has me completely dumbfounded! You were ever far beyond being the very special unpredictable wonder of it all! Nothing in the wild, or in a cave would ever have harmed you... The very soft shadow of yourself, smile, and attitude, whenever in a cave, or anywhere with me on a desert vista, denoted from you only love and compassion for all living things. You were always a most generous, and gracious soul! "There need be no good-byes for us babe! You are ever to be seen looking back down from the wild ducks that fly South each winter/fall from Alaska at the time of every, Indian Pongoniff!"

Disonga; The Full Moon; The Blue Moon!

Disonga, (Dzunukwa, Tsonoqua,) or, in fable and fact may actually have something more to do with the full moon phase in infractions, implications, and demanded wanton adherence, somewhat helpful to more explain the high strange plaiting? What ever more is written here concerning Disonga, or any other strange anomaly of the witchery women sort, or any other Gods or obscure Goddesses worshiped of yore still possibly wanton today with any number of growing out of proportion high strange requirements; for time and space, not enough here will be said of them aside from what immediately pertains/applies as I am sure by now that most all readers still with me well understands where all of this is jargon is going to end if them wanting to agree with me or or not! If or not agree, regardless I intend to further investigate all pro-to-type and unorthodox mythological pictographic art, statuary, etc., as may similarly evidence the ugly/beautiful hag, Disonga, that is still revered powerful in Native American Apache Indian Tradition, Disonga is to them the wicked Blue Ogre Colored Women, that becomes at will the dread or a beautiful effigy depiction of, Disonga!

Disonga is portrayed graphically, as the most likely terrible equivalent example of all European neophyte fables that is at all relative, such as is the favored fairytale character known as, the wicked Old Witch of Any where, and Every where, as is similarly personified in the fable story of, Hansel and Gretel! Disonga is also a much just the same ugly or beautiful depiction as becomes the Hawaiian equivalent or her, that is the highly fabled, Madam Pele, or, the dread Island Goddess that dwells within the fire flames of the volcano on The Big Island of Hawaii.... Disonga just as Pele, is believed to be able to, SHAPE SHIFT at will, also into either a beautiful women, or a much haggard troglodyte of a no name type effigy! If in any way to fact any of this has a wanton influence on American wild man, or even anything found similar as them as yet we have no real way to know? Nothing is absolute, but when considering the demands and extremes of many primitive societies in regard of horses plaiting, unorthodox belief, worship, etc., who is to say that an abstract fear or a negative or positive influence or much similar may not merit considerations in effigy adherence, and/or an allegiance to fabled entities such as Disonga, Madam Pele, The Blue Moon and The Southern Cross, and countless other Moon Goddesses as are/were, Isis, Diana, Ester, She of The North, Sirius, etc! We are going there next! Humankind is only as mysterious as the mystery of his thoughts. There is Sooo much to know! Sooo much more than even full volumes would write. Every page, every new idea, everything thing conjectured, even suspicion-ed ever writes a separate book within contemplation! Remember, books are not always the last and final word to anything? Books after all are written to be re-written, as there is nothing written that cannot be erased and updated! What I wonder as I write, what exactly would, FRAZIER, the mentor of all passé anthropology write similar of his genius work titled: The Golden Bough, have to say that might opt to more explain the plaiting? Perhaps in that awesome book we have missed something very important and pertaining to it? I will have a look? He was the master of occult relativity to all unorthodox sociology and psychology, archeology, traditions an customs of wild populations, and human sort sexual dimorphism of the body and spirit.... Frazier was more than a discriminating writer! Java Bob would throe his hands into the air?"

The Blue Moon!

The popular song titled, "Blue Moon," has forever had me puzzled of its applications? Exactly what was intended in the song to suggest the color blue?

I myself have never observed the color at any moon phase, except sometimes under the right conditions during late after noon during day light when it seems to have appeared in subdued white and gray implications, the blue moon phase however has been recorded, as I have discovered that it actually does but very rarely occur, but not often!

The last blue phase noticed by astrologers happened twice, close dates apart, the last one was recorded in year 1999, lasting approximately 90 days, happening 3 times over the winter months of January – April. The first time span astronomically recorded was twice again similar, in 1915 (86 years apart!)! What sets a blue moon apart from any other; there results many a strange, uncanny, and highly unexpected happening, as for example when it happens that many large and small animals, and sizable flocks of birds, turn up mysteriously dead, and/or are sometimes found floating in world rivers, etc., while at the same time any number of strange animals large and small are found wandering far from their expectant home haunts, and some others all at once show up at the darnedest places! I only mention this, because in future the blue oddity may prove to have a more founded importance. It is interesting however that the color blue signifies the insistent countenance color of the haggard, blue lady witchy-women, who is often as not personified as a same depiction similar of the same stark blue colors often described when anyone attests to have experienced a close encounter of a,UFO, etc. What does the color blue have to do with anything? There are described blue bright night stars and the floating plankton seen at sea at sight is much seen in that color...

Strange Blue Creatures of the Deep!

When at open sea in the coldest waters of the North Pacific, at late night, when are proclaimed the we-hours of the 24, from the deck or bridge (20') of a low slung ship underway while slowly slicing its way only a few feet (7') above the water surface; far below perhaps at two fathoms or so down, often as not can be seen close to the surface what ever looks to be the high strange deep bright blue color similar of Disonga, and UFOs, constantly floats by; to be seen, are various undetermined, and unknown small, and very large creature sized plankton, or better noticed and believed to be in some cases, very large strange sea creatures as are squids, etc. Sometimes these larger if able would measure twenty or more square feet, and ever floating up with them are many, many, thousands of much smaller sea creatures, all of them fast flitting together, as if all were in an incredible intended erratic kaleidoscopic fish school of sorts, flying fast past your already confused imagination, all of the while you unable to remotely figure out what the heck exactly is all of this strange sea-life passing from bow to stern under your straining hull ? One old veteran sea-dog once explained it to me as best could by saying, "that stuff lad, that blue color there, is nothing but the effervescent light being given off for the reason, up from the trapped radiation prevalent of today's sea-world abrupt the creatures? To some wild imaginations there has even been claims; suggestions of human like forms of that size sometimes seen flitting by under water with the almost magical kaleidoscope of sea life... O'course all of that is but a fantasized observation of Bourbon or Gin on the rocks?

In the old days of the later 1950s when I was there, we sailors sailing on the Tin Cans from the North Pacific to the South, thought all of the various mixed hues of blue passing by the fantail at night were evidence of Giant Kraken, or huge squads, and/or huge octopus!

I believed then and now that some of the sea life we saw is still unknown even today? What I still wonder is why they all choose to surface only after dark? You'd think just the opposite unless for some reason it also has something relative to do with the moon?

Perhaps in the dark of night without the glare of the sun light, they figure that by the light of the stars and moon, they could more easily see to feed; somehow the moon light seemed to bring them top-side?"

Color Blue?

"What anyone know of the color purple?"

"Cold sky babe, blue heaven and you and I, and everything under foot, is hard lava, pebble rock, and sticker brush... why complain, we haven't fallen into a hole or pit yet! Never anywhere is there rock turf harder or more forbidding than it is on the Kona side sea coast of Big Island Hawaii! "Even the goats there are trying to weave a hammock!"

(The above an excerpt note written while Beach Combing and exploring alone for six weeks off the Kona Coast, 2004! Plenty sharks there along the Kama ma Highway!)

The sea truly is a wonder... There are many unknowns down below coming up only at late night! I have much sailed my share, and I have many times been witness of this blue color display as said, all high suspect of being deep sea creatures? It has nothing to do with plaiting, but the same blue persona is an interesting like description anomaly best seen on the darkest of moon lit nights beneath an erratic changing cloud cover.

PART THREE

"Krakens, and/or what else?"

Log: Sailing:

Off the coast in sight of the light-house at sea, just west of land fall where begins the incredible mountains of Olympic peninsula! "Giant squids (?), some excessively huge, are well documented deep down off the shores of Seattle and Bremerton! Ever some are suspect of being more than just gigantic and possibly larger beyond recent discovery. As said, many times I have realized and pondered that same mystery? Everything below the surface is fast passing by close up top-side to the surface of the ships forward way... Last to be seen are some many of the largest, floating in a final swirl past the ships fantail, where sometimes the unfortunate have been cut to-shreds in the whirling water action of the ships powerful and fast propelling screws!

Sharks follow after all night in the feeding spree of trash over-board and the bounty of all natural disaster! I loved the sea when I was there, and sometimes I hated its isolation, but every captain good and bad alike needs a provider, and the ocean was ever that! Where sailing in fair weather is best, is off Australia towards New Zeal to include some covert vistas hidden in the South Pacific... "Yeah, Java Bob, we truly are drifting this time on a flat ocean of reminisce! Put on three kinds of bad coffee... make yours tolerable, MK's better, and mine just about perfect! Cowboys and we pirates got no problem with that connection... Stale is stale, as stale, is UN-sanitary, says Darrel Miller! George Seboldt, and Swear-in Peg-leg would rather fight than switch?"

"Purposeful Plaiting!"

"Why do anything be want'n to need accomplish such useless braids on horses?"

Yeah, why? Sailors Kathy Seavey, have always plaited everything! Caps, hammocks, sweaters, Turk's heads, monkey fists, and have tied and re-invented endless clever knots, etc., the list goes about everywhere! Heck, the Spanish Vaqueros and Pirates sailing with them long ago taught all Old World seamen how to braid whips, whip line, plait canvas, braid useful horse tack, and most important braid, Huang Yu's in in typical Chinese style, and Olga's blond, hair to much resemble Patty Sasquatch! Now that would be plaiting with a purpose...

But that not so either until after the ancient Chinese had long cornered the reputation along with Eurasian wild man and braided women and men far prior to the sojourn of, Attila the Hun, 4th Century B. C. was it, who's men plaited mega baggage including children, etc., onto their mounts! Probably wild hominids became proficient at plaiting via all of them? Monkey see, and monkey do! And the feral people still with us are much much more than them! Collectively the eccentric vagabonds much influenced world tapestry... Plaiting has always been with man! From sailors and horsemen women learned embroidery and knitting skills. Somewhere wild man gets right into the middle of all of this as they sailed anciently with all early voyagers and vagabonds that were the wilder men that brought them to our shore! Bob, we are back to sea again, you can join the scuttle-but and applaud, or groan and write your own account! Either way, your coffee was the very best that I had on that unforgettable day! Thanks for all memories! I have often seen all of these above described blue anomalies, including a Blue Whale, a Nair, and many common ones, once seen forty strong huge devil fish, and much more long forgotten when sailing off the

276

mouth of Puget Sound, via further north off wild, Wrangle AK., when heading towards all Alaskan Ice flow, where once we encountered a magnificent Polar Bear, far out to sea a-top an Ice Burg; and had watched from there many times the strange anomaly of the blue plankton.. Countless times we stared into that frozen water like watching for fish in a barrel, when sailing all cold waters of the North Pacific. "Flying fish" were ever to become a familiar sight, and sometimes, "chow," after flipping themselves against the hard steel bulkheads abrupt the ships galley where we gathered them on the calmer mornings, next to fry them on the grill whenever we could? "Flying fish at night as said, often pounded hard against the side of our ships lower level bulk-heads before landing side by side amid the death throws the many next to be taken to the ships galley! When the blood, guts, and ships debris was dumped, sometimes the water churned aft almost to be a gambling frenzy as the vicious schools of brown, gray, blue, hammer-head sharks, hammered after the spoils... especially the sharks were thick of numbers when in all far waters of The South Pacific down and beyond the, Sulu Sea, and the lower Philippines, where as said, at that time there still did exist multiple types of fearsome ethnic feather clad wild hominids! Why all of this Bob, (?) well, all South Sea Peoples plait just about everything possible including the upper gunwales of their famous out rigger canoes, before applying the hot tar like pitch to its hull than when cured will turn the sea water almost indefinitely... Plaiting Bob, sure as hell it was mentioned! Yeah Bob, we are drifting far aft of the subject for a last time!

Once I believed to had actually seen what is known as a giant squid, shortly after having just seen a tremendous very large find-winged sea skate, perhaps in access of twenty foot long, off the Straits of, Juan' D' Fuchsia, some many miles off Bremerton WA.,

"Westward it swam, towards the vast Pacific sun down! According to ship mate, Tom Shrusbury, "Don, It may actually have been one of those very huge and long fabled, Kraken that was after that winged monster...? It looked to be more than just a massive squid, we never knew! Young sailors at sea are sometimes naïve, and ever dubious and powerful dreamers! However never once had I saw a, Mermaid, as also recently did attest life long now retired sea-fairer Gene Sheller, of Lake Havasu, AZ., that once long ago had left me with the impression that he did (?), but as it is somewhat covert known, portions of the Inland Sea World just off the Seattle WA., water front, has been documented to be perhaps evidence some of the deepest oceanic depths yet to be investigated within the Northern Hemisphere. If wrong, I stand corrected... Captain Scheller, Ship, USA Nonsense, certainly should have some sort of an idea, as he and I were the best ever, A, # 1, Smelt and herring fish swallowing contest winners of the WEST-PAC fleet and hamburger eating contest that ever staggered down Pike St., Seattle convinced somehow to believe that he'd once actually seen a Mermaid with blue plaited hair? What I still wonder Scheller had you been drinking to have me thinking that ? "No, dammit he said, for the last time I don't believe in the wild man or Mermaids, and because of your wondering about witches and all of stuff, we have missed the liberty boat! Here, have another green apple! I got two pants pockets full, and my shirt full all of the way down to my navel!"

Zakynerous Cave Idaho, 2003

"The Night Stalkers!"

"Why concern about hominids in caves in a horse book? Well, long before being aware of plaiting or kumiss, I had long wondered how it was possible for cave dwellers to get enough protean during winter to stay alive especially when the herds of game animals as deer and elk have moved to lower elevations? How would they get enough animal protean void of meat, unless of course somehow it was being obtained from domestic range stock being left on the open range pending the next late season round-up sometimes extended into late November, or December? Well, with all of that considered there would be plenty of off protean as milk if one had the advantage, as there was often considerable numbers of horses and cattle within eye sight distance of particular seldom visited caves were we were finding hominid evidence, however as yet at the time I had not more than slightly pondered the notion; however I had already considered the cattle if not horse kumiss as I had long known of horse milk and its use in Asia. I continued to ponder this possibility and slight theory using field glasses to examine the stock, but from a distance of course there was no real way to reasonably validate my theory, even if some animals at times to retrospect had looked suspect of recent suckling, as some few had trailing behind them colts or aging heifers left over from spring calves that are sometimes insistent and continue to nurse far longer than the natural requirement! I didn't know either then exactly what I was looking for or was expectant, but nevertheless highly considered the all obvious, as it is a fact that cattle exactly like humans in the case of a nursing; if a nursing child is allowed consistent at the breast, and extends the effort at the mothers compliance to continue to furnish milk, the natural process continues almost indefinitely. In particular known scenarios women have encouraged siblings to nurse and up to and past five years, and some even longer! This is not as common today was as passé, but it is still well known in regions of the world as Africa and northern Europe. As said, at no time could I get close to these restless cattle for an educated look, but I really did wonder the high possibility! Probably I was already correct, and now as I write today I am investigative-adamant of the fact, as when I had first began cutting plaited horse mane samples off from the 135 Hinck Ranch horses, I was not all that surprised that we were sometimes finding what looked like hardened estrous milk; a white cream colored thick textured mares milk that was sometimes entwined at places within the braided hair! Wow, of course when discovering this I was excited, but for all naïve witness with me, to think them at the very beginning to be able to believe this was already difficult; the though of feral people suckling the kumiss at night was almost to far from most lay persons imagination to cope with, but it was finally agreed that unless the animals teats had not to fact been handled prior, or during plaiting, there was no other plausible reason for the milk to be in found in the braids! How else would it be possible?

Tonia, prior to all of this without my knowing had already began investigations into ancient horsemanship up from the historical times of, Attila, and inquired their plaiting customs, ancient natural animal husbandry, breading, etc., which had included some interesting mention concerning kumiss and its human use abrupt horses, etc. So, naturally at that point in time I was already aware, eager, and ready to be convinced of the kumiss (Mare's milk!) connection to feral human needs, aside from logical conclusion already had that wild hominids as perhaps Sasquatch ever needful of nourishment were the only ones capable and intelligent enough other than Homo-sapiens able to be doing it! Estrus milk was being precariously left behind from the creatures milk wet fingers when in use when they next did the plaiting! What's for dinner suddenly became much more than exciting and takes on a whole different meaning? For dinner Charley, we got, clabbered horse milk kumiss, made in goat skin bota bags that was/is still a primitive yogurt of a sort derived from cattle/horses! This in places of the world can include a mixture and extracted blood, and what ever else can easily be milked/taken from any number of wild and/or domestic goats, sheep, Lamas, Alpacas, and whatever, as the list reads endless in the possibility where animals are more than plentiful every where over the vast corn belt farm region of South East Ore-Ida! Wild man is there and thrives about every where similar where there are abundant farm crops and produce available most year around. The endless tall silage corn fields of what is called The Gem Valley (Ore/Ida/Neva!), and far beyond in every direction are just one short measure of feral man's almost endless extended home-range, including all many unlikely places had along the snake infested willow tree and sage brush covered banks of the wild Snake River, where all fall harvest foods found within that region are endless as include, potatoes, onions, cabbage, barley, oats, grain, long abandoned orchards left from pioneer settlement, farm yard fruit trees, etc. Sometimes all foods mentioned and more are available any where after the fall harvest for the taking as late year as, January and February! All that for anyone UN-knowing is to be considered, as well as are all far adjacent secluded Owyhee River bottomlands where are found fresh water tributaries and potable water springs, river duck ponds, and any mega number of contemporary irrigation ponds, abundant large tracts of edible cat tail reed, all various wild berry bushes, and much, much, more including various small game animals, game and trash fish, large carp and succors, domestic and wild water fowl, including geese, swans, egret, loons, and all western descriptions of up-land game bird populations, including mega numbers of Chinese pheasants, quail, etc! Well, I'm sure by now you get the picture! You and I could if wanted easily survive well fed and in complete seclusion if clever almost anywhere over the Gem Valley.... Why not feral wild hominids?

What better habitat to be had anywhere could any desperate feral, or pseudo civilized human(?), or an all knowing wilderness wise, tough Ho-BO, recluse, or any wilder personage to the imagination of any sort in dire need or want of survival ask for? Anyone, even myself if necessary could easily become the literal king of all desert jungle cantaloupe, onion, and all cherry and vast corn crop land adjacent in every direction abrupt all south eastern Ore/Ida/Neva? Wild man definitely are to be found here as particular oral treasure depositions in my latent collections well attest all probability, not to mention all recent plaiting and kumiss explanations had above to further flaunt the truth! Of late I have thought to wander over one particular interesting flood plain river bottom during a late fall, say October, and to do it much short of creature comfort baggage, being almost as naked of artifacts as Sasquatch need exist, as a literal in-land beach comber by comparisons, in order to better understand their life style and to possibly find them? Anyone want to join me? Long years prior to all explained above, I had been telling some of the local ranchers a small part of this theory, and some had agreed, however the hardest persons to convince for the most part (Until of late!) has been my close-net ranch family relatives. Mega numbers of mule deer, and some much smaller numbers of low land white tail deer frequent the river bottom vistas of all Owyhee River, and some many uninterested farm residents have not once seemed to have even one clue of the later spices of white tail! This mentioned to exemplify how easy it is for anything extremely elusive as is a white tail deer let alone a clever man to avoid human detection! "Wild hominids by their obvious natural ability have become their own special forces! We can learn a great deal from their sojourn....

Sanctuary!

Any similar semi-urban land mass, river bottom Island, or beaver pond brush pile, and/or small forest extension, can easily suffice as viable wild man habitat, and "him" ever remain completely elusive via a simple indisposed life style, especially this so, if ever without the irritating demands and encroachments of selfish humanity, and the irritation of barking dogs! What really defines the high stress and confusion of today's toy-prone humanity, opposed to wild man's obvious simple needs, has to be true peace and serenity, of ever being lost in a regional sanctuary without the unwanted requirements and unwanted demands of all unacceptable mechanical noise! "The wind for a maid, and the moon for a butler, and perhaps the sun for a particular comfort after sun rise, has to be the expected lament of the Wild Man while watching the sun depart in the west at the promise of all rain-bows end? Believe me, Sasquatch/feral people do exist, and until the end of time will continue to plait the manes of horses for what ever more found reasons that may surface? With them in all probability, very, very, long ago plaiting for unexplained/explained reasons had became an innate requirement somewhat expedient of the many, many, hardships of their misunderstood existence. If this conjecture theory manuscript does not touch upon some of the plausible reasons, "then figs grow on Yowie trees, and the Sasquatch eats the cherries from off the banana bushes, while Java Bob does a wild dance to entertain his mashed potatoes, and Ron Roseman sings with the Beatles!"

Sasquatch Exists!

"Excerpts of Neil Hinck!"

Where is the proof? All of this wild notion of feral man, kumiss, plaiting, etc., for most persons perhaps is peculiar indeed, however while I was writing only a short while ago, some latent thought kept prodding at my awareness as if to be telling that I had needed to remember whatever it was that at the moment seemed of such a great importance? What had I over looked; what was it that I keeps wanting to be remembered that is so insistent of my attention? Most of us have all experience similar? Why, what, and.... (?), and so I leaned back into my chair where my head touched the frizzy white hair fluff of the mountain-goat skin given me by Neil Hinck when last time with him at the N. & N. Oregon Ranch... "Neil Hinck was talking in his colorful off the wall expressions, and sometimes serious humor... We had just won World War Two, he was home from the Army, and he had wiped down his trusty rifle for his last time while explaining to me .... "Don, these Sasquatch or what ever they are (?), are not one bit concerned about us in the in the least! I believe that they are around here too....But if you wanna see one, you gotta hold your head *just right*, the bastards are probably around here sometimes during the day, as at times I have found strange things missing in the after noon that I know'd was there on that morning... What sort of stuff? Well, once it was a pair of hoof pincher s.... You know, the nippers that we use to trim the horses hoop before we shoe em! And I lost a good pocket knife! No one else but me was around that day but me either... Remember I told you about the elk story back there in Wyoming... Well, they are real! Norma (His wife..) has been hard to convince... I don't think she wants to know? Better I guess that she won't... Those guys... Well, just like you say they are for some reason hanging around my horses?"

After as explained, when later I and Neil's daughter had first became witness to the kumiss found enmeshed into the cut braids, my thoughts went at once back to the open range, and to the horses that were ever back there loosed over the vast high desert mountain regions of all or most all of Idaho and Montana, that were usually within rifle shot of many little known hidden caves. Enough horses during had in memory during my sojourn along with update knowledge had from Onya's research of the fascinating Eurasian Steppe Mountain deserts of all upper China-Mongolia, Kurdistan, Tibet-Bhutan, and the Southern and Northern extremes of Russian Siberia, where explained is also the place of giant God bears of wild Kamchatka; and now the mares milk/kumiss being found on Neil's ranch, and a smattering knowledge of the many exciting Asian nomadic desert populations past and present known over all Eurasia, some many of their ongoing customs and definite adherence to kumiss, that in some extremes has been mixed with blood.. (That is far superior in nourishment, minerals, and animal protean by comparison than is straight nomad clabbered milk, or primitive yogurt!), ... my interest in this cattle-horse kumiss had been re-fired at once first time realized when found in the plaited manes at the Hinck Ranch, as eight years earlier, long before having any remote knowledge of braided manes, kumiss, in fact any of this stuff, as was explained somewhere, I already had high suspicions of range cattle being somehow milked by the wild feral populations!

All of it made logical sense! I myself or even you would have thought of it... and so the discovery of kumiss on the Hinck property was no real or of a great surprise! However back then I had no real idea or even one clue how anything or any one could think to easily bond with any rangy animal aside from roping it, and next tying them down hard and fast?

I had no real proof of anything really, and so for the time mostly just put the thought aside and slept on the idea, as if had completely forgot it.. Now all at once with all new exciting first hand evidence had along side the plaiting to include kumiss, I was overwhelmed... "but who really, in the honorable name of Molly B' Damn was ever going to believe it? Who, especially in bias America could be easily convinced that wild hominids were actually plaiting the manes of horses (For one possible reason to console them!), in order for another partner with them, be able to sometimes access their estrous milk, and especially believe them to be able to do this UNLESS first having needed to successfully bonded with them (As said!), for one more good reason, "in order to be able next to suckle at turns, at their already forming estrous milk, and just possibly next be able to accomplish slowly riding, or walking them for entertainment around the enclosed holding pens, etc?

I was beside myself, and suddenly reasoning all of I the strange anomaly, and much, more? Well, even after all of that said, and this manuscript presentation, who important to wild man studies academic or maverick would actually consider to allow the theory? Most naïve persons of today, would not even believe that a Brown Recluse Spider could bite them on the ankle or could even be able to kill them... or even would they probably doubt the dirt being shoveled on top of them that is loudly mashing in the top their coffin! The mind set of today general naïve populace at large it seems is extreme erratic, unorthodox, and confused beyond comparable to even colorful rollmop blathering, and/or one short paraphrased truthful example statement that might read: Well hell, I don't read! I don't care! And I sure as heck don't want to learn nothing about plaiting, kumiss, history, the far west or anywhere, and especially anything having to do with wild people as they just do not exist!

Anyway, they just don't, and that is all and much more than I want to say about it! Lets go down to the theater and watch the movie called, The Walking Dead!

Indeed! Strange Things Happen!

Incredible Avenues of Unexpected Discovery!

"In retrospect of the kumiss, the milk, cattle, horses, plaiting, all of it, back to the year, 2003 – 2012! By spring 2003, now I realize that I had already aspired to the Crux of what it would take to be able one day to completely understand at least the kumiss, if not yet back then even remotely the plaiting, as I had not as yet even heard of Plaiting prior to year 2004... (More will be explained in its place of how all of that came about!) ... or all of the continuing high strange happenings yet to be had five years later since 2008, and continuing on the Hinck, Jenson, as well as at other ranch/farm areas where I have already been, and will return, etc.).... and I'd been able to understand and reasoned the kumiss, etc., (Had done it!) without even knowing I'd been aware!"

"The Crux!"

("Meaning here!")

"One possible answer of what it would take to begin to explain the strange kumiss milk protean that I would later find in year 2008. "The milk mixed into the plaiting found on the Hinck Horses!") "Wow! All of a Sudden, another Very Interesting Crux Inspiration?" "Believe it or not... even as I write this minute, I have suddenly had another probable answer come to me that will perhaps even more be able to explain the plaiting, than I unknowingly have conjured back in time from the year 2003, when as yet, "back then," as said, I had no remote idea what so ever either, that plaiting was an issue, or had even existed as an anomaly on American horses! My part answers to follow came only minutes ago, from (?), inspiration probably unrealized that I already had I guess, just now for a second time (?), "but not until I had actually began to write this exact page of the manuscript! And, SO, that inspiration/answer, (Ironically that inspired explanation!) begins here, and now, right here on this very page, this moment, without future edit, "as I am suddenly experiencing what seems curious promptings from (?) retrospect via, "De'Ja'Vue," or, what amounts too: much exiting recall, to more be able to explain a very high strange discovery, had myself, Debby Brown, Hawaii, and retired New York, detective, John Doitch, back in spring, year, 2003; the discovery was the unexpected find of a dead Black Angus heifer calf, that had been dropped, stuffed down, under, and deep down within all massive huge lava (Basalt) boulders that were then everywhere around to be seen, at the bottom most sand floor place, of a deep dry Idaho desert lava rock canyon water way, where we had come to re-explore a particular interesting cave!"

The heifer we discovered had its neck broken in a very precarious, and curious way, as at first it was hardly noticeable, until I finally jumped down into the deep boulder enclosure in order to remove a bright numbered, plastic Stock-man's ear tag, still there to be seen, that was easily visible if/when standing above. Where the calf was placed ("Placed? Looked that way?) laying flat down on its side, (Head to the East!) and seemingly to all opinion, had been stashed for some covert (?) reason, deep as possible between what was every where to be seen over the area, are endless massive, very huge lava boulders of various descriptions; this discovery was made early April, (From memory April, 15th?) of the very same year (2003!) of my wife's untimely death, had her five months later, on, August 17th, ("I only mention this as the dates of early April, and, late August, may have a specific significance later, if told more of the story?) The calf carcass had already began to rot, Tammy was first to find it from its rank odor, and from all evidence we estimated that it had been there for perhaps two weeks (Since perhaps, April 1st?), and the whole picture amassed, looked at once almost to had been impossible, or improbable, definitely very unlikely for the animal to had fallen on its own, after having needed to climb on and over many huge nondescript boulders and difficult terran to had even arrived to the place of where it was then laying (Look Peaceful!) in that position on its own as was in a picture perfect position that was agreed, all looked very much just as if the calf were purposely stashed there somehow with further intentions (?)! There was an identification tag with a number visible and to easy to read left clipped to one ear.. I collected the tag (Still have it!) and located the local ranch authorities to learn the owner, "called him," satisfied his curiosity, learned the animals missing history, and was right on top of time and date assumptions, etc. The owner had agreed that the young cow calf, (A female!) likely could not easily have arrived to the location where found on its own, but had no more problem with that, or idea how? He was awe struck at our story, thanked us, etc!

There is much more of the end of that story and much more to do with its ramifications explained within all collective books of the, "Sasquatch Trilogy." For openers, it was to later be found more absolute evidence of continuing Idaho wild hominid activity. All of that story's high strange happenings had been resolved by a more than incredible grand Finley by the first week of October.... Photographs exist to be able to more define and explain it.

Shortly after October due to local earth quakes and tremors much of the canyon boulders were re-arranged beyond description. If it weren't for Tammy Brown's keen nose, likely we would had past the carcass by thinking it was something obvious that I already well understood! Women as I have long ago discovered, and have said as much many times, are often a real asset to exploration. Tammy was an exceptional inquisitive girl and an interesting critic. I have long ago lost track of her, but several years ago I received a short letter from her explaining that her interest since in wild man curiosity has pretty much convinced her that they exist! Tammy where are you? We could use you in another discovery. Remember adventure for its own sake will forever need a few good men and women! Aloha!

More Confusions?

"Short excepts had of MK Davis on the Roger Patterson Film, and much more:

Regarding Sasquatch... And just as MK Davis has just this day pointed out to me over the phone: "Don, its no use! What ever the first thought accredited or thought moot academic on the seen of anything thought to do with Bigfoot has to conclude... anything that he has to say about anything.... anything at all... the entire Bigfoot community will swallow it hook, line, and sinker! If him actually correct, that's great! But if him wrong well, ... as you well know, there is always very much left to consider! Sasquatch just don't act like Patty did and normally just all at once walk out in front of a large groups of people as had happened that is now well able to be proved from the many enhancements taken from off the original Patterson Film! And remember that you and I both know exactly the actual reasons why Patty was out in the open where she was and was able to be photographed!"

PART THREE

"Private Library!"

Log: May 31, 2012 – A short reprieve.

Written while much involved in plaiting investigation and discovery...
Probably I was consuming all known to help UN-orthodox venom release?
"My recent snake bite, and my strange revelation!"

Kumiss! Plaiting! Range Cattle! Kumiss, and milch cows!

It is well past midnight, I write in desperation ever wanting to complete this sorry jargon and to get it off as soon can to the publisher before I actually self-destruct from a recent dread Brown Snake Bite! The rascal bit me on the ankle some nine weeks ago on March 28th, and so I am that far away and several days further in want of at least a short nap or no sleep at all! The excruciating pain in my swollen foot keeps me red eyed, sleepless, and much sick from medi- cines, and as restless as the local wolves and elk while reclused here another time at Lima, Montana, the pain is horrific! Not here wanting sympathy, but next said all is a warning to any further interested... Never dare to take off your cowboy boots! Any boots! Die with them on! Spiders and dangerous snakes are universal! Dammit, but I really am miserable! And all doctors just as myself, are next to helpless, or not also hopeless to do much about it? To my knowledge as yet there is no known antidote for Brown snakes or recluse spiders? Since yesterday from the tension and high stress of constant pain I have re- initiated more painful Shingles had over most of my back and chest! Anyone who has ever had them knows what I am experiencing! Where really do I go from here...Alone in Siberia Montana all doesn't look good! I swore that 2012 would be a year without further physical stress or injury... probably this continuing sojourn of horse plaiting will inspire additional reason to want to live... Admittedly I am concerned for my future...

Log: Private Journal - June 1, 2012 - The Strange Intuition!

Or was it all a bad dream?

"Don, the doctor said, snake poison can really effect your sleep! For a while do not try to drive too much, and get plenty of rest! Call us if you need further help! You are in for many months of misery...." Tonight the moon shines down in all its clear sky splendor since the last snow fell two days ago leaving more than a foot of the blasted stuff on my leaky roof! As explained, since a child I have regularly watched the moon, and now with the horse plaiting anomaly a temporary priority, the full moon phase ever needing observed, and the local range cattle by the many hundreds returning back from the mountains., and all important research wanted to be accomplished before June 8th when I meet Mk Davis and the others at the Portland Airport where after we drive another time Northern California to re-explore important high mountain areas of Bluff Creek. My great concern for all ramifications of my snake bite will I truly be able to make the climb...? Well, I just returned back into my cabin house with a last midnight arm load of fire wood before had paused for a minute watching the wind whip the night clouds fast past the bright moon, giving the impression to the all seeing eye of Diana, that looks down as if it were a flash -light looking toward the west! A large skunk with its white tail held high as if it were a main sail bid me ah-do from across the road! "Montana is for the wild animals and

"It was Very Strange! Very strange?

Third one that I have witnessed!"

exiled humanity... Actually I have always liked skunks, magpies, etc., most all animals that others don't, don't want to, or will not? All evening I had been pondering all first importance of this manuscript, my struggling life, its message, and more important in my present discomfort, and my needed determination and accelerated exhilaration to want at all to continue to complete this document just as soon as can... I just stumbled through my cabin door with my fire wood, suddenly I am experiencing a very peculiar sort of, De' Ja' Vue, had probably from all past sojourn all is very peculiar indeed.... All of this is probably the result of the antibiotics and the snake venom... My continuing varied confusing thoughts follow over the page ahead... I wrote that day to aid and abet my discomfort... What ever, much having to do, or otherwise having to do with plaiting, cows, horses, all of this strange anomaly was suddenly much on my mind to include a recent discovery of what was a very strange cattle mutilation found and photographed only last fall while in Washington state and exploring along the Carbon River with "plaiting expert," Becky Butello... After words of the discovery we had several conversations over the phone more trying to help solve or explain the mystery?

"It was Very Strange! Very strange? Third one that I have witnessed!"

The cattle mutilation connection to the plaiting or any of this if indeed there actually is one, may not be so for several reasons, (?) however the ones (2nd!) that I have seen, both were domestic milk cows, each with their milk bag (Utters!), cut directly in half; "each were both an equally divided, hind section of the utter removed, leaving the second half that was nearest to the head connected to the carcass or hide!" At this time I am fairly sure that we are now onto something concrete that might actually begin/help to explain one or more, but not all of the abstract reasons for the plaiting? In spite of the fact that the first found was "a heifer" stashed deep down into an Idaho canyon (All very strange, Year, 2003!), was also a female, and it was what is called dry, as it was not as yet fully matured enough to calf either (to bear young!), and so that rules out any chance for anything to have killed and carried it to where is was stashed intending milch, but still the dead animal was a female?" At the Hinck Ranch, more than once, and repeated often to me by them all, Neil, Norma, daughters, everyone in family had told me over and again "that long years before my acquaintance, one of their prize mares was horribly mutilated, and when found it had every large bone broken in its body! (?) All of the many pastured ranch horses had circled around the pathetic heaped crumbled mass and would venture any closer! It looked to all of us just as if something had picked up the horse and carried it high up into the air and then just dropped it like a bunch of smashed bananas! What Neil had asked me... "What can actually pickup a heavy horse like that and take it all of that distance into the air, and just let it drop? That would take something like a helicopter or something or other, wouldn't it? We got no idea Don, but that had really happened!" All of the Hinck family of four persons had all agreed to the story! "Neil continued: Then back a few years ago some of our ranch hands just up and quit the job... Just like that they walked off, without giving us one bit of warning! They'd said they just that day seen something that was just too strange too even believe, describe, or even wanted to try to explain...! What ever is was, it was some kind a terrible human looking creature! It kept breaking down the fences around there over and over again, and it did stuff like that until they finally saw it! Yeah, no

285

fooling, they all just up and quit! I guess t was because they were all afraid! None of them ever came back!" This was not the first that I had heard a similar story, and incidentally the other three told me had also originated in Idaho!

Log: "UFOs?"

> I really have no real Idea as yet to make of all of that? But...all of that stuff had above in the account of the supposed dropped horse, is indeed truly very strange! However the Hinck horse was actually killed and what happened will always remain... what has now become at best a forgotten mystery. Understand, that I am not at all here suggesting that plaiting has anything to do with UFOs, as I know nothing or have little to say about outer space in particular, however I myself on several occasions have seen unidentified objects, and each sighting was ever different from the other and happened a considerable number of years apart... Twice I have seen the after math of cattle mutilations, and was described the details of another that had also happened some ten years or so ago ironically on the same Jenson ranch property as where today is tethered Hink! Back about year 1979 my hunting partner and I came haphazardly on to other unexplained bloody mess of a large nondescript domestic dog found skinned and done to much similar as were the cows, but not quite enough the same either, as Eben Wolters then (Coeur d 'Alene, Idaho) with me had agreed with me that it all looked to him to be possibly the works of sick cultists, satanists, or much similar persons so ascribed, as this mess included a left behind pair of blood soaked white gloves, a knife, and a peculiar long length of knotted cord, and the dog had been left tied to the fence in a notable fashion of intended unsavory expertise. Hardly was that any UFO!"

Log: Fall, 2011 – Cattle mutilation: Carbon River, Washington, with Becky Butello!

> The single cow mutilation that Becky Butello and I found today was again the luck of happenstance when we accidentally stumbled onto a part carcass of a strangely slaughtered milk cow! Becky was first to see the dead cow! Before us in plain sight, just a few yards from the rivers edge lay a part cattle mutilation minus most all of its body parts and head! The carcass lay almost covert as it was partly concealed by the surrounding brush! When stretched its length it went perhaps seven foot long! All of it, hide, one half part of its udder; everything was strangely left as if hair brushed and immaculately clean! Everything looked completely void of blood, and exactly like had been explained had been done to the Hinck horse, this hide had also been very carefully dropped directly onto the bare ground of a mud and dirt surface! Strangely, not one morsel of that hide or parts, had more than one visible spot of dirt anywhere on it! That fact of no dirt or blood left behind, was almost as surprising as was the discovered cow remains! It was ever obvious that the cow had been very carefully skinned leaving behind only the part udder dead center cut as if for some reason it had been carefully dissected, and next left incredibly clean almost to suspect it had been vacuumed! Every cut done to the hide and remains looked professional; not one single small piece morsel of meat left was left anywhere on flesh inside of the hide! That in itself is almost next to be impossible unless one is a very capable skinner as are seasoned taxidermists, etc. The utter especially looked as if all had been done by a very sharp scalpel, or even a lazier! (?) I have skinned many, many, an animal and have not seen similar! Even before pondering any part of the, hows, whys, etc., of all of

the above and all more to follow, first we need explore what it would actually require for any-thing, or anyone, to have accomplished any of this animal to man, creature to animal, bond-ing, etc, in the first place? Anyone who has ever tried to run down the family cat, bird, or, pony very well understands the difficulty, let alone wild and domestic horses, cattle to hominid bonding; plaiting on horses, and finally become adapt at kumiss extraction, etc., and how is any of this possible? To want to accomplished plaiting on any horse there definitely need be an acute and pleasant animal bonding been done first, especially urgent would be if wanting to in any way milk the horse. In my opinion plaiting is the direct avenue had to accomplish the milk-ing of a horse. Even between a trusted owner/trainer, doing this with a horse would be difficult to do! (?) Horse milk is every a little sweeter, and richer in animal protein as is cows milk! "Conclusion, if could be one, plaiting definitely has a direct association with wild hominid need of animal protean, food, and survival!"

THE WAY THIS BOOK GOT STARTED!

Mixed Yarns, and Important Blather! Horses! Plaiting! Kumiss! Bonding! It all began with the plaiting mysteries? More on Disonga, and the color Blue, preparations for advanced high strange anomalies... Pagan worship, and first mention of cave experiments mentioned, and much general and unsavory reflections to more understand all further intelligence projections considered of wild hominids, or. the whole nine yards, and more!

Just like Tonia Brown had always said:

"For me Don, the horses had always been coming!"

Me too, as life long I have admired horses... Never had a lot of time for them, was bucked off a few of them at various rodeos, and when younger made myself a horse's-ass on any number of them in other ways, and for a long time while exploring the western deserts have much watched the wild mustangs and other semi domestic range stock horses and cattle threw field glasses ever interested in finding plaiting, etc. Well, ironically by late fall 2004 a most curious thing happened when a local Montana cowboy (Jim!) who had just arrived back Eurasia-Mongolia-Kurdistan, without notice all at once appeared at my cabin door, excited and befriended me with wild Mon-golian horse stories, including explaining important plaiting comparisons had him most recently of Asian-Steppe horses, and North American horses, and as a result of his visit my interest had began! (The above story to be continued in its place.)

The color blue:

"The color blue is more than just an accidental color in use as a wanted anomaly! Before we get hammered into all of the high strangeness yet to come next in Jim's particular case scenario, there is space here out of necessity for just one more short reflection on the rare blue moon phase descriptions, and upon the Ware-Women effigy description of, The Blue Lady, Disonga, and one small part of her possible reflective importance, had relative of an incredible almost to be beyond belief short open case cave story that happened to the author with three other witness present, all back as far as nine years ago! All of this next explained is but one more high suspect load of fire fuel, if not absolute spark-ignited of significant abstract proof of the high possibility and reasonable thought validity of my moon-phase theory-opinion, of an on-going obscure, and much latent ido-latrous fetishism moon-struck probability abrupt fear and resolute compliance abrupt particular subscribing wild hominid populations that ever ascribe to the effects of the full moon, viruses an-cient pagan sort worship, or similar? Wow, how next to tell all of the rest of this all more than ex-hilarating and all true account? The far side of Disonga is at her best when fully described in the uncanny pending manuscript to be titled: The Twilight Zone Chambers, where we visit many of the strange sister caves of, Zak Cave Idaho. I will grant you that all of this next to be explained is most incredible and almost beyond easily belief but actually happened, and was witnessed both going and coming by the same people, Paul Wright, Rex burg Idaho. Lewis Chandler, Pocatello Idaho, and, John Doitch, New York, City, all were witness with me to attest this extremely strange event that took place both early spring and mid summer, 2002. Because of all this highly strange event and its unexpected outcome, nothing will ever surprise me again having to do with the intel-ligence of wild man, (Sasquatch hominid), compared to us Homo sapiens in a One on One physi-cal, and/or mental interaction between them! The ramifications of these two separate purposeful visits to Zak Cave next to be explained, the last done in a re-assessment, are still latent and much important to all intentional creature to human intellect and logistic comparisons and further con-jecture. This next explained, and much done since, and prior, have me much more than convinced and aware of all human inapt understandings of a great man unexplainable happenings. Today's people for a most part just do not seem to care?

The Disonga Effigy Story Results!

All of this story is true. It is intended to be only a partial explanation of a very mysterious and extraordinary event that took place spring and summer months of year 2002. Much more having to with all of this odd anomaly was to occur without prompting several more times and all of them many months apart. All of that will be further explained in up coming book titled; The Twi-light Zone Chapters! For reasons unknown, my life even as I write, continues almost weekly with all new, and ever strange and unexpected events. As said, this story is to be re-told over again when added upon and written in,

"The Trilogy, Twilight Zone Chapters! Wait for!

Assuming that by now all reading have had a skeptical good look at Disonga in the photo. Section? Well, story short, year, 2002, Paul, John Doitch, Lewis Chandler, and Myself, placed that very same picture portrayal that you have seen of Disonga painted on the hard shiny surface of a four, by four, inch. slab of white bathroom tile. We left this pictured effigy standing up-right about an inch deep, stuck in soft sand face showing in the middle of the cave floor in front of a rather elaborate offering of bait food and various useful items as would be cigarette lighters, canals, plas-tic toys, shiny coins, etc., everything done that day was recorded on film, ever we expectant if for-tunate, for another incredible creature to crew interaction between us... Upon return some four weeks later, all food offering had been ravished and left to my surprise left rather tidy? Everything was gone except for the blue colored effigy on tile of Disonga, that had not been touched. What exactly did all of that tell us? I was especially interested to see if the several deer bones brought into the cave and put with Disonga in a purposeful arrangement would be disturbed. They were not? Bones of that type were well known to the cave-dwellers, as there were also many found similar all through out the grotto; each of the ones brought in had been carefully placed in studied shamanistic arrangement that was somewhat pseudo reverent, each facing another direction as, North, South, East, West, had done all of this by the use of a compass and flash light, etc. All of these caves are absolutely as dark as darkness ever gets! For anything, or anyone to see at all required at least a good light, lantern, or candle, and we had them all.

I had done this to see what would happen to the bone display and to Disonga, ever curious to find out if indeed the creatures would recognize the effigy enough to identify in any way with the picture, pick it up, handle, destroy, etc. Everything was done the same with much thought and care. I had been intent to put all foods of the offering in a slightly difficult position, so that in order to get to them, anything that need reach over, or far, past Disonga, and if careless, or not very careful, it would be very easily have knocked her over. Everyone had agreed that this would surely happen if not carefully done. Satisfied that Disonga had been observed, respected with in reason, untouched, etc., I opt to return out of the cave, leave nothing more behind until I would return back again in a few weeks after flying to Honolulu to visit my wife's doctors, family, etc., planning to return back to the cave in six weeks. Upon return we re-entered the cave to re-evaluate and leave more food, etc., and everything had been taken except Disonga. I next made the last minute abscission somehow prompted (?), intent to exit the cave room, leave no food this time, take out the effigy picture of Disonga, and most important completely rake, and fox-tail brush the sand floor of the room smooth and clean-emasculate, leaving absolutely nothing at all, and return back again in a few weeks time completely to re-do the exploratory effort. There were then many new caves been recently discovered, and we had plenty to keep us more than busy! So, the boys, including a new witness then with us, (Now five!) with, Ken Bear Iddins, AK.

Back for More!

Third time back, the last visit to Zak Cave with the intent to re-place food, Disonga, etc. This time we had a sizable amount of food, heavy packs with everything possible thought necessary to think to entice the cave hominids into action. We entered the room blackness on stomachs dragging our packs behind on ropes, flash light first, held out front to lead our way. At once when arrived, all crew became stark silent, in awe, and extreme surprise at what was stark visible... Right there at the very same exact place and exact spot where before first time had been put and last time retrieved Disonga, was another new and exact same bone pile of much similar deer bones all placed in the exact same numbers, etc; everyone of them stood the same way facings as, N., S., E., W., etc, just exactly as I had done before! The presentation was in every way exact, and as much shamanistic in suggestion as had been mine! The only thing different was there was no effigy portrayal of Disonga... What was also absolute and far beyond high strange, was that there was not one single foot or hand track to be seen left over the sand anywhere! How indeed... How could anything or anyone know to do such a thing, and do it all in genius exactness as explained, do it in complete pitch-black darkness, be able to allow the exact number of same animal bones to be used, know the precise four in number exact same compass directions abrupt the original display, complete the duplication in the exact center most portion of the room, and then what's more, leave not one bit of new evidence to prove that they had ever been there at all? Definitely the creatures (If allowed called that, for a better description-identity, as none back then had any far extended idea of what we were experiencing, etc, and they in true fact may in time indicate that faction, as with my many plaster casting (Some have been already posted on www.artistfirst.com

talk radio! Among them collectively of note: are ever multiple numbers of four separate possible identities! Yes, one could be horrible, another complacent or docile, etc, others well, it is highly plausible that particulars of them could at time be absolutely beyond dangerous! However thus far to my opinion they exist as a much mix-matched relict feral wild-man hominid, all if not some looks much the same as looks, "Patty Sasquatch," but definitely for reasons as were previously explained, Not All?) We departed the cave after leaving all new food and artifacts. Interactions continued and were cast and before and after the fact filmed without further Disonga involvements. The Disonga mystery continues...The creatures know something! I know much less! The plaiting continues! What really have the secrets of the dark shadows on the moon besides the rabbit? We should pay close attention, as wild hominid attention weather any know it or not, walks with us beyond all shadows of dark forest and grotto! It is to be remembered, that we completely had raked and hand brushed clean the entire cave room. It had been left immaculate! Anything at all that would have entered the room, even a cave rat, mouse, or wild cat, etc., would ever need have left its evidence! Sasquatch are in the shadows and may be following you!

Monkey Island!

"A Needed Reprieve!"

"After all of that, Java Bob, we do need a reprieve! Lets all take time out for a few laughs, and Sail as far off as possible to some wild uninhibited Island of the South Pacific, where there are also many unexplained anomalies as wild-man populations, and well known much more! So, hoist the anchor and we are restless off to where in the story next we will be fast drifting "Ass-Backwards" towards all flitting Sea Hawks flying high above the infamous Bengali Island, the home-base port of call, reproduction center, and strange winter-quarters of all southern dread Sea Snakes, Macaque monkeys; and after a short stop there before we escape to the port-quarter of Layette Island, Philippines....it is to be remembered, don't anyone dare mess with another monkeys monkey!"

Log: Adventures on, Layette Island, Philippines!

"Ode to ship-mate, Tom Shrewsbery, addressed then, any where Louisiana?

There was only born one all American proud exceptional Louisianian rascal as was Tom! By the late fifties guys like Tom and I had already became an endangered species... We first realized this while stalemated on the jungle Island of Layette, Philippines, hiding together high up in a jungle tree where we were being to be literally eaten sober by mega hordes of far best described vicious biting-stinging red fire-ants..... This was after us having ran desperate from a pack of wild Morrow and Huck, jungle bunny, bandits hard after our hides, and excited wantin' to own for the taking our already empty Navy Ships Company, Colt .45, Automatic Pistol, exactly the same sort as the one that had been stolen earlier that morning from of the duty belt of a John Snell then at the moment a sleep walking watch-stander on the Quarter deck of the USS, Good-Ship can't yet divulge its real name! Tom and I at the time were already long-time Over the Hill, and ever in dire need to be anxious to be back to the sanctuary of the ship, as we both at the moment were somewhat concerned for our life, all of the time having brought along an unwanted highly agitated, extremely ugly to the bone, ever was it an open mouthed, teeth showing, loud screeching, desperate shrill spouting, highly stupid, belligerent, dirty smell-

ing, highly obnoxious Spider monkey! For space, I will need spare you all the rest of the story, but believe me its end is more than interesting.... What, really, that was wanted said, for what is worth Java, there actually is quite another truly wild unidentified sort of a feral hominid (One or more?), yet to be found still unrealized wandering over some many of approximate seven thousand plus more Islands that comprise the Philippine South Pacific Archipelago …

NEXT UP!

The More Than Incredible Happened!
Lewis Chandler There Really Are Best Kept Secrets!

"Back to reality, horses, plaiting, caves, wild man, and moon light, hardship, and misery!"

Log: Xmas Eve, December 24th, 2003.

One day before Christmas!

On the telephone with companion Paul Wright: "What the heck do you mean Don, you/we are going caving on Xmas or New Years Eve...? I'm not! Not me! What's up? What the reason? Hell man, everywhere is frozen! No wonder I live sixty five miles away from you... You are going alone...! So, Merry Xmas! I'm eating Ham!" Paul was Wright, actually his last name was also Wright, however if he wrong or even right, often as not he had little patience with what he though were my wild idiosyncrasies! In this separate assumption he wasn't always alone... "Ever With You Don There Was The Challenge... Said by Tonia Brown!" I, say... every new adventure of merit usually begins with a sharp-prod with a sharp stick from its beginning! Actually there are no tomorrows in exploration. Today is now, and now is when you do it! The good guys, and incredible Gals are still around, but they are getting very hard to find, and, when realized, some many never get the credit! "The pity!" And then, there was the "Zak Cave Adventure, had, "New Year's Eve, 2003," party of four in company... And O' course. well yeah, this is a True Story, and to begin the excitement, "there actually was one very large unexpected wild brother of deception wandering along with us quite UN-seen, that twice that night left anther definite hand impression in the cave dust for us all to experience on that unforgettable night! The trip had been founded/determined upon my request that the four of us committed were going to venture down into the deep confines of Zak Cave, in order to be there a the stroke of mid-night, regardless of the weather then being down to a miserable forty degrees below zero! Come blizzard, deep snow, high stress, much difficulty, or what ever... We all were going to do it, and we darned well did it too! I was just certain that season because of all prevailing bad weather conditions that there was a very good chance to possibly experience one or more living relict hominids on that night already hold-up in the cavern! The weather was beyond terrible, and we even almost got our car hopeless stuck in deep snow trying to arrive close there! This experience and the horrific one sited by Donald Massey, collectively proved to be another reason of many others to need be explained in the Trilogy Manuscripts! There will be no exaggerations in these documents. I write what truths are here somewhat in desperation, ever hopeful that I will have time enough before my last sun down to complete them? Writing for me is difficult, as besides experiencing disturbing dyslexia, being half blind in one eye, missing several typing fingers from mishap, having many more obvious priorities and misgivings, wanting to return back to my love of fly fishing, canoeing, sailing, and hunting, etc., I write only dutifully as an aging derelict at that disadvantage. For my contesting honesty I am not popular with the pseudo Bigfoot community, or have I ever cared, "and it is truly ironic that in some small measure I also write for them, as among them are also some many true adventurers, that like myself only want recognize the complete truth of wild hominids for there historical human fact! It is only going to be a matter of time when what I have written may make a difference. Till then the Hell with it, and so I will be on with it!"

My life long sojourn of discovery was not completely a waste, as I encountered a lot of wonderful UN-sung human wonders of our world...! Oh, to be able to catch just one irritating horse fly in my hand! Don Massey had done that once!"

"THE surprise PARTY!"

New Years Eve, year, 2004, Ken Bear Iddins, "Red", Myself, and another unnamed, wanted insisted anonymous. On this night we experienced an extraordinary large wild hominid something or other (?), that if for no other express reason, would be enough reason for the importance of the experience to be continuing all of the books now slated that will one day God willing, finally comprise the all new revised, "Sasquatch Trilogy!"

"Paul Wright, earlier year 2003, with me exploring in Zak Cave!"

Forget the rocks, Paul? He has never! "Don he said, what in the name of heavy lead. and rocks... What the heck have you got in these heavy packs? Rocks, iron, bisques, plaster, lunch, water, or what? Even a camel couldn't drag and carry this stuff! It must weigh more than sixty pounds!" ("It did!") Often as not because of ongoing experiments, all plaster and casting material, included water needed in dry caves, we always did need to pack rather heavy... This day we were all crying the maximum load, everything possible required to be able to feed, and/or tempt any wily cave creature encountered; make all necessary plaster castings, etc., ever it was necessary, and needed was particular hardware, cameras, lanterns, fuel, plenty enough water in gallon jugs (Eight pounds to the gallon!), etc. ...I was forever thinking of new ideas to increase our chances for an incredible discovery, and today we actually were carrying rocks (Paul was still unaware!) that would prove the unexpected importance of them in the future! Later, when I finally had explained my intentions with the rocks, "all crew after-shock of seeing them dumped from the packs, became anxious and willing... The rocks experiment alone that was being implemented could write in future another rare and much interesting and puzzling book, as some of the suspected ramifications are still being watched for today, and it has been ten years!

"Yeah, Paul, Rocks!"

"What, you mean....rocks? You mean real rocks? BIG rocks... you mean these are actually real rocks in these packs....?"Yeah, they are round shaped heavy river rocks that are all painted in several different colors of paint? Rocks my Ass, Don, you are a kilt, dead....! "Hey wait a minute...You are not kidding! I can actually smell the wet paint! You are... What the heck, you are not kidding these are PAINTED Rocks?" Paul for the moment was not a happy camper... It wold take several pages to explain the great difficulty to have carried and drug the heavy rocks to where we had arrived at the moment...

Yeah Paul I sad, some of the heavy stuff in your pack actually is heavy rocks... Rocks of all colors, some silver, a few red, black, but most are painted bright Gold, just like the fillings in your teeth, and the rocks in your head! I couldn't get Paul to laugh! The others with us were the same! "My head, man you must be kidding me? Heck, I should have joined the Marines, or the, French Foreign Legion, at least I'd get to eat, and be paid something for my miseries! Are you planning to go it alone, or what? I'm taking a break!" Come on Paul, we heard some strange sound ahead! Ron and Lewis are right behind you prodding us along! "Heard something what? Now that is in-corrigible... No, I'm not crawling another inch! I'm sitting here wishing that I were somewhere else like, maybe singing in the Congo-chorus with the smallest Congo pigmies, or looking for Ron Roseman at his Gentleman's Club in Siberian or Tibet where there are none....! Or maybe being on my way to Honolulu.... Or, gone to The Big Island Hawaii.... Now something like that would make more sense! When did you say you are going there again? Wow, that should give us a real break.... At least they got No Caves there do they? What? They have lots of caves? What is that desert place called the .... The Ca-hue, or, Kangaroo Desert or what? "(Kahu Desert!)" "Hey, did we or someone hear that small loud noise or what...? Listen....?"They all listened....! Paul rifled through my pack, and then another.... "Dam-it Don, I looked, and there are painted rocks in all of these packs! Why are they most all painted gold and silver? What are we trying to prove...? What has painted rocks got to with anything? Man this is all just plain crazy? Now I fully understand what you told Ron and I, when you met us at the Spokane Air-Port.... And, I can remember every single word that you said.... "After today guy's, you may learn to hate me, but you will never for-get the experience! Well, sure as hell, today I really do hate you... and THIS is no Mega Fun Party experience extraordinaire....! This is an unadulterated, stupid lava-tube cave door-way into hell and misery! It's always all of us just one foot step after another behind or ahead of the next idiot, or, Bob-Cat.... Did you see those big cougar tracks back there where we first came in? We are not alone! Those cat tracks didn't leave! What the hell are we planning next? Really, why Don, why have we brought in all of the painted rocks? Man it better be good!"

(See Twilight Zone Chapters, 2014!)
None crew, but two, ever quit, and WE all fired them!

("Things happen! People happen! No one gets to run wild forever in the mountain deserts, forests, ever chasing legends, fantasy, and dreams.... Adventure finally becomes a literal financial drain, on One's pocket book, energy, time, etc. The Old One's dwindle, and the most valued are seldom replaced. No one funds most mavericks in the field! Books that I have written have been found in the Montana dump! Adventure is simply in ones blood!")

Log: Horses, Caves! Excerpt from real life exploration!

Perhaps this next will give the reader a more personal glimpse of exploring logic, just as if he/she had been with us, etc., before the author had at all realized that plaiting was a reality mostly gone on unrealized before fall, 2004, as yet before then plaiting in my case was com-pletely unknown with the exception of a little known then obscure book hardly as yet been in-troduced in America written in Russia by, Dmitri Bayanov sometime prior to the year 1975 (?), titled: "On The Trail of the Russian Snowman!" So, until well into the year, 2004, I had no founded expectations of plaiting being done to any horses anywhere, except in pseudo places of mountain Russia described by Bayanov. More will be explained of the Russian book when we pick up where left off pages ago with the story account of, Montana Jim, where is explained that in the fall of 2004, he had unexpectedly come to my Spencer, Idaho home after having just returned back from Mongolia. As said, many of these caves that we are describing were located within close proximity of local ranch stock cattle and horses left long season to wander all desert mountain open range. I had always wondered since having first read Dmitri Bayanof's book about year, 2000 that domestic ranch stock as horses and cattle just might for some reason have something to do with what was being described to me at my Spencer Idaho Trading Post Bigfoot Report Station of what back then was being described to me as local Sasquatch? I had closed the Report Station Store by late fall 2004 about the time when I had first met "Montana Jim" and had first learned first hand of plaiting! Since then I have continued to this day to watch all moon phase, and ever the instinctive movements of most all of the larger wild big game animals.

Strange Anomalies To Some Exaggerations?

Various Moon Phase, Full Moon, Crescent Moon, Blue Moon, Sliver and Silver Moon!

"Human sacrifice, head-hunting, voodoo, cannibalism, witchcraft, etc. This is much evident over the vast sea world of all far South Pacific Islands, Africa, Borneo, Java, The Caribbean, All West Indies, etc. Head hunting was outlawed in all Southern Ocean Lands of the South Pacific, about the year, 1966. Early reminiscent humanity as was Cro-Magnon man also reverenced sacred what is the, Crescent Moon Phase and an evidenced belief in a revered, Moon Goddess, or, what was believed the Sliver Crescent represented her all seeing night eye. It is reasonable from cave depictions that they must have realized very long ago a theoretical all possible next world, or even a neither world of pre-existence? With a very little imagination; when having a close look at the Sliver Moon, it becomes easy to realize this fable belief. The moon definitely effects much more than has been probably studied including ones daily intellect in certain ways; that is but conjecture of course, but from watching many animals and man's peculiarities perhaps there is something to it?

A Preview to animal Mind Power!

"Similar of Shen, etc?"

Log: Lima Montana, January 15, 2012. The important Deposition of animal trainer/breeder, Jesse Johnson!

"Don, she said, all wild animals and tame, definitely have many unexplained communications between them, as well as with particular humans! This is not necessarily any particular acute mental telepathy either!"

(Jesse's deposition to be continued below.)

Note:

Even the suggestive body language of humans, when/if only seen at a long distance has its own relativity to animal and human communication. First time encountered strangers on any wilderness trail at most any reasonable distance can tell at once each other intentions and something about them. Wolves, coyotes, dogs, cougars, etc. at a long distance well know at once if or not them safe, in dire threat of a rifle, etc., anytime whenever encountering a human simply by all obvious body language. The unspoken communication uncanny between fur trappers, animal trainers, skilled hunters, pet owners, and all higher animals as wolves, cougars, etc., between man has long been accepted. Some of the lesser intelligent fur barriers as, mink, martin, fisher, and especially the legendary wolverine ever out smart even the shrewdest hunter until he can finally identify their fatal habit.

Log: "First a few words about Jesse...

Her story is as incredible as it is meaningful. She is a much traveled person, however opts by choice to live a simple. happy, productive, lifestyle. She could have walked right off from the pages of a 16th Century wilderness adventure novel. Her uncanny animal experience explained ahead has direct ramifications to help one contemplate the extraordinary animal-human bonding possibilities that would be all necessary between horses and man, or what ever it is that is plaiting their manes. Ahead when we access "Shen" I will also attempt to explain extended conjecture to magnify all logical cause and effect of man and animal bonding. No one completely understands all humankind, or even their cherished family pet. Look into any strangers eyes, and especially into the eyes of any wild or tame animal: for the most part most people haven't really got one clue to all pent-up latent perceptions or anything of their possible intentions. The surprise of misinterpretation may even get you or someone killed! Often over the media comes another tragic story of a pseudo tame exotic animal attacking its master. There are no written rules to the animal world behavior. What is most important within Jesse's deposition, are the direct and abstract associations realized of all the unknown powers that be among animals and man. Powers that are much evident and in effect as exemplified by all high strange plaited manes being left on many world horses. More on mind power when we access the innate indications associated with Chinese Mind Power, or Shen! "Jessie's Deposition continued from above. "Don, perhaps I never told you... But, long before I moved here,

I raised four wolves. We also had several mixed breeds of wild dogs and animals with them. Animals as coyote-dogs, various sled dogs, malamutes, Siberian huskies, etc. One in particular was a beautiful white female wolf-dog, ironically she played regularly for many hours at a time with a large wild, Black Bear! Yeah, a real bear! Why are you laughing? Yeah, no kidding, the bear one day just all at once showed up on the property, and without more incident joined all the dogs and wolves as if he were family! Surprisingly that bear remained harmless with us for a long time! It was almost as if it were tame! Yeah, I know all of this is very strange, but the bear ever stayed harmless for about two months, until finally because of my concern for all children, I allowed the bear be trapped by the Montana Fish and Wildlife Service! It was humanely captured in one of those big barrel type catch cages. No kidding, the Montana Fish and Game became very upset at me; ever claiming that it was illegal to have in possession any mixed domestic wild animal as would be a coyote-dog, wolf-dogs, any wild wolf, coyote, badger, bob cat, etc! Yes, at the time, I had all of fifty-six ("Yeah, 56!") mixed dogs, wolves, coyotes, etc! Yes, I had actually raised all of these animals all at the same time! Yes, It was crazy how the wolf-dog would play with that bear! It would charge, and charge again, and again, over and over at the Bear! Always the two of them were in comical animal play! The bear each time would sorta sit back on its rump and sorta sling the dog quite far-off to its one side, just like when tossing a ball by using only the base of a hand like is a base part of its paw! Yeah, not once did it ever hurt the dog! The dog seemed to love the bear! I kept all of these dogs housed and tethered in a close net circle, but still we had all of them tied a considerable distance apart on long chains! The Bear would choose to get right into the middle of all of them and sleep the night quietly inside all of that chained amassed animal confusion! Never once had he bothered any of them! Yes I know this is all very unusual! But, "We All," animals and man just seemed to have what I can best explain was somehow some sort of an unspoken and accepted tolerance for the other, or what might have been a collective humanistic-animistic agreement established somewhat as if automatically between us... if any of that makes any sense? Well, that's the best that I can explain it! Yes, I realize that dogs, wolves, coyotes, etc., are all natural enemies! And that is very true! And all of that especially SO when considering all bears! Normally the smallest dog can easily run a bear up a tree! But somehow, none animal ever bothered the other? They all got along beyond belief! Probably Now-a-Days, any New, or Old Report Filed, revealing anything future claimed to be true of past existing, or present running wild coyote-dogs, strange wolves, half wolves-coyotes, wolf-dogs, etc., and/or anything thought to be hybridize like that... "All blame of such animals by anyone, and especially the Fish and Wildlife Experts, will all be claimed to have happened as the direct result of persons just like myself! You can't tell me that is not possible for all wild canines to hybridize in the wild! Things like that just happen! Exactly how we all had bonded so incredibly is really not more explainable, but we just had naturally all done it!"

"Wow, Jesse, that's some story!"

Log: December 9th, 2011 -

"The Full Moon and the strange braiding of horses' manes?"

This manuscript documentation began from where I am staying today as a house guest with, "Bob, and, Patti Reinhold," at "Sweet Home Oregon." The week-end abrupt us was the beginning and end of a historical, "Eclipse of the Moon," academically explained to climax Saturday night, December 10th. This rare "Eclipse" is not to re-occur similar for many years to come. Up to this time since the fall of 2004, I have been doing much arduous and extensive investigations of all realized encounters where still might be found as told me, still remaining evidence of any high strange unexplained intricate horse mane plaiting being done to the hair manes of horses. This strange braiding, (explained plaiting), continues as a long unsolved mystery? In order to further investigate, I next need journey 600 miles by late night across Oregon State to investigate two separate ranch land settings each located some twenty miles or so south of, "Nyasa," each property located approximately 15 miles distance from the other along the lofty tangled brush and deciduous tree covered banks of the famous, Owyhee, and Ore-Ida, Snake Rivers. First stop will be to visit, Phil, and his mother, Norma Jenson, as for several years running they have experienced ongoing and repetitious plaiting of their horses' manes! It is my hope that abrupt all Full Moon Eclipse now diminishing, that just possibly all new plaiting evidence may have already began, or will begin happening enough to more attest my full moon theory pos-

sible? Believe it or not, I even wrote it down before had arrived at the Jenson's; I highly do expect to find new plaiting going on when arrive tonight at Phil's! I just know its happening! How? I just know! Much more to be explained on moon theory outcomes as all pertains. Even if not agree, anyone still reading with me must allow, that it is my firm opinion that the unexplained high strange plaiting is all being accomplished by some sort of an unrealized human entity, that I call instead of Sasquatch, Bigfoot, etc., prefer, Wild Man! And with that said, I am ever adamant, and logical explanations for reasons why continue... So be it all possible, Molly b' Damn, is probably wandering with them?

"Neil Hinck," Adrian, Oregon.

His Blazer horses are much a part of this documentation!

Until his demise, 2008, Neil came hard riding into this century from the last, as the real article pier cowboy horseman, a man ahead of all time, if ever there was one, exemplified notably as an exceptional humble seasoned wrangler, front and center applauded, all unintended, well recognized by all of today's world wide cowboys similar! Neil was as if ever a well renowned and highly accomplished Vaquero, horse trainer/breeder, if ever was one! His credits included many notable Hollywood efforts, to include admirations from famous persons as was last century's fabled, Hal-dago*, and the famous "Los Vegas" magician, Doug Henning. His invincible self as a successful trainer and breeder-originator of the world famous, Hinck Blazer Horse strain, writes its own ongoing historical note.

Neil was the horseman's horseman! He and I had bonded upon meeting as if we both were two unmanageable horses! Neither of us had ever been fenced, or tethered! His extraordinary ranch life accomplishments was far beyond most persons imagination.

If there are horses Anywhere Up Yonder, Neil definitely has been put in charge of the wildest mustangs! I miss you old buddy! If it were possible that anyone were born, "half a horse," you are the one! "It seems that over the vast ranch lands of all wild Ore-Ida, that the "Night Stalker's," as I opt to call them ("Unrealized wild man!"), seem to much single out your horse strain where ever they remain corralled? Perhaps it is the reason of their highly intelligent, cooperative, and easily approachable nature? What ever the reason, who really understands to be able to say or

Figure 52. Neil Hinck.

---

* Hidalgo, in a movie by that name, a paint mustang ridden by Frank T. Hopkins against purebred Arabian *al-Khamsa* horses in the late nineteenth century "Ocean of Fire" race across the Arabian desert. Neil Hinck is said to have been trained for distance riding under Frank Hopkins. Some researchers dispute whether that race across the Empty Quarter of Saudi Arabia ever really happened or was merely Frank Hopkins' fiction, but any dispute over the facts of Frank Hopkins casts no aspersion on Neil Hinck's horsemanship. [ed.]

understand, exactly what strange mysteries or unexpected inanities wader under the dark night moon light more able to accomplish extremely humanistic intricate plaiting?" "If a thing it is not the obvious, then it is the contrary!" - Sherlock Holmes.

"Every opinion has its disadvantage. If this treatise is wrong, lets hear a better assumption. This very day I was offered a ridiculous suggestion that perhaps the plaiting is being done by an unknown flying something like would be a human humming bird, as it never leaves tracks, or by invisible spirits, shape shifters, pixies, fairies and trolls, and the like! Who really is all that crazy? What is amazing is the extremely naive population of wannabe moderns that fail to even realize man's ancient history! What is to say that a plausible reminiscent example of humanity has not cleverly continued to live right along side us in parallel to this very day! In all societies there has ever existed an unaccounted for small outcast population. Not the place here to access all of that, but that is exactly relative to what I believe. They have existed since earliest times within all generations. There are actual records of them in ancient texts and scripts. Hear me out before you toss aside this manuscript. What meaningful if not frightening, or even friendly, may be waiting just out side your cabin door on any given dark night might highly surprise even the most ardent stubborn critic minded among you! Mice play when the cat's away! What say Erich Von Daniken .... "Absolutely no one, who puts forward a new theory has any claim to be embraced, kissed and congratulated, but the very least that he can reasonably expect is, that his theory will be seriously examined and discussed..." -Erich Von Daniken.

" World Geography!"

"Horses Are Everywhere!"

Wild and domestic horses roam far and wide over the USA and Canada, and especially vast territory of Ore-Ida-Nevada, across the Owyhee Desert bad-lands, up from the "Paiute Indian Reservation at Pyramid Lake, north as far as the Duck Valley Indian Reservation at the confluence of Ore-Ida, Nevada; and from there include all further range and ranch lands of western Montana, Idaho, Oregon, Washington, Utah, Colorado, Wyoming, and some of the High Sierra California high mountain wilderness up to approximately where today is called Bluff Creek, and southward in California far abrupt the Arizona-New Mexico Bad lands of Texas, Baja Calif., etc. All region is but only some many of the extensive river ecosystems to be found within this vast expanse, today popularly known as, "The American Great Basin Wilderness that includes The Great Basin National Park! All vastness described where rural is ever an endless high mountain desert country, all of the way down to the Pacific Ocean Shores. And all of it possible in future to much more excite continuing unexplained horse plaiting being done more able to further astonish/attest the incredible truth of the all high strange anomaly! Everywhere in the world occurs an all much similar full moon phase! Eurasian steppe and North American High Desert Mountain Longitude and Latitude are much similar also. Before getting whole heart idly into all Lunar factors, traditions, customs, etc., after considerable studies in conjunction I have concluded that the bulk of Russian, European, and most all Asian claims of similar horse plaiting as is being accomplished within all wild mountain regions of the Caucasus, Urals, Himalayas, etc., far places as Mongolia, Bhutan, Kurdistan, etc., almost to the limit of possibility, most every location mentioned is well centered mainly within the same much similar elevation, longitude, latitudes, seasonal weather expectations, etc., as have the western portion of the USA and much also of Canada. Have an educated look at your world map to discover a whole new range of plausibility! Not the space here either to elaborate all of the reasons, but much within this observation with a little imagination of the reader has the author also realizing possible ramifications to why, where, and what purpose that said Sasquatch (Wild Man!) actually chooses to predominate the far west northern regions of all remaining wild North America? As far as allowed to date by pier academic research it is believed that predominately wild man populations as are Sasquatch/Bigfoot, etc., mostly frequent the far mountains and forests of the Inter-Mountain West, including the West Coast Ocean Forests of North America. No doubt from all collective sightings this is true, with the exception that predominately my personal discoveries evidencing wild man in found in mountain and desert regions have continued to border on areas directly adjacent to productive farm crops, and/or much plentiful small, and large game populations. The smaller game, and up-land game birds, water fowl, etc., all the more important... Of course where there is extensive domestic crop food, there are also milk cows, considerable horses, many sheep, and ever domestic and feral wild poultry, ducks pigeons, etc. Exactly there is naturally the easiest place to observe plaiting being done on domestic horses. Wild man is ever most safe in urban wilderness as no one remotely expects him! There are endless places within rural ranch and farm lands, adjacent forests, and endless deciduous tree covered river bottoms, reed covered irrigation systems, wild duck and goose pond sanctuaries, etc. where any intelligent Ho-BO, including myself if wanted to could easily exist... Joe Stromer, still the literal Indiana Jones, of The Black Rock Nevada Desert, well knows that there are still a few places in many a canyon wall where a wild man can crawl! Joe and I both attest that the unless they are stopped soon your good old B.L.M. will soon have destroyed them all... Soon there will be wilderness where we will be allowed to enter!

Ray Crowe, my good friend that disdains my free spirit writing. Ron Roseman, ever we lost together in Florida, etc., and, MK Davis, everywhere out of necessity between Mississippi and California at times has needed share with me weed-patch room, # 126, and many others ever amazed if not confused at all my blather I insist in spite of most everyone knowing that darn well know that I have been just about every where, even if I have not ever claimed to have already done that? Yeah, Ray, this part of the book probably is unimportant, unnecessary, and will be somewhat repetitious? Bob Schmalzbach should have written at least a part of the Preface to explain all pending confusion! What is important for you to understand old pals, is that with your help and continuing assistance others, diligent critics, and credible investigators alike in time (Collectively speaking!) we may all finally get to the stark truth of all this matter?"

Update: Ray Crowe, January 17th, 2012. "Just today I received a complimentary copy of, "Ray's new revised book addition titled, "Shaman from the East!" (ISBN #, 9781468078305) "I have past times read all the original manuscript, and as now have only taken the time to thumb slightly through all new book, however it looks to be entertaining, and an excellent educational read! Ray's magical writing form, is exactly that! He overwhelms everyone in variations of opinion, "and ever bottle caps our intuitive agreeable conclusions exactly safe as they always stay in his waste basket! Ray, when realizing that when last with you I was impossible; Ray would always tell me... "Well Don, if don't believe me, then ask "Fred!" Fred was Ray's pet Gold Fish, that ever well realized that if a fish kept his mouth shut, he would never get into trouble! Rays late wife "Theata, and I, were the best of friends! Year 2004, as promised Ray, we named a special wind swept stark beautiful Idaho Mountain Cave for her! On the same day, Ron Roseman with detective John

Doitch, N.Y. City, caught and rescued a lost and confused small wild raven chick from sure death that had been accidentally ousted from its nest! After ward I became its mother and hand fed the baby chick at my cabin where finally after seven dedicated months I opt to teach Bird Theata to fly, as it was time to let her back to nature. All of that another story for a special book that perhaps I will never the find the time to write? Anyone alive is ever a candidate for sudden death! What is for dinner in future might be anyone? Recently while kayaking a part of the Arizona Colorado River with pirate, Gene Sheller, Lake Havasu City, we short-stopped on an Island experiencing wild pigs! What's next for dinner Gene Sheller, or up problematic with Johnny Foxx? We need try again 2014 to explore that impossible AZ. River! Hello to wild Mark-us!

A Reprieve

Log: Siberia Montana - "To much wind, and not enough vodka!

(?) MK Davis, because of you, this becomes a difficult deposition manuscript! I'm alone and frozen again in room #126 at Lima Montana! I wish that you were along to be miserable with me and to re-argue any part of our aborted adventure to a warmer sojourn! As soon I'm out of fire wood I'm out of here to somewhere after March 1st? You will here about it! No, you are too late now to re-join the effort! MK, of late has been very sick... He's too tough to admit it.

Plaiting!

What Done it?

"Only a very high intelligence abrupt anything could accomplish it!"

Such intricate handy work of which I now have more than fifty samples would require to any imagination, much extreme dexterity, much tenacity, and need have a definite purpose, and if available the expertise of very small and dedicated child, if not also very dainty nimble fingers! All of it overwhelms all reason! Not once in ten years have I yet found one foot track of evidence! Never once has been left any real clue to what had done it... other than of course, the ever high suspect evidence of thick textured, hard dried mares milk, found braided tightly into the crises-crossed strands of the plaited mane! What, really, do any think are the good reasons to have anything opt to labor so intensely, and be able-handed and steady enough to do it by the dark light of a questionable moon? The challenge to solve the mystery is beyond exhilarating, and far beyond simple fascination. Once solved there will be a reckoning of embarrassment embellished within the alleged main stream Bigfoot community! What more say anyone?"

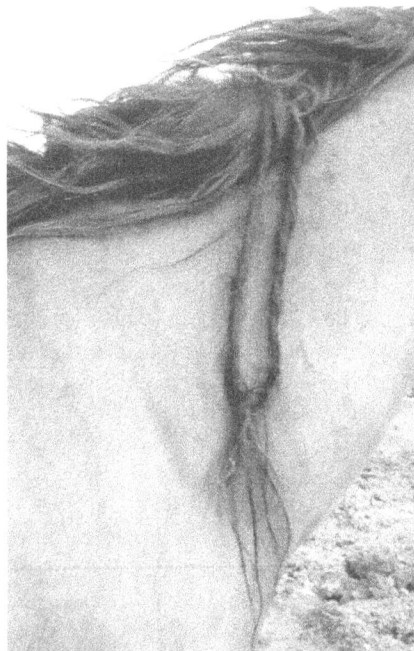

Figure 53. A distinct loop formed with two strands of about equal thickness, joined below, and with most of the ends appearing to be trimmed.

"Montana Common Sense!"

"Don, what pray-tell is a valid Bigfoot community?"

Log: Deposition: Sage Brush, Darrel Miller, and, cowboy pal

Sage investigator, Seboldt George, and Peg-Leg Swartz, we are all seated and yapping together down here at the, Yesterdays Cafe, the pride of Dell Montana! When cowboy/biker friend, Darrel Miller, opt to put local common sense this way.... "Don he said, that Bigfoot Community, where ever it is (?), must be One Hell of a Crowed place full of Fools! Since for as much time as all of them seem to spend hashing nothing important over and over again on the Net, they all must spend very little time out in the woods? Good thing that you are not popular with the rest of them... If you were, the whole damn flock of crazy bastards might show up here in Montana trying to re-classify our wolves and elk! That guy on television from ISU Pocatello, Idaho that we had to listen to together on location at the Ohio Bigfoot Conference, 2007.... Well if you ask me, he is far short of common sense, and as full of beans as ever was my first-grade teacher's leakiest bean-bag! He told one flock of lies, after more lies after another! As you well know, one lie is a lie, as a lie is a lie! Get him up here next spring and we will tie him to one the trees up on Pine Top for that big bear to pawnder! You know, those big bear evidence claw marks that I saw on one big tree up there was big enough for the Montana Grizzly King! Naw, George said, the new Montana Law Says that you can't tie a horse to a tree, or probably even any Horses Ass? Probably all of that don't make much sense either, but then again maybe it would be better if we just introduced him to the local red ants, or took him out, One Way to the County Dump?"

"Peg leg said... Yeah, Nope, and, Yep!"

The Full Moon During December

Log: December 11, 2011. "Nyssia Oregon!"

"This Is Where This Last Fifteen Months Of Close Moon Phase Research Had Began!"

Because of the pending, "Full Moon Eclipse continuation, I am now on my way fast driving the 600 miles across the state of Oregon, traveling, West, to East from Sweet Home Oregon, to investigate the rich ranch and farm lands near the burg town of, Nyssia, that are long famous for their exceptional produce, livestock, etc. I'm going to where I now have high suspects that just possibly during all of the bright moon lit nights all past week, and the few bright nights still ahead all during the continuing, Full Moon Eclipse, that likely as not, once again as before, all new plaiting may have already began on the, Jenson property, or possibly the N. & N. Hinck horse ranch?"

Update: This moment as of ten minutes ago it just turned midnight March First, 2013, and I am winding down the manuscript half frozen in my Montana Cabin House! The research for now is over... tomorrow I send this confusion out to its publisher! What pseudo corrections are not accomplished from here down we will just need to deal with it! Remember this is a theory only, but the plaiting to date since Dec. 2011 has not failed!

Theory Only?

Some of it now founded in fact!

The full moon phase is but only one part of the authors conjecture to explain the pseudo workings of all night stalking wild hominids of either gender. There is of course no feasible way to know if indeed it is being done by male or female or both, and I am reasonably sure when all considering it is taught mother to teenager, followed by all younger children. The adult male had early on learned plaiting at his mothers heals, and later when became mature is expectant to wander more or less as a provider/protector/scout, all of the while being free to seek out numerous companion mates. Their continuing existence depends much on procreation,, and because of obvious evidence found in one particular cave room, I have plausible reasons to believe they care intensely for the safety of their young. All Sasquatch (wild hominids) likely out of dire necessity and habit are highly phlegmatic, and it is reasonable that planned parenthood with them is exactly as all nature requires that most animals except bears need birth in spring. That said, it is my opinion that the female is likely the best candidate to be doing the plaits.

Neil Hinck The Barbarian!

"The Catalyst!"

We sat eye ball to eye ball... Neil the rascal, and I the pirate!

"OK, he said, what is this crazy wild man theory idea anyway that has to do so much with my plaited horses? What are they? "Even if all my new idea and the or human like after my horses... Feel free to have a look around anytime you want! Let us know if find anything were a stark auto suggested reality to Neil, after a third cup off coffee, and with our feet up, aging old, "Neil" finally admitted that he had once encountered an actual wild man one time while hunting elk in Wyoming south of "Jackson Hole!" "Yeah Don, the critter looked strong enough to pick up an elk! And it did to! We chased the rascal for a long ways, and he never once put the thing down! We finally let him have it! Anything that hungry deserved it! And there was the time at the gate in Idaho... I'll write you that story and all details... I got to agree, there is something human like after my horses... Feel free to have a look around anytime you want! Let us know if find anything were a stark auto suggested reality to Neil, after a third cup off coffee, and with our feet up, aging old, "Neil" finally admitted that he had once encountered an actual wild man one time while hunting elk in Wyoming south of "Jackson Hole!" All of what she had just described in somewhat more detail, was much similar to expectations, except this time, all new plaiting was done much more elongated enough to extend double length of the horse's mane that measures approx. 14 inches, now extended to a crazy long, "28!" Yeah really, how is something like that possible?" Well, there is one part answer explained below, but that explanation is separately as overwhelming as the plaiting! God only knows, how, why, who, or for sure what purpose all of this is being done? The elongation method will be partly be explained in its place.

Log: January 9th

Another exciting update phone call to all of this came this afternoon. I definitely do need to be heading back to the Oregon Ranch Lands, however it is ironical that when I had departed for Arizona last week, January third; on the very same date and time, all of this new stuff had just been taking place! I had no real way of knowing for sure that all of this would happen so soon, or I may had gone there instead? Maybe not? It's important that for a while I continue to watch each new full moon phase! Last nights phone call had explained, "that Phil had only that night again noticed that all new braiding had started all over again on the horse, "Hink, exactly as it was, on the eve of when the moon was in its upward half-phase heading towards its full zenith... Only, this time the new and additional braid was but obvious to had been done on a second attempt, intended as it were, perhaps to re-plait, or cleverly add upon more length to one of the Previous plaited Braids, only this time all new was done also much elongated! This elongation is being done by only one observed founded explanation, done by, believe it or not, by cleverly and very carefully cutting off and using long portions of extracted horse tail hair, cut/taken from off a same horse, or possibly at times, taken from another horse, that has also already been plaited cleverly into another elongation mode! done repetitious, "then in due time I guess, the tail probably could be finally pulled off?

Neil Hinck had passed away shortly prior to all This elongation, is ever being done artistically, with much clever difficult expertise, enough so, that all of it is hardly noticeable to the eye, except in the case of the ones that have been already discovered/observed that were all previously obvious! All of this was elongation was first time discovered how done, after having noticed that a particular long braid already had explainable multicolored horse hair additions its length, etc! Fall 2009, "Brenda Hinck, Neil's Veterinarian daughter," put into my hands a complete, somehow pulled, or severed off, tail from a horse, a complete black horse tail length was looking back at me that she explained she had found laying amiss out in the middle of the pasture without one more clue to which horse out of 130 plus horses then grazing the pasture land, that it had peen pulled off from? The extracted tail remains a mystery and is now in my plaited hair collection. Best that I can figure from all tail evidence, the tail has two separate obvious hand holds amassed (Mashed down sort of tightly at two locations...) within its total length, what is at once obvious to anyone holding on to it in a purposeful double hand hold position, just as if say that it were still attached to the horses ass, and one was wanting or intending to be hanging onto the horse, as if wanting to hold it back, or wanted to be pulled along on your two feet behind, etc. The two deep set double hand holds along the tail length, are both definitely very well deep a mashed impressions, deep-set permanently into the tail hair! Another way said, there are two distinct hand holds, both well positioned in place, each exactly located where one would require ones hand hold onto the tail would be, if when wanting to be pulled, or be running close behind!

If so, that was actually being of this, and so the existing horse count at the time was uncertain, however from memory then I had been told the count was in excess of 135 head? Spring 2010, "Debby Hinck and I," spent most of a full day very closely examining all of the horses on the ranch and found over forty (40!) female horses plaited! The majority were fillies and mares! Predominately fillies, horses about to drop their first colt! All of these fillies had a heavy waxy consistent white colored es-tress milk substance already forming in their teats, that would sooner or later become complete milk protean food for all new borne colts... We found some evidence of this thick waxy milk substance, "hard set, mixed-braided, crises-crossed into some of the plaited manes, ever suggestive that what ever had braided the manes, had also at some point in time, recently been down at the teats probably in order to suckle all possible milk protean? A wild assumption you say... Well people all over the Eurasian World still doing exactly that, especially after the birth of the horse, when after the mares milk becomes very sweet and pleasant to the taste. Where do anyone think comes mares milk? Asia today still relishes mares milk, and yogurt made from it! I have first hand knowledge of at least three separate persons that have suckled horses, and in one particular case had to be stopped, as the colts were not getting enough milk! Ice cream made form mares milk is beyond excellent! What more need be said? Snails, es cargo, lobsters, crabs, even slugs, worms, Beatles, bugs, larva, lice, etc. become suspect of a much lesser food! Try mares milk sometime if any can get the chance, and report the outcome! The conquering hordes of, "Genghis Khan," swore by it... and probably also swore at it? Apparently wild man is mesmerized by it? It almost is as if the estrus horses have an abstract bonding attachment, to the cause and effect of possible wild man suckling, etc?

Never once on a morning after all evidence of plaiting having been done, etc. has any horse ever once seemed ancy, or to had been excited or in high stress. Never one single foot track of what done it has been found... Never, not one!" To be kept in mind, "approximately every 28 days a full moon phase appears around the world," Long realized if not understood as explained, bright moon light highly effect the outcomes of man and many animals such as dogs. Every one has heard dogs etc., howl at the moon? During the recent full moon phase at the time of all recent plaiting being done at the Jenson's December 2011, the two dogs belonging to their close neighbors, "Marvin and Diane Hollens," also my close friends, living on the Owyhee River edge of the Jenson place; Diane told me.. "Well Don, our two dogs acted very strange at that time, and had refused for two days to even leave our front porch! Both just sat there shivering as if confused, frightened, etc? These dogs remember were both strangely attacked down by the river about one year ago... Remember, you saw them, both were badly bittern over the head and on the anus! Both bled profusely, and both needed medical attention. There were multiple bits all over ones back about the size of golf balls! Very deep bites! "Dolly even needed a transfusion!" Yes, I have examined these dogs earlier, and the scars are obvious. This attack remains an unexplained happening, and may, or may not have anything to do with the strange plaiting, as during the month of September 2011, close near by to the Hollens Home, I encountered running ahead of my car, a very large black wolf, the biggest that I ever saw, running fast across the property. As I say, the wolf was the largest that I have ever seen! Our Montana wolves by comparison are wimp pups!"

Java Bob!

"Don your book content is drifting!" Not necessary, "Java Bob... As just like all justified exploring manuscripts, yours, mine, everything written worthwhile, constantly needs to be re-written with all new updates, etc, "just as if you might say again... "Don, damn it, everything here is just as if all were ever being written, "Back Ass Wards!" That is completely true Java, when considering all necessary updates, etc! This story will not be complete until all is finally eventually found conclusive... Bob, believe me, we both need help! Heck, it takes fifty bucks just to print out your rough copy! Probably after all its written, it will go into the crypt o trash bucket? Doubt everything, or believe nothing...What often counts is the unwanted outcome! No one likes to be proven wrong!

"Bob Schmalzbach, (Java Bob!) this is the place where intelligent minds gather together to resolve or pass over past thought unsolvable problems! To be sure however, ever keep on your kaleidoscope skepticals!" A slight added upon, paraphrased, excerpt, taken from the writings of, Old buddy, -Ray Crowe!"

Remember, this sort of important perhaps thought dubious topic is much time consuming, and very hard to explain intelligently in manuscript in order for all others to comprehend regardless of however exhilarating and exciting all of it may be to the author. Much unexpected and ever unnoticed goes on during all dark nights! There is no solution to a great many things of the unexplained. Sometimes the solution is to leave things just exactly as we found them; that however is not the true nature of the curious. Only a person with the brain half the size of a walnut would doubt all of what has been discovered ever 2012 possible! We truly are into the age of the miraculous. Ray Crowe always told me, "Don, if still are in doubt, just ask old Fred! ('Fred was his and my aging gold fish friend, around for decades ever silent of opinion for may a disagreement over expectant questionable food and drink! My pirate self fond of the exotic, while old buddy Crowe opts for mashed potatoes and !) About all that truly can for now be said of all of this "horsing around contemplating plaiting is, well critics, all of this is the complete truth explained here just exactly as I have discovered it. Got better answers (?), well if SO, help us, "Molly b' Dammed!"

Log: Paiute Indian Reservation, Pyramid Lake, Nevada, 2011.

Deposition input was had today from two candid members of the Northern Nevada Paiute Indian Tribe, located at Nixon, Pyramid Lake. Much the same high strange anomaly had been noticed by them been done to some of the reservation wild mustangs! ("For what ever the reason they said, this sometimes happens. This has been long noticed been done on some of the longer manes of our wild mustangs!" What they asked me, what did I think were the reasons? "We have no idea of what does it? Sometimes during hot summer, we see stuff like that hanging down when the horses come down to the lake for water! Our boys see it and tell us its maybe done by the Water Babies?"

"Water Babies, all just another part of our undecided Wacky World!"

"It just so happened that I knew a little something of the legendary Pyramid Lake Water Babies, and all was helpful to realize more needed confidence. Native peoples as is well understood, often hesitate to rely on neophyte attitudes able to comprehend their native traditions. They are ever surprised whenever meeting a "white man" that is earnest of interest and none opinionated of all semi-covert traditions."

"It is to be noted that much similar to all of the above described plaiting has long been reported (I had heard of it before from the Nevada Paiutes when a guest of my late friend, Chief Smoky when at "Ely," Christmas week, 2005.), and much similar has mysteriously long taken place on many horses far distance apart at many extended world wide locations from China/Mongolia, deep into Northern Russian Siberia!"

"This manuscript is the result of real life discoveries wanting more truth to think to have found part viable answers able to more explain what in the hell high strange something is actually braiding these horse manes! As said, many sample plaited photographs are included. "You look...

you tell me if can what else done it? All photos are undeniable evidence to attest the strange anomaly. Never in my research have I need stretch the truth. However accepted, the truth eventually ever writes its own indisputable history. My creditability even after I pass this life, relies entirely upon my written word, compared along side all other many strange collective expedition artifacts, and/or are witnessed in any past, or further unfinished manuscripts left behind that will further attest this treatise. No matter what anyone doubt. This document is but one incomplete truth so help me, I swear by the long red hair of, "Irish, Molly be Damned!"

Critics And Discoveries

"He who protest too long, protest too much! Where were any of you when dedicated academics or mavericks made a new discovery?

"For what it is worth, and you have word on it... everything written in this manuscript is the result of real life discoveries wanting more truth to think to have found part viable answers able to more explain what in the hell high strange something is actually braiding these horse manes! As said, many sample plaited photographs are included. "You look. You can tell how much really is still left today completely unrealized, untold within our highly confused technical, and ever Wacky World, yet to be discovered and realized accepted. I continue awestruck at the many, many, possibilities. Here to follow is more of the incomplete story. Most of it is strange-excitement. During the adventure the reader becomes only but slightly introduced to the wild and wacky world of horses!

Neil Hinck if still alive would continue to sail with me on this continuing voyage of uncanny mystery, as when alive he became much interested to understand exactly what high strange was gong on with his many Blazer horses? "Don, I just don't know what, but something just is not right about all of this stuff being done to my horses!" A rare photograph is included picturing Neil Hinck, casually examining a long length of tightly braided three strand plaited mane still attached to one of his horses. All photos are undeniable evidence to attest the strange anomaly. Never in my research have I needed to stretch the truth. However accepted, the truth eventually ever writes its own indisputable history.

Neil was the horseman's horseman! He was an incredible person and trainer. He even managed to fully train to ride a full grown wild African zebra. Upon its acquisition, Neil was hired and in six short weeks trained it to be ridden double, as requested from the famed Hollywood Los Vegas highly acclaimed magician, Doug Henning, who was next

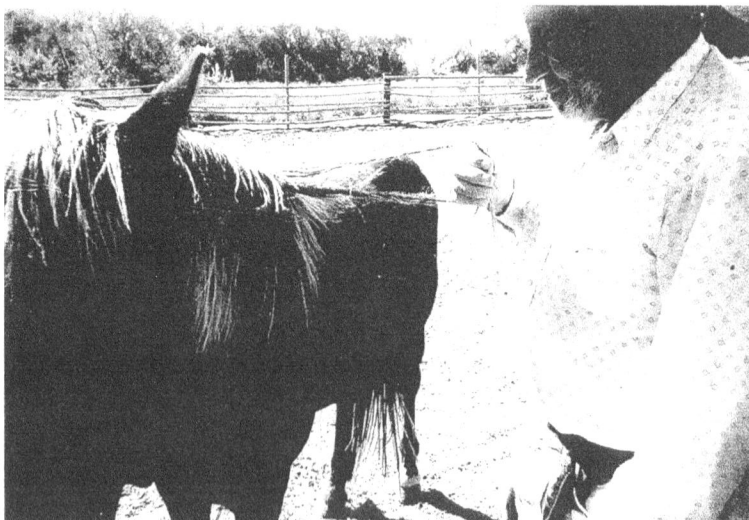

Figure 54. Neil Hinck checking out the length of this loop! Where did the extra come from? Perhaps tail hair braided in to extend the mane?

306

to be seen riding the zebra mounted with his wife televised from Los Vegas sometime during the late 1970s. As said, Neil had accomplished this in just six short weeks time! He later bought that zebra and kept it on his Oregon ranch for 13 years.

"A Dubious Manifesto!"

The more you study the subject the more you realize there has to be a much long founded thought ethical reason/purpose for what is being done. Considering all moon phase high regard, the mega effort and obvious adaptability of the anomaly, could it be that the Plaiting The Result of an Unknown Extremely Primitive Religious Connection dating back to the very first beginning of man's realized identity towards animals as was touched upon when explaining ancient Mesopotamia? It is to be remembered that Mesopotamia was long gone history before later surfaced ancient Egypt! Animal fetishism and related adoration is hardly a new thing. Its semblance even carries over into present day practices of recognized witchcraft and similar. The fabled "Great Owl" revered annually at "Bohemian Grove California," should realize anyone fully aware of its manifestations something to highly consider. Man and animals definitely are an equally relative acceptance. Man's animal pets are often more adored/treasured, or much similar treated as should rate the expected affection shown to a human child. Truth be known, some dog/cat, etc., pets are even treated somewhat much better! Exactly what are the implications of extreme pet-love unto almost humanistic identity-sacrifice? I am not psychoanalytical, but there are indeed strange affections far beyond my understandings. It is not here the space to further evaluate all of that, "but in all truth I have made discovery while exploring particular Idaho/Montana Cavern-Caves, suspect wild animals proven to having been tamed: have found wild man and animal tracks together; made plaster casts of the anomaly to prove all viable track evidence, to firmly offering of/or a tribal repentance-fetish allowance, and/or a wantin' forgiveness or new recognition? Perhaps such customary plaiting ever intended/thought to had been an expectant abstract tithe payment of sorts, ever to be expressed through, "very special physical hand-mental indulgence, done in what is thought to have been a particular and special way, offered at the beginning of a, Full Moon Phase, monthly, seasonal, whenever; all plaiting done as is in a special offering, perhaps as a direct result of an abstract though direct reverence to a long past, almost to be forgotten, very primitive and ancient religion? Wow, that said, we need a reprieve!

"What of blind Customs!"

Traditions/Blasphemy/Idolatry, etc.

"Custom is very strong, even among the desperate, the forgotten, abandoned, the forbidden, and unwanted, and the divided! What, really, do we understand of all past primitive societies, and especially of their outcomes? Wild populations have always existed unexpected in all regions of the world ever evident in all past generations. Read all of what has been documented considered gospel, in countless various world testimonials. The 800 years long lasting, "Roman Games, held in the Dread bloody Arena," accomplished ever brag-full as written in various recorded history accounts, as can be read complete in the invincible book titled, The Martyrs!" The sojourn period was said to have annihilated any number of people who believe that wild pets such as a wild Cat in this case scenario/more possible as ermine, etc (?), are more than likely hunting-traveling along side them! ("Them..." Sasquatch, etc., by any name allowed?") What better hunting companion than say, a paranoid bob cat or blood thirsty weasel by the light of the moon, or in the complete stark darkness of a mountain cave could better hunt you down a meal? To catch a rat "The night eyes of cats are legendary, as well as in places of the South West, wild man today is sometimes called by the name, "Cat People," in direct reference as is claimed, "due to their extreme night vision ability! Even some of their eyes Don, would frighten you, as they resemble the eyes of a human cat!" Yes or not, much more is slated to be written of that eye anomaly in manuscript, The Cavern of Zakynerous!

What If?

Yeah, what if really...

"Give a thought?"

Following is a complete unfounded ever possibly much questionable conjecture equation. The sum of its suggestion is not expected to be easily accepted. As all of its plausibility rests as yet an unfounded discussion/decision, ever all up for grabs, if not completely thought to be thinking way far too distant out of the box? However all speculation was inspired of the author when on night field effort when fully realizing all extreme difficulty now ever necessary (as it all was/is), to have ever reasonably accomplish such a highly magnificent intelligent display of ongoing unexplained intricate plaiting. Beyond genius and expectations of human ability; under all circumstances, "ever all plaiting was done completely covert, under the unimaginable high stress and extreme duress of all personal gamble of unwanted detection! Collectively all total accomplishment perhaps amounting to a pseudo tribal expressive awareness if you will allow... A much physical expos-ay if any can allow that comparison? An indisputable individual expressive physical and mental tenacity display of primitive art done through difficult braiding! All of it very difficult efforts, that in every case scenario results in an ultimate personal expression of wanting compassion, possibly to be considered as a completed reverence adorned to all higher powers that be however conceivable (?), via much difficult physical and mental human/animal/horse persuasions, etc! Yes indeed, this is very strange plaiting, most discovering it thinking its completions rather useless! What, really, can be its purpose? Do any other person other than the author think it possible that there just might be direct ramification, of self-expressive sacrificial offerings being done through difficult hand craft indulgence, as if perhaps all done ever respectful of an ongoing realized or not, "abstract penitence-prayer, an acute awareness if you will," or be it a physical expose of dedication effort wanted realized? A Full Moon recognition difference done to a higher deity as perhaps a, "Moon Goddess," or what ever belief (?), via the participation evidence all obvious via the results of much useful hands!"

Ever such an expression all hopeful, as well as perhaps a personal admittance/offering of/or a tribal repentance-fetish allowance, and/or a wanting forgiveness or new recognition? Perhaps such customary plaiting ever intended/thought to had been an expectant abstract tithe payment of sorts, ever to be expressed through, "very special physical hand-mental indulgence, done in what is thought to have been a particular and special way, offered at the beginning of a, Full Moon Phase, monthly, seasonal, whenever; all plaiting done as is in believe that wild pets such as a wild Cats in this case scenario/more possible as ermine, etc (?), are more than likely hunting-traveling along side them! ("Them..." Sasquatch, etc., by any name allowed?") What better hunting companion than say, a paranoid bob cat or blood thirsty weasel by the light of the moon, or in the complete stark darkness of a mountain cave could better hunt you down a meal? To catch a rat "The night eyes of cats are legendary, as well as in places of the South West, wild man today is sometimes called by the name, "Cat People," in direct reference as is claimed, "due to their extreme night vision ability! Even some of their eyes Don, would frighten you, as they resemble the eyes of a human cat!" Yes or not, much more is slated to be written of that eye anomaly in

"What if Moon Phase and Plaiting indeed, actually has something responsive to do with an ancient primitive religion or similar? Look for a future book, The Cavern of Zakynerous!

Could it be a special offering, perhaps as a direct result of an abstract though direct relict wild populations of unwanted, Post Relict" Eurasian Humanity, at the historical time living much along side them and in parallel now all long extinct?"(Prayer Beads; Sacraments; Tithes; Denial; Confessions; Self Percussion: Omission; Compassion, Etc. "Could plaiting do you think in any way result similar? All much too abstract of course some would insist, but what else about all of this strange anomaly is not? At least think hard about any part of it as it may be one plausible answer where there seems no other?")

QQQQQ!

"All of that conjecture written so far Don, is just not possible... ?

What in the name of hell have you been drinking man? Are you smoking something or what? What exactly are you thinking Mon... ? "Rum Mon, rum... Jamaica rum Mon, if had some? As I am sure by now that if any all knowing pseudo critic intellectuals are still reading that most unintelligent will opt to wanna quickly trash this manuscript? If that be done (?), "well then, return back to your Moot Conclusions of world wide wandering night marauding Pixies, Fairies, and Goblins? Doctor, Erick Von Daniken, and even, my old friend of late, the pseudo Open Minded, anthropologist, Grover Krantz, and, Honolulu's beloved, University of Hawaii, anthropologist-investigative author, and, Haunt Radio Host, ever he was expressive/informative of all Oahu Island high Cryptic Matter, the late, "Glen Grant," ever locally famous for his many Spooky Books, and especially for his invincible, Late Night Halloween Walks, done by Moon Light, ever the participants investigating all magical "kahuna revelations" and similar "Ka-Pu," all persons now mentioned by now surely would have opt to have heard me out, and each probably likely as not would have added wanted informative if not questionable comment. I was several times guest interviewed on Glen's Honolulu Haunt Book Store location, allowed flaunted my then current book, and was ever more than fascinated and highly rewarded of the many opportune spooky stuff real life story accounts and insights then to be had of all Hawaii!"

"ALOHA!"

What but very little do any of us actually think to know to explain any part of unrealized human spooky stuff possibility and how much more indeed is still out there to discovered, lets have a look? Again, do any others reading think with me that it is at all plausible that some of this unexplained plaiting may have a direct baring associated to an all but forgotten very primitive religion? Ask the Winter Wind, if not the Moon? One Montana Ishmahachie Crow Interpretation, All of the above may be true, said Old Man Winter to The Man in the Moon! What damn fool in his right mind by any logical notion would opt to repetitiously braid the manes of horses? Why would he do this for any plausible reason? And especially if need done under frozen winter conditions and always on much uncertain terms as dim moon lit nights, and barely be able to have accomplish the highly unbelievable, almost impossible, and most incredible? We both have seen "them" do it! But Moon, as you well know, all of our, High Wind, and, Mysterious Light Mysteries, are not solved either! Earth Man it seems, just does not get it! Humans say they hate Winter, and winter is ever necessary! And as for Moon Light! We, the Indians say: "the Moon is always there for us to guides us at night when the Sun has long gone to sleep! We much honor the Sun. But the Moon need stay awake all night to guide the Sun into each new day and to show the Sun where to best warm our Earth! Our wonder of inspiration comes from the Moon. Our strength comes from the warmth of the Sun. The Great Moon-donen is our friend of compassion! When we die our spirit drifts with our "Totem" very high towards the sky far places near our wonder friend the Moon... while the Sun as you know continues to warm, and crumble our bones! Some ancient peoples worshiped the Moon as the Corn God, some still may? In New Mexico, and in places of, Arizona, near to where is, "Sedona," as you say you well understand the almost magical terrain there; there are still many possibilities of stone and fetish worship, etc. Stay simple! The Moon is simple! The sun is simple! Man is the only difficult confusing entity! The obvious is often not the most simple solution! Sometimes the obvious hides many secrets. The moon shadows never reveal all of the story of the dark night. During the day, the sun often reveals all dark happenings of a secretive night! Be aware of the moon... its reasons are beyond the imagination. Believe what you want to, but ever be kind to the animals."

Sage Concepts

That idea, all of that religious conjecture, of course needs much, much, more study and definitive positive identification! Perhaps in due time there will be found exciting conclusive answers when all moon phases are well reasoned by prominent authoritative astrologers and anthropologists, ever searching for the viable past belief of the pseudo intellect Neanderthals, ancient man, etc. Well understood today from various petroglyphic indications of cave paintings, etc., it is all evident that ancient Cro-Magnon Man highly revered the Sliver Shaped Crescent Moon Phase, that is this night all evident even as I write, January, 24th, 2012," believed by them to depict, The Ever Watching Eye of the, "Mother Goddess!" Apparently the Cro-Magnons had some idea of a pre-existence (?), or some hope for a hereafter?" Ancient deities as were believed to had been Gods and Goddesses as was, "Odin," were considered Gems from Heaven! Various animal and bird effigies, totems, Idols, etc., why not then also include the latent intellect of wild man, if indeed we rationalize that wild hominids have been with us living in parallel on earth ever since it seems the dawn of time? Why couldn't he have also well realized some sort of a primitive acceptance of a religious nature? Perhaps, and just perhaps, plaiting of horses' manes actually has something stark, real, and definite to do with a decisive unrealized reverence abrupt anything what ever possible anyone think then, or now, that opts to perceive; to actually represent one's creator?"

Log: Letter to Ray Crowe!

"Old friend, why I am writing all of this, "none of it particularly of your interest really," is because as you know there is just too much relative, reliable, and plausible evidence in pre-

history, much historical data, Biblical references allowed, etc., much, much, collective accumu-
lated information, had from all world sources, all of it much evident via viable documentation
insight. etc., "if not all of it probable proof to attest that ancient man ever lived right along
side, "true wild man," in parallel existence, as far back in time as is today accepted by science
that man had existed since the earliest beginnings! If Biologically accepted, ever beginning
with, "Genesis," all humans early on, had revered, "even if not all accepted," the stark actuality
of a, "Supreme-Being," or perhaps later recognized many when considering, "Pending Idolatry,
as is Moon, Sun, and similar described worship, etc., closely follow the pattern of the later. The
following is somewhat said from memory as you have past time written and impressed me in
your invincible, "Track Record Magazine! As you say Ray; "This is the place where intelligent
minds gather together to solve unsolvable problems with impossible answers!" - Ray Crowe

"Miss You old Buddy, like it or not! Why we tolerate the other, is because we are both always right! See you in June, when you are with Ron Roseman at Bob and Patty Reinholdt's at Sweet Home, Oregon...

More Moon Options

"As late as the 16th, and 17th, century, "Ming Dynasty, China," "Kuan Yin Goddess," or "Moon Goddess," or, "Goddess of Compassion and Mercy," She is still admired by that name, and "Her Goddess Effigy" is highly revered today when she is intricately and reverently carved from only the Finest Jade available, or the Jade that is called, "The Finest Gem Stone From Heaven!"

The Moon in Kwagiulth Tradition

"The Moon's High Regard"

In the Kwagiulth Indian nation tradition, the moon is artistically depicted carved in wood, or painted on the front of a drum; "what is the central human face surrounded by a solid rim, that represents, "The Man in the Moon!" The depiction usually combines the central face effigy adorned with a third color, that is predominately done in blue. The round-rim painting, or if a cross watching carving is made up of four separate human figures all to be seen facing each other, "From The Four Traditional Directions." Pictured is each of them holding up five fingers held up-right palm facing forward, just as if all of them were wanting to represent welcoming hands. This highly revered Traditional Kwagiulth Design is based on an Old Bella Bella Indian Style Mask effigy, that was originally painted on a hide drum that can be seen in a New York City Museum. What also is of note, is that the four human figures surrounding the Central Larger Male Figure, all of them face directly across from the other, and each of them are directly opposite of the other; this collectively represents a same exact double take of only two (Not four as looks!) persons facing that is an exact depiction of the other opposite; with the exception that two are male, and two a same female. Other words, there are two exact same male and female figures carved facing each twice, done exactly to depict a same gender face, all representation, two definite exact same pairs of two personages, that as said are two separate male and female faces, ever both painted or carved depictions of a same face facing "eye ball to eye ball" directly across from the other. Or representative of only One female, and One male face each represented twice! "Probably all wel-come hands described represent a much similar message as represents the, "Chinese Jade Carved

Moon Goddess of Compassion mentioned above," if indeed welcome in this case can be abstractly accepted to be, "Mercy First, Before Human Judgments!" Much in this is to be considered much representative of moon inspiration. The Moon Goddess representation takes on many perspectives beyond all pseudo Christian understandings and allowance. An Indian Totem Pole still to be seen in one far corner abandoned Church yard of the berg town of Lima Montana, Miraculously it still exists with authentic depictions of West Coast Fetish Adherence. It has ironically not as yet been desecrated by the neophytes! Its silent projections I intend to further investigate."

In the mythological traditions of some tribes there are believed to be existing related races of strange people that are never seen during the day; "these ugly ones come out only at night from their hidden caves and roam at night doing their mischief... These are the dread bat Indians with human bodies and bat like wings. They sleep in gloomy forests and dark outcroppings of the rock... The red man's philosophy of elemental creatures like that is often based much on an intense and often stark contact with all nature, cause and effect of such metaphysical legionary conjecture? Frightening is frightening of what ever if not the same in all peoples! What say anyone more to explain wild man, or plaiting? To have even suggested pixies, fairies, etc., borders on insanity! What has happened to all logical imagination opposed to wanton fantasy; as for example concerning all considerations of all various phases of the moon that very likely as has been touched upon may have something significant to do with it? Our world is hardly yet the Twelfth Planet Either, or AVATAR, but definitely trying to explain plaiting is an exciting side trip even if we get nowhere

A Wild Man Language?

"Ever a Possibly!"

All next is written somewhat repetitious Ray, but necessary all of it, as much more now needs explained! All of what is now being discovered done to American horses (for now!) can be best explained as said; "all has been done in my opinion by, a long mixed ancient remnant population consisting of unrealized wild feral hominids! Hardly is any of it; none of it is being done to any idiotic wild stretch of the imagination, by any sort of over looked ape-entity! There is very much story here! Some intelligent imagination, if not a reasonable belief, is all necessary to fully understand any real part of it! In one remote second hand story first time explained to me, December 2011, and ironically the same surface again, January 2012, "both depositions similarly attest/explain, an all possible, much similar wild man language, somewhat much relative to all continuing story, by two separate stable comparisons, incredibly both had heard a much same vocalization as will be described, without the other ever having at any time one conferred with the other, neither acquainted, and both attest the same exact described vocalization was heard thousands of miles apart... Texas, and Washington State! Various wild man encounters in areas near to horses attest to have heard within ear shot, (recorded on an existing private tape recorder) are heard the spoken words, best defined in sounds interpreted as, "Allote Nashoba (Wolf!), "Babosk, or, Baboska (Food?)," and, "Adena (?), (Spelling?), as well as various other words undefined ever possible to emulate remote, Oriental expressions, and/or more Native American abstract vocalizations, thought possibly more ancient, "Hidatsa-Crow," however all much corrupted if that, and/or various, "Choctaw Indian words, "that are all also of high suspect of mixed interpretation in some opinion. What this indicates is just but another of high suggestive indications that what ever unknown biped wanders undetected it surely has some sort of a meaningful language. It is here for me to write, that indeed if man like creatures with opposed nimble fingers and thumbs, by the light of the moon, or at any time are actually able to do this intricate braiding, it is not beyond the realization that they could also easily accomplish plaiting rope lengths, baskets, sleeping mats, primitive sandals, even weave primitive clothing, etc., and any number of other possibilities. If say that any of them had primitive foot wear, then they would leave no visible high suspect tracks at times of soft ground, etc. Never once however to my knowledge as yet, has any plaiting been found recently accomplished when snow Who, How, When? To attempt it would surely give away the obvious! All tracks of everything are undeniably left in snow. There just may be as of all various mixed/similar reports more than several different large and smaller examples of wild man all relative was fresh on reports more than several different large and smaller examples of wild man all relative wandering restless under "Old Moon-Donon?" the ground. To attempt it would surely give away the obvious! All tracks of everything are undeniably left in snow. There just may be Who, How, When? as of all various mixed/similar reports more than several different large and smaller examples of wild man all relative wandering restless under "Old Moon-Donon?" as of all various mixed/similar reports more than several different large and smaller examples of wild man all relative wandering restless under "Old Moon-Donon?" the ground. To attempt it would surely give away the obvious! All tracks of everything are undeniably left in snow. There just may be Who, How, When?

Wow Don, Come On!

"Hey Critics!"

"If by now anyone reads completely in awe, still in disbelief of wild man by any name; well if So, you are far Short of having extensive reasoning and common Sense. Both are actually wonderful gifts awarded us from experience and the intellect! Not what done it Charley? But rather how done it, and what are the useful reasons why?" It is obvious, that no man as we think to know ourselves could accomplish a similar plaited mane! You couldn't do it, I can't do it, and so far neither can anyone else that has claimed to have tried! Thus far top experts at braiding as Becky Butello, Washington State have tried it to no avail. None person so far has even one small clue to the extreme difficulty! Especially this would prove next to impossible in cold weather. Last week when "Norma Jenson" called me reporting the plaiting, the night temperature was plus 33 degrees Fahrenheit! Again the high question? What is the purpose of the plaiting? Answer that, and we have many answers! Thus far, zilch, nada, tilt?"

Australia & The Southern Cross

Perhaps even when we have finished all comparisons to be had over North America, we should next access all world wide hominid intellect! So far the humor of tenacity and the considered intellect of wild man is much to be noted here if not further explained. In this particular case scenario of plaiting, dexterity, etc., all intellect of them seems much more than just simple, uncanny, elusive, clever, inventive, ever all is incredible if not much admirable!

"Down Under, to...

The Vast, Never-Never Land, Out Back, of all Australia, where hopefully future I intend to re-confirm my Moon Theories by needed contact with my extraordinary investigative, "Good-on-ya Mate, Yowie guide, and nonsense mate, David Jennings," find, "Terry Roscoe, Phil O' Meley," and perhaps bonfire cook with them over prawns on the barbie, somewhere within the Vast 'Phillaga Scrub Forest Ranch Lands, and do it also with, "Tony Healy, David Nimbin," and an invincible exploring man that is at least two parts Yowie, "Paul Compton." Just perhaps maybe year 2013, or sometime soon or about then, we can have another "hard look see" at the mixed kangaroo and Australian horse populations just in case any importance has been Skipped Over or had their hair plaited in Southern Moon Light Abrupt Northern Confusions?"

"The Obvious"

"Oriental Considerations! And the overlooked

possibility of the obvious!"

"The Wild West Remaining That Is The Wild Man's Best Abode!"

(Montana/Idaho/Nevada/Oregon/Washington Utah/Wyoming, etc.)

"Let's just call it the far west! All of the above area mentioned, and all further West, North, South, and East, and beyond of where ever else conclusive evidence has been found? Of course to many urban Americans many, many, Western States remain completely oblivious to all understandings. Many persons will never travel over them extensively enough to at all understand the vast now remaining over looked wild country; the character of the local inhabitants, and especially all of its vast semi-domestic, wild, and even feral animal population on the rise exemplified by feral pigs, loosed serpents, etc. What possibly can any of all of that have to do with the strange plaiting being done to horses?

Well, after much study, and many, many, arduous miles accomplished to looking for plausible answers to how, why, when, and what over looked anomaly just might be the reasons for all of the strange unexplained plaiting of horses' manes? It had only recently dawned on me that predominately it was obvious that the bulk of repetitious Wild Man Sightings was being reported within a much close proximity of exactly where ever much plaiting going on! Anywhere where is to be found many opportune domestic animals, range cattle, milk cow's, goats, sheep, and horses! I had long ago miscued by not having prior realized this; And Especially So was Another Most Obvious fact overlooked; Right There in Plain Sight in front of my anxious scissors busy cutting off the Braided Mane Samples from off the "Oregon Hinck Ranch Horses," the abundant food was the most likely the good reason for all of this high strange plaiting being done! Wild man simply needs to eat and so remains in the area! In other words, Anywhere At All where is to be found much abundant food within any given ranch and or farm land, where there is highly much predominate animal protein to be had from all various farm stock as, snatched small animals as pets, rabbits, pigeons, cow, and of course Much Horse Mare's Milk long known as kumiss!

"What the Hell, Tell It Like It Is!"

The mega number of persons besides the author that actually has believed wild man of any sort could actually be suckling milk protean from wild and domestic horses besides myself includes, the late Neil Hinck, Tonia Brown, and, Marion Monroe. Bob, and Patty Reinholdt, Becky Butello, Norma, Debby, and Brenda, Hinck, Phil, and Norma Jenson, Paul Wright, Var Harris, Bear Ken Iddins, "Red", Sherrie Stallman, etc. The list goes on and on, and for what it is all worth, four in number local Montana cowboys are continuing in firm belief while in complete awe of my support! I have found persons within the confines of the pseudo remaining, "Wild West," that have repeatedly accomplished suckling mares milk from the teats of horses held within their corral! All participants say that the horses don't seem to mind their efforts, and some of them in fact might welcome-encourage the close association? The kismess milk is said mild, sweet, delicious, and some intend to continue the pursuit. Now what anyone think of that? Drinking horse milk has been an accomplished custom and tradition over all Mountain Steppe Eurasia since the dawn of Earliest Man! "Yeah, we know all idiot critic... Milk comes from the grocer; and chocolate milk comes from brown cows!"

"What Proof?"

"Proof of What? Horse Milk? Estrus milk? Where? Mares milk is found repetitious Mixed In Within The Tightest Examples of Braiding being done of the Manes! Among my very best extracted plaited mane samples, are some obvious visible hard dried milk evidence; (That is left behind mares milk!), that were put there "however done," by some type of nimble fingers when the plaiting of the hair was being accomplished! And who or what do any think is holding the horse still and content while braiding the mane, while one accomplice or more perhaps drinks his turn at the milk? Not at all that hard to believe is going on! "What's difficult to understand is exactly how any wild anything could easily bond' with any horse enough to have it cooperate? What power of control? What logic? Well, just consider what is purposed next when considering mind power opposed to favored telepathy? Before we go into pseudo telepathy, "probably little considered is the geographical fact that all or most of high steppe China, Russia, Tibet, Mongolia, etc., most of all wilderness Eurasia, mountain desert steppe, etc., all of this mystical land when considered, is almost or exactly much the same to description in high Mt. elevation, prototype terrain, endless river ecosystems, urban and semi-primitive life styles possible, etc., as has much of the expectations and ranch world conditions found over much of the vast American West. "Wild man populations there and here seem to require a much similar like world of survival activity. Plentiful urban and wild food varieties including and range stock is exactly where best exists wild man. I'm sorry but today's farm and ranch lands are a literal utopia for an extended food chain than ever before in world history, and if any have an educated look, close adjacent to most all sightings and close encounters is not all that far distant from cultivated or natural good tucker!" Phil Jenson, at the Nyssia Oregon Ranch, 2011, explained to me that over the span of five years, 1995 –2000, "he estimated lost, or unexplained, approximately fifty lamb-sheep, goats per year, and only a few could be evidenced had been taken by coyotes, etc. only recently fall 2011, Phil lost two more of his most prized goat lambs, without even one suspect trace of how or when? The reason why is obvious. Its long been believed over Eurasia that suspect wild man populations prefer the young of goats and sheep. Easy prey, easy to transport, impossibly good tucker are sheep and goats when eaten hot and directly right from off the Bar-A-Be Mate, as is well established in all places of vast

Out-Back Australia where mutton prevails when comparing the all alleged Yowie to our pseudo American Sasquatch!"

"Australia's Aust'y Mates!"

"Might see you another time when Down Under in the Pilliga Scrub, 2013, or in a near future guide, David Jennings, as the critics here are about to self-destruct, and or belch blather to throw out much of this thought illogical conjecture! Its the pity that So Many, many, of these bias Yanks, are so damn much naive! Its much just as if it has been written in out dated text's exactly what will, and or will not be accepted to be believed according to popular pier rubbish!" Barbecue "No" shrimps on the Barbie for the "Unbelievers," and many large Prawn's for all of the rest of the best! All of that regardless is Good Tucker Mate... "Good on Ya David Jennings!" "Stand under The Southern Cross while anxiously waiting for me to soon be planning to be sending you another wild something!"

"The Chinese, Mind Power?"

"Shen"

"The Chinese word for, Mind Power! Hardly it is considered telepathy either, when considering all of the innate influence of the in tune spirit, all human reflection, determined passion, and all learned horse sense possibility. Horses aren't for everyone; and all people are not a-kin to horses! The Velcro has his special talent, the sailor has his boatswain bird logic, grog, salt pork, and sea biscuit, "while the night wind ever keeps many hidden secrets close-net and under the dim-light night stars including the high strange mystery accomplished of the plaiting being done of world horses! What more can be said of this obvious mind power? The wild, Dub-Tu Monks of Bhutan, claim to perhaps realize animal mind associations with man mind-set the best? Something very powerful, "little known," that is as if "magical," actually controls and accomplishes to be tending their Asian pack animals...Believe it or not, animal and man under abstract and controlled conditions, can combine efforts beyond all supposed telepathy!"

"THE INVISIBLE CHINESE!"

Posted message, "Joss House," China Town Winnemucca Nevada, 1881:

"The Gods can fully manifest their strength and ability through the spirit even to the most distant places..."

"The wisdom and knowledge of the Gods far exceed what man know!"

("Perhaps all above a compared passion that is ever there for allowed for only you or a chosen effort?")

"As above said, was posted on the wall of the historical, "Chinese Joss House," center of, "China Town, Winnemucca, Nevada 1881," population then at "400," with few women. All gone by 1955."

316

("The meaningful plaque can be read on the second floor wall of the "Humboldt County Museum at "Winnemucca, Nevada." The two plaques had remained for many years on the second floor catching dust, until at my prodding, finally all message had been deciphered by "Grey-Ling the Cat" from China") Other ancient obscure Chinese artifacts have been discovered found and overlooked from the Nevada territory.")

Much high strange and of anthropological importance thought out of the box has long been over looked over the vastness of all high desert America. It is time that we allowed at least one viable part of it, as in my opinion if the truth of particular muted discoveries were allowed public, much truth would already have been allowed surfaced! Check out the captive Nevada Desert Mustangs for yourself...Some many will be discovered to have the strange plaiting! How who done it? Yeah, how?"

"Shen?"

"Mind power as is here being considered sited in order to be able to fully determine all possibility abrupt from all earnest Night Stalker's discoveries as myself, ever fully welcome any intelligent open minded critic opinion, as it is in this particular high strange plaiting equation; we may all like it or not soon require applause each others full intuitive suggestion! If mind power is not telepathic, then how can we ever think to explain it? Perhaps there are multiple clues in the Chinese Sage Words above, "strength, ability, and spirit? However I do not think to even come close to define it beyond my separate personal intuition. The spirit of unrestricted genius is all relative to wild fools; and all fools are often the direct relatives of spirited geniuses, etc. Several places in the manuscript I may try another time to add rational to all of what follows?"

"Spirit"

"What think we ops to explain in laymen terms One's Spirit? The human spirit! A spirit? Not everyone's spirit of mind unto human and animal interaction is exactly the same! Makes one think doesn't it? What spirit refers and comprises the support association to the Xmas Spirit! One's spirit! Or, the spirit of Saint Lewis, etc? Perhaps there is something all relative in even that Xmas, city, and human, spirit consideration? "IF," say, an animal as is a horse were to feel from a humanistic personage, any person, a stranger, or an accustomed thing recognized, or, unrecognized; anything of a realized closeness, "a oneness of spirit," a shadow indication from a well recognized past allowed comradely, and / or a particular pleasure, a feeling of security, or even a similar surprise acceptance, as is abrupt possible whenever one for example enjoys the brushing of one's hair; an affectionate arm around the shoulder; the feeling of unconditional closeness, expecting trustful expectations; the feeling and spirit appreciation of perhaps prayer, or a reprieve answered in the manifested support spirit of an honorable past pride; or the presence of all high spirited the spirit of man or beast. Trouble is, we can't all compromise, or dictate one to the other all of the strength of genius and success, wild or constrained spirit response; nothing founded is written expectations; as is in and the power within the spirit to insure one's future through caution and preparedness; the emotional concepts of one's soul, the desire to know and learn more, the high complacency of consolation, call it a spirit that is in the full trust of another; the spirit of adventure, or the spirit determination to want to conquer the unknown! What exactly admits a spirited horse? What abject really is explained a low spirited animal? The spirit of unrestricted genius is all relative to wild

317

fools; and all fools are often the direct relatives of an spirited adjournments, etc. Several places in the manuscript I may try another time to add rational to all of what follows?"

Us! We are all fools to think we understand everything wild spirited, or to be able in every case to easily explain the spirit of man or beast. Trouble is, we can't all compromise, or dictate one to the other all of the strength of genius and success, wild or constrained spirit response; nothing founded is written on the wind! There is always the new spirit of adventure. Try to imagine the actual ability eminent to be able to braid any untethered horse mane by the dark of the moon on a wind blown night! To say that he Devil made them do it is as worthless as the long tails on a lawyers jacket!" us! We are all fools to think we understand everything wild spirited, or to be able in every case to easily explain the spirit of man or beast. Trouble is, we can't all compromise, or dictate one to the other all of the strength of genius and success, wild or constrained spirit response; nothing founded is written expectations; as is in and the power within the spirit to insure one's future through caution and preparedness; the emotional concepts of one's soul, the desire to know and learn more, the high complacency of consolation, call it a spirit that is in the full trust of another; the spirit of adventure, or the spirit determination to want to conquer the unknown! What exactly admits a spirited horse? What abject really is explained a low spirited animal? The spirit of unrestricted genius is all relative to wild fools; and all fools are often the direct relatives of an spirited adjournments, etc. Several places in the manuscript I may try another time to add rational to all of what follows?"

On the wind!

There is always the new spirit of adventure. Try to imagine the actual ability eminent to be able to braid any untethered horse mane by the dark of the moon on a wind blown night! To say that he Devil made them do it is as worthless as the long tails on a lawyers jacket!" on the wind! There is always the new spirit of adventure. Try to imagine the actual ability eminent to be able to braid any untethered horse mane by the dark of the moon on a wind blown night! To say that he Devil made them do it is as worthless as the long tails on a lawyers jacket!"

Log: Deposition!

Becky Butello, Puyallup, Washington!
"Don, WE Have More Than Forty Hair Braids!"

"All of this just does not make sense or seem possible! I realize that you are a life long impossible romantic dreamer, and a self-funded unlikely adventurer, but this stuff is all far beyond anyone's wildest dreams! Anyone can criticize what's here, but any negative opinion will not change the truth! I'd really like to go with you to visit that Hinck property! There has got to be something very strange going on there?"

Deposition:

December 12, 2011. "Becky Butello, Puyallup WA."

"Don, I tried and tried very hard to duplicate those braids in any way, and I just could not do it even when a standing still in a warm room right along side of the hair sample model we had *with the horse main and all. I could never had braided all of that stuff like that so tight, so small, and so intricate! I tried several times for several days... I did it for hours at a time by day light in my home, and I just could not do any of it like that or even unsimilar! The dexterity required to do all of that tight uniform plaiting is beyond the imagination to have accomplish it. It would take the tiny-est and nimblest of fingers to do it, fingers much, purpose? What ever done it was very adapt and strong! Much care was intended to braid each of those manes...and they are all done so even! To even separate the plaits, most anyone would need to cut them apart! You much, more able than mine! Wow Don, all of this stuff is incredible! No wind could ever be doing all of this! Anyone believing any thing like that is just not looking! As you well know the wind can tangle a horse's mane to be unmanageable, but it could never do something like that! I have seen some of your more recent pictured samples; and you have sent me about forty so far, and all of them are awesome! The ability to even hold the crossed hair braids in place as tight as they are to do the plaiting would take someone of considerable strength, and with much determination! What ever, how ever it all has been done, it is almost beyond the human strength and endurance, and for what just can't easily separate them! I just can't believe all of this! Every braid is beyond incredible!"*

"IS THERE A CHINESE CONNECTION TO WILD MAN?"

"In my opinion, yes, there is a definite Asian/Chinese entity wild man connection possibly through the blood lines of the fabled Yeron, Yeti, Snow-man, Alma, etc... All ancient Eurasia-China, Tibet, Mongolia, Bhutan, considered, etc. in my belief is where they originated, as there is considerable thought circumstantial artifact, vocalization, evidence much relative to all world physical examples abrupt American hominids (?), especially this writes probable since the viable research-discoveries of, Gavin Menzies, in his incredible research continuing documentary books as is, "1421, The Year That The Chinese Discovered America, and 1405! Yeron as Yeti, Alma as man, and documented, Russian Zanna, and her son Kuwitt, Bluff Creek California Patty, The Wisconsin Ice Man, etc., are but just a few of the obscure remnant entities of a possible type brought early to America as a labor force, etc?" It is highly possible the "Wisconsin Ice Man, and Bluff Creek California Patty," were direct relatives of what is explained above. In time perhaps through DNA, conjecture, proven fact, etc., "all of it for now but muted deceptions," the inevitable will be shouted from the roof tops! That not most likely happen either, "as what for example what should be expected of the law, etc., as seems to had been over looked in 1968 when had been realized the massacre case of, "The Wisconsin Ice Man," all of that to be much further explained of his human side (but not all story complete) in a short paragraph below... "Wouldn't you think if, The Ice Man, Patty, or anything/anyone even wild and uncivilized believed high suspected of being human, especially when was known to had been shot and killed would requisition a follow-up police investigation? Much, much, indeed, is yet left on the Human Side of the Sasquatch Plait to further be digested by earnest academics and all concerned! Are we all to be remembered as perhaps unconcerned compliant extensions of, "Fiddlers on the Roof," where is the justice?"

"Why would any doubt that there to fact could be a humanistic Chinese Wild Man as Yeron or much similar; a living connection to wild man all historical as mentioned above? For over thirty years I have believe and written that anciently wild humanistic entities as Sasquatch from Asia as suggested had likely sailed to North America with the earliest possible World Circumventing Orientals as were ever the Invincible navigating Chinese long before the Ming Dynasty 1405 -07, and/or even much prior than the navigating little realized Eurasian European horde that had sailed with them far, far, ahead of the Notable Icelandic Raiders (All Vikings, etc.) that had had in essence been late comers to had reached main land America, and likely when the Chinese did arrive they brought with them what is today refereed to as, wild man *Sasquatch*, likely all much relative of Alma, Yeron, Yeti, Yowie, etc. Ancient customs, religions, totems, and fetish-ed traditions much sailed with them. What do any think to understand of the traditional dragon like heads proceeding the Norse Adventures on their Viking Ships? And early on as I am suggesting wild man was brought with them if for no other reason as working slaves. Ever American wild man are in my opinion, our Asian Sasquatch equivalent…as I firmly believe explains them; that will be found in time, that at least a notable percent of all *Sasquatch* blood is from all mixed captured Asian hominid blood lines. There is way too much of that Possible Theory Here, and not this the place to continue it, but even as I write tonight, December 22nd, 2011; approximately two weeks prior, or about that time period, Adamant-viable-Rumors" within the Pseudo Informed Academic Bigfoot Community, "would have it believed, that recent DNA tested flesh, said taken from an alleged Wild Juvenile Sasquatch and its Mother, has positive test results, Claiming, Mother Human, and its Father as yet undecided! What make of that? O' course this for now non but a rumored alert, but I have no doubt that in time similar or more resolute may result. For some reason everything within the au-thoritative Bigfoot community found positive, ever results negative! Ever reasoned why?"

"The Wisconsin Ice Man, 1968!"

"Bluff Creek Patty Sasquatch 1967?"

"Wow, I find all of the above extremely interesting if not exciting, just as Ivan T. Sanderson wrote much stark over looked information of The Wisconsin Ice Man in May 1968 issue of, "AR-GOSY" magazine, in reference of him human after having further investigated all Ice Man-human possibility! Paraphrased next verbatim as best as can: Sanderson - "This body under ice, The Ice Man, is definitely human! It was shot through the back of the head, and both eyes were blown loose from the entry of the large caliber bullet! The body had been alive within the last five years…

(Continued below…)

The Ice Man & Bluff Creek Patty Sasquatch!

"Think about it! Ice Man, 1968, minus five years, "year, 1963 -1964," and/or includes claims of, Patty Sasquatch, "1967," the last considered date and year, "1967," was the alleged exact dis-covery date of, "Bluff Creek California Patty Sasquatch hominid!" Patty was an obscure Sasquatch alleged discovered single handed by, "Roger Patterson/Bob Gimlin, and she was never to be seen again! Does it seem ironic, that just shortly after that discovery date, that in year, 1968, The Minne-sota Ice Child, if could be called that (as will next be explained), had also walked out into the world and next also fast vanished into Canadian History Oblivion, or where ever it may still be frozen on ice today? What say anyone more able to explain all of this possibly forgotten anom-aly?"

320

(Continued from above)

A last excerpt part taken from the 1968 deposition of Ivan T. Sanderson: ...and the Ice Man he said, "indeed may not be a fully grown adult specimen, and so instead, should perhaps be called, "The Wisconsin Ice Child?"(Where is this missing "Ice Child" today? Just perhaps we unknowingly have over looked by complacency at least one clue left long behind closed doors year 2007?) Yeti, - Alma, - Yeron, - Snow - Men, - Sasquatch - Etc.

"Bigfoot FROM the frozen wild lands of all CHINA-AISA," and there are a great many!" Your casts Don, are just to much human to be Sasquatch!" There were even suggestions flaunted 2004 and probably since over the Net by Pseudo Authorities that I was faking my plaster casts by using the damaged fingers and cropped-thumb of my left hand! Many of my more than incredible much varied hand casts evidence broken or frozen-off fingers, frost damaged broken toes, and or damaged body parts in including on prize evidencing a broken fore arm and wrist. I suppose the ironic fact of my damaged hand through accident had led idiotic bias critics into a rage of discovery oblivion! Late year 2004, shortly after the Bigfoot seminar held at Bellingham Washington, with the internet help of M.K. Davis: I had Davis carefully post a good photograph flaunting well cast evidence of my entire my hand destruction. I did this in an effort to rebuttal all continuing flack past and future; but in spite of that, the result was concave, as the harmful opinion had already been cast in stone...I was not to be believed! The horses' Asses have Prevailed! The public is stuck with programmed academic allowance of exactly what, when, and who if anyone other than them are allowed to make a possible new and contrary discovery, etc. As if it is, that the popular opinionated academics are allowed to decide among all peers, who will be allowed to announce their genius! Next they dictate all fraud and fact to the ever b lay persons will continue to want to believe.

The pity of it all is, that the needed truth often remains under covers many years behind, or it is never to be realized. Time apart from misled importance can result everything stultified, stagnated, obliterated, mavericks strangled! February 7, 2012 M.K. Davis and I posted online images of some of the most controversial castings with our broadcast of the world wide talk radio show www.artisfirst.com for anyone to appreciate. As luck would have it, that night we had a record breaking 135,000 listeners! What was revealed by the casts I still hope to have reviewed by intelligent academic opinion from Other Than Only I.S.U! The show is only one hour long. To fully explain all high strange anomalies was not covered. What is there I am sure as were others viewing much more than was expected. To fully appreciate each of them; by close examination, anyone half intelligent can easily determine that the hands in question are each one un-similar, dissimilar, each a paradox to the other, and all collectively represent several possible descriptive hominids all living in parallel-harmony in a same cave environment! Case in point, "there just may be Don, more than several, if not four different descriptions of wild man Sasquatch? When I write all books of the slated, "Sasquatch Trilogy," my name Ron Roseman, Becky Butello, Bob and Patty Reinholdt, and many others of my personal admiration for them, Will Really be Mud!" As said, Perhaps there are four separate relative kinds of relict Sasquatch ("wild feral hominids") roaming over North America?

Ever since my first cast taken on Mt. Harrison, Idaho fall, 1980, and all further evidence continuing to date with mega more casts and artifacts discovered, including all ongoing and event recent oral confirmations of existing wild populations had opinion divulged by indigenous peoples, I continue in high suspects that definitely there is as yet an unfounded Oriental Connection I hope future to explain/prove of at least a base part of all historical and theoretic importance in regard of the continuation-and future protection of American Sasquatch. My early manuscripts 2001-2003, prior, and to date here, only partly explaining some of this; that in my opinion, Sasquatch by what ever the name, had for one Originated in North America as an Oriental base example of Wild Human Yeti Snow Man Type, ("The Abominable Snow Man, all another story if relative?") and/or much similar, and are very likely by now where existing as a mutated miss/match gene pool into more than several peculiar identities! This notion "up" from all high suspect evidence had from particular ongoing physical descriptions to include frozen winter lands extending over many wild reaches of all high desert America! Some many of them smaller; many believe-described adults, are said to be much, much, less than are the gigantic species, as is the typical prototype usually ascribed by some many to exist in the Pacific North West. Not so, as there are also very large, probably only a few very huge Sasquatch wandering over places of wilderness Idaho and Montana. And if any can/will can believe it or not, from past and current witnessed vocalizations, often as not have been described/heard (Word indemnifications!) spoken sounds to likely attest a part corrupt language of mixed Asian with semi-defined much supposed Native American indications!

"And Yes, Var Harris, that is more truth, and yes, blathering academics, and all stammering bug-eyed couch potato critics... I have myself been fortunate to have heard some of what has been described myself! As said, in my opinion from casts and other fresh evidence taken from a variety of distant locations, there is probably perhaps at least four or more separate Sasquatch representative examples, all related however in a much mixed varied all finely proving different DNA gene pools, if that can be had future to completely confirm them? All of that theory not here the space or place to further discuss it, but all of it is believed to be of relative importance to help explain all strange horse plaiting being done via the stark and undeniable fact of high Sasquatch intelligence... From endless comparative reports and many credible depositions, etc., I am especially firm in that theoretic consideration, "as well as much influenced by what has been had from all continuing incredible exploring crew interactions with a small population of cave dwelling hominids! Very much , much, more of this adventure all explained ahead in other up-coming Trilogy manuscripts. (Descriptions and photos of casts taken, artifacts discovered, vocalizations witnessed, fresh evidence encountered, etc., all of that and much more of unsuspected important has often been completely over looked when if only all had been discovered by proficient/resourceful mavericks unheralded by perhaps envious professionals?

For some long time I have been much roosted for my stark insistence that wild man Sasquatch was human, and that he also was not in any remote way related to any of the extinct great apes! My incredible plaster casts taken from North West Desert Cave Locations were even used/explained via Tongue in Cheek blatherings by particular bias academics as early as 2001! My casts were said then by I. S. U. associate professor Jeffery Meldrum to be nothing more than mere fakes of humans...! Yeah Don, all of them are incredible! But I am sorry, all of your casts as good as they are, are all of them just to much human to be sort of a true Sasquatch, etc! 2012, is not over, or is 2020! I may be around "that long" to watch all bitch and male dog fights? What ever that so, or no, believe me, it is definitely wild feral man by what ever name he is yet to be concluded that is plaiting the hair manes of North American horses!"

Back To School?

Meldrum's academic disapproval-disappointment said publicly 2004 to front row peers and spectators at Bellingham, Washington, was exactly what I had ever wanted to hear! I had long realized the general popular assumption then that Sasquatch was none other than a hold over thought to be long extinct great ape of some kind such as, Gigantopithecus! Nothing in my options for the past thirty years was further from the truth! By the year 2001, when first meeting Meldrum in his lab at Idaho State University, Pocatello, I for a time actually thought that we were on friendly terms, and later when him explaining to me the acclaimed Skookum Cast, and was further from the truth when later bringing him a more than incredible actual Juvenile Sasquatch Ass Cast, early year 2004; the casting had from a sandy body length dug sleeping hole found with others deep within an Idaho cave. (It was more than incredible, can anyone imagine? The complete story related in slated Trilogy book, The Cavern of Zakynerous) Meldrum had to say about the cast: "Don, this is truly incredible! Yes, it much looks to be the real thing! I have never seen anything like it! Where did you get it? It is probably the only one of its kind?" And shortly after that, during the same spring some weeks before the Bellingham Conference,

I took to his lab for his opinion "a truly strange flesh and bone artifact," that to this day February 2012, still remains undecided for certain in mixed opinion and remains much controversial (!), and sadly now the strange evidence rests Miss-Placed somewhere (?) swept some untold under the dark rugs of Who ever is the academic or researcher who knows for sure Where in the hell it is hidden, Why being kept, and When, or "If" I will ever get it back? The politics of the Bigfoot community does not include the author. All that I want to know is...

Where is the Hand of Unknown Origin Now?

That's A Good Question!

"It will surface! And if not badly harmed, may match others? Maybe that is the reason for its disappearance!"("?") This difficulty of the lost hand is completely due to my own Naive Nature, fool-hearty Negligence, poor judge of character, and earnest desire to have had the artifact officially appraised, etc., comprising going on 10 long confusing Years of, Good Old Buddy Comradely Allowance, abrupt all "Bloody Bastard Pirate Sad-Set Pseudo Bigfooters," along with few high Narcissistic Ego-Maniacs leading the pack with ever a Moot big Mouth! The documented hand of unknown origin among lay critics and interested academics has become known by the name -title: (given it by the late Tom Biscardi), officially as, The Hand of Unknown Origin? Initially I had a Contract Agreement with Tom, believed being able to retrieve the Hand upon Request, but that has all somehow also gone By the Way-Side? Legal formations in future may become necessary to rite the problem? The hand aired (Long term posted!) over Internet Radio for several years running since 2004, and it still may be seen by assessments of the shows archives? If interested search up the Tom Biscardi Internet Radio Show archives*,. and have a good look! And remember, Just as Ray Crowe Cautions, always Keep on Your SKEPTICALS whenever reading anything read in The Track Record, realized said contrary to intentions, or appears to be too good to be true, concave, converse, and/or stems from All suspect Cross

---

* The link www.tombiscardi.internetradioshow.com appears not to be active at the time of this publication, but the reader could search for renewed availability.

Eyed Opinion!

Tom got the hand from me fall 2004, posted my credit very small case, the hand became one important visual leader of his show presentations, and since then Thank-You, the flesh and bone artifact has vanished from my recovery! August 2011, Tom informed me that he was "onto the problem," and was incorrigible that "We/He" would get If back! (Q?) If the hand has not some stark importance to do with hominid considerations, then what is the good or bad reason for all of the delay in its return? Last told by third hand informants was, that the strange anomaly was being kept locked-up in the Lab of Melba Kitchen (?), who ever, or, what ever she has anything to do with anything? I can't even get her to answer her lab phone? Perhaps in time, and just perhaps not, we can realize much more from the hand? For now, all of The Rest of That Story needs be on kept on hold with the author... As I have cautiously kept covert a few little known possible plausible facts surrounding all high suspects of its unfounded importance. Its end discovery truth will probably need go to my grave with several other incredible discoveries (All as much...) equally of a highly skeptical nature, etc... Is of unfounded importance the correct word for Deliberate Caution M.K. Davis, or what can be said better? We each well understand the blatant nature of most all know it all humanity! As I have said, when first conferred with Meldrum I had thought to had been on friendly terms. I was excited at that time having unexpectedly only recently made many new, ongoing, and exhilarating puzzling discoveries within Idaho/Montana mountain desert caves. I had even offered that Jeff opt to join my venture; explore with me. I had then much respect for his anatomical expertise. My advice since has become, have no mentor except one's self! Learn to criticize only the true importance of what little you can prove. When we are gone our secrets go with us! Wild man is no secret as, I know Damn Well that they Exist!

Log: Today Was No One's Day in The Sun!

(Bellingham Washington, 2004)

Regardless of any future generated repercussions ahead, on that day 2004, at the Bellingam Symposium I held on to my guns! Wild Man what ever it turns out to be definitely is human! By then I had only seen one viable example of a feral hominid at a distance of perhaps 100 yards, fall season, year 1982, while climbing with my late wife, Marion Monroe near top most summit of Mt. Index Washington, where today comprises the off bounds Seattle water shed. I had not taken but two plaster casts prior to that time, one in Idaho on Mt. Harrison, and another near the Idaho border of Utah, near where today on the road map is, Devil Lake, an interesting namesake for an area where suspect wild men of yesteryear were said to had been especially numerous? The plaster casts being examined that day by Meldrum and his coverts at Bellingham, were indeed un-similar in some respects to many of the ones then on display tables had by the public. And so naturally I took a good look at the casts, and many of them of note actually did to me also look abstractly very much human. Note: the casts that I had allowed Meldrum were not any of them said either to had been bogus casts of flat wooden foot floppers as are often my high suspect of some many others sometimes allowed. No names mentioned here, as I am not of that Ilk... But Some Much of Pure B. S. wanted us believed today, has me much proud to be realized eccentric! True, a few good men, and a few truly discovered Wilder Man Tracks, all flouted without restrictions to what is allowed conclusive, and what is not! With that, we have a win-win situation! To date Sasquatch has not walked out on to the stage for anyone's close inspection with the exception of, The Wisconsin Ice Child, and, Bluff

Creek Patty Sasquatch! Where really aside from I. S. U. is all of the authoritative opinion? Send in the clowns, we got em every kind! There are a great many in and out of the Bigfoot community!"

"The truth, is the truth, is the truth, like it or not!"

But as a result of all wrongful opinion in my now Closed Case Scenario Sojourn, and much future similar discredit of myself and others unjust for their efforts, all ridicule still to this day comes back to haunt all of us On Both Sides of the Coin with the complete irregularity of noticeable and rude avoidance of person. This is a complete fallacy regardless of personality differences, as very much can be learned even from the gravest of human errors! Aren't we all – ALL sometimes guilty of occasional unintended misinterpretation... True Bigfoot exploration is far, far, beyond the popular entertainment nonsense allowance of Hollywood movie, Harry & The Hendersons!"

In Zakynerous Cave!

Horses were often semi-wild wandering the open range lands of Idaho and Montana, and easily to be seen within eye sight of particular feral hominid discovery cave sites... Long before my first realization of horse plaiting I had wondered if indeed wild populations had a working relationship of any kind for any reason with the loosed domestic stock. Ever so many range animals are unaccounted for during all fall and spring round-ups! What we were experiencing in various caves was actually the left evidence of unsuspected wild feral humanoids, or, hominids much relevant in many ways and the needs of present day Homo-sapiens, at least this so in the case of food high in animal protein. First time discovered by us was the evidence of them residing at least part time during coldest winter the deep confines of particular hospitable caves. This claim has raised not a few negative eye brows, on as many a naive critic, hardly any of them either truly covert fellows, ever adamant, if not purposeful, that my reputation and all crew as well be forever squelched as viable investigators simply because of my thought moot, unproven, speculative conjecture theories, thought all of them to be illogical assumptions, or similar of that in broadcast academic opinion. Even had been expressed harmfully behind my back were words to the effect that my crews had exaggerated our discoveries, made bogus castings, etc! However this documentation be written as ragged as it is, it is still believed to be the best Logical Theory to be had of the moment of None Existing Better Solutions? Perhaps very soon, much, more will be found to better explain all things even not written here that will write more logical if not all conclusive! As I understand, with me separately in this effort writes highly acclaimed Sasquatch investigator and author, Bobbie Short, and Ray Crowe, and likely write several others? There is very much here to consider.

Mega Mysteries!

Definitions of Shen. The horse named Hink! Hominid/human telepathy versus creature/human common Sense and all obvious discernment interaction response. Animist and human mimicking of birds, animals, and man. Eye color of the wild man retina much distinctive and all separate in its hominid pupal irregularity? The peculiar outcome of hominid and combined horse sense! The bias Void of Human Critic Common Sense via misunderstanding himself and Hominid

325

Intentions, and most horses collectively. The ability of anything, or anyone to accomplish walking any considerable distance completely backwards, day or night, and ever able to do this in a purposeful and much deceptive straight-line... (Reverse track-way natural deceptive walking; heal ahead backwards first, "rather than toe ahead, and be able to go to any place desired where it appears that it had just Traveled From, instead of having Gone Forward To (?), instead of having just waked backwards from a place, where it actually had just walked backwards from! (Walked deceptive backwards!) And to expect to do this often as a matter of necessity quite naturally, as is required abrupt all wilderness obstacles, sticks, rocks and boulders, down timber, etc., all mentioned (and even more endless obstructions possible!) able to avoid mishap and injury when Being in Pursuit from encroaching Humanity, all necessary accomplished from only the use of One's Instinctive Intelligent Memory, and after only just One Single Eye to ground eye Glance! Humans as we allow ourselves cannot walk haphazardly, or purposely, "Quick, Quick (!)," to any place far ahead and meaningful to anywhere! This last could have been written first, and all first above could have been written last? Either way we much need to have another look into the physical and mental workings and extended possibilities of Shen. In Shen study here we are not in any way assessing illogical telepathy, As That as a Subject is all quite another unsolved issue I wish not to b e involved, however I do believe that Most All of us have some of this Natural Ability up from our latent recall, but without more study in its regard to Sasquatch field interactions with man, I have observed nothing of it, know nothing of it to compare, however there will be touched upon ahead at the conclusion of the book some very striking all new considerations, and all new expectations future unto much unorthodox, if not far beyond the expected and uncanny, hominid to wild and domestic animal sort of interactions! Our first interest here remember, is to be able to pseudo explain a new theory of the reasons for the plaiting of horses.

Beyond the wildest imagination...

There is much, much, more yet to be explained that I cannot!

That I can do any justice at all to more explain my separate theories, depends much upon the readers imaginative and comparative ability, an his determination to thoroughly explore with me the highly improbable, the exhilarating, and/or if not ever thought impossible? We are launched 2012, into, A New Awesome Age of The Thought Unthinkable!

The clever and invincible author, Lloyd Pye, writes, paraphrased from the title of his book, "Everything You Think You Knew is Wrong!"

It is true, some people have a difficult time to understand even the most reasonable assumptions via common sense... Common sense in this day and age, in many respects continues almost unknown and uncommon! With no hardship comparisons, how can anyone today fully appreciate all human comforts, freedoms, wilderness, wild populations, etc., My day, Your day, To-day everything of past importance seems to be over looked! Wild man has no problem with that... His world only has changed in his need to stay elusive. Once Caged ("Heaven Forbid!") he is instantly extinct... and all realize it!

If not, they would have already been exterminated much as were the aboriginals of Australia, etc! Man kills or destroys everything that he does not understand or wants not to deal with!

Expect the unexpected!

Have hard at look at your horses on all bright lit nights...

Anyone still convinced that The Wind had Plaited these Manes, absolutely Does need much Magical Help from some unknown Magic. Something?

The open ended conclusions shared in part this chapter are highly plausible and will, "Stark-Shock" all logical considerations already had with the much thought illogical! All conjecture "there" is most difficult! Never till now has anyone dare write that message. True or false, a highly strange video long covert till now reveals that reasoning. Everything suggested there is also very new to my consideration-reasoning, and all of it's message Much, much, to early to fully reason all functions...But if we truly earnest in this wild endeavor then we must consider all things... Wanting to realize-believe it or not, M.K. Davis just as myself has no choice? We plainly do fully reason all functions...But if we truly earnest in this wild endeavor then we must consider all things... Wanting to realize-believe it or not, M.K. Davis just as myself has no choice? We plan summer 2012 to further investigate all video and deposition claims of the matter? If all said is nil naïve to belief; found null and void; if hoaxed; if deceptive; if I further criticized for my audacity to write its stark preview, then who more rejected than I dare subject the academic critic, and pour more fuel onto the lay critic fires? If the video evidence at all true, then we have just begin with the fun and confusion of all Bigfoot community on another run to nowhere! And if the video true... Absolutely No One has even One Valid small Answer to all Wild Man Stark Possibility!

NOTE:

(Please don't read next at once to the end of the book before completing all natural Line Ups of the manuscript confusions! This is a very difficult sojourn to write and to edit. All matters ahead further dictate all belief outcomes. I much need all readers help and input to secure this mystery Case Closed! I much need to further investigate and document more horses in the field, as I truly do hope to one day resolve this plaiting mystery. Sometimes the most obvious is easily over looked. Seek and you shall find? What more say anyone of this strange anomaly? The limit is we shall see I way, way, over the moon! The moon is at the head of the rainbow! See you in the stars! Discover all night life excitement... All wild hominids know well that you are there!

Log: "The horse named, Hink!"

"Wow! Today I discovered another strange plait on Hink!"

A full moon has just re-occurred... all is most ironic to secure if not found more of my the theory? This next to be explained below could write a whole another separate manuscript!"

327

Hink!

Log: November 11, 12, 13, 2011, and now today as I write it is the 14ᵗʰ

"I am now four days into investigating in the Jenson, and Hinck Ranches, the first located, east bank of Owyhee River, Oregon, and the Hinck Blazer Horse Ranch, located close near by to the famed, Snake River, East bridge vicinity of Idaho along the Oregon border, near by to the berg town of Adrian, Oregon. All continued story is a necessary retold account for content unto reminisce investigation..."

"ANOTHER HINCK BLAZER HORSE MYSTERY!"

Log: December 11, 2011 - Plaiting

Realizing that over the past night there was a historical moon eclipse and realizing all of its possible ramifications in the belief of the full moon having to do with the plaiting of horses, I decided to drive the 600 miles from Sweet Home, Oregon to the Jenson Ranch located near the confluence of the Owyhee and Snake Rivers along the Ore-Idaho border. It was late night when I arrived. I was told by Phil Jenson that a new braid had been noticed being done only that same morning on the right side of Hink! It had just happened since the beginning of the new moon phase... "Yeah, he said, for sure a bright moon like that would make the braiding much easier! No I have no idea exactly when all of this new had began, but it was very recent! I must leave for a few days. I will be back on Thursday. Likely by then the braid will have been finished. Perhaps you should stay a while and more will happen? Yes, this is all very strange! Never once as yet have I ever found even one strange track!"

Figure 55. Hink in braids. Photo Jenson.

Log: December 14, 2011: Three days later

Only minutes ago Norma Jenson and I went to feed and inspect the horses. I had stayed away from Hink and the other animals so as not to muddle the situation of any new possible plaiting. The outside temperature today is, plus 33 degrees. To our surprise, there are now three intricate new braids neatly done on Hink's right side, opposed to all of what was done last time on her left side. I could easily imagine that if one were to want to ride the horse bare back, it would be easy to do by using the elongated plaited mane as a primitive hand held neck reign much as one would do when using the reins of a bridal. I easily approached Hink up to about one yard distance of her braids but was unable to cut off them off. She was not particularly nerved from all past plaiting. What ever is the contact it must be gentle or pleasant. It truly is difficult ti imagine anything as uncanny as this. What ever powers that be that control these horses needs to be a direct identity allowance. It is beyond human reason. I am now waiting for Phil to return. I hope when he does we can get'er all done before I need to leave tomorrow. I would like to add the recent plaiting sample to my collection that now numbers about fifty! If I have that many, then how many indeed are out there in the world unnoticed, etc. We sometimes fail to realized that any new thing discovered is but only that moment in time; one short sojourn on the human clock. Think of the mega everythings that are left un-

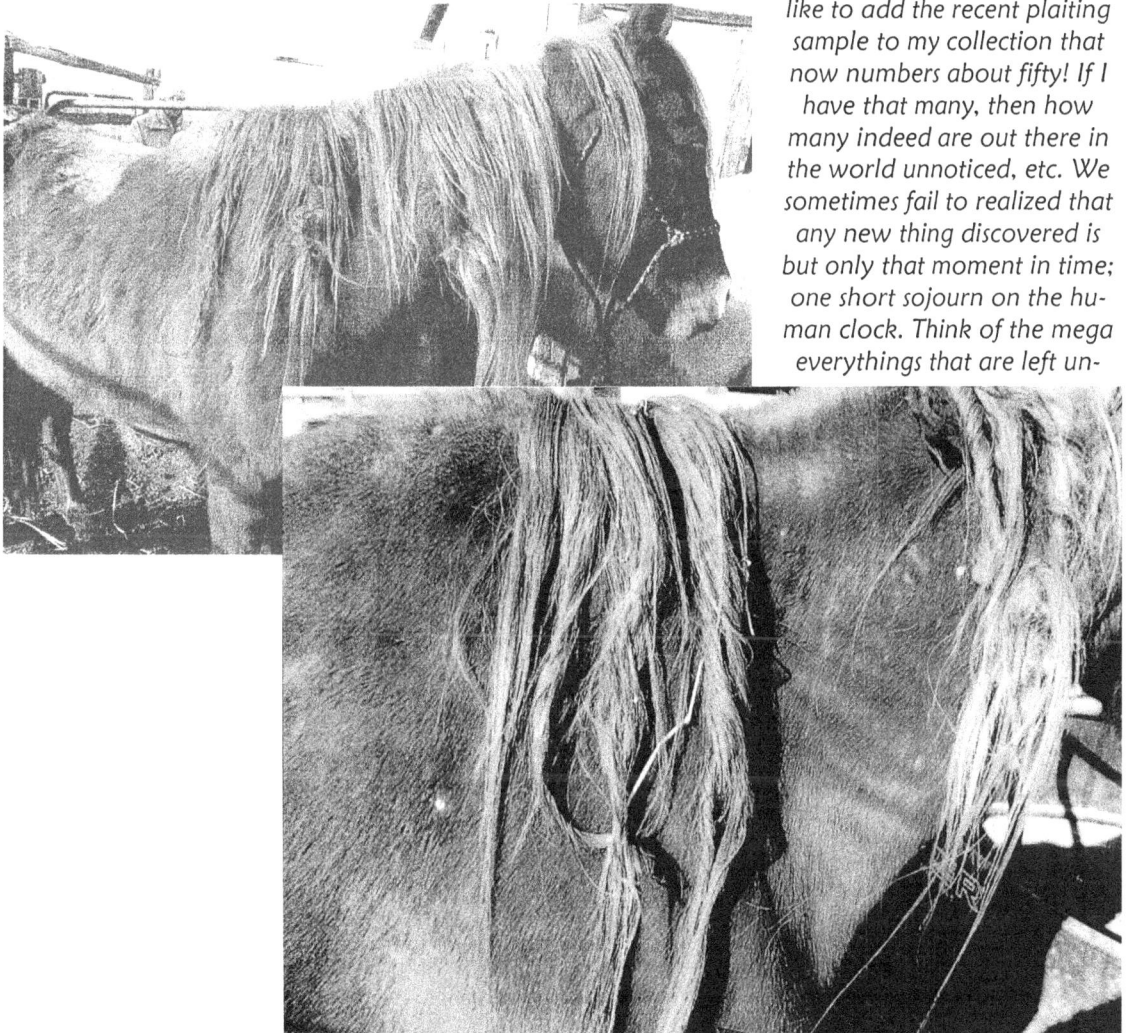

Figure 56. Hink with three new braids on the right side.   Photo Jenson.

329

known. Our short time on earth actually touches little. On any dark night anywhere perhaps thousands of horses world wide are plaited and some possibly ridden? We examine that likely anomaly somewhere ahead when we again finally meet. Montana Jim!"

"Hink"

(A mare!)

She was named for the invincible and famous wrangler, Neil Hinck, who sold her to the Jensen's about years 2009 (?), and since then the horse has been plaited any number of times. She was one of the forty horses that I had documented plaited year 2007 when examining the 137 horses then on the Hinck property. At that time Brenda Hinck and I counted in access of forty plaited horses, most all of them were mares with colts or fillies about to drop their young. The other horse today on the Jenson place is a white Arabian mare. She unlike the previous other white mare that died only recently of natural causes had also for a long time been repetitious plaited. More of that experience will also be explained. One account in particular is beyond interesting.

Since first discovery of plaiting being done to the Hinck horses two years prior to the year, 2007, numerous times I had returned by the invitation to the Neil Hinck, and Norma, Blazer Horse Ranch investigate their select herd of registered Geldings, Mares, and Stallions, that at one time not all that long ago had numbered at 250, however when I first went there the count was down to about 150. Norma told me early on without any realization of the importance, "that for at least thirty years Don, I have been cutting off those same strange type braids and just threw them away thinking no more about them than they were sort of peculiar? I had no idea of how it got done that way, or anything of what might be their importance? Now after learning all of this I will cut them off for you in the future and save them!

You know, for a long time towards evening, I have sometimes felt a little uneasy when feeding the horses! It was just a feeling as if someone or something were looking at me from across the road in those trees, but I never really though all that much about it! We have had a few strange things happen though. About 25 years ago when we lived north of here towards Emmett Idaho, One of our horses looked as if it had been picked up and next dropped from high above the ground? How ever happened it broke every single bone over its body! All of the other horses would not go near it! They just all stood around it watching it! Neal had no idea what happened! That sort of bothered us! The girls will remember? Any way, have you any idea Don what that was all about?" No, I had no idea then, and I don't now, but was thinking about the strange incident that had also happened at the Jenson ranch only a few years ago when one of his calves was found lying in the snow with its eyes, ears, vitals, etc., all blood and body fluids completely drained and leaving a sizable gaping hole evident in one area of its neck as if it had eaten from the inside out... None of this has ever explainable by anyone including the local veterinarian, and/or the Government trapper, etc. All evidence was sent to the University of Idaho lab. At Caldwell for answers no conclusion was ever made?

Strange things happen. The Jenson and Hinck properties seem to have their share. "Phil further told me (2011) that only recently within the past six months that two of his prized young hair sheep lambs had vanished without a trace from behind his fenced pasture close to the house without leaving one clue?" It has long been the consensus that wild man populations over Eurasia and China favor sheep. Why be that tradition any different here? Phil further told me, "that from year

1995 – 2000, we lost all of 50 or so lambs per year ("50 per year!") and found some evidence of coyotes, but very little. Coyotes killed some of the lambs, but not all...the fish and wildlife, game warden, government trapper, and the vet. found not one more conclusive clue! Things still happening in and around the Jenson place. Only last night, December 13th, 2011, Diane Hollins, a friend and close neighbor living now on what was once the Owyhee River edge of the Jenson property, told me that shortly before my arrival on that same evening before dark she heard a rather strange unidentified loud howling sound coming from not all that far away from her front door, and so brought her two pet dogs inside to be out of harms way. Coyotes and wolves eat small dogs. Today she described the sounds again saying that it had been disturbing, however she was sure that it had only been one animal. Norma Jenson then with us during the conversation ironically said that she had also recently heard an unusual howling coming from about the same vicinity.

Not that is has anything to do with the plaiting, wild man, moon phase, or anything relative, but only six weeks ago when I was last time at the Jenson property, one late night about ten P. M. while driving the hay-field dirt road at a distant say perhaps 300 yards from the Hollins home; all at once fast crossing the road in front of my head lights ran an extremely large black colored

Figure 57. Brenda Hinck with scissors to trim 'tangles' out of the manes. For years these were just dismissed as annoyances and thrown away without noticing there was a pattern to their occurrence.

wolf, "as anxious an animal as I have ever encountered on the run, including a bolting deer," to be best compared to the graphic picture of a fleeting Gray Hound Dog or African Cheetah stretched out leg-length as is seen painted running on the side panels of a Gray Hound Bus! Wolves are not completely uncommon or impossible to encounter especially in Owyhee County Oregon, but the size of that wolf made Montana wolves look like puppies! Time allowing I plan to return to the Owyhee river drainage."

The Famous Neil Hinck Blazer Horses

"Neil, Norma, Debby, and Brenda"

A Brief History

"The N & N Hinck Ranch"

< Adrian, Oregon, 2009 >

"Over 40 years of plaiting Don! Never could figure it out?"

"A slight Hinck Family History"

All of this high strange plaiting, similar, and even more, as has been long explained over the many pages of this book, had gone on at "The N & N Ranch," for well over 25 years! It had even happened even earlier on Neil's horses long before changing the Ranch location from where he had moved from, Emmett, Idaho after leaving Wyoming ....

Neil

"Don, he said, this crazy stuff has gone on steady around here for a very long time! I can't really remember when we had first noticed it? I have been running these horses around in circles for over forty years, and it seems to me that it all started even before we left our Ranch in Wyoming!"

"The Blazer Champion Stallion, Rambo Santana"

Probably Neil's favorite horse was Rambo Santana, with stud service offered year 2009, @ $1,000.00! By the year 2009, Neil had experienced more than 70 years of breeding and training almost every type of equine (Horses!), including training first and only time ever accomplished, before or since; "Neil upon the request of the famous, Los Vegas Strip magician, "Doug Henning .... Single handedly he trained the world's only known adult wild Zebra, tamed it, and broke it to be ridden-double in just six short weeks' time!" As said, this had never been done before, or to my inquiry ever again since! To had accomplish this is just about impossible! Henning wanted the Zebra trained to become a needed part of a pending magic show! It just so happened that I had actually had watched the show before ever meeting the Hinck's! "Henning rode bare back on the wild Zebra accompanied by his wife! Neil's veterinarian daughter Debby said, "Don, Our Dad actually is Half Horse! He constantly studies them! He ever knows exactly how a horse thinks! What actual part of the horse half that he is, depends on the moment, situation, and the time! Dad is able to mentally identify with a horse, just exactly as if he were also a horse himself, more than anyone I have ever known!"

The U.S. Calvary, & The Man, Hal dago! *

"Truly Neil Hinck was a paradoxical man, truth known, somehow he probably was actually half horse...? During the 1930s, the real life man depiction in his high boots and flesh; "the very man who actually was the colorful cowboy projected in the Hollywood Movie, "Hal dago," visited Neil when still a boy, at his Wyoming Property, in order to compliment him for his rare, natural ability, with American Army horses! The family had made a part of their living raising remount horses for the U.S. Calvary... Neil was determined at the early age of 9 years, "to create a useful horse, that would be a horse friendly to humans, and at a same time be instinctively determined to win at any race, just as much as would be wanting any anxious dance partner, boxer, or a gymnastic competitor, etc., and ever as well be a more than an invincible, willing, hard bent beast of burden! Neil accomplished that dream, in the creation of the famous Blazer Horses! The colorful man gave his all to create the very best natured and useful horse possible that the world would ever see!" Since his demise in 2009, at the time of this writing 2011, the Blazer Horse Stock has dwindled down to a sad count of perhaps 25 head! The Neil Hinck, N. & N, Blazer Horse Ranch and it latent legacy lives on now only in the reminisce of myself, his friends, wife and children .... So Be it Neil, the Horses are Coming, and in its way, this book actually needs be dedicated to you!"

"Last Wish"

"Neil old friend .... I am sure one day that we will ride together again! Break biscuits, drink sage brush tea, and set up camp another time, under some awesome and exhilarating high desert Owyhee sun down ....! Where I am sure old buddy, your family, and all your headstrong friends, will be waiting there for you!"

"And, remember this other wild man, that hasn't forgotten you!"

"Ishmahachi – "From the vast land of Idaho/Montana, that is still the place of the mountain lion!"

"Always Expect The Unexpected!"

The Horse Named Hink!

Log: Author @, One O' Clock A. M., December 15th, 2011-

"Writing while waiting for Phil Jenson's return back to the Jenson Ranch Oregon, while experiencing more of the incredible!"

---

* See footnote p. 297 [ed.]

PART THREE

Meanings and Identity?

Log: Moon Phase Logic?

The latest plaiting done was all relative to the recent Lunar Eclipse, with a full moon phase that began December 10th-12th. The eclipse is said not to reoccur for many years, and was easily viewed from the Ore-Ida ranch regions. As said, the Jenson and Hinck properties are both locations close to the confluence of the fabled Snake, and Owyhee rivers. Phil has now returned, and for another time explained to me that the strange braiding had began as he said on the eve of the moon eclipse. I checked Hink last time Wednesday morning three days after arrival Sunday and found to my amazement four new braids. (Included are pictures.) On my way driving from the Jenson place to Montana I passed by the remaining Hinck stock, and threw field glasses could detect that there were two more additional new braids been done on two of the Blazer mares, but because of their play-full frenzy and all running ah-muck I could not get close enough to them for a picture. It is now December 16th, and I have arrived back to Siberia-Lima-Montana, where I found the water barrels in my cabin frozen solid to three feet! As I have written, Norma had several times explained to me that the plaiting had been going on for more than thirty years, and until I had called her attention to its uncanny importance she was oblivious to the anomaly, but true to her word she had continued to cut off the braids and had saved many for me. After taking part in the mystery by the year 2009, she was more than curious. However as good as all of the cut braids were for my collection there was no real documentation of when cut, being done etc., no moon phase connection, or had she any way to had known of that interest! Through precarious care of how to best cut off the braids, little or no note of the predominating horse gender, etc., I was just very grateful for all of her dedication. With limited time and the great distance apart of 450 miles there just was no realistic way that I could be at all times or enough on the property. As many times as I have gone there; as many miles as I have traveled in this effort, the tally is unfathomable! Such dubious research has few piers, many critics, is a passion quite like no other, and is a separate fascination of Cryptozoic investigation, and mostly raises doubting eye brows among today's growing numbers of the much naïve generation. To establish an accepted rapport with today's younger ranchers o/ever suspicious and of high suspect to/of all strange motives, etc., is often far beyond difficult, even with close friends and family... People just do not want to deal with what they think not to understand, or is imagination in today's world a working part of all blind bias. People are actually afraid and very quick to blindly criticize what they cannot easily accept. My most difficult effort of late has been to find persons of a true curious nature willing and anxious to explore the unknown. Ever there are a thousand reasons, and mostly financial or time consuming why the pseudo interested cannot continue with all importance. True exploration has always included a lonely Supper for One without Candle Light. There are no words to express the appreciation and exhilaration of a dutiful tight mouthed trail mate! I have been most fortunate to have had a considerable many. Once hooked by the obvious high adventure of the truly strange, one seems to do a little less fishing! Adventure is where you allow it, and it has forever it seems found ways to had discovered me.

Log Continued: Norma Hinck.

What is the normality example of today's intelligent but innocent society!

Yes she said, "I found many a braid, many a time, and just cut them off and threw them! Nothing much to it all I thought! I just figured it was all being done by the wind, or maybe done when the horses rolled around in the pasture! Yeah Don, I actually did think that it was sort of odd, but had no real idea or time to consider all of what it was? We just cut them off, threw them, and paid little attention!

The Gate?

Never got all of the story, but the strange happening had left a definite impression on Norma Hinck!" Do you really think that it is being done by wild people? Ask Neil, have him tell you all about the one, the wild man or something like that, that, he once saw and chased in Wyoming! You know Neil wouldn't lie to you... The darn thing picked up part of his elk and just carried it off! Then there was the time way back when several years ago when we lived on the other place in Idaho... This was a strange thing that happened with our fence gate... Have Neil tell you about that too... Then there was the killed horse I told you about out in the pasture... None of our more than 150 horses would go any where near to it! The girls will remember all of that... Have them tell you." Yeah the wind does it! Most will also admit that when it happens the wind has hardly blown for many days, etc!" I was awe struck, and found all of this complacency at first hard to believe; hard to believe that anyone could be so unaware of such a high strange ever obvious humanistic anomaly being done as are continuing finely done tight long braids found on a considerable number of horses, and many of them even elongated longer than the original mane hair? But when realizing that several others had told me much the same story, or very similar, I just had to allow it? Most persons while engrossed in their busy long day of demanding ranch chores, etc., had not bothered to closely examine the plaiting, or might had been to tired to care. Still I find that almost as awesome as is the plaiting! Such complacency is the norm and will be repeated over, and over again!

Plaiting Comment

Neil Hinck

All said just prior to Neil's Passing.

"Well Don, I actually had noticed the braids... but I didn't think to understand any of it! But yeah, I was curious... Don't know exactly why, but I chose to ignore them... Both my adult daughters, Brenda and Debby had cut them off many times... It was always difficult to brush out the manes! I even had thought to crop the manes... I don't know what I thought... What does a cowboy know about such stuff? All of this wild man stuff that you say, "they done it," is not actually all that much of a surprise either! I have seen plenty of strange unexplained stuff many times! Yeah, just like Norma told you, I did see a wild man once over in Wyoming when hunting elk up in the Wind Rivers (Mts!) close to where I was born... We were hunting elk! Come into the house and I will tell you about it!"

335

Things happen; phones ring; someone wants to buy a horse! I never get but parts and pieces of Neil's wild man story! After that conversation and a few others, Neil was ever adamant that I was onto something and offered his help! At the time he was a sick man. His daughters and wife though, took a while to convince... but they only somewhat joined the effort. All my efforts were much too late. The high strange anomaly of plaiting is not recognized by everyone for its importance. Often as not I have been asked, "what is the reason that you even concern with all such matters as this stuff? You would think that finding over forty plaited manes in just one short day on a single ranch, as had happened back in 2007, would have lit the mid-night fuse on fire! It has been just barely three years since Neil's demise and today 2012, the World Fabled Blazer Horses are all but extinct... My hats off to you cowboy! Up the canyon you have gone where the sun-down meets the sky...

(To be continued.)

(A 2012 Reminiscence-Review.)

Log: Nyssia Oregon - "December 9-12, 2011"

As said, I arrived to the Jenson's late Sunday night December 11, two days after the week end eclipse on the 9th! I was met by Phil explaining to me even before out of the car that recent plaiting had began! The braiding he said started the night of December 8th! "As far as I can tell Phil said, it started about the same eve as the moon eclipse. That bright phase is still now! The new braid on Hink is rather short, but I expect that it will somehow get much longer? All looks to me like it is not yet finished? Seems that it doesn't always happen in just one night! Perhaps you can stay a while and see what more might happen? I will be gone for a few days on the truck, so will see you in a few days."

(Continued from above.)

"More Importance of the Hinck Horses! Explanations of what we found on the forty plus plaited horses, etc."

<2007 – 2010>

Because of horse sales, the herd had diminished in numbers to approximately 137 by late October 2009. With the help of Brenda numerous times I visited their ranch horses, those years as above, through examine and count the plaited horses 2007, predominately the braids were done mostly on the pregnant fillies then in estrus and about to drop their new born colts. Few studs or geldings at that time had been messed with...? And what was most curious, on some of the black, or better said, the darker hair colored braids (where all could be more easily detected) had been left "Mares Milk, (Or, Kumiss!)" where it looked like all braiding efforts had included high evidence of kumiss left on the braids where had been working fingers! Nothing else could had left the milk dried there in that way if not left by braiding hands! NOTHING... Brenda was very surprised, and I could see at once that she really wanted nothing further to do with it beyond admitting a same opinion! It was all just almost too much for her to grasp! All of these many years had passed, and an entire family never the wiser to all of what was going on right before their very eyes! Earlier that same morning when conversing in the house, Brenda had been very skeptical and reluctant of my thought to had been wild assumptions, I had to all but challenge her to even accompany me out into the pasture, but now all of a sudden she admitted how puzzled, fascinated, and confused, or even convinced that she had become! "Yeah Don really, what else other than someone or something on two legs could do anything like this? And the milk? Could it be possible that someone is drinking milk from these horses? Do we really think so? That would be more than incredible if not almost impossible?"

"KUMISS"

Or, mares' milk, may begin to be naturally produced in a pregnant horse just prior to birthing! It first forms into a very thick white substance somewhat unlike pseudo expectant prototype mares milk. It can be best described as a very sweet tasting, very thick white cream. People over all vast Asia have long centuries been highly nourished by kismess, and it is still popular and in use today. It has becomes my projected theory that very likely wild man by what ever name, or whatever the hominid is (?) that does the plaiting, "is also is suckling this milk protein!" What ever is braiding the manes has the use of opposed fingers and thumbs and could easily fondle or do what ever to all other desired places of the horse. We also found on that day, numerous curious unexplained white large and smaller spots, all of them much similar of destructive acid burns! But these were only found on the top most parts of a horse's back at the place of the withers, (where normally is placed a saddle). This high strange acid like anomaly was only found on the fillies! (Pregnant horses!)

No plausible answer for any of this actually, unless all of it is just exactly as what it looks to be... It looked to me to be possibly very strange high acid body fluid, or a much similar body excretion? acid. Definitely all of it was very strange, and to date and prior I had never heard of it mentioned before? Well Brenda, what do you think of all of this, and do you think that it at all possible that our creatures are even likely riding the horses, or even leading the horses around the pasture at night by using the plaited elongated manes, much the same as One might use say a leadrope, or would use the reigns of a bridal? Could the acid-stuff or what ever it is (?) be being left behind at the seated place, or where ever, what ever, had last sat and left this white what ever? No idea had either of us? Still all is a mystery and completely unreal to further imagination? I have not seen it again. Anyone Know? Brenda had little more to say! She was astonished, overwhelmed, and bamboozled, and has remained silent ever since? I have not seen or conferred with her again, as she does not reside at the Hinck Ranch property. Our meeting was circumstance, both were visiting. However she was ever adamant, amazed and startled of our discovery day together, and I am sure if need be she would agree to write for us her deposition. All Neil's daughters much loved him... So be it Neil, you were A # One!

"A NEW MOON PHASE, and,

AN ALL NEW MYSTERY!"

("Update continued from above!")

One month later!

337

PART THREE

Log: January 8-11, 2012.

Another incredible unforgettable Full Moon Phase!
Tonight you could just about reach up and grab the stars!"

Author writing wile again on road heading back to Montana after having kayaked an eventful portion of Arizona Colorado River with pal, Gene Schiller, Lake Havasu City, Arizona. I am now at Pocatello Idaho, January 9th, 2012 – Norma Jenson was just on the cell phone telling me... "Yes, she said, all plaiting has happened again! We can't believe it, or at all understand how it is at all possible? No tracks left behind again, nothing at all! No evidence, or idea at all what's doing it? Remember those long mane braids that were done on Hink in December? Well, the plait that you considered-said that its shape much resembled the shape of the moon eclipse has now been further extended and is on the opposite side of the horse and with it are a lot more of much smaller braids!

How many plaits are now on the horse? Well, I don't really know? There are just a lot! Perhaps... maybe all of them are about eight inches long or so?" "I guess that I really should have measured them? Did you say the mane before plaited measured 14 inches? We just can't believe any of it! John (Phil's brother visiting from Guam.), will take pictures. Phil will bring them down tomorrow when he meets you at the Fort Hall Idaho Indian Reservation truck stop... I will watch closely to see what more if anything happens?"

I met Phil the next day at Fort Hall and got the photos. They are included in the Figures below.

Log: Meet John and Cheri Jenson! 2012

(John and his wife Cherie's visited Phil and Norma at the property year 2011, prior to the following account. While there Cheri had a very strange plaiting adventure. All that important story ahead!

What is also ironic to the story, is the fact that at about the same exact date of the month 28 days later during February, in regard to the full moon phase just over during January, at the time when all plaiting had been done already described (19th – 12th, 2012), quite by happenstance, John was again for a second time with his brother Phil exactly when all plaiting was being done again. However all next described was not being done to the same horse as was experienced earlier by Cheri 2011! Because of John's close association and duel experiences he was much impressed and remains confused in awe! This time with him there along with Marvin and Diane Hollins there were all of five persons present to further attest the 2012 experience. John's comments, had second hand, are most interesting.

John – "Both Cheri and I were completely unaware of the importance, or even of the real fact of the matter of the plaiting either... What happen last time here in 2011 to Shari had completely boggled my mind! It was incredible, unbelievable, uncanny, and very strange, and definitely raises many questions! We still very much wonder what done it?"

(John is a scientific investigator explorer stationed in Guam, North Pacific Islands. He is very qualified in observations of the unusual. His credits would write all another interesting story. The Hollins, the same. Marvin and Diane are inexplicable in honesty and character.)

338

Figure 58. Cheri holds out a very long loop twisted into Hink's mane. This is over twice the length of the mane hair. This extra length had to come from somewhere. Photo John Jenson.

Cheri's Story

Last time (First time!) there during summer 2010, "Cheri, then completely unaware of all experimental importance going on between Phil, Norma, and myself; she had been daily riding what was corralled then, a beautiful white mare! (This horse was not the same white horse that is presently tethered on the Jenson property 2012!) She could not help but noticed an obvious, though ugly, and curious, entanglement of the horse's mane! Next she said paraphrased, for lack of a recording: "All entanglement was a very long and confusing! All of the white mane, was much tightly twisted tangled, and looking as if all was somehow braided? It was a complete hanging mess! Almost all of this I was thinking, would be difficult, or completely next to impossible to unravel, but I decided to try it! All of it turned out to be a very difficult...and to do it took a long time; being most of t a mixed multiple conglomeration of very hard to decide how to think to untangle all tight and elongated knots? All collectively to be described, best said would be, all of it was simply a sizable long length of indecisive messed-up hair!

How in the world it got that way (?) I could not imagine?

Wow, what a miserable, tangled, horse hair mane! Yeah, I was thinking that it was rather odd, but then also I thought that it was not all that important? I unraveled every bit of it as best I could and then brushed it out not thinking any more really about it... We planned to catch the plain an fly out the next morning, and I was wanting to ride the horse one more time before departing for Guam... when we all went out to the horses, to everyone's great surprise and awe, "all of yesterday brushed out mane as described; EVERYTHING... everything, every plait had been re-braided again! I could not believe my eyes, and I still can't believe it? Everyone *there was a witness! That sort of thing just has to be almost impossible? I had no idea of Don's interest in the plaiting? No one had said one word about it!"*

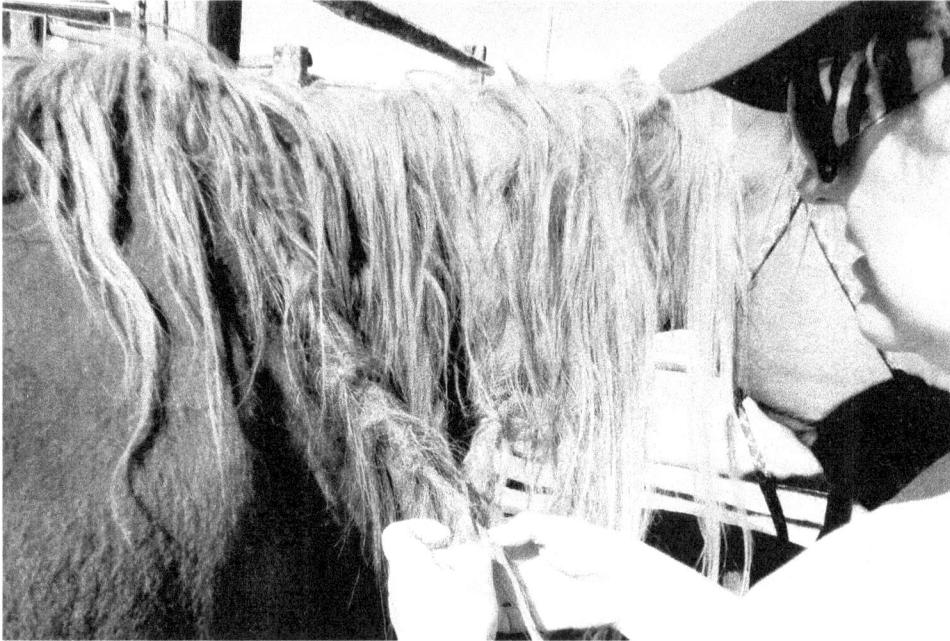

Figure 59. Cheri examining Hink's braids wondering: "How in the world it got that way?"
Photo Jenson.

(More update on all of this, when and if, or as when can recount? "Actually it was a very good thing that Cheri had unraveled the plaits, or we would never have realized the all of the much more high strange! Not one bit of wind had blown on that night, or particularly on any other night significant to any separate story thus far aired within the manuscript. Fairies, elves, ghosts, all of that, etc., is complete B. S.!)

New Moon Phase!

Every 28 days, 13 times a year as everyone knows, there begins a new moon phase, comprising of approximately seventeen days and nights of a full and or half moon phase on both sides of the ever ebbing and soon diminishing full moon. This pseudo semi-calculated, results that there are somewhere around 15, or perhaps, 17 nights of bright, or partly dimming bright visibility nights, or, approximately 204 nights of the year when it would be somewhat possible to see by moon light well enough to even think to be able to attempt to plait a horse's mane... In other words, with an approx. calculation of perhaps, 161 dark nights, that is about, 2/3rds of the year, the night sky is at least partly a bright-lit moon, that is provided of course, there are more dark nights ahead than lit, "if say, all is heavily overcast, etc?" That tally amounts to approximately, bright nights, about, 66% of the year, OR, when any Wild Anything, man or beast, can wander Wide Eyed if wanting to, under the bright night stars! "It is also most interesting that almost every claim of an alleged Sasquatch having been seen to be peering/peaking threw a night window, almost every one has occurred on the darkest of Moonless Nights!"

LOG: UPDATE! January 14ᵗʰ, - February, 28ᵗʰ, 2012.

"All of this is more than incredible!"

It is now only nine days until the next full moon phase. Of late, since all of this strange plaiting, I nightly ponder the night sky. Exactly how to begin this segment of the mystery has me much in retrospect of the year, 2009 and years prior, when so very much was happening on the Neil Hinck Ranch! So much then perhaps taken for granted, that I hardly made the extended effort, or did not completely photograph, or document any real part of it, as to exact moon phase dates, etc., or let alone always get (as explained!) any needed exact information from Norma Hinck, of how, when, conditions, etc., she had cut off all of the braid samples that she had so faithfully saved for me, etc! At that time I had before me a herd of select and famous Blazer horses in access 135 head, Neil himself to confirm with, and his daughter, Debby and always his good wife Norma to invite me in to the house for a snack or a cup of coffee. All that much is changed now. As said, Since Neil's passing the ranch has dwindled to nothing. The bulk of the horses have been sold for ridiculous prices. Norma and Debby married, etc., everything, and everyone changes. Almost magical after over forty years of dreams and hard work was born a wonderful and select breed of Blazer Horses! Anyone further interested in the magical breed and all history, need only to spend a moment on the internet to research them. It would be well worth it to be able to fully understand what we are dealing with here. It has occurred to me that because of the incredibly gentle special breed that they were, extremely easy to approach, etc., may have been another good reason for all of the extreme plaiting being done to them? The magnificent herd is now down to less than 25 head or so? Last time that I tried to count them through my filed glasses as, late December 2012. It was difficult as the wonderful horses that they are were all hard running in all directions fast around the pasture. After having departed the Jenson's, and on my way out I looked at them a last and to my notice was at least two of the horses having new braids! Exciting as all was, with dwindling day light, time running out, and all horses playful, there was no real opportunity to further conclude them. "Perhaps Neal, that was our last horse race moment together in proxy-retrospect...Damn well old buddy, you were there! For all that I know there will never be written after me any more, or all of the rest of the almost magical Hinck Horse history? I had always wanted to own one of the Blazer horses, but rolling stones gather no moss... Everything has always been a matter of finance. Wanderers just get along towards the next sun down on our Shanks Pony, or clever named canoe to collect another memory! Had she lived, I had promised Tonia Brown 2011, one of the Hinck mares, and its new colt... So be it Neil, nothing is ever over till it's all over! Your life and times as I knew them were Just & right!"

Log: January 17th, 2012 - "A most difficult explanation!"

Phil Jenson and I meet at Fort Hall Idaho.

Before me as I write are five recent photographs given me by, Phil Jenson just four days ago, Friday 13th, over, Blackfoot Indian fry bread had on the Fort Hall Reservation. No real significance to the legendary time and date, but that particular Friday the 13ᵗʰ had not been Phil's best day either, as he only that same morning lost his wallet and all of his effects. I was grateful as was he that we met together. Things happen! Phil operates a long haul truck. On his way towards Montana points he scheduled our meeting as he had important pictures for me taken only one day earlier Jan, 12ᵗʰ, as was all explained above of new and recent Hink plaiting. The photos he said were all of them recent updates, etc. All absolute and much new startling evidence of plaiting been done to his horses, and most important to me, all of it during a visible full moon! Its definitely very hard to write all of this, but hear me out for pertinent descriptions unto further possible understandings?

Only the unimaginative will not understand my excitement with these photos, and most of them are not reading this. The pictures Phil provided (Figures 52, 53, 56, and 57) are each dated and self-explanatory. Many of them feature the red Hink, his first recent photo is dated, January 9th, 2011, Right side facing showing old plaiting been changed new again, etc.

Log: Phil Jenson Explanations

Note:: all following is slightly paraphrased for full understandings.

This is but words of description had on location. The actual pictures are in Figures 53, 54, 56, and 57...... Phil here is doing the explaining: "This first photo Don, plainly shows the plaiting that you first saw when you were on the property December 2011. The long twilled braid resembling a looped-circle, as if hand hold of sorts, almost it looks just as if all plaiting was fully intended to be the emulation of a full moon eclipse, and with a little imagination all braids are pictured here are very much the same, just as well as are all the rest of smaller tangled hard braided very tight knots, etc. Everything plaited has been left just exactly as you said to leave them. We have done nothing, nothing at all to change them.

"The second photo of course is also of Hink, taken one month later, January 11th, (2012), almost to the day after one months time, each exactly done the same at a full moon! We developed the photos on the January 12th, and so when meeting with you on the 13th, everything is very recent. What is important and most uncanny here is, the fact that this second photo of Hink, has him standing this time Left Side Facing, fully exposing on that same side (Right side facing in December!) the very last plaited braid mentioned as was to be seen previous on his Right Side! Now with the all full moons, that New Braid somehow has been re-fashioned for a better description...Into, or is now, a much longer, much re-worked plaiting, that is at least, Two Times longer than is the horses actual mane that measures only about, 14 inches long! The new plaiting is now realistic hanging down to perhaps, 28 inches in length! How is anything like that at all possible?"

"This last one Don, is the most incredible, as it exposes Hink again standing Right Side Facing, on January 12th, with what must be up to about ten or more various plaited knots, and all braids done to all manes at a very same location exactly where before only the two braids back on December 11, 2011! Any way, all of this is beyond logical reason. The last photo shows Hink, standing together with the white Stud, both eating from the same hay bale and feed trough where can easily be detected done on Hink's neck, the new plaited much elongated, 28 inch long braid as is described above. That last picture was taken January 9th, and clearly attests all of what had been done, on, or slightly before that date!"

In Time There May Be Written Another Sequel?

The plaiting on the Jenson property and many others I am sure is hardly over? Enough is written here to challenge anyone's imagination to think to make new discoveries future and want to tell about it. The plaiting in time will be explained. Just possibly this manuscript will be helpful, and maybe not? If this not the answer, other explicit books will be written. The persons to be involved might surprise you! We are now into a new misunderstood world of unexplained logic... By that I mean, "it seems that more and more people do not seem, or even realize how, or want to bother to think, or even ponder deeply. The computer age has changed the past few generations into an instant gratification public, many of our youth are suddenly frustrated with ever demanding expectations of instantiations answers, ever they believe to only be found upon demand over the Net! Once found, most forget the equation, dates, histories, persons, places, and things, etc., almost as instantaneously as they appear! In future there may result new theoretic classes of within world universities new theoretic classes constructed to teach people to re-think their thinking... "Why memorize such stuff Don...? Heck, anything that we need to know is on the internet! You Old Man, "am" a dinosaur! You don't even know what is going down!" ("Am?")

"Ode To The Night Stalkers,

and, Molly b Damn?"

(All horse Plaiters, and all Worthy Eccentrics'!)

Bob Schmalzbach, Ron Roseman, Bob Reinholdt, M. K. Davis, Don Monroe, and all many others thought eccentric, or lost in the fair winds of all time, and fast running while ever daring to be thinking out loud!

"The Tide is Out lads!

Our Ship is Launched!

All crew are confused!

Who among you dare navigate...

Far, far, beyond the reef we go.... Perhaps we will see, Exunda?"

I slumber, and shudder on grog, and sleep in confusions till all tomorrows, when all good pirates as myself will sail far beyond all critical canon danger and the further jab of the judgment sword! There are many worlds within ours yet to be explained and filmed, if not already plundered beyond belief by the critics! Horses, Ships, Men and Mice... All flesh under the moon shutters at the unexpected, and the unknown! The Night Stalkers, and Molly, and I, don't even think about such mishaps or dangers, do we? The strange powers that be, are far beyond the reason of most common men and women... Explorers are not common?" After all is said and done, the intelligent rascals upon any far vista, are in charge of their own travel, success, failure, and destiny! Why should any think to deny that we understand very little of many things? There remains very much more to further investigate... Yes, and in time there are plausible answers! Real men sail lighthearted to all new horizons where all magic ever becomes happenstance! Success is sometimes hidden in failure! Adventure discovered is every man's advantage! Don't look for dreams in only the stars, they will return to haunt you, and in time even sometimes find you! Learn to learn from all that there is to be understood! The final great adventure of life will probably begin on the very day of one's final demise! Be prepared before you sail to batten down all open hatches, trim all sail, as I assure you lads we are headed for a storm, and there is nothing at all that we can do about it! There is a full moon above, and the boatswain bird at the mast has predestined our course! There is danger on every frozen dark snowy windy night; the water as cold as the heart of an owl, or what becomes a scorned women! Look to the stars for all answers, and you will never find them enough, as stars hide in the misty-haze when all storms take command! All truth is in the discovery of literal truth itself! So be it all good sailors, and the youthful, beautiful, Molly be Damned, or should she have chosen to had actually sailed with us other than in a sailor's dream, to the place where all horses, condemned men and women are safe? The best that I could do was to name this strange plaiting anomaly and its folly after you, as it is written and believed fair Molly, that you will surely be Damned? But not I say, before the allegiance is scorned of all ridiculous critics abrupt yourself, and all legion in numbers of my ilk, that dared in life to have sailed to where few others had gone before! The First of them will be last, and the Last of them will be first, and I will be darned, or damned, if any of that really matters at all...? Java Bob Smallsbach, M. K. Davis, and myself, and many more good men and women wanted to be overlooked by the dominating self-righteous, Damn well Know that WE have always Dare Think right dab-square in the middle of the box, or Completely far out of it Until all truth has finally Pulled us Up by our boot straps!" "Shame often becomes the truth! The truth often precedes the shame! The shame is that the few moot critical of anyone seem to never actually have all of the answers either! So be it!" – Author

Plaiting

"This quest is an exhilarating moment in time!"

I have hardly the time or opportunity alone to resolve it!

A plea to the uncommon man; the resourceful women; the intelligent critic; the able open minded academic; anyone reading interested having horses, goats, sheep, or other of the larger live-stock. Have a close look at each of them. I have considered much more has been done "to or with" domestic animals than has even been considered? No matter anyone's opinion, think long and hard about all of this high strange horse plaiting being encountered! I have spent a life time out of doors among animals in many facets of experience, and they continue to more than amaze my reason. We only need to appreciate them. Animals can be understood. Early life I was a considerable trapper. Animal behavior and intelligence is not up for grabs... Many animals far excel human understandings of even ourselves in some respects, and certainly we do continue to learn from them! A pile of common ants is often over looked for human guidance and logical wisdom. If for no more reason than the sake of new discovery do some extensive research for yourself. Anything at all, all at once seems possible during the dark shadows of the night!

Twits!

Say about me what you want about my research and theory... but keep your opinions to yourself, if cannot find better answers? Intelligent, diligent, research-investigators, do not have time for all moot nonsense, and or the blather off unintelligent, non-field-participating think-tank critics!

The plaited horses are coming, and even the nameless horses' asses, who already well realize exactly who they are; those idiots that expound most unrelievedly; who expect the urban public or anyone to believe that Pseudo Elves and Fairies are to blame for the plaits... who have long fallen off the log of reason... Or if not, all with much less common sense than an English Twit Swoosh, will soon be wanting off! I have a difficult time to even believe that any reputable printer would even publish such rubbish?"

All of Chapter One was a notable original trip, or was it a wild and improbable moon light ride? Chapter two will open new doors to much more of the unimaginable! Glad to have sailed and explored with you mates... Australian Yowie are slightly mentioned ahead... However when there 2006, I heard not word of plaiting... To think of it, I actually didn't even to think to ask David Jennings! Anyone Down Under on their way to do the Spring Warwick Gathering, please have a look... And especially look at the Shelia horses! Just the horses! Good on ya Mate, be down soon to put some prawns on the barbie!"

We Are Nowhere?

What the heck...! We are somewhere, and nowhere?

"Open Line Friday The Thirteenth, 2012!"

Log: A Phil Jenson request!

("A Needed Author Disclaimer Interview of Creditability, etc!")

"If you don't like it, don't read it... And, damn well don't criticize what ever you have not already read, understood, or intelligently considered! Phil liked that, because he has been much active in the book..."And Critic Stupidity amounts to Critic Narcip-ipitty! There is no time in serious exploration to "kowtow" to "obvious wannabees!" Ever notice all pseudo gang-bangers, and obvious moot critic ethics (?), "or especially their noticeable prototype ethnology?" Everyone of them wear a definable ethnographic ugly lost by self-damnation uniform thought original but ever revealing! If I am describing you, then you know exactly who you are! Silence is golden, and sometimes just plain cowardly, especially if anyone afraid to be saying all of it to your face! (Phil liked that too!) If one has nothing to say positive or productive, then you are not welcome in Lima Siberia Montana, or any where near the Jenson or Hinck properties!"
"Well Understand that Phil is my nephew, and everything documented in this manuscript is predicated upon absolute proof of discovery; credible witness, and viable photographic proof in every case scenario with any number of existing horse hair artifacts available for inspection upon serious arranged appointment!

Almost always to date, "by gosh and by golly," there has been at least One, or More than One person as a creditable witness actually on farm location during each new discovery; close examination, etc. And/or, another person had been on the ranch/range whenever was cut off plaited mane samples. My (hair-mane) collection to date numbers at perhaps fifty to sixty, of which most are laid out in the Plaits Gallery section seen earlier. And also consider all the new evidence to be had via recent photographs taken by Phil and John Jenson."

Log: January, 2013; Thad Mauney and Suzette Brantley in the Stillwater River Valley, Montana.

Out on the back roads sniffing for a breath of un–or a lot less–polluted air we were driving down the Stillwater River above the town of Absarokee, Montana, and spotted three horses by the pasture fence, so we stopped to friend them up. As before, Suzette had them all hugging up in a just a couple of minutes. Thad hung back quietly to give them time to get comfortable, then joined in. These horses are on the ranch pasture, with headquarters most of a mile down the road. A little farther down is a small settlement called Beehive, named for Beehive Rock, which has not so much as a post office or store; humans are sparse up here.

Yep!, one horse had loops, two of them, braided in the mane. We returned a couple of weeks later and they were still in place. Mostly they lay on the right side, but the stiff wind occasionally blew one of them over to the left. (The wind was rolling rocks around on the second visit.) For reference, our initial visit was about third quarter moon, a week after fullness.

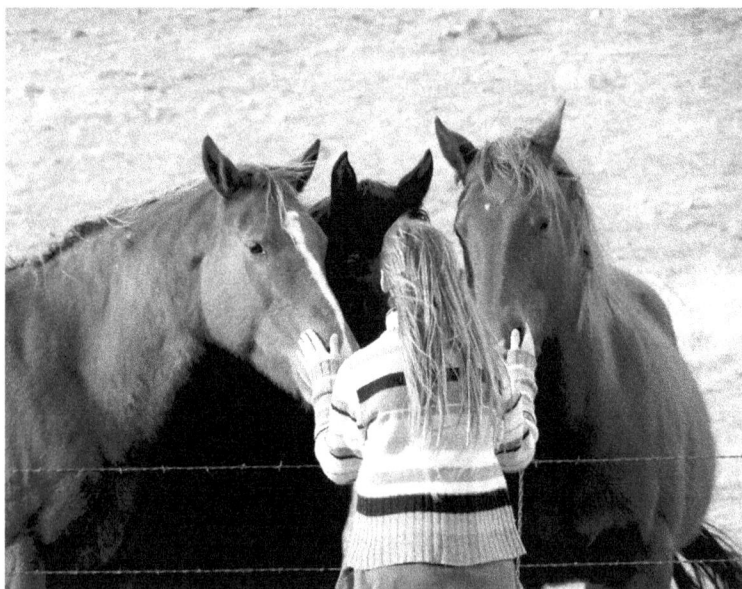

Figure 60. Suzette gets in a group hug with the horsies. Braids? Yes!   Photo T. Mauney, January 9, 2013.

Figure 61. Two loops on this horse!   Photos by T. Mauney.

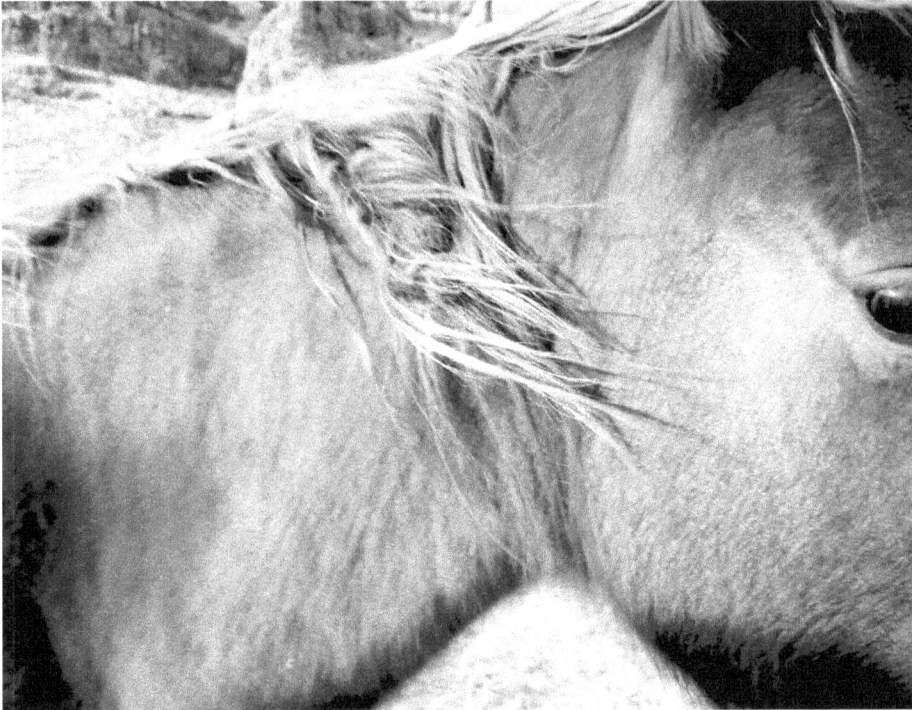

Figure 62. These loops are set just a few inches apart on the neck. Again, the forward strand seems thicker than the rear strand. January 25, 2013.   Photos T. Mauney.

Figure 63. Braids flying in the wind. Stillwater River of Montana, near Beehive Rock. January 25, 2013. Photo T. Mauney.

Figure 64. This is a soft silky mane. We noticed that the sides of these loops twist in opposite directions out from center in both cases. They are tied at the bottom but we did not investigate the knot in detail.   Photo January 25, 2013, T. Mauney

More Shen?

"Plaiting, and Mind Power?"

"Wolves and Coyotes, or Much More than Wild Bears may be at Our Door... Here in Siberia-Montana during coldest winter, almost anything may be welcome...? Strange stuff happens here far beyond simple plaiting! Anything goes... and most people Did!"

Is Mind Power, Abstract Persuasion? Animal bonding, intuition, animal fetish infatuation, you name it? All mind power can hardly be explained as simple telepathy?

"If indeed wild man is responsible for the plaiting, then what is the direct avenue of contact allowance accomplished between them and all horses to make this everywhere possible? In Chapter One we touched only but slightly upon Chinese Mind Power, or what is known as, Shen. If that not a beginning of all logical considerations of unexplained powers that be, and not be hypothetically all more considered to be a realistic positive option; abrupt all pseudo reasonable/unreasonable difficulty and hard-conjured logic perhaps little considered or even realized; at best most difficult even with much shared collective thought to find viable and plausible answers, to How, and more important, WHAT had done it, well toss away the book, because with reasonable understandings of ourselves, and the high influence within expected outcomes, others similar in persuasive abilities realized or not; well, we all often share a bit of mind power via much, or little, insistent and demanding persuasion! Guilt or purpose in humans, food or pleasure as from petting a cat, patting a dog, or the known ways of bonding with a horse, etc. Persuasion at least in the temporary sense is possible in all animals!"

Options!

All Logical Considerations of Options...

Some persons are not at all logical! Some will not consider anything other than what is thought by the masses as gospel? And the highly bias and predigests will allow no options other than what they or their piers allow! Sometimes finding an option, becomes the only option! Ahead is further explained animal logic, something perhaps much more over looked than has already been suggested, especially this is so if anyone relates to all of what was said in the invincible deposition given us by Jessie Montana's Johnson when she explained in her own words the uncanny animal associations abrupt her highly mixed wild pack of dog-coyotes, coyote-wolves, and dogs, etc., and their unconditional acceptance of a large Bear! (Please feel free to contact the author if have more plausible ideas, helpful information, comment, misconceptions, or exhilaration had from any part of this manuscript. What ever anyone agrees, disagrees, allows as a comparative, or what, would be happy to hear from you.)

Animal Perception and Discernment?

I have often had wild animals as, moose, dogs, deer, coyotes, rabbits, feral cats, and once even a wolf come to my door, etc., and what is ironic, each time I had known them to be there prior to having actually seen them. Perhaps a part explanation for all that is the result of animal expectations, and creature response had at the place where I reside during winter here in Siberian type wilderness Montana. During winter I always expect animal visitations. What then should we consider does say a moose, wolf, etc., think to relate to human expectations? Animals definitely can read man's intentions. In many unexplained ways pets can easily detect when a person is hurt, miserable, lonely, distraught, etc. Part of mind power in man or beast needs be much relative or similar as are vocal expectations, physical displays, observability of danger, etc. via obvious body language, expectations and or disappointments abrupt rewards, etc. Latent persuasive expectations as are realized in acute fear, deliberate and/or unexpected rejection, moot expectations gone mis-understood, etc. much, much, more is to be considered open ended ahead when we assess the keen mind set of horses in interaction with man. Animals are actually very much like humans.

More Shen!

I don't pretend to fully understand beyond superficial all that there is to realize from the al-most magical mind power of the mysterious Chinese mind control known as, "Shen," but by sim-ple comparisons of known animals and man, and what can exactly be more explained is the ever manifested acute ability of the alleged almost metaphysical unexplained, human Sixth-Sense, that in effect is probably much relative in abstractions to the powers of particular Chinese mystics if not Shen? Not here the place to further attempt to explain it, but the power of the mind in the ex-treme is crypto-documented in the vastness of all Bhutan-Himalayan Mountains, as among the wild Dubtu-Fakers; they are renowned to be able to create the fabled Mind Creatures, (Somewhat supposed in some regard to be the equivalent of the fantasized Genie of the Arabian Knights?) and sometimes the viable creatures are said to be accomplished in multiple numbers! If that be true at all, then anything at is possible? What think to explain Gut Feelings that transpire? A much similar application to a supposed sixth-sense ability might be the much the same sort of mind-set interac-tion avenue had with man and animals that is alleged sometimes working in our favor in such simi-lar cases as when can often easily be detected say an alley cat or anything at all walking light footed quietly across our cabin porch, or perhaps all at once be able to fast open a closed door in high expectancy that someone or something is out there unannounced, and to fact via one's Gut Feeling we are not all that surprised that they are!

Discernment!

Or, by an extended Sixth Sense application as when we are in tune with our surroundings, and are sometimes able to discern an important thing, or an eminent danger as is a poisonous snake, or anything unwanted that is a human threat laying in wait when traveling late-night on a dark trail, or to be able through discernment to realize anything similar to be true that happened of much similar nature of one another; being very hard to explain the like outcome, amounting collectively to another uncanny ever hard to explain multiple story, almost the very same in con-tent and occurrence as was next revealed or only recently told to us, etc.

Inconclusive-Conclusive!

Come-see Come-saw! So-so, mind power?

All of this astute mixture amounts to a definite human intuition ability, most eminent at the time of what ever, etc. What ever actually was/is the cause and effect of things relative to Shen and or to a Sixth Sense, etc. (?); and if added upon much more by certain unexplained phenomena, and all further ramifications of intelligent field logic, it all becomes the necessity of much further logical, and even some illogical conjecture! I only write this last pseudo explanation because of all of "IT," as was said with some insistence... All of "it" was done by particular inspiration, etc. within all explanations experienced, "it" was there in most all situations explained above, and so the crux of the matter, and "it," by any further explanation is perhaps much to be realized for its vital importance, if anyone be truly able to understand any real part, or hopefully all of what will be next conjectured-considered for viable explanations and answers, as we as yet have not at all assessed the moot idea of creature mental telepathy!

"Q"

Wild Man!

Without fire or an understood Language?

Madness?

Perhaps, and just perhaps... Who knows really what is what? all irrational down-beat pace, in a much diligent positive (not negative) quest for viable wild man answers. Chasing obscure man like creatures in fur coats through deep woods and grottoes to prove them what ever they are or are not is one thing, but to be ...... Well critics man your skepticals and pencils! This next conjecture will chock off your perception, and hi-ten up your scoff!

It may read impossible, but what really in human thinking, if not including deep reasoning, is not often at first implausible, until finally sometimes becomes completely viable? It is to be understood here, that I am not concerned that any reasoning part of the following question be true or false. I only submit it in an effort to shake off the cobwebs, and add needed fuel to a dead fire of moot thought and think-tank blather; add fuel to the positive fire that in time may spark from it much needed rational thinking, up-smartly from an all irrational down-beat pace, in a much diligent positive (not negative) quest for viable wild man answers. Chasing obscure man like creatures in fur coats through deep woods and grottoes to prove them what ever they are or are not is one thing, but to be able to understand the mechanics and mentality of pseudo wild man thought beasts, we must first let them think to have cornered us! e to understand the mechanics and mentality of pseudo wild man thought beasts, we must first let them think to have cornered us!

I assure you, wild man is highly intelligent. If anyone doubt that, they are the lesser. As said, I have encountered examples of hominid Sasquatch on three separate occasions over a span of twenty-six years (1982 - 2006), and each time have compared them with myself and the success, and each time they not me became evasive! In one respect by allowing themselves to be observed, they not I were in command! Wild man is a free spirit. Humankind as we think ourselves is a wanna-be!

This next is a wild question asked with much unfounded conjecture, and perhaps needs a wanton tongue in cheek to its end, as I agree it is completely out of sync even when considering all ramifications of fantasy of Pandora's Box, and all possible hidden tigers of the mid-night hour that prowl beyond the sun down; and it will probably be thought by most to have been at best an irrational concern-equation, or perhaps the realistic concerns of a very much-live-alike hard-existing, forgotten, cold and homeless wild desperate hermit vagabond? Wild man of this century has to be much like above described... their life has to be beyond difficult!

"Question?"

Does the ability to be able to plait the mane of any strange horses at anytime have something almost magical to do with human mindset's power much similar to all written previous, however needs much more of the abstract understanding to easily understand it beyond everything and anything here experienced or already explained? And if so, is the braiding partly accomplished by an acute accepted awareness of animal to animal-hominid statuesque that becomes perhaps as if a bonding of rank via a control pattern that is instantly established repetitious between hominid and horse whenever confronted? Is it possible that any given horse at the hominid command may submit its allowance upon demand that is the result of all close net bonding allowed with what little are the understood animal expectations of receptive pleasure next had without demands, as might be exemplified as would be a thing comforting to a horse, "as say the pleasant brushing of its long mane, etc.," and/or by doing this or any number of comforting things, all the while, be able in that way to hold the animal at bay, while accomplishing to plait its mane, or suckle at its estrus milk? This indeed may be one plausible answer to at least explain how a horse might be approached, bonded, and even as I write it may be occurring between whatever entity anyone accepts could be doing it, as the plaiting continues if any want to condone it or not. The price of truth is fact! The fact of truth, we just have to look for it and to recognize the ever obvious. Is it also to abstract to suggest that at times when wild man is temporally or permanently existing in urban ranch surroundings, that during these times when the intricate plaiting is being done, etc., that a part of the effort perhaps even abstract in purpose to the player, is being done out of a tradition all hopeful and meaningful to be wanting humanistic connection between them and us, in a real or fantasized belief and concern, that perhaps by plaiting the manes, all most difficult to do on horses; this done every single time in an extreme exact braided art form, "that finally somehow via obvious humanitarian and high human intelligent realizations via all art form observations, that one day perhaps "they the feral man" will eventually be discovered and allowed to be human! And the next thing (Although this could likely never happen?) "they" be finally welcomed back to re-enter the human race!

All of that above for sure is a highly wild and unfounded auto suggestion, but are we truly intelligent enough to be able to recognize the possible complexity and real significance of the strange plaits, and if so, be able to further understand all possible simple-signal-plea within them, "that is ever all possible, even if not thought probable, and they also somehow to be realized a much primitive long misunderstood sign of wanting empathy? Has, do any think, "has wild man after some many thousands of endless lost centuries, finally came to realize over and again for some obscure reason probably not even fully understood within himself, "a needed desire to want to further identify his kind with today's humanity, or abstractly through his limited language of plaited art, that in certain terms might be an unrealized desperation and much curiosity about us, think to need out of latent animistic-human attachments through DNA etc., want to come home? If so, we need this century to be ashamed...

A Dubious Manifesto In Review?

Indeed this is a dubious manifesto! The story is unwanted, as it is just to much for most persons to deal with, or even to want to bother to comprehend any part of it! Why Don bother with such things? Yeah, why? Its price of toil and sweat to had written it need enter oneself into the judgment realms of madness... as the average citizen critic is hardly average either in his narcissistic assumptions of superiority, not he is all that much different really from the bias academic abrupt all of the unexplained. Remember this is an exploration adventure, a conjectured discovery trip intended to comprise the unexplained; a chance to enter and understand the ever unfamiliar... here we need leave the comforts of reality behind to travel through relative understood reality, at all times however we will remain in the comforts of logical conjecture, thought, and understood explanations, etc. Everything to follow will come right out of everyone's familiar book of life understandings. -Johnny Foxx.

If it's not mental telepathy, then What is it?

Evaluate if can, all previous conjecture, etc., in order to easily comprehend all next? As, in my opinion this strange plaiting is not being accomplished by any simple mental telepathy! Not telepathy at least in the true sense of telepathy as is explained by metaphysical academics. I am not here referencing pseudo telepathy as is presently thought to be being accomplished between man and sea animals, etc., as all of that is still another separate avenue of sorted speculation and theory that I have yet to need explore, as at this time I do not fully ascribe to animal mental telepathy being anything yet proven to be more than a highly interesting project with few probabilities. Rather instead I am highly suggesting a notable intensified acute man to animal intuition, that is actually an expectant allowance done perhaps best explained by abstract animal justifications, through the undeniable and recognized dominating control abrupt human observation ability ever leading to successful horse to human interaction, etc., between them that still perhaps be insisted by some many lay-scholars, to be an absolute manifest example of something as complicated as remote animal telepathy. My explanation of telepathy and theirs are not the exact same thing, however both are much relative in all logical considerations. Each if were possible to apply, either one has no more or less a needed amount of simple animal instinct control, etc. If I'm wrong, animals in the wild are not telepathic, but they can read our intentions... In the case of what ever fits the description of wild horses; in my opinion just like cats, all horses are wild, as it is a known fact that if any are to be ridden, then each and every needs first to be broke by a capable buck-a-rue!

EPILOG

Though my home is now refurbished as an all but forgotten western dwelling, with cracked and damaged glass and deteriorating wood frames windows, an iron stove, and hammock bed, it shall not stop me from laying bare my adventures of discovery. Indeed the wild wind and breeze, the frost of night, the ice below my steps, the rhubarb now frozen in my front has inspired me from Siberia, Montana to wield my pen...

The Bard in the Cabin, DLM.

THE END

Table of Subsections

Table of Subsections

Table of Subsections

Table of Subsections

Table of Subsections

Table of Subsections

Table of Subsections

Table of Subsections

Table of Subsections

Table of Subsections

www.ingramcontent.com/pod-product-compliance
Lightning Source LLC
Chambersburg PA
CBHW082350270326
41935CB00013B/1570